Missionaries in Persia

Missionaries in Persia

Cultural Diversity and Competing Norms in Global Catholicism

Christian Windler
Translated by Pamela E. Selwyn

I.B.TAURIS
LONDON • NEW YORK • OXFORD • NEW DELHI • SYDNEY

I.B. TAURIS
Bloomsbury Publishing Plc, 50 Bedford Square, London, WC1B 3DP, UK
Bloomsbury Publishing Inc, 1359 Broadway, 12th Floor, New York, NY 10018, USA
Bloomsbury Publishing Ireland, 29 Earlsfort Terrace, Dublin 2, D02 AY28, Ireland

BLOOMSBURY, I.B. TAURIS and the I.B. Tauris logo
are trademarks of Bloomsbury Publishing Plc

Originally published in Germany as *Missionare in Persien*, Böhlau Verlag, 2018
First published in Great Britain 2024
This paperback edition published in 2025

Copyright © Christian Windler, 2024

Christian Windler has asserted his rights under the Copyright,
Designs and Patents Act, 1988, to be identified as Author of this work.

For legal purposes the Acknowledgments on p. x constitute
an extension of this copyright page.

Series design by Adriana Brioso
Cover image: 'Alī-Qulī Bēg, ambassador of Shah 'Abbās I at the Roman court.
Detail of the frescoes in the Sala Regia of the Quirinal Palace in Rome, 1616.
(© Giovanni Ricci-Novara)

This work is published open access subject to a Creative Commons
Attribution-NonCommercial-NoDerivatives 4.0 International licence (CC BY-NC-ND 4.0,
https://creativecommons.org/licenses/by-nc-nd/4.0/). You may re-use, distribute,
and reproduce this work in any medium for non-commercial purposes, provided you
give attribution to the copyright holder and the publisher and provide a link to
the Creative Commons licence.

Bloomsbury Publishing Inc does not have any control over, or responsibility for,
any third-party websites referred to or in this book. All internet addresses given
in this book were correct at the time of going to press. The author and publisher
regret any inconvenience caused if addresses have changed or sites have
ceased to exist, but can accept no responsibility for any such changes.

A catalogue record for this book is available from the British Library.

Library of Congress Cataloging-in-Publication Data
Names: Windler, Christian, author. | Selwyn, Pamela E., translator.
Title: Missionaries in Persia : cultural diversity and competing norms in
global Catholicism / Christian Windler ; translated by Pamela E. Selwyn.
Other titles: Missionare in Persien. English
Description: London ; New York : I.B Tauris, 2024. |
Includes bibliographical references and index.
Identifiers: LCCN 2023029254 (print) | LCCN 2023029255 (ebook) |
ISBN 9780755649365 (hardback) | ISBN 9780755649402 (paperback) |
ISBN 9780755649372 (pdf) | ISBN 9780755649389 (epub) | ISBN 9780755649396
Subjects: LCSH: Catholic Church–Missions–Iran–History–17th century. |
Catholic Church–Missions–Iran–History–18th century. | Discalced Carmelites–Missions–Iran–History–
17th century. | Discalced Carmelites–Missions–Iran–History–18th century. |
Missionaries–Iran–History–17th century. | Missionaries–Iran–History–19th century. |
Iran–Church history. | Iran–History–16th–18th centuries. | Iṣfahān (Iran)–History.
Classification: LCC BV2240.I7 W5613 2024 (print) |
LCC BV2240.I7 (ebook) |DDC 266/.02355–dc23/eng/20231117
LC record available at https://lccn.loc.gov/2023029254
LC ebook record available at https://lccn.loc.gov/2023029255

ISBN: HB: 978-0-7556-4936-5
PB: 978-0-7556-4940-2
ePDF: 978-0-7556-4937-2
eBook: 978-0-7556-4938-9

Typeset by Integra Software Services Pvt. Ltd.

For product safety related questions contact productsafety@bloomsbury.com.

To find out more about our authors and books visit www.bloomsbury.com
and sign up for our newsletters.

Contents

List of Figures	viii
Acknowledgments	x
List of Abbreviations	xi
Glossary of Latin Terms	xii
Introduction	1

1 The Short Arm of Rome: The Curia, Superiors, and Missionaries — 13
  The Holy Office and the Congregation of the *Propaganda Fide*:
  Aspirations and Obstacles to Enforcing Papal Primacy — 15
    Limited Financial Resources — 16
    Jurisdictional Conflicts and Personal Networks — 18
    The *Propaganda Fide* and Claims to Secular Rights of Patronage — 20
    The *Propaganda Fide* and the Privileges of Religious Orders — 23
  The Discalced Carmelites: Dysfunctional Institutions and
  Internalized Discipline — 25
    From a Community-Based to a "Monarchical" Form of
    Governance? — 27
    The Missions as Sites of Particular Law — 30
    From Election to Appointment from Above: Provincial
    Vicars and Priors — 31
    The Uses of Visitation — 33
    Internalized Discipline and Self-Empowerment — 35
  Maintaining Proximity from a Distance — 38
    Conditions and Practices of Correspondence — 39
    The Cultivation of Personal Relationships — 42
  "Stepmother" or Protectress? Missionaries and the *Propaganda Fide* — 47

2 In the Shadow of the Shah: The Safavid Empire as an Arena for Catholic
  Mission — 59
    The European Powers in the Safavid System of Imperial Rule — 60
    The Safavid Practice of Power, between Inclusiveness and Orthodoxy — 65
    Global Actors: The Armenian Merchants of New Julfa — 70
    Omens of Conversion or Machiavellianism? — 74

3	Christian *'ulamā*? Missionaries and Muslims	79
	Missionaries at the Safavid Court	83
	Diplomatic Assignments	84
	Translators and Interpreters	88
	Disputations as Expressions of Religious Patronage	92
	Missionaries and Shi'a Scholars	95
	Shared Knowledge Cultures	95
	Learned Disputations	99
	Disagreement and Personal Respect	103
	Medicine, the Belief in Miracles, and the Administration of the Sacraments	105
	Priesthood, Medicine, and Miraculous Healing	108
	Miraculous Healing in Interreligious Competition	110
	Rituals of Salvation and Healing	112
	From Social Proximity to Conversion to Islam	116
4	Among "Brethren," "Schismatics," or "Heretics"? Missionaries and Armenians	123
	"Good Correspondence" and Sacramental Community with Rediscovered "Brethren"	127
	Welcomed as Fellow Christians	127
	Communication with the "Ignorant"	129
	A "Great Friendship": The Discalced Carmelites and Vardapet Moses	131
	"We do not need you": New Practices of Confessional Disambiguation	134
	Wide Networks	135
	Confessional Agitators with Rome's Approval	137
	"He Always Disputes Furiously": The Dominican Paolo Piromalli	137
	The Discalced Carmelite Élie de Saint-Albert and the Formation of a Catholic Armenian Community in New Julfa	139
	The Armenian Clergy Draws Boundaries	144
	Accommodation and Dissimulation	150
	Trade Networks, Mobility, and Confessional Affiliation: The Sceriman Family	151
	Leaving the Armenian Church "in Its Heresies"	157
	Almost Orthodox	163
5	As Christians among Muslims: Missionaries and European Laypeople of Different Confessions	167
	European Laypeople in Isfahan and New Julfa	169
	Economic Activities and Social Practices	170

	Institutional Conditions of "Great Freedom"	174
	Missionaries among Themselves	177
	Affiliation with an Order, Geographical Origin, and Claims to Secular Rights of Patronage	178
	Members of Religious Orders and Episcopal Authority	181
	Transconfessional "Friendship" and "Good Correspondence"	185
	Help along the Way	185
	Paying One's Respects	188
	Useful Services: Transporting Mail	191
	Knowledge and Relationships	193
	Alms, Gifts, and Loans	196
	Shared Religious Practices in the Diaspora	199
	Celebrating Mass in Private Homes	201
	Mixed Marriages	204
	Baptisms and Godparenthood	206
	Caring for the Dying and Funerals	210
6	Local Interconnections and Observance: The Missionaries in Conflict with the Norms of Their Order	219
	The Discalced Carmelites: Unsuited to Mission?	221
	Local Social Integration and Observance	223
	Courtiers Not Missionaries?	224
	Contested Signs of Social Distinction	227
	"Friendship" and "Good Correspondence" with Laypeople	232
	All-Too-Worldly Business	235
	Roman Norms	236
	The Subsidies from Rome	237
	Local Economies	239
	The Mission as a World Turned Upside Down: Justification Strategies and Cultural Relativization	251
7	Undesirable Outcomes: From Mission to Enlightenment?	257
	Doctrinal Disambiguation	260
	Truth Claims and Limits to Norm Enforcement: The Practice of Avoiding Decisions	269
	Normative Orders outside the Church	278
Conclusion		283
Notes		293
Sources and Bibliography		348
Index		376

Figures

Cover image: ʿAlī-Qulī Bēg, ambassador of Shah ʿAbbās I at the Roman court. Detail of the frescoes in the *Sala Regia* of the Quirinal Palace in Rome, 1616. Photo: © Giovanni Ricci-Novara

1 Giacomo Cantelli, "Regno di Persia," 1679 (from *Mercurio geografico* [...] *[Rome, 1692]*, vol. 2, map 172). David Rumsey Map Collection, www.davidrumsey.com   12

2 Rome, Collegio di Propaganda fide (from Giuseppe Vasi, *Delle magnificenze di Roma antica e moderna libro secondo [...]* [Rome, 1752], plate 40 [detail]). Deutsches Archäologisches Institut, Abteilung Rom, Bibliothek, K 551 × rara (1,2)   18

3 Plan of the Discalced Carmelites' house in Isfahan, n.d. (probably seventeenth century) (AGOCD, 233/d/15bis). © 2017 AGOCD, reproduced with the kind permission of the AGOCD, all rights reserved   61

4 Factory of the VOC in Isfahan (from Cornelis de Bruyn, *Voyages [...] par la Moscovie, en Perse, et aux Indes orientales*, 2 vols. [Amsterdam, 1718], vol. 1, plate 107 [detail]). ZB Zürich, Alte Drucke und Rara, NR 83   62

5 Paintings inside the *Čihil Sutūn* in Isfahan: Shah Ṭahmāsp I (r. 1524–76) offers the Mughal emperor Humāyūn refuge at his court. Photo: © B. O'Kane/Alamy Stock Photo   64

6 Cross stones (*khachkar*) in the Armenian cemetery of Julfa on the River Arax (from Francis Rawdon Chesney, *The Expedition for the Survey of the Rivers Euphrates and Tigris [...]* [London, 1850], vol. 1, plate 9). ZB Zürich, AR 242   68

7 Holy Savior Cathedral in New Julfa. Photo: © Christian Windler   71

8 Paintings of scenes from the life of Christ in the Holy Savior Cathedral in New Julfa. Photo: © Diego Delso, under CC BY-SA 4.0, via Wikimedia Commons   73

9 Fol. 24v of the "Morgan Bible" with explanations of the illustrations in Persian (1 Sam. 14:37–45 and 15:2–9). © The Morgan Library & Museum, New York, MS M.638, fol. 24v. Purchased by J. P. Morgan (1867–1943) in 1916   76

10	"Image of the World Square" (*Maidān-i Naqš-i Ǧahān*) in Isfahan (from De *Bruyn, Voyages*, vol. 1, plate 75). ZB Zürich, Alte Drucke und Rara, NR 83	80
11	*Čahār Bāġ* Boulevard in Isfahan (from De Bruyn*, Voyages*, vol. 1, plate 79). ZB Zürich, Alte Drucke und Rara, NR 83	80
12	Allāhwerdi bridge in Isfahan (from De Bruyn, *Voyages*, vol. 1, plate 78). ZB Zürich, Alte Drucke und Rara, NR 83	81
13	Title page of the Arabic translation of Euclid's *Elements*, printed by the *Typographia Medicea* in Rome in 1594. ZB Zürich, Alte Drucke und Rara, 3.19	98
14	Palazzo Sceriman on Rio del Gozzi in Cannareggio, Venice. Photo: © Christian Windler	156
15	Gravestone of Jacques Rousseau in the cemetery of New Julfa. Photo: © Christian Windler	172
16	Pocket watch produced by Pierre-Didier Lagisse in Geneva for the Persian market, ca. 1675, (a) face, (b) back of the movement with signature. © Patek Philippe Museum, Geneva, Inv. S-179	174
17	Gravestone of Jean Malom in the cemetery of New Julfa. Photo: © Christian Windler	217
18	Map of the Jesuit settlement in New Julfa, n.d. (ARSI, Gallia, 97 III, doc. 94, fol. 284r). © Archivum Romanum Societatis Iesu	250
19	Title page of the Arabic translation of Filippo Guadagnoli's *Pro Christiana Religione Responsio* (Answer in Favor of the Christian Religion), printed in 1637. UB Basel, FB IV 4	267

Acknowledgments

The author would like to thank Fr. Antonio Fortes Rodríguez OCD, Fr. Oscar Ignacio Aparicio Ahedo OCD, Fr. Angelo Lanfranchi OCD, and Marcos Argüelles García for their warm reception and competent advice at the archives of the Discalced Carmelite order in Rome. I am no less indebted to the staff of the archives of the *Propaganda Fide*, the Holy Office, and of all the other archives and libraries whose holdings I consulted. Many thanks to Christoph Riedweg and Michele Luminati, who ran the *Istituto Svizzero di Roma* during the years of my archival research, for the opportunity to live at the Villa Maraini during several stays in Rome. The author also has fond memories of his times as a guest scholar at the University of Münster in the autumn of 2016 and exchanges with colleagues there, especially Barbara Stollberg-Rilinger, André Krischer, and Ulrich Pfister. Sundar Henny, Alexander Keese, Kim Siebenhüner, Henning Sievert, and Hillard von Thiessen all offered valuable comments and suggestions that helped the author to improve the original German manuscript. I received important inspiration and assistance from my academic staff, and would like to thank Nadine Amsler, Mathilda Knoop, and Daniel Sidler for their extensive research in libraries and archives in France, the Netherlands, and Switzerland. Particular thanks go to Nadine Amsler for her numerous comments on the entire German original manuscript, drawing on her research on the Jesuit missions in China. Her sympathetic and perceptive criticism provided much food for thought. Comments by Daniel Sidler, Samuel Weber, and Philipp Zwyssig proved equally useful during the revision of the manuscript.

The book you have in your hands is a shorter and much revised version of the German original, and the author thus owes a debt of gratitude to even more people. Nadine Amsler, Regine Maritz, and Samuel Weber provided essential support in shortening the German text and reviewing the English book manuscript. Allison Silver Adelman carefully edited the English manuscript, while Marina Stone meticulously controlled all the footnotes. Last but not least, I am very grateful to Pamela E. Selwyn for her careful translation of the revised text into English.

Abbreviations

AAV	Archivio Apostolico Vaticano
ACDF	Archivum Congregationis pro Doctrina Fidei, Rome
Acta	Acta Sacrae Congregationis de Propaganda fide, APF
AGOCD	Archivum Generale Ordinis Carmelitarum Discalceatorum, Rome
AN	Archives Nationales de France, Paris
APF	Archivio Storico *de Propaganda fide,* Rome
ARSI	Archivum Romanum Societatis Iesu
ASFI	Archivio di Stato, Florence
ASPD	Archivio di Stato, Padoa
BA	Biblioteca Ambrosiana, Milan
BAV	Biblioteca Apostolica Vaticana
BL	British Library, London
BNF	Bibliothèque Nationale de France, Paris
CP	Congregazioni Particolari, APF
DAAG	Directorate of Archives and Archeology, Goa
EIC	East India Company
IOR	India Office Records, BL
MAE	Archives du Ministère des Affaires étrangères, La Courneuve
MEP	Archives des Missions étrangères de Paris
Mss. fr.	Manuscrits français, BNF
n.a.f.	nouvelles acquisitions françaises, BNF
NA	Nationaal Archief, The Hague
SC	Scritture riferite nei Congressi, APF
SO	Sanctum Officium, ACDF
SOCG	Scritture originali riferite nelle Congregazioni Generali, APF
St.St.	Stanza storica, ACDF
VOC	Verenigde Oost-Indische Compagnie

Glossary of Latin Terms

baptism *in articulo mortis* baptism "at the point of death"

bigamia simultanea "simultaneous bigamy," the crime of entering a second marriage while the first marriage is still valid and the spouse alive

bishop *in partibus infidelium* a bishop "in the lands of the unbelievers," in this case a nonresidential or titular Latin bishop of a diocese in the Near East

casus reservatus a sin that can only be absolved by a higher church authority, i.e., a bishop or, in some cases, the pope

communicatio in sacris sacramental community, in this case between Catholics and Eastern Christians or Protestants

consultor an expert who gives a nonbinding advisory opinion in a procedure at the Holy Office

devotio domestica domestic devotion, in this case the devotional practices of religious minorities restricted to their home

donati the lay brothers of a religious order, in this case the Discalced Carmelites

dubium, pl. *dubia* a question ("doubt") on church doctrine addressed to the Holy Office

dubia circa sacramenta "doubts" concerning the proper administration of the sacraments

excommunicatio latae sententiae an excommunication incurred *ipso facto*, which comes into force automatically, although no church authority is aware of the offense and no sentence has been passed

facultates the competencies and rights assigned to clerics, in this case the missionaries

formula scribendi the rules governing the correspondence of the members of the order with their superiors, established in the Society of Jesus

ius scribendi the right of a regular cleric to correspond with the superiors of his order

litterae annuae the annual letters that each Jesuit mission, college, and province were required to submit to the superiors

nihil esse respondendum "there shall be no answer," a formula used by the curial congregations to avoid taking a position on controversial issues

ordinationes the directives by which the visitors clarified rules at the end of a visitation

plenitudo potestatis "the plenitude of power," the supreme jurisdiction and the supremacy over law claimed by the papacy

potestas absoluta "absolute power," as opposed to power subject to law (*potestas ordinata*)

primatus honoris the "primacy of honor" attributed to the bishop of Rome as the successor to St. Peter, to be distinguished from the primacy of jurisdiction claimed by the papacy

Propaganda Fide *Congregatio de Propaganda Fide*, Congregation for the Propagation of the Faith

Rituale Romanum the "Roman Ritual," published in 1614, regulating the ritual functions performed by a Roman Catholic priest

suspensio a divinis the suspension of a cleric from the exercise of the powers of orders

Introduction

I must not neglect to mention that the missionaries move throughout the entire Orient in their own habits; among the common people there they are considered physicians and surgeons, who treat the sick for the love of God; they pass for dervishes, that is, men detached from the world and devoted to the veneration of God and the service of their neighbors. The fact that they generally confirm this reputation with a rather pure and orderly way of life renders them agreeable to the Mohammedans.[1]

The man who described Catholic missionaries in Persia in these words was Jean Chardin, a French jeweler who, after living in Persia for several years, published the first version of his travel account in 1686. This work appeared in numerous editions and translations into various languages and thus became the most important source on Persia in the European Enlightenment. When he published the account, Chardin was living as a Calvinist refugee in England. His travelogue was strongly influenced by his experiences as a religious refugee, and he contrasted religious toleration in Persia with persecution in Catholic France. In his work, Chardin promoted an understanding of religion in which godliness depended on the individual believer's sincere veneration of God and resulting way of life. He contrasted this conception of religion, which he encountered in his contacts with the Islamicate societies of the Near East, with the Catholic confessional church's commitment to institutionally bound regularity.[2]

Despite his negative experiences in Europe, Chardin's view of Catholic missionaries working in Persia was by no means wholly negative. During his sojourns in Persia in the years 1666–7, 1669, and 1672–7, Chardin enjoyed the hospitality of the Capuchins and the Discalced Carmelites in Isfahan on several occasions. They were among his most important informants on the country, and they introduced him to local contacts, although they were well aware that their guest was a Protestant. Chardin in turn acknowledged these services and was prepared to respond in kind when the occasion arose. In his work, he testified to the diverse social roles that missionaries assumed on the ground. He described them as men of God who lived withdrawn from worldly affairs, as bearers of medical and scientific knowledge and as local experts who could open doors and introduce him to useful contacts.

Chardin's comments on and relationship with Catholic missionaries in Persia lead us to key questions for a novel history of Catholic missions. This book tells this story not as a history of expansion but instead centers the missionaries as local actors operating at the intersection of divergent systems of norms. It directs attention to the members of various religious orders who saw themselves as pioneers in the universal mission of their church, but who did not bow submissively to the demands of the Roman Curia. Rather than focusing on the Jesuits, as most studies of early modern missions in Asia have done,[3] this book considers the whole range of religious orders present in Safavid Iran: Augustinians, Discalced Carmelites, Capuchins, Jesuits, and Dominicans. Special attention is given to the Discalced Carmelites (the male Italian branch of the order reformed by Teresa of Ávila), who found it particularly challenging to reconcile their active lives as missionaries and envoys in the service of the papacy with the requirements of a contemplative mendicant order.

This book draws on the heuristic potential of microhistory to show how early modern global Catholicism confronted, and was shaped by, cultural diversity and competing normative demands in multiple ways.[4] It uses the interactions between Catholic missionaries in the Safavid Empire and the superiors of their orders and the Roman Curia as a lens through which to deconstruct the notion of a uniform Tridentine Catholicism as a myth created during the nineteenth-century conflicts between the Catholic Church and the new nation-states.[5] Instead of simply juxtaposing Europe and Asia as monolithic entities, the book highlights the coexistence of competing normative systems and their impacts on the experience of both the missionaries on the ground and the societies of Catholic Europe with which they stayed in touch.[6]

In early modern European societies, religious, social, and common good-oriented norms competed and conflicted with each other. It was only during the period of the Atlantic Revolutions around 1800 that the coexistence of these different systems of norms was fundamentally reorganized. In Europe and the Americas, reformers and revolutionaries claimed to privilege political norms oriented toward the common good over alternative religious and social normative frameworks, thus disentangling, and more clearly demarcating, the various social fields with their respective normative demands.[7]

Despite the move toward less ambiguity as a result of confrontations with the churches that emerged from the Protestant Reformations, different systems of norms continued to coexist and intermingle within early modern Catholicism. Thus, for example, in their rejection of a worldly way of life, the religious orders distinguished themselves from Roman court society and the Curia, but even within the Curia, there was a virtually inherent diversity of and competition between norms due to the dual spiritual and secular nature of the papacy.[8] The rights of patronage or protection that secular Catholic rulers asserted over the churches of their dominions and the missions, the influence of these rulers, which extended as far as the Roman Curia, and the privileges of the religious orders gave early modern Catholicism a composite and polycentric character. Not dissimilar in principle from particular law in secular "composite monarchies," the privileges of the local churches and the orders meant that the practices of alignment with the *one* prince of the Church were decisively shaped by the agency of subaltern actors.[9]

Safavid Persia, in turn, was not the monolithic Shi'ite "theocratic state" historians once imagined it to be.[10] At the beginning of the eighteenth century, two centuries after the Safavids rose to power, around one-third of their subjects were still Sunni

Muslims, and even a segment of the political elites had converted only superficially to Shi'a Islam.[11] To legitimize their rule, the Safavids appealed not just to Shi'a Islam but also to key figures in the Abrahamic prophetic tradition and to pre-Islamic Persian and Turkish-Mongol history.[12] Together with their antagonism toward the Ottomans, which the Safavids shared with the papacy and secular Christian courts in Europe, the inclusive character of their imperial rule, especially under Shah ʿAbbās I (r. 1588–1629), created the preconditions for the reception of Catholic missionaries at the Safavid court and for their establishment in Isfahan and its Armenian quarter of New Julfa starting in the early seventeenth century.

The study of the missionaries' experiences in this context contributes to the enterprise of provincializing early modern Europe.[13] Indeed, in the Persian missions, the centrality of Rome as the norm-setting authority in missionaries' everyday lives was profoundly called into question. This was not just a result of the adverse conditions under which missionaries, the superiors of their orders, and the Roman Curia communicated over great distances. The fact that missionaries in seventeenth-century Asian empires participated in local societies from subaltern positions also clearly contributed to the "de-centering" of the Roman authorities. As Jürgen Osterhammel has shown, in their descriptions of the Asian empires, European observers at that time resorted to negative othering less often than they searched for similarities and equivalences. It was not until the period of the Atlantic Revolutions that the inclusive Eurocentrism of the Enlightenment was replaced by an "exclusive Eurocentrism" that took European superiority "as axiomatic."[14] While they hoped to convert the Persians to their faith, in the seventeenth century, Catholic missionaries did not differ from secular visitors from Europe in viewing the Persians as heirs to a glorious past.[15]

In this respect, Catholic missions to Asia differed starkly from the missionary enterprises in the Americas. Unlike in the sixteenth- and seventeenth-century Americas, European "expansion" in Asia rarely resulted in conquest and the takeover of political power. In the sixteenth and seventeenth centuries, the power and influence of the Portuguese, and later the Dutch and English, in Asia were largely limited to maritime spaces, while on land they interacted with locals from a subordinate position.[16] Their inferiority found symbolic expression in the ceremonial practices to which their agents and envoys of various ranks and status—including Catholic clerics—had to submit at the courts of Persia, the Mughal Empire, and China.[17] By participating in Safavid court life, missionaries from the distant European "province" contributed to establishing the host court as a political and cultural center.

Such conditions contrast sharply with the conventional narratives about the missions, which, starting in the sixteenth century, were shaped by the Catholic Church's claims to universality. In the context of Iberian expansion and opposition to Protestantism, the Latin term *missio* took on its double meaning of spreading the faith among non-Christians and intensifying it among Christians. According to this understanding, the term contained the aspiration to change entire societies.[18] As such, missions throughout the world became a central pillar of the identity of the papacy, religious orders, and secular Catholic rulers.[19] They could be portrayed as a triumph over the Protestant churches, which only began to dispatch missionaries overseas on a larger scale in the eighteenth century.[20] Viewed from this perspective, missionaries were the spearhead of a new, confessional Catholicism, one that drew increasingly narrow boundaries around what was considered orthodoxy. Congregations within the Roman Curia such as the Holy Office and the *Propaganda Fide* established in 1622, which institutionally underpinned papal claims to *plenitudo potestatis* in doctrinal matters or missions, were meant to project the image of a more strongly centralized confessional church.

Contemporaries, by contrast, were aware of the challenges associated with missions across the globe. The image of missionaries was accordingly ambivalent even within the Church: even those orders, like the Society of Jesus, that had expressly enshrined the apostolate as a central task in their constitutions regarded missionary activities not just as the fulfillment of a duty but also as potentially perilous for the observance of the order's Rule.[21] The varied, new local forms of ecclesiastical practice that emerged from the overseas expansion of Catholicism ran utterly counter to efforts to more clearly establish the requirements of the Catholic confessional church. While missions all over the world were central to the self-fashioning of Counter-Reformation, confessional Catholicism, missions also increasingly led Catholic clerics to interact with diverse societies, which fostered processes of pluralization.[22] Clerics who set out to win over souls for the "true religion" turned into local actors who built their reputations by defining their social roles in accordance with the expectations of the host society. In Persia, the missionaries failed from the very beginning to gain large numbers of new converts and instead cultivated "friendship" and "good correspondence" with Muslims and Christians of various denominations (Roman Catholics, as well as Armenians and Protestants). More and more, this practice was at odds with the increasingly rigid ways of understanding Catholic Christianity as exclusive of any other faith.

As a consequence of European expansion to America, Africa, and Asia beginning in the late fifteenth century, encounters with previously virtually unknown cultures acquired an unprecedented intensity. When the problematic consequences of mass baptism, as practiced in the early period of Iberian expansion in the Americas, were recognized over the course of the sixteenth century, Catholic missionaries in America and Asia contributed to a new body of knowledge whose aim was to facilitate more individual forms of inner conversion that were not limited to the formally correct performance of church rituals.[23]

Missionaries differed from other intermediaries in that they not only encountered people from remote cultures in everyday interactions but ideally were also able to influence them in the transcendental dimensions of their lives. In commercial or diplomatic exchanges, knowledge of the other and trust in their future actions could be reduced to those aspects that were immediately relevant for human coexistence. The permanence of such relationships depended upon whether the actors could reach an agreement about the rules that applied in the specific situations in which they interacted with one another.[24]

In the context of missionary activity, however, the processes of knowledge accumulation went deeper. The consequences of these processes were accordingly also farther reaching. Thus, starting in the second half of the seventeenth century, contrary to the intentions of the people who had gathered it, knowledge about the "heathen" societies in Asia increasingly challenged the Church's certainties. The great

Asian empires did not fit into the category of barbarism but were instead experienced as at least equal to European societies. The engagement with non-Christian cultures promoted by the Catholic missions thus decisively contributed to relativizing European certainties, a process that Paul Hazard described as a "crisis of the European mind." Particularly in the wake of the so-called Chinese rites controversy, it ultimately seemed impossible to reduce the unknown to the known and Chinese religion to Catholicism: "Nothing now remained but to acknowledge the existence of an entity with which no terms could be made, yet an entity at once strange and majestic."[25]

The starting point for the debate over rites and the resulting destabilization of European certainties was the local ritual practices that church actors, first in China and later in Europe, regarded, depending on their viewpoint, either as permissible or as backsliding into idolatry. The wide-ranging resonance of these controversies contributed early on to an increased interest in the history of the missions to China. The scholars who began to study missionary activities within local sociocultural contexts shifted their attention to practices of adaptation or accommodation, while still focusing mainly on the missionaries. Since the 1990s, studying missions from the perspective of a history of expansion has given way to an exploration of Chinese Christian communities. The practices of these communities are now understood as the expression of specific forms of Christianity that emerged from interactions between locals and missionaries.[26] Associated with this historiographical shift is a focus beyond the courtly urban milieu of the male *literati*, for example, to include rural Christian communities[27] and the female-dominated domestic sphere as well.[28] These developments have also led to the insight that the priests working in the context of the Catholic missions were "more than just missionaries of the Christian faith," since they assumed diverse social roles on the ground.[29]

The same development toward a history of local forms of Christianity has also become evident in research on other regions of Asia. Ines G. Županov has written of "tropical Catholicism" in South India, a practice of adapting Tridentine Catholicism to local conditions.[30] In the Near East, Bernard Heyberger's work on Christians in the Syrian provinces of the Ottoman Empire is representative of the growing research focus on local Christianities that has been underway since the 1990s in this context as well. Since converting Muslims was forbidden, missionaries in the Ottoman Empire had to content themselves with proselytizing among Eastern Christians. These contacts led to a heightened sense of religious difference among Eastern Christians as well as to a standardization and simultaneous internalization of their religious identities, which were not too different from the processes in contemporary Europe that scholars of confessionalization have described.[31] At the same time, however, the practices of sacramental community (*communicatio in sacris*), which continued to shape the relationships between Eastern Christians and Catholic missionaries at the end of the eighteenth century, illustrate the limits of these processes of confessional disambiguation.[32]

The multiplication of studies on different settings also allows for a reevaluation of the interactions between missionary practices and cultural transformations in Europe. Recent research has postulated that the Chinese and Malabar rites controversies were "geographically, chronologically and epistemologically part of larger processes."[33] This book takes up this challenge and analyzes these sorts of transformations within global Catholicism from a Near Eastern, Persian perspective.

Compared to the missions in China, Japan, India, and the Ottoman Empire, the activities of Catholic missionaries in Persia have received little attention from scholars.[34] This may be in part because, within the master narrative of Catholic expansion, the Persian mission could only be viewed as a failure. Initial hopes to convert Persian Muslims proved to be in vain. The missionaries hardly fared better among the Armenians who became the main target of the mission because of the prohibition on missionary activities among Muslims: only a small segment of Armenians agreed to enter into a union with Rome. In 1714, more than a century after the arrival of the first missionaries, there were four Catholic churches in New Julfa, the Armenian quarter of Isfahan, the imperial capital of Persia. Three of them—belonging to the Jesuits, the Dominicans, and the Discalced Carmelites, respectively—mainly served the approximately 100 Latin Christians (known as Franks) there. The fourth church was that of the Armenian Catholic parish, which was under the patronage of the Armenian merchant family Sceriman and had about ninety members. Given that there were some 30,000 Christians living in New Julfa at the end of the seventeenth century, this was a miniscule number. Even the fact that the Scerimans, one of the leading, globally active Armenian merchant families of New Julfa, supported the union with Rome cannot disguise the Persian mission's lack of success from the perspective of conversion.[35]

However, precisely the aspects that make the Persian missions appear unattractive from the standpoint of a history of expansion also make it a worthwhile object of study if we turn our attention instead to the multiple social roles of clerics and their entanglements with local society. Several peculiarities set the Persian mission apart from other missions in Asia. First, members of several orders (up to five at times) of different origins were present at the same time in the same place, namely, the imperial capital of Isfahan and its Armenian quarter of New Julfa. Second, the small size of the European diaspora and the mutual interdependence of its members facilitated close contacts across confessional lines. The resulting multivocality of the documents affords us a unique opportunity to reconstruct the local entanglements and diverse social roles of the missionaries.

The Discalced Carmelites were dispatched to Persia by Clement VIII (Ippolito Aldobrandini, r. 1592–1605) in 1604 and arrived in Isfahan in 1607. There they encountered the Portuguese Augustinians, who had come to Persia in 1602 and considered the mission there to be under the patronage (*Padroado*) of the kings of Portugal in their *Estado da Índia*.[36] Challenging such claims of secular rulers was a central aspect of the politics of Clement VIII, whose significance for the history of post-Tridentine Catholicism has been made increasingly clear by recent scholarship. With the help of his nephews Pietro Aldobrandini and Cinzio Passeri Aldobrandini, additional confidants, and the congregations of the Curia, the pope sought to consolidate his hold on the Church at the expense of the College of Cardinals, to strengthen the rights of the Church and push back the influence of the Iberian powers.[37] In this context, the Persian mission of the Discalced Carmelites was *the* project in the field of foreign missions. It was conducted not under Spanish or Portuguese auspices but directly from Rome by members of an order that had been founded by Clement VIII immediately before he sent them to Persia. This policy was continued by the Congregation for the Propagation of the Faith (*Propaganda Fide*), which was established in 1622 by another reformist pope, Gregory XV (Alessandro Ludovisi, r. 1621–3), against the resistance of the Iberian powers.[38] Like Clement VIII, the members of the *Propaganda Fide* were initially convinced that Persia would prove a fruitful field of endeavor, thanks to the mission of the Discalced Carmelites.

In the first decades of the seventeenth century, relations with the Safavid Empire occupied an important place in papal self-presentation, as evident from the pictorial program of the *Sala Regia* in the Quirinal Palace commissioned by Paul V (Camillo Borghese, r. 1605–21). Together with the emissaries of other non-European rulers, the ambassador of Shah ʿAbbās I is depicted as paying homage to the papacy's claim to universal jurisdiction (cover illustration).[39]

The conflict between the Curia and the Portuguese *Padroado*, the competition between the various orders, and the rivalries between the secular Catholic courts finally led to a situation in which five different orders as well as secular priests from the French *Missions étrangères de Paris* were active at the same time in the small space of Isfahan and New Julfa. The Portuguese Augustinians and the Discalced Carmelites were followed in 1628 by the French Capuchins and in the middle of the century by the Jesuits. By supporting the missions of these two orders, Louis XIII (r. 1610–43) and Louis XIV (r. 1643–1715) compensated for the weak French commercial presence in Persia and the Gulf region. Until the arrival of a secular envoy in the early eighteenth century, the guardian of the Capuchin mission in Isfahan was considered the French king's agent at the Safavid court. The Jesuit mission was dependent on the order's Lyon province but was also under Polish protection. In the 1680s, the Dominican Sebastian Knab, archbishop of Nakhchivan, founded a settlement of his order in New Julfa, which was associated with the Roman reform congregation of Santa Sabina and thus, like the Discalced Carmelites, was relatively closely connected to the Curia.[40] Aside from the Augustinians, Discalced Carmelites, Capuchins, Jesuits, and Dominicans, individual secular priests from the French *Missions étrangères* were also active in Isfahan and New Julfa in the late seventeenth and early eighteenth centuries. Members of religious orders also established themselves for a time in other cities, especially Shiraz (Discalced Carmelites), Tabriz (Capuchins), and various ports on the Persian Gulf (Discalced Carmelites). In the 1620s, the Discalced Carmelites and the Augustinians also settled in Basra. Although this town was ruled by a local dynasty at the time and later conquered by the Ottomans, the Discalced Carmelites and the Roman Curia treated the convent there as part of the mission to Persia. In the late seventeenth and early eighteenth centuries, some priests from the *Missions étrangères* lived in Hamadan as part of the retinue of the French bishop of Babylon (Baghdad).[41]

Due to the unusually large presence of regular and secular clergy in the same location—Isfahan and New Julfa—the lack of success in conversions was already quite striking for contemporaries. While clerics could not avoid the sobering conclusion that the mission to Persia must be regarded as a failure, their accounts, together with those of laymen such as Jean Chardin, open up perspectives on the multiple social roles occupied by missionaries in their relations with various local actors. Clerics and laity alike integrated into local society and maintained relations with the court and people of varying status and religion.

With its decentering perspective, the present study follows recent work on local forms of Christianity in Asia and the Near East. By concentrating on the missionaries as local actors, it also sets its own very specific emphasis. The investigation focuses on the practices of the missionaries in their capacity as mediators between differing normative systems rather than on the practices of the indigenous Christian community in interaction with European clerics. The history of the Catholic missions told here is thus not one of a transfer of confessional ecclesiastical practice from Rome and other Western European centers to Persia. Instead, the focus has been placed on the missionaries as actors embedded in local and translocal relationships who gave their actions meaning as they worked through each specific local interaction.

With its focus on the Discalced Carmelites, the book highlights an order relatively close to the Curia. Yet this relationship to the papacy points to a significant characteristic of Catholic missions in the early modern period: even after the establishment of the Roman *Propaganda Fide* in 1622, the missions remained primarily a matter for the individual orders. The limits of the papal mission are further borne out by the fact that the papacy's preferred instruments in the Persian mission, the Discalced Carmelites, did not evolve to become an actual missionary order. Both the number of religious active in the missions and their proportion relative to the overall personnel of the order remained consistently low.[42]

While the secretaries and members of the *Propaganda Fide* themselves were very much aware of their dependence on the orders, the state of relevant source materials and limited access to the archives of the orders have led researchers to overemphasize the role of the Roman Curia over that of the orders. One exception is the Jesuits, who, thanks to their well-organized and accessible archives, have been the subject of countless studies exploring the order's scope of activities especially in the missions, which as such have come to be closely associated with the Society of Jesus. To the extent that the relevant archival sources have been preserved and made accessible, it is clear that the missionaries of other orders also mainly corresponded with their own superiors, to whom they were responsible by virtue of their vows. Thus, while this book examines the social roles of missionaries in their local contexts, it studies them primarily as members of religious orders.[43]

Apart from the documentation in the *Curia generalizia* of the Discalced Carmelites and the Society of Jesus in Rome, the author consulted a multiplicity of sources of varied origin, notably the holdings of the archives of the *Congregatio de Propaganda Fide* and the Holy Office. The responses to the challenges of living with tensions between different normative systems differed according to the order, the individuals involved, and the point in time, as reflected by the correspondence between missionaries on the one hand and superiors and the *Congregatio de Propaganda Fide* in Rome on the other. These epistolary exchanges illuminate the relationships of missionaries with Armenians and European Christians of other confessions, as well as their relations with the Muslims with whom they communicated at court and in scholarly venues. Despite the missionaries' tendency to convey the impression that they were faithfully fulfilling the norms of the Church, the *Propaganda Fide* had to deal with a plethora of deviant behaviors, as the records of the congregation show. The Holy Office played a key role in clearing up doubtful cases (*dubia*) relating to sacramental practices and church doctrine that were brought to the attention of the Curia. The dossiers of the *dubia*, preserved in the archives of the Holy Office, offer important insights into the treatment of deviating practices by missionaries as well as the Latin and Armenian laity. We must consider, however, that the scope of the archival holdings of the *Propaganda Fide* and the Holy Office mainly reflects the differing reach of the two congregations and less the relative importance of individual missions on the ground. In the case of the missions to Persia, the archives of both curial congregations document the Discalced Carmelites and Dominicans sent directly by the papacy relatively well, whereas their holdings concerning the Portuguese Augustinians, French Capuchins, Jesuits, and priests of the *Missions étrangères de Paris* are far more fragmentary.

Like most studies of foreign missions, the present work relies overwhelmingly on archival materials originating in the activities of the leadership of the order and the Curia. Since the missions in Isfahan and New Julfa were abandoned during the turmoil after the toppling of the Safavids in the eighteenth century, they lacked the institutional continuity into the nineteenth century that might have ensured the preservation of local archives.[44] The surviving source material ought to be taken with a grain of salt. The documents in the Roman archives offer insights into everyday missionary life only when local actors turned to their superiors and to the curial congregations for various reasons, or when these superiors or congregations sought information about circumstances on the ground, for example during visitations. The image of local practices conveyed by the archival holdings of the order superiors and the Curia is thus not merely fragmentary; these documents consistently measure local practices against the expectations placed upon missionaries from Rome.[45]

Sources produced outside the conflicted area between local practice and ecclesiastical norms are comparatively rare but provide important alternative insights. Worth mentioning in this context are the travel accounts of Protestant authors such as Adam Olearius, Engelbert Kaempfer, Jean-Baptiste Tavernier, and Jean Chardin. All of them maintained close relationships with missionaries, whom they met not just as followers of other faiths but also as fellow Christians and compatriots.

*

This study is divided into seven chapters. Chapter 1 elucidates the conditions and practices of communication between the Roman Curia, religious superiors, and missionaries within the context of early modern processes of institution building. With the deconstruction of older notions of secular "absolutist" rule, the study of ecclesiastical institutions has also been placed on new foundations. How effectively could the Curia actually monitor and direct missionaries acting far away from Rome? How did the missionaries use the institutions of the Curia and their religious orders? To what extent could the Curia and the order's superiors expand their reach thanks to the demands of actors on the ground? Moving away from an approach oriented toward the Curia, the chapter places equal attention on communication within the orders, for the study of which the archive of the Discalced Carmelites in Rome provides unusually rich sources. It offers insights into the coexistence within early modern

Catholicism of differing systems of norms, which in turn interacted with foreign cultures in the missions.

Chapter 2 introduces the Safavid Empire under ʿAbbās I and his successors as an arena of Catholic mission. It shows how the conflicts with the Ottomans and the inclusive domestic strategies of rule since the reign of ʿAbbās I created favorable conditions for Persia's interaction with European courts and trading companies, as well as for the reception of the missionaries. Yet, contrary to older narratives, the chapter locates relations between the court and European actors within the Asian context into which the Safavid Empire was integrated. Furthermore, it points to the importance of the Armenians of New Julfa as a main target of the Catholic mission, and it shows how the global entanglements of this local Christian minority through its commercial activities opened up new possibilities for Catholic mission. The final subchapter demonstrates how the inclusive nature of Safavid rule fed images of a philo-Christian court and how the Roman Curia began to base important decisions on this fiction, which proved surprisingly long-lived.

The three chapters that follow explore the interactions between the missionaries and Muslims, Armenians, and laypeople of European origin, respectively. When the Augustinians and the Discalced Carmelites arrived in Isfahan in the early seventeenth century, they turned first to the ruler and his court (Chapter 3). While their plans for alliances and hopes to convert Shi'a Muslims were soon thwarted, the missionaries did manage to gain access to the court. The missionaries' disputations on points of religion and philosophy with Shi'a clerics polarized them on questions of dogma, yet fostered a degree of familiarity between people who respected each other's standing as scholars. Beyond the narrow circles of the court, Persian Muslims appealed to the missionaries as healers. Did they attribute the missionaries' capacities in this field only to their presumed medical knowledge or also to their ability as men of God to bring about miracles?

The elevated status of some missionaries framed their activities among the Armenians (Chapter 4) and the small European diaspora (Chapter 5), who lived as *ḏimmī* (non-Muslim "protected persons") under the authority of the shah. In both cases, relations of "friendship" and "good correspondence" went hand in hand with the othering of Armenians and Protestants as "schismatics" or "heretics" and introduced a considerable degree of ambiguity, even in religious practice. When the Augustinians and the Discalced Carmelites first arrived in Persia in the early seventeenth century, favorable assumptions, further nourished by a friendly reception by the Armenian clergy, facilitated *communicatio in sacris* (Chapter 4). Starting in the 1630s, both sides articulated confessional differences more clearly, while the missionaries cultivated close relations with Armenian families who were active in trade with Catholic commercial hubs from Western Europe to the Philippines and adapted their religious practice to the places where they were staying. Chapter 5 analyzes relations between Catholic missionaries and laypeople of European origin who operated in conditions of mutual interdependence. As with the relations with Armenians, social proximity managed to blur clear-cut confessional differentiations up to the eighteenth century.

Chapters 3 to 5 also inquire into the multiple social roles that missionaries played in their interactions with people of different confessions and religions. Their services as religious specialists can be viewed against this backdrop. The chapters ask how participants attributed specific meaning to the religious rituals, including the sacraments, that the missionaries performed in local contexts. What did the coexistence of diverse normative frames of reference mean for the actions of people who had been sent by their superiors to spread *the* one and only truth? How did they reconcile their church's demand for confessional unambiguity with local practices that showed a relatively high degree of tolerance for ambiguity?[46]

Against this backdrop, the relationship between the integration of missionaries into local sociocultural systems and the norms of strict observance, whose implementation was demanded by the religious orders, remains to be explained (Chapter 6). As members of a contemplative, mendicant order, the Discalced Carmelites faced a special dilemma: their constitutions did not allow for the sort of accommodation practiced by the Jesuits. Missionaries were not to become involved in worldly affairs or engage in trade and finance. Yet in their interactions with the Safavid court, the Carmelite friars had to adopt signs of social distinction, for example, riding horses, carrying arms, or keeping enslaved people. The neat lines of demarcation that the orders and the Roman Curia were trying to draw flew in the face of the material constraints on the ground, most notably insufficient funding from Europe. Missionaries grappling with chronic underfunding responded to local demands for worldly and spiritual services to secure the long-term survival of the mission.

Finally, attention turns to the repercussions of the integration of missionaries into local contexts for the Catholic Church as such and its place in the European societies of the seventeenth and eighteenth centuries (Chapter 7). To what extent did exposure to foreign cultures cause Europeans to relativize their own certainties, and how did the Roman Curia respond to such undesirable outcomes? In connection with this, the chapter takes a fresh look at the decision-making processes at the Roman Curia. It explores the issue of *communicatio in sacris* with "schismatic" or "heretical" Eastern Christians and shows that the Roman Curia responded with a strategy of decision avoidance when it recognized that it would be unable to enforce the very decisions that the true doctrine of the Church would have demanded. Clear-cut papal decisions on controversial questions of missionary practice—controversies over the Chinese and Malabar rites and the practice of sacramental community—only started to be made from around 1700 onward. The chapter interprets this new decision-making strategy as a result of the growing awareness at the Roman Curia of the challenges posed by cultural diversity, the resulting diversification of missionaries' social roles, and the public controversies relating to these issues. It places the doctrinal clarifications during the pontificates of Clement XI (Giovanni Francesco Albani, r. 1700–1721), Benedict XIII (Pietro Francesco Orsini, r. 1724–30), and Benedict XIV (Prospero Lorenzo Lambertini, r. 1740–58) in the context of the processes of disambiguation in which the Church, finding its authority under attack, gradually withdrew into an all-the-more vigorously defended core religious arena, distinct from "profane and civil society."

Figure 1 Giacomo Cantelli, "Regno di Persia," 1679 (from *Mercurio geografico [...]* [Rome, 1692], vol. 2, map 172)

1

The Short Arm of Rome: The Curia, Superiors, and Missionaries

Catholic missions were closely associated with early modern institution-building processes. The post-Tridentine Church's efforts to assert its contested claim to universality by disseminating its faith among non-Christians and intensifying belief among Catholics dovetailed with papal efforts to centralize important decisions at the Curia and the expansion of the papal bureaucracy. Roman congregations such as the Holy Office and the *Propaganda Fide* paid close attention to the formalization and standardization of their procedures in order to lend legitimacy to their decisions. The papacy justified its claim to the *plenitudo potestatis* by invoking a universal responsibility based on salvation history and divine and natural law in a way that became a model for secular princes claiming absolute power, as Paolo Prodi has demonstrated.[1]

However, while the pope, as head of the Church, claimed a symbolic authority that was in principle far more absolute than that of secular rulers, this could not obscure the inner diversity and the "layered" and "composite" structure of early modern Catholicism.[2] This inner diversity profoundly shaped missionary activities, as will be shown in this book. In the present chapter, I will reflect on the extent and limitations of institution building at the Roman Curia and in the order of the Discalced Carmelites.

As Wolfgang Reinhard has shown in his pioneering research, in the early modern Roman Curia and the Papal States, institution building and personal networks complemented each other as factors of political integration. The deconstruction of the concept of absolutism further called into question the assumption that the actions of the newly established Roman congregations were guided by impersonal, bureaucratic rationality. Today's discussions foreground the role of personal networks and the competition or congruence, as the case may be, of various social, religious, and common-good-oriented norms in a given situation.[3] As rulers in an elective monarchy, the popes were even more dependent than hereditary princes on competing noble kinship groups, to which they themselves belonged.[4] These families were, in turn, linked to competing secular rulers, who, in the struggle for primacy in Catholic Christendom, sought to influence papal elections and the popes' exercise of office.[5] Within and outside the Papal States, relations between the Roman Curia and subordinate actors functioned similarly to those that secular princes maintained with their vassals. In both cases, efforts at better integrating the periphery were structured by personal networks.[6] Despite its claim to universality, in terms of its jurisdictional activity the post-Tridentine papacy was a largely Italian institution. As a result of both a lack of resources and the legal constitution of the Church, its capacity to act remained limited even on Italian soil.[7]

Given the material limits of papal power, the role played by the deployment of symbolic resources was all the more important in affirming the papacy's universalist claims. In this sense, the dispatch of the Discalced Carmelites to Persia in 1604 and the framing of this event at the Roman court as a papal mission were tied to efforts to strengthen the pope's position in church governance.

Yet, not unlike the Portuguese and the Spanish Crowns, the religious orders defended their position by citing the privileges that they had been granted. Clement VIII tried to solve this problem by recruiting "his" missionaries from a community that had only arisen during his pontificate. With the founding of the Italian congregation of Discalced Carmelites in 1600, not only all Italian convents of this order came under the protection of the pope but also all those to be founded in the future outside of Spain.[8] That is why the Discalced Carmelites of the Italian congregation seemed better suited than members of other orders to promote missionary activities as a dependent arm of the Roman Curia.

We will have to keep these considerations in mind when we survey both the curial institutions and the order of the Discalced Carmelites. In the process, actors who adhered to differing sets of norms will come into focus: first, the curial bureaucracy as part of Roman court society; then, a religious order whose members claimed to have renounced worldly honors and riches and yet often acted within the "world," not least in their communications with the Curia. According to the most recent scholarship on social elites, institution building and personal networks were not opposites but rather complementary aspects of the processes of political integration. In this chapter we will see whether this also applied to an order whose members had vowed to renounce status and rank. To what extent did regular clerics rely on personal relationships when they addressed their superiors? What conventions applied when they had to address a curial congregation or its individual members?

The aim of better integrating peripheral actors was associated with both the expansion of the curial bureaucracy and the formation of institutions within the order. Yet in both cases we have to ask how long the arm of Rome actually was.[9] To what degree did strengthening the authority of curial congregations and the superiors of the orders also depend on the demands of subaltern actors and consequently on "empowering interactions"?[10] Since its foundation in 1622, the *Propaganda Fide* had become a source of protection alongside the superiors of the order. Did this affect the relations of regular clerics with their own superiors?

The Discalced Carmelites as well as the Jesuits and other communities were founded in the sixteenth century as a result of the widespread sense of dissatisfaction with the existing state of the Church. This raises the question of whether members of a reforming order might have set limits to their duty of obedience to the *Propaganda Fide* by invoking not just the privileges of their order but also their own specific system of values and norms, which was rooted in the transcendental. The discussion of these issues leads us, finally, to the question of how the persistence of competing normative systems within early modern European Catholicism influenced the interactions in missionary territories and what repercussions these contacts, in turn, had in Europe.

The Holy Office and the Congregation of the *Propaganda Fide*: Aspirations and Obstacles to Enforcing Papal Primacy

In the course of the sixteenth and seventeenth centuries, the Catholic Church drew the boundaries of orthodoxy increasingly more narrowly in order to distance itself from the churches that emerged from the Protestant Reformations. The insistence on confessional norms also had consequences for relations with Eastern Christians, Muslims, and "pagans," since it limited the willingness to tolerate divergent practices among potential converts. At the Roman Curia, two congregations of cardinals were at the forefront of enforcing the new orthodoxy and orthopraxy in this field: the Holy Office and the *Congregatio de Propaganda Fide*.

The Holy Office (now the Congregation for the Doctrine of the Faith) was created by Paul III (Alessandro Farnese, r. 1534–49) as a tribunal directly subordinate to the pope and reorganized as a congregation by Sixtus V (Felice Peretti, r. 1585–90). The new institution embodied the papal claim to uniformly define doctrine and ecclesiastical discipline and to enforce them as universally binding. Apart from judging and punishing deviations, the Holy Office also examined the questions posed to it in the form of doubts (*dubia*). Since its archives were opened in 1998, early modernists have focused great attention on the Holy Office as an Inquisition court, inspired by the broad public interest in spectacular trials such as that of Galileo Galilei.[11] In contrast, research on its role in handling *dubia* has been limited to case studies, which historians have only begun to integrate into more general surveys.[12]

In both of its roles, we encounter the Holy Office as a body whose actions were marked by efforts to lend legitimacy to its decisions by formalizing procedures. The handling of *dubia* revealed this concern with establishing orderly procedures, especially in linking the decisions of the cardinals and the pope to the opinions of the *consultores*, who examined the concrete case in the light of the universally valid principles of church doctrine and discipline, as well as previous decision-making practice. The cardinals and, ultimately, the pope were, however, free to make decisions that diverged from the advice of the *consultores*. The pope's independent decision found its legitimation in the power vested in him as the vicar of Christ. As we will see in the course of this study, however, cardinals and popes could not act in a manner untethered from their specific social and cultural environments.

When the *Congregatio de Propaganda Fide* (now the Congregation for the Evangelization of Peoples) was established in 1622, it was a sign of the will of Gregory XV to assert papal primacy in the missionary field and to use the missions to legitimate his claims to primacy.[13] Like the reform of the procedure for the election of a new pope, which took place at the same time, the foundation of the *Propaganda Fide* was a project of reform-minded cardinals and scholars in the Curia who defended the primacy of religious and ecclesiastical norms against the interests of secular rulers. Both reforms were intended to help the papacy assert itself as a superior, spiritual power vis-à-vis the secular princes—chief among them the king of Spain. Both projects were supported by the so-called *zelanti*, who gathered in the *Accademia dei Virtuosi* during the years 1621 to 1623 under the leadership of the cardinal-nephew, Ludovico Ludovisi. A leading member of the circle and confidant of the Ludovisi pontiff, Francesco Ingoli, became the first secretary of the *Propaganda Fide*.[14]

The main aim of the new congregation *de Propaganda Fide* was to convert the infidels, "heretics," and "schismatics." It was also charged with supervising the activities of missionaries among the Catholics who lived under the rule of "heretics" or "infidels," as well as Greek Rite Catholics in Italy. The founding of the congregation was part of the efforts to make Rome *the* central site of missionary knowledge, replacing the previous points of origin of the missions under the patronage (*patronato*) of the Iberian powers. Like the secular courts in Western Europe that aspired to rule over non-European societies, the Roman Curia recognized the instrumental and symbolic importance of acquiring knowledge about conditions on the ground, for decisions could only be adapted to the local contexts if the decision-makers possessed appropriate insights. At the same time, the accumulation of knowledge helped to lend decisions a veneer of legitimacy. However, in its effort to document conditions at the sites of mission as thoroughly as possible and to apply this knowledge to decision-making, the congregation faced a variety of difficulties.[15]

Three sets of problems will be addressed here: the limited financial resources of the *Propaganda Fide*, the jurisdictional conflicts between the *Propaganda Fide* and the Holy Office, and finally the conflicts resulting from the fact that the newly created papal institution challenged ancient law—the rights of patronage of secular rulers and the privileges of orders.

Limited Financial Resources

The *Propaganda Fide*'s limited resources contrasted strikingly with its sprawling remit. Although scholars have paid little attention to its finances thus far, the *Propaganda Fide* clearly shared three characteristics with other Roman congregations: a very modest financial position in comparison, for instance, to the budgets of rich cardinals; dependence on funding from the Papal States and, in a few cases, from other Italian territories; and the high proportion of resources that were expended in Rome. Viewed against the background of the existing research on papal finances, these findings are hardly surprising, but they do shed new light on the role of the *Propaganda Fide* and the Roman Curia overall in promoting the missions.[16]

According to Volker Reinhardt's study of the finances of Scipione Borghese, cardinal-nephew of Paul V, "private interests and undertakings intended to promote the family of the pontiff, its status and elevation" took precedence over "efforts directed at the overall spiritual and political duties of the papacy."[17] In fact, the revenues and outlays of a cardinal-nephew from a family in the process of rising into the Roman aristocracy vastly exceeded those of the future *Propaganda Fide*. While the average revenues and expenses of Scipione Borghese between 1605 and 1633 amounted to 225,003 *scudi* and 224,556 *scudi* per year, respectively,[18] the revenues of the *Propaganda Fide* between 1651 and 1709, according to its *bilanci*, ranged from 21,158 to 25,745 *scudi* per year, and its outlays from 19,027 to 29,335 *scudi*, with no clear upward trend over the years. And yet the *Propaganda Fide* was still better funded than the Holy Office, whose average annual revenues between 1633 and 1678 amounted to just 7,978 *scudi*, with expenses of 8,243 *scudi*.[19] During his pontificate, Paul V gave monetary gifts of 1,095,130 *scudi* to his family, in addition to many donations in kind, as well as lucrative benefices to his cardinal-nephew.[20] Even Alexander VII (Fabio Chigi, r. 1655–67), who at the beginning of his pontificate ostentatiously excluded his kinsmen from the government, spent some 620,000 *scudi* in 1659 just to support his nephew Agostino Chigi on the occasion of the latter's marriage to Maria Virginia Borghese.[21] In contrast, the *Propaganda Fide* had a capital amounting to just 610,196 *scudi* in 1651 and 748,289 *scudi* in 1693. As in secular monarchies, the ceremonialism of the Roman court that was aimed at elevating the pope's position barely concealed the fact that it was wealthy noble kin groups rather than the emerging institutions that set the financial tone.[22]

In the context of this courtly economy of favors, the *Propaganda Fide* depended on donations from families in the Papal States with close ties to the papacy. To be sure, in 1622 Gregory XV promised the congregation a tax of 500 *scudi* each on the cardinals' rings. It was no longer the heirs, but the cardinals themselves, who had to pay this tax when their new dignities were conferred upon them. However, as Giovanni Pizzorusso has emphasized, the symbolic importance of this tax outweighed its material significance. While some cardinals turned the payment into an act affirming their loyalty to the papacy, non-Roman cardinals refused to pay, citing the privileges of their local churches. More important for the accumulation of the congregation's capital were the donations and legacies of individual cardinals, above all those of Antonio Barberini Sr., brother of Pope Urban VIII (Maffeo Barberini, r. 1623–44).[23] Like the building of churches, legacies in favor of missions were well suited to deflecting criticism and increasing the reputation of the donors and their families. While they represented a limited financial burden, they offered all the greater gain in symbolic capital, as they documented the dedication of the donors to a central concern of the post-Tridentine papacy.

The use to which the *Propaganda Fide* put these proceeds was reflective of their origins in the Papal States: the lion's share of its financial resources was invested in the city of Rome. Some 40 to 50 percent of expenditures served to stage *missio* as a papal enterprise in Rome, where the *Propaganda Fide,* together with its *Collegio Urbano* and the *Tipografia Poliglotta*, was housed in a purpose-built palace on Piazza di Spagna designed by two highly respected architects, Gian Lorenzo Bernini and Francesco Borromini (Figure 2). The prestigious building, along with other projects, such as the paintings in the *Sala Regia* of the Quirinal Palace or the *Fontana dei Quattro Fiumi* on Piazza Navona, helped to represent in courtly and urban spaces the papacy's universalist claims, of which the missions had to be considered the expression par excellence.

Behind the baroque facade of the palace on the Roman Piazza di Spagna stood an institution that financially supported only a small portion of the missions from its *stato temporale*. The Persian mission was a typical case: although Clement VIII had launched it as a papal enterprise, the Discalced Carmelites were dispatched with funds from their own order. In 1655 Pope Alexander VII transferred control over these funds to the *Propaganda Fide*. This, along with the fact that the Discalced Carmelites subsequently received no additional funding, contributed to their estrangement from the Curia. In eighteenth-century Persia, only the Dominicans of the reform congregation of Santa Sabina and the bishops of Isfahan, who were recruited from either the latter order or the Discalced Carmelites, received subsidies from the *Propaganda Fide*'s *stato temporale*.

Figure 2 Rome, *Collegio di Propaganda Fide* (from Giuseppe Vasi, *Delle magnificenze di Roma antica e moderna libro secondo [...]* [Rome, 1752], plate 40 [detail])

The Augustinians, Capuchins, and Jesuits, in contrast, had to rely on their secular patrons, the kings of Portugal, France, and Poland. Only rarely did the congregation contribute funds to the Capuchin missions, and any payments of travel allowances or subsidies were extremely modest when compared to the needs of the recipients. The *Propaganda Fide* sent its monies to places where the patronage of secular rulers left gaps for activities by the Curia. Foremost among them were parts of the Ottoman Empire, followed by Armenian communities in Poland as well as Ireland and Scotland. Otherwise, in place of the curial congregation, it was actors whose influence the post-Tridentine papacy sought to limit that stepped into the breach: secular patrons and protectors as well as religious orders. What all missions had in common, however, was that their funding was insufficient to sustain the settlements. For that reason, the settlements themselves had to generate a more or less large proportion of their resources, as I will show for the Persian mission.[24]

Jurisdictional Conflicts and Personal Networks

Upon its establishment in 1622, Pope Gregory XV gave the *Propaganda Fide* a wide remit in all aspects of mission. This assigned the new congregation a field of endeavor that was already partially occupied by the Holy Office. The founding of the

Propaganda Fide was thus followed by protracted conflicts over how to delimit its areas of responsibility. In the sixteenth and seventeenth centuries, such conflicts tended to arise wherever the spheres of activity of new, specialized congregations overlapped with those of existing institutions.

Attempts to clarify competences began immediately after the founding of the *Propaganda Fide*, when Gregory XV authorized the Holy Office to decide on the granting of the *facultates*—that is, the assignment of the various competences and rights of missionaries: the *Propaganda Fide* submitted the application to the Holy Office and had the *facultates* issued to the missionaries. The decision on the *facultates* was routine business for the Holy Office, as evident from the nearly always slim files, the almost complete absence of personal data, and the formula "with the usual faculties" used in the decisions. From the perspective of the performance of authority, it was precisely this routineness that constituted a significant part of the meaning of these decisions, since they gave the Holy Office repeated opportunities to reassert its primacy over the *Propaganda Fide*.

Of far greater relevance was the competence to settle questions concerning controversial aspects of church doctrine and discipline. The Roman authorities were presented, in the form of *dubia*, with opinions and practices whose compatibility with the established doctrine and discipline had kindled doubts. The petitioner expected the matter to be settled in such a way that it served as a guideline for the faithful. The presentation and resolution of a *dubium* helped to give shape *in actu* to papal assertions of definitory power. The author of the *dubium* was never punished because his request for clarification laid bare a willingness to be consistent with church teachings. Among the petitions, the *dubia circa sacramenta* took center stage because of the importance the Roman Church placed upon the sacraments as signs of divine grace, whose salvific effects were contingent on their correct administration by a priest or exceptionally (as in the case of emergency baptism) by a layperson.[25]

Beginning in the sixteenth century, the emergence of new Catholic churches outside Europe created a need to settle many questions. While the Curia's dealings with the *dubia* underscored its claim to ultimate decision-making power, the *dubia* themselves also reveal the scope of action available to actors outside the Curia, who introduced their own ideas and contributed to the diversity of ritual practices. In their sheer numbers and frequent repetitions, the *dubia* suggest the difficulty of reconciling local practices with the norms of the Roman Church. We may also ask to what extent, in practice, examining the *dubia* mutated from a process of creating clarity to a channel for articulating diversity and ambiguity.

In the missions to both China and the Eastern Christians, the competition between two congregations—the Holy Office and the *Propaganda Fide*—helped to dynamize the controversies. Ever since its founding in 1622, the question of the new congregation's relationship to the Holy Office arose on a number of occasions when *dubia* arrived from the missionary territories. The *Propaganda Fide* repeatedly formed *ad hoc* committees to examine controversial questions. In 1625, this included charging a congregation of theologians with studying and responding to a book written by Persian Muslim scholars against the *Truth-Showing Mirror*, penned in the Mughal Empire by the Jesuit father Jerónimo Javier de Ezpeleta y Goñi. Following this *Congregatio Persiae*, the *Propaganda*

Fide installed additional committees to clarify missionaries' *dubia*. Nevertheless, it would be inaccurate to speak of jurisdictional conflicts without considering the connections with the Holy Office. While the secretary of the *Propaganda Fide*, Francesco Ingoli, was the driving force behind the assertion of the jurisdiction of "his" congregation, some cardinals belonged to both dicasteries and used the resources that these dual memberships offered them according to their personal logic. Since 1632 and 1633, respectively, both the Holy Office and the *Propaganda Fide* were subject to the authority of a nephew of the reigning Pope Urban VIII as secretary or prefect. While on an institutional level there were two separate jurisdictions, on a personal level the congregations were closely intertwined. Close connections also existed on the level of the experts who made up the committees appointed by the *Propaganda Fide*. Unlike the Holy Office, with its staff of *consultores* and qualificators, the new congregation did not have a fixed circle of specialists to scrutinize the *dubia*. The committees formed by the *Propaganda Fide* thus consisted mainly of qualificators from the Holy Office, who were, however, supposed to perform their duties as experts on behalf of the *Propaganda Fide*.[26]

Jurisdiction was ultimately decided by Alexander VII, who in 1658 forbade the *Propaganda Fide* from discussing the *dubia*. The practice that now took hold corresponded to the procedure that had already been used to bestow the *facultates*. The *Propaganda Fide* conducted the correspondence with missionaries while the Holy Office deliberated on the *dubia*. Accordingly, it was the *Propaganda Fide* that referred most *dubia* from the missions to the Holy Office. The focus was on matters of ritual practice raised by the missionaries and occasionally other persons from the places of mission. Despite the decision made by Alexander VII, the coexistence of the two congregations continued to create a situation in which the Curia spoke with two voices on important matters.[27]

Such processes suggest that the institutional structures were still less fixed than the arguments mobilized in the jurisdictional conflicts might lead us to believe. Those involved deployed institutional rationality and personal logic in different ways. If we are to believe the first secretary of the *Propaganda Fide*, Francesco Ingoli, the conflicts between the *Propaganda Fide* and the Holy Office should be characterized as jurisdictional conflicts. The secretary sought to position the *Propaganda Fide* as a body responsible for all mission matters. Meanwhile, the cardinals partially bridged these contradictions by dint of their dual membership in both congregations: while Ingoli defined his social status and radius of action at the Curia through his position as secretary of the *Propaganda Fide*, well-connected cardinals had the opportunity to act, depending on the situation, as members of the *Propaganda Fide* or the Holy Office.

The *Propaganda Fide* and Claims to Secular Rights of Patronage

In his *Relazione delle Quattro Parti del Mondo* of 1629–31, Francesco Ingoli referred to the "political affairs of princes" as the main obstacle to the rapid spread of the Christian faith. He was referring here mainly to the rights of patronage of the kings of Portugal and Spain, which he believed hindered the appointment of new bishops and the sending of missionaries, and set the monies intended for the Church aside for other purposes. Ingoli then issued a scathing critique of the missionaries recruited from the ranks of the regular clergy. Far from the eyes of their superiors and bishops, they reveled in their "sensuality" and their stinginess; many were ignorant and did not live upright lives. Instead of spreading the Christian faith, their comportment drove away potential converts.[28] Ingoli thus addressed two fields in which tenuous legal claims stood in the way of the efforts of the *Propaganda Fide* to impose itself as the sole authority over the missions: the rights of patronage of the Spanish and Portuguese Crowns, and the privileges of the religious orders. Behind Ingoli's critique was a fundamental question: Were the pope and the curial congregation bound by ancient law, or could they suspend or even revoke it by citing the absolute papal *plenitudo potestatis* grounded in the history of salvation and divine and natural law, if the service of God's Church demanded it?

In the sixteenth and early seventeenth centuries, the missions in America and Asia had largely been shaped by the conditions that the Iberian powers created based on the rights of patronage the papacy had bestowed upon them. Asia belonged to the part of the world that Alexander VI (Rodrigo Borgia, r. 1492-1503) had assigned to Portugal in the 1494 Treaty of Tordesillas. Based on the papal privileges, the kings of Portugal claimed patronage over the missionary churches there: the right of the Crown to present the pope with candidates for the archdiocese of Goa and the episcopal sees corresponded to its obligation to disseminate the Christian faith and build churches. Many conflicts arose from the fact that the papal bulls issued in the sixteenth century to establish the archbishopric of Goa and its dependent dioceses did not draw their external borders to coincide with the territories of Portuguese rule but kept them open in the hope that missionaries would be able to conquer new souls well beyond the areas under formal Portuguese control.[29] The settlement of Portuguese Augustinians in Isfahan in the name of Philip III of Castile as king of Portugal (r. 1598–1621) in the early seventeenth century was associated with Portuguese claims to patronage over the missionary churches in the Safavid Empire. The royal coat of arms on the facade of the convent underlined their dependence on the Portuguese Crown. As in Japan, China, and broad swaths of Southeast and South Asia, in Persia, too, the claim to the *Padroado* was extended to a territory that never came under Portuguese rule.

Starting in the seventeenth century, these secular claims clashed with ideas of papal supremacy, which were first affirmed with the arrival of missionaries from the Discalced Carmelites in Isfahan in 1607. The establishment of the *Propaganda Fide* in 1622 further exacerbated the latent conflict. To be sure, the new congregation was supposed to respect the rights of patronage of the Spanish and Portuguese Crowns, but in practice it tended to limit these to those territories under the effective secular rule of the kings of Spain and Portugal. While the Spanish territories in America were *de facto* largely off limits by virtue of the *patronato real*, over the course of the seventeenth century new opportunities opened for the congregation in Asia. Since only a tiny part of Asia fell under Portuguese control, and Portuguese influence in Asia was substantially weakened by competition from other European powers, most notably the United Provinces of the Netherlands and England, the issue of the enforceability of Portugal's rights of patronage arose with increasing frequency. Ingoli argued in his *Relazione delle Quattro Parti del Mondo* that where the Portuguese did not rule—especially in China and Japan—bishops and archbishops could be appointed by the pope independent of the *Padroado*. With the appointment in 1632 of two bishops for the dioceses of Isfahan and Babylon (Baghdad), the *Propaganda Fide* affirmed that Persia and Mesopotamia did not belong to the *Padroado*, a fact that had already been claimed when the Discalced Carmelites were sent there almost three decades earlier.

Beginning in the 1630s, the *Propaganda Fide* faced similar challenges to Rome's primacy from the French Crown. At first, the Curia tried to use the installation of French clerics to undermine the *Padroado*. This was a risky strategy because the ecclesiastical policy of the French Crown did not differ fundamentally from that of the kings of Portugal. When the weakening of Portuguese influence left a gap in the Catholic missions, it was less the Curia than the French Crown that stepped in. This became evident in East Asia starting in the second half of the seventeenth century.[30] Yet the founding of the Capuchin and Jesuit missions in Isfahan (in 1628 and 1647, respectively) had already proceeded in concert with other French initiatives in various corners of the world, where commitment to the "true faith" legitimized French claims to supremacy. As an *éminence grise* in the shadow of Cardinal Richelieu, the Capuchin Joseph de Paris played a key role in sending his order's missionaries to Persia.[31] This mission was part of an enterprise by French Capuchins under royal protection that primarily targeted the Ottoman Empire. The dispatch of missionaries served the aim of strengthening the French Crown's political influence: the guardian of the Capuchin mission in Isfahan served as an agent of the French king at the Safavid court. In 1634, using Crown funds, the Capuchins purchased a residence located in the immediate vicinity of the shah's palace. Although Père Joseph sought and received legitimation from the *Propaganda Fide*, the settlement of French members of his order planted the seeds of rivalry not just with the Portuguese Augustinians but also with the Discalced Carmelites. Like the Augustinians under Portuguese patronage, the French Capuchins and later the Jesuits in Persia largely evaded the authority of the *Propaganda Fide*—less through open defiance than by regulating their affairs as much as possible without recourse to Rome and avoiding correspondence with the congregation.

French influence extended to the secular clergy, including the two dioceses in the area. The episcopal see of Babylon was held by a French cleric starting in 1637, when Urban VIII had given his assent to this clause as part of a donation agreement with Élisabeth Le Peultre, the wealthy widow of the childless Antoine de Ricouart, *conseiller au Parlement de Paris*, who agreed to offer 120,000 *livres tournois* (about 40,000 *scudi*) to the diocese in return. Until Isfahan acquired its own bishop in 1693, the bishops of Babylon were also apostolic vicars of that diocese. However, it was not until the 1680s that two vicars, François Picquet and his successor Louis-Marie Pidou de Saint-Olon, fulfilled their residential obligation and began working from Isfahan and Hamadan to solidify French influence. When they moved to Persia, they were accompanied by priests of the *Missions étrangères*, who worked together with the *Compagnie des Indes orientales* to expand French influence.

French claims to the protection of the missions in the Safavid Empire were only formalized in the early eighteenth century. These treaties mirrored stipulations in the capitulations of the Sublime Porte, which at once legitimized the preeminence of the Most Christian King within Catholic Christendom and justified the practice of overwhelmingly peaceful relations with Muslims. Like the capitulations of the Porte, the treaty that the envoy Pierre-Victor Michel negotiated with the Persian court in 1708 contained protective provisions for all Catholic Christians, regardless of origin. Unlike the Iberian patronages, French protection of the missions and Catholic Christians in both the Ottoman Empire and Persia lacked a basis in canon law. Instead, these claims derived unilaterally from the Ottoman capitulations, and in Persia from the treaty of 1708.[32] The struggle to get the French protection recognized was thus fought out above all on the level of everyday interactions and through symbolic communication, as we will see.

Suffice it to say, at this point, that even without a comparable basis in canon law, French protection was no less a challenge to papal primacy than the claims of the Portuguese Crown derived from the *Padroado* had been. If the *Propaganda Fide* wished to assert its jurisdiction on the ground, it had to rely on the practices of indirect influence: at times, it may have seemed expedient to challenge the claims of the Portuguese Crown by promoting French clerics. More promising overall, however, was the deployment of regular clerics with a more direct relationship with the Curia: first the Discalced Carmelites and later also the Dominicans, who belonged to the Roman reform congregation of Santa Sabina. Unlike the bishops of Babylon, who had to be of French origin starting in the 1630s, as per the donor's provisions, the Latin bishops of Isfahan appointed from 1693 onward belonged to these orders exclusively, which set limits on Portuguese and French claims and was intended to assert the jurisdiction of the *Propaganda Fide* in Persia.

The *Propaganda Fide* and the Privileges of Religious Orders

The jurisdiction of the *Propaganda Fide* was limited not only by the rights of patronage bestowed on the kings of Spain and Portugal but also by the ancient law of religious orders, both in the form of privileges and customary rights.[33] Traditionally, the popes had preferred specific orders for certain mission territories, granting them more or less extensive privileges. In the context of the Spanish patronage, the mendicant orders acquired privileged positions in the Americas and the Philippines, while the Society of Jesus was at the forefront under the Portuguese *Padroado*. The Roman Curia retained limited opportunities for influence by extending similar privileges to rival orders. When the Augustinians were sent from Goa to Isfahan, this occurred within the context of Clement VIII's opening of the missions under the Portuguese *Padroado* to the mendicant orders—the Franciscans, Dominicans, and Augustinians.

Efforts in the wake of the Council of Trent to regulate the faculties of dispensation and absolution more strictly and link them to the church hierarchy led to conflicts with the orders. When the *Propaganda Fide* was founded, the Roman Curia abandoned the practice of granting permanent privileges for certain mission territories and orders in favor of issuing *facultates* for a limited time and following more uniform criteria. The *facultates* were meant to improve the preconditions for conversions or to prevent people in confessionally mixed milieus from turning away from the Catholic Church, for example by giving absolution to "heretics" or offering dispensation from the strict application of canon law.

The rules for granting the *facultates* were laid out more precisely in the years 1633 to 1637 within the framework of the Particular Congregation *super facultatibus missionariorum* established by Urban VIII, which was composed of members of the Holy Office and the *Propaganda Fide*. The Particular Congregation elaborated five universally valid formulas and four that applied in special cases. It defined the missionaries' *facultates* of dispensation from ordinary canon law most broadly where the secular authorities limited or forbade the practice of the Catholic faith or where other circumstances made access to parish priests and bishops especially difficult. Based on the *facultates* bestowed upon them, missionaries enjoyed authority that, in Europe, was restricted to higher church officeholders, particularly with regard to granting dispensations and absolution. Where distance or other factors made recourse to the Curia impossible, the missionaries were even authorized to grant absolution in cases otherwise reserved for the pope himself. Thus, even within the framework of the new rules, the mission territories remained areas of particular law, removed from ordinary church jurisdiction, where Tridentine norms could be enforced only to a limited degree.

In early modern societies, legitimacy was derived from ancient law. Consequently, the Roman Curia's challenge to the privileges of orders—much like that posed by secular monarchies to the privileges of the nobility—met with resistance from those affected. Unilateral decisions by the Curia had boundaries imposed by processes of negotiation that exhibited clear parallels to the relationship between secular rulers exercising their *potestas absoluta* and the estates that insisted upon ancient rights. In a protracted struggle, the Curia had to attempt to enforce the new regulations against contrary claims. In the process, it was more concerned with defining its own competences *in actu* by making decisions on concrete matters than with refusing requests for dispensation. The broad privileges granted by the popes obstructed efforts to regulate the missionary activities of the orders. The obstacles were lower in the new mission territories such as Persia. Like secular princes in their territories, Clement VIII deployed the bestowing of privileges to gain the loyalty of the Italian congregation of Discalced Carmelites, which he had founded. Subsequently, the order also cited these privileges to support its social status and legal position.[34] In this respect, too, we can see striking parallels to the behavior of secular actors: like aristocratic families, the religious orders defended their own ancient rights, on the one hand, while also using their relations with the highest granter of favors to acquire advantages and privileges and to improve their position in relation to their peers, i.e., the other orders. At least initially, the newly founded Italian congregation of the Discalced Carmelites was particularly dependent on maintaining good relations with the Roman Curia.

The established orders had a wider scope of action. In their dealings with the *Propaganda Fide*, the Jesuits were especially adamant in defending the right of their general to send, transfer, and recall missionaries at his own discretion. In 1629, shortly before the convocation of the commission *super facultatibus missionariorum*, Urban VIII had reaffirmed the Society's privileges. Under such conditions, the only hope was to convince the order's superiors to adhere to the formulas developed by the particular congregation when preparing the *facultates* for the missionaries they themselves sent out. In 1643, the general of the Jesuit order accepted the new formulas for his missionaries. The Jesuits, however, reserved the right to send, transfer, and recall missionaries independent of the *Propaganda Fide*.

The *Propaganda Fide* had to rely on the personnel reservoir of the orders to staff the missions, and on the authority of the orders' superiors to implement its authority over the missionaries. In a 1657 memorandum that paints a pessimistic picture of what had been achieved since 1622, the secretary of the congregation, Mario Alberizzi, could not help but acknowledge the continuing importance of the regular clergy for missionary recruitment. The unity of organization and governance in the orders led to shared attitudes and interests, which favored their activities. After reluctantly acknowledging their significance, Alberizzi offered an extensive critique of the orders. He accused them of claiming individual missions for themselves alone and excluding other orders or even clerics of the same order but from different provinces, as well as of preventing the ordination of native priests. The picture Alberizzi painted of relations between the *Propaganda Fide* and the orders was similarly negative: while the well-organized orders (especially the Jesuits) obeyed only their own Rule and wished to remain independent of the congregation, in the less strictly organized communities each member sought to live without being subject to the superiors and the Rule. Visitors were no help, Alberizzi said, because it was nearly impossible to find secular priests for this task, and the members of an order were so suspicious of other orders that many were not willing to answer to them. According to Alberizzi, the Curia's attempts to rectify this state of affairs were ineffective because the orders insisted on their privileges and appealed to secular princes.[35]

The Curia's dependence on the regular clergy had already been manifest in Clement VIII's missionary mandate to the Discalced Carmelites. The fact that the pope recruited "his" missionaries in 1604 from the newly founded Italian congregation was met with surprise both within and outside of the order; after all, the reform of the Discalced Carmelites inspired by Teresa of Ávila and Juan de la Cruz was strongly oriented toward a contemplative way of life.[36] The extremely scant personnel resources similarly complicated the deployment of this order for the Persian mission, seeing as in 1604 the Italian congregation could only draw from its convents at Genoa, Rome, and Naples. On the plus side, unlike the established missionary orders, the newly founded congregation of the Discalced Carmelites did not enjoy extensive privileges and was more dependent on papal favor. Together with the orientation toward a largely new mission territory, the choice of the order was symptomatic of the practical limits of the papal claim to primacy.

The Discalced Carmelites: Dysfunctional Institutions and Internalized Discipline

The reorientation toward mission confronted the Discalced Carmelites with new challenges, with regard not only to the order's contemplative orientation but also to its organization. To be sure, the Discalced Carmelites had adopted a constitution from the mendicant orders that connected the individual convents to provinces and oriented the members' affiliation toward the provinces and the overall order. In an order dedicated to withdrawal from the "world" and to a contemplative life in the collective framework of the convents, however, there was no provision for individual members living in tiny communities scattered across vast distances. This, however, was precisely the situation of the Persian mission and subsequent undertakings. In this section, I will therefore explore the efforts to build functioning organizational structures to ensure that the order's scattered members pursued common goals and adopted a shared behavioral code.

The orders were no mere objects of papal policy; rather, they participated actively in the early modern processes of institution building. Thus far, however, research in this field has concentrated on the Society of Jesus. Since historians have not yet studied the governance of the order of the Discalced Carmelites, it seems appropriate here to proceed from studies of the Jesuit order and, based on them, to inquire into the peculiarities of institution building among the Discalced Carmelites.

The missionary mandate in the order's constitutions tasked the Society of Jesus with preserving unity among its members who were dispersed across the world. The constitutions provided for a strictly hierarchical structure and the absolute obedience of members to their superiors.[37] Because of this comparatively centralized structure, its self-understanding of representing an elite, and the integration of contemplation into *actio* in the world, the Society of Jesus has been described as a "'modern' type of order."[38] The controversies surrounding the "monarchical" constitution of the order, which began with the founding of the Society of Jesus,[39] have further contributed to a particular scholarly interest in how it functioned, making the Jesuits the best-studied order by far. What Hartmut Lehmann still characterized as "a kind of absolutist rule in a supranational association of persons,"[40] however, was also subject to the limitations characteristic of early modern rule over long distances more generally, which has led scholars of secular configurations of rulership to abandon the paradigm of absolutism. According to Markus Friedrich's seminal research, local events "could only rarely be simply controlled by regulations and instructions." The superiors remained dependent on the willingness of actors on the ground to cooperate and not to instrumentalize operations to benefit themselves. Not only was the disciplinary power of church actors over the laity restricted, but the internal practice of even the apparently "most modern" order can only be grasped from the perspective of a specifically early modern understanding of authority.[41]

While clear parallels can be drawn to secular configurations of rulership, some characteristics were specific to the ways religious orders functioned: on the one hand, religious orders styled themselves as independent from the worldly obligations that personal networks spawned; on the other, they used specific practices of internalizing values and norms that guided action. Within the Society of Jesus, personal entanglement lacked the legitimacy it possessed in the "world." Even in the Society of Jesus, the bureaucratic procedures of personnel administration, with their declared aim of doing away with the logics of entanglement, nevertheless ran up against obstacles. Personal connections between men from the same region or country played an important role among the Jesuits as well.[42]

Such a dynamic of entanglement, which could weaken the authority of the order's leadership, ran up against order-specific practices for internalizing shared values and norms. The constitutions defined adaptation to place, time, and persons as a guiding principle of the Society of Jesus. Although this left considerable scope for different modes of action, the underlying spiritual foundations and aims were universally binding.[43] The Society met the need to adjust to specific circumstances while preserving the unity of the order by seeking to make members internalize the order's principles through many years of study and the practice of spiritual exercises: in this way, members of the order scattered across the globe were supposed to make their own decisions in the spirit of the order and arrange their lives accordingly. Instead of demanding blind obedience, the superiors were supposed to win over the will of the members, which was rooted in individual conscience.[44] This process contained an inherent tension, however, which we will need to keep in mind.

In comparison to the Jesuits, the conditions and practices of communication within the Discalced Carmelite order have scarcely been studied. Thus far, the literature has focused on the Spanish origins of the Teresian reform, especially on Teresa of Ávila herself,[45] on the beginning of the Italian congregation of the order around 1600,[46] and on the order's French provinces.[47] As a reformed mendicant order, the Discalced Carmelites differed in two respects from the Society of Jesus with regard to the issues addressed here: First, the Teresian reform obligated the Discalced Carmelites not to contemplation in the "world" but to contemplation in withdrawal from the "world." To what extent the papal missionary mandate could be reconciled with this orientation remained a subject of debate on all levels of the order's hierarchy, from the friars in Persia to the order's superiors, as will be discussed in more detail in Chapter 6. Second, while members of the order vowed to strictly observe the communal rules, which restricted their individual scope of action, the competences of the superiors remained tied to the congregation (represented in the General Chapter) and those of the *praepositus generalis* to the *Definitorium generale*. Thus, for the Discalced Carmelites, the question of the extent of the duty to obey and the limits of "absolute" authority arises in the context of the communal participation of all members rather than in that of "proxyship," as was the case with the Jesuits.

These considerations lead to the questions that will occupy us in what follows: Were there similar signs of evolution toward a functional hierarchization and centralization of decision-making among the Discalced Carmelites? What role did calls by the Roman Curia to reform the regular clergy play in this? Following upon the research on the Society of Jesus discussed above, questions also arise regarding order-specific disciplining practices among the Discalced Carmelites. To what extent was external discipline exerted through subordination and control in institutional structures supplemented by attempts to influence individual behavior by internalizing the order's specific mission? Did the internalization of the community's values and norms lead to unwanted dynamics of self-empowerment that could unfold particularly in a mission setting?

From a Community-Based to a "Monarchical" Form of Governance?

Inspired by mendicant orders, the Discalced Carmelites blended network-based governance with communal forms of governance, in which the chapters served as the focus of decision-making on various levels—the convent, the province, and the order. Officeholders were not only obliged to listen to advice from the friars but also required to seek their consent on a number of matters, as well as to submit to the chapters, which assessed their performance.[48] To a far greater degree than in other orders of the confessional age, especially the Jesuits, the prerogatives of the order's leadership thus remained tied to the will of the entire community. In the case of the mendicants, the rejection of a "monarchical" form of governance signified the dedication to poverty and humility and the rejection of worldly markers of social distinction. The return to these values was at the heart of efforts to reform the mendicant orders founded in the Middle Ages, and this included the Teresian reform of the Carmelite order. The constitutions of the Discalced Carmelites correspondingly also restricted the use of the honorific titles that helped to establish internal hierarchies of rank in other orders. Officeholders remained friars; ideally, what set them apart from other members of the order was merely the functions they performed and not any particular quality of rank.

The General Chapter was considered the highest embodiment of the community, and consisted of the superiors, the provincials, and two elected representatives of each province of the order. Between 1605 and 1743—with a brief interruption between 1665 and 1671—it met every three years and thereafter every six years. Until 1703, the missions were also, in theory, supposed to be represented in the General Chapter, but in practice special regulations were in place that will be described below. The *praepositus generalis* and the definitors, who oversaw the order's everyday activities, were elected by the General Chapter for terms of just three years between 1605 and 1743 (except between 1665 and 1671); before and after that, they served six-year terms. In 1611, the order revoked the possibility of a one-time reelection of a *praepositus generalis* immediately following his term in office.

Apart from the short terms of office of the superiors, additional competences helped make the General Chapter rather than the *praepositus generalis* or the definitors the highest decision-making body: according to the constitutions, it was the General Chapter that was invested with the ultimate power to decide on the founding and dissolving of missions, provinces, and convents; to enact, revise, and interpret the constitutions; and to make additional resolutions that would remain in force until the next General Chapter took over. While among the Jesuits, the participants in the General Congregation—comparable to the General Chapter of the Discalced Carmelites—were primarily responsible for conveying information, among the Discalced Carmelites the procurators participated directly in the decision-making processes thanks to the competences of the General Chapter.

In this respect, the contrast with the Society of Jesus could scarcely have been greater: among the Jesuits, the General Congregation elected the general not for three or six years but for life. Also unlike the Discalced Carmelites, the Jesuit constitutions expressly stated that General Congregations were to be convoked as rarely as possible and, as a rule, only to elect the general of the order upon the death of his predecessor. This corresponded to the imperatives of what was practically possible under the communicative conditions of the early modern period, but it also reflected a self-image in which the individual members of the order were subject to an extensive functional hierarchy with an eye to the "greater glory of God." While the superior general of the Jesuits, after election to a lifetime position, became the "starting point of all power within the order," the *praepositus generalis* of the Discalced Carmelites remained bound by the resolutions of the General Chapter, which met regularly. Not only did the General Chapter make major policy decisions, for example regarding the orientation of the Italian congregation toward the missions, which any Chapter could then challenge again; the General Chapter also consulted on individual cases that were sent to Rome from the various mission settlements. Moreover, the *praepositus generalis* was not a single monarchical authority, as was the case with the general of the Society of Jesus, but was instead integrated into the collective decision-making body of the *Definitorium generale*, whose members were part of the order's leadership and accordingly, like the general of the order, became the addressees of correspondence from the settlements far from Rome.[49]

Such structures clashed with the papacy's skepticism about collegial forms of church governance and the increasing efforts of the Roman Curia to subject the regular clergy to its directives and, to this end, to strengthen the authority of the orders' superiors. These efforts were justified in terms of the necessity to rectify abuses and enforce observance, and began with the reform decrees of the Council of Trent and the establishment of a specialized curial congregation by Sixtus V (*Congregatio super consultationibus regularium,* later the *Congregatio episcoporum et regularium*/Congregation of Bishops and Regulars).[50] Viewed from this standpoint, the Society of Jesus rather than the mendicant orders was considered a well-governed community, even by those who disapproved of the Jesuits' independence from the curial congregations. Although the founding of the Discalced Carmelites was in itself a response to calls for a reform of the regular clergy, starting in the mid-seventeenth century the order came under increasing pressure to adapt its government to a "monarchical" model.

The aim of better governance legitimized papal interventions in the working of internal decision-making processes, as is evident from the conflicts surrounding the extension of the tenure of the *praepositus generalis* and the definitors from three to six years. This measure was intended to strengthen the position of the superiors at the expense of the General Chapter, which would now only convene every six years. Although Alexander VII, who sought to bolster the spiritual power of the papacy after his election as a candidate of the so-called *squadrone volante*, had already made this demand, it was only under Benedict XIV (1740–58) that it could assert itself in the long term against resistance within the order. Benedict XIV encouraged the extension of tenure as part of a reform of the regular clergy by gathering representatives of the order and asking them to devote serious thought to the measure. He mentioned the possibility of acting based on the authority of his office but formally allowed the order's own decision-making process to take its usual course. The General Chapter followed the papal recommendation with forty-eight of fifty-four votes.[51] Still, the Discalced Carmelites' form of government remained much less "monarchical" than the government of other orders. In the case of the Dominicans, for instance, the reforms adopted in the seventeenth century meant that, with very few exceptions, the General Chapter was only convened to elect the master general to his lifetime position, making this old order much more similar to the modern Jesuits.[52]

The Missions as Sites of Particular Law

The extension of tenure to six years did not simply correspond to the tendency toward a functional hierarchization of the orders' governance as a means of enforcing observance. It was also a response to changes in the order of the Discalced Carmelites since the establishment of the Italian congregation under Clement VIII: the congregation, initially limited to Genoa and Rome, turned into a network composed of various provinces across the whole of Catholic Europe except for the Spanish monarchy, as well as several missions in Persia, India, and Palestine, in addition to territories under Protestant rule in Europe. Accordingly, attendees of the General Chapter had to undertake long and costly journeys. This also meant that the provincials and their *socii*, or the procurators of the missions, were torn from their convent communities for several weeks or months (or, in the case of Persia and India, for well over a year), and were thus largely prevented from cultivating those practices of a contemplative life deemed essential for a Discalced Carmelite. Such structures were dysfunctional for both practical and spiritual reasons. As a consequence, the procurators of the missions in the Orient were present at just six of the thirty-one General Chapters held between 1608 and 1701. In 1703, the *Definitorium generale* therefore resolved that the missions in Persia and India should no longer send procurators and *substituti* to the General Chapter. Two other measures adopted at the same time show that, these spiritual concerns notwithstanding, the main aim was to strengthen the authority of the order's superiors: on the one hand, the priors of the convents at Isfahan and Goa would thenceforth no longer be elected by the conventuals but rather appointed by the *praepositus generalis*, and on the other, the definitors obliged the provincial vicars in Persia and India to adhere to the ratio stipulated by the *Definitorium generale* when distributing subsidies to the various settlements.[53]

The resolutions of 1703 marked the culmination of a long-term process that had steadily increased the *praepositus generalis* and the *Definitorium generale*'s competences in the governance of the missions. In 1620, the need to adapt to local circumstances had already caused the General Chapter to grant the *Definitorium generale* the competence to offer dispensations from the constitutions and to award the provincial vicar in Persia a corresponding *facultas* that surpassed his ordinary jurisdiction.[54] This meant that the governance of the missions was in large part transferred to the definitors and the general of the order and that the provincial vicar appointed by the *Definitorium generale* and later the *praepositus generalis* gained more power at the expense of the convent community. These adjustments ran counter to the general norms of the order, for which reason the General Chapter hesitated to bow to the exigencies of the situation. In 1638 it extended the authorization from Persia to Goa and the entire mission to the Orient.[55]

However, the fact that until 1703—despite the very obvious dysfunctionality of the practice—the order demanded that the missions in Persia and India be represented by a procurator of their own at the General Chapter reveals the great degree to which the Discalced Carmelites considered collective decision-making, and therefore the requirement that all settlements be represented at the General Chapter, to be a cherished characteristic of their order. Critics had repeatedly pointed out the disadvantages of having to send a procurator to the General Chapter.

What all attempts at rectifying the obvious dysfunctionality of the order's constitution ultimately had in common was their confirmation of the missions' specificity as sites of particular law. By empowering the *Definitorium generale* to grant dispensations from the constitutions on a case-by-case basis and granting the corresponding *facultas* to the provincial vicar in Persia, the General Chapter distanced itself from a form of governance in which the chapters played a leading role as decision-making bodies on various levels. This development was completed with the decisions of the definitors in 1703, when all forms of representation of the missions at the General Chapter were abolished and the authority to appoint priors was removed from the convent community and transferred to the *praepositus generalis*. Does this mean that we can speak of central control? As I will show, the decision signaled instead a shift on the local level from the convent community to an appointed officeholder, who for his part acted locally. At the same time, the abolition of representation at the General Chapter curtailed a possible connection with Rome.

From Election to Appointment from Above: Provincial Vicars and Priors

Until 1703, the missions of the Discalced Carmelites were headed both by an official appointed by the superiors—the provincial vicar—and by the priors who were elected by the local convent communities. In what follows, we will begin by exploring the relationship between the provincial vicar and the convent communities, then trace the path from the election of the priors to their appointment by the superiors of the order. In both cases, we need to ask about the significance attributed to the participation of the convent communities in the governance of the order. This challenged the acceptability of "absolute" forms of rule in a community shaped by both its members' duty of obedience and the grounding of authority in the order's laws.

The provincial vicar for Persia and India was responsible for important aspects of the order's governance, particularly decisions regarding the transfer of clerics between the different settlements, the administration of their finances, and negotiations with the court in Isfahan. He was initially appointed by the *Definitorium generale*, and beginning in 1638 by the *praepositus generalis*. Following the customs of the order, his term of office was short—three years—but was often extended for a second term. The provincial vicar usually lived in Isfahan, but he was also responsible for the other settlements in Persia and until 1689 those in India, which had been founded from Isfahan. The provincial vicariate, which despite relevant efforts never became its own province of the order, was itself composed of two priories, Goa and Isfahan. The latter in turn comprised additional settlements in Shiraz and Basra. Because of the enormous distances between the settlements, however, the provincial vicar could not exert the authority of his office both in Persia and in India at the same time. The *Definitorium generale* took the necessary measures in 1689, when it instructed the *praepositus generalis* to appoint two provincial vicars in the future, one for Persia and another for India.[56]

In an order that made important decisions dependent on the consent of the community of the order, the wide-ranging competences of the provincial vicar clashed with those that the priors, subpriors, and *discreti*—officeholders who in the seventeenth century were mainly elected by the conventuals—had claimed for themselves. Whether this led to conflicts or resulted in some kind of rapprochement depended upon the personalities of the parties involved as well as the circumstances. For example, in 1657 the prior of the convent of Isfahan, Denis de la Couronne d'Épines, brought his complaints about the provincial vicar at the time, Felice di Sant'Antonio, before the definitors and the *praepositus generalis*. Friar Denis's arguments and the resolution of the order's leadership show that even officeholders remained members of the community dedicated to poverty and humility and were expected to adjust their leadership style and way of life accordingly. It was unacceptable for the provincial vicar to separate himself from his confreres by particular signs of social distinction. According to the prior, the provincial vicar ruled "absolutely" and did not maintain "the poverty and humility" cultivated by his predecessors. Even in the city he rode on horseback, accompanied by a servant.[57] In light of the provincial vicar's "all-too absolute and despotic mode of rule," the superiors should send a visitor to restore order.[58]

The administration of the convents' finances also gave rise to complaints against the provincial vicar. The constitutions of the order set strict limits on superiors' competences in this regard, stipulating that the convent chapter had to be consulted for any larger expenses. Did the power of disposal over all assets of the missions in Isfahan, Shiraz, and Basra lie with the provincial vicar, as Friar Felice had ordered when he was still visitor general before taking over this very office? To be sure, Denis de la Couronne d'Épines argued that "fairness and reason" favored sharing worldly assets among all the houses. This should, however, be arranged in such a way that no individual had "full and absolute power over everything."[59] Although the *Definitorium generale* on several occasions affirmed the competence of the provincial vicar to transfer assets from one settlement to another, it now supported the prior rather than the provincial vicar: in 1658 it admonished the vicar to distribute the subsidies immediately after receiving them according to the needs of the various settlements, retaining for himself only the sum needed to cover his travel expenses. He needed to account for this distribution to his successor as visitor general and provincial vicar, a practice that had apparently not always been followed up to that point.[60] The definitors thus used the complaints to more clearly establish the subordination of local officeholders to the order's leadership as well as their ties to the convent community. This was also a decision against the "absolute" rule that had given rise to complaints against the provincial vicar.

The participation of the convent community in the governance of the order was also expressed in the manner in which the elections of the prior and subprior were organized up to 1703. In 1620, the definitors had decided that the prior of the convent of Isfahan should be elected by the conventuals.[61] Henceforth, the matter of the extent to which the friars who did not live in Isfahan (or Goa) were authorized or obliged to participate in the elections became a topic of discussion. In 1630, the *Definitorium generale* determined that they, too, belonged to the two convents in Isfahan and Goa, where they enjoyed the passive franchise and, when sojourning there, also the active franchise.[62]

In 1703, the *Definitorium generale* transferred the authority to appoint the prior of the Isfahan and Goa convents to the *praepositus generalis*, the same person who already had the authority to appoint the provincial vicar. This decision was, nevertheless, not simply a response to difficulties with the practical implementation of rules that were oriented toward the geographically circumscribed conditions of the time of the Italian congregation's founding and not toward mission. In fact, it also signaled a decisive step toward a constitution in which subaltern actors were instructed to participate by means of petition. The governance of the order was thus aligned with models favoring the kind of functional hierarchy and central control that already prevailed in other orders. When the missionaries in Persia learned of the new arrangement, they issued an objection to the appointment of their prior by the *praepositus generalis*, though without success. According to the *Definitorium generale*, this was a wise decision by the General Chapter, which it neither could nor wished to alter.[63] Rule from a distance remained an illusion under early modern conditions, however, if it did not garner at least some measure of acceptance from those affected by it. When appointment by the order's leadership replaced election by the conventuals, this did not prevent the men so appointed from using their remaining leeway on the ground independently. Such dynamics are evident in the Persian missions in connection with the dispatch of visitors, who were sent to check on the subordinate officeholders' conduct of office and the way of life of the conventuals. That is why I will look more closely at the visitations here.

The Uses of Visitation

In their various guises, visitations were part of the usual arsenal of early modern rule from afar in secular and ecclesiastical contexts.[64] In both cases, visitors were generally assigned extensive powers. Among the Discalced Carmelites, the visitor had the right and the duty to inspect all relevant documents, question convent members about adherence to the order's constitutions, record complaints of violations, and admonish the guilty and impose suitable penances. The visitor was required to report especially severe breaches to the *Definitorium generale*. The definitors sent the first visitor to Persia in 1620. The *praepositus generalis* instructed him, and later visitors, to pass on information from Rome, end abuses, and keep the leadership of the order apprised of local conditions. The directives the visitors composed at the end of the visitation were known as *ordinationes*. Proceeding from the instructions received, these covered a wide range of problems. The *ordinationes* thus corresponded, on the one hand, to specific standpoints in the debates conducted in the broader context of the order—especially on the question of the relationship between *contemplatio* and *actio*; on the other hand, they were the outcome of personal contacts between the visitor and the people he met on the ground.

Despite the extensive competences of the visitors, there was no lack of misgivings about their efficacy. In his *Relazione delle Quattro Parti del Mondo* of 1629–31, Francesco Ingoli accused the commissioners whom the superiors had entrusted with visiting the orders' settlements in Asia of abusing their expansive competences and engaging in simony by selling appointments and the spiritual graces granted to them.[65] The missionaries also raised objections. Beginning in the 1630s, visitors general were frequently given the office of provincial vicar following completion of their visitation.

Under these conditions, the visitors could use their *ordinationes* to influence the orientation of their own future conduct of office. This led to conflicts with the convent community, as we saw in the case of Felice di Sant'Antonio, who as provincial vicar was accused of taking excessive liberties with the finances entrusted to him. The right length of the sojourn was key. If a visitor had no previous connection to the settlement he visited and remained there only a short time, he was vulnerable to accusations of making decisions without sufficient knowledge of the local situation. Other criticisms, in contrast, referred to excessively long sojourns by visitors. Stays of several years in a convent, which occasionally occurred, represented an additional financial burden on already-underfunded settlements.

Much like local actors in secular contexts, the missionaries used the communication channels established by their superiors, including the visitors' reports, to further their own interests. Intervention in local affairs by visitors from outside awakened fears among those whose position meant they had something to lose, and expectations among those who had lost out in local conflicts. While some accused the visitors of lacking local knowledge, others may have placed hopes in their impartiality and nonentanglement in the local context. Those unwilling to accept the outcome of a visitation and the visitor's *ordinationes* could still plead their case in letters to the *praepositus generalis* and the *definitores*. In many instances, the visitations accordingly did not resolve local controversies but rather transferred them to a higher level. In that case, those who could mobilize connections in Rome to support their viewpoint were in the better position.

The archives of the *Curia generalizia* contain a number of correspondences that provide insights into the dynamics of a visitation. If the friars had differences, the visitor was ideally supposed to arbitrate and reconcile the parties. In practice, each side sought to win over the visitor. If they succeeded, they were sure to arouse the disapproval of those who had lost out, who might then appeal to the order's superiors in Rome. While from the Roman perspective the visitations served to investigate local life in the order, they also created channels of communication that clerics on the ground could use to convey their own issues to Rome. Thus, when the visitor, Vicente de San Francisco, arrived in Isfahan in 1621, he received a memorandum in which, alongside requests for books and devotional items, the local friars listed matters that had previously met with little response from Rome.[66] The friars also associated the arrival of a visitor with the hope of overdue subsidies or other financial support. When this failed to materialize or the visitation lasted too long, they experienced it as a financial burden. Complaints about this implied a more or less explicit criticism of the outlays that a visitor had caused, in contravention of the spirit of the order's constitutions. In 1661, the provincial vicar, Felice di Sant'Antonio, complained that instead of promoting the missions, the visitor sent by the superiors had done nothing but stir up unrest and play the fiscal official. With his fiery temper and lack of experience, he had sent only ominous reports to his superiors and at the same time spent hundreds of *scudi* that belonged to the mission.[67] While we know that the visitor was supposed to test the abovementioned complaints about the provincial vicar's financial conduct, it is understandable that the vicar would seek to discredit him precisely on that point.

The outcome of visitations depended largely on whether and how the visitors were integrated into the local context. Like a nonlocal commissioner dealing with secular officeholders, the visitor of an order could do little if the communities closed ranks against him and demonstrated their observance of the Rule. Matters were different when the friars were on bad terms with each other and sought to gain support for their various positions. This was just what Girolamo di Gesù Maria did as provincial vicar in 1675, when he requested that the leadership of the order recall unwanted fellow friars. Because it was so difficult to gain insights into conditions on the ground from faraway Rome, his report, delivered by the procurator of missions in Persia along with the visitor general's account, was intended to put the superiors in a position to safeguard "peace" and "observance" in the missions.[68] Armed with local "knowledge," a visitor sent from outside could execute the commission of the superiors. Faced with the reports and *ordinationes*, which sanctioned particular positions in conflicts on the ground, all that remained for the defeated party—in this case Ange de Saint-Joseph, whom the prior pushed to resign from his office—was to petition the superiors he knew.

Beyond individual cases, it is difficult to judge how efficient the visitations were as instruments of the order's superiors. What is striking is that many complaints in the *ordinationes* were repeated over decades, as we will see in more detail below: breaches of the rules in connection with contacts to the court or "friendship" and "good correspondence" with the laity; the use of symbols of social distinction, e.g., horses and servants; and the all-too-worldly business dealings that secured the continued material existence of the settlements.[69] "Laws that are not enforced"[70] were not just a structural characteristic of early modern secular administrations. Yet the orientation of the religious orders toward transcendental values lent the obedience of their members a specific quality, which we need to keep in mind in comparisons with secular configurations of rulership.

Internalized Discipline and Self-Empowerment

As instruments of rule from afar, the institutional structures of the order of the Discalced Carmelites proved largely dysfunctional within the situation created by the papal missionary project. The tiny communities in Asia could not be governed by the same rules as the order's convents in Europe. Neither could members of the community participate from Asia in decisions about the order's affairs within the General Chapter, nor did the order's leadership possess the means to intervene more than selectively in the functioning of the settlements in Persia and India. If the Discalced Carmelites in Persia nevertheless acted as members of their order and despite integration into diverse local contexts remained true to the order as such, it was not because of efficient institutional structures. The question of which factors maintained cohesion within the order must be posed differently, especially with respect to the missions. Apart from the forms of personal interconnection, which played a central role in secular processes of political integration, we need to turn our attention above all to those practices through which norms were internalized to such a degree that a member of the order knew what to do in a particular situation, even if far away from the watchful eyes of superiors. The techniques of self-examination specific to the order as well as the practices of correspondence served this purpose. Because letters took so long to arrive, correspondence was less effective for coordinating action than for communicating general guidelines and a sense of affiliation, as I will demonstrate below.

Techniques of self-examination and the internalization of norms as factors in the cohesion of religious orders in the early modern period have mainly been studied for the Society of Jesus. With the practice of the spiritual exercises, Ignatius of Loyola provided the members of his order with a means to attain an awareness of their own vocation and to internalize their calling to spread the Christian message to as many souls as possible, wresting them from the banner of Satan and gathering them under the banner of God.[71] The internalization of this calling was intended to put Jesuits in a position to make the right decisions on their own and adapt to varied conditions without losing sight of their actual mission. The exercises thus pursued the aim of "producing an unprecedented degree of internalization of the order's and the Church's specific values and behavioral norms," as Wolfgang Reinhard explains.[72]

The spiritual exercises adapted the practices of contemplation and self-sanctification in poverty and abnegation of the world that the mendicant orders had long cultivated to the specifically Jesuit practice of contemplation in action. The spirituality of the Discalced Carmelites, in contrast, was oriented, in the manner of the late medieval mendicant orders, toward reconciling the demands of the *vita activa* with those of contemplative life in the convent, with the former being subordinate to the latter. This left little room for release from the norms of outward discipline under mission conditions, which in the Jesuit case could be adapted to local requirements and especially to foreign cultural contexts. The tensions between the demands of the *vita contemplativa* and those of *actio* remained correspondingly acute throughout the existence of the Persian missions. It was in this area of tension that the assessment of one's own behavior and that of one's fellow friars operated; conflicts were nearly always described as the results of differing orientations toward the demands of the *vita contemplativa* or *actio*.

Spiritual exercises held similar importance for the Discalced Carmelites as they did for the Jesuits. Despite differences in the orientation of life within the order, the Carmelite form of exercise—inward, silent prayer—may also be understood as a means of internalizing the order's values and norms beyond the constraints of external discipline. The objective of moving from personal gnosis to finding the right path to participate in divine grace was no less central to Discalced Carmelite spirituality. Like the exercises of Ignatius, the daily practice of inward prayer prescribed by Teresa of Ávila was intended to develop the capacity of members of the order to orient their lives toward God through contemplation of Christ's suffering.[73]

The central role that the founders of the Italian congregation of Discalced Carmelites accorded to inward prayer, and to the practice of the *vita contemplativa* more generally, especially in the context of mission, is evident from the instruction that the first provisional head of the congregation, Pedro de la Madre de Dios, offered the members of the order sent to Persia in 1604. He described the long journey as a "practical study of theology." He instructed the missionaries to read the New Testament and speak of it with humility, so that each of the friars could learn from his fellows. At other times they were to speak of the secrets of the faith, so that all would be of one mind as regards their faith and instruction, this being especially important when dealing with infidels. Pedro de la Madre de Dios began the instruction with the admonition to strive during the journey "to acquire the spirit and virtue they are lacking for such a great undertaking." Apart from regular confession and communion, they could achieve this through inward prayer, for which the fathers and brothers, as in the convent, were to reserve one hour each morning and evening. As soon as they approached their destination, they were to reserve time at noon and in the evening to examine their conscience. They were to pray the rosary while doing so. They were to use the rest of their time to give thanks to God, dedicate themselves to other spiritual exercises, and "sometimes speak of the lands, people, and towns they were traveling through to enlighten themselves about everything."[74] In the superior's instructions, the acquisition of secular knowledge about the countries and people was mentioned last and was presented as subordinate to the contemplative aspect of the journey. The journey through the "world," a potential peril to their salvation, was to become a practice that would help the friars arrange their lives in accordance with the order's values and norms.

To summarize: Discipline and the enforcement of norms were social processes which, while building on the constitutions and the competences of the order's officeholders stipulated therein, were in practice supported and thus shaped by the whole community and its individual members. They occurred under the material conditions of the early modern period, which left great scope for the dynamics of local societies. The religious practices and more generally the individual and collective coping strategies by actors on the ground were correspondingly diverse, particularly in the mission field. What could have been regarded as a violation of norms from the standpoint of confessional rules and canon law might be part of societal normality in a non-Catholic environment. This normality makes an appearance in the archival holdings of the orders and curial congregations mainly when outside observers or local actors expressed dissent.

We should not underestimate the factors of inner cohesion that turned the orders into communities able to operate in global contexts despite their clearly dysfunctional institutional structures. If the Discalced Carmelites in Persia—much like the Jesuits in China or other missions well beyond the reach of any secular Christian authority—remained loyal to "their" orders, this was a function not of the efficacy of institutional structures but of the fact that they had internalized their community's values and norms. The efficacy of such processes of internalizing values and norms, which ideally included a willingness to die for the faith, constituted the strength of the religious orders.

By guiding members of the order to examine their consciences and orient themselves toward the service of God, such procedures were at the same time expressions of an individualization process that freed the conscience from external constraints. That is why J. Michelle Molina has underlined the importance of Ignatian spiritual exercises in constituting a new individual beyond the context of the order.[75] Put in such broad terms, the hypothesis requires further empirical scrutiny. What we can say, however, is that among both the Jesuits and the Discalced Carmelites, spiritual exercises aimed to afford the meditator insights into his personal role in God's plan for salvation and to put him in a position to make an individual decision to dedicate his life to serving God.⁷⁶ These practices had the potential to lend transcendental legitimacy to individual behaviors. In no order did this liberation of the individual conscience go as far as it did among the Jesuits, as their roles in the conflicts over the Chinese and Malabar Rites illustrate. Silvia Mostaccio has accordingly described the extent and also the limits of the duty of obedience in the individual conscience of a Christian as a particular quality of Jesuit culture.⁷⁷

Unlike the Jesuits, the Discalced Carmelites played no prominent role in missionary controversies. They did, however, also tend to justify deviant behavior by citing higher values. In the tension between the *vita contemplativa* and *actio*, missionaries from this order also argued that they should be exempted from the rules of strict observance outlined in the order's constitution to enable them to save as many souls as possible. By countering the accusation of deficient observance with the argument that cultural differences might require deviation from apparently fixed norms, they were participating in processes of cultural relativization that will be addressed in more detail below.⁷⁸

When it came to the possibilities for legitimizing deviant behavior, bureaucratic structures like the *Propaganda Fide* were less encumbered by risk than the religious orders. However, they offered nowhere near the integrative potential of the orders as communities of shared values. A lack of institutional resources on the ground meant that the *Propaganda Fide* was a bureaucratic "superstructure" with a limited capacity to enforce norms. As regards the relationship between the Discalced Carmelites and the *Propaganda Fide*, we need to ask in this context how far disobedience toward a curial congregation remained legitimate for members of the order, who legitimized their disobedience precisely by citing their duty to their own community, whose system of values and norms was rooted in the transcendental.

Maintaining Proximity from a Distance

When superiors and curial congregations alike sought to bind subaltern actors to shared goals and behavioral norms, they found themselves faced with the difficulties that geographical distance engendered. Since early modern social relations were overwhelmingly based on personal contacts, missionaries also confronted the problem of how to create and cultivate close personal relationships, at least indirectly, over long distances. The "human media"⁷⁹ that the constitution of the order provided for were only partially equal to the challenge: the visitors were supposed to represent the authority of the superiors but sometimes became the voices of local actors, while participation in the governance of the order within the General Chapter proved impractical for missionaries. Because they were embedded in the local context for long periods, it is difficult to view the local officeholders appointed by the order leadership—the provincial vicars, and, depending on the exact moment in time, the priors—as efficient instruments in long-distance relationships. For that reason, written correspondence became the primary medium for cultivating relationships between the superiors and clerics on the ground. We will therefore begin by examining the instrumental and symbolic aspects of written correspondence. In the second section of this subchapter, the interpersonal dimension of the letter takes us to the question of practices for cultivating personal relationships.

Conditions and Practices of Correspondence

Letters facilitated contacts between missionaries abroad, the leadership of the order, and the Curia. They fulfilled a variety of functions, in which instrumental and symbolic aspects were closely intertwined. Letters conveyed information, but especially in the case of correspondence within orders, it would be shortsighted to reduce our analysis to their contents alone. In the Society of Jesus, regular correspondence, standardized in its external form, style, and content by the *formula scribendi*, equally served to strengthen the sense of belonging among members scattered across the globe. The "edifying letters" in particular served this purpose, with their processing in the form of the *litterae annuae* being, according to Markus Friedrich, "an eminently bureaucratic process that in many cases resorted to the ... routines and procedures of administrative communication."[80] In the case of the Discalced Carmelites, too, the question of how order-specific role models were conveyed both internally and externally takes us from the letters of members and the use of reports by superiors (for instance in relations with the Curia) to the publication of individual accounts and the preparation of histories of the Persian mission as part of the order's broader history.[81]

In all of these processes, as Markus Friedrich has stressed for the Jesuits in Europe, "systemic limits" fundamentally restricted "information-based authority," supported by "second-hand information." Even in the Society of Jesus, which was especially consistent in promoting letter writing, the functionality of an information system based on correspondence ran up against constraints: it was tied to the willingness of the order's members to cooperate in generating knowledge. It also proved difficult for the order's understaffed and underfinanced Curia to cope with the flow of information dictated by the *formula scribendi*.[82]

Finally, the letters written by the regular clergy also had an interpersonal dimension that has received far too little attention from scholars up to now. The retreat from the "world," as expressed in the ideal of nonengagement, contrasted with the face-to-face cultures of the early modern period. When studying correspondence within orders, we need to examine the creation of proximity from a distance through letter writing and the cultivation of personal relationships within this normative context. The following remarks thus take us from the instructions of the Discalced Carmelites concerning correspondence to the material conditions of postal communication and the resulting writing techniques, to the question of the cultivation of personal relations between missionaries in Persia and their superiors through the epistolary medium.

The instructions sent along with the missionaries to Persia in 1604 by the first acting head of the Italian congregation of Discalced Carmelites, Pedro de la Madre de Dios, already contained detailed descriptions of the content and practices of dispatching the correspondence that the missionaries were to conduct with their superiors during their journey to and their sojourn in Persia.[83]

As much as they differed from some of the subsequent instructions for visitors with respect to the issue of how far the contemplative way of life should be adjusted to the needs of mission, the authors of the first instructions and the visitors both sought to integrate the far-flung settlements into regular correspondence networks with the leadership of the order. In 1621, the visitor general, Vicente de San Francisco, stipulated that the friars gather every Saturday so that each might report on what he had heard over the course of the week and what had happened to him. One of the friars was to write down anything noteworthy so that this might be sent to Italy at the next opportunity. The *ordinationes* issued by the visitor of 1621, moreover, reveal the intention to keep parallel channels of information open so that alternative assessments and those that might not have been approved by the superiors on the ground might reach Rome. To this end, every friar was to write to the *praepositus generalis* at least twice a year and report on those matters that called for improvement as well as anything relating to the "good governance and progress of the mission." The visitor forbade the superiors of the convents to read these letters even if the friars wished to show them their missives.[84]

Such rules for correspondence gave superiors the opportunity to gain a better picture of conditions on the ground by comparing information of varied provenance. In practice, however, the requirement to report and correspond could create an undesirable dynamic: it was an invitation to bring local conflicts before the superiors of the order and to seek their protection for particular interests. Missionary correspondence thus followed rules that conflicted with the general Rule of the order. For example, the constitutions forbade regular members to compose, send, and receive letters without the consent of their superiors. Similarly, the General Chapter sought to prevent unjustified appeals to the superiors against the judgments of subaltern officeholders.

In an effort to deliberately effect the "double- or multi-stranded nature" of the correspondence, the specific instructions for missionaries recall the Jesuit system of information studied by Markus Friedrich. There, too, the very redundancy of the reports appeared to ensure the appropriateness of the information, while contradictions and deviations represented "an opportunity to test the truth." As to the right to contact the order's superiors, however, a clear contrast emerges: while the Jesuits generally limited the *ius scribendi* of simple members of the Society in order to protect its hierarchical structure,[85] the Discalced Carmelites obliged all missionaries, regardless of whether or not they held office, to report on the state of the missions. Furthermore, contrary to what the constitutions stipulated, the missionaries' correspondence was not to be checked by their immediate superiors. In fact, ordinary missionaries frequently wrote directly to the *praepositus generalis* or individual members of the *Definitorium*. Such practices expressed the involvement of the entire community in its governance.

The correspondence between missionaries on the ground and the superiors of the order was shaped in large part by the material constraints of mail delivery. The order's leadership and the Curia depended on functioning postal services if they wished to guide and coordinate the activities of their subordinates. In their correspondence with the Near East, they could not resort to the services of postal enterprises, which in Europe had significantly accelerated the mail since the sixteenth century. The missions usually lacked the funds to hire the paid couriers used by the trading companies. The mission couriers were the missionaries themselves when they had to travel from one settlement to another or were on their way from or to Rome. In this way, they could also offer postal services to people outside the order, including those of other confessions, and in return could expect them to take their letters along when necessary.[86] In part, however, the missions depended on highly unreliable middlemen to dispatch their mail: in the early 1660s in Isfahan, where the Jesuits had only recently arrived, they sometimes even had to resort to their greatest rivals, the Capuchins, to deliver their letters.[87]

In the best-case scenario, for instance when letters were delivered directly by missionaries traveling through the Ottoman Empire by land, mail between Rome and Isfahan took a good six months. The problem was not simply the slowness of transport but also uncertainty about whether the letters would ultimately reach their intended destination. Church institutions and trading companies assumed that letters would go missing or that their couriers would suffer excessive delays. For that reason, the VOC sent news of exceptional importance from the Netherlands to the Near East in up to four copies via Marseille, Venice, and Livorno, while the VOC's outposts in Persia generally prepared two or occasionally three copies of each letter.[88] The instructions of the Discalced Carmelites also stipulated that letters be sent in duplicate or triplicate.

Complaints about missing letters from their superiors run through the correspondence of missionaries of various orders. Important news was therefore frequently recapitulated in a series of letters in order to ensure that the information would be conveyed even if individual letters were lost. The importance that senders accorded a piece of information is evident not least from how often they mentioned it in their correspondence when they were unsure of whether the addressee had received it. For example, the letters that the Discalced Carmelite Felice di Sant'Antonio sent to the definitors in 1670 and 1671 revolved continually and in very similar formulations around a single topic, in this case his claim that the election of Ange de Saint-Joseph as prior of the convent of Isfahan was invalid. In this context, Friar Felice repeated with similar frequency his complaint that there were too few missionaries.[89] Alexandre de Rhodes even treated the existential matter of the transfer of the returns from the endowment capital of the Jesuit mission in Isfahan and of the endowment capital itself from France to Persia with tireless insistence in nearly all of the letters he wrote to the general of his order between 1656 and 1660. His later letters summarize the most significant contents in such a way that the addressee could understand them without any knowledge of the previous letters.[90]

If unexpected situations arose that the existing normative texts did not consider, the missionaries were left to make their own judgments. Delays in information exchange created an argument for demanding that superiors on the ground should be given the competences needed to facilitate speedy action; if they were not granted such authority, the insufficiencies of correspondence provided an excuse for unauthorized practices. Since two years could pass before an answer arrived from Rome, the Discalced Carmelite Felice di Sant' Antonio argued, he as provincial vicar should be permitted, with the consent of the prior of the convent of Isfahan and the two most senior missionaries, to send back to Europe "those who disturbed the peace and quiet of the missions." The occasion for this suggestion was a freshly arrived missionary who had by all accounts refused to demonstrate the requisite obedience and in particular to stay anywhere that wine was not available in profusion.[91] After consulting with the oldest friars, the provincial vicar eventually sent the missionary in question back to Italy without waiting for an answer from Rome.[92]

If letters were of limited use as a means of effectively coordinating actions on the ground, why did all participants nevertheless invest such effort in cultivating regular correspondence? Under the circumstances, correspondence served primarily as a means of rendering account. Letter writers tried to interpret their actions in the local context in accordance with the norms that they shared with the addressees. The symbolic meaning of the letters as signs of the fulfillment of duty and devotion by subordinates, and protection and concern on the part of superiors, thus trumped their function as media for conveying information and for preparing decisions by the order's superiors. On an instrumental level, the absence of replies challenged the missionaries' dependence on their superiors. On a symbolic level, the lack of correspondence was considered a disheartening expression of weakened affiliation with a shared "body," as the Jesuit Aimé Chézaud put it.[93] The Discalced Carmelite Ange de Saint-Joseph made a similar argument: experience showed that in the minds of their superiors, the missionaries "practically lived in a different world." In three years in Isfahan, they had received just two letters from the superiors of their order.[94] Among the regular clergy, too, a masterly example of the epistolary art was deemed a sign of the labor and effort invested in cultivating relationships. In an early modern culture of gift exchange, unanswered letters were accordingly interpreted as a failure to respond to the services missionaries performed through their informational letters and consultation of their superiors. As signs of a lack of respect, they also reduced the social capital of honor of those compelled to wait in vain for a reply.[95]

The Cultivation of Personal Relationships

Letters served not only to convey information that was important from an instrumental standpoint for senders and addressees alike. Information, as well as the media used to communicate it—letters or people who delivered them personally to the recipient— also contributed to the creation and particular configuration of relationships. Early modern people capable of writing therefore sent many letters that appear insubstantial at first sight and yet were highly relevant from the symbolic perspective of cultivating relationships.[96] To what extent did this also apply in the context of religious orders, where the expected renunciation of the "world" manifested itself in an ideal of nonengagement? More than other communities, the Discalced Carmelites understood entry into the order as a profound break with the commitments of personal relationships in the "world." The symbol for retreat from one's worldly family was relinquishing one's family name and, in most cases, also one's baptismal name.[97] But how far did social practice correspond to the ideals of the order? Did renunciation also apply to personal relations in the context of the order itself? According to Adriano Prosperi, families whose sons entered the Society of Jesus could regard this as the definitive loss of a family member, which resulted in conflicts between the family and the order.[98] Studies less dependent on internal documents of the order suggest that this finding was not universally applicable: sons of the Borromeo family who entered the Theatine order continued to be integrated into the strategies of the family, which since the time of

Carlo Borromeo had relied in particular on the symbolic and material resources of the Church.[99] Parents and siblings of a Jesuit engaged in missionary activity could also use his service to elevate the reputation of their kinship network.[100]

Repeated resolutions by the General Chapter and the definitors of the Discalced Carmelites in opposition to members of the order having recourse to persons from outside the order also reveal the importance accorded to the break with worldly entanglements and the perception of such entanglements as a looming threat to the life of the order. One of the questions that the visitors to the Discalced Carmelites were expected to ask the priors and friars referred to possible kinship obligations.[101] In 1644, the General Chapter forbade members on pain of excommunication *latae sententiae* to seek the protection of princes and other persons outside the order in matters affecting the life of the community.[102] By 1623, the General Chapter had, conversely, forbidden the definitors, the procurator general, priors, and all other members of the order from attending to the business of persons from outside the order in Rome without the permission of the *praepositus generalis* or the most senior definitors.[103] Both decisions were subsequently affirmed regularly by the General Chapter. In the second half of the seventeenth century, measures within the order were propelled forward by papal efforts to strengthen discipline and observance, which also targeted the mobilization of protectors from outside the order in internal matters.[104]

While we could easily add to the list of such measures, it is difficult to grasp the social practice of personal entanglement, the significance of which is suggested by the repeated resolutions of the order's leadership and the Curia. The remarks that follow should therefore be understood as an initial approach to the problem. Based on a series of episodes, we will first address relationships in the "world." Then we shall turn our attention to the role of correspondence in cultivating personal relationships within the order.

As we will see below, national affiliations played an important role in structuring relations between clerics and laypeople. In early eighteenth-century Isfahan it was not just French Capuchins and Jesuits but also Discalced Carmelites of French origin who, because of their national affiliation, cooperated with the envoys of the king of France at the Safavid court.[105] There is, in contrast, only very occasional evidence that kinship ties affected the Persian missions of the Discalced Carmelites. The following case, however, seems to suggest that this may be a distortion that owes more to the nature of the available sources than reality. In 1712, the Discalced Carmelite Chérubin de Sainte-Thérèse, a native of the diocese of Lyon, used his position to assist a number of his close relatives, who were wealthy merchants, in their efforts to intensify French trade with Persia. The beneficiaries included his brothers, brothers-in-law, and nephews who were active in trade and, as citizens of Lyon, in some cases also held municipal office. Following the custom of his day, the family was to send some younger members, nephews of the Discalced Carmelite, to the Near East as commercial agents. The suggestion survives, tellingly enough, neither in a letter penned by the friar himself nor in the internal correspondence of the order, but instead in a letter from the coadjutor of the bishop of Babylon to the superior of the *Séminaire des Missions étrangères*.[106]

Moreover, kinship ties also existed between individual members in the Persian missions of the Discalced Carmelites. In the case of Sebastiano di Santa Margherita, such relationships affected the performance of his office as bishop of Isfahan, since he was accompanied at his various domiciles on the Persian Gulf by his brother Giacinto di Santa Teresa, also a Discalced Carmelite. In 1755, at the death of the bishop who had appointed him as his vicar general, Friar Giacinto took possession of not only the man's personal effects, but also his pontifical regalia. The order's superiors submitted a list of three possible successors to the *Propaganda Fide*, including his brother, who, however, was only third on the list. The curial congregation for its part categorically rejected such a succession, since the Council of Trent and canon law detested "any impression of hereditary succession" in ecclesiastical benefices "and even more so in episcopal office."[107] The successor to Sebastiano di Santa Margherita, Cornelio di San Giuseppe, also a Discalced Carmelite, took on Cesario di Sant'Antonio, a nephew who belonged to the order, as his secretary in 1773, that is, after his return to Italy. His *Memorie* show that, back in his native Lombardy, he attended important family events, especially weddings and funerals. As bishop he even had access to his own financial resources to assist his relatives. For example, he topped up the dowry of a second-degree niece with 3,000 *lire*, retaining the annual interest of 4 percent for himself for the rest of his life.[108]

While the deployment of kinship relations is rarely documented, a study of internal correspondence in the Discalced Carmelite order shows that here, too, letters played a central role in cultivating personal relationships. As in the "world," the meaning of many letters can be understood only in terms of their existence and form rather than their contents. Letters of congratulation on the occasion of an appointment or election were sent not only by convent communities but also by individual friars on their own behalf. In 1630, a Discalced Carmelite told the general newly elected in 1629 that he had written to him via various routes, and although the letters contained nothing substantial, he would be disappointed to learn that they had not arrived, since he had wanted to let him know of his pleasure at the news of his election.[109] Discalced Carmelites who had affairs pending in Rome often wrote to individual members of the leadership whose personal ties led them to expect a positive response to their requests. In 1621, Juan Thadeo de San Eliseo asked his former companion Paolo Simone di Gesù Maria, who had become a *definitor* of his order, to be "a good advocate of the [Persian] mission," for he was "its foundation stone" and was "obligated to aid it with his blood and his life."[110]

Upon entering the order, the friars were supposed to leave the obligations of national and regional allegiances behind them. In practice, however, this form of personal entanglement seems to have enjoyed the greatest acceptance within religious orders. Contrary to the stated aim of dislodging the logics of entanglement, in the Society of Jesus the assistants of the provinces in Rome became intermediaries between their compatriots and the general of the order. Thus, Aimé Chézaud corresponded from Isfahan with the *praepositus generalis* and the *assistant de France* in Rome, attributing to the latter a mediating role with the general of the order. The Discalced Carmelites had no office on the leadership level comparable to that of the assistants. When it came to forging close personal relationships in distant Rome, however, national and regional relationships were central here, too. The Discalced Carmelites couched such relationships with their superiors and other trusted individuals in the language of patronage, as the correspondence preserved in the archive of the *Curia Generalizia* in Rome shows. Although the constitutions restricted the use of honorific titles as an expression of retreat from the world, the order-specific affirmation of humility and obedience in the service of God and the Church assumed forms that emphasized devotion to the person of the addressee and thus resembled the secular rhetoric of patronage. When clerics referred to themselves as their superiors' "most humble servants and sons in Christ," they not only lived up to the self-image of the order but also described their personal status toward the recipient in the specific situation.

In 1678–9, the Discalced Carmelite Fortunato di Gesù Maria wrote a letter to the procurator general of the order to complain about the most recent *ordinationes* of a visitor but also to apply for permission to return to Europe. He did so using the terms "grace" and "favor."[111] Having received no reply, in late April 1682 he petitioned the provincial of his Sicilian home province, Bernardo Maria di Gesù, of whose election he had just been informed. He combined his congratulations as a "son" of this province to his "prelate and father" with the request that the provincial might aid him with his prayers and his petition to the *praepositus generalis* and the General Chapter of the order, so that he might be granted permission to return. At the same time, he promised to serve the province "as a son" with all of his might and to remain indebted to the provincial as his "servant." In a letter of the same date, Friar Fortunato complained to the procurator general that he had received no reply to his letters from any of the superiors of the order. At the end of September 1682, the friar reminded the provincial of his request to enable him to return to his home province. In a letter to the procurator general written at that same time, he reiterated his complaint about the lack of response from the superiors of the order, which left him with the impression that they had given up on the mission.[112]

After Bernardo Maria di Gesù was himself elected procurator general of the order in May 1683, Friar Fortunato once again resorted to mentioning their regional bond: the election contributed to the "glory" of the province of the order and the "honor" of the Kingdom of Sicily. Friar Fortunato combined congratulations to his compatriot with a request that the procurator general might seek to obtain permission for him to return. Europe offered more opportunities to serve the order than "these idle countries of Barbarians." The new procurator general had already provided him with so many pieces of evidence of "favor and grace," which he would never forget.[113] About four months later, another letter to the procurator general from his home province followed, with the aim of obtaining proof of "his grace and favor." By appealing to their shared origins, Friar Fortunato now sought both to mobilize the protection of the definitors against the unpopular prior Élie de Saint-Albert, urging them to send a provincial vicar and visitor after several years of vacancy and to receive permission to return at long last.[114] The fact that the leadership of the order left letters unanswered for years at a time meant that the friars felt themselves abandoned "without any comfort" in "their exile." Friar Fortunato claimed that, as a result, all of them wanted to return to their home provinces; he himself hoped that his compatriot would show him this favor.[115]

Letters could only partially replace the direct personal contact that was considered an especially effective form of communication in the early modern period. In secular contexts, it could, for instance, be advantageous for petitioners to have someone they trusted carry letters to the ministers or the monarch in person.[116] The same applied to friars who wrote to their superiors. This is evident in the archives of the Discalced Carmelites from the parallel correspondence with the *praepositus generalis* and with a *definitor* better known to the petitioner or another member of the order who was believed to have influence over the leadership. After the Discalced Carmelite missions were placed under the jurisdiction of the *Propaganda Fide* in 1655, Casimir Joseph de Sainte-Thérèse in Basra sought permission to return to his province because his vow meant that he owed obedience to the superiors of the order alone. To this end, he wrote to the general of the order and one of the *definitores*, who like him also came from the order's Flemish province and to whom he had already been writing regularly. Friar Casimir Joseph wrote to his compatriot, who had just been confirmed in his office, as a "most humble son and servant," which he wished to remain for the rest of his life. He hoped that his compatriot's favor would help enable him to return home. Casimir Joseph also used his letters to cultivate relationships with other individuals, sending them greetings to this end. One month later, Casimir Joseph wrote again to the general of the order and his compatriot among the definitors; he hoped that he would support his petition "with his protection and authority." Once again, he asked his compatriot to convey greetings to the superiors and confreres he knew in Rome.[117]

The small gifts that missionaries occasionally sent along with letters to the leadership also helped to cultivate these relationships. In the 1650s, the Discalced Carmelite Barnaba di San Carlo regularly corresponded from Basra with Isidore de Saint-Joseph, procurator general of the order from 1647 to 1653 and a *definitor* from 1653 to 1659. Apart from passing on news from India and the Near East, the services he provided to Isidore from the port city of Basra included sending him exotic products such as a balm he had acquired from a Persian traveling to Mecca. As long as he remained in Basra, he would not cease to send Isidore items from India and Persia that were available in the port city. Six small crucifixes along with a letter from Rome were deemed signs that the *definitor* to whom Barnaba had written remembered the poor friar.[118]

When Barnaba di San Carlo held out the promise to transmit information and procure exotic products, he was offering his superior participation in his specific cultural capital as a middleman in foreign lands in a manner reminiscent of the gift-giving practices of consuls, for example.[119] Contrary to their claims to have left the "world" behind upon entering the order, the logics of personal entanglement embedded in an economy of gift exchange influenced the relationships that missionaries cultivated with their leadership through the medium of correspondence. Thus, alongside the administrative and edifying aspects, their correspondence also contained an interpersonal dimension that is no less important for an understanding of the relations between members of the order and their superiors. The correspondences reveal which practices of personal entanglement were considered consistent with the norms of the order: while the national and regional connections made within the context of the order itself were addressed explicitly, relationships that referred to the parties' origins in the "world" can only be extrapolated indirectly.

Conversely, it was considered entirely inappropriate to involve persons from outside the order to obtain favors that affected life in the order. The holdings of the archive of the *Curia Generalizia* accordingly lack any evidence of Discalced Carmelites in Persia trying to draw upon relatives as intermediaries and intercessors with the leadership of the order. Yet this is precisely what Felice di Sant'Antonio did in his dealings with the *Propaganda Fide*, bypassing his superiors in the order. The cleric, known in the "world" as Giuseppe de Cunto, came from a noble Neapolitan family. In 1662 his siblings petitioned the *Propaganda Fide* for the first time to call him back to his province. They asserted that they needed their brother to arbitrate a dispute over an inheritance, a duty frequently fulfilled by regular clerics because of the disinterest in worldly affairs attributed to them. While the *Propaganda Fide* merely acknowledged the request in 1662, another attempt nine years later proved successful. Because Friar Felice had already served the missions in Persia for thirty-seven years, in 1671 his relatives in Naples requested that the *Propaganda Fide* call him back to his home province. The *Propaganda Fide* granted the Discalced Carmelite the corresponding *facultas* and instructed its secretary to see that the order's superiors implemented the decision. Felice di Sant'Antonio faced criticism within the order for his conduct. He sought to defuse it by thanking his superiors for the permission, thus reinterpreting it as a decision made within the order. He regretted that the superiors of the order had not themselves granted permission, as he owed the order far more than he did his kinsmen. Because of the choice to involve the *Propaganda Fide*, the severe lack of missionaries in Persia, and his age, he claimed he was very uncertain about what to do.[120] Permission had been given, however, and in the end, the cleric used it to return to Italy. The leadership of the order had invoked this very danger—that members would seek to gain decisions in their favor from the *Propaganda Fide* "through friends and persons well-disposed to them"—when Pope Alexander VII placed the Discalced Carmelite missions directly under the jurisdiction of the *Propaganda Fide* in 1655. The method adopted by the Neapolitan cleric thus leads us to the question of how the regular clergy cultivated relationships (and not just in personal matters) with a curial congregation that was part of Roman court society and thus followed social norms from which the religious orders expressly distanced themselves.

"Stepmother" or Protectress? Missionaries and the *Propaganda Fide*

The comparatively close ties to the Curia distinguished the Discalced Carmelites' Persian mission from the older missions under the patronage of the Iberian powers. This proximity found expression in the instructions for correspondence that Pedro de la Madre de Dios sent along with the friars as the first acting superior of the Italian congregation in 1604. Their correspondence was to always contain letters to the cardinal-nephew, Pietro Aldobrandini, and Cardinal Cinzio Passeri Aldobrandini, another nephew and confidant of the reigning pope.[121] Discalced Carmelites of the Italian congregation were actively involved in the efforts to establish the *Propaganda Fide* as the curial congregation responsible for the missions.

In fact, among the Persian missions of various orders, only the Discalced Carmelites and, starting in the late seventeenth century, the Dominicans of the Roman reform congregation of Santa Sabina as well, corresponded with the *Propaganda Fide* with any regularity. Assuming that the missionaries' letters implied the symbolic performative acknowledgment of a claim to authority, the differing intensity of the correspondence reflected more or less marked reservations about the curial congregation. The heads of the *Missions étrangères de Paris* accordingly tried to prevent the bishops of Babylon François Picquet and Louis-Marie Pidou de Saint-Olon from corresponding directly with the Roman Curia. Picquet was instructed to send his letters for the *Propaganda Fide* to the procurator of the *Missions étrangères* in Rome rather than directly to the congregation.[122]

The willingness to respond to questions from the *Propaganda Fide* differed widely, and the state of information in the congregation depended upon missionaries' willingness to engage with the body. For example, in 1664 only the Discalced Carmelites responded to the *Propaganda Fide*'s request to the procurators of the various orders for information about the number of missionaries in Isfahan and the possibility of increasing it. The procurator of the Augustinians sent his excuses with the statement that the order had no linguistically qualified priests; the Jesuits did not reply, and as to the Capuchins, the secretary of the *Propaganda Fide* was uncertain about whether they even had a settlement in Isfahan.[123] The fact that since 1693 the *Propaganda Fide* had mainly recommended the Discalced Carmelites of the Italian congregation and in one case a Dominican of the congregation of Santa Sabina to the pope for appointments as bishops of Isfahan was connected to this comparatively close relationship of the two orders to the Curia and led to a further increase in correspondence.

Despite their relative closeness to the Curia, after the founding of the *Propaganda Fide*, the General Chapter and definitors of the Discalced Carmelites affirmed their own jurisdiction with measures of symbolic significance. As early as 1623, the General Chapter resolved that those who went on missions must swear an oath of loyalty to the superiors of the order.[124] The *Definitorium generale* recognized the risk that members of the order could bypass their superiors and turn to the new congregation instead. For that reason, in 1629 it demanded that members of the order could only pursue business with the Curia via the procurator general of the order and with the consent of the general.[125] Vehement criticism of the *Propaganda Fide* and the Roman Curia more generally crystallized around Alexander VII's 1655 resolution to place the order's missions directly under the *Propaganda Fide* rather than the leadership of the order in matters both secular and spiritual. The timing of the resolution was no accident: Alexander VII took it right at the beginning of his pontificate, when, by spectacularly excluding his kinsmen from government, he sought to establish the papacy more decisively as a spiritual power.[126] Accordingly, the decision to open a mission would no longer lie with the leadership of the order but with the curial congregation responsible for the governance of missions. The pope also withdrew decisions about the choice of seminarians for the mission seminar from the *praepositus generalis* and obliged them after six months to take an oath before the prefect of the *Propaganda Fide* promising to go on a mission. The procurator of the order had to apply to dispatch missionaries and acquire the permission of the *Propaganda Fide*. The friars also could not leave the mission without its express consent. The power of disposal over the order's revenues earmarked for the missions, particularly the endowment of Baron of Cacurri, of which we will hear more soon, passed to the *Propaganda Fide*. Subsidies for the missionaries were now paid out by the procurator of the order on instructions from the prefect of the *Propaganda Fide*. Fixed sums were set aside for travel; similarly, the *Propaganda Fide* decided upon the amount allotted annually to each cleric. The *praepositus generalis* retained the authority to appoint provincial vicars and visitors.[127]

Alexander VII's resolution of 1655 was just one of a series of measures taken in the mid-seventeenth century that questioned the assets of the regular clergy. Since the pontificate of Clement VIII (1592–1605), the many small convents in Italy in particular, which seemed not to offer the prerequisites for observance, became targets of curial reform efforts. In his 1652 bull on the enforcement of monastic discipline, Pope Innocent X (Giovanni Battista Pamphilj, r. 1644–55) dissolved 1,624 small convents in the Italian territories with up to twelve clerics, about one quarter of the total number. To be sure, this drastic measure was partially reversed in 1654 after protests from those affected, their patrons, and the communities that benefited from their services; 22 percent of the closed convents reopened.[128] However, accusations of a lack of adherence to the Rule remained, and future pontificates offered repeated occasions for curial interventions in the life of religious orders.

Thus, in 1655, when Alexander VII placed the Discalced Carmelite missions directly under the *Propaganda Fide*, relations between the regular clergy and the Curia were already tense. In the years that followed, they bore the additional burden of the interventions into the internal constitution of the order addressed above—the pressure to extend the period of office of the general of the order and the *definitores* from three to six years. In this context, the superiors of the order and the missionaries in Persia responded with the specific arguments of a reform order to the papal resolution. Viewed from the standpoint of their values and norms, members of the order expressed vehement criticism of the *Propaganda Fide* as a bureaucracy and as part of Roman court society. As to financial administration, the leadership of the order emphasized the disadvantages that arose from dependence upon officeholders "in whose antechambers much time was wasted." They knew of clerics who depended financially on the congregation and had gone there up to twenty-nine times before receiving an audience. When the *Propaganda Fide* selected the missionaries, there was a danger that the seminary would be filled with "restless clerics" who wished to avoid obedience to their superiors and thus sought to influence decisions by the curial congregation in their favor "through friends and persons well disposed toward them." Since nobody knew the men under him better than the general of the order, it was proper that he alone should also decide on their appointment and removal. As "sons" of their order, the good clerics did not wish to submit to the curial congregation.[129]

The missionaries in Persia aimed their objections in a similar direction. One of them even went so far as to attribute the pope's resolution to "inspiration by the Devil," who sought to disrupt the good that the missionaries were doing.[130] The provincial vicar, Felice di Sant'Antonio, who gathered the missionaries in Isfahan to discuss the innovation, spoke of sons who were losing their beloved fathers and teachers; he believed that the *Propaganda Fide* lacked the requisite knowledge of local conditions and feared delays in the decision-making process. The friars would prefer to return to their provinces rather than depend upon the *Propaganda Fide*. None of them had sworn an oath of obedience to the congregation.[131] More plainly than their superiors, the missionaries thus stressed the conditional nature of their duty of obedience as members of the order: according to their vows, they owed obedience to the legally constituted authorities of the order. The order was the "good mother," the *Propaganda Fide* a "stepmother" to whom he would never turn, wrote a friar from Basra. He owed "sacred obedience" to the order; when he had gone to Basra, he had done so with the intention of remaining "under the obedience of his holy order and its superiors." For that reason, he asked for permission to return to his home province. If the superiors of the order could no longer guide them, the friars would make use of "what Nature teaches them to be legitimate."[132] Being placed under a congregation to which they had taken no vows thus justified the clerics' own decisions to abandon their mission.

The correspondence with the superiors of the order following the brief of 1655 reveals patterns of perception according to which the Discalced Carmelites as members of a reformed mendicant order assessed the Roman Curia from afar. The statements reflect the discomfort they felt with the secularization of the Church that had led to the reform of the Carmelite order in sixteenth-century Castile.[133] By invoking a system of values and norms rooted in the transcendental realm, even simple friars believed they could reject the decision of a curial congregation, and indeed of the pope, without violating their duty of obedience. The fact that their direct subordination to the *Propaganda Fide* had been ordered by a pope who was also seeking to break with the nepotism of his predecessors played no role here. In 1658, Barnaba di San Carlo wrote to a *definitor* of his order that the Discalced Carmelites did not wish to be dependent on the *Propaganda Fide* in either spiritual or secular matters: in spiritual matters because "nobody gives away what he does not have"—"those gentlemen" (that is, the members of the *Propaganda Fide*) seem to care for everything "the world craves"—and in secular matters because the congregation would let them die of starvation.[134] Subordination in financial matters to the *Propaganda Fide*, wrote Friar Barnaba, amounted to usurpation by "such a rich pope" of revenues that a very poor order had legitimately possessed for many years and managed for a sacred purpose.[135]

In this view of the curial congregation, the ills of the "world" in the form of the pursuit of riches and social distinction were associated with the "unbearable slowness" of a nascent bureaucracy. In Rome, as at the courts of secular rulers, the growing importance of bureaucratic procedures did not, in fact, render close personal relationships superfluous. Rather, those affected experienced the time-consuming efforts of petitioners or their proxies to have their problems heard as essential features of a nascent bureaucracy. The orders found an answer to this challenge in the institution of the procurators, who served as institutional mediators with the papal bureaucracy. They were expected to have legal knowledge and above all experience with the procedures of the papal institutions. The procurators were responsible for cultivating personal relationships with decision-makers as well as representing the orders in trials and performing economic tasks.

On paper, being placed under the *Propaganda Fide* by the brief of 1655 should have resulted in profound innovations for the Discalced Carmelites. As violent as the immediate reactions of those affected may have been, in practice the effect of the papal decision did not correspond to what the wording of the brief would lead us to believe. Members of the order continued to administer the funds intended for the missionary seminary and the Discalced Carmelite missions separately from the *stato temporale* of the *Propaganda Fide*. They had to account for the money to the curial congregation but otherwise acted largely autonomously, so much so that the *Propaganda Fide* later occasionally referred again to the disbursement of subsidies and travel funds as a duty of the order's superiors.[136] Moreover, after 1655 the *Propaganda Fide* neglected to conduct regular correspondence with the missionaries that might have given shape to the new competences on the ground.

For the *Definitorium generale* and the General Chapter of the Discalced Carmelites, the papal decision of 1655 offered an occasion to highlight the order's missionary engagement. In 1659 and 1662, during the pontificate of Alexander VII, the General Chapter put the question of observance of the Rule in the small monasteries on the agenda, in keeping with the papal reform projects. In 1665, it similarly instructed the missionaries, but more particularly the superiors of the missionary settlements, to report frequently to the *Propaganda Fide* about the successes of the missions.[137] At the same time, the *Definitorium generale* continued to articulate norms that treated the activities of missionaries as a matter for the order. The *praepositus generalis* still decided on the dispatch of missionaries, who had to acquire the permission of the general of the order if they wished to return to Europe, although the consent of the provincial vicar sufficed in extremely urgent cases. In 1739 the *Definitorium generale* set down these competences in the constitutions of the order, which were revised at that time.[138]

The *Definitorium generale* expressed its entitlement to run the missions with particular clarity in the 1683 instructions for missionaries in the East, which, proceeding from the individual decisions issued over the years, codified the rules governing the conduct of the friars. Tellingly enough, they were more consistent than previously in considering the mission's specific needs. This included making language studies compulsory and loosening internal norms that apparently hindered missionary activities, for example stipulations concerning activities outside the cloister. By adapting internal norms to practical circumstances, the definitors upheld their own authority in mission matters toward the *Propaganda Fide*. In the 1683 version, the instructions did not include any explicit reference to the *Propaganda Fide*, thereby implicitly affirming the missionaries' exclusive obligation to their superiors within the order. Only the prohibition—which had already applied internally in the order—on "intervening in the business of the laity" was now affirmed with reference to the regulations of the congregation.[139]

In a later version of the instruction adopted by the definitors in 1719, the authority of the *Propaganda Fide* in various matters advanced to a place alongside that of the order's superiors but did not supersede it. In keeping with the terminology of the curial congregations, the heads of the individual missions—in Persia, the provincial vicar—were now referred to as prefects. Their election was assigned to the *praepositus generalis* "or" to the curial congregation. The prefects were only allowed to return to Rome with the permission of the *praepositus generalis* "and/or" the congregation.[140]

The striking alternative competences likely attenuated the compulsory nature of the instruction. It had become clear early on that the coexistence of the leadership of the order and the *Propaganda Fide* could lead to undesirable latitude for the missionaries. Wherever the procedure introduced in the 1630s for granting the *facultates* was applied, there was a danger that missionaries would use it to call the authority of their superiors into question. A draft for a general instruction, which was probably written in the 1640s at the *Propaganda Fide*, therefore prescribed that the *patenti* were to be sent out not by the congregation, but by the superiors of the order, in order to underline the continuing subordination of the regular clergy to their superiors in all matters that did not apply directly to the mission.[141]

In fact, subaltern actors did not experience the emerging central bureaucracies in the secular and ecclesiastical realm simply as authorities that restricted their sphere of action. Curial congregations acting on the pope's behalf could offer symbolic capital and protection, which made them attractive even to those who largely evaded their grasp. Discalced Carmelites had sought to use these resources even before 1655. The *Propaganda Fide* availed itself of such opportunities to enforce its jurisdiction. In 1640, Denis de la Couronne d'Épines, who would later baptize countless terminally ill children of Muslim parents, complained to the secretary of the *Propaganda Fide*, Francesco Ingoli, that the observance of the Rule demanded by the superiors of the order impeded missionary work.[142]

In 1655, in his dealings with his fellow cleric at the convent of Isfahan, Pierre de la Mère de Dieu, the Discalced Carmelite Felice di Sant'Antonio worried that conflicts from his order might spill over to Rome. He asked the *praepositus generalis* to remove the cleric from Persia but to ensure that he not travel to Rome, where he might spread false claims about the opportunities for the mission in Persia that the Discalced Carmelites were neglecting. As a missionary coming from Persia, he might impress the cardinals, although in Isfahan not only the Discalced Carmelites but also the Capuchins, Augustinians, and Jesuits made fun of him. In order to prevent the friar from addressing the *Propaganda Fide*, it would be best if the *praepositus generalis* did not immediately relieve him of missionary duties altogether but, instead, transferred him for the time being to the convent on Mount Carmel.[143]

Such episodes, of which many more could be cited here, offer hints of the ways in which subaltern actors used the curial institutions. However, they provide only limited answers to the question of how important the *Propaganda Fide* became in the everyday lives of missionaries. Two manuscripts written by the last bishop of Isfahan, the Discalced Carmelite Cornelio di San Giuseppe (known before entering the order as Carlo Amatore Adeodato Reina), provide further insight.[144] As autobiographical documents by a Discalced Carmelite they are unique, at least for the Persian mission. They reveal a man who closely observed and participated in everyday social life in the places where he lived. At the same time, they offer evidence of the relationships that Cornelio di San Giuseppe cultivated in Rome. Like his brethren who had resisted subordination to the *Propaganda Fide* after 1655, Cornelio di San Giuseppe criticized the congregation for the ways it used its procedures for the purposes of maintaining power and influence. Despite such criticisms, however, he, too, mobilized the resources of the nascent curial bureaucracy, at times successfully.

In order to better understand the Discalced Carmelite's observations, we first need to consider a few aspects of his biography. Carlo Amatore Adeodato Reina, born in Milan in 1710, took minor orders in 1726 at the age of sixteen while a pupil of the Jesuit College of Brera. Three years later, in 1729, he entered the novitiate of the Discalced

Carmelites in Milan, where he took vows the following year. After studying theology in Bologna, he was ordained to the priesthood in 1735. In 1736 the provincial sent him to Rome to the missionary seminary of San Pancrazio, where he took his vows for the missions to which the general of the order sent him at his own request in 1738. The Discalced Carmelite had stressed his preference for mission over the contemplative life in a "holy desert" of his order. Indeed, his autobiographical account reveals a cleric who found the *vita activa* more to his liking than life in monastic seclusion. He certainly seems to have had no misgivings about contact with people of different cultures and religions, as we will see in more detail below.[145]

Friar Cornelio arrived in Basra in 1739 at the age of twenty-nine, and from 1743 to 1745 he lived in Isfahan. In 1745, the provincial vicar of the Discalced Carmelites found him suited to head the mission in Bushehr because of his knowledge of Turkish, Armenian, Arabic, and Portuguese. In the years that followed, he lived in Bushehr and other trading posts in the Gulf region and Mesopotamia. In 1758 he was appointed bishop of Isfahan. After his consecration in Cagliari, Sardinia, in 1759 and a longer sojourn in Rome, he traveled to Basra in 1762. Since the wars in Persia prevented him from entering his diocese, he lived from 1762 to 1771 under the protection of the agents of the English and Dutch East India Companies in Basra, on Kharg Island, and in Bushehr. After the English East India Company evacuated Bushehr in 1769, signaling what seemed to be the abandonment once and for all of the last factory of a European trading company in Persia, and Cornelio di San Giuseppe was forced to settle outside his diocese in Basra, the *Propaganda Fide* granted his request for permission to return home in 1770. The Discalced Carmelite left Basra in early March 1771 and traveled via Baghdad and Aleppo to Rome, arriving at the end of October 1772. Although he retained the title of bishop of Isfahan and some of the associated revenues until his death in 1797, he never returned to his diocese.

While Cornelio di San Giuseppe gave an account of his life in the *Memorie cronologiche che puonno servire a meglio sovvenirmi de varii altri incidenti di mia vita*, which he wrote on the basis of old diaries after returning to his native Lombardy, in his *Centurie* he described and commented upon countless episodes that he had experienced himself or heard about from others.

The biting critique of the worldly riches of the Roman court and the ignorance of the cardinals is particularly striking. In one *centuria*, for instance, Cornelio di San Giuseppe gives voice to a cleric who delivered a sermon in which he allegedly admonished the cardinals not to be indignant about missionaries' requests for subsidies, since they only desired a very small part of their own wealth. Unlike Jesus with his disciples, the pope and the cardinals were incapable of granting the missionaries the ability to perform miracles and thus relieving them of the necessity of begging for subsidies from Rome. Who if not the missionaries with their efforts at conversion had provided the cardinals with all the money, palaces, and rich sources of revenue? A single one of these sources of revenue would suffice to secure the living of all the missionaries, while all together they were not enough to finance the splendor of the cardinals.[146]

In another *centuria*, Cornelio di San Giuseppe addressed the dysfunctional nature of information-based bureaucratic rule from a distance, which justified disobedience in the light of higher values and objectives. He gave the *centuria* the form of a letter sent by an unnamed missionary bishop (himself?) to the *Propaganda Fide*: he would act in contradiction to the congregation's intentions if he were to blindly follow its orders. The cardinals and the secretary were too far away to judge certain matters, which could only be verified on the ground. He asked them not to attribute his disobedience to a lack of respect; his intention in informing the congregation was instead to prove his perfect devotion. Knowing the facts of the case, the prefect and cardinals, as well as the secretary, would doubtless agree with him, even if this ran counter to the suggestions of their subaltern officials.[147]

If we are to believe the *Memorie cronologiche*, the *Propaganda Fide* played only a minor role in the author's life. In 1738 he and his companion received the *patenti* in Genoa from the *praepositus generalis*. He only begins to mention the curial congregation more frequently in the *Memorie* after his appointment as bishop of Isfahan. Only now did he also obtain an annual remuneration of 200 *scudi* provided by the *Propaganda Fide* rather than his order. After being consecrated as a bishop in Cagliari in November 1759, Cornelio di San Giuseppe lived in Rome for six months, from December 6, 1759, to June 2, 1760. There he stayed with the Discalced Carmelites, first in Santa Maria della Scala, and later in Santa Maria della Vittoria. After his first papal audience, he spent the month of December 1759 making visits, especially to members of the *Propaganda Fide*. On January 6, 1760, he celebrated a pontifical mass in the *Propaganda Fide*'s church; on this and the following days, he remained for lunch with the secretary and servants of the congregation. On January 21, 1760, he attended an "academy of poetry in various languages" by the students of the *Collegio urbano*, including an Armenian from New Julfa whom he had sent to the college the previous year. The events mentioned in the *Memorie* were mainly those that gave him an opportunity to cultivate relationships at the Roman court—to the *Propaganda Fide* and the superiors of the order but also to the Roman aristocratic family Colonna on the occasion of a daughter's entry into the Discalced Carmelite convent of Regina Coeli. As during the first two weeks, Cornelio di San Giuseppe spent the final two weeks of his sojourn in Rome, after a farewell audience with the pope, making countless visits and return visits.

During the period when Cornelio di San Giuseppe lived as a bishop in various Persian Gulf ports, the *Memorie* mention the *Propaganda Fide* only very rarely. This was in keeping with the very sporadic nature of correspondence with the *Propaganda Fide*. During his stay in the Persian Gulf from 1762 to 1771, Cornelio di San Giuseppe wrote to Rome a few times a year and only seldom received letters from the congregation. In 1767 the bishop lamented from Bushehr that he had not received a single letter from the *Propaganda Fide* in some two years, although it must have received at least three missives from him during the same period, which in itself was not exactly evidence of an abundant exchange. The more or less punctual transfer of the annual subsidies of 200 *scudi* from Rome was correspondingly unreliable as well.[148]

In the *Memorie cronologiche*, the *Propaganda Fide* features centrally only in connection with the inquiry into the union of the Nestorian patriarch with Rome. Bishop Cornelio di San Giuseppe claimed that he had negotiated it together with the local bishop in Baghdad on his return journey. During his second sojourn in Rome (October 25, 1772, to February 28, 1773), just after returning from the Persian Gulf, he used this inquiry as an icebreaker to address his personal concerns. The request for permission to celebrate the pontifical mass outside his diocese and for the continued payment of his subsidies of 200 *scudi* annually as bishop was based on the dispensation from the obligation to return to a convent of his order, which Alexander VII had imposed upon bishops recruited from the religious orders who left their dioceses. Cornelio di San Giuseppe had to spend a good deal of time waiting in antechambers in the hope of gaining an audience with the *Propaganda Fide*. These concerns now largely overshadowed mission affairs.

Along with his correspondence with the *Propaganda Fide*, Cornelio di San Giuseppe's *Memorie* offer important insights into the ways in which a missionary and bishop cultivated relations with the Roman Curia. While the author's notes on his audiences with the pope stressed the degree of favor shown him, he portrayed the *Propaganda Fide* as a bureaucracy whose officials did not shy away from undermining the graces bestowed upon him by Pope Clement XIV (Lorenzo Ganganelli, r. 1769–74). When he visited Stefano Borgia, secretary of the *Propaganda Fide*, bearing "the pope's most favorable rescript" in support of the further payment of his subsidies, Borgia congratulated him upon a grace that no one before him had been granted. He did not, however, know how the prefect, Cardinal Giuseppe Maria Castelli, would respond to his method of bypassing the *Propaganda Fide* and going directly to the pope. As secretary, he was naturally obliged to bow to the pope's wishes and present the matter to the next congregation. This congregation, however, according to Cornelio di San Giuseppe, was never convened, and although he asked several times, he received nothing from the secretary but "fine words in the Roman style." After putting him off for more than a month with promises, the secretary finally issued a document assuring him that the subsidies would be paid for two years and that this would be extended if he returned to his diocese.[149]

Directly following the election of Pius VI (Giovanni Angelo Braschi, r. 1775–99) in 1775, Cornelio di San Giuseppe traveled to Rome once again. After initially being denied the personal audience he sought and, after many difficulties, only managing to have his subsidies extended for one further year, he finally gained direct access to the papal audiences once again. In his own words, he had done everything alone and trusting in divine providence, which had opened doors for him so that he might lie prostrate directly at the feet of His Holiness. The letters of recommendation from the archbishop of Milan, Count Firmian, and other distinguished persons, in contrast, had earned him nothing but "fine words and useless offers in the Roman manner to render him every service in their power." While Cornelio di San Giuseppe emphasized the pope's role as the highest divinely inspired giver of grace, the *Propaganda Fide* and above all its lower officials appear once again as (ultimately surmounted) obstacles to attaining what in his view Clement XIV had already granted him in 1770 along with permission to return to Europe: the continued payment of his episcopal subsidies.[150]

In fact, the *Propaganda Fide* stopped paying the subsidies on February 17, 1776, but then in June of that same year they granted Cornelio di San Giuseppe the "grace" of one additional year of payment, with the express note that they no longer had any obligation to him beyond that time.[151] The bishop was nevertheless able to draw his subsidies until the end of his life—another twenty years—thanks to a decision that Pope Pius VI made at the beginning of 1777, bypassing the congregation, "particularly with a view to the intercession of the imperial-royal court of Vienna."[152] The decision, communicated by the Secretariat of State to the secretary of the congregation, was no longer fundamentally challenged before the bishop's death. This did not, however, gain Cornelio di San Giuseppe a good reputation in the *Propaganda Fide*, from whose perspective the payment of subsidies to a nonresident bishop was "inappropriate and irregular."[153]

The story of Cornelio di San Giuseppe could be read as a conflict between the efforts of a bureaucracy, the *Propaganda Fide*, and its officials, over the enforcement of universally applicable legal norms, on the one hand, and the absolute papal power to bestow grace ascribed to divine will on the other. The pope's authority as the highest bestower of grace was constituted not least through the granting of individual favor—exemption through dispensation from universally binding norms.

The bishop's story shows that a man who, by his own account, was an extremely weak actor, could under certain circumstances effectively press his interests at the Roman court even in the late eighteenth century by using the latitude created by the coexistence of several norm-giving authorities—the order, the curial congregation, and the pope. Cornelio di San Giuseppe, who had also learned in the Persian Gulf how to secure protection across confessional boundaries, retained his episcopal title and revenues until the end of his life, that is, for twenty-five years, despite being far away from his diocese. As a bishop he was dispensed from his obligations as a member of the regular clergy, especially the vow of poverty. This calls into question two ideal figures of the Catholic reform movement: the bishop who fulfills the pastoral duties of his office in his diocese, and the member of the regular clergy embedded in the discipline of his order.

In their efforts to enforce the norms they had formulated over great geographical distances, the Roman Curia and the leadership of the orders faced problems similar to those of early modern secular authorities. In many respects, the solutions they proposed were also similar: an expansion of bureaucratic structures in combination with the intensification of personal ties. For their part, the missionaries did not behave very differently toward their superiors in the order and toward the Curia and its representatives than subaltern actors did on the periphery of secular configurations of rulership: they obeyed the Curia as a matter of principle, relied on the privileges of their order, and attempted to use connections to higher authorities as resources in their local sphere of activity. Writing about relations between the missionaries in South India and the leadership of the Society of Jesus, Ines G. Županov has noted that in the case of disputes on the ground, the fathers consistently claimed to obey instructions from Rome while interpreting what their duty of obedience meant in different ways depending on the situation.[154]

The study of relations between missionaries in Persia and the *Propaganda Fide* confirms these observations. Attempts to assert authority from Rome ran up against local efforts to coopt external resources, which also created an interest in cultivating reciprocal contacts. In the ecclesiastical context, too, these contacts implied empowering interactions. The extent to which these contacts strengthened the power of ruling authorities remained dependent on the specific circumstances. Under certain conditions, empowering interactions facilitated the *Propaganda Fide*'s access, while leaving wide latitude and opportunities for local actors to instrumentalize the symbolic and sometimes material resources of the congregation for their own purposes. This state of affairs strictly limited efforts to assert papal sovereign rights over the regular clergy as actors in foreign missions. More than the curial congregations, the superiors of the orders intervened in the everyday lives of missionaries, who in turn felt primarily committed to the order. The superiors of the order remained the "fathers," the *Propaganda Fide* an unloved "stepmother," who largely left the missionaries to their own devices. The regular clergy nevertheless expected that the *Propaganda Fide* would occasionally provide useful protection, without binding them to any farther-reaching duty of obedience. This duty was limited by the personal nature of vows to the superiors of the order and by the presumption that the authorities would act lawfully in keeping with the order's constitutions. The rejection of an "absolute" understanding of authority referred not just to the relationship between the order and the curial congregation; around 1660 it was also confirmed internally by the *Definitorium generale* as part of the conflict between the convent community and the provincial vicar studied here.

In the early modern period, "absolute rule" suffered from an acute legitimacy deficit in both the secular monarchies and the ecclesiastical context. By invoking papal responsibility for the world rooted in the history of salvation and divine and natural law, the Roman Curia could only partially compensate for this shortcoming, as relations between the Discalced Carmelites and the *Propaganda Fide* show. The aspirations of the latter to work toward the propagation of the faith also generated competition within the Catholic Church. As members of a reform order dedicated to strict observance, the Discalced Carmelites confronted the *Propaganda Fide* as an institution embedded in Roman court society, and occasionally even the "rich pope." They did so out of an aspiration to live by their own system of values and norms distinct from the "world," a system rooted in the transcendental, and thus superior to all other systems of values and norms. At the same time, the study of correspondence as a medium for cultivating personal relationships has shown that despite this aspiration, even a reformed mendicant order could not wholly resist the secular logics of entanglement. The order was influenced not just by outside ecclesiastical actors but also by secular authorities. This could also be documented for kinship ties in individual cases.

The internal diversity of early modern Catholicism, with its competing jurisdictions as well as systems of values and norms, also influenced the contacts that missionaries cultivated in foreign societies. In what follows, attention turns to the various social roles that the Discalced Carmelites and the members of other orders—the Augustinians, Capuchins, Jesuits, and Dominicans—played in Persia in their dealings with Muslims, Armenians, and laypersons of European origin. In the process, we will need to consider the degree to which the emergence of competing confessional churches in Western Europe shaped their experiences, which in turn influenced the situation in Europe. First, however, we will introduce the preconditions that the Safavids created for the activities of Catholic missionaries in their empire.

2

In the Shadow of the Shah: The Safavid Empire as an Arena for Catholic Mission

In the sixteenth century, contacts between Europeans and Persians were few and far between. Europeans showed little interest in the region. What information was available was fragmentary and chiefly secondhand. European observers combined this small store of empirical information with the knowledge about ancient Persia that they had inherited from the Greeks and the Romans. Few Europeans traveled from India to the fort on Hormuz, which had been in Portuguese hands since the early sixteenth century, and onward into the Persian Gulf and the heartland of the Safavid Empire. Portuguese interests focused mainly on the coastal towns on the Persian Gulf, as is evident from the surviving written accounts and maps. The envoys the Portuguese governors of Hormuz and the viceroys of the *Estado da Índia* sent to the Safavid court beginning in 1514 received little attention in Persia. Contacts with other Christian courts remained episodes at best.[1]

This situation of mutual indifference ended around 1600. News of the successes of ʿAbbās I's troops against the Ottomans that were reaching the European courts fostered projects of an alliance with the shah. A variety of European expectations came to focus on the Safavid Empire. At the court of Philip III, king of Castile and Portugal, and at the Roman Curia, hopes arose of realizing a twofold dream: military victory over the Turks, the enemies par excellence of Christendom, and the conversion to Christianity of large numbers of Muslims.[2] Around the same time, from the Indian Ocean, the English and Dutch discovered the Safavid Empire as a potential trading partner.

On the Persian side, Shah ʿAbbās I (r. 1588–1629) was similarly searching for allies against the Ottomans. Moreover, his politics of empire-building created the structural conditions needed to enhance and solidify contacts with European courts and trading companies, as well as to attract Catholic missionaries. Indeed, Shah ʿAbbās I consolidated monarchical rule over a vast socioculturally and religiously heterogeneous empire, not only by expanding bureaucratic institutions and a mercenary army but also by integrating the various population groups into the court networks.

This chapter demonstrates how the inclusive nature of Safavid imperial politics facilitated the settlement of Catholic clerics starting in the early seventeenth century. It begins by placing the Safavids' relations with European powers within their own imperial system of rule. Contrary to older narratives of European expansion, the

Safavids did not show any preference for relations with Christian powers but situated themselves within an Asian context. The second subchapter shows that the inclusive character of Safavid imperial rule was a necessary condition for the survival of Christian minorities and the establishment of Catholic missions on the ground. The Armenians of New Julfa were by far the most economically significant local Christian community. Their situation illustrates the limitations as well as the potential inherent in the status of *ḏimmī* (non-Muslim "protected persons") under Safavid rule. Their story began in 1605 with their forcible resettlement from Julfa on the Arax to a suburb of the imperial seat of Isfahan, which came to be known as New Julfa. This district soon became the center of one of the most remarkable success stories of early modern global business. The third subchapter introduces these well-traveled and globally connected merchants, who soon attracted the zeal of Catholic missionaries. The final subchapter will show how the inclusive nature of Safavid rule under ʿAbbās I nourished Western European images of a philo-Christian court and indeed the vain hopes of a rapid conversion to Christianity. The Roman Curia began to base important decisions on this fiction, which proved surprisingly long-lived.

The European Powers in the Safavid System of Imperial Rule

The shared conflict with the Ottomans provided the Roman Curia with a first opportunity to make contact with the Safavid court. A few weeks after the victory over the Ottoman fleet at Lepanto (1571), Pope Pius V (Antonio Michele Ghislieri, r. 1566–72) called upon Shah Ṭahmāsp I to take advantage of the situation and wrest from the "tyrant of the Turks" the territories in Mesopotamia and Assyria that he had unjustly occupied by force. The papal breve constructed the aversion to a tyrant who had grabbed foreign land without regard for human or divine law as a shared point of reference that transcended religious differences. In 1592, Clement VIII then appealed to ʿAbbās I to join the fight against the "tyrant of the Turks," a ruler possessed of all the vices, a tyrant who recognized neither respect for oaths nor good faith. In light of the Ottoman conquest of Crete, in 1646 Innocent X called once again for a joint battle against "the tyrant of the Turks and most important and relentless foe of the entire globe and the [Persian] royal house."[3] The Roman Curia suggested that the common struggle against the Ottomans would be a "just war" because this enemy neglected the norms that formed the basis of any relationship between princes, regardless of religious differences.

The Roman appeals to the shah were motivated by the information received in Western Europe about the military conflicts between the Safavids and the Ottomans. In fact, these conflicts moved ʿAbbās I himself to seek relations with Christian courts that were hostile to the Ottomans. Against this background, persons of varying rank, religion, and origins gained influence as intermediaries. The most illustrious among these middlemen were the English brothers Anthony and Robert Sherley. They brokered relationships between Christian courts and the court of ʿAbbās I well before the Augustinians and Discalced Carmelites arrived in Isfahan. In 1599, the shah sent Anthony Sherley and a Persian envoy to Europe, where they were supposed to drum up support against the Ottomans and improve the conditions for the sale of Persian silk. The younger brother, Robert, remained in Persia. In 1608 he in turn was entrusted with negotiating agreements against the Ottomans on the shah's behalf.[4]

Given this context, it is unsurprising that the Augustinians and the Discalced Carmelites received a warm welcome when they arrived in Isfahan as envoys of Philip III and the pope in 1602 and 1607, respectively. In 1602, ʿAbbās I promised the Augustinians a building that had previously housed foreign envoys, where the friars could install a chapel. The Augustinians later purchased neighboring houses and had a church built in the middle of the complex, which was completed in 1622.[5] In 1609, the shah similarly gave the Discalced Carmelites a house for their use, in which they could live as his long-term guests. This house had also previously served as accommodation for envoys from foreign courts. It was surrounded by a large garden, was well supplied with irrigation and good drinking water, and offered ample space for workshops and a stable for horses. After initially using the main hall as a place of worship, in the 1630s the Carmelites erected a new church with five altars (Figure 3). Both the Augustinians and the Discalced Carmelites would live in the buildings allotted to them by ʿAbbās I until they abandoned their missions in Isfahan in the 1750s.[6]

The missionaries were followed by the English and Dutch East India Companies. In 1617, the English East India Company opened a trading post in Isfahan, where the shah granted them a palace directly adjacent to the bazaar. Against the backdrop of conflicts over the Portuguese presence in Hormuz, the Company received extensive privileges. Aside from customs privileges in Bandar ʿAbbās, freedom of trade throughout the

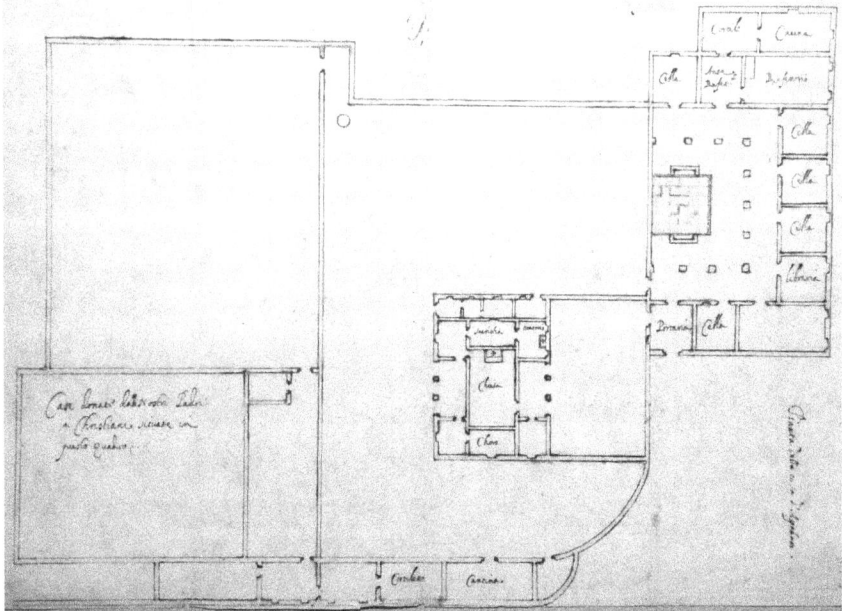

Figure 3 Plan of the Discalced Carmelites' house in Isfahan, n.d. (probably seventeenth century) (AGOCD, 233/d/15[bis]). © 2022 AGOCD

empire, and freedom of religion, these included the recognition of the Company's agent in Isfahan as a judge for the internal affairs of the English "nation." Shortly after the English, the Dutch *Verenigde Oost-Indische Compagnie* (VOC) was granted similar privileges and established trading posts in Isfahan and Bandar ʿAbbās (Figure 4). The VOC became the most important European trading partner of the Safavids, ahead of the English East India Company. The two companies' trading posts in Isfahan survived with varying success until the mid-eighteenth century. At that time, the focus of their activities shifted from the imperial court to the Persian Gulf. Unlike the Dutch and English East India Companies, the French *Compagnie des Indes orientales*, which also received privileges from the shah in 1665 and 1673 shortly after its foundation in 1664, did not organize its activities in Isfahan in a factory but integrated merchants of French origin established in Isfahan into their business as agents. Its attempt to establish a *comptoir* of its own in Bandar ʿAbbās ultimately failed. The business activities of the *Compagnie des Indes orientales* fell well behind initial expectations, and not only in Persia; it ceased operations because of debt in 1706. After the toppling of the Safavids, Persia was of only marginal importance for the *Compagnie des Indes* that was newly founded in 1719. Beginning in 1742, the Company pursued its trading activities in the Persian Gulf from Basra.[7]

The Persian rulers' tokens of favor toward missionaries and merchants should not be interpreted as signs of a preference for stable relations with European powers. Rather, European–Persian relations must be understood as part of a multi-actor constellation in which standards were set locally and European actors occupied a

Figure 4 Factory of the VOC in Isfahan (from Cornelis de Bruyn, *Voyages [...] par la Moscovie, en Perse, et aux Indes orientales* [Amsterdam, 1718], vol. 1, plate 107 [detail])

subordinate position. Persian trade relations were oriented primarily toward South Asia, rather than the Levant, Western Europe, or Russia. The occupation of Hormuz in the early sixteenth century allowed the Portuguese to control and tax shipping and trade between Persia, the Persian Gulf, and India, not Europe. In the early seventeenth century, when the first Dutch and English ships docked at Persian ports, this offered ʿAbbās I new export channels for Persian raw silk and, in the absence of a fleet of his own, the opportunity to play these European rivals off against the Portuguese. With English support, he wrested the island of Hormuz from the Portuguese in 1622.[8]

The expulsion of the Portuguese from Hormuz and the rise of Bandar ʿAbbās to the most important harbor in the empire contributed to breaking Portuguese control over the sea route between India and the Persian Gulf and opening it up to European *and* Asian competitors.[9] This did not, however, give the English and Dutch East India Companies the outstanding importance that older economic histories have accorded them.[10] In the first half of the eighteenth century, Armenian kin networks still proved the equal of European trading companies, and the English East India Company courted their cooperation intensively starting in the 1680s.[11] Even more than the role of the Armenians, scholars have long underestimated the importance of Indian merchants and financiers in trade between Persia, the Persian Gulf, and South Asia. Europeans who traveled to Persia in the seventeenth century, in contrast, were quite aware of their presence in Isfahan, estimating the numbers of Indians living there at 10,000–15,000. The Venetian Ambrogio Bembo spoke of 12,000 Indians—both Muslims and "heathens"—all of them wealthy merchants, who possessed their own market in Isfahan, where they sold Indian textiles in large quantities.[12] As imprecise as these estimates and all other available contemporary figures on the population of Isfahan and New Julfa may have been, they nevertheless contrast impressively with the number of "Franks" living there, 100 people at most. Together with the Armenians and the East India Companies, the Indian diaspora helped to integrate the Safavid Empire into the commercial and financial networks of South Asia. Similarly instructive for locating the foreign economic entanglements of the Safavid Empire is the fact that the Dutch and the English East India Companies, like the Portuguese before them, pursued their business from South Asia as intra-Asian actors, while the exchange of commodities between Persia and Europe was of only secondary importance.[13]

As in the field of economy, the significance of Western European actors within the political foreign relations of the Safavid Empire remained quite limited overall in comparison to that of the Ottomans, Mughals, and Uzbeks. While ʿAbbās I's reception of the Augustinians and Discalced Carmelites was widely noted in Catholic Europe, the Safavids' interest in relations with Christian courts was selective and depended very much on the dynasty's relationships with its Asian neighbors.[14] In many cases, little attention was paid to "Frankish" delegations at the Safavid court. After the peace treaty of 1639 with the Ottomans, the Safavids relied even less on the Christian powers as a counterweight to the Turks. Where the Safavids saw themselves in the imagined hierarchy of powers is illustrated by the paintings in the *Čihil Sutūn* in Isfahan, where ʿAbbās II (r. 1642–66) and his successors received foreign embassies, held audiences, and hosted hundreds of guests at banquets. In this central site for the performance of power, the scenes portrayed referred exclusively to the emperor's relations with his

Asian neighbors, the Uzbeks, and Mughals, while depictions of the Europeans were relegated to the outer walls.[15] Nothing represented the imperial aspirations better than the portrayal of the Mughal ruler Humāyūn as a refugee who had sought sanctuary from his foes at the Safavid court (Figure 5).

As a result of this self-perception, since the sixteenth century, the style of negotiation practiced in relations between the Portuguese and the Safavid court was marked by the subjection of Christian envoys to local normative prescriptions and an absence of reciprocity. Beginning in the early seventeenth century, the new European actors entering the scene—the missionaries who came to Persia in the name of the Roman Curia or the French king, as well as the agents of the English and Dutch East India Companies—adapted to this negotiation style.

Like the Ottomans and the Mughals, the Safavids understood their relationships with Christian rulers as unequal states of dependence, and diplomatic ceremonial was organized accordingly. Envoys received at court were supposed to bring gifts that could be understood as tribute payments. In return, they could expect accommodation and food upon arrival and during their entire stay. When they departed, the shah had the envoys presented with vestments of honor, which he saw as an expression of his own superior position. This was given visual meaning by staging the rituals before the courtly audience. When the Dominican Antonino Tani arrived in Isfahan in 1665 bearing letters from the pope, the Holy Roman Emperor, the king of France, the Republic of Venice, and the grand duke of Tuscany, the shah insisted for that reason on receiving the friar in a public audience "with the greatest possible solemnity" rather than in a private meeting. The Dominican had previously put in a request to

Figure 5 Paintings inside the *Čihil Sutūn* in Isfahan: Shah Ṭahmāsp I (r. 1524–76) offers the Mughal ruler Humāyūn refuge at his court

that effect because he feared that he could not compete in a public audience with the ambassador of the Grand Mughal who was present at the same time and had arrived with a large retinue bearing magnificent gifts, whereas Ferdinand II, grand duke of Tuscany (r. 1621–70), had only given him plants as gifts for ʿAbbās II, few of which had survived the long journey.[16] If Friar Tani was fortunate enough to get an honorable reception in spite of such disadvantageous conditions, this was because ʿAbbās II was keen to seize this opportunity to humiliate the envoy of his imperial rival by showing favor to the modest Christian cleric. The Dominican was all the more suitable for this purpose since ceremonial usually treated the envoys of Christian rulers very poorly in comparison to Muslims, not just the ambassadors of the Grand Mughal.[17]

These hierarchies were characteristic of the Safavids' imperial system of rule. In Isfahan, all intermediaries in the service of Christian princes, whether laymen or clerics, participated inadvertently in courtly ceremonial choreographies that were meant to humiliate them. According to the chronicle of the court scribe Iskandar Bēg Munšī, reverences attributed to the pope played a particular role in the staging of the shah's superior position. While he deemed contacts with Christian courts worthy of only brief mentions, his concluding assessment of the "world-beautifier ʿAbbās" includes an extensive alleged "translation" of a 1624 breve by Urban VIII. A comparison between the Farsi version and the Latin original reveals significant changes of meaning: while the Roman author cited the "protection of the world and the human race" as a particular characteristic of papal dignity, the authors of the "translation" quoted by Iskandar Bēg Munšī turned it into an encomium of ʿAbbās I. In the new text, the pope addressed the shah from a subordinate position. He praised him as "the refulgence of infinite divine grace and the refuge of all mankind" and as "a king who is the model and source of guidance for people throughout the world, and particularly for the Vicar of Christ Our Lord at Rome." Because ʿAbbās I surpassed other monarchs in grandeur, majesty, and dominion, all human beings had to pray for the perpetuity of his reign. For that reason, he, Urban VIII, regarded it as his duty to have prayers said in his churches asking God to grant ʿAbbās I long life and His assistance. If even the pope, whom Iskandar Bēg Munšī calls "the greatest of the Christian rulers" and "the caliph of the Christians," lauded ʿAbbās I to this extent, then his enviers, the author of the chronicle asserted, could not dismiss his praise of the ruler as the kind of artificial elaboration indulged in by secretaries.[18] The two versions of the papal breve stand for the opposing world views that the Catholic clerics who were sent to Isfahan in the early seventeenth century had to negotiate. While they arrived with the mission to broker an alliance against the Turks and convert more souls to the Catholic faith, the clerics could not avoid participating in interaction rituals that staged the shah's superiority.

The Safavid Practice of Power, between Inclusiveness and Orthodoxy

ʿAbbās I's efforts to forge closer relations with Christian powers and the tokens of favor he offered to missionaries were elements of a politics that aimed to integrate a broad array of sociocultural and religious groups into his system of imperial rule. Like all early modern rulers, the Safavids ran up against structural limits to the enforcement of their claims to power. The picture of a "theocratic state" with "totalitarian tendencies" that Roger Savory drew in the 1970s[19] is thus now considered outdated. To be sure, Safavid rule was inextricably linked to the enforcement of Twelver Shi'ism. In the early sixteenth century, Ismāʿīl I tried, at times with extraordinary brutality, to force the then largely Sunni population under his control to convert. But he left an ambiguous legacy to his successors, who had to contend with the reservations of an originally Sunni majority whose adherence to Shia Islam remained questionable. At the beginning of the eighteenth century, one-third of the Safavids' subjects were still Sunnis. Securing their loyalty was all the more important since they generally lived in regions bordering the territories of Sunni powers. There were also Christian, Jewish, and Zoroastrian minorities. In comparison to the Sunni Muslims, they were far fewer in number. Nevertheless, in the Caucasus, that is, the frontier zone with the Ottoman Empire, the Safavids also had to rely on good relations with the local Christian populations. Under such conditions, inclusiveness on the model of earlier Islamic empires was a precondition for the longevity of Safavid rule. Indeed, during the reign of ʿAbbās I, inclusive practices of rule facilitated an unprecedented consolidation of the shah's power.[20]

This inclusive model of rule had been in the making since the early days of the dynasty in the sixteenth century. During his rise to power, Ismāʿīl I (r. 1501–24) was still dependent on the *qizilbāš*. These were largely Turkish-speaking communities who owed loyalty to Ismāʿīl in his capacity as *šaiḫ* of the Sufi brotherhood, which gave the new dynasty its name and provided the troops necessary to enforce its rule. Their leaders, however, held on to significant authority in their respective domains and at times refused fealty to the shah, instead supporting rival members of the ruling family in their struggles for power.[21] To counter their influence, Ismāʿīl I had already tried to strengthen this precarious power base by recruiting an elite of Shi'ite scholars (*ʿulamā*) who owed their material advantages and respected offices to his patronage.[22] In addition, during his long reign (1524–76), Ismāʿīl's successor, Shah Ṭahmāsp I, began to recruit young Georgian, Armenian, and Circassian boys, who were trained as loyal servants of the ruler (*ġulām*). In so doing, he introduced a custom that the Ottomans had already practiced in the form of the "child levy." The Safavid *ġulām* were also overwhelmingly boys of Christian origin whose conversion uprooted them and bound them to the shah. Because of their early integration into the ruler's household, they sometimes had a close personal relationship with their master.

Despite these efforts to broaden the dynasty's support base, when Shah Ṭahmāsp I died in 1576, the *qizilbāš* were still influential. How dangerous dependence upon them could be became evident between 1576 and 1590 in the military conflicts over Ṭahmāsp's succession, when the *qizilbāš* backed competing members of the ruling family. Once ʿAbbās I had eliminated his rivals, he established a system of rule based mainly on the appointment of royal slaves, the *ġulām*, to key positions in the household, army, and administration. Together with an elite of Shi'ite scholars, the *ġulām* helped the shah to shake off his dependence on the *qizilbāš*. ʿAbbās I integrated different groups into his system of rule and played them off against each other: apart from the *qizilbāš*, the *ʿulamā*, and the *ġulām*, this also included communities with no previous ties to the court, chief among them Sunni Kurds, whom he obligated through marital connections. Together with the royal slaves of mostly Christian origin, the Christian Armenians of Julfa also formed part of a new Caucasian elite, which Shah ʿAbbās I and his successor Ṣafī I (r. 1629–42) used to extricate themselves from dependence on the qizilbāš. With their commercial activities the Armenians contributed to alleviating the chronic silver shortage and financing the new military and administrative order.[23]

Following a pattern that also shaped early modern European monarchies, officeholding on the highest level was associated with the integration of the periphery through patron–client relationships. The inclusion of a plethora of different groups in court networks implied a high degree of religious heterogeneity. Thus, despite their conversion to Islam, the ġulām in many cases did not break off ties to their Christian kin networks. The Georgians, while reputedly quick to convert, nonetheless clung to tenets of the Christian faith and practices. Their opponents never tired of pointing out this Christian background. Religious identities mattered even less in the shah's familial relations. He married women of non-Shi'ite origin in order to bind Sunni and Christian kin groups that were influential on the periphery of the empire to his ruling house.[24]

Furthermore, beyond the learned Shi'a milieu, the conversion of the originally Sunni population to Twelver Shi'ism often remained superficial. A nominal profession of faith could suffice as a sign of loyalty to the ruler for the purpose of assuming office at court or in the provinces. The fact that even the highest officeholders were not always Shi'ites shows that personal loyalty to the ruler was ultimately more important than a shared religion. According to Rudi Matthee, the rulers, despite their at times extremely brutal treatment of dissent, preferred on other occasions to integrate those living on the margins of the empire into court networks, thereby enabling them to operate close to the center of power. Even toward the end of Safavid rule, when a doctrinaire version of Shia Islam had become the dominant force at court, one shah still chose a Sunni grand vizier.[25]

Inclusivity manifested itself not just in the integration of elites of extremely diverse backgrounds but also in the legitimation of imperial rule. The monarchs did not rely solely on a religious program defined by the millenarianism of the Sufi brotherhood from which they had emerged as well as Twelver Shi'ism. When Ismāʿīl I conquered Tabriz in 1501, he also reclaimed for himself the pre-Islamic title of "pādishāh" ("master king"). References to pre-Islamic Persian history had their place in the rhetoric of the Safavid court chancery along with allusions to the key figures of the Abrahamic prophetic and Shi'a traditions. Notions of justice, kingship, and social order also drew upon the (not only Islamic) Turkish-Mongolian history of Central Asia. Political philosophy and ethics followed the works of Greek antiquity in Arabic translation. During the reign of ʿAbbās I, the system of rule centered the imperial court in an unprecedented manner, and the shah had himself portrayed as the custodian of a plural political, religious, and cultural legacy. This diversity rooted the ruler's imperial claim to superiority in God's plan of salvation.[26] The splendid expansion of Isfahan into a capital city may be considered the material expression, still visible today, of this imperial understanding of rule. The gigantic square laid out at its center bore the telling name "Image of the World Square" (Maidān-i Naqš-i Ǧahān) (Figure 10, p. 80).[27]

Yet despite his commitment to inclusive strategies of rule, ʿAbbās I did not end the persecution of Christian subjects. The mass deportations from the Caucasus he ordered in the context of the war with the Ottoman Empire meant great sacrifices for those affected. Contrary to some assertions, the shah's decision to deport the population of the commercial city of Julfa on the River Arax in 1605 was initially unconnected to policies of protection for the merchants of Julfa (Figure 6). The deportation was organized haphazardly since it was triggered by a sudden deterioration of the military conflict with the Ottoman Empire.

Although the deportation would soon give rise to the founding of the prosperous Armenian quarter of New Julfa, the merchant families from Julfa did not have an easy start in Isfahan. It was not until several months after their arrival that ʿAbbās I provided them with the land where New Julfa is now located. Only from this moment onward can the shah's measures be read as serving the dual aim of consolidating his power economically, based on his connections with the Armenian merchants, and strengthening the financial foundations needed to support a mercenary army and a paid bureaucracy.[28]

The privileges that ʿAbbās I granted the merchants from Julfa—religious freedom, tax exemptions, self-administration, and their own courts to resolve their community affairs—corresponded to the significance of the trade networks that they had already built up in their previous home in the Caucasus. These privileges created the basis for New Julfa's ascendance as a center of expansive trade networks stretching from Western Europe across Persia and India to East Asia. These interventions benefited an

Figure 6 Cross stones (*khachkar*) in the Armenian cemetery of Julfa on the River Arax (from Francis Rawdon Chesney, *The Expedition for the Survey of the Rivers Euphrates and Tigris [...]*, vol. 1 [London, 1850], plate 9)

elite that played an important role in cementing monarchical rule. Accordingly, New Julfa accepted only the wealthiest of the Armenians deported from the Caucasus. The rich merchant families established in New Julfa were not merely the protagonists of trade; they also acted politically as representatives of the Armenian community.[29]

The protection ʿAbbās I afforded wealthy Armenian merchants contrasted with the persecution of other Christian communities, whose members were strongly pressured to convert. The majority of the deported were settled in rural regions under difficult conditions. Those artisans and other poorer Armenians of lower social status who were resettled in Isfahan lived together with members of other Eastern churches (especially Georgians, Chaldeans ["Nestorians"], and Jacobites) in various quarters, where they constituted a minority among the Muslim population and took no part in the privileges of the Armenians in New Julfa. Shortly before his death in 1629, ʿAbbās I issued a decree directed at all non-Muslims without exception, giving any *ḏimmī* (non-Muslim protected person) who converted to Islam the right to inherit the entire property of those relatives who had not converted. Henceforth, this law would represent a serious threat to the cohesion of Armenian families.[30]

ʿAbbās I was a master at pitting the competing groups around him—Christian missionaries and Armenians as well as *ġulām* and Shiʾite *ʿulamā*—against each other.[31] His successors were less successful at integrating these varied actors into one system of rule. While Ṣafī I (r. 1629–42) had essentially continued a policy that afforded Christians a certain measure of protection, his death brought growing uncertainty for the Christian community. The Armenian merchants of New Julfa also suffered under growing tax burdens. In the years 1655 to 1657, most Christians, with the exception of the missionaries and representatives of European trading companies, were forced to leave the majority Muslim quarters of Isfahan and settle in New Julfa and other suburbs. The fact that attempts were now made to force the Jews to convert to Islam is indicative of the mounting pressure on religious minorities.

Such measures were closely associated with the Shiʾa clergy's consolidation of power and influence. Starting in the 1690s, measures were introduced that increasingly humiliated Christians and restricted their sphere of action. Decrees issued by Shah Sulṭān Ḥusain (r. 1694–1722) once again worsened the legal status of the Armenians in New Julfa. There were to be no more direct grain deliveries to New Julfa, so that Armenians had to purchase it in Isfahan instead. Furthermore, they were no longer allowed to sell food to Muslims and had to pay higher taxes.[32]

Even under Shah ʿAbbās I, the scope of action of the Christian minorities and missionaries had already been subject to repeated and unexpected challenges. Nevertheless, the frequency of such measures in the second half of the seventeenth century suggests that the legal and social discrimination against religious minorities was increasing. In the process, the dominant influence of the Shiʾite *ʿulamā* was directed not just against non-Muslim minorities but also against Sufis and Sunni Muslims. Religious boundaries were drawn more sharply and gained significance in everyday life. Tijana Krstić has therefore suggested that the confessionalization paradigm be deployed beyond Western Europe to analyze processes in the Ottoman and Safavid Empires that pointed in a similar direction.[33] This study will not be able to supply a direct answer to the question this raises, namely, whether the history of Western Europe is linked to that of the Ottoman and Safavid Empires in the parallelism of processes of confessionalization and state formation. It needs to keep the question in mind, however, of how far the changes discussed in this chapter narrowed the missionaries' scope of action.

What is certain is that it was only the anarchic conditions that followed the toppling of the Safavids in 1722 and the attendant economic decline of Persia that challenged the existence of the missions as such. At first, the Catholic clerics, like the Armenian merchants of New Julfa, managed to reach a rapprochement with the new rulers. In 1742, one Augustinian, three Discalced Carmelites, two Jesuits, and one Dominican were still living in their houses in Isfahan and New Julfa. Two Armenian priests tended to the Armenian Catholic parish. Only the Capuchin convent was abandoned.

The actual turning point for both the Armenians and the Catholic missionaries came later, toward the end of the reign of Nādir Šāh (r. 1736–47). As a successful military leader, he had formally restored Safavid rule in the late 1720s before advancing from regent to ruler in 1736 and trying to establish an imperial order in his own name. This included a new practice of religious inclusivity, which integrated Twelver Shi'ism into a Sunni-dominated context and also placed the Christian communities under the protection of the shah. In the 1740s, however, when the need for increased funding for the troops sparked resistance in various parts of the empire, Nādir Šāh also terrorized the populations of Isfahan and New Julfa to enforce the payment of exorbitant contributions. Years of anarchy followed the 1747 murder of Nādir Šāh.[34] Now, for the first time, the missionaries also became the targets of violent attacks and plunder. One by one, the Augustinians, Jesuits, and Discalced Carmelites abandoned their missions in Isfahan and New Julfa. In 1769, just one Dominican remained in New Julfa, where he looked after the long-abandoned house of the Discalced Carmelites. Latin Catholics now only occasionally traveled through Isfahan and New Julfa. The last two Latin bishops of Isfahan, the Discalced Carmelites Sebastiano di Santa Margherita (bishop from 1751 to 1755) and Cornelio di San Giuseppe (bishop from 1758 to 1797), no longer resided in Isfahan or New Julfa, but in the commercial centers of the Persian Gulf. There they tended to small communities of Catholics of varied origin, most of whom had arrived with the trading companies. In 1771 Cornelio di San Giuseppe even abandoned the Near East entirely. He never again returned to his diocese, although he kept his title until his death in 1797.

Under ʿAbbās I, inclusive strategies of relatively strong imperial rule had created favorable conditions for the economic success of the Armenian merchants of New Julfa as well as for the establishment of Catholic missionaries. In the eighteenth century, these conditions faded away, and both groups eventually left Persia.

Global Actors: The Armenian Merchants of New Julfa

As a consequence of the policies of ʿAbbās I, upon their arrival in Isfahan Catholic missionaries encountered an Armenian community shaped by the wide-ranging commercial networks of its leading merchant families and their ability to interact with varied cultural contexts. While deportation from the Caucasus also entailed enormous sacrifices for the wealthy mercantile families, the extent of privileges and favors granted to these families in the years that followed clearly distinguished New Julfa from the other Armenian communities in the Safavid Empire. This special status corresponded to the significance that the wealthy Armenians from Julfa attained as merchants and financiers under the reign of ʿAbbās I.

New Julfa did not just flourish economically; as an episcopal see, it also became the most important ecclesiastical center in the Safavid Empire, rivaling Etchmiadzin, where the catholicos of the Armenian Church resided. ʿAbbās I promoted this development as part of a policy to bolster the central function of Isfahan as an imperial residence in every respect. The jurisdiction of the bishop of New Julfa extended to most of the Safavid Empire, and also included the Armenian communities on the Persian Gulf, in India, and in Southeast Asia (Figure 7). Protracted jurisdictional conflicts marked his relations with the catholicos of Etchmiadzin. The catholicos refused to accept limits to his own jurisdiction and, when it seemed opportune, tried to make use of his relationships with the Catholic missionaries and with Rome to put pressure on the bishop of New Julfa.[35] As a consequence, as we will see in Chapter 4, relations between the catholicos of Etchmiadzin and the papacy were tainted with ambiguity until the end of the seventeenth century.

The Armenian merchants of New Julfa inserted themselves into the most diverse contexts in Asia and Europe and were able to use the business opportunities that opened up in the process. Apart from their own language, they generally also spoke Persian and Turkish, and many were conversant in Italian, French, and other European languages as well. In trade networks, knowledge that helped the merchants navigate

Figure 7 Holy Savior Cathedral in New Julfa

the globe was most precious. An Armenian-language handbook of currencies, weights, and measures "from the entire world," published in Amsterdam in 1699 at the expense of a rich merchant from New Julfa, is evidence of the demand for this kind of information in this milieu.[36]

The far-flung entanglements of the extended Armenian families were also reflected in material culture. In 1674, when the French jewel merchant Jean Chardin was entertained in New Julfa, he was served spirits from Russia and France as well as liqueur from Italy. Armenian merchant families provided European-style silverware for their European guests. Murals from the Safavid period in Armenian houses in New Julfa reveal a clear preference for European motifs; those depicted often wear European dress, and the cityscapes and landscapes adopt a European aesthetic, especially in the application of perspective.[37]

The Western European influence is also evident in the decoration of the churches in New Julfa. Armenian merchants purchased panel paintings by Italian and Dutch masters for the churches of New Julfa. In contrast to the previous abstention from figurative painting, the interior walls of churches were now commonly adorned with extensive picture cycles of mainly biblical content. While the composition of many pictures can be traced back to Dutch prints, their execution can rarely be attributed to specific masters. To be sure, individual painters from the Netherlands were active in seventeenth-century Isfahan and New Julfa, but to the extent that names appear in relation to the pictorial cycles in the churches of New Julfa, we learn that Armenians adapted the Dutch prototypes. The decoration of the Holy Savior Cathedral, which can be dated to the 1660s, is associated with the name of a certain Yovhannes Mrkuz. According to Jean Chardin, the man who commissioned the paintings, the merchant Ḥwāǧa Avetik, had become convinced during his travels to Italy that figurative paintings in a church were especially pleasing to God. After his return to New Julfa, he managed to implement this project against the resistance of the bishop and the monks. Chardin asserts that at the time of his sojourns in Persia (that is, in the years 1666–7, 1669, and 1672 to 1677), the paintings remained the subject of intra-Armenian controversy. The reason was that, in contrast to Armenian tradition, the depiction of Christ's human nature was now at the center of church decoration (Figure 8). As in the Syrian provinces, the increasing spread of Western modes of depiction in the churches of New Julfa impressively illustrates cultural exchange that did not necessarily culminate in conversion.[38]

Along with the presence of Catholic clerics in Persia, the trade networks of the Armenian families of New Julfa created the conditions for this exchange. The activities of these families were not rooted in the organizational form of the privileged trading company but in the cohesiveness of large kinship networks and the reputation of their members as honorable merchants. Armenian customary law aimed to ensure that family assets were kept together in the male line after the father's death. The father's fortune was distributed equally among his male heirs, who remained linked to one another, with mutual liability, under the authority of the eldest male member of the extended kin network. To the extent that they lived in the same place, this also preserved the spatial unity of the household. An essential part of this kin organization was securing the cohesion and financial stability of geographically widely dispersed trade networks.

Figure 8 Paintings of scenes from the life of Christ in the Holy Savior Cathedral in New Julfa

Sometimes, for example in the case of the Sceriman family, about which we will hear more later, these networks were truly global in scope. In the early eighteenth century, the Scerimans' kinship network consisted of at least twenty partners belonging to three generations. About half of them lived in New Julfa, while the others had settled in Venice, Livorno, Surat (India), and smaller trading centers in Asia, or were traveling at the family's expense.[39]

While the merchants of New Julfa conducted business mainly through the ties between the members of extended families, they also drew on the instrument of the *commenda*, which joined the capital of the great merchants domiciled in New Julfa to the abilities and manpower of their commercial agents from Western Europe to East Asia. These agents were not employees; instead, they could keep a portion—between one-quarter and one-third—of the profits as payment. Thanks to their participation in the commercial success of these ventures, some of the *commenda* agents were able to go into business for themselves after a time, which favored the dynamic expansion of the trade networks and the emergence of new commercial centers.

The ties based on kinship and *commenda* in turn facilitated business by ensuring the necessary trust. They helped foster a marked geographical diversification and, with it, risk reduction and adaptation to altered conditions, the importance of which became evident after Shah Sulṭān Ḥusain was toppled in October 1722, signaling the end of a cooperation that had been advantageous for both the Safavid dynasty and the Armenian merchants. While the Armenians were able to reach some degree of agreement with the new Afghan rulers, the wealthy merchants were among the main victims of the arbitrary demands for contributions in the 1740s, which Nādir Šāh enforced with the utmost brutality. These developments put an end to New Julfa's role as a hub of trade networks extending from East Asia to Western Europe and also called into question the continued existence of the small Armenian Catholic community there.[40]

Thanks to the broad geographical diversification, the decline of New Julfa did not mean the end of the trade enterprises that had thus far been centered in Persia. By the seventeenth century, some Armenians had invested large parts of their capital in European centers of trade and finance. As the Russian Empire gradually opened up for trade, the Armenian merchant firms of New Julfa successfully tapped into the new markets in Russia and the transit routes to Northern and Western Europe. After the fall of the Safavid dynasty, the privileges of the tsars offered favorable conditions that encouraged rich merchants to settle in Russia.[41] Within the same context of geographical diversification and risk reduction, others shifted the focus of their activities to South Asia. While scholars disagree on the extent to which Armenian merchants cooperated with the European trading companies in India, there is no doubt about their ability to use the opportunities that the growing European presence offered. Armenians familiar with local conditions performed important services in India as middlemen for the Portuguese, Dutch, and English.[42]

This diversification also had important consequences in terms of religion, as it put the merchant families in closer contact with other forms of Christianity: Russian Orthodox, Catholic, and Protestant. Armenian families who shifted the focus of their activities to territories under Catholic rulers tended to cultivate contacts with Catholic missionaries. A notable example was the Scerimans, who, since the reign of ʿAbbās I, had been one of the leading families in New Julfa, from where they engaged in trade with Italy, among other lands. When they moved their base of operations to Venice around 1700, they profited from the fact that, as converts to Catholicism, Italian authorities considered them supporters of the Armenian Church's union with Rome. Quite strikingly, the Scerimans had begun to show this preference starting in the 1640s, when the first changes began to appear in the local power structure that would eventually threaten the relatively privileged position of the Armenian merchants of New Julfa under Safavid rule.[43] The merchants' need to diversify their networks opened up new possibilities for Catholic mission.

Omens of Conversion or Machiavellianism?

Persia attracted the attention of the Catholic courts in Rome and Madrid at a time when the inclusive nature of Safavid rule was especially pronounced. European observers saw in this characteristic of rule under ʿAbbās I signs of an impending conversion to Christianity. This was a misperception based on a confessional understanding of religion. In Rome, this idea remained in place for some time and influenced decision-making until around 1630, despite contrary reports about actual practice on the ground that portrayed ʿAbbās I as a Machiavellian ruler.

In the late sixteenth century, Pius V had sought common ground with Shah Ṭahmāsp I in their shared aversion to attacks on human and divine law by the "tyrant of the Turks." By 1601, Clement VIII, in a breve he sent along with the Jesuits Francisco Costa and Diego Miranda, proceeded from the assumption that ʿAbbās I was inclined to convert to Christianity. The pope even addressed one of the shah's wives as "our dearest daughter in Christ" because of her Georgian origins.[44] This idealized image of a philo-Christian Safavid court resulted from the selective reading of accounts of the presence of Christians at court and the shah's signs of respect for the Christian faith. It originated in intelligence that had arrived in Goa and Europe in the 1580s via the diplomatic mission of an Augustinian, Simão de Morães, acting on behalf of Philip II as king of Portugal. The flow of information suddenly became broader but also more contradictory with the lasting establishment of the Augustinians and Discalced Carmelites in Isfahan in 1602 and 1607, respectively. Some of the missionaries soon vehemently contradicted the image of the shah as a philo-Christian potential ally. Nevertheless, the positive reports about ʿAbbās I still formed the basis for decisions that the *Propaganda Fide* made in the first decade after its founding in 1622.

The benevolent gestures with which the shah received the Augustinians and the Discalced Carmelites were initially interpreted as signs of the ruler's religious proximity to Christianity. In 1602, Aleixo de Meneses, archbishop of Goa, had the Augustinians Jerónimo da Cruz and António de Gouveia present the shah with a book containing depictions of the life of Christ, because he had been informed of "how much affection the shah has shown for the matters of Christianity." ʿAbbās I seemed to confirm this impression with his curiosity about the "secrets" of the Christian faith represented in the book and his request that all of the illustrations be explained in Persian marginal notes. In his 1606 chronicle of the Augustinian Congregation in India, Friar Felix de Jesus reported such news and other information on the obliging treatment of his brethren. According to this portrayal, the permission to build a church in Isfahan was more than an opportunistic gesture toward the envoys of a potential coalition partner; it was also a hint of the possibly imminent conversion of the shah and his subjects.[45]

The choice of gifts that the Discalced Carmelites presented to ʿAbbās I in January 1608 was telling. They included a rock crystal cross, a copy of the *Salus Populi Romani* icon of Santa Maria Maggiore in Rome, a painting of St. Michael, the four books of the New Testament in Arabic translation, and a lavishly illustrated thirteenth-century Bible, alongside an Arabic edition of Euclid's *Elements*. Guiding this selection was the notion that the shah was about to convert to Catholicism. The Arabic translations of the Gospels and Euclid's *Elements* (Figure 13, p. 98) documented Rome's role as a center of printing in non-European languages, since the books were most likely the editions of these works published by the *Typographia Medicea* in Rome. ʿAbbās I accepted these gifts with clear signs of appreciation. He had the illuminated manuscript now known as the Morgan Bible inscribed with explanations in Persian (Figure 9).[46]

Alongside news of demonstrations of favor by the ruler, which were interpreted as harbingers of his imminent conversion, reports that could have dampened such hopes also arrived in Europe early on. Contradictions between accounts written by the same cleric show the degree to which their content was influenced by both the context of the interaction on the ground and the relationship with the addressees of the reports. This is particularly striking in the case of the Discalced Carmelite Juan Thadeo de San Eliseo, whose later position as an interpreter and translator at the court

Figure 9 Fol. 24v of the Morgan Bible with explanations of the illustrations in Persian (1 Sam. 14:37–45 and 15:2–9). The picture Bible, created around 1250 for Louis IX of France (r. 1226–70), came to Isfahan as a gift from Cardinal Bernard Maciejowski to ʿAbbās I. © The Morgan Library & Museum, New York, MS M.638, fol. 24v. Purchased by J. P. Morgan (1867–1943) in 1916

will be discussed in more detail in Chapter 3. After his first sojourn in Isfahan from 1607 to 1608, the Discalced Carmelite Paolo Simone di Gesù Maria, in a letter of 1608 or 1609 to the *praepositus generalis* of the order, painted a rather positive picture of the emerging possibilities for the mission. His companion Juan Thadeo, by contrast, emphasized ʿAbbās I's intention to convert as many Christians as possible to Islam. In a relation concerning the morals of ʿAbbās I also composed in 1609, Friar Juan Thadeo paired enmity against the Christians with sexual proclivities (polygyny and homosexuality) to create an image of a ruler from whose lusts nobody—boys, girls, or married women—was safe. This picture was further substantiated by the rulers' violations of the commandments of his own religion—the accusation that he consumed pork and wine. ʿAbbās I was described as a man without religion, guided in matters of faith, as in all government business, by his will alone.[47] It was not love of and an inclination toward the Christian religion but "mere interest and reason of state" that determined ʿAbbās I's relationship with the clerics, two other Discalced Carmelites noted in 1609.⁴⁸ In later reports, Juan Thadeo de San Eliseo wrote far more positively than he had in 1608–9 about his conversations with scholars and his reception at court. The new tone corresponded to the altered position of the Discalced Carmelites, who had built up relationships at court and won the shah's respect in the meantime.

How the Curia perceived the Persian mission and made decisions only partially followed the reports that arrived in Rome. In 1622, the *praepositus generalis*, Domingo de Jesús María, himself a member of the *Propaganda Fide*, presented the congregation's other members with the printed relation on the "martyrdom" of five Muslim converts to Christianity who had been baptized by the Discalced Carmelites.⁴⁹ Thus, in the year of the *Propaganda Fide*'s founding, the Discalced Carmelites' Persian mission acquired its own martyrs, which would assign it a worthy place alongside the Asian missions of other orders. At the same time, these events showed that in Persia, too, there could be no question of converting the Muslim population.

Nevertheless, it was not such news that determined the newly founded congregation's perception of Persia. Cut off from direct contact with its missionaries in the field, in the first decade of its existence the *Propaganda Fide* experienced the Persian mission in its own way—as it was supposed to be, not as it actually was. Although most accounts written by missionaries in the 1620s suggested different conclusions, the congregation's consultations and resolutions were largely based on information that affirmed the image of clerics being welcomed with open arms. The secretary of the congregation, Francesco Ingoli, added various approving marginal notes to a report by the Dominican Gregorio Orsini explaining why the dissemination of the Christian faith was so easy in Persia: there they were free to preach the truth of the Gospels and the errors of the "Mohammedan faith." The Persians shared with the Christians "many principles and various opinions."⁵⁰ Since the path to convert Muslim Persians was open, Ingoli argued for the appointment of a Latin bishop in Isfahan. Thanks to the presence of a bishop, those willing to convert would find their way to the Latin rather than the Armenian rite. The bishops of Isfahan and Baghdad appointed in 1632 were accordingly sent to Persia with the dual mission of winning over the "king of Persia," his court, and other "persons of authority and knowledge" to the truth of the Gospel, and encouraging the "heretical" or "schismatic" Christians to unite with Rome.⁵¹

The *Propaganda Fide* and its first secretary, Francesco Ingoli, thus took particular note of information that helped to justify the missionary plans and thereby to legitimize the congregation. The Persian mission of the Discalced Carmelites, one of the few undertakings under the comparatively direct authority of the *Propaganda Fide*, was especially well suited to the awakening expectations of the recently established congregation's success. To be sure, voices that warned against such excessive expectations were also raised in Rome: the papal breve for the shah, as Pietro Della Valle, a Roman nobleman who had lived in Isfahan from 1618 to 1621, noted in 1632, should be limited to "exhorting the king to retain his friendship and correspondence with His Holiness and all Christians and grant his favor to the bishops sent to Persia and all of the Christians subject to them." To expect the shah to build and furnish a church was akin to "demanding that the pope build and furnish a mosque in Rome."⁵²

The missionaries mostly described the respect that the shah showed them and the practices and objects associated with their faith as harbingers of his imminent conversion or as an expression of Machiavellian opportunism based on reason of state. Individual reports, however, suggest that such gestures should be interpreted within the context of a culture in which godliness was not tied to exclusive claims of a confessional nature. We cannot say what exactly was behind each individual report by missionaries who claimed to have publicly called upon the shah to convert to the "true faith." Did the Augustinian António de Gouveia actually dare to demand before the assembled court in 1602 that the shah abandon "the false law" he had followed thus far and instead adopt "the true law of Christ"? Reports of this kind catered to expectations of the missionaries' role as potential witnesses to faith, and there is good reason to doubt that they cited these dialogues faithfully. The shah's response as cited in the chronicle of the Augustinian Felix de Jesus is striking, however; according to the friar, the shah had replied that "his faith was good *too*, and he could achieve salvation within it."[53] To the Augustinian and his readers, the notion that there might be more than one road to a godly life could only appear as an "error," especially when the other religion in question was Islam. If we accept that Felix de Jesus reproduced the shah's reply correctly, we can also interpret it in a different way: what follows will demonstrate that the shah's answer, and his show of respect for Christian practices and the objects associated with them, should be understood as expressions of an inclusive understanding of religion, which allowed for a higher degree of ambiguity and plurality than did the confessional churches of early modern Europe. Such attitudes of relative tolerance for ambiguity were characteristic of premodern Islamicate societies.[54] Alongside the inclusive strategies of Safavid imperial rule, they paved the way for the settlement of Catholic missionaries in Safavid Iran.

3

Christian ʿulamā? Missionaries and Muslims

Starting with the Iberian overseas expansion, Europeans categorized the societies they encountered outside Europe hierarchically. This in turn formed the basis for instructions in the missionary handbooks that outlined the appropriate ways to make contact with local people. If we follow the Jesuit José de Acosta's influential *De procuranda Indorum Salute* (On how to bring about the salvation of the Indians) (1588), the inhabitants of the Asian empires, with their permanent governments, laws, fortified cities, respected magistrates, prosperous trade, and written cultures, belonged to the highest category of non-Christians and therefore, like the Greeks and Romans, were to be called to the Gospels in the manner of the Apostles.[1] For Acosta, this meant that any element of these cultures that did not contradict Christianity should be respected. The friendship and trust of the potential converts were to be gained with modesty, and the local authorities respected.[2]

The missionaries who began arriving in Isfahan in the early seventeenth century followed a categorization and approach similar to Acosta's. Except in matters of religion, they met local culture with great respect. From the outset, the Discalced Carmelites expressed admiration for the material culture of the capital city of Isfahan. In 1609, Friars Redempto de la Cruz and Benigno di San Michele described the "Image of the World Square" (*Maidān-i Naqš-i Ǧahān*), which ʿAbbās I had laid out near his palace, as larger and more beautiful than any other in the world (Figure 10). The shah had erected accommodations for foreign merchants that brimmed "with royal splendor and grandeur." Their opinion of the boulevard (*Čahār Bāǧ*) constructed on the orders of ʿAbbās I to connect the Armenian quarter of New Julfa with Isfahan via the Allāhwerdi bridge—one of the most splendidly embellished, according to the authors—was equally euphoric (Figures 11 and 12).[3] Philippe de la Très Sainte Trinité, who spent a few months in Isfahan in 1629–30 and a few weeks there in 1640, was receptive to the aesthetic value even of the mosques, especially the Shah Mosque.[4]

The reports by Discalced Carmelites were not the only ones to contain implicit and explicit comparisons suggesting that the material culture of Isfahan was at least equal to that of European cities. The Capuchin friar Pacifique de Provins, who founded his order's settlement in Isfahan in 1628, stated that ever since ʿAbbās I had chosen Isfahan as his capital, it had become "the most pleasant place to live under the sun."[5] Alexandre de Rhodes, one of the first Jesuits to arrive in Isfahan in 1648, used similar words: "It is one of the largest and loveliest cities I have seen anywhere in the world."

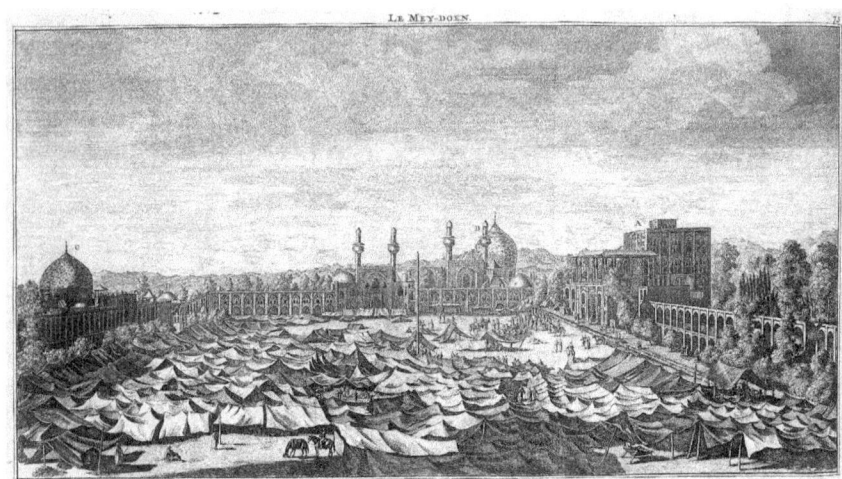

Figure 10 "Image of the World Square" (*Maidān-i Naqš-i Ǧahān*) in Isfahan (from De Bruyn, *Voyages*, vol. 1, plate 75)

Figure 11 Boulevard (*Čahār Bāġ*) in Isfahan (from De Bruyn, *Voyages*, vol. 1, plate 79)

Figure 12 Allāhwerdi bridge in Isfahan (from De Bruyn, *Voyages,* vol. 1, plate 78)

The French Jesuit's points of comparison were Paris and Rome, which were not the superiors of Isfahan: "In the center of the city is a beautiful rectangular square [Image of the World Square] like the Place Royale in Paris, but a good deal larger; it is twice the size of the Piazza Navona, which I saw in Rome."[6]

While preexisting notions about Asian empires conditioned the missionaries' approach, their favorable perceptions of Persia were also fashioned by the ways in which the clerics were received at the court in Isfahan. This chapter will take a closer look at the social practices underlying their descriptions. When they first arrived in 1602 and 1607, respectively, the Augustinians and Discalced Carmelites primarily addressed the ruler, Shah ʿAbbās I. They would request his permission to settle in Persia, but that was not their only goal. In Madrid, Goa, and Rome, the dispatch of the clerics was associated with hopes not just of an alliance against the Ottomans but also of converting many Muslims and indeed the shah himself to Christianity, as noted in Chapter 2. The express mandate to cultivate relations with the court distinguished the missions in Persia from those in the Ottoman Empire. There, the court was deemed out of bounds for Catholic clerics, for which reason the practices of indirect contacts on the highest level (for example, through the French ambassadors and their dragomans at the Sublime Port) aimed to create latitude for activities outside the court, among the Eastern Christians and the Latin diasporas. In Persia, by contrast, aside from the ruler, the ʿulamā close to the court were among the first contact persons for missionaries. The friars conversed with Shiʾa scholars not just about religion but also about ancient philosophy and other fields of knowledge.

Since the Roman Curia's first efforts to make contact with the shah, the shared enmity toward the Ottomans had shaped perceptions of the Safavid Empire. At the time of ʿAbbās I, these contrasted markedly with the negative characterizations of the Ottoman Empire, which had replaced older, inclusive categories in the wake of the Reformation and Catholic reform.[7] Secular and clerical European travelers alike not only recognized Safavid Persia as the site of a splendid material culture but also described a flourishing intellectual culture. Although education and scholarship were cultivated equally in the Ottoman Empire, assessments of the Safavid Empire were far more positive. The military conflicts that disrupted relations with the Ottoman Empire were absent here. Through the reception of ancient authors, the Ottomans, who had sealed the decline of the Byzantine Empire with the capture of Constantinople, were associated with the descendants of the nomadic, barbarian Scythians, while the Safavids were associated with the Persian rulers of antiquity.[8] For the missionaries reared in the tradition of Italian humanism, the focus was less on the descriptions of the Persian kings as Asiatic despots in the work of Herodotus than on the image of Persia presented by Xenophon, whose *Cyropaedia* characterized Cyrus as a virtuous and wise monarch.[9]

The notion that the shared opposition to the Ottomans implied a rejection of an illegitimate "despotic" mode of government is evident in political writing from as early as the sixteenth century, for example in the works of Giovanni Botero. Mission accounts picked up this line of argument. They contrasted the "tyrant" of the Turks, who degraded his subjects to the status of slaves and disregarded all the rules of law in interactions between princes, with the ruler of Persia, referred to as a king, whose rule thus appeared legitimate, despite the difference of religion. The "miserliness" and "arrogant tyranny of the Turks" contrasted with the "agreeable and polite disposition of the Persians" and the "order and security of their government," according to a certain Jean de Montheron, who accompanied the bishop of Babylon, the Discalced Carmelite Bernard de Sainte-Thérèse, to Isfahan in 1640–1.[10]

Starting in the second half of the seventeenth century, reports on the Persian political order grew progressively gloomier. This corresponded on the one hand to actual changes in the practice of rule under the successors to ʿAbbās I, in which the living conditions of the Christian minorities deteriorated, and on the other to changing patterns of perception among European observers. Their positive assessments increasingly referred to a past golden age, while the image of the present was marked by despotism and the decline of the social and political order.[11] Raphaël du Mans's 1660 *État de la Perse* is but one example of the increasingly negative representation of Persia by European authors. Unlike Giovanni Botero, the Capuchin now described the government of the realm as "despotic." The king possessed "absolute command … over the life and death" of all his subjects, whom he could exalt or humiliate with equal ease. In court cases, an individual with no knowledge of the law decided in favor of the highest bidder; there was no aristocracy even in name only, and tax collectors took from the poor as they saw fit.[12] Despite his dependence on the Capuchin's information, Jean Chardin qualified the despotic nature of Safavid rule by associating despotism primarily with the court. He further contradicted reports stating that the king concentrated landownership in a despotic manner and praised the low taxes paid by his subjects.¹³ Meanwhile, in 1728 the Jesuit Tadeusz Juda Krusiński' published his *Histoire de la dernière Révolution de Perse* on the most recent history of Persia. Within its pages the Afghan conquest and the toppling of the Safavids in 1722 stood for the ruin of a once-flourishing empire as a result of the immorality of the eunuchs who had seized the reins of government.¹⁴ In eighteenth-century European political writing, the reign of Nādir Šāh (r. 1736–47) was depicted as the very epitome of Oriental despotism.¹⁵ When the last Latin bishop of Isfahan, the Discalced Carmelite Cornelio di San Giuseppe, left Bushehr on the Persian Gulf in the retinue of the English in 1769, he said that he had done so to avoid "falling victim to the wrath of those barbarians."¹⁶

As in other Asian empires, such perceptions provided the foundation for more or less extensive adaptations to the local social structure. For that reason, the practices of cultivating relationships on the ground that the missionaries pursued and the comportment they adopted should be viewed against this backdrop. We will turn first to contacts at court, where the Portuguese Augustinians and French Capuchins, in particular, performed diplomatic duties on behalf of Christian courts, while individual missionaries also entered the service of the shah as translators and interpreters. Building on this, in a second subchapter, I will explore relationships between the missionaries and Shi'a scholars. I will analyze the Catholic clerics' participation in a knowledge culture rooted in antiquity and show that while the religious disputations exposed the dogmatic divide between them and Shi'a scholars, the same practice also allowed them to share in a culture of sociability with their Muslim counterparts. Third, I will examine healing practices in broader segments of the Muslim population. Here we need to elucidate how much demand there was among the Muslim population, not just for the medical skills of some missionaries but also for the capacity to work miracles, which Muslims attributed to them as men of God. At the end of the chapter, I will explore the case of two Augustinians—singular in the history of the Persian missions—who, as a result of their social integration into local society, broke with their order and the Church and converted to Islam. These were exceptionally rare cases. Similarly, however, the hopes of converting numerous Muslims to Catholicism, which the friars drew from the respect shown them and the symbols of their faith, were destined to be disappointed.

Missionaries at the Safavid Court

The clerics who arrived at the Safavid court beginning in 1602 were given direct access to the ruler. This might appear surprising, considering contemporary practice at Western European courts and the missionary experiences at other non-Christian courts, but we now know that the practice of conviviality fundamentally distinguished Safavid court ceremonial from that of the Ottomans. Ottoman ceremonial glorified the *majestas* of the sultan by increasingly restricting his public appearances. The outer walls of the Topkapi palace and a whole series of internal gates separated the interior space of the sultan's court from the city. The Safavids, in contrast, rehearsed the obligations of ruler and subjects through rituals emphasizing the hierarchically organized personal proximity between the ruler and a select circle of his subjects.

The expansion of Isfahan into an imperial residence starting in the reign of ʿAbbās I (r. 1587–1629) was intended to locate the ruler's accessibility within an earthly vision of heavenly paradise in expectation of the return of the *mahdī*. Accordingly, the "seat of power" (*Daulathana*) was connected via a building (*ʿĀlī Qāpū*) designed as both a gate and a palace with the gigantic, generally accessible "Image of the World Square," which formed the center of the new urban complex (Figure 10, p. 80). Unlike the Ottoman court, where Christian envoys could interact with the sultan only very rarely and in highly formalized acts, at the Safavid court the shah's *majestas* was expressed through occasions of choreographed sociability. For instance, foreign guests (including missionaries) might be invited to banquets over which the ruler presided in person and where a surfeit of food and wine was served, accompanied by music, dancing, and other entertainment.[17]

The ruler's accessibility made it easier for Catholic missionaries to contact him. At the same time, it facilitated misunderstandings: the Augustinians and the Discalced Carmelites based their initial expectations of conversion not least on the fact that they were not merely given access to the ruler but were even permitted to convey their position to the assembled court. The fact that the actions used to represent the shah's superior position resonated far beyond the palace walls because happenings at court were so widely visible also had an impact on diplomatic practice. It contributed to the European courts giving preference in their relations with the Safavid court to agents who were not perceived as the alter ego of their monarchs. Members of the regular clergy fell into this category.

Diplomatic Assignments

In 1602 and 1607, the Augustinians and the Discalced Carmelites arrived at the Safavid court as envoys, respectively, from Philip III and the pope. They were expected to subordinate their missionary activities to the aim of getting ʿAbbās I to commit to the struggle against the Turks. While the political dimension of the papal commission soon waned in importance for the Discalced Carmelites, the Augustinians in Isfahan remained existentially bound to the interest of the court at Madrid (later Lisbon) and the viceroy of the *Estado da Índia* in Goa in maintaining a permanent agent at the Safavid court. The same applied until around 1700 to the guardian of the French Capuchin settlement founded in 1628, who was also supposed to act as his king's agent at the Safavid court.

For the court at Madrid and the viceroy of the Portuguese *Estado da Índia* in Goa, the permanent presence of their own agent at the court in Isfahan in the early seventeenth century was all the more important as relations with the Safavids were strained at a time when the Portuguese had occupied Hormuz, and the English and Dutch were beginning to prove themselves serious rivals in shipping and trade on the Indian Ocean. The Augustinian convent in Isfahan was therefore financed from Goa in the king's name "in the service of God and His Majesty." In exceptional cases a layman might be sent to the Persian court to lead negotiations in the prior's stead. Yet, even then, the latter was supposed to advise the former with his knowledge of the language and local conditions and assist him with contacts at court.

Upon the recommendation of the archbishop of Goa, the Augustinian Aleixo de Meneses, in 1608 Philip III ordered that two Augustinians should always follow the shah whenever he left Isfahan. They were to represent his interests with the shah, inform themselves of all necessary circumstances, and in this way compensate for the absence of an ambassador. Because of his experience and the apparent favor of the shah, Friar Belchior dos Anjos, who had already accompanied a secular envoy to the Safavid court in 1604, was selected for this task. In the 1610s, Belchior dos Anjos and other Augustinians corresponded with the court in Madrid from Persia as agents without ambassadorial status. They sent information about ʿAbbās I's military campaigns against the Ottomans and his relations with foreign courts, as well as the silk trade, the conflicts over Hormuz, and the English advance into the Persian Gulf.[18] The activities of the Augustinians were conditioned by the composite structure of the Spanish monarchy, which included the Crown of Portugal starting in 1580. The friars acted more within the context of the Portuguese *Estado da Índia* and less that of the overall Spanish monarchy. When Philip III sent García de Silva y Figueroa, a secular envoy reputed to follow the interests of the Crown of Castile, to Persia, Friar Belchior dos Anjos participated, in agreement with the viceroy in Goa and the governor of Hormuz, in the efforts to undermine this mission. The ambassador of Castilian origin was held up for more than three years in Goa and Hormuz. Although he arrived in Goa in October of 1614, he was not able to obtain his first audience in Qazvīn until 1618.[19] In his correspondence with the Council of State in Madrid, Friar Belchior dos Anjos gave the impression that he was acting in consultation with García de Silva y Figueroa but not without heavily criticizing the latter for the great expenses he had caused and casting doubt on his skills. Because of his status as a clergyman, the Augustinian presented himself as the better servant of the king; what was needed in Persia was "an intelligent person, who costs little and writes a good deal to the court [in Madrid], to India, and Hormuz."[20]

The conquest of Hormuz in 1622 by the troops of ʿAbbās I with the support of English ships signaled the weakening, but not the end, of the Portuguese presence on the Persian Gulf vis-à-vis its European and Asian rivals. In 1630, the *wazīr* of Shiraz granted the Portuguese the right to set up a factory in Bandar-i Kung and gave them half of the customs revenues there. In practice, Portuguese revenues remained well below those promised in 1630.[21] In 1650, the Portuguese *Estado da Índia* lost the port of Muscat, which the Omanis then used to threaten the remaining Portuguese settlements. In this context, the Augustinians repeatedly played an important role in negotiations with the Persian court. Success would also have financially benefited their convent in Isfahan because the Crown had promised them part of the revenues from Bandar-i Kung.

In 1695, when ships belonging to the imam of Oman pillaged Bandar-i Kung, the preconditions for a Portuguese alliance with the shah seemed to be fulfilled. The governor of Lār offered to help negotiate a treaty, in which support from ships of the *Estado da Índia* was tied to the fulfillment of the Portuguese claim to half of the customs revenues from Bandar-i Kung. The viceroy in Goa sent Gregório Pereira Fidalgo to Isfahan to ratify the treaty, but opponents of the agreement gained the upper hand and the diplomatic mission failed.[22]

This failed mission is interesting nonetheless because it documents the division of tasks between the participants particularly well. According to instructions from the viceroy in Goa, Gregório Pereira Fidalgo's role as ambassador was to obtain the ratification of the treaty by the shah and in the process to emphasize through ceremonial his superior rank to the other Christian envoys present in Isfahan. A role outside diplomatic ceremonial was reserved for the Augustinian António de Jesus. He was supposed to advise the ambassador and prepare for his journey from Bandar-i Kung to Isfahan and his reception at court. Because of the friar's knowledge of local customs, the ambassador was to follow his advice, "as this cleric is so experienced, you must always adapt precisely to his accounts."[23]

Friar António was indeed in Bandar-i Kung when the ambassador arrived. According to Pereira Fidalgo, the division of labor corresponded to the viceroy's instructions: while he himself attended to the appropriate ceremonial, the Augustinian made sure to insist on payment of the Portuguese portion of the customs revenues. António de Jesus earned high praise for his services as adviser and negotiator in 1696–7. The king instructed his viceroy to thank the friar, who had been appointed prior of his convent in October 1696, for his efforts in the negotiations.[24] The viceroy never got the opportunity, since almost simultaneously with Peter II's letter, he also received news of the Augustinian's conversion to Islam. The very knowledge that had made António de Jesus a suitable adviser to and negotiator for the Portuguese ambassador would also enable him to build a new existence in the service of the shah.[25]

Gregório Pereira Fidalgo was the last ambassador of the viceroy of the *Estado da Índia* at the Safavid court. As had been the case before his dispatch, the correspondence between the viceroy and other Portuguese officials and the Persian court was conducted wholly through the factor of Bandar-i Kung and the Augustinians in Isfahan. António de Jesus's successor as prior, António do Desterro, was soon deemed a similarly well-informed intermediary and agent. We know that this role was assigned to him from instructions to the commander of the fleet in the Persian Gulf and from the viceroy's correspondence. Thus, in March 1709 the Council of State of the *Estado da Índia* in Goa opposed the dispatch of an ambassador. Negotiations with the shah were to be handled instead by António do Desterro, whose "intelligence" and thorough knowledge of that court were thought to be more efficacious than that of "any other person."[26]

Although António do Desterro never attained any diplomatic rank, he nevertheless remained *the* key figure in all negotiations between Goa and the Persian court. The instructions regarding cooperation with the Augustinian given to the commander of the Portuguese fleet in 1709 were repeated in later instructions to the commanders. To enable the Augustinian to perform the role intended for him, he was to receive copies of all letters to the shah, and the friar would insist upon a quick response to them. The viceroy frequently corresponded with the Augustinian prior directly about these commissions. According to him, the Augustinian was well respected at the court in Isfahan and "did the business of state there."[27]

Such deployments of members of the regular clergy as agents of the Portuguese Crown in Persia were not isolated cases but corresponded to a practice that the viceroys of the *Estado da Índia* had already cultivated on the Indian Subcontinent in the sixteenth century, for instance at the Mughal court. The guardian of the settlement of French

Capuchins in Isfahan founded in 1628 would perform similar tasks in the service of the king of France. From the 1650s until his death in 1696, the longtime guardian Raphaël du Mans played an ambivalent role as a contact who put his knowledge of the local culture and language at the service of Europeans of varied origin while also acting as a confidant to the shahs who reigned in this period. From the time of François Picquet's sojourn in Isfahan during the years 1682 to 1684, in his capacity as agent of the king of France, the guardian of the Capuchins had competition from the bishop of Babylon, who was also the apostolic vicar of Isfahan until the appointment of a bishop there in 1693. When Picquet arrived in Isfahan in 1682, he was received as the ambassador of Louis XIV.[28]

In the early eighteenth century, secular envoys began to take precedence over clerical ones. In 1708, Pierre-Victor Michel negotiated a treaty regulating relations on the French-Ottoman model, which was intended both to create the basis for the expansion of the activities of the *Compagnie des Indes* to Persia and to ensure the protection of the king of France for the missions.[29] In the background, French clerics continued to intervene in the conduct of business: even before his arrival, Michel corresponded with two Jesuits and two Discalced Carmelites. Together, the four clerics worked against the influence of "enemy nations," among which they numbered not just the English, the Dutch, and the "heretical Armenians" but also the Catholic Portuguese. Friar Basile de Saint-Charles used his connections at court to ensure that Michel would be conducted to Isfahan and appropriately received there "with all honors due to the title of an ambassador."[30] After Michel's departure, his consular functions were transferred to clerics of French origin. Louis-Marie Pidou de Saint-Olon, bishop of Babylon, was appointed consul in Isfahan and Basile de Saint-Charles vice-consul. In 1718 another French secular envoy arrived in Persia in the guise of Ange de Gardane, Sieur de Sainte-Croix.

Unlike the Capuchin Raphaël du Mans, who had acted without diplomatic *caractère*, Pierre-Victor Michel and Ange de Gardane combined their personal claims to status with the functions of diplomatic representation. In 1708 Pierre-Victor Michel tried to transfer Louis XIV's claim to precedence over the representatives of all other Christian rulers from the Ottoman Empire to Persia. He demanded the right to appear before the shah bearing his sword because the king of France was the mightiest monarch in Christendom. He was not permitted to do so and instead had to make do with a written declaration that no ambassador had ever been admitted to an audience wearing a sword. The question of precedence vis-à-vis the Dutch then arose when he was received by the grand vizier (*i'timād ad-daula*): since the representative of the States General had been served his meal on gold plates, Michel refused to eat from porcelain dishes, but this effort proved equally in vain. Given the seniority and economic superiority of the Dutch and English East Indies Companies in trade with Persia, his successor, Ange de Gardane, was equally unable to enforce his monarch's precedence over the republican and thus—within European princely society—vastly inferior United Provinces.[31]

The relations of the Portuguese and French Crowns to the Safavid court clearly reveal the advantages of deploying members of the regular clergy. At a time when Portuguese power politics was running up against ever tighter restrictions, the Augustinians in

Isfahan, who were integrated into local society and mastered its language and customs, represented a comparatively efficient and inexpensive alternative to the dispatch of temporary secular envoys, who were unfamiliar with local conditions and had to be accompanied to Persia by a fleet that was actually urgently needed to protect Portuguese possessions in India and shipping in South Asia.

Above all, however, deploying intermediaries whose status meant that they were not considered the alter ego of their ruler within European princely society avoided the ceremonial problems that the French envoys, Michel and Gardane, encountered. Because of their personal vows of humility and poverty, regular clerics could not engage in the secular rivalry over status. Their use as diplomatic actors thus removed concerns about enforcing claims of rank; without any loss of honor for the monarch who dispatched them, regular clerics could dispense with the kind of prestige spending incurred by secular envoys. This was all the more important since envoys at the Safavid court not only faced difficulties when they sought to enforce claims of rank over European rivals. In addition, they had to submit to local ceremonial that underscored the superior position of the shah. While Catholic courts thus preferred to entrust diplomatic missions to regular clerics, the fact that they were present in Persia with their East India Companies offered a different solution to the Protestant States General and the king of England. To be sure, both endowed these companies with privileges and granted them monopolies based on which they exercised a wide range of prerogatives in their settlements, including criminal jurisdiction. From the standpoint of a European princely society shaped by aristocratic values, representatives of trading companies involved in diplomatic missions nevertheless did not hold the status of unlimited proxies for their rulers. Not unlike the representatives of the companies on the West African coast that Christina Brauner has studied, their counterparts in Persia could claim to represent their rulers but were "by no means compelled" at all times "to worry about upholding their representative role," which they could deploy flexibly as a resource.[32]

For their part, regular clerics could play the role of the ruler's agent (but not his representative) in certain situations or where necessary could return to their "true" vocation as men of clerical estate. The Augustinian Manuel de Jesus did the latter in 1690 when two employees of the VOC complained to him of the Portuguese resistance to a VOC trading post at Bandar-i Kung. He responded that, as a "member of the clergy," he did not involve himself in such matters.[33] The Augustinian's arguments recall the strategies of women in European court diplomacy, who in their capacity as intermediaries also alternated between different roles. They performed diplomatic tasks, but the prevailing social conventions also allowed them to evade responsibility when necessary, in this case relying on their gender rather than their clerical status.[34]

Translators and Interpreters

The mandate to cultivate relationships with the court allowed individual missionaries to grow into a role as translators and interpreters at the Safavid court. The precondition was the linguistic skills they had acquired since arriving in Persia. The translation of and commentary on the texts they were expected to deliver led to commissions to assist less linguistically skilled visitors from Europe, whether envoys, agents of trading companies, or those traveling on their own business. Two key figures here were a Discalced Carmelite, Juan Thadeo de San Eliseo, in the 1610s and 1620s and, in the second half of the century, a Capuchin, Raphaël du Mans. Their activities at the Safavid court will be explored and compared in what follows.

After arriving in Persia in 1607, Juan Thadeo de San Eliseo devoted himself to studying Persian, Arabic, and Turkish. His priorities in learning these languages reflected the orientation toward the court and the Muslim elites, in keeping with the commission he and his companions had received from Clement VIII. In 1609, the friar reported that he could now speak, read, and understand Persian. He understood just a little Turkish and was diligently learning Arabic because this language was important for perfecting his Persian and understanding the Quran.[35]

Against the background of his successful efforts at making contacts at court and in learned circles, in the 1610s Friar Juan Thadeo adopted a missionary strategy dedicated more to the example of Christian perfection than to the refutation of "errors" and "ignorance." Because of their appreciation for the purity of the Christian religion and its servants, the Persian Muslims would ultimately recognize their own errors and turn away from them. Such missionary strategies presupposed a long period of coexistence with people of other faiths. They combined efforts to communicate religious content with services of immediate practical use for the shah.

The Discalced Carmelite composed several works in Persian and translated an explanation of Christian doctrine as well as biblical texts into that language. To do so, he relied on the help of three mullahs and a rabbi for the translations. The rabbi prepared a Persian translation of the Psalms based on the Hebrew text, which the friar amended using the Latin Vulgate. The mullahs, for their part, helped edit the Persian versions of the texts. In 1618, Friar Juan Thadeo presented the Persian translation of the Psalms and an Arabic translation of the Gospels to ʿAbbās I. While the Persian translations were prepared under the direction of the Discalced Carmelite, the Arabic version of the Gospels was that of an edition published in Rome in 1590–1 by the *Typographia Medicea*, a copy of which the shah had already received as a gift in 1608. This time, the Discalced Carmelite kindled ʿAbbas I's interest in printing. Juan Thadeo de San Eliseo hoped that the shah's request to procure an Arabic-Persian printing press from Rome would lead to the dissemination of Christian literature and that this miracle of technology might win the shah over to Catholicism. The printing press was finally brought to Isfahan by some Discalced Carmelites, who arrived in December 1628 or January 1629. No products of this printing press have survived; apparently, the conditions to keep it operational were lacking in Persia.[36]

For the Discalced Carmelite Juan Thadeo, the fulfilment of the shah's wish was in keeping with a relationship strategy that was only indirectly expected to culminate in successful conversion. This included activities as an interpreter and translator at court, which are especially well documented for the years 1619 to 1621. Friar Juan Thadeo was always present in those days when ʿAbbās I received the Spaniard García de Silva y Figueroa. The shah passed letters from the ambassador and other guests to the Discalced Carmelite, who first summarized them verbally and then prepared a written translation. When the friar himself presented letters from Christian courts that had been sent to the Discalced Carmelites, he was also asked to translate them personally into Persian. According to eyewitness accounts, ʿAbbās I completely trusted the friar's translations. After some ten years in Persia, he was capable, for example, of spontaneously translating a letter from Philip III in Spanish—his mother tongue—into Persian during an audience.[37]

For the latter half of the seventeenth century, we have ample documentation of the position of the Capuchin Raphaël du Mans at the Safavid court. In his case, too, an outstanding knowledge of Persian is evidence of his affiliation with court society and learned Muslim circles. In his 1660 *État de la Perse*, the Capuchin compiled an impressive wealth of information about the beliefs and customs of Persian Muslims, which, like his linguistic abilities, served as a knowledge basis for his contacts. His text pays scant attention to the Armenians, however, and he also felt no need to learn their language. The political dimension of their mission on behalf of the French Crown meant that in Persia, the Capuchins, in contrast to the broad social basis of their missions in Europe, mainly cultivated contacts with the court and the Muslim elites. Acquiring proficiency in the Persian language had thus been foremost in their minds ever since establishing themselves in Persia in 1628.

Like the Discalced Carmelite Juan Thadeo de San Eliseo had done before him for a time, with his services as interpreter and translator Friar Raphaël gained the particular trust of the three shahs who reigned during his nearly fifty-year sojourn in Persia from 1647 to 1696. The first evidence of his activities as a translator to the court stems from 1654 to 1655. Meanwhile, interpreting services that brought him into personal contact with the shah are first mentioned during the stay of the French jewel merchant Jean-Baptiste Tavernier, a Huguenot, at the court of Isfahan in the winter of 1664–5. According to Tavernier's account, the Capuchin was summoned to the court amidst preparations for Christmas services. When business had been concluded to the shah's satisfaction, he invited the friar, Tavernier, and three Dutchmen to a banquet with musical and dance entertainment, during which Raphaël du Mans once again interpreted for Tavernier and the other "Franks."[38]

The Capuchin's relationships at court were already so good by 1665 that people began to suspect that he was playing more into the hands of the shah than the Christian envoys. In May of that year when a Dominican, Antonino Tani, arrived in Isfahan bearing letters from the pope, the emperor, the king of France, the Republic of Venice, and the grand duke of Tuscany, he was compelled to dispense with the services of the Armenian provincial of the Dominicans in Nakhchivan, whom he had brought along to Isfahan in the capacity of dragoman. Instead, he had to make do with the Capuchin. The shah had informed him that he would accept no other interpreter, the Dominican reported to Grand Duke Ferdinand II. On the third day after his arrival in Isfahan he received a visit from Friar Raphaël, who inquired after his well-being, his clients, the business he was supposed to negotiate, and the gifts he had brought. The Capuchin recorded all of this for the Persian court.[39]

The Capuchin's proximity to the ruler was confirmed two months later when two envoys from the king of France and three from the *Compagnie des Indes orientales* arrived at court. Once again, Friar Raphaël was enlisted to interpret and translate. Since the envoys were not familiar with either the language or the customs of the court, their contacts to the court were dependent on the abilities and good will of the friar and other intermediaries. What made matters more difficult was that the king's two aristocratic envoys and the three representatives of the trading company, merchants by trade, mistrusted one another. When the shah did not grant them all the privileges they had expected for their trade in Persia, the envoys from the *Compagnie* blamed the Capuchin, who as an interpreter could say whatever he wished.⁴⁰ While distrust of interpreters was a topos of travel literature, it is striking that suspicion here fell not on a foreign dragoman, but on their "own" interpreter, who was guardian of a mission under French protection.

Friar Raphaël retained his position as interpreter, translator, and intermediary in the service of the shah for the rest of his life. In 1673 he acted for a second time as interpreter for a delegation from the *Compagnie des Indes orientales,* who negotiated a confirmation of the privileges granted in 1665, albeit for only three years.⁴¹ In connection with the reception and negotiations of Ludwig Fabritius, ambassador to Charles XI of Sweden (r. 1660–97), in the years 1684–5, the legation secretary, Engelbert Kaempfer, even spoke of the Capuchin as the "royal interpreter," whom he described as "a thoroughly learned man highly respected at court" whose role was to translate and elucidate the texts the envoys of European princes presented to the shah.⁴²

Although the function of "royal interpreter" never culminated in an appointment to an official position or a formal title, Europeans who sought access to the court had to defer to the Capuchin's position of trust. This applied even to representatives of the VOC who, against the background of Franco-Dutch conflicts, feared the French Capuchin's close relationship with the local court. As an intermediary in the service of the shah, the Capuchin found himself confronting the VOC's ambassador in Isfahan, Joan van Leene, who was supposed to negotiate a new trade treaty with the shah in 1690 and resolve various disagreements that were straining relations between the trading company and the Safavid court.⁴³ On July 24, 1690, Friar Raphaël sought out the VOC ambassador to pay him the honor of the first visit. This was, however, not just a gesture of "good correspondence" that a member of the European diaspora owed to a visitor of high status; rather, the point was to prepare the ambassador for the ceremonial expectations of the Persian court. During additional visits before the audience on September 14, 1690, and subsequent treaty negotiations, the Capuchin took on the task of convincing the Dutch to compromise with Persian expectations. For example, he recommended that the ambassador ask the shah's forgiveness for an attack on the island of Qeshm ordered by a *commissaris directeur* of the VOC and the prohibited export of cash aboard a Dutch ship on behalf of an Armenian client.⁴⁴

A comparison between the activities at court of Juan Thadeo de San Eliseo and Raphaël du Mans points to the different conditions that missionaries faced over the course of the seventeenth century. To be sure, until his death in 1696, the Capuchin Raphaël du Mans was embedded in the activities of the shah's court in a way that no other missionary had been before him, nor would be after him. The activities of the Discalced Carmelite Juan Thadeo de San Eliseo as translator and interpreter in the early years of his order's mission, in contrast, were more strongly imbedded in a specific missionary strategy of developing close contacts with Muslim elites with the ultimate aim of conversion. ʿAbbās I had awakened such hopes with his policies aimed at integrating heterogeneous actors into a system of imperial rule. Over the second half of the seventeenth century, the increasingly dominant influence of the Shi'a 'ulamā and the more sharply drawn religious boundaries did not exclude the Capuchin Raphaël du Mans from the court. They did, however, force him into a practice of extensive adaptation, which left him far more vulnerable than Friar Juan Thadeo to accusations that he had abandoned his actual vocation as a religious and a missionary.

Disputations as Expressions of Religious Patronage

If missionaries gained the ruler's trust as translators and interpreters, it was primarily because of the practical utility of their work. The Islamic understanding of the history of salvation, which included Christian revelation, while deeming it imperfect, created a further precondition. Above all, however, the presence of missionaries at court responded to the inclusive strategies that 'Abbās I deployed to consolidate his power. A segment of the Catholic missionaries adapted their conduct to the fact that scholarship was becoming an important foundation for reputation and influence in this context. Disputations at court served to dramatize the power of the shah as well as the prestige of scholars there.

While consolidating their power, the first Safavids had made use of "their" Sufi brotherhood and suppressed the other, once influential, brotherhoods. They combined the millenarianism of the *qizilbāš* and the Shi'a Islam of learned 'ulamā in a conflict-laden religious dyarchy. Learning had long enjoyed high prestige in Persian Islamic culture. Starting in the early sixteenth century, however, the rise of the dynasty and its orientation toward Shi'a Islam allowed the Shi'ite 'ulamā to attain a degree of political influence that far surpassed that of Muslim scholars in the contemporary Ottoman and Mughal empires. While a native Shi'a clergy emerged thanks to the support of the Safavids, the question of the legitimate exercise of political rule as a proxy for the "hidden" imam, which was central to Twelver Shi'ism, also contained a subversive potential, for the Shi'a clergy could conceivably withdraw their support from the shah and claim its share in the exercise of power.[45]

The strong position of the shah under 'Abbās I was expressed in many ways. One of them was his ability to display his imperial status by building a prestigious Friday mosque on the main square of Isfahan, his new capital city, despite strong misgivings among the 'ulamā over whether Friday prayers were permissible during a time of waiting for the twelfth imam or *mahdī* (Figure 10, p. 80).[46] At the expense of the millenarianism of the *qizilbāš*, a space was opened for a comparatively broad spectrum of theological and philosophical positions. Crucially, from the shah's perspective, this diversity did not question his claim to imperial rule but rather affirmed it. Under court patronage, a group of scholars, which Henry Corbin has referred to as the "Isfahan School," sought to achieve a synthesis between Shi'a theology, mysticism, and ancient philosophy. Apart from their broad interest in ancient Greek philosophy, these scholars were also prepared to grapple with pre-Islamic Persian and in some cases even ancient Indian traditions.[47]

Up to the reign of Sulaimān I (r. 1666–94), representatives of this circle of scholars held numerous offices and influenced the theological and philosophical debates. At the time of ʿAbbās II (r. 1642–66), the range of different positions was able to evolve once again under the ruler's direct patronage: the shah cultivated the acquaintance of Sufi dervishes and philosophically trained scholars on the one hand, while on the other staging himself as a Shi'a ruler at celebrations commemorating the 680 Battle of Kerbela, where the Prophet's grandson had met his death. He moved these celebrations, which helped to create a Shi'a Muslim identity, to a newly built hall on the palace grounds. Given the potential danger posed by clerics' claims to participate in secular rule in the expectation of the hidden imam, ʿAbbās II continued the efforts of ʿAbbās I to integrate a broad spectrum of scholars of varying affiliations into the court network. This spectrum narrowed significantly in the final two decades of the seventeenth century. Among the ʿulamā, those who clearly distanced themselves from Sufi mysticism and placed less importance in ancient philosophy gained the upper hand.[48]

ʿAbbās I tolerated disputations between representatives of different positions. Some of these were even held in his presence as part of a politics of religious patronage. Disputations were components of a practice of symbolic communication intended to bolster the ruler's authority through demonstrative inclusion. The knowledge culture of the Shi'a ʿulamā paved the way for this practice, as it recognized the autonomous search for truth using the tools of the human intellect. It appreciated mathematical, scientific, and medical learning and promoted the active reception of the ancient canon of knowledge. The inclusion of Catholic missionaries in the local practice of disputation was thus not simply the result of foreign policy expediency—the hope of winning over Christian courts for the fight against the Ottomans—which made it opportune for ʿAbbās I to treat the Catholic missionaries more or less circumspectly.

In 1621, ʿAbbās I hosted a disputation between two Discalced Carmelites—Juan Thadeo de San Eliseo and Visitor General Vicente de San Francisco—and the Protestant agent of the English East India Company, his chaplain, translator, and two additional Englishmen. Two days previously, the Englishmen had accused the Catholics of idolatry, which inspired the shah to invite the friars and the Englishmen to debate in his presence. He questioned the rivals about their positions on fasting and good works, the veneration of the cross and images, free will, and the antiquity of the Roman Church and papal primacy.[49] This followed the practice of intra-Muslim disputation.

According to the Discalced Carmelites, the disputation was largely a dialogue between the shah and the two friars, whose arguments the Englishmen had trouble countering. In contrast to the friars, who spoke Persian, the agent of the East India Company and his chaplain depended on their translator. The shah for his part had Juan Thadeo de San Eliseo translate and explain the Englishmen's arguments. Because of the one-sided nature of the sources, we cannot be certain whether the disputation in fact turned out to be as successful for the missionaries as they made it out to be. What is clear from the accounts of the Discalced Carmelites, though, is how they fell back on intra-Muslim arguments to make their position as Catholic Christians appear plausible to the shah. Thus, they argued not in terms of the Christian controversies of the confessional age but instead justified Catholic doctrine and practice by constructing parallels to Shi'a positions, while suggesting that the Englishmen were closer to the Sunni Ottomans.

The friars found it most difficult to defend Catholic practices around the treatment of images and the veneration of the cross, the English criticism of which had provided the occasion for the disputation. In front of the shah, who was intrigued by the Protestant accusation of idolatry, the friars made their point in agreement with the decrees of the Council of Trent, by posing the rhetorical question of whether the shah and his people might perhaps be called "idolators of seals or earthenware stones" because of their use of clay prayer beads (*muhr*) and rosaries. The question was cleverly posed insofar as this was indeed a Shi'a practice controversial within Islam. The Discalced Carmelites anticipated the answer: naturally this was not the case, since those praying did not venerate these objects as gods but used them out of reverence for the earth in which their ancestors and great men were buried. The justification for the Catholic treatment of images they provided on the basis of the decrees of the Council of Trent picked up this interpretation: one did not venerate the images as if they were gods, nor did one expect intercession from the pictures themselves at the Last Judgment. Rather, one venerated what the images represented. At the same time, the pictures helped to recall the virtues of the saints, so that they might serve as models.

According to their own explanations, at least, the missionaries found it easier to defend the Catholic position on the other points. The friars defended fasting by referring to the consonance between the religious laws of Catholics, Muslims, Jews, and "heathens," which the shah and his courtiers for their part had affirmed based on Mosaic Law, the Gospels, and the Quran.

The questions of free will, the antiquity of the Roman Church, and papal primacy ultimately gave the friars an opportunity to draw parallels between the English and the shah's chief Islamic opponents, the Ottomans. In the matter of free will, the English thus agreed with the Turks, who also denied human free will. The Turks and the English asserted that God was the author of everything, good and bad. The Discalced Carmelites took up a debate here in which Twelver Shi'ism in fact supported a position closer to that of the Catholic Church. When it came to the antiquity of their church and the primacy of the pope, the agent of the East India Company claimed that the English were the original Christians who therefore did not need to submit to papal primacy. The Discalced Carmelites once again responded by suggesting to the shah a comparison with the Turks, noting the previous English obedience to the pope: just as the Turks had granted the caliphate to ʿUmar instead of Ḥusain, the English denied obedience to the pope as Christ's vicar on earth.[50]

The disputation took place against a background of present-day politics: the intensified English presence in the run-up to the 1622 capture of Hormuz, during which English ships would come to the aid of the largely land-bound Persian troops. Under these circumstances, the Discalced Carmelites drew a line between the denial of free will and everyday actions: this was the reason the English, who knew neither conscience nor fear of God, were pirates whose word could not be trusted. The Discalced Carmelites contrasted this with their own example of a good Christian life.

In this form, the disputation of 1621, in which the shah claimed for himself the role of arbitrator in intra-Christian disagreements, represented an exception. At the same time, however, the manner in which the Discalced Carmelites argued before the shah using the terms of Shi'a Islam reveals their connection to a practice of disputation with Shi'a scholars that had supplied them with the necessary familiarity with intra-Muslim arguments. The Persian missionaries considered this practice to be a specific characteristic of their mission, which set it apart from conditions in the Ottoman Empire.

It is, rather, to the Jesuit mission at the Mughal court in India in 1580 that we must look to find a parallel to the practice of disputation that the Augustinians and Discalced Carmelites encountered in early seventeenth-century Persia. The two Mughal rulers Akbar (r. 1556–1605) and Jahāngīr (r. 1605–27) allowed the Jesuits to build churches. They appreciated the clerics as agents of information about their society of origin and, like ʿAbbās I, were interested in certain aspects of European material culture—e.g., firearms, clocks, and paintings—with regard to their practical use and the symbolic dramatization of their own power. In this context, they invited the Jesuits to disputations at which, with the broad participation of scholars of various religions—Hindus, Parsis, and Jains, alongside Muslims of various stripes—they represented and performed their imperial claims to power. For Akbar and Jahāngīr, what the Jesuits, proceeding from a confessional logic, could only regard as harbingers of impending conversion or—when it failed to materialize—as the outcome of Machiavellian opportunism, was also a component of a policy of religious patronage.[51]

When Akbar called Jesuits to his court to explain the most important Christian texts, this also expressed a search for God that took the ruler away from Sunni orthodoxy but not toward Christianity. In keeping with local religious cultures, which proceeded from a broad set of manifestations of divinity and similarly varied forms of veneration and godly ways of life, Akbar and those in his immediate environment appreciated the missionaries as men of God without adopting the specifically Christian dogmas, especially the notion that Jesus was the son of God.[52] Akbar's and Jahāngīr's religious patronage improved the status of their non-Muslim subjects to a degree unique among the early modern Muslim empires. At the same time, they created the framework within which one of the Jesuit missionaries, Jerónimo Javier de Ezpeleta y Goñi, could write and circulate theological treatises in Persian, the language of the Mughal court.[53] The Discalced Carmelites also brought one of these works, *The Truth-Showing Mirror*, to the Persian court, where it became the subject of debates with Shi'a scholars. This further illustrates how diplomatic assignments and the missionaries' services as translators, interpreters, and intermediaries at court prepared the ground for their contacts with the local scholarly elite. The missionaries considered such a rapport to be the key to any attempts at conversion. The following subchapter will explore this relationship.

Missionaries and Shi'a Scholars

Shared Knowledge Cultures

Soon after their arrival in Isfahan, the missionaries understood that the Shi'a scholars were part of a highly respected and influential elite. This encouraged the Catholic clerics to seek out and cultivate contacts with the ʿulamā. Missionaries hoped this would gain them respect and open additional doors. Their reports thus point both to the potential utility of their activities for the Church and to a capital of honor that retained its transcultural importance beyond the local context. The Discalced Carmelite Juan Thadeo de San Eliseo was among the first missionaries to associate with the 'ulamā. While his first reports of 1608 or 1609 scarcely found a good word for the Persian Muslims, neither about religion nor philosophy or the "secrets of nature and good reasoning,"[54] his later accounts were far more positive. In 1616 he told the *praepositus generalis* of his order that he increasingly encountered respect and good will among the learned Persians. The disputations with scholars gave the Discalced Carmelites an opportunity to preach regularly before Persians at court.[55] In a letter to a fellow Carmelite in Rome, he underlined the high regard and respect that the friars enjoyed at court: "There is no grandee at this court or minister of the king with whom we do not cultivate friendship. All of them esteem and honor us to the highest degree."[56] Friar Juan Thadeo was among the missionaries who managed to establish contacts at the highest level over a period of many years. Following the example of Persian scholars, he claimed the honorary title of "Mīr," as is evident from the inscription on his personal Persian seal. At the court of the shah, Juan Thadeo de San Eliseo offered his services as an intermediary thanks to his language skills; at the same time, he sought to live up to the role model of a scholar. This included not just translating into Persian biblical texts and Catholic theological literature but also engagement with the religious and intellectual preoccupations of his Muslim contacts and opponents. The list of manuscripts that Friar Juan Thadeo took with him upon his return to Rome in 1629, after a good twenty years in Persia, affords an impression of this dual orientation: Persian and Arabic translations of Christian texts on the one hand and the Quran, a volume of ʿAlī's sayings, and a collection of Islamic law on the other, along with a mirror for princes and a moral treatise with a commentary in Persian.[57]

Friar Juan Thadeo had the Italian traveler Pietro Della Valle partake in his connections with Persian scholars. Della Valle's journal contains a note about his visit to "our friend," a certain Ḥusain Qulī Mīrzā, which he undertook in 1617 together with the Discalced Carmelite. Della Valle described the mullah as a "man of letters" who led a modest life "wholly devoted to his studies and matters of religion, far removed from all thoughts of and involvement in affairs of state."[58] The Italian traveler thereby attributed modes of behavior to the mullah that Catholic regular clerics claimed for themselves, in keeping with Christian humanism. He described the mullah as a member of the republic of letters whose only shortcoming was a lack of knowledge about the true faith.

Later texts by Discalced Carmelites continued to present Persia as a place of learning. The authors suggested to the superiors of the order that the choice of new missionaries be suited to these local conditions. When the procurator, Felice di Sant'Antonio, presented the missions in Persia and India to the General Chapter of the Discalced Carmelites in 1649, he lauded not just the beauty of the city of Isfahan but also the cultivation and knowledge of the Persians, which the missionaries had to live up to. The clerics who were sent to Persia should be learned because the Persians cultivated knowledge, maintained public philosophical universities, and were highly interested in mathematics and astrology. One could reap a rich harvest with the sciences provided one proved capable of "teaching the truth of faith through the truth of natural matters."⁵⁹

In the prologue to his *Gazophylacium linguae Persarum*, printed in Amsterdam in 1684, the Discalced Carmelite Ange de Saint-Joseph likewise saw Persian authors as equal in eloquence and knowledge to European men of learning. Only the fact that "a people educated in so many disciplines" followed "the darkness of a superstitious law" aggrieved him. The *Gazophylacium* was intended to put missionaries in a position to wrest the Persians from the "darkness of their law." To this end, the work included not just translations of Persian terms into Latin, Italian, and French but also a wealth of information about the population, institutions, economy and society, culture, and natural conditions. While Ange de Saint-Joseph was convinced that the Persian Muslims, as "infidels," did not participate in the truths that God had revealed through his son, his works express admiration for a society in which learning was held in high esteem. In his eyes, the Persian scholars were not "barbarians." Instead, precisely because of their high level of education, they were worthy interlocutors when it came to communicating Christian revelation. In his *Gazophylacium,* Ange de Saint-Joseph expressly refers to Persian medicine, in particular, as the equal of European medicine.⁶⁰ His translation of the pharmaceutical text of Muzaffar b. Muḥammad al-Ḥusaini aš-Šifāʾī under the title *Pharmacopoea persica* was proof of this esteem for the medical knowledge of the Persians, whose goodwill he hoped missionaries would gain with their equal abilities.⁶¹ The friar published his works after returning to Europe. This followed controversies among missionaries in Persia in which Friar Ange had been accused of a deficient observance of the Rule, to which he responded in the letters to his superiors by emphasizing the importance of paying attention to education and language skills when selecting clerics. If a friar was unable to present his standpoints in the language of the local scholars after spending several years in the country, he and the secrets of his faith would meet with contempt. A cleric, in contrast, who was capable of conversing with Persian scholars as their equal, would earn their "infinite" esteem.⁶² The selection of missionaries should thus create the preconditions for their recognition by local scholars as men of equal status.

The arguments among the Discalced Carmelites opposing the order's primarily contemplative orientation were bolstered by experience in other Asian kingdoms. In China, for example, the Jesuits used their conversations with Confucian *literati* to make a name for themselves as (Western) men of letters. Accordingly, the fathers conducted their debates less as controversial disputations than as convivial dinner conversations, with the aim of reaching an agreement wherever possible. In the Chinese mission, it was considered common sense that the communication of religious truths depended upon successful communication in the fields of mathematics and the natural sciences.⁶³

Like some Jesuit priests at the Chinese imperial court, but without civil servant status, the Capuchin Raphaël du Mans also won respect at court and in the learned milieu with his knowledge of mathematics and astronomy. Tavernier, for example, praised his mathematical knowledge and wrote that several courtiers possessed astronomical instruments that the Capuchin had made with his own hands.⁶⁴ Shi'a clerics, including those from other Persian cities, visited the learned Capuchin in his convent in Isfahan.⁶⁵

The Jesuit Jacques Villotte relied on the attractions of the unfamiliar when he set up a kind of cabinet of curiosities in his order's house in New Julfa. In 1699, two German Jesuits stopping in Isfahan on their way to India exhibited the curiosities they had brought with them from Germany. This exhibition reportedly attracted "all of the distinguished persons" from Isfahan and New Julfa to the Jesuits' house. It is also said to have accustomed the "gentlemen of the court" to continue visiting the Jesuits in large numbers even after the departure of the two priests. The guests were received in a room adorned with engravings, astronomical charts, and maps intended to astound the visitors.[66]

While the natural sciences, mathematics, and medicine offered access to the powerful, as in the Mughal Empire, shared references to ancient philosophy were deemed the most suitable point of departure for learned discussions intended to lead to the truths of the Christian faith, especially the incarnation of the word of God in Christ and the Trinity. The missionaries won respect with their ability to conduct learned

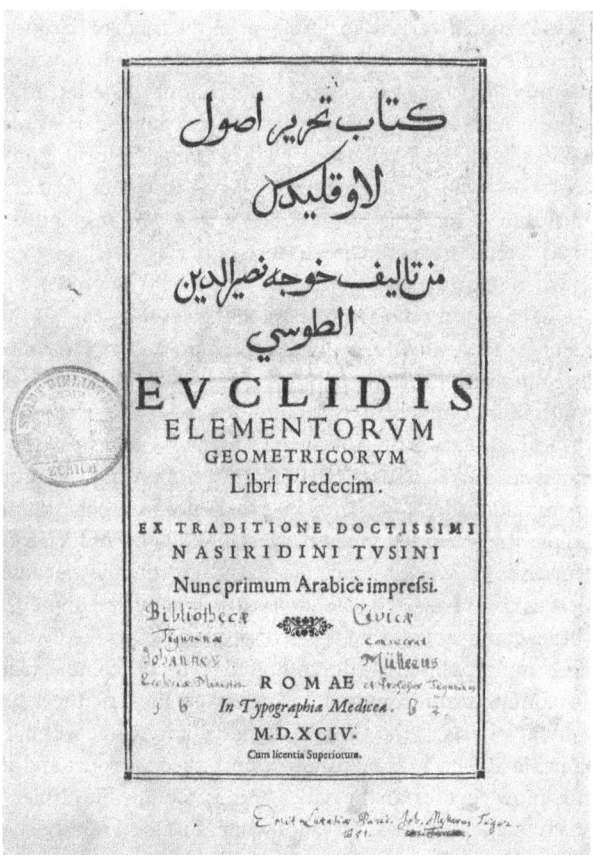

Figure 13 Title page of the Arabic translation of the *Elements* of Euclid printed in 1594 by the *Typographia Medicea* in Rome

conversations about the works of the ancient philosophers. In this way, the humanist curriculum taught in colleges and universities in Europe benefited the mission. In Rome, the very choice of gifts that the Discalced Carmelites brought to present to ʿAbbās I on their first journey to Persia relied on shared esteem for the knowledge of Greek antiquity: in addition to the gifts of Christian content, Cardinal Cinzio Passeri Aldobrandini sent along the Arabic translation of Euclid's *Elements* printed in 1594 by the *Typographia Medicea* in Rome (Figure 13). In Persia, Juan Thadeo de San Eliseo noted that of all the books one could send, those about "the secrets of nature," astrology, philosophy, and history were most appreciated.[67] In 1621, the Discalced Carmelite Próspero del Espíritu Santo requested editions of the works of Aristotle and Plato because their observations were cherished by the Persians and were held up as if they were holy. When the Discalced Carmelites were allowed to settle in Shiraz in 1623, the ḫān of the city asked them to procure the works of Aristotle and Plato in Greek or Latin along with an Arabic translation of the Bible and Arabic–Latin dictionaries for the local "university" (*madrasa*). Friar Próspero recommended the fulfillment of this wish to the *praepositus generalis* and the *Definitorium*, since the Discalced Carmelites could gain access through education.[68] In fact, the leading representative of the learned circle known as the "Isfahan School," Mullā Ṣadrā Šīrāzī (979/1571 or 1572 to 1050/1640 or 1641), was teaching in those days at the *Madrasa-i Ḫān* in Shiraz, which Allāhwerdi Ḫān (governor of Fars province from 1003/1594 or 1595 until his death in 1021/1612) had built for him. Like his teacher Mīr Dāmād, Mullā Ṣadrā Šīrāzī contributed significantly to developing the connections between Greek philosophy and Shi'a Islam. If what Próspero del Espíritu Santo wrote is accurate, contacts with the missionaries awakened the desire among certain Shi'a scholars to gain access to the original ancient texts instead of working with Arabic and Persian translations and commentaries as had been common up to that time.[69]

Learned Disputations

Apart from shared interests in Greek philosophy, travelers both clerical and secular described the practice of disputation and controversy as a dominant trait of Persian knowledge culture. In one of the very first reports of the Augustinian mission published in Europe, in 1606, António de Gouveia stated that the Persians "were mad about argumentation and disputation," wasting no opportunity to engage in it day or night.[70] One can find assertions about a specific culture of disputation over the entire period of the Persian mission's existence. This characterization was part of the effort to dissociate the Persians from the Turks. Even Protestant travelers, none of whom was educated in theology, reported being challenged to religious debates.

The inclusive political strategies of ʿAbbās I and some of his successors opened spaces for such discussions. Debates on religious matters, for example between Shi'a *ʿulamā* and Sufi dervishes, were conducted not just in mosques and madrasas but also in coffee houses, marketplaces, and central squares, where Sunni Muslims, Christians, Jews, and Zoroastrians could be present alongside Shi'a Muslims.[71] Missionaries able to speak the language tried to profit from these circumstances.[72]

We can gain insights into their role in such debates from the correspondence of the missionaries, as well as from the letters that Pietro Della Valle wrote to his learned friend Mario Schipano, a medical doctor in Naples, which were later published in edited form. For Della Valle, the private and public disputations were part of a knowledge culture that linked Persian and Western European men of letters:

[T]he Persians, as men most eager for knowledge, many of whom are conversant in philosophy and other sciences, are not only happy to receive and read our books but also gladly speak and debate in private and public about matters of faith, as I have myself seen on several occasions; they do not cultivate the rigor of the Turks, who refuse to listen.[73]

In a later letter, Della Valle describes an event of April 1621, when he and the Augustinian Manuel da Madre de Deus visited the house of a distinguished Persian acquaintance, Mīr Muḥammad ʿAbd al-Wahhābī, and found various guests conversing there, including a scholar. As usual, they immediately began to discuss religious matters. Unlike the Turks, the Persians permitted others to say whatever they liked against them, Della Valle explained. On this occasion, they disputed those three points around which controversies with Muslims mainly revolved, namely, why the Christians did not accept Muhammad and the Quran after the prophets and the Old and New Testaments, whether the Gospels and the other Christian books were falsifications of the word of God, as the Muslims asserted, and whether the Catholics could be considered idolators because of their treatment of images.[74]

After the disputation, Pietro Della Valle composed a brief *discorso* summarizing the Catholic arguments on these three points. With the missionaries' approval, in September 1621 he presented the treatise with a dedication to his host, Mīr Muḥammad ʿAbd al-Wahhābī, and asked him to read it together with the scholar who had been present at the debate. In fact, high-ranking Shi'a clerics felt compelled to commission a rebuttal to Della Valle's apologia, which was composed by Sayyid Aḥmad ʿAlawī and apparently circulated in numerous copies. The mention of Sayyid Aḥmad ʿAlawī by name is instructive in that it allows us to place the controversies on the Muslim side in the context of the scholarly circle that Henry Corbin called the "Isfahan School." Sayyid Aḥmad ʿAlawī was the cousin, student, and later son-in-law of Mīr Dāmād (Mīr Muḥammad Bāqir Astarābādī, d. 1041/1631–2), who as a teacher in seventeenth-century Persia was mentioned in the same breath as Aristotle and al-Fārābī, was a confidant of ʿAbbās I, and influenced the "Isfahan School" more than virtually anyone else well beyond the reign of that shah and his own death.[75]

Pietro Della Valle had written his text in ignorance of the works that the Jesuit Father Jerónimo Javier de Ezpeleta y Goñi had composed in Persian for the mission in the Mughal Empire. Knowledge of the latter had reached the Shi'a scholars of Isfahan by 1622, if not earlier. Ezpeleta y Goñi's *Truth-Showing Mirror* also became a subject of controversies between Catholic and Shi'a clerics. In the years 1622 to 1625, the Discalced Carmelite Próspero del Espíritu Santo told of a mullah who instructed the friars in Arabic and Persian and requested a copy of Ezpeleta y Goñi's work. The Shi'a scholars then sent the pope a rebuttal to this work, which, like the response to Della Valle's apologia, was written by Sayyid Aḥmad ʿAlawī. How leading Muslim scholars understood their relationship to Christianity is evident from the responses to Della Valle's text and the *Truth-Showing Mirror*, which were couched in a tone of learned controversy. They contrasted present Christianity with an early Christianity whose purity had been restored by Quranic revelation. On the one hand, Sayyid Aḥmad ʿAlawī sought to find evidence in the Old and New Testaments of Muhammad's coming prophethood, which he as a Muslim considered the completion of divine revelation. On the other, he accused the Apostles and Evangelists of having distorted the "true" revelation of God to the "prophet Jesus."[76] Such arguments were not new but belonged to the established repertoire of Muslim–Christian controversy: from the beginning, Muslim authors had accused the Christians of incorrectly interpreting or even falsifying biblical texts in order to explain the differences between the Islamic and Christian traditions.[77]

The opponents in Isfahan shared an intense engagement with the other side's sacred texts, that is, the Quran and the Bible, respectively. Apart from the list of manuscripts that the Discalced Carmelite Juan Thadeo de San Eliseo brought to Rome, this is evident from the Persian writings composed by the first guardian of the Capuchins in Isfahan, Gabriel de Paris, and the Jesuit Aimé Chézaud. In 1635, Gabriel de Paris explained in a letter to the *Propaganda Fide* that the missionaries engaged in philosophical and theological discussions in an attempt to gain the respect of scholars, so as to move the conversation toward questions of the Trinity and the redemption of humankind through Christ's death.[78]

A work that Friar Gabriel wrote around 1634 and dedicated to a qadi who had helped the friars purchase a house, and who had invited him to speak about the Ten Commandments in the presence of other scholars, gives some hints of how the Capuchin intended to approach Muslim scholars. According to his account, those present asked Friar Gabriel to commit his observations to paper. In the process, he expanded his remarks on the Ten Commandments into an introduction to the Christian faith. Characteristically, he preferred to speak of "divine" rather than "Christian faith." Proceeding from the shared convictions of Muslims and Christians—for example the belief in the unity of God—the Capuchin explained Christ's special mission as redeemer and his nature as the son of God. While the treatise aimed to demonstrate the necessity of believing in Christ for salvation, the author nevertheless conceded that Muslims had partial access to God's revealed truth, emphasizing, for example, that it was unnecessary to stress the unity of God when speaking to Muslims. Alongside biblical texts, Friar Gabriel quoted verses from Persian poets and referred to Socrates, Plato, and Aristotle, whom he acknowledged as part of the consistent body of knowledge shared by the addressees of his treatise.[79]

The missionaries only partially recognized the significance of the intra-Muslim debates that were touched upon in the practice of Muslim–Christian controversies. The two Persian-language volumes in which the Jesuit Aimé Chézaud refuted Sayyid

Aḥmad ʿAlawī's remarks against Ezpeleta y Goñi's *Truth-Showing Mirror* contain suggestions that references to ancient Greek philosophy were controversial among Shi'a clerics and defined specific positions. The Shi'a cleric had asserted that important passages in the Bible were forgeries. In an epistle prefacing the work that Father Chézaud addressed to the son of the late author, the Jesuit declared his respect for his opponent's theological and secular learning, his knowledge of the original Hebrew texts, and the moderation evident in his work. Typically enough, following the example of Ezpeleta y Goñi's treatise, in the first part of his work Chézaud dramatizes a conversation over several days between a missionary, a mullah, and a philosopher. At first, the last of these assumes a skeptical intermediary position before finally being persuaded by the missionary's arguments. This is likely how Chézaud believed the disputations should have proceeded, which he himself had conducted primarily on the status of Jesus as the son of God. Chézaud's work, too, reveals a sound knowledge of Judeo-Christian and Islamic literature as well as ancient philosophy. In the process, he also referred to the Quran in order to demonstrate the truth of the Bible: in the course of the discussions, he referred the mullah who claimed that the Gospels had been wholly falsified to a number of passages in the Quran that had been borrowed from the Bible as proof of the latter's veracity; the Quran itself stated that books revealed by God had already existed at the time of Muhammad.[80]

Chézaud's mode of argumentation was nothing new. Since the beginning of the Persian mission, the possibility of proving the truths of the Christian faith using Islamic texts had encouraged missionaries who possessed the necessary language skills to study the Quran. In 1617, the Discalced Carmelite Redempto de la Cruz noted that just as the Gospel said that Christ was the word, and the word was made flesh, Muhammad stated in his book that Christ was the word, the soul, and the spirit of God. If Muslims wanted to know the truth, they could easily recognize it in Muhammad's words. However, this argument had undesirable implications: the admission that the Islamic tradition participated at least partially in the Christian truth. Redempto de la Cruz anticipated the response to such objections when he stated that nobody should be shocked if he sought to prove the Christian understanding of the divine filiation of Jesus using the Quran.[81]

As in the case of Gabriel de Paris, Aimé Chézaud's writings in controversial theology emerged from his presence at court and participation in learned circles where he sought to gain respect with his nontheological, in this case mathematical, knowledge. Before Chézaud was sent to Persia in 1653 he had been active in Syria, where he began to study Arabic and Armenian in 1639. In Persia, the Jesuit was also one of the missionaries who delved most deeply into Islamic texts and the one who drew the most radical consequences from the absence of conversions: in 1661, the cleric advised against continuing the disputations with Muslim scholars because they merely served to harden the adversaries' positions and to "alienate them from our holy faith and embitter them."[82] For that reason he relocated the mission to a part of the city directly adjacent to the Armenian quarter of New Julfa, where most Christians lived. There the Jesuit fathers ran a school until the mid-eighteenth century, with which they primarily sought to satisfy the demand for education among Armenian notables and the small European diaspora of various confessions.

Disagreement and Personal Respect

Did Chézaud's rejection of disputations mean that the participants were not just irreconcilable adversaries but also personal enemies? It is true that the disputations never ended in conversion in either direction but rather reinforced both parties in their respective positions. At the same time, however, they were part of social contexts in which missionaries and Shi'a clerics became better acquainted with one another. Missionaries who claimed to be learned acknowledged the Shi'a *doctores* as members of an equal estate with whom they sought to interact as social peers in the hope of attaining a comparable rank in local society. In this regard there are parallels to the relationships that Jesuits in China built with the local *literati*. In order to welcome their guests appropriately, the Augustinians and Discalced Carmelites set up a reception room in their convents known as a divan. Della Valle's journal and letters mention a practice of reciprocal visits among "friends" of equal rank. Contrary to our present-day tendency to view Islamicate societies as wholly defined by religion, early modern missionaries working to establish relationships with the local population could consistently rely on the existence of sociocultural subsystems that were less permeated by religion than others. This was the case in medicine, mathematics, and the natural sciences, as well as in the study of ancient philosophy. In their relations with the court, it emerged that religious discourses could claim widely varying importance in different situations. Religion played a specific role in the various subsystems. Religious discourses were by no means always "more important and more correct than nonreligious ones," and the religious norm was far from asserting itself in all areas of life.[83] The missionaries could enter the domains less defined by religious discourses largely unencumbered by their status as Catholic clerics if they had something else to offer their interlocutors: the prospect of an alliance against the Ottomans, skills as translators and interpreters, or knowledge of medicine, mathematics, or ancient philosophy that was of value in the local context. Language here was characteristic of the asymmetry that typified these contacts. In Persia, China, and Mughal India, it was always the missionaries who had to use the language(s) of the local scholars.

In the disputations themselves, the opponents at least conceded that both sides shared a search for the truth of divine revelation and a belief in one and the same God. In this way, Christian positions could stand alongside the varied intra-Muslim approaches to Islam, such as they were formulated by Sufis and Shi'a clerics, for example. It was a practice of conversation on matters of faith, in which participants treated each other with courtesy, built on mutual recognition as truth-seekers. In the literature of theological controversy, the refutation and firm rejection of "errors" went hand in hand with avowals of personal respect toward the opponent.

Persian and Arabic-language lessons, in particular, established rapport between missionaries and Shi'a clerics. Just as Juan Thadeo enlisted the cooperation of three mullahs and a rabbi for his Persian translations, Shi'a scholars placed themselves at the disposal of Catholic clerics as language teachers and copied Arabic and Persian manuscripts for them. The debates of the 1620s about the *Truth-Showing Mirror* began with the request for a copy of this work by a mullah who gave Arabic and Persian lessons to the Discalced Carmelites. In 1630, the *Definitorium generale* granted the friars permission to study languages with a mullah, though the superiors of the order were not completely comfortable with this decision, admonishing the missionaries instead to use one of their own for this purpose wherever possible if he possessed the requisite skills.[84] In fact, it is highly likely that the Shi'a scholars also harbored hopes of converting the missionaries with whom they were in contact. These relationships were also criticized as part of a social practice that took the missionaries away from an exclusive emphasis on their role as members of an order.

In relationships across religious boundaries, differences of faith could have a more or less strongly divisive effect. When missionaries found themselves in trouble, relationships with Shi'a scholars could also open an escape route. This occurred in the case of the Augustinians, when their right to use the buildings the shah had given to them was challenged after the death of ʿAbbās I. The plaintiffs were the heirs of the original owners, who had been expropriated by the shah. In this situation, a mullah who had taught Persian to some of the friars intervened at court on the Augustinians' behalf. He helped the friars to compose a memorandum and recommended that they present it personally to the shah. At court the Augustinians had the support of the *dārūġa,* the highest judge of the city of Isfahan (a Georgian convert to Islam), who was instructed by the shah to render them justice.[85] In 1648–9, a Shi'a scholar who had been cornered by the Capuchins during a disputation took his opponents before the *šaiḫ al-islām,* who sent the clerics to the *dārūġa,* who in turn forbade them to preach to Muslims, including the scholarly elite. The guardian of the Capuchins, Valentin d'Angers, for his part, sought the advice of a judge with whom he was on friendly terms. The latter advised the friar to appeal to the *dārūġa,* who now indeed went back on his decision in a final verdict and affirmed the previous practice, that is, the permissibility of religious discussions with scholars and the ban on any further missionary activities among the Muslim population.[86]

Behind what Aimé Chézaud perceived as a failure in 1661 were the measures against the indigenous Christians in Isfahan beginning in the 1650s, as well as the looming narrowing of the spectrum of religious debate in Persia, which affected not just relations with missionaries but also intra-Muslim relations. Aimé Chézaud's decision did not signal the end of disputations. Later reports, however, mention such conversations in passing, sometimes in connection with the express comment that they had not proved successful. Reports by the Discalced Carmelites from the early eighteenth century no longer express any expectation of converting Muslims in this way. Some of them describe the willingness to debate religious questions as an expression of simple curiosity and the wish to display erudition rather than the intention to draw any religious benefit from it. Others report, without any negative undertones, on the frequent visits of Persian notables to their convent. In 1721, the provincial vicar of the Discalced Carmelites wrote that these notables enjoyed their conversations with him, which he described more as an expression of social esteem and less as part of efforts at conversion in one direction or the other.[87]

In comparison to the first half of the seventeenth century, scholarly contacts with local elites did not merely occupy a less important place in missionary correspondence to Europe. The writings of the Capuchin Raphaël du Mans also show how opinions of Persian scholarship grew gradually less positive against the background of changes in European knowledge cultures in the second half of the seventeenth century. To be sure, his *État de la Perse* also stressed the high status that scholars enjoyed in Persia in comparison to his French homeland. The Capuchin, however, increasingly regarded the orientation toward antiquity as a deficit when compared to the progress being made in France, especially in the field of mathematics.[88] He continued all the while to cultivate close contacts with Shi'a scholars, whom he received at the convent and used as sources of information. This was, incidentally, how he was able to procure descriptions of the schools, mosques, and markets of Isfahan for Engelbert Kaempfer, the learned secretary of the Swedish envoy Fabritius. On the same occasion, the Shi'a cleric who had prepared the descriptions also brought Kaempfer a letter from the friar. These services of a local scholar as a sort of messenger working on behalf of a Christian missionary may be viewed as an indicator of everyday forms of contact beyond this particular instance.[89]

In relations with the Safavid court, even in the 1680s learning was deemed capital that conferred respect and opened doors. At the same time, it was associated with the expectation that one could display one's own superiority. The choice of gifts that Louis XIV sent the shah in 1683 or 1684 via François Picquet, bishop of Babylon, betrayed such hopes: aside from technically sophisticated clocks and several volumes of pictures of the king and the dauphin and views of the royal palaces and the city of Paris, they also included astronomical instruments. These had not been chosen in keeping with ecclesiastical condemnations of heliocentric notions; in fact, one of the instruments showed the movement of the celestial bodies according to the Copernican system.[90] Did the French court hope to impress Persian court society by displaying the latest in astronomical knowledge? If we are to believe Engelbert Kaempfer, it was unsuccessful, and the "precious *astrolabia* and astronomical *instrumenta Copernicana*" were regarded as "African monsters" and not appreciated because the Copernican worldview was unfamiliar to Persian scholars.[91]

Against the backdrop of the decline of the Safavid Empire and changes in how Europeans positioned themselves over the course of the eighteenth century, derogatory descriptions of the Persians became more common in ecclesiastical correspondences and reports. In the 1760s, the last Latin bishop of Isfahan, the Discalced Carmelite Cornelio di San Giuseppe, while still falling back in his *Centurie* upon the distinction between the Turks and the "more studious and astute" and "less barbaric" Persians, turned to these now in order to warn the missionaries against engaging in disputations with Persian scholars.[92] The role model of the Persian scholars, which had shaped missionaries' relations with their Muslim surroundings since the early seventeenth century, was tied to conditions that no longer existed in the 1760s: to the pluralism promoted by the inclusive political strategies of ʿAbbās I on the one hand and to European perceptions of Persian culture as equal to their own in nonreligious matters on the other.

Medicine, the Belief in Miracles, and the Administration of the Sacraments

The missionaries especially cultivated relationships with the court and a scholarly elite whose prestige they aspired to. Yet they also entered into contact with broader segments of the Muslim population. Their perceived skills as healers appealed to men and women of all social ranks. When the Augustinians and Discalced Carmelites settled in Isfahan in the early seventeenth century, they soon noticed that Muslims also visited their churches. In 1605, the Augustinian Belchior dos Anjos reported that many "Moors of both sexes" were coming to his order's little church, most of them out of curiosity, but some of them also because of illness. They begged the friars to heal them by praying to Christ on their behalf and reading aloud from the Gospels over their heads. "By the grace of God" some of these people were actually healed, he noted. All of them venerated the images of the saints and kissed them with great respect.[93] After his first sojourn in Isfahan in 1607-8, the Discalced Carmelite Paolo Simone di Gesù Maria reported similar experiences: Persian Muslims visited the church out of curiosity, bowed to the Gospels, and sometimes brought along the ill for the friars to lay the Gospel on their heads.[94]

Around 1700, the Jesuit church is said to have belonged to the "rarities" in Isfahan and New Julfa that were visited by persons of various religions "with pleasure and amazement." The fathers accordingly adapted the furnishings of their churches to the expectations of local visitors: according to a travel account published in 1707, the Jesuits had laid out a carpet in the church that could only be walked on barefoot. They had done so because the Persians observed this custom in their mosques and "considered it very disrespectful to appear in a house dedicated to God wearing shoes."[95] We know that in the Augustinian church women and men were spatially separated, as in the mosques, that the church was "painted in vivid colors according to the Persian custom," and that the vaulted ceiling and the women's gallery were entirely gilded.[96]

In the early period of the Persian mission, the clerics still hoped that visiting the church might be a first step toward conversion. Thus, the Discalced Carmelite Paolo Simone di Gesù Maria reported in 1607-8 that the friars could teach the sacred faith to those visitors who asked questions. No one had been converted thus far, however; he believed that the Persians were waiting for one of "their grandees or their mullahs" to take the first step.[97]

For the Augustinians and Discalced Carmelites who came to Persia in the early seventeenth century, it was an unaccustomed experience to discover that the objects (including the sacramentals) and rituals of their church were venerated by Muslims and that they themselves were respected as men of God by people of another faith. Seeking the reasons why the hopes of conversion that derived from this behavior remained almost wholly in vain, the missionaries focused on the shah's "Machiavellian" fixation on reason of state as well as Islam's alleged permissiveness toward human vice, particularly in the sexual realm, which converts would have been forced to abandon.

There were, however, other explanations for the visits, too: in the Near East, Asia Minor, and the Balkans in the early modern period and in some instances up to the recent past, some monasteries and other Christian places of worship attracted numerous Muslims seeking a cure for physical ailments. In some places, sacred spaces were used jointly by Muslims and Christians. That it was usually Muslims who visited Christian holy sites and not the other way around is evidence that Islam, in its various orientations, integrated the older Christian revelation into its own understanding of the history of salvation.[98]

The fact that the acceptance of Catholic objects and practices by those of other religions was rooted in an understanding of the sacred as not exclusively tied to a single religion is stated most clearly in the account by the Calvinist Jean Chardin cited in the introduction. Some missionaries, however, had realized even earlier that these phenomena could not be explained using the confessional categories of their church. Pietro Della Valle, for example, reported around 1620 that because of his knowledge of the country, the vicar of the Discalced Carmelites "did not think it bad" when, during a visit to New Julfa, Shah ʿAbbās I kissed the relics presented by the Armenian priests and laid them on his head, and even broke the bone of the female martyr Ripsime with his own hands in order to present the vicar with a piece of it.[99] In 1621, the Discalced Carmelite Próspero del Espíritu Santo, while attributing the respect shown by the Muslim population to missionaries wearing the habits of their order primarily to the clerics' personal qualities, also recognized a religious component, since he reported that his Muslim traveling companions kneeled down together with him to pray.[100]

Various authors mention the Muslim demand for Christian objects and rituals: the Venetian Ambrogio Bembo, for instance, accused the Armenians in Isfahan of trading in Catholic devotional articles and even selling them to Muslims, along with images of the saints.[101] For the author, this was yet more evidence of the opportunism of the Armenians, who adapted their confession to circumstances, but it also documents a demand for Catholic devotional objects across religious divides.

Hopes in the efficacy of Christian sacred spaces, objects, and rituals manifested themselves particularly when people were seeking a cure for serious illness. Here, too, Jean Chardin proves an attentive observer, who was however unsparing in his confessionally tinted criticisms of the Catholic clergy. According to his account, Muslim Persians believed that "the prayers of all people were good and efficacious," for which reason they sought out "the devotion of persons of different religions" in cases of illness or other problems. When they resorted to supernatural remedies for sickness, they did not associate the sacred solely with representatives of their own religion but also turned to gentiles, Jews, and Christians. The Christians then read aloud from the Gospel of St. John used during the mass over the bodies of ailing men, women, and children. Chardin accused the missionaries of doing so even more than Eastern Christians, although, since the Persians understood no Latin, this could only be viewed as a "magical act," thus profaning the Gospel. Despite corresponding remonstrations, the missionaries did not abandon this "evil practice" because they hoped for material rewards or respect.[102]

Church documents confirm that such practices increased the missionaries' social standing among the Muslim population. Yet these practices were controversial within the Church. In the following section, I will explore the heated discussions that accompanied them. These focused on the contested issue of the relationship between medicine, priesthood, and miraculous healing; on the place of missionaries in an interreligious field of miraculous healing; and on the salvific and healing power of baptism and the potential desecration of this sacrament.

Priesthood, Medicine, and Miraculous Healing

On the one hand, the Catholic Church recognized medicine as a science based on natural causality, and on the other it postulated that God or the Devil could intervene in worldly affairs at any time, either personally or through intermediaries. Based on the sacrament of ordination, priests were considered the instruments par excellence of God and agents of divine wonders. Their separation from the rest of society as the clerical estate, in contrast, had meant that since the twelfth century, the priesthood had come to be regarded as fundamentally incompatible with medicine. While in the early days of monasticism medical assistance for the sick was still considered an essential element of *caritas* for priests, since the Council of Clermont (1130) there had been increasing regulations limiting the study and practice of medicine by clerics. In 1215, the fourth Lateran Council forbade priests from performing surgery, especially when it involved burning and cutting. In 1234, the various prohibitions became part of the decretals of Gregory IX (Ugo/Ugolino di Segni, r. 1227–41) and thereby of canon law. The practice of medicine by priests now required an explanation based on the individual, exceptional situation, which could be used to justify a papal dispensation. Despite this practice of dispensation, over the course of the late Middle Ages, new training opportunities at the universities conspired to turn medicine into a secular science separate from the priesthood that also distanced itself from the less prestigious practice of surgery, which was defined as a craft.[103]

Among the regular clergy, however, some exceptions remained permissible. The pharmaceutical activities of both male and female religious were scarcely affected by the rigid restrictions. In the early modern period, the preparation of medications for the sick continued to be understood and practiced particularly by the missionary orders as part of the imitation of Christ.[104] When it came to the practice of medicine and surgery, misgivings were directed above all against overstepping the boundaries to the secular world associated with caring for the sick. When a physician joined an order, the community's interest in his knowledge and skills frequently outweighed any canonical reservations. In the early 1550s, the Society of Jesus in Rome employed two laymen for the medical treatment of members but dismissed them in 1553 after the entry into the order of a respected doctor and the acquisition of a papal dispensation, although the Jesuits continued to consult secular physicians when necessary.[105]

The missions were granted privileges allowing priests to practice medicine. In 1576, Pope Gregory XIII (Ugo Boncompagni, r. 1572–85) bestowed a general dispensation upon the Jesuits in case there were no other physicians available. In 1641, a particular congregation of the *Propaganda Fide* defined rules for the provision of dispensations. No dispensation was required "in case of necessity," which allowed for a broad scope of interpretation. Various circumstances could favor the granting of a dispensation: the possibility of contributing to the mission's revenues, the goodwill to be gained thereby, and easier access to the homes of infidels and the chance to make friends of the powerful, who would use their authority to protect the missionaries from persecution. Nevertheless, in principle the *Propaganda Fide* rejected the granting of dispensations. Only in exceptional cases should a priest with the necessary abilities be granted a dispensation: he had to practice medicine free of charge, not perform operations, and only work where no physician of secular estate was available.[106]

In the Persian mission, the arguments in favor of practicing medicine clearly retained the upper hand. One option for reconciling its advantages with the reservations of canon law was to entrust the practice of medicine and surgery to a lay brother or layman. However, it was by no means only lay brothers or laymen who engaged in medical practice. In 1618, Della Valle praised an Augustinian friar in Isfahan who had advised him during an illness and was in his view "the best physician in this country."[107] François Pétis de la Croix attributed his recovery from a severe fever in 1674 to the care of the Capuchin Raphaël du Mans. When subsidies failed to appear from Europe, the practice of medicine and surgery also offered a source of income. In 1724, the vicar of the Discalced Carmelites in Isfahan survived by practicing surgery. A Jesuit lay brother and a priest, Tadeusz Juda Krusiński, after offering them successful medical treatment, gained the respect of the new Afghan rulers who brought down the Safavids in 1722. Finally, when treating ailing Christians, medical and pastoral care were closely intertwined: when the Augustine prior in Isfahan took an ailing Catholic Georgian merchant into his convent in the early 1740s, he offered him medical and pastoral care until his death. In his testament, the man made the prior his executor, instructing him at the same time to use a bequest to say requiem masses for him.[108]

One cleric whose medical activities in Isfahan are particularly well documented was the Discalced Carmelite Ange de Saint-Joseph. In 1674 he tended to the dragomans of the Venetian Ambrogio Bembo and two friars, all of them seriously ill. But he also treated Persians, whose language he understood perfectly. After returning from a fourteen-year sojourn in Persia, the friar, a man "educated in medicine and many sciences"[109] according to Jean Chardin, published a Latin translation of the mid-sixteenth-century pharmaceutical work of Muzaffar b. Muḥammad al-Ḥusaini aš-Šifā'ī under the title *Pharmacopoea persica*. It includes a long foreword in which the friar justifies the usefulness of his translation and general medical knowledge for the missionaries based on his experience in Persia. Medical knowledge was "the true and indeed only key to houses and hearts," offering protection in places where there were no consuls, envoys, merchants, or ships from Europe; it was not uncommon for Muslims to give alms to the missionaries out of gratitude. The Discalced Carmelite defended the compatibility of medicine and priesthood using numerous examples from the Old and New Testaments and Church history. Even the Church fathers had not disdained "to contemplate and practice this most noble art."[110]

Based on his awareness of the significance of medical expertise, the author explained that he had combined his study of the Persian language with that of medicine, mathematics, and astronomy. Missionaries had the best chances of conversing with the learned elites of the Safavid Empire if they were able to communicate mathematical and scientific knowledge. While mathematics offered access only to a small minority and mathematical treatises engaged the mind so violently that no room remained for religious arguments, medicine could penetrate people's hearts and souls. Medical practice was well suited to gaining the goodwill of the Muslim authorities, which made missionary activities possible in the first place. The hope of bodily healing moved non-Catholics to beg the missionaries for help when they fell seriously ill. Friar Ange describes how he used such opportunities to combine medical care with Christian instruction.[111]

In actual practice, the lines between the duty of every priest to minister to the sick and wounded on the one hand and their medical treatment on the other were as blurred as the lines to magical practices. For the sick and those around them, belief in the healing power of church rituals and of magical practices not sanctioned by the Church coexisted closely with faith in the abilities of physicians, surgeons, and apothecaries. The healing practices corresponded to the varying explanations for the causes of illness: natural causality or divine or diabolical intervention.[112]

In the practice of missionaries in Persia, too, ambiguity in the treatment of illness had not yet been swept aside by a single discourse; instead, the very same person undertook actions directed at salvation and healing that aimed to meet varied expectations. Friar Ange's introduction to the *Pharmacopea persica* reveals this close connection between a belief in miracles and medicine and the simultaneous attempt, typical of the post-Tridentine Church, to Christianize the magical practices that the Church opposed as superstition: the missionaries were to recite exorcism prayers to the sick children of infidel parents, but instead of an amulet they were to use "the words of the Gospel" and offer them the sacrament of baptism if they seemed likely to die. The Carmelite friar Denis de la Couronne d'Épines managed to baptize thousands of terminally ill children in this way. Such "successes" were rooted to a large degree in the polysemy of the acts the missionaries performed. While the Discalced Carmelite Matteo di San Giuseppe was extolled by his acolyte during their walks through the streets of Bandar ʿAbbās as a "physician, who distributes remedies free of charge for any ailment," thereby winning the hearts of not just the English and Dutch but also the infidels, and baptized hundreds of children, these encomiums pointed to the ambiguity of the remedies (*remedia*), which were to be understood both as sacraments in the sense used by the Catholic Church and as medical remedies.[113] As we will see, however, the ambiguity of the *remedia* was already present in the ecclesiastical understanding of the sacraments themselves.

Miraculous Healing in Interreligious Competition

In his *Gazophylacium linguae Persarum*, Ange de Saint-Joseph describes the spiritually and physically healing power of holy water as a great mystery of the Christian religion. Most children were cured when the priests read the Gospel over their heads, but above all when they poured water over them. Any child who died after being washed with this water entered Paradise.[114] The assignment of both spiritual and physical effects to the Church's sacraments was not specific to the Persian mission. The notion that the sacraments could also heal the body corresponded to the understanding of miracles as manifestations of divine intervention.

Against the background of Protestant critique, following the Council of Trent the Church sought to draw a clear line between true religion and diabolically inspired superstition. The Council had accordingly subjected the recognition of miracles, defined as extraordinary events not explicable by natural causality, to certification by the local bishops. This accorded a central place to the medical scrutiny of absent natural causality and led to a sharp decline in the number of miracles recognized by the Church.[115] The experience of miracles among the faithful, like the clergy's treatment of miracles, was by no means congruent with the restrictive practice of the Roman Curia in beatification and canonization processes; thus, in the seventeenth century, miracles remained "virtually an everyday occurrence"[116] in Catholic regions. On the one hand, the preconditions were created by precarious living conditions and omnipresent threats to human existence as well as the limits of scientific knowledge. On the other hand, the everyday nature of miracles and expectations of miracles was associated with the activities of church actors, who understood and presented themselves as the intermediaries of divine grace. When clerics worked miracles, this was considered "proof of closeness to God." Clerics who could drive out demons and work miracles demonstrated the "truth of the Catholic confession in general and the efficacy of priestly ordination in particular."[117]

Miracles therefore became more frequent in situations of confessional competition, in which, according to the understanding of the post-Tridentine Church, the servants of God and the Devil struggled for the souls of men and women.[118] In these contexts, miracles were signs of divine intervention mediated by the Church, while magic was the expression of a pact with the Devil, of which non-Catholics were accused. In the practice of exorcism, the struggle with the Devil found a ritual form codified in the *Rituale romanum*, which was reserved for priests. It was no coincidence that it assumed special significance in liminal confessional and religious situations.[119] The Catholic Church also saw confirmation of its claim to be the true Church of God in the healing power of its rituals. The power to work miracles, however, was attributed not just to the sacraments and other church rituals but also to a variety of objects. These included relics of the saints and sacramentals, whose mass dissemination was intended to strengthen the cohesion of the Catholic Church in Europe and beyond in the face of manifold threats.[120]

The inner and overseas missions were liminal situations par excellence. Few sources document the competition that missionaries faced from Muslim healers even among the Christian population in Persia with as much clarity as the *Centurie* of the last Latin bishop of Isfahan, Cornelio di San Giuseppe. They show that, in practice, the faithful distinguished far less clearly between miracles and magic and among religious specialists of varying origins than the bishop might have wished. In the *Centuria quinta*, probably written in 1767 in Bushehr, Cornelio di San Giuseppe describes, among many other events that he had experienced personally in the Near East since 1739 or heard of from other missionaries, how Catholic Armenians also sought help from Muslim "sorcerers" in emergency situations. These "sorcerers" sold talismans to the "gullible people," wrote spells to elicit love or hate, brought good luck, or located lost objects, and were paid to use their arts to heal sicknesses.

Cornelio di San Giuseppe did not deny the efficacy of the work of Muslim healers, which could not be explained by natural causality. Instead, he believed it revealed the intervention of the Devil. Thus, for example, he recounts how Anna, wife of Arutiun Sceriman, the head of the Armenian community in New Julfa, had suffered since the birth of her son Sarat from an ailment whose cause and name nobody had been able to identify: a cold fever that forced her to cover up in all manner of warm clothing even in the greatest heat of summer. After suffering for seven years during which neither medicine nor prayers in the Catholic Church had brought any relief, she followed the advice of other Armenian women who believed her sickness was the result of an evil spell and agreed to call one of the "sorcerers" to the house without her husband's knowledge. The "sorcerer" had moved throughout the house with a book in his hand and then unearthed two bones bearing a Persian inscription, which he stated were the cause of her sickness. He had the bones burned and the ashes scattered in the river, whereupon Anna was immediately cured. Hearing this, the missionaries explained to Arutiun Sceriman that his wife's conduct was "illicit and prohibited." As a "good Catholic" Arutiun shouted at his wife and instructed the servants never to let anyone like that into the house again. When Anna fell ill with the same ailment nine months later, the "sorcerer" returned to the house: he explained that the cause of her relapse was a third, undetected bone. He had come to locate this bone and restore the sick woman to complete health. This time, the sorcerer was sent away and Anna remained ill.

In another case, an Armenian in New Julfa whose black beard had turned white overnight from misfortune suffered from colic, which made him fear for his life. He suffered in this terrible condition for many months, receiving no relief from the remedies of his priest and doctor (according to the phrasing, they may have been the same person). Finally, his wife, a "schismatic" Armenian, convinced him to call in a "sorcerer" since she believed he was under an evil spell. As a God-fearing Catholic, the Armenian had his priest inscribe the Gospel of John on a piece of paper, assuming that if he held it in his hand, he would be doing no wrong. When the "sorcerer" entered the sickroom, he immediately fell into a rage and asked those present why they had called him if they did not trust him. As evidence of his powers, he wrote out the Gospel of John in Armenian, a language he did not know. Cornelio di San Giuseppe regarded the story—which he said was strange but true, as he could attest as the Armenian's confessor—as confirmation of his assumption that the acts of the Muslim "sorcerers" were works of the Devil, which the missionaries had to combat. This was very difficult, however, because the belief in such "witchcraft" was deeply rooted among the Armenians, "especially the women, who are very superstitious by nature."[121]

In a social environment where the belief in intervention by supernatural forces for good or ill was not associated exclusively with a particular religion, the missionaries needed to prove their superiority over their competitors, whom they condemned as servants of the Devil. Apart from Muslim "sorcerers," Cornelio di San Giuseppe's *Centuria quinta* mentions an "Indian charlatan" who had arrived in Isfahan and performed all manner of miracles in the public squares for money with his "devilish art."[122] As "instruments of God," the Catholic priests stood in the way of the "sorcerers" as "servants of the Devil." Miraculous healing was said to have improved the standing of missionaries within local society: in an account written around 1640, an Augustinian described how, since the first years of his order's mission in Isfahan, Muslim men and women had often brought their sick children to Friar Jerónimo da Cruz to be blessed. The children had miraculously recovered, and everyone began to call Friar Jerónimo a saint.[123]

Rituals of Salvation and Healing

While the missionaries promised all sorts of remedies for physical healing, they also offered rituals, such as reading the Gospels and praying over invalids as well as baptisms, that appeared to guarantee a last-minute cure. In both Persia and the Ottoman Empire, such rituals gave the missionaries access to people who would otherwise scarcely have sought them out.[124] In contrast to Chardin's report cited above, the accusation that this removed these acts from their Christian context of meaning and therefore "profaned" them was not in the foreground of Catholic debates about their permissibility. The focus was, rather, on the fear that those terminally ill individuals who survived after all could desecrate the sacrament of baptism through "apostasy," that is, continuing to practice the religion into which they had been born.

The hope of Muslim parents that their dying children might be healed allowed the missionaries to perform rituals that they considered baptisms. Faith in the missionaries' medical skills became combined here with the expectations placed in the healing power of the rituals they performed. From the 1620s onward, the correspondence of the Discalced Carmelites contains references to baptisms of terminally ill children of Muslim parents. One account of 1634 illustrates how the attribution of medical knowledge facilitated a boy's baptism. The Discalced Carmelites offered to a Muslim, a "friend" and "acquaintance of the house" who asked them for "bodily medicine" for the ailing foundling he had taken in, to pray over the dying boy in his house and help him to the best of their ability. The prior and another friar found the boy *in extremis*; the prior gave him the "water of salvation," i.e., baptism. Almost immediately thereafter it had pleased the Lord "to call him to Paradise."[125]

While the first such rituals were products of happenstance, starting in the 1640s the Discalced Carmelites, followed by the Capuchins and Jesuits, discovered baptisms of children at the point of death as a field in which they could finally register tangible successes among the local population. This was particularly welcome after their initial hopes of converting the Persian Muslims and a union with the Armenian Church had dissipated.

The clerics were aware that parents who feared for their children's lives did not expect them to administer a specific Christian sacrament. In a report on hundreds of baptisms performed in the years 1646–50, the Discalced Carmelite Denis de la Couronne d'Épines expressly stated that Muslim parents sought healing for their terminally ill children from the missionaries and not baptism as understood by the Church. Friar Denis's account begins in September 1646, when the friars were called to a young boy who had been ill for some time and would in fact die the night after his baptism. In this case, the baptism was preceded by rudimentary religious instruction: despite the presence of family members, they had whispered to the boy about the soul and the Christian faith and had noticed his willingness to be baptized. Between the baptism and his death the following night, he had neither acted nor spoken against the faith. Beginning in 1647, the Discalced Carmelites, especially Friar Denis, increasingly expanded their baptismal activities. In 1647, they christened 95, in 1648, 120, and in 1649, 375 sick children; in addition to the children of Muslim parents, they also included a few children from Jewish and Zoroastrian families.[126]

In a 1656 report, the Discalced Carmelite Alessandro di San Silvestro mentions that the friars had christened more than 1,000 dying children in their church in Isfahan up to that date; Friar Denis had baptized another 2,000 children in the city and the surrounding villages, and the other friars about 900. The (Muslim) parents brought their ailing children to the convent so that the friars might bless them and read the Gospels over them and say prayers. Of himself, Alessandro di San Silvestro wrote that since he was known to possess medical skills, people not only brought their children to him in the convent but also called him from all quarters of the city to administer physical remedies and read the Gospels aloud in their presence.[127]

Alessandro di San Silvestro boasted of having baptized a total of 2,916 terminally ill children. This number is published in an account that the procurator of the missions in Persia and India, Valerio di San Giuseppe, presented to the *Propaganda Fide* in 1671. According to Friar Valerio, the Persian Muslims were very devoted to "the holy Gospels and the other devotional practices or, more precisely, to the prayers the Church tends to recite over the sick." In connection with their services for the sick, the missionaries were assured of special appreciation from the Muslims of various ranks and sexes, who recognized them as *padri* consecrated to God, who were not subject to the usual reservations concerning the "unclean" members of other faiths. Muslim women, who are otherwise virtually never mentioned in missionary accounts, also make an appearance here: Valerio reports that women and men alike had the friars lay their hands on their heads, although Muslims were generally highly superstitious and never allowed anyone "from outside their sect" to touch them, so as to avoid becoming unclean. According to Valerio, in Isfahan it was not just ordinary folk but also "the grandees" who sought out the friars. Even the grand vizier had called one of the Discalced Carmelites to his house to recite from the Gospels and say prayers over his ailing son.[128]

The Jesuits and Capuchins followed the example of the Discalced Carmelites. When the Jesuits saw that children were going to die, they also baptized them in the hope that they would act in heaven "as intermediaries for the salvation and conversion of their parents."[129] The Capuchin Gabriel de Chinon reported that the missionaries afforded the children "the grace of baptism" before they died "under the pretext of healing their ailments, to which end they read the Gospel over their heads."[130] Despite his positive assessment, the friar harbored no illusions about the differing expectations of parents and missionaries. However, this was also the point that drew criticism. While the provincial vicar of the Discalced Carmelites, Dominicus a Sancto Nicolao, for instance, believed that Friar Denis was acting properly, he acknowledged that his predecessor in the office of vicar believed that the Church had no right to baptize children without their parents' consent. The Dominican Paolo Piromalli, who presented himself as a custodian of strict observance of confessional rules in other matters as well, adopted a particularly critical position. In light of this reproof, Friar Dominicus hoped that the Discalced Carmelite procurator general in Rome would intercede with the *Propaganda Fide* to obtain permission for the practice.[131] Shortly thereafter, Stefano di Gesù, visitor general of the Discalced Carmelites, submitted these proceedings as a *dubium* to the *Propaganda Fide* and the Holy Office. He was troubled not by the lack of parental consent but rather by the small number of christened children who unexpectedly survived and, despite baptism, were not raised as Catholics.[132]

The decisions that the Holy Office reached on such *dubia* in the seventeenth century affirmed the validity of the baptisms administered by missionaries as well as the misgivings expressed by Stefano di Gesù. Christenings were permissible if the priest had every reason to believe that those being baptized were about to die. Such decisions helped to justify the practice of baptizing non-Christians *in articulo mortis*, which remained widespread in missionary territories into the twentieth century.[133]

The Holy Office's decisions in favor of such baptisms rested on an approach that largely failed to consider the broader meaning that the ritual assumed on the ground. The sacrament, administered with formal correctness, was thus only profaned if the baptizands survived and, in the absence of a Catholic upbringing, became apostates. In Rome, too, however, doubts about such an approach were being raised by the seventeenth century. They were expressed, for example, in a papal nondecision of 1683 on whether clerics should accede to requests by Muslim or nonbelieving parents to baptize their children in the hope of recovery from an illness or an evil spell. While six cardinals voted no and five yes, Innocent XI decided against responding to the *dubium*: "nihil esse respondendum" (nothing is to be answered).[134] Although the focus remained on the danger that children who recovered after all would "fall away" from the faith, the nondecision of 1683 may also have been influenced by unease about the possible reinterpretation of the sacrament of baptism on the ground, which threatened to profane acts sacred to the Roman Church. The nondecision, which was not communicated as such, did nothing to change the fact that the missionaries were inserting a sacrament of their church into a social context in which the sacred was not defined along the lines preferred by the Roman confessional church.

*

The Discalced Carmelites, who baptized several thousand dying children from Muslim families in the 1640s and 1650s, had every reason to count this as a success. On the one hand, like the Capuchins and Jesuits who followed their lead, they would have been convinced that they were indeed securing eternal life for the children. On the other, in the gray zone between medicine and miracle, healing practices were among the acts that increased the missionaries' social prestige across religious boundaries. Their successful integration into local sociocultural frames of reference was certainly tied to the missionaries' role as religious specialists, who participated in the aura of the sacred and could thus join the specialists of other religions as healers.

In this context we should recall Jean Chardin's statement, cited in the introduction to this study, that missionaries, in the combination of expectations of healing and salvation that were projected onto them, were associated with dervishes, and respected as "men detached from the world and devoted to the veneration of God and the service of their neighbors."[135] Among the role models available in local society, that of the dervish may possibly have more closely approximated that of the missionary than that of the scholar, since it was after all closer to the mendicant orders' dedication to a life of poverty and unworldliness. A report about the Capuchins by the Jesuit Jacques Villotte echoes Chardin's assertion that the missionaries were associated with dervishes because of their way of life and their clothing.[136] When Cornelio di San Giuseppe, listing the various types of dervishes in his *Centuria quinta*, mentions first those who earned their keep by practicing medicine with herbs and seeds, speaking "certain words" over the sick, and hanging small capsules with texts inside them around their necks, it is reminiscent of the salvific and healing practices of the missionaries.[137]

Other stories in the *Centuria quinta* suggest that similar ways of life and perceptions engendered social proximity and situations of competition in Persia as well. Thus, the bishop told of an order of dervishes that, like the Carmelite order, claimed to have been founded by the prophet Elijah. One of its leaders had once visited the Discalced Carmelite convent in Isfahan, showing "great respect and veneration" for the images of the Virgin Mary and the prophet Elijah in the church and referring to the Carmelites as brothers of the same religion because of their common founder. The story began with the veneration that the prophet Elijah enjoyed in Islam, especially among mystics, because of his struggle against the priests of Baal. These circumstances, which were apparently unknown to Cornelio di San Giuseppe, lend a certain plausibility to his account, the content of which is not substantiated elsewhere. From the time of his own stay in New Julfa (1743–5), Cornelio di San Giuseppe reports on a dervish who had been recommended to him by his predecessor. This dervish was in the habit of visiting the Discalced Carmelites, who sought to keep him as a "friend" by offering alms or gifts of bread, rice, or fruit from their garden. In fact, "our friend the dervish" protected the Discalced Carmelites from the hostilities of other dervishes.[138]

Despite similarities in their ways of life and the perception others had of them, the role model of the dervishes nevertheless held scant significance for how the missionaries positioned themselves in local society. In contrast to scholarly status, the Catholic clergy in Persia never explicitly claimed this role model, for instance with respect to the selection of suitable missionaries. This was probably because Sufism was becoming increasingly marginalized under Safavid rule. The first Discalced Carmelites had already correctly recognized that it was the ʿulamā rather than the dervishes who enjoyed the respect of ruler and court. The image of dervishes as charlatans and servants of the Devil who were sometimes disdained even by Muslims was influenced not least by the Shiʿa ʿulamā in their conflict with the Sufi orders.[139] For that reason, the role model of the dervish was ill suited to gaining respect for missionaries within local society.[140]

From Social Proximity to Conversion to Islam

The orientation of missionaries toward the role model of the scholar entailed an adaptation to local sociocultural frames of reference that, because of the attendant deviations from observance and adherence to confessional rules, met with reservations within the religious orders as well as the Curia. It is striking, however, that between the early seventeenth and the mid-eighteenth centuries, only two Catholic clerics in Persia took the step from social proximity to conversion. As exceptions in the history of the Persian mission, the conversions of the Augustinians Manuel de Santa Maria (1691) and António de Jesus (1697) therefore caused a great sensation among Christians and Muslims alike, not least because António de Jesus had been the prior of his order's convent in Isfahan.[141] These conversions were explained in different ways: Was the problem debts the friars had incurred because of their lavish way of life and relationships with women, in contravention of their vows, as the Christians claimed? Did they have a religious conversion experience, as Friar António alias ʿAlī-Qulī Ǧadīd al-Islām himself asserted in his Persian-language treatises? While Manuel de Santa Maria was said to have regretted his apostasy in retrospect, ʿAlī-Qulī Ǧadīd al-Islām cemented his reputation as an orthodox Shiʾa Muslim by participating in the controversies against Christianity and the Sufis in a number of Persian-language treatises, thereby taking the side of the Shiʾa *ʿulamā* in intra-Muslim controversies as well. Immediately after his conversion, there was thus already talk of his becoming a "scholar of the Quran" and preparing a book against the Christian religion.[142] His successor as prior, António do Desterro, declared that he had spoken with both converts often, "nearly always about religion." While ʿAlī-Qulī Ǧadīd al-Islām, as a "clearly bad" person, refused to see reason, the other man realized his error but could not resolve to travel to Europe or India, despite receiving the money to do so.[143]

Because of the role that Friar António alias ʿAlī-Qulī Ǧadīd al-Islām played as an intermediary in the service of the shah after his conversion, his biography is better documented than that of his companion, who disappears from the historical record sometime after converting to Islam. In the following I will pursue Friar António's activities as an intermediary following his conversion. The case is particularly interesting because the reflections within the Augustinian order about why the two men converted offer insights into more general aspects of the relations between the missionaries and their Muslim environment.

At the very moment when King Peter II of Portugal (r. 1683–1706) instructed the viceroy of the *Estado da Índia* to thank António de Jesus for his services negotiating the alliance with the Safavids, disquieting news arrived in Goa from Persia: the friar, who had just been appointed prior, "had relinquished the true law of Christ in favor of the false dogmas of Muhammad."[144] In fact, António de Jesus converted in 1697, married a Muslim woman, and served between around 1701 and 1721 as translator and interpreter for European languages to the shah, replacing the Capuchin Raphaël du Mans, who had died in 1696. In this capacity he played an important role on the Persian side in negotiations with the envoys and agents of Christian rulers. In 1702, "the renegade Friar Antonio, now called Aly Guilibeque," is mentioned again in the files of the Council of State in Goa because of his involvement in correspondence that was intended, like the negotiations that immediately preceded his conversion, to pave the way for a joint action against the imam of Oman.[145]

Because of his position as translator and interpreter to the shah, ʿAlī-Qulī Ǧadīd al-Islām was considered a knowledgeable and influential intermediary, whose goodwill was courted by secular envoys and clerics alike, including his successor as prior of the Augustinians. The convert acted, for example, as an *interprète du roi* for both Pierre-Victor Michel's French delegation in 1708 and for the negotiations between Gratien de Galisson and the court in Isfahan in 1712. Galisson, coadjutor of the bishop of Babylon, thus believed that he must be brought over to their side with the promise of monetary rewards.[146] In fact, ʿAlī-Qulī Ǧadīd al-Islām became the French bishop's most important intermediary with the Persian court. During frequent visits, he supplied Galisson with information on the progress of the business that he had brought forward, explaining to him, for instance, why the decrees in favor of the missions promised to him in the audience with the shah had not been drafted immediately. ʿAlī-Qulī Ǧadīd al-Islām not only conveyed confidential information to the bishop concerning the situation of the Dutch and English but also hinted at the intrigues of the regular clergy against him and the priests of the *Missions étrangères*. In this way, ʿAlī-Qulī Ǧadīd al-Islām proved himself both a well-informed and a trustworthy intermediary. Galisson concluded that the convert was "wholly devoted to France" and could therefore not bear the partisanship of missionaries for the (Protestant) English.[147]

It was precisely on mission affairs that Galisson consulted the apostate. When ʿAlī-Qulī Ǧadīd al-Islām visited him on May 31, 1712, Galisson took the opportunity to tell him of the Discalced Carmelites' desire to build a church on the foundations of the church structure begun by Élie de Saint-Albert in New Julfa, which had been demolished in 1694 after a court decision handed down to the Armenians. This church would replace the house chapel, which had become too small. ʿAlī-Qulī Ǧadīd al-Islām outlined how the friars should proceed. If we are to believe Galisson's reports, even Prior António do Desterro tried to win over the apostate. By his account, in 1711 the prior attempted to persuade him with the promise of large sums of money to promote Portuguese wishes regarding the missions to the shah and his ministers in order to convince the Roman Curia to appoint him bishop of Isfahan. Unlike the Frenchman Galisson, the Portuguese Augustinian was apparently unsuccessful in his efforts to gain the convert's goodwill.[148]

The conversion of António de Jesus took place against the backdrop of his integration into local frames of reference. His linguistic qualifications and cultural knowledge enabled him not just to exchange his status as a member of the regular clergy and agent of the king of Portugal for a position as a paid translator and interpreter in the shah's service but also to change sides in theological controversies. The reflections within the order about the two conversions and how to prevent further members from following suit thus aimed to improve the selection of missionaries and the appointment of priors, and especially to draw clear lines of demarcation between the spheres of clerics and the laity of other faiths. Observance of the Rule was tied to life in a religious community and adherence to enclosure. For that reason, according to an internal memorandum, at least four members of the order should live together with the prior in Isfahan. Every effort should be made to ensure that the missionaries left the convent only in groups and never at night and that by no means should they seek personal entertainment with or stay overnight at the homes of Muslims or "heretics." They must also avoid playing games with "heretics," inviting Muslims or "heretics" for meals, or accepting invitations from them. They must not serve wine to Muslims, except for a few "grandees." A side entrance to the convent garden was to be sealed because it brought only "destruction" in many spiritual and secular matters. Muslims must not be engaged as servants, and Armenians could only be hired if they were at least twenty-five years old.

The practices of "good correspondence" also included the participation of Christian clerics and laypersons in Muslim feast days. On this subject, the memorandum stated that the friars should no longer wish the Persians a good holiday on Muslim feast days or during the month of Ramadan; the only exception was the Persian new year's festival, which was not associated with a religious creed and was observed by Zoroastrians and Christians as well. Apart from the fact that it was an "unspeakable abomination" to tell the Persians "to enjoy rituals they should be running from," it was also "a matter lamented by true Catholics that some of them uttered this pestilential greeting."

The apostasy of António de Jesus occurred as a consequence of the missionaries' dependence upon influential and wealthy Muslims. After converting, the friar married the sister of a certain "Mīrzā Phagi." The order's internal memorandum of 1700 shows that the Augustinians in Isfahan remained beholden to the good will of the convert's father-in-law. That is why the author dared not risk a break: while the prior and missionaries were never to enter the father-in-law's house and were to avoid "any particular friendship with the Mohammedan in question," they were not to forbid him access to the convent when the friars were at home. The friars could continue to present him with occasional gifts from the garden and convent. Similarly, they were not to deprive him of the profits he made from selling carpets or other objects on the convent's behalf. They could also offer him a glass of wine but never a bottle of wine to take home with him.[149]

The two Augustinians' sensational conversions thus led to discussions of the ways in which missionaries integrated into local society. Beyond the context provided by these cautionary tales, such modalities of integration hardly ever show up in the sources. They include practices of social exchange with Muslims and "heretics," marked by reciprocal invitations to eat and drink, play games, and converse; participation in the local calendar of festivities, including specifically Muslim feast days; and economic interconnections and dependencies.

*

Despite social proximity, the religious boundary between missionaries and their Muslim environment usually remained stable to the extent that no conversions occurred in one direction or the other. At the same time, the Catholic clerics participated in a culture that assigned them a lower but autonomous and legally secure status as Christians. Proceeding from their duty to cultivate contacts on the highest level, they assumed various tasks that in some cases took them away from their religious mission. Yet, as in other mission territories, these activities were justified by the fact that they made the mission enterprise possible in the first place or secured its continuation. The practices of accommodation associated with such activities also contrasted starkly with the demand for strict observance of the Rule, since the Jesuit practice of exemption from external discipline in everyday life was foreign to the orders that predominated in Persia. Missionaries who cultivated especially close contacts at court were reproached, both within their order and in the rivalry between different orders, for acting like courtiers. When Jean Chardin accused the clerics of losing sight of the purpose of their mission because they were distracted by their secular functions, he was taking up similar critiques that had been voiced within the Church. According to the Calvinist author, the missionaries in Persia had been able to settle there not only thanks to the political utility that the Safavids could draw from their diplomatic mission but also because they had gained access to people of all walks of life with their knowledge of new astronomical instruments and medicine.[150]

The presence of missionaries at court likens Persia to other great Asian empires, in particular the Indian Mughal Empire with which Persia shared a common religion and language. Moreover, the way in which some missionaries gained respect by adapting to local role models also recalls Jesuit missionaries in China. Like the latter, the friars in

Persia were "more than just missionaries of the Christian Faith."[151] Unlike some Jesuits in China, none of them held court office, but for a number of decades in the second half of the seventeenth century, a Capuchin attained a position of trust that led the Europeans who had contact with him to describe him as the "royal interpreter." Over a period of several decades, European visitors to the Persian court could scarcely avoid Raphaël du Mans. Not even the representatives of the Dutch East India Company were able to sidestep him.

When cultivating relationships, missionaries to Persia drew on local role models to gain respect while remaining committed to their clerical estate. The high esteem in which they held Persian erudition translated into affinity with Shi'a scholars (*ulamā*), who, once they had made contact with the court, became their most important connections and adversaries. The friars recognized in them an influential and highly regarded elite with whom they shared knowledge and a cultural practice—a knowledge of the authors of Greek antiquity and the practice of disputation and controversy as a means of attaining truth. Moreover, the *ulamā* could be seen as a social role model that appeared to resemble the missionaries' clerical status. Because of the increasing marginalization of the Sufi orders under Safavid rule, the dervishes, in contrast, did not become a role model for the regular clergy, despite commonalities in their lifestyle and the ways in which Persians perceived them.

Thousands of baptisms of terminally ill children offer evidence of the missionaries' integration into social contexts in which the assessment of the godliness of a given lifestyle depended only partially on the religious confession. Muslim parents not only placed their hopes of a cure in the clerics' medical knowledge but also, despite religious differences, put their faith in the power of the rituals that Catholic clerics performed as men of God. Against the background of the persecution of his fellow Protestants in France, the Huguenot Jean Chardin praised this local practice as the expression of a view of religion that associated godliness more with a genuine veneration of God and the ensuing way of life than with adherence to the norms of the official church. From a confessional standpoint, however, this could only be denounced as "error." The Dominican Gregorio Orsini, for instance, denounced it as such in a report he presented to the *Propaganda Fide* in 1626 after a sojourn in the Safavid Empire. With regard to the "schismatic Armenians," he castigated those "pitiful creatures" (*homunciones*, literally "little men") who excused conversion to Islam with the argument that human beings justified themselves before God, not by faith in Jesus Christ but by good works, which culminated in the claim that Jews, pagans, Christians, Muslims, and all other people could be saved if only they behaved well and did not harm their fellow humans. In Italy, even children and the simplest folk realized how "unreasonable" such claims were.[152]

From the standpoint of local society, we need to ask to what extent such practices should be regarded as expressions of an understanding of the sacred not tied solely to a specific religion or confession. In his work on the Syrian provinces of the Ottoman Empire, Bernard Heyberger has emphasized the importance of a "common deposit of faith," which the Christians of various churches there shared with one another as well as with Muslims and the Druze.[153] The missionaries, however, had difficulty understanding religious cultures that were not expressed through the uncontested authority of "sound doctrine."[154] While older literature on the Ottoman Empire stressed the strictness of boundaries, since the 1990s scholars have devoted more attention to the diverse forms of exchange between religious and ethnic groups. This research revealed the permeability of religious boundaries in everyday life.[155]

Following such conclusions, Thomas Bauer has suggested that before the nineteenth century, the Islamicate societies of the Near East were characterized by a relatively high degree of "tolerance of ambiguity." Only in defensive interaction with Western cultural norms did these societies arrive at the extreme forms of rejection of ambiguity and pluralism that tend to be considered intrinsic to them today. Referring to Europe, Bauer highlights the intolerance of ambiguity of Cartesian rationalism and of the Enlightenment, while he argues that during the Baroque period, "European literature reached its peak with regard to tolerance of ambiguity."[156] The present study proceeds instead from the hypothesis that the formation of distinct churches since the Reformation and the process of confessionalization had already produced a boost in disambiguation that caused Christian Europeans to perceive the religious cultures of Islamicate societies as increasingly alien. This led a Calvinist refugee like Jean Chardin to compare conditions there favorably with the repression in his homeland, while, at least in their correspondence with the Curia and the superiors of their orders, missionaries condemned the lack of neat boundaries as "error."[157] At the same time, Chardin's assertions take us to the question of how far contacts with foreign religious cultures and the dissemination of the resulting descriptions in Western Europe fed resistance to the strictures of confessional commitment. This resistance can be observed, for instance, in justifications of practices of confessional indifference, which may have been more widespread there than the German-language literature on confessionalization, in particular, has long been willing to concede.

4

Among "Brethren," "Schismatics," or "Heretics"? Missionaries and Armenians

In 1604 the Discalced Carmelites Juan de San Eliseo and Paolo di Gesù Maria received new names. Before they left for Persia, Pope Clement VIII added to their names those of the Apostles Judas Thaddeus and Simon. Thus Juan de San Eliseo became Juan *Thadeo* de San Eliseo, and Paolo di Gesù Maria was renamed Paolo *Simone* di Gesù Maria. According to Church tradition, these two disciples of Christ had been active in Armenia and Persia where they had been martyred by the infidels. For the friars, the names were at once aspiration and obligation: their obligation to complete the work of Simon the Zealot among the Persians and Judas Thaddaeus among the Armenians derived from the pope's claim to primacy as the successor to St. Peter. The reference to Judas Thaddaeus thus also implied a contrast with the Armenian Church, which traced its position as an autocephalous, apostolic church to the work of the Apostles Judas Thaddaeus and Bartholomew.

Yet the post-Tridentine Church did not see itself in direct opposition to the Eastern churches. When it intensified its efforts at a union between the Eastern churches and Rome starting in the late sixteenth century, it framed the endeavor as a reconstruction of a common past. The Eastern communities were viewed as vestiges of the oldest churches in Christendom. The inner-European confessional controversies gave rise to efforts to document the common ground between the Eastern churches and the Roman Church that separated them from the Protestants. This was the intention of the Jansenists Antoine Arnauld and Pierre Nicole when they addressed the clergy of the Eastern churches via Charles Olier de Nointel, French ambassador in Constantinople from 1670 to 1680, while composing their work against the Protestant notion of the eucharist *La perpétuité de la foi de l'Église catholique touchant l'Eucharistie*. In New Julfa, the Capuchin Raphaël du Mans directed their letters to the Armenian bishop, who responded to their query in 1671 together with other clergy and laymen (including the *kalāntar* or head of the community). In the East, the Capuchin friar and his sponsors discovered churches that, unlike the Protestant "innovators," had since late antiquity preserved the core truths of faith, especially the doctrine of the real presence and transubstantiation as well as the seven sacraments. The Roman Church and the Eastern churches, in contrast to the Protestants, therefore shared the same "apostolic tradition."[1]

Members of the reform orders, in particular, considered the secluded lives of Eastern Christian monks to be relics of the early eremitism whose values they themselves aspired to renew. Traveling in the Near East gave them the opportunity to visit the key sites of the biblical history of salvation and introduced them to a past that they regarded as part of the history of their own orders and of the Roman Church. They were aware of such commonalities as a result of the study of Church history, which assumed a prominent place in the educational program of Christian humanism. At the same time, the clerics who entered into contact with the Eastern churches wished to make them see the "error" they had committed in breaking away from Rome. They derived the mission to return them to the path of salvation from the contrast between the idealized images of early Christian monasticism and the dire conditions they believed existed in the present.[2] Depending on the situation in which they interacted with Eastern Christians in everyday practice, they perceived them as either lost—and now rediscovered—ignorant brethren, schismatics, or heretics, as we will see in what follows.

But first we need to look briefly at the previous history of relations between the Roman and the Armenian Church. In the history of schisms, the separation of the Armenian Church from Byzantium and Rome occurred rather early on, in the wake of the Christological debates of late antiquity. To be sure, the nonparticipation in the Council of Chalcedon (451) could still be attributed to Armenia's location on the edge of the Sassanid Empire rather than to any fundamental doctrinal differences. Beginning in the sixth century, however, the Armenian Church followed its Alexandrine counterpart in rejecting the position of the Council of Chalcedon, according to which Christ's divine and human natures coexisted "unconfusedly." Their Greek and Latin adversaries therefore referred to the Armenians as "monophysites," whom they accused of recognizing only one, inseparable divine nature of Christ. The Armenian Church for its part stressed not the unitary nature but the permanent oneness of the divine and the human in Christ. These differences became associated with the controversies surrounding the relationship between Byzantium and the churches on the margins of the empire, since the Council of Chalcedon also postulated the primacy of Constantinople over the other Eastern patriarchates.[3]

The Armenian Church at first distanced itself from Byzantium but not to the same extent from Rome. When close contacts arose in the context of the First Crusade (1096–9), the Armenians' relationship with Rome, unlike that with Byzantium, was not burdened by memories of persecution. Because of the martyrdom of the Apostles Peter and Paul in Rome, the Armenian Church also considered that city to be an especially holy place, along with Jerusalem. It thus made sense to accord the pope a place of honor among the patriarchs as bishop of Rome; this was expressed, for example, in the Armenian *vitae* of Gregory the Illuminator, which attribute his consecration as catholicos to Pope Sylvester I (314–35).

The Latin Crusaders brought welcome support against the Muslim Seljuks and Byzantium. At the same time, their advance signaled an intensification of contacts between the Armenian and Latin clergy and laity. Depending on the context, doctrinal and ritual differences could lead to accusations that the other side was persisting in error. In the Latin view of the Armenians, the focus was on two divergent practices in particular: the use of undiluted wine during the mass and the celebration of the birth of Christ together with Epiphany on January 6—both issues that would remain central into the early modern period. The Armenians contradicted the Roman claim to primacy by describing Christendom as consisting of different autocephalous churches, each with its own patriarch. Union accordingly meant neither subjection nor conversion, but merely a recognition of the *primatus honoris* of the "patriarch" of Rome as the successor to St. Peter. One practical difficulty of negotiations over union lay in the limited prerogatives of the catholicos vis-à-vis the bishops: a catholicos might be willing to enter a union, but actually bringing about the union depended on the assent of the bishops of the various local churches.[4]

Given the decentralized nature of the Armenian Church, contacts between individual local churches and Latin missionaries could lead to partial union. They heightened the confessional conflicts—all the more so as they came about against the backdrop of ecclesiastical and political conflicts. This applies in particular to the Dominican mission in the Caucasus, which since the fourteenth century had encouraged the Armenians of Nakhchivan to enter a union with the Roman Church and which remained influential into the early modern period. The Armenian *Fratres Unitores* were a community associated with the Dominicans, who were eventually integrated into this order in 1583. Unusual within the broader context of medieval and early modern efforts at union was the adoption in Nakhchivan of the Latin rite, which the Dominicans were allowed to celebrate in the Armenian language.[5]

The Council of Florence (1439), to which Pope Eugene IV (Gabriele Condulmer, r. 1431–47) invited the catholicos of Sis, Constantine VI, remained the most important point of reference for post-Tridentine efforts at union. Constantine VI sent a delegation of the bishop of Aleppo and other clerics who agreed to a union. However, years later, the ratification and implementation of this decision by the Armenian Church, which was divided on the matter of union, were still pending. The eventual reestablishment of the see of the catholicos in Etchmiadzin in 1441 was a clear signal that the Armenian Church rejected the union efforts at that time.[6]

The early seventeenth-century Roman Church was thus not unacquainted with the "monophysitical" Armenians. The fact that the dogmatic differentiation between the Armenian Church and Byzantium or Rome had developed since late antiquity meant that around 1600, both sides essentially could resort to old stores of knowledge about why their rivals should be understood as an unorthodox Christian church. The reciprocal excommunications in connection with the reception of the Council of Chalcedon lived on in church rituals. Thus, the Armenian Church venerated Dioscorus (d. 454), the patriarch of Alexandria deposed as a "heretic" by the Council of Chalcedon, as a saint. Similarly, the Armenian liturgy commemorated the condemnation of Pope Leo I (440–61), who had excommunicated Dioscorus. The unsuccessful efforts to unify the churches, most recently those of the Council of Florence, were always also accompanied by dogmatic disambiguation and delimitation. The latter would be repeated in connection with the post-Tridentine Catholic Church's attempts at union.

From the Roman perspective, union meant turning away from "errors" of doctrine as well as recognizing the primacy of the pope. In the wake of the Council of Trent, the concept of the "Oriental rite" made it possible to express the special status of the Uniate Eastern churches within a largely Latin Catholic Church in legal terms. Cleansed of "errors" and "abuses," the Uniate churches retained their own legal personality within the framework of their subjection to the pope. To what extent deviant liturgical practices and law were expressions of "schism" or even "heresy" was determined in individual decisions, which meant that the politics of the Roman Curia ultimately remained contradictory: the same prerogatives could be granted to certain churches and denied others. While the pope in principle claimed the authority to issue universally binding norms, in practice he recognized particular canon law in many matters.[7] That Uniate Eastern Christians were to retain their own rites was among the principles that the curial congregations repeatedly recalled. Separation was rehearsed and emphasized through the practices of symbolic communication, for instance when Catholic Armenian priests were forbidden to celebrate mass wearing Latin vestments. Latin missionaries were permitted to hear confessions from Eastern Christians, but were only to administer the sacraments of community, especially baptism and marriage, in cases of emergency (*in casu necessitatis*, i.e., if no priest of their own rite was available). The Roman practice of respect for the "Oriental rites" as it developed in individual decisions was formalized in Benedict XIV's 1755 encyclical *Allatae sunt*. The notion of the "Oriental rite," however, did not imply a recognition of autonomous churches, but rather the validation of deviant practices based on the Latin rite as it had been reformed in the wake of the Council of Trent, thus underlining the superiority of the Roman Church.[8]

The Armenian Church was thus a subject of many controversial theological debates with origins in late antiquity. Yet the Catholic clerics sent to Persia starting in the early seventeenth century were largely unprepared for the unfamiliar circumstances, which they discovered only gradually. The first subchapter takes us from the reception of the missionaries upon arrival by the Armenian clergy to the "great friendship" that the Discalced Carmelites cultivated in the 1620s with Vardapet Moses (catholicos of his church from 1629 until his death in 1632) and a community of Armenian monks in New Julfa. It explores how the missionaries perceived and dealt with differences of doctrine and ritual practice. The focus here is on the question of whether they intensified their contacts with Armenian clerics beyond the social practices of mutual respect that contemporaries called "good correspondence" and also arrived at practices of *communicatio in sacris* that implied reciprocal recognition as brothers in Christ.

The second subchapter illuminates the processes of confessional disambiguation that began to emerge in the 1630s. The Armenian community was characterized by wide networks, whose cultivation also included relations with Rome. Despite a distance of some 3,500 kilometers, the conflicts in Lviv's Armenian community over the appointment of a new archbishop there reached New Julfa. The subchapter will then explore how individual missionaries on the ground called for adherence to confessional rules, and were granted protection in Rome as a result, and to what extent the Armenian clergy for its part drew clearer boundaries.

The third subchapter is devoted to practices of accommodation and dissimulation, which even in the late seventeenth and eighteenth centuries remained oriented more toward ambivalent coexistence than confessional opposition, thus limiting the tendency to confessional disambiguation. Attention here focuses on the relationships between missionaries and Armenian merchant families, some of whose members, because of their mobility as traders, lived under Catholic authorities or at least cultivated close relationships in Catholic countries. The aim is to demonstrate how their far-flung activities, which extended from Western Europe to East Asia, helped to create space for efforts to unite the churches that went hand in hand with a high degree of confessional ambiguity.

"Good Correspondence" and Sacramental Community with Rediscovered "Brethren"

Welcomed as Fellow Christians

Like the Portuguese in their first contacts with the Thomas Christians in South India, the Augustinians and Discalced Carmelites in the Safavid Empire had the initial positive experience of encountering, in a non-Christian environment, the Christian Armenians who welcomed them as brothers in faith. The Augustinian Belchior dos Anjos, for example, recounted how he and his companion Friar Guilherme de Santo Agostinho were met outside Julfa on the Arax in 1604—just before ʿAbbās I deported the city's population—by numerous Armenian priests who had come to lead them to a church in Julfa consecrated to John the Baptist. There they welcomed the friars after a few prayers. The Augustinians' suggestion that they attend the Armenian mass and that the Armenians attend their mass was joyfully accepted, according to their account, for they were the first "Frankish brothers" ever seen in that country. Three days later all of them proceeded to mass at St. George's church in Julfa. After the mass, the Augustinians joined the priests and asked them questions about their faith. While, according to the report, the Armenians recognized the pope as the head of the Church, they insisted on their own rites, which they traced back to Gregory the Illuminator. As for the articles of faith and the sacraments, the Augustinians could, however, detect no errors in the answers translated by the interpreter. In the Augustinian's account, the differences were limited to ritual forms, which he believed to be those of the Greek Church. The friar made no mention whatsoever of Christological differences, and under these circumstances there was no question of whether his presence at an Armenian mass was acceptable or had to be rejected as *communicatio in sacris*.[9]

While Belchior dos Anjos conveyed an image of the Armenians as "nearly orthodox" Christians who diverged from the Roman Church more in outward forms than in doctrine, we nevertheless need to ask to what extent he and his companion Guilherme de Santo Agostinho were in a position to understand the unfamiliar environment. The language barrier and their lack of knowledge of the other church limited communication. The two Augustinians were forced to rely on an interpreter for their conversations with Armenian and Georgian clerics. Friar Belchior's account of a discussion with Georgian priests shows that he was aware of the resulting consequences for an exchange on complex theological matters. The Augustinians had discovered no errors, "for the interpreter was unfamiliar with the terms that could have revealed any."

We should also be skeptical of the knowledge of differences that divided the Eastern churches: Belchior dos Anjos was unaware, for example, that the Armenians particularly distanced themselves from the Greek Church, whose rituals he thought he recognized in those of the Armenian Church. He and his companion had believed that the Armenians were so closely aligned with the Greek Church in this regard that they would not deviate from them. At the same time, the Augustinian claimed that it was only fear of the Turks that made the Armenians continue to obey the patriarch of Constantinople; otherwise, they would have been prepared to recognize the pope as head of the Church.[10] For Belchior dos Anjos, this recognition implied the effective submission to a superior jurisdictional authority, but his interlocutors may simply have meant a position of honor as "patriarch" and bishop of Rome.

Together with his companion, Belchior dos Anjos thus approached these fellow Christians without the knowledge to effectively assess whether their religious practices aligned with the orthodoxy of the Roman Church. Against the background of their friendly reception, the Augustinians showed no hesitation about correspondence even in the sacramental arena. When the Armenians deported from Julfa on the Arax arrived in Isfahan in 1605 together with Catholicos David IV (1590–1629), the friars not only helped them to erect a church for the catholicos but also presented him with one of their two chalices, a gift of high symbolic value, which implicitly signified the acceptance of the Armenian sacrament of the mass.[11]

The Armenian clergy's reception of the Discalced Carmelites in 1607 largely corresponded to that experienced by the Augustinians three years before. On their way to Isfahan, some fifteen Armenian priests accompanied Paolo Simone di Gesù Maria and his companions in procession to the church in Ardabil where they attended a mass in which the congregation prayed for the pope. The Armenian priests seemed like Catholics to the Discalced Carmelites "because they spoke well of Your Holiness and everything else we told them of the faith."[12] From Isfahan, Juan Thadeo de San Eliseo informed the *praepositus generalis* of his order that thus far, the Discalced Carmelites had "discovered no heresy or schism among the Armenian people." The Armenians said that since the time of Gregory the Illuminator they had acknowledged the pope "as head of the entire Church."[13]

When the Capuchins Pacifique de Provins and Gabriel de Paris arrived in Isfahan in 1628 to establish a settlement of their order there, the Armenian laity and clergy welcomed them just as warmly as they had the Augustinians and the Discalced Carmelites. The Augustinians, Discalced Carmelites, and Capuchins all described rituals with which the Armenian clergy honored them in their shared capacity as Christian priests: that is, not simply by gestures of "good correspondence" such as reciprocal visits but also by receiving them with hymn-singing priests holding crosses and censers, inviting them into the church (even for celebrations of the mass), and clothing them in precious surplices. Pacifique de Provins emphasized that the Capuchins were received at the monastery of Bishop Khachatur "not as foreign men of a different religion, but as angels." The Capuchins reciprocated with invitations to their first mass and the banquet that followed in the house provided for them by the shah thanks to the intercession of an influential Armenian merchant.[14] Such practices of "good correspondence," which included the sacramental arena, were part of a strategy of mission that the Discalced Carmelite Juan Thadeo de San Eliseo described as follows in 1608–9: One need only cultivate good relations with the Armenians, celebrate mass in their churches, and invite the Armenian clerics in turn to celebrate in the missionary churches. This would gain their affection and, if they harbored errors out of ignorance, they would discard them.[15]

Communication with the "Ignorant"

As Bernard Heyberger has stressed, the missionaries in the Syrian provinces in the early seventeenth century were convinced that the roots of "heresy" and "schism" lay in the ignorance of the Eastern Christians.[16] The ignorant were not truly "schismatics" separated from the Roman Church, let alone "heretics." The missionaries' task was to open their eyes to divine truth in the spirit of Christian charity, thereby leading them to the path of salvation. To this end they had to make personal contacts and gain the trust of those in need of instruction.

Signs of close social relations between the Discalced Carmelites and the Armenians of New Julfa were emerging by 1616–17. Among those mentioned are leading Armenian merchants referred to by the honorary title of *ḥwāǧa*, who later also appeared as middlemen and competitors of the East India Companies. In 1616, the head of the community (*kalāntar*) of New Julfa, Ḥwāǧa Safar, a wealthy merchant, and his brother and future successor in the office of *kalāntar*, Ḥwāǧa Nazar, stood as guarantors for a loan with which Juan Thadeo de San Eliseo financed the erection of a wall surrounding the order's cemetery outside the city.[17] From the diary of the Italian traveler Pietro Della Valle we learn that in 1617, on the way back from a ride to this cemetery, Friar Juan Thadeo took him to pray at an Armenian church in New Julfa also built by Ḥwāǧa Safar. The prayer in the Armenian church was embedded in a practice of "good correspondence" that also included visiting the homes of Armenian notables. While riding out on another occasion a few months later, the Discalced Carmelite and Della Valle visited the homes of the *kalāntar* and his brother, "the first men and heads of all Julfa," as well as another Armenian notable, "a very courteous man, very well disposed toward us Franks."[18]

The Discalced Carmelite Dimas della Croce, who arrived in Isfahan in 1618 after a two-year sojourn in Baghdad, specifically sought to offer his clerical services to the Armenians. At the end of 1618, the friar reported to the procurator general of his order in Rome on his language studies, which had already enabled him to hear confessions in Armenian. When the Discalced Carmelites went to the churches and homes of Armenians, the latter showed them much deference, even more than they did their own clerics, and asked for the friars' blessings. Dimas della Croce asked the procurator general to help him obtain a papal license to celebrate the mass in Armenian because this would further increase the Armenians' goodwill toward the missionaries. The request, which the *Propaganda Fide* denied in 1627, was accompanied by the suggestion that such celebrations of the mass should take place in Armenian churches as well. Through "communication in spiritual matters" one could gradually correct "abuses" in the Armenian rituals and gain the Armenians' good will.[19]

According to the provincial vicar of the Discalced Carmelites, Pietro Della Valle's marriage to Maani Gioerida [Ǧuwairī], daughter of a Nestorian father and an Armenian mother, contributed to more members of Eastern churches than had previously coming to the mission church. These new churchgoers also turned to the Discalced Carmelites in matters relating to canon law (marriage dispensations and the like). The friars, according to the vicar, accommodated them in such matters so as to gradually guide them toward obedience to the pope. The cemetery laid out in 1616 outside the city was intended to offer a suitable place of burial not just for the Discalced Carmelites and the Catholic laity but also for "schismatics." In this way, they could at least "reap in their final hour the benefits they had missed in life." Juan Thadeo de San Eliseo relativized religious differences against the backdrop of close contacts. He noted that the well-educated Armenians were less different from Catholics than many people thought; at the same time, he stressed their willingness to recognize the primacy of the pope. The "simple folk," on the other hand, lived in extreme ignorance but also showed such good will that they could easily find their salvation.[20]

Della Valle's letters to his friend Mario Schipano in Naples provide us with more details. While not wholly unproblematic because of the way they were edited for publication, they nevertheless offer deeper insights into local practice. Della Valle refers repeatedly to relations between the Discalced Carmelites and the family of his wife, Maani Gioerida, who leaned toward union with Rome following her marriage. The traveler shared with the friars the narrative of Armenian ignorance that excused deviations. His wife's religion consisted of "little more than the constant profession that she was a Christian, a knowledge of the most necessary prayers, and, by tradition, confused notions of religious precepts and sacred history."[21]

In 1619 Maani's sister Laali married an Armenian notable from New Julfa. Confessional distinctions played a subordinate role in this marriage as well. The description of the Latin and Armenian religious services on the occasion of the wedding shows how the Discalced Carmelites participated in the ritual, which elided both the canonical forms of nuptials and the question of the confessional allegiance of the parties involved in order to accommodate the Armenian notables. The events began on a Saturday morning with a mass in the Discalced Carmelite church, where the bride made her confession and took communion. Then the bride was led to New Julfa, where Armenian priests performed the wedding ceremony in the main Armenian church. Even if we believe Della Valle's assertion that the officiating priests were good Catholics, the choice of the main Armenian church is evidence of a practice that did not distinguish clearly between Catholic and "schismatic" places of worship.[22]

The missionary reports solidified the purported ignorance of the Armenians, which was used to justify such practices, into a topos that would be raised repeatedly until the end of the Persian missions in the eighteenth century. This topos made procedures that otherwise fell under the prohibition of *communicatio in sacris* appear permissible. In the absence of ill will, and with "abuses" and "errors" being attributed solely to a lack of more thorough instruction, one could not actually speak of "schismatics" or "heretics." In this case, sacramental proximity had to be understood as a means of eradicating "abuses" and "errors." The missionaries in Persia thereby anticipated the response to criticism of their practices. In fact, in the *Ordinationes* at the end of his 1621 visitation, Vicente de San Francisco reminded the Discalced Carmelites in Isfahan that Paul V had not only not granted them permission to celebrate in the churches of the "schismatics" but had also been rather outraged by the very suggestion.[23] In 1630, the *Definitorium generale* felt compelled to instruct the friars to use their cemetery outside the city solely for the burials of Catholics. This instruction was part of a whole series of orders against practices of *communicatio in sacris*: the missionaries were not to allow the Armenian priests to celebrate the mass in the order's churches with unleavened bread (*azyma*). The missionaries, in turn, were not to celebrate in the churches of the "schismatics," nor were they to attend their worship services.[24]

A "Great Friendship": The Discalced Carmelites and Vardapet Moses

The Discalced Carmelites' close proximity to the Armenians of New Julfa, which Della Valle had documented, continued throughout the 1620s. In 1621 they preached on holidays in Italian, Farsi, and Armenian. In 1623 they ensured regular catechesis in Italian, Farsi, Arabic, and Armenian. In those days they enjoyed a "great friendship" with Vardapet Moses, who would become catholicos of the Armenian Church in Etchmiadzin in 1629 and who died in 1632. As vardapet, Moses was a priest of great theological learning and reputation who lived as a monk, comparable to the *hieromonachoi* of the Greek Orthodox Church. Seventeenth- and eighteenth-century sources in Western European languages often refer to the vardapets as bishops because they held the powers of visitation and excommunication that, according to the Latin view, pertained to bishops.[25]

According to the accounts of the Discalced Carmelite prior, Próspero del Espíritu Santo, the relationship with Moses began when one of the friars met him during an exorcism at an Armenian church. This blossoming friendship included gestures of "good correspondence." For instance, the vardapet and his companions were accommodated at the Carmelite convent in Isfahan following a dinner at the home of the captain of the Dutch East India Company (a Calvinist). The relationship went far beyond such signs of respect, however. Quite remarkably, the vardapet and his companions participated in the divine office of the Discalced Carmelites and subsequently invited them to New Julfa, where Moses received the prior of the Discalced Carmelites as a papal representative at a service in his church. Vardapet Moses, who is said to have supported union with Rome, wished to celebrate mass in the church of the Discalced Carmelites; the latter, in turn, would be able to celebrate mass in his church. This did not come about because Moses refused to make a formal confession of faith, arguing that his Armenian opponents would otherwise declare him a heretic and divest him of the authority he enjoyed among the people. The prior of the Discalced Carmelites, in contrast, attended the consecration of a vardapet, holding his hand above the head of the cleric together with Moses, a clear signal of sacramental community.[26]

Following the visitation of his order's missions in Persia and India, from which he returned to Rome in 1627, the Discalced Carmelite Eugenio di San Benedetto reported on Moses and other vardapets around him to the *Propaganda Fide*. His description was informed by the idea that Eastern Christian monasticism was a continuation of its early Christian predecessor, which the Latin reform orders aspired to revive. The vardapets led lives of exemplary strictness and enjoyed a reputation of saintliness among the Armenians. They preached, taught, and dispensed the sacraments in the countries and cities inhabited by Armenians, who had previously fallen into grave errors for lack of instruction. While the visitor's description of their way of life and activities suggested parallels to Teresian reform and the apostolate of the Discalced Carmelites in Persia, he interpreted the reception that the vardapets offered the missionaries as signs of their willingness to unite with Rome. They spoke positively of the Catholics, he noted, and invited the Discalced Carmelites to all their festivities and ceremonies, giving them pride of place there. The vardapets tended to refer to the "Franks" and Armenians as "two dear brothers" who had grown apart and now had found each other again "with incredible joy."[27]

More precise indications of the social dimensions of relations between the friars and monks in New Julfa may be drawn from the writings of Dimas della Croce from 1631 and 1632, in which he tried to persuade the *praepositus generalis* of his order that these practices were consistent with the observance of his order's Rule and would help to convert the Armenians. If the Discalced Carmelites dined outside their convent during their regular visits to the monastery in New Julfa, they did so to "maintain and promote community," for like Catholicos Moses and the vardapets, the monks were "very well-disposed" toward them. From time to time they gave the Discalced Carmelites "good alms," such as a batch of flour, and at every opportunity and every important transaction they helped them greatly, which the friars repaid "with signs of good correspondence and charity" when the Armenian monks visited their convent in turn.[28]

The *Propaganda Fide* welcomed the gestures and declarations of Vardapet and future Catholicos Moses as hopeful signs. They were in keeping with the image of a successful Persian mission, which the Congregation famously also cultivated with regard to the Muslims in the early years of its existence. In 1625 the secretary of the *Propaganda Fide*, Francesco Ingoli, was prepared to receive Vardapet Moses's declarations as an approval of union with Rome. He recommended that the pope bestow pontifical vestments upon the vardapet as a sign of the recognition of his dignity. He also understood the suggestion of reciprocal celebrations of the mass in each other's churches as a suitable means of affirming union; the vardapet and his priests would overcome the remaining "errors" thanks to regular communication with the Discalced Carmelites. The profession of faith remained a precondition, however.[29] While the *Propaganda Fide* set aside the call for abjuration and absolution and thus the portrayal of union as conversion, it insisted upon the written profession of faith and its scrutiny in Rome as a prerequisite for recognizing bishops and access to the joint celebration of the mass.

The relationship remained unclear from the Roman perspective, despite a willingness to assume that Catholicos Moses and Bishop Khachatur of New Julfa aspired to implement the union resolved at the Council of Florence. As Rome saw it, the adoption of the resolutions of the Council of Chalcedon should have occurred at a synod convened by the catholicos. The response of the catholicos to this expectation was ambivalent: On the one hand, Moses stated that it was impossible to adopt the decisions of a council—Chalcedon—that had been convened by a Roman emperor hostile to the Armenians. On the other, he denied the differences between the Armenian and Catholic understandings of the dual nature of Christ and emphasized that relations between Roman and Armenian Christians should be marked by charity, not quarrels.[30]

With the instruction penned by Francesco Ingoli in 1632, the *Propaganda Fide* charged the newly appointed Latin bishops of Isfahan and Bagdad, Juan Thadeo de San Eliseo and Timoteo Pérez, with the special task of winning over Catholicos Moses, "who was so close to adopting the Catholic faith."[31] By having 1,000 images of St. Gregory printed to give to the missionaries, the Congregation made use of the saint most revered by the Armenians as an "illuminator" and symbol of a church tied to Rome by the shared Nicene Creed. When the catholicos died in 1632, the ambiguity surrounding his relations with the Discalced Carmelites and Rome remained unresolved.

A statement that a member of a delegation from the English East India Company attributed to Bishop Khachatur was characteristic of how the Armenian clerics with whom the Discalced Carmelites cultivated friendships in the 1620s understood their relationship with Rome. When asked in 1628 by members of the delegation about his view of the "pope of Rome," the bishop of New Julfa reportedly answered "that he was a great bishope and that he loved him because he professed the name of Christe, and noe otherwise did he beleef him to be then another religious man."[32] Such a definition at once opened up possibilities and set limits—possibilities for the cultivation of social and sacramental proximity to clerics who referred to a papal commission, and limits on a union that would have included the recognition of the superiority of papal jurisdiction.

In contact with missionaries on the ground and with the Curia, however, the Armenian clergy arrived at a heightened awareness of their own identity as distinct from the Roman Church. The efforts at union implied a preoccupation with everything that divided the two churches. For that reason, starting in the 1630s the controversies of late antiquity around the dual nature of Christ increasingly determined how the Armenian or Roman "Other" was treated. This matter will be examined in more detail in what follows.

In social relations in Isfahan and New Julfa, the practice of "friendship" and "good correspondence" coexisted with efforts at confessional disambiguation. In their dealings with the Roman Curia, Catholicos Moses and Bishop Khachatur stressed that they loved the Discalced Carmelites and other clerics as "legitimate brothers." They recalled the harmony that had prevailed between Pope Sylvester and Gregory the Illuminator; in the present, as adherents of the Church of Christ, they loved the other followers of Christ. At the same time, they demanded of Rome that the Armenian clerics and merchants be treated equally well and complained that the Catholics referred to them as "heretics and schismatics."[33]

In their correspondence with the *Propaganda Fide*, the missionaries had to adapt to their own church's growing demand for adherence to the confessional rules. On the one hand, Dimas della Croce, who had praised the celebration of the mass in the Armenian churches and "communication in spiritual matters" more generally in 1618, continued to cultivate "good correspondence" with the Armenian high clergy in the 1630s. Thus in 1634, he congratulated the new catholicos, Philip, successor to Vardapet Moses, on his election and presented him with a devotional item. On the other hand, Dimas della Croce now condemned the deficient confessional clarity of the Armenians as one of their "errors." In a letter to the prefect of the *Propaganda Fide*, Cardinal Antonio Barberini Jr., he wrote that the Armenians were "very obdurate in their errors," which included the "pestilential" assertion that any Christian nation that professed the mystery of the Holy Trinity and Christ's nature as the son of God was on the path of salvation.[34]

With these statements, Dimas della Croce was reacting to the change of heart that the secretary of the *Propaganda Fide*, Francesco Ingoli, had been undergoing since the 1620s. In 1625 Ingoli had still perceived Vardapet Moses's declarations as affirmations of union and supported the suggestion to celebrate mass in each other's churches. In 1643, in contrast, in a response to several *dubia* regarding relations with "schismatic" Armenians that had been submitted by missionaries in Persia, he categorically opposed practices of *communicatio in sacris*.[35] Ingoli thereby defined a position consistent with a confessional self-understanding. Accordingly, the Holy Office had already decided in 1637 that Armenian penitents must be refused absolution if they did not make a confession of faith in the form stipulated by the Holy See and instead merely declared that they believed what Pope Sylvester had believed[36]—the very pope who, according to a Latinophile Armenian tradition, had allegedly ordained Gregory the Illuminator during a visit to Rome.

"We do not need you": New Practices of Confessional Disambiguation

In 1698 three vardapets from New Julfa complained bitterly about the Catholic bishop of Isfahan, Élie de Saint-Albert. They summarized their complaints in a letter addressed to "the beloved and loyal Signor Agha and the other Armenians" in Italy. These men were to present the letter to those who oversaw the missions and, if possible, to the pope as well. The vardapets accused the bishop of calling the Armenians heretics, schismatics, and ignorant. The bishop, they reported, denied the validity of the Armenian mass, which he called just as useless as their church's other sacraments. In particular, he very publicly reperformed the baptism of all those who had been previously christened by Armenian priests. He permitted people excommunicated by the Armenian clergy to take communion. He stole the dead from the Armenian priests to bury them himself, forbade the faithful to keep the fasting commandments of their church, and granted marriage dispensations to third-degree relatives, which was forbidden by the Armenian Church. According to the vardapets, this behavior contrasted sharply with previous relations between the missionaries and the Armenian clergy: they had always "cultivated friendship with all missionaries" and "honored one another in brotherly charity," and visited the convent. Other missionaries continued to show them great affection; they had always lived in peace with them and were not complaining about them. Élie de Saint-Albert, however, had brought some likeminded men with him to New Julfa, causing a scandal there and disrupting the peace and tranquility of the Armenian community. Instead of supporting Armenian priests and admonishing the faithful to obedience, he had sown great hatred, appealing to the pope in all his actions.[37]

As the three vardapets saw it, as Armenian Christians they could not be the object of Christian mission because they had already accepted the divine nature of Christ and the Nicene Creed. The vardapets met the missionaries as Christian priests and thereby called into question the justification for their mission: "Fathers, we are Christians; we have the true priesthood and do not need you."[38] The differences in the practices of Catholic clerics described by the three vardapets in 1698 are affirmed in several places in the body of sources on which this book is based. Beginning in the 1640s, the tendency toward confessional disambiguation that marked the post-Tridentine Church did actually have individual proponents in the Persian missions as well. This same attitude can be observed at that time in missions toward the Eastern churches in the Syrian provinces or in the controversies surrounding the Chinese and Malabar rites. Even before then, the wide networks of the Armenian Church had already led to conflicts in other zones of contact influencing the situation in Persia, as we will see in the following subsection. The sharper demarcation lines on both sides are all the better documented since they contrasted with previous practice and thus met with resistance on the ground. In all these matters the authors of the 1698 letter referred to clear differences between Élie de Saint-Albert and his companions on the one hand, and the other missionaries on the other. The latter were still willing to accommodate the Armenian truth claim, which went back to the Council of Nicaea, far enough to avoid conflict. The vardapets from New Julfa for their part sought the understanding of the secular and ecclesiastical Catholic authorities in Italy and seem to have placed their hopes in the pope himself.

Wide Networks

The reception of missionaries by the Armenian clergy was determined by local rationalities as well as by the wide networks of the Armenian community. Clergy and laity alike understood cultivating contacts with the missionaries as an opportunity to increase their relational capital. This opened doors for the Catholic clerics but also meant that they were drawn into local disputes that were initially more about secular power and influence than doctrinal matters.[39]

Like the prelates of other Eastern churches, starting in the early seventeenth century the Armenian high clergy hoped that contacts with the Roman Curia and secular Catholic courts would offer support against Muslim authorities and opponents within their own community. While in 1605, after the deportation of the Armenians from Julfa on the Arax, Catholicos David IV staked his claim to the highest office in the Armenian Church from New Julfa, his coadjutor Melchisedech remained in Etchmiadzin. A conflict thus emerged between New Julfa and Etchmiadzin that would mark the Armenian Church throughout the seventeenth century. The Armenian communities were oriented toward competing dignitaries, who for their part relied on their relations with Rome when dealing with adversaries within the church: David IV accordingly at first cultivated good relations with the Augustinians, and in 1607 he even pledged obedience to Pope Paul V and his successors.[40]

While David IV did not break off relations with Europe, his coadjutor sought backing in the intra-Armenian conflicts and against the shah by contacting the Roman Curia and repeatedly issuing professions of support for union with Rome. These contacts with Rome gained in significance when Melchisedech was forced to flee to Poland where, shortly before his death in 1627, he ordained Nikol Torosowicz, the son of a wealthy merchant, archbishop of Lviv. In so doing, he placed himself above the rights of the local community to suggest a candidate to the catholicos. The appointment split the Armenian community of Lviv and thereby became the point of departure for a conflict in which Torosowicz sought support from union with Rome. Thus, it was at first not differences of religious doctrine but the conflict between two factions within the Armenian community of Lviv that led to challenges to the authority of Moses as catholicos and Bishop Khachatur of New Julfa as visitor to the Armenian communities in the Polish-Lithuanian Commonwealth.[41]

While King Ladislaus IV of Poland (r. 1632–48) took the side of Torosowicz's Armenian opponents in Lviv, those geographically more distant and less familiar with local circumstances tended to understand the disputes over the archbishop's appointment as a confessional conflict. Since neither the king nor the Latin archbishop of Lviv joined his side, Torosowicz traveled to Rome in 1634 as a Uniate archbishop (as he was now referred to) to drum up support against his adversaries in Lviv. During his nearly one-year sojourn in Rome from 1634 to 1635 he sought to negotiate the conditions of a union of his church with the *Propaganda Fide*. In his 1632 profession of faith before the nuncio in Poland, he had made it a condition that all the rites of his church that did not exclude union with Rome should retain their validity. This demand notwithstanding, once in Rome, he saw himself compelled to bow to the Curia in almost all disputed points. In a particular congregation of January 30, 1635, the theologians appointed by Urban VIII to examine his concerns, along with the apostolic datary and four cardinals of the *Propaganda Fide*, refused to accommodate the Armenians in Poland on matters of liturgy. Because the Armenian liturgy contained many "errors," the pope could order Torosowicz to repeat the creed in the form recently prescribed for Eastern Christians.[42]

The particular congregation of January 30, 1635, was followed in the same year and in 1636 by additional congregations of similar composition, which examined other questions of the Armenian liturgy. These consultations and the decades-long controversies surrounding the union of the Armenians in Poland-Lithuania contributed significantly to the *Propaganda Fide* and the Holy Office developing their own decision-making practice. In the process, rites that deviated from Latin practice were increasingly identified with heretical doctrines. For example, the admixture of some water with the communion wine was described as a sign of turning away from the "monophysite heresy" and adherence to the Roman notion of the dual nature of Christ and was thus imbued with a theological meaning previously absent from missionary perceptions.

Within the Armenian clergy, too, the appointment of Torosowicz as archbishop of Lviv and the subsequent decades of conflict around the union of the Armenians in Poland-Lithuania heightened the sense of confessional particularity. The fact that Bishop Khachatur of New Julfa intervened personally in the conflict in Lviv on behalf of Catholicos Moses in 1630–1, suffering the most severe hostilities from the Catholic clergy there in the process, strained his subsequent relations with the missionaries in Persia.

Events became interlocked at various levels on both the Catholic and Armenian sides. Nikol Torosowicz gained the protection of the *Propaganda Fide* by accepting the conditions formulated by the particular congregation of 1635. They had set unambiguous confessional points of reference that were controversial in relation to the Armenians, which the Congregation itself, but also confessional agitators among the missionaries, would increasingly use for orientation. The missionaries found that emphasizing confessional orthodoxy gained them favor and protection in Rome. The following section will examine these interactions using the two best-documented cases as examples.

Confessional Agitators with Rome's Approval

In the 1640s, individual missionaries in Persia began to question the previous practice of Christian commonality with the Armenians, according to which "errors" were regarded more as a consequence of ignorance than an explicit rejection of the "true" faith. Contemporaries were already associating the decisive turn toward confessional controversy with two specific clerics, whose services in this area had earned them the particular favor of the *Propaganda Fide* and appointment to relatively high office—high, at least, in comparison to other Persian missionaries of the time: the Dominican Paolo Piromalli (1591–1667) was appointed archbishop of Nakhchivan in 1655 and bishop of Bisignano (Calabria) in 1664, and the aforementioned Discalced Carmelite Élie de Saint-Albert (1643–1708) became bishop of Isfahan in 1693. Both men encountered great resistance on the ground, and both were adept at presenting how they handled it to the Roman Curia as evidence of their particular devotion to the Church.

"He Always Disputes Furiously": The Dominican Paolo Piromalli

In 1631, the *Propaganda Fide* dispatched Paolo Piromalli to the Dominican province of Nakhchivan in the Caucasus, where he was to head the seminary established on the Congregation's initiative in 1623 to aid in reforming the church of the Catholic Armenian archdiocese. The distant province in the Caucasus had already attracted the interest of Roman reform efforts in the late sixteenth century. In 1583, the Armenian *Fratres Unitores*, who had been connected with the Dominicans, were integrated into that order. This integration began to take shape in 1614 with the dispatch of Paolo Angelo Cittadini as vicar general, accompanied by four other Dominicans of European origin. Although he had instructions to avoid controversy, Cittadini came into conflict with the Catholic Armenian archbishop, who did not share his Tridentine notions and whom he therefore sought to replace with an Italian Dominican. When Urban VIII named Cittadini as the Armenian archbishop's coadjutor in 1626, he tied the right to succession to this appointment, thus removing the local electoral body's right to suggest a successor. This body consisted of sixteen clerics (including eight Dominicans) and eight laymen and had previously held the authority to recommend a candidate to the pope. Ultimately, however, the papal decision could not take effect because Cittadini died before he was able to assume office as archbishop.[43]

Because of this background, by the time Paolo Piromalli reached Nakhchivan in 1632, the local Armenian clergy was already upset about outside intervention. Soon after his arrival, the Dominican fell out with his Armenian brothers in the order as well as the archbishop. In the letters he sent to Rome, he portrayed himself as an uncompromising advocate of Tridentine orthodoxy. He attacked the ignorance and way of life of the Armenian members of the order and criticized the archbishop's administration of office. Letters with such content, however, were intercepted by Piromalli's opponents, who therefore placed him under arrest until the general of the order could decide his fate.

The pugnacious priest used his time of incarceration (1632–4) to learn Armenian. While the general of the Dominican order tried to resolve the conflict in 1633 by ordering Piromalli's release but calling him back to Rome, the priest received sufficient backing from the *Propaganda Fide* to continue his activities in Nakhchivan. In the memoranda he presented to the *Propaganda Fide*, Piromalli painted a picture of an Armenian Church whose errors in matters of faith were mirrored by those in other fields of knowledge.[44] In this way, the Dominican acquired a reputation in Rome as an expert on the Armenian Church. The *Propaganda Fide*'s support is evident in the fact that, among other things, it sent Piromalli to Lviv in the 1630s to mediate between Bishop Torosowicz and the Armenian community, and that after a sojourn in Rome in the early 1640s it entrusted him with negotiating with Catholicos Philip about a union of the Armenian Church with Rome. Piromalli, however, helped instead to exacerbate the conflicts.

In the 1640s, Piromalli spent some time in Isfahan, where he was active as a controversialist author and an unwavering preacher who could express himself well in Armenian. He found support from the Augustinians, while the Discalced Carmelites and most Capuchins turned against him. Piromalli's relationship with the Capuchin Valentin d'Angers was especially fraught. The two men brought their conflict before the *Propaganda Fide*, where they traded mutual accusations. Piromalli claimed there was a "great schism" between the Capuchin and the other missionaries with regard to observance of the Rule. Furthermore, Valentin d'Angers wanted to perform marriages without the approval of the episcopal vicar general (the Augustinian José do Rosário), because the council resolutions had not been published in Isfahan, as he incorrectly asserted.[45] The Capuchin responded to these accusations by asserting that Piromalli's controversial conduct had ruined the missionaries' relationship with the Armenians. How could one have anything to do with a man who "always disputes furiously" and insults those with whom he speaks?[46]

The conflicting statements formed the basis for the *Propaganda Fide*'s assessment of Piromalli's conduct. Various voices made themselves heard. While the *Propaganda Fide* valued a firm commitment to confessional orthodoxy, the body worried at the same time about the potential damage caused by Piromalli's brusque conduct. In 1644 the cardinals responded to his report on his disputations with the Armenian "doctors" by calling upon him to avoid public disputations because they did more harm than good.⁴⁷ In 1654 the *Propaganda Fide* nevertheless decided to propose that the pope appoint Paolo Piromalli archbishop of Nakhchivan. Alexander VII followed the Congregation's recommendation in 1655. In so doing, he not only decided in favor of a personality who had proven highly controversial on the ground but also, like Urban VIII before him in 1626, ignored the right of proposal of the local clergy and laity.

The Discalced Carmelites in Isfahan were alarmed by the news of Piromalli's appointment as bishop of Nakhchivan: Piromalli was "a far too violent and vehement spirit," the Discalced Carmelite Denis de la Couronne d'Épines wrote to one of his order's definitors. He was the cause of "the great deterioration in relations and aversion of the Armenians" to the missionaries.⁴⁸ And indeed, the brief archiepiscopal tenure of Piromalli, who only arrived in his province in July 1657, was marked by bitter conflicts with the Armenian Dominicans and laity, who accused him of seeking to introduce many new, Tridentine, ceremonies. For that reason, the *Propaganda Fide* sharply rebuked Piromalli in 1660, at a time when he had already left his archdiocese. The criticisms were based on written and oral complaints that had reached the Congregation. One of the complainants, the Dominican Silvestro Bendici, argued that the *Propaganda Fide* should adopt a different approach to avoid conflicts with the Armenian clergy: The Congregation should allow the missionaries to refrain from mentioning the Uniates' duty to receive the sacraments solely from Catholic priests. The sacramental community with the "schismatics" should thus, while not formally approved, nevertheless be tolerated.⁴⁹ Paolo Piromalli had better chances with the *Propaganda Fide* than did those who presented such proposals, since he had gained a reputation as an expert on the Eastern churches and a proponent of Tridentine orthodoxy. Despite the conflicts that had encouraged him to leave his ecclesiastical province in the Caucasus, the Dominican was appointed bishop of Bisignano in Calabria in 1664. His path thus took him from Latinizing the Armenians of Nakhchivan to attempting the same with the *Italo-Greci*: Bisignano was among the Calabrian dioceses with significant Greek rite communities, which starting in the second half of the sixteenth century were being strongly pressured to give up their specific liturgical practices and to submit to the authority of the local Latin bishops.

The Discalced Carmelite Élie de Saint-Albert and the Formation of a Catholic Armenian Community in New Julfa

The vehement reactions to Piromalli's methods among the clerics of Isfahan should not obscure the fact that he spent only a brief time in the capital and never returned to Isfahan after his appointment as archbishop. The Discalced Carmelite Élie de Saint-Albert, in contrast, was active in Isfahan and New Julfa from 1677 to 1699. Thus, like his fellow friars Juan Thadeo de San Eliseo and Dimas della Croce, he belonged to a group of missionaries who remained in the Safavid capital for many years and who acquired outstanding language skills during this time, which assisted them in their various activities at court or among the Armenians. In the process, however, Élie de Saint-Albert broke radically with his predecessors in his approach to religious differences. At the same time, his order's settlements received additional personnel: in 1693 there were four friars and one lay brother in Isfahan; at the time, five Discalced Carmelites lived in the newly founded convent in New Julfa—taken together, this was more personnel than ever before. The activities of Élie de Saint-Albert were a thorn in the flesh of the Armenian clerics who forced him to leave New Julfa twice—in 1681 and 1694—while tolerating the Jesuits' activities there since the 1660s. Both times, Élie de Saint-Albert owed his return to decisions that the shah made with respect to his relations with the Catholic courts. The Discalced Carmelite and those around him claimed to have introduced previously uncommon missionary practices. In a *Vita* and a detailed travel account, the lay brother Francesco Maria di San Siro described Élie de Saint-Albert, his companion of many years and later bishop, as an exemplary protagonist of strict confessional orthodoxy. He did so in a hagiographic style that emphasized how this bishop, who had "died not without the reputation of saintliness," broke with "heresy" and the practices of accommodation cultivated by other missionaries.[50]

Élie de Saint-Albert prepared for his mission in the Near East by studying controversialist theology and Arabic at the *Seminario di San Pancrazio*, the Discalced Carmelite mission seminary in Rome. After arriving in Isfahan in 1677, the friar first learned Persian and then moved to New Julfa in 1679 to study Armenian. With his move, he followed the aim long discussed in his order to live as close as possible to the Armenian and Latin Christians since they hardly attended the church in Isfahan.

Élie de Saint-Albert received support for the settlement in New Julfa from the Armenian merchant family Sceriman, which in light of the deteriorating living conditions of the Armenian minority at that time was diversifying its mercantile connections and investments in various directions, especially in Italian cities. In 1679, the family left a small house at the friar's disposal. Later, they built a small church in which Élie de Saint-Albert and a vardapet celebrated mass according to the Latin and Armenian rite, respectively. In 1691 the family financed the construction of a convent in New Julfa with a larger church consecrated to the prophet Elijah. The Discalced Carmelite left the smaller church to Catholic clerics of the Armenian rite. Henceforth, this church served as the focal point of the small Catholic Armenian community, which arose in the 1680s following a formal profession of Catholic faith by eleven male members of the Sceriman family. The social proximity to the missionaries, as already expressed in the 1646 profession of allegiance to union with Rome by Ḥwāğa Sarhat, head of the Sceriman family, led to the emergence of a congregation whose confessional profile was sharpened by the controversies of the 1680s and 1690s. Ḥwāğa Sarhat's sons, Zaccaria, Marcara, Michele, Gasparo, and Murat, became the most important sponsors of this congregation, which the missionaries therefore generally referred to as the "Sceriman church."

The author of the *Vita* of Élie de Saint-Albert attributed the Sceriman brothers' decision to build the Discalced Carmelite convent and church to the spiritual utility that resulted from the gatherings in their houses, which were attended not just by their relatives but also by numerous other persons, along with their children, who were dependent upon the family. Before dinner, Friar Élie would introduce those present to the mysteries of the Catholic faith; this proved more efficacious than the sermons because in this setting he could address the doubts that his listeners presented. The relations with the Sceriman family also led to the establishment of a school. The unusually close contacts with the Armenian laity are confirmed by the reactions of critics within the order who objected to Friar Élie's dinners and overnight stays outside the convent as innovations not in conformity with the Rule.

The author of the *Vita* also lauded the role played by Élie de Saint-Albert in the celebration of the jubilee year pronounced by Alexander VIII (Pietro Vito Ottoboni, r. 1689–91) on the occasion of his election as pope in 1689, which, owing to the slowness of the mail, was only announced and celebrated in New Julfa in 1691. If we are to believe the author of the *Vita*, the jubilee celebration became the source of growing polarization. The vardapets now often challenged the friar to disputations, but because of their "ignorance" always lost, much to their disgrace. As "heretics" they nevertheless clung obstinately to their "errors." The deliberate use of the term "heretics" referred to a difference over the fundamental truths of faith and not simply the rejection of the papal claim to primacy. It was in keeping with the manner in which Élie de Saint-Albert had orchestrated the conversion of the Armenian vardapet Michael in the Discalced Carmelite church in New Julfa in 1689. At his behest, the vardapet made a detailed profession of faith in which the "errors" of the Armenian Church were corrected point by point.[51] This staging as a conversion contradicted the mission strategy previously practiced in New Julfa, which explicitly had not presented union with Rome as a change to a different church.

Élie de Saint-Albert's suggestion that the *Propaganda Fide* grant the vardapet the rights and privileges of the missionaries and bishops who depended upon it, so that he might exercise episcopal authority over the Armenians and ordain priests, pointed in a similar direction.[52] The installation of a Catholic Armenian bishop would have meant abandoning the attempts to win over the Armenian Church as a whole to union with Rome. In predominantly Catholic Poland-Lithuania, efforts to found a Catholic Armenian parallel church upon the authority granted by Rome had already been made in 1689 when the pope issued a decision extricating the Armenian archdiocese of Lviv from its ties to the catholicate of Etchmiadzin. In the Ottoman Empire, unlike in Catholic Poland-Lithuania, it was not until the confirmation of Abraham Petros I as patriarch of Cilicia in 1742 that Benedict XIV created an Armenian parallel hierarchy separate from the jurisdiction of the catholicos and united with Rome. The *Propaganda Fide* did not go that far in Persia. In 1693, it merely proposed that the pope appoint Élie de Saint-Albert as Latin bishop of the diocese of Isfahan, which had previously been under the bishop of Babylon's authority as apostolic vicar. This step alone proved polarizing, as demonstrated by the incidents in the wake of the appointment, which was announced in 1694. While the Scerimans used the occasion of the Discalced Carmelite's appointment to build a larger church, the Armenian bishop of New Julfa, Stephan, understood the papal decision and the construction of the church as challenges to his own authority. He set the head of the Armenian community (*kalāntar*), the most important notables, and the vardapets against Élie de Saint-Albert, whom he reportedly never referred to as bishop. According to the *Vita*, the Discalced Carmelite responded by laying the foundation stone for the church and holding a Corpus Christi procession through the streets of New Julfa—two acts that the Armenian clergy could not help but regard as provocations. The Armenian bishop finally achieved the destruction of the newly begun church and the expulsion of the Discalced Carmelite from New Julfa, both ordered by the highest Muslim judge.

As described by the author of his *Vita*, Bishop Élie de Saint-Albert orchestrated his return to New Julfa three years later on orders from the shah as a triumphal procession through the entire quarter. A Portuguese ambassador, Gregório Pereira Fidalgo da Silveira, had intervened in support of his return and permission to rebuild the demolished church, presenting the shah with relevant letters from Innocent XII (Antonio Pignatelli, r. 1691–1700) and the grand duke of Tuscany.

As Latin bishop of Isfahan, Élie de Saint-Albert wielded only limited jurisdictional authority over the Uniate Armenian Christians. In 1705 the pope accordingly refused to allow him to ordain Catholic Armenian priests.[53] Élie de Saint-Albert's efforts to bring the Catholic Armenians closer to the Latin Church nevertheless had consequences for relations with the Armenian clergy. The fact that he went a good deal further than intended by the curial congregations also played a role here. Thus, the profession of faith that the Armenian vardapet Michael made to him in 1689 included the recognition of all of the definitions and decrees of the Council of Trent. The *Propaganda Fide*, in contrast, had decided in 1631 that the Uniate Eastern Christians were not subject to Latin canon law, except in matters of doctrine, when Eastern Christians were explicitly mentioned or when the rules, by their very nature, had to be understood as universally valid.[54]

In his correspondence with superiors of his order and the *Propaganda Fide*, Élie de Saint-Albert urged that "the Armenian Church be brought into closer conformity with the Latin Church."[55] As bishop of Isfahan he presented the *Propaganda Fide* with a revised version of the profession of faith issued by Rome for the Armenians, in which he had clarified several points "necessary for the recanting of their heresies." This draft, too, revealed the will to depict union with Rome as a formal conversion from "heresy" to the "true faith." Like Paolo Piromalli before him, in the process he went beyond the usual more or less clear rejection of a number of ritual practices whose symbolic content was not always understood, such as the admixture of some water in the communion wine.[56]

Such an approach was responsible for the extreme reactions to his presence in New Julfa. In the account of his expulsion from New Julfa in 1694, Élie de Saint-Albert himself cited the *kalāntar*, who had visited him with the initial intention of mediating: Was it true that the pope had sent the missionaries to convert the Armenians? They were already Christians, after all, and had baptism and the other sacraments. According to his own account, the Discalced Carmelite answered that he represented the one orthodox Church, from which the Armenians had split off. The Armenian mass contained so many sacrileges that no true Christian could participate in it.[57]

In this way, acceptance of union with Rome became tantamount to deserting the Armenian Church, which unsurprisingly exacerbated the conflicts within the Armenian community. Not even all members of the Sceriman family agreed with the bishop. One of the five Sceriman brothers quarreled with his siblings and sided with several Armenian clerics who also supported union with Rome instead of with the Discalced Carmelite. Contrary to Élie de Saint-Albert's assertions, the family's recurring refusal to pay his promised stipend as bishop after his 1694 expulsion from New Julfa cannot be explained solely by the persecution they suffered at the hands of Armenians who rejected the union with Rome. While the Scerimans distanced themselves from the bishop, they maintained their relationships with the missionaries of other orders. Such relations were all the more important for the family because they were preparing at the same time for the permanent settlement of some family members in Venice, and thus for life in a new Catholic environment. While the Discalced Carmelite Basile de Saint-Charles complained in 1705 that the Scerimans no longer ensured the livelihood of the friars of his order and the bishop, a Dominican praised the family's "good deeds," which allowed for the construction and decoration of his order's church in New Julfa and the construction of a comfortable house for the friars.[58]

Élie de Saint-Albert polarized people within his own order and beyond. As visitor general, Agnello dell'Immacolata Concezione chided the friar in 1684, and not just for his close contacts with the Armenian laity, which he regarded as violations of the order's Rule. While Élie de Saint-Albert was "very learned and virtuous," he was also unsuited to the office of prior, since he "thought very highly of himself, but was hated by everyone."[59] In 1694 Élie de Saint-Albert asserted that the missionaries of all orders had "admirably" stood by the Discalced Carmelites when he and his companions were expelled from New Julfa.[60] In fact, by no means had all of them signed the report he sent to Rome at that time: the signatures of all the Jesuits, Capuchins, and Dominicans in New Julfa as well as Louis-Marie Pidou de Saint-Olon, bishop of Babylon, and François Sanson, a priest of the *Missions étrangères* close to Pidou, were missing. The report that the prior of the local convent sent to the *Propaganda Fide* after Élie de Saint-Albert's departure showed that not even all of the Discalced Carmelites in Isfahan approved of "their" bishop's practices: the bishop had made many enemies among the Armenian clergy in New Julfa. After his departure the prior had thus visited the vardapets, who professed their "great friendship." One of the vardapets had returned his visit and told him that it was better to live in unity.[61]

As in the case of Paolo Piromalli, the *Propaganda Fide* occasionally referred to Élie de Saint-Albert's "excessive zeal" as deleterious.[62] Overall, however, it seems that in their relations with the Curia and the superiors of their orders, clerics could present a narrowly conceived confessional orthodoxy as a sign of their proper performance of duty, to the detriment of their local rivals. Pope Innocent XII appointed Élie de Saint-Albert a bishop in 1693 after he, like the Dominican Piromalli before him, had portrayed himself as a zealous campaigner against "schism" and "heresy." Élie de Saint-Albert's approach, about which the vardapets complained bitterly in 1698, was not simply rooted in his personality. Rather, the controversies he unleashed were embedded in relations between the missionaries and the Roman Curia, which was increasingly less inclined to accommodate local notions and practices. The missionaries managed to adapt to these changes. While individual clerics like Paolo Piromalli and Élie de Saint-Albert brought the confessional controversies to their areas of activity, others adapted to the expectations they assumed were held by the recipients—the superiors of their orders and the curial congregations—only in the reports they wrote. This included the willingness to suffer hardship and persecution from the "infidels," "schismatics," and "heretics" because of their devotion to the Church. We will need to keep this in mind when we rely largely on missionary accounts to explore the boundaries that the Armenian clergy purportedly drew.

The Armenian Clergy Draws Boundaries

When the three vardapets from New Julfa complained about Élie de Saint-Albert in 1698, they referred explicitly to the person of the bishop. It is also striking that they wished to present their complaint to the secular and ecclesiastical Catholic authorities in Italy, preferably to the pope. This, along with express references to their "friendship" with the other missionaries, contradicts the image of a consistently acute confessional conflict. Practices of "good correspondence" and a shared awareness of brotherhood in Christ persisted alongside the drawing of boundaries under the influence of conflicts, such as that with the Discalced Carmelite Élie de Saint-Albert.

Among the Armenians, contact and discussions with Catholic clerics were initially characterized less by the desire for controversy than by curiosity about each other. Khachatur, bishop of New Julfa from 1623 until his death in 1646, who disputed with the "Frankish" friars in Lviv in the early 1630s, used this experience as an opportunity to improve his own knowledge of theology, philosophy, and languages.[63] Closer contact with Catholic clerics also awakened the Armenian clergy's interest in the printing press. After returning from Lviv, Bishop Khachatur established the first printing shop in New Julfa. The books printed there between 1638 and 1642 were not devoted to controversy with the Roman Church but were works that belonged to the basic library of a priest: an edition of the Psalms of David, a book on the lives of the Church fathers, a missal, and a breviary. The same was true of the books produced by a vardapet from New Julfa whom the bishop sent to Western Europe in 1639 with instructions to learn the art of printing and acquire the necessary equipment to improve the quality of printed works. Under the suspicious eyes of the Curia, the vardapet printed some 1,050 copies of an Armenian-language psalter in Livorno before bringing his printing paraphernalia to Persia in 1646. There he printed a calendar in 1647. He had to abandon plans to print a Bible, perhaps because of hostility from the copyists in the scriptoria, who feared competition from printers.[64] Such initiatives emerged from the context of contacts with Latin clerics but were not yet expressions of sharp confessional disassociation. Apart from the choice of titles printed, this is suggested by the fact that in 1640 the Capuchin Blaise de Nantes recommended to the superiors of his order that they assist the "good bishop" (referring to Khachatur) in overcoming technical problems by speedily dispatching an experienced printer who also knew how to manufacture paper and by sending Armenian type, which would help to make him a "friend."[65]

The Armenian Church historian Vazken S. Ghougassian describes Khachatur's tenure as bishop of New Julfa as the beginning of a golden age in which the monastery of the Holy Savior, the center of the prelate's activities, became a site of higher education, literature, and the production of printed and manuscript books and ecclesiastical art. When he returned from Lviv in 1631, Bishop Khachatur focused his attention on the monastery school. He not only sought to attract as many pupils as possible but also changed the curriculum, perhaps with borrowings from the curricula of the Jesuit colleges. The pupils were instructed in grammar, rhetoric, philosophy, natural sciences, geometry, music, and theology. The pupils and later teachers at the monastery of the Holy Savior included Simeon of Julfa, the author, among other works, of an Armenian grammar used well into the eighteenth century, a treatise on logic, and a commentary on Proclus Diadochus, a fifth-century neo-Platonic author. In the last-mentioned work Simeon addressed not only the writings of Armenian doctors of the Church and ancient philosophers such as Plato and Aristotle but also the works of Roman Catholic doctors like Albertus Magnus and Thomas Aquinas. In the second half of the seventeenth century, the monastery of the Holy Savior maintained a school that prepared merchant sons from New Julfa for careers in trade in addition to a school that trained future clerics. Khachatur's successor, David of Julfa (bishop from 1652 to 1683), continued his work. David had already headed the school since 1647. Ghougassian attributes to him the training of a new generation of monks, who distinguished themselves through their learning and their role in defending the Armenian Church against Islam and Catholicism. Three of his pupils would serve as catholicos of Etchmiadzin.[66]

As long as the Catholic clerics did not intervene directly in its sphere of activity, the Armenian clergy did not draw sharp boundaries. The Armenian clergy claimed responsibility for baptisms, weddings, and funerals, that is, for the rituals that marked the key moments in a Christian life. In situations of "good correspondence" it tolerated contacts between the faithful and missionaries. The latter preached in Armenian, heard confessions, and gave communion in exchange for tolerating the practices of *communicatio in sacris*, as we will see in what follows. A limit was reached especially when the missionaries wanted to settle in New Julfa, which is when the Armenian clergy came to regard them as rivals. In the 1630s and 1640s, the Discalced Carmelites and Capuchins therefore dispensed with settlements in the Armenian quarter. Nevertheless, such plans sometimes met with the approval of Armenian notables. When the Capuchin Gabriel de Chinon, two Discalced Carmelites, and three Jesuits settled in New Julfa in 1652 under the pretext of wanting to learn Armenian, they did so with the support of the *kalāntar*. He even invited the Jesuit Aimé Chézaud to stay at his home in 1653 after the Jesuit received the shah's permission to found a settlement in the Armenian quarter in addition to the mission in Isfahan, already approved in 1647. At the same time, the *kalāntar* protected the two Discalced Carmelites. In light of the Armenian bishop's prohibition on sending children to the friars for instruction, the Discalced Carmelite Balthasar de Santa Maria still had great hopes in 1653 that the wealthy Armenian merchants who did business with Europe would want their sons trained in European languages.[67] Their support was all the more important because the incursion into the Armenian quarter provoked fierce resistance from the clergy. In 1654, the provincial vicar of the Discalced Carmelites, Felice di Sant'Antonio, managed to extract the two missionaries from his order just in the nick of time, while the Jesuits and Capuchins were expelled from New Julfa at the instigation of the Armenian bishop. The transfer of the Jesuit mission from Isfahan to New Julfa in 1661 and the running of a school was more successful—at the price of dispensing with controversial demarcations and "enticements" of the faithful, as will be outlined below.

Élie de Saint-Albert overstepped all of these boundaries. It is therefore hardly surprising that the Armenian clergy had him expelled twice, while at the same time the Jesuits and Dominicans as well as the priests of the *Missions étrangères* were permitted to remain. Moreover, Bishop David of New Julfa and his vicar and successor Stephan (bishop from 1683 to 1696) generally restricted Armenians' contacts with Catholic clerics. In 1679, the year when Élie de Saint-Albert settled in New Julfa, they forbade mixed marriages with Catholics and formally excommunicated those Armenians who attended Catholic churches.[68]

As bishop, in 1686 Stephan reactivated the printing shop that Khachatur had founded in New Julfa in 1636. Unlike in the 1630s and 1640s, its production was now firmly oriented toward the needs of controversies with Catholic clerics. Works directed at the "errors" of the Roman Church were printed in—by local standards—large editions of 500 copies. Some of these were old works by doctors of the Church opposing the reception of the Council of Chalcedon and the teachings of the "duophysites," while others were treatises written in the context of current controversies with Catholic missionaries.[69]

If Armenian clerics increasingly distanced themselves from Catholic missionaries, it was not simply in response to methods like those used by Élie de Saint-Albert. As in the early decades of the seventeenth century, the drawing of boundaries and attempts at rapprochement by Armenian clerics also arose from inner-Armenian conflicts. The conflicts between the bishop of New Julfa and the catholicos of Etchmiadzin continued to play a decisive role. While New Julfa, promoted by the ruling Safavid dynasty, became an economic, religious, and cultural center, Etchmiadzin was on the empire's periphery, far from the court and also from the rich merchants who financed ecclesiastical institutions in New Julfa. The fact that the bishop's opponents also had close biographical ties to the Armenian quarter was typical of the central significance of New Julfa. When Jacob of Julfa was elected catholicos of Etchmiadzin (1655–80), David, the bishop of New Julfa, rebelled. Jacob had lost out to the latter when the episcopal see of New Julfa was filled and had to leave the city in 1650 or 1651. In 1658, Jacob IV traveled to Isfahan to visit the local community as a catholicos and have his election confirmed by ʿAbbās II. In order to weaken his opponent in New Julfa, he created several independent bishoprics in his jurisdiction in 1659, thereby restricting Bishop David's authority to the Armenian quarter. In 1660 he partially revoked these decisions, only to separate a diocese from New Julfa again in 1663. In light of this approach by the catholicos, the community of New Julfa used its connections at court to encourage the shah to forbid such changes.[70]

Catholicos Jacob IV also cultivated relationships in Rome as part of his conflict with his adversaries within the church. In 1662, Paolo Piromalli presented the *Propaganda Fide* with a letter from him in which he professed his devotion to the pope and requested his help in combating the "oppressors of the Armenians." In 1663, a report by François Pallu, bishop of Heliopolis, reached Rome: Jacob IV had revoked the excommunication of Pope Leo I and condemned Dioscorus and now wished to travel to Rome.[71] Jacob IV died in Constantinople in 1680 on his way to Rome. Before his death he made a Catholic confession of faith before the patriarchal vicar, Gaspare Gasparini.

Jacob IV's two successors as catholicos of Etchmiadzin also had conflicts with the bishop of New Julfa. They thus remained an ecclesiastical authority for Armenians from New Julfa who themselves struggled with the local bishop as well as a focal point of Roman hopes of union. Catholicos Nahapet (1691–1705) received Catholic clerics in a manner recalling the practices that had encouraged hopes of union in the early days of the Persian missions. In 1692, Jacques Villotte and a fellow Jesuit used a sojourn in Yerevan to pay the catholicos a visit and attend the consecration of a vardapet in nearby Etchmiadzin. Out of respect for the Jesuits, the catholicos is said to have dispensed with the otherwise usual renewal of the excommunication of Pope Leo, the Council of Chalcedon, and the "duophysites." At the same time, he brought in the Catholic Armenian bishop of Erzurum, Aaron, who had been expelled from his diocese, as one of the four co-celebrant bishops. Villotte commented that such gestures indicated that God had "imperceptibly guided the Catholicos to complete union with the Roman Church."[72] Even with regard to sacramental acts such as the mass and the consecration of a cleric, the differences were once again outweighed by the reciprocal awareness of Christian commonalities.

The protracted quarrels between the bishop of New Julfa and the catholicos of Etchmiadzin came to an end under Alexander I of New Julfa (1705–14). As catholicos, he enabled the bishop of New Julfa to consolidate his jurisdiction and extend it to the Armenian communities in India and Southeast Asia. The new peaceful relationship between the bishop and the catholicos was accompanied by a clear disassociation from the Catholic missionaries. Thanks to the consolidation of ecclesiastical jurisdiction, the bans on visiting their churches and sending children to their schools could be implemented more effectively. Catholicos Alexander I then received decrees from the shah and the local Muslim authorities drawing sharper lines between the Armenians and the "Franks."[73]

At the time of Alexander I, the image of the Armenian clergy in missionary reports gained a new coherence and was now dominated by an impression of harsh hostility. On the Armenian side, Catholicos Alexander I promoted a similar break with the practice of ambiguous affiliations as the *Propaganda Fide* and the Holy Office had long been demanding on the Catholic side. The catholicos used the institutions of his church and his influence at court and with subordinate Muslim officeholders to implement such rules. Complaints initially came mainly from the Capuchins in Tabriz. A segment of the Armenian community there backed a vardapet who supported union with Rome and had asked the pope to grant him episcopal competences. The catholicos therefore threatened the Armenians who attended the Capuchin church and who sent their sons to the order's school with excommunication.[74]

The continued existence of the missionary churches henceforth became more dependent on the protection that the representatives of Catholic courts, above all the king of France, asserted at the Safavid court. In 1708, the Capuchins in Tabriz benefited from the intervention of the French envoy Pierre-Victor Michel. While his chief task was to negotiate a trade treaty with Shah Sulṭān Ḥusain, this treaty, analogous to the capitulations of the Sublime Porte, also contained protective stipulations in favor of all Catholic Christians, regardless of origin. This did not mean that the conflict was ultimately decided in the missionaries' favor, however. In 1711, the bishop of Babylon reported that Alexander I had succeeded in getting the edicts of 1708 revoked in favor of the Capuchins of Tabriz and having other edicts with the opposite effect enacted.[75] In the name of His Most Christian Majesty, in 1712 Gratien de Galisson, for his part, attained the revocation of the decrees against the missionaries and the confirmation of the promises made to Pierre-Victor Michel in 1708.[76]

The rapid succession of contradictory and only partially enforced decrees was also a sign of the progressive disintegration of monarchical authority. Barnaba Fedeli di Milano, bishop of Isfahan, summarized the impression of extreme uncertainty in a letter to the prefect of the *Propaganda Fide* in February 1722, shortly before Isfahan was captured by Afghan troops. On the one hand, he reported that all matters affecting the missions had been satisfactorily regulated by the decrees that the shah issued after being presented with letters from the pope, the emperor of the Holy Roman Empire, and the king of France. On the other, the bishop doubted the efficacy of these decrees. God alone knew whether they would ever be enforced, since nothing lasts and the law follows money. The picture of the decay of the legal order drawn by Bishop Fedeli was no stereotype but reflected conditions in the late Safavid Empire.[77]

The Afghan invasion of 1722 and the fall of the Safavids did nothing to alter the confrontation between the missionaries and the Armenian clergy. While the upheaval seriously disrupted business for the merchants of New Julfa, the Armenians enjoyed privileged treatment from the new rulers in comparison to their other non-Afghan subjects. In this context, the Armenian clergy obtained a judicial decision in 1727 that prohibited all Armenians from visiting the missionary churches. The Catholic clerics were forbidden to teach and preach to Armenians. The Scerimans managed to obtain a judicial declaration that the ban was limited to those who had converted after the Afghan invasion. This nevertheless narrowed the field of missionary activities once again. The immediate occasion for the Armenians going before the Muslim judges was the ordination of an Armenian priest by the Latin bishop Fedeli, which the "schismatic" Armenians labeled a usurpation of their bishop's jurisdiction. In fact, this ordination signaled a significant legal and symbolic step toward the formation of an Armenian Catholic parallel church. Bishop Fedeli undertook it because of a lack of Armenian Catholic priests who could run the Sceriman church.[78]

The despotic rule of Nādir Šāh (1736–47), whose main victims included the wealthy merchants of New Julfa, represented a watershed moment. The ruler became an arbitrator who determined the opportunities for one side or the other to develop. In 1740, Filippo Maria di Sant'Agostino, bishop of Isfahan, sent the *Propaganda Fide* a detailed account of the difficult position of the missions as a consequence of the hostility of the catholicos. On Maundy Thursday, the bishop and the superior of the Jesuit mission had been compelled to make the long journey to the court in Teheran. There, they had to engage in a disputation with three vardapets about the primacy of St. Peter and the authority of the pope before Nādir Šāh's son.[79] There was no longer any question of "good correspondence"; in the disputation with "heretics" (rather than "schismatics"), the competing truth claims clashed starkly. Gone was the missionaries' empathy for the adversity that their confessional foe had suffered at the hands of the Muslim authorities. For example, in 1745 the Discalced Carmelite Sebastiano di Santa Margherita reported on the following "advantageous events": Nādir Šāh had received the "heretical Armenian patriarch, the oppressor of Catholics," with insulting words, unseated him, had his beard and ears cut off, and sentenced him to prison, flogging, and a high monetary fine.[80]

There is much indication that the contacts between the Armenians and the Latin clergy, which had become closer with the dispatch of missionaries starting in the early seventeenth century, produced tendencies toward stronger confessional disambiguation within both camps at this later stage. This was nothing fundamentally new: early efforts at union had already led to more precise definitions of the differing positions. Since the sixteenth century, however, the Catholic Church had taken on a new, confessional quality in its confrontations with the churches that emerged from the Protestant Reformation and had drawn narrower boundaries around what it considered orthodox. The European powers, on the one hand, increased the scope of missionary efforts in new geographical spaces and intensified them to a previously unprecedented extent. On the other, they provided the missionaries with ideal images of confessional orthodoxy, which coexisted on the ground with the practices of "good correspondence" in secular and spiritual matters.

The setting of boundaries remained unmistakably tied to certain persons and contexts and by no means consistently affected relationships between missionaries and locals. On the Catholic side, a few firebrands were especially prominent, but they could reckon with the favor of the Roman Curia in the form of appointments to comparatively high office. On the Armenian side, conflicts within the church— particularly between the catholicos and the bishop of New Julfa—opened up room for the cultivation of contacts with the missionaries and the Roman Curia. At the same time, there was a danger of missionaries' being drawn into conflicts that were initially more jurisdictional than confessional in nature.

As in their relations with Persian Muslims, the missionaries found themselves confronted in their relations with the Armenian laity and clergy with a religious culture that associated the godliness of a life less with a specific confession than the European churches of the confessional age preferred. To be sure, among Armenians, as well, reciprocal excommunication and condemnation as "heretics" were rooted in the Christological disputes of late antiquity. It is striking nonetheless that the shared quality of being Christians shaped interactions in the Persian missions well beyond the first contacts in the early seventeenth century. This is evident even in sources from the late period of these missions. Once again, the writings of the last Latin bishop of Isfahan, the Discalced Carmelite Cornelio di San Giuseppe, prove especially illuminating. The bishop thus writes in his *Memorie cronologiche* of the "political friendship" he cultivated with the "schismatic archbishop" of New Julfa, whom he had already met as a simple priest. When he sent a former pupil of the *Collegio urbano* to serve as parish priest of the Sceriman's Catholic church in New Julfa in 1769, his recommendation had the desired effect on the prelate, since he demonstrated his good will on every occasion.[81]

Meanwhile, even at the time of Cornelio di San Giuseppe, relations with the Armenian clergy were not limited to a "political" friendship, that is, one demanded by opportunistic considerations. A memorandum he prepared for the *Propaganda Fide* shows that the "friendship" also extended to the administration of the sacraments. The author wished to know whether it was permissible for the promotion of "peace" and "friendship" for the missionaries to supply the "schismatic" Armenian priests with communion wine, candles, and liturgical objects. Were they allowed to lend an Armenian priest their chalice or provide him with communion wafers? Cornelio di San Giuseppe then asked about the validity and permissibility of the ordination of a

Catholic priest by the Armenian bishop. Since New Julfa was without a Catholic bishop for a time after the death of Filippo Maria di Sant'Agostino in 1749, the "schismatic" bishop of New Julfa had ordained an Armenian Catholic priest. The prelate allowed the Catholic priest to pour water into the chalice and to render obedience to the pope instead of the catholicos. While the ordaining bishop spoke the names of the "heretics," the man being ordained spoke the pope's name in their place.[82]

Cornelio di San Giuseppe sought to learn from the *Propaganda Fide* how these and other practices involving *communicatio in sacris* should be regarded. Tellingly—doubtless in the knowledge of the questions he could expect regarding the orthodoxy of his own conduct—he dispensed with submitting his memorandum to the Congregation and instead filed it among his personal papers. The *dubia* of Cornelio di San Giuseppe, like his *Memorie cronologiche*, show that under certain circumstances, both sides were still inclined toward a shared "good correspondence" among Christians. To the dismay of the curial congregations, practices of *communicatio in sacris* that ran counter to confessional clarity remained a fixed component of this "good correspondence." The bishop thus used a different language toward the *Propaganda Fide* than he did in his unpublished manuscripts. In a report on conditions in Persia and the missions there that he presented to the Congregation at the end of 1772, the non-Uniate Armenians became "our enemies, the Armenian heretics," who often conspired against the missionaries.[83] In this account, danger to the continued existence of the mission in New Julfa also came from the Armenian bishop, even though the Discalced Carmelite described that selfsame person in his *Memorie cronologiche* as "well-disposed in every instance" toward the priest of the Sceriman family's Catholic church. The conventions of speech in contact with the Roman Curia that become tangible in such contradictions determined the ways in which missionaries described their relations with the Armenian laity and clergy. Their reports to the Curia nevertheless reveal a practice that was defined far less by confessional disambiguation than the curial congregations and individual agitators on the ground might have wished.

Accommodation and Dissimulation

Although Élie de Saint-Albert was loath to admit it, his confessionally divisive methods were controversial even among the other members of his order in Isfahan. As we have seen, in 1694 none of the Jesuits, Capuchins, or Dominicans in Isfahan and New Julfa signed his account of the expulsion from New Julfa. Nor did Louis-Marie Pidou de Saint-Olon, bishop of Babylon, or François Sanson, priest of the *Missions étrangères*. Interestingly, neither the Jesuits, Dominicans, Pidou de Saint-Olon, nor any priest of the *Missions étrangères* were faced with expulsion. While Élie de Saint-Albert portrayed himself as an unswerving proponent of confessional orthodoxy and was therefore viewed in Rome as a suitable candidate for the episcopate, most of the other missionaries adhered to practices that facilitated "good correspondence" with the Armenian clergy and afforded them access to the leading Armenian merchant families. As highly mobile actors, these families were interested in increasing their relationship capital and thus also their social capital in terms of contacts with missionaries from

Western Europe, while remaining at the same time disinclined to commit themselves to an extent that would have implied a break with their own clergy.

This is where the observations that follow begin. They take us from the connections between the cultivation of relationships, mobility, and confessional affiliation, which I will address using the example of the leading Armenian Catholic family of New Julfa, to the justification of practices of *communicatio in sacris* by the missionaries. I will also pursue the question of the extent to which the friars' practices exhibited differences specific to their orders. In the history of mission, accommodation is associated with the Society of Jesus. To what extent does this finding, which emerged from studies in other Asian contexts, especially China and South India, apply to Persia? Or in other words, were the cases of Paolo Piromalli and Élie de Saint-Albert typical for the Dominican and Discalced Carmelite orders, respectively?

Trade Networks, Mobility, and Confessional Affiliation: The Sceriman Family

Since the early days of the Persian mission, there had been calls to offer trade advantages to those willing to enter into a union with Rome. In 1630, the *Propaganda Fide* promised Armenian Catholic merchants from New Julfa trade privileges in the Papal States and corresponding intercession with the Catholic princes. In 1653, when two Discalced Carmelites faced opposition to their settlement from the Armenian clergy, they placed their hopes in the *kalāntar* and the merchants. The merchants, a letter noted, had understood the advantages to be gained from "good correspondence" with the European clerics: the mediation of missionaries had helped many traders to recover goods believed lost owing to the misconduct of their agents.[84] In 1700 Pietro Paolo di San Francesco, bishop of Ancyra, who had traveled to the Safavid court as a papal envoy, suggested that only those Armenians who had made a profession of Catholic faith be allowed to enter the Papal States. The Curia should recommend that Venice, the grand duke of Tuscany, and the Holy Roman Emperor confiscate all goods belonging to Armenians if they did not accept union within a specific period of time, for only self-interest would lead them to what religion and the soul never could.[85] In 1712, a French Discalced Carmelite proposed to the prefect of the *Propaganda Fide* that he encourage the king of France to offer a free trade privilege to those Armenians whose status as Catholics was confirmed by the missionaries.[86]

In this case, the main aim was to gain advantages for the Sceriman family, because it was the most important pillar of the small Armenian Catholic church in New Julfa. The family controlled a powerful trade network extending from Western Europe across the Mediterranean region to Russia, Persia, and East Asia. Its history takes us from the strategies of globally diversifying its networks (which *also* implied a social proximity to the Catholic missionaries) to efforts at recognition as part of a Catholic elite in a new location in Italy. Using the history of this family as an example, in what follows I will illuminate the links between mobility in trade networks and confessional orientation and also show the potentially negative consequences of a turn to Rome that was perceived as conversion.

In the second half of the seventeenth and the early eighteenth century, the Sceriman family was one of the driving forces in opening up Russian markets and

Russian transit routes to the Baltic and North Sea region. At the same time, the Scerimans cultivated ties to the English East India Company. Yet it was the trade relations with Italian cities, notably Venice and Livorno, that the Sceriman family established over the course of the seventeenth century that proved decisive for their relationships with the missionaries in Isfahan and New Julfa and support for union with Rome.[87] Armenian merchants from Julfa on the Arax, who we know had already been active in Venice in the 1570s, helped to turn the city into one of the most important transshipment points for Persian silk. By the 1610s, the Scerimans owned a house in Venice where commercial agents and family members could stay. By the first half of the seventeenth century, the Scerimans had invested substantial sums on the Venetian capital market to diversify their financial risk. Gasparo Sceriman, the fourth son of Sarhat, who had announced his support for union in 1646, spent longer periods in Venice, Livorno, and Rome in the 1650s and 1660s. In 1692, his brother Murat's two sons were living in Livorno and Venice. At that time, Gasparo Sceriman sent Basilio, one of his five sons, to Rome to enter the *Propaganda Fide's Collegio urbano*, thanks to letters of recommendation from the superiors of the Jesuits and the Discalced Carmelites and the bishop of Babylon, Louis-Marie Pidou de Saint-Olon. The family had just revealed their favor toward the Jesuits by financing their new church; the Discalced Carmelites owed them a house in New Julfa and the funds to support two or three missionaries. As Bernard Heyberger has shown, the entry of a son into the *Collegio urbano* was among the strategies that Eastern Christian merchant families used to strengthen their networks in Italy.[88] In fact, Basilio Sceriman had a brilliant career there. He was ordained as a priest in 1707. In 1714 the senate of the Venetian Republic included him among their four recommendations to the pope for the appointment of an auditor in the Roman *Rota*, an honor for the Sceriman family even though Clement XI ultimately chose not Basilio but a scion of the patrician family Foscari. Thanks to the efforts of his protectors in Rome, Monsignor Basilio did at least acquire the title of *protonotario apostolico*, and he was governor of various cities in the Papal States starting in 1718. In 1751 he became *chierico di Camera*, a member of the *Camera Apostolica*, i.e., the most important administrative body in the Papal States, which was responsible among other things for finances. In 1766 he was promoted to dean.

His studies in Rome and the subsequent *cursus honorum* took place in the context of the family's reorientation toward Italy. In 1692, along with young Basilio, the Scerimans transferred 200,000 Venetian ducats to Italy, where the *Propaganda Fide* was supposed to ensure a safe and profitable investment. The family spoke of settling in Italy with their business for the long term. Through the mediation of the *Propaganda Fide*, 100,000 ducats were invested in Rome with the *Congregazione lateranense*. The Scerimans invested a further 100,000 ducats in Venetian annuities, to which end they asked the *Propaganda Fide* for a letter of recommendation to the nuncio in Venice so that he would intervene to secure them a preferential interest rate of 5 percent in wartime or 4 percent in peacetime.[89] This was only part of the at least 890,000 ducats in all that the Scerimans invested in Venetian annuities in the 1690s. The utility of these investments lay, on the one hand, in their comparative security at a time when the family's assets and social position in Persia were endangered, and on the other in a surplus of symbolic capital that was associated with the privileges that the Venetian senate granted the Scerimans in exchange.

In 1698, Gasparo Sceriman left New Julfa to settle in Venice permanently with his son Stefano. More members of the family followed. Venice became the new center of the Scerimans' far-flung networks, while the family members who stayed in New Julfa continued to cultivate this hub of Armenian trade networks and played an important role in coordinating the activities of the *commenda* agents in Asia into the 1740s.[90] In the first decades of the eighteenth century, the Sceriman brothers in Venice mainly traded in gemstones but also in silk and woolen cloth. At the beginning of the century, three of Gasparo's nephews settled in Livorno with the support of their fathers, Murat and Michele. There they dedicated themselves to the trade in raw silk from Persia, luxury textiles from Tuscany, coral, and precious stones. They also engaged in lucrative financial business in Venice and Livorno. The family maintained additional branches in Rome, France, the Netherlands, Moscow, Constantinople, India, and the Philippines. Moving to Italy had the advantage of protecting the family fortune from being inherited by a relative in New Julfa who had converted to Islam, as well as from the chaos that followed the Afghan invasion of 1722. Those members of the family who remained in New Julfa suffered greatly from Nādir Šāh's demands for contributions in the years 1745 to 1747. After their failed flight to Basra, the family heads, Pietro and Leone, were forced by imprisonment and maltreatment to request money from their agent there to pay the tribute imposed upon them. Nādir Šāh's attacks and the anarchic conditions following his murder in 1747 not only led to the departure from New Julfa of all remaining members of the Sceriman family but also sealed the ultimate downfall of the Christian suburb as a hub for the Armenian trade networks.[91]

Starting in the late seventeenth century, the Scerimans used the union with Rome to increase their privileges and prestige. In 1696, Innocent XII bestowed Roman citizenship upon them in recognition of the usefulness of their commercial activities and their zeal "for religion and the Catholic faith." At the same time, he exempted them from import fees and gave them free housing in the lazarettos in the Papal States' two most important ports, Ancona and Civitavecchia. The pope commended the family, their servants, and their goods to all the Catholic princes; the ecclesiastical dignitaries were to provide them with "every assistance and favor."[92] In 1699, the family received the title of counts in the Kingdom of Hungary from Emperor Leopold I (r. 1658–1705). When they settled in Venice, the Scerimans cited both the honorific titles they enjoyed in Persia and their recognition by the emperor and the pope.

The files of the *Propaganda Fide* show how a globally active Armenian merchant family relied on its relationship with the Curia to gain advantages from the Catholic powers for its business in South and East Asia. Thus, around 1670, Gasparo Sceriman sought the permission of Louis XIV of France to travel at his own expense on ships belonging to the *Compagnie des Indes orientales*. According to a resolution by the *Propaganda Fide*, the nuncio was to seek an audience with Jean-Baptiste Colbert in Paris to this end.[93]

Part of the *Propaganda Fide*'s intercessions on behalf of the Scerimans were directly linked to the family's services to the missions, such as the transfer of subsidies for the missionaries, the provision of loans, or the forgiveness of their repayment. When

Pietro Sceriman declared himself willing to ensure the transfer of the annual financial allocations for the missionaries from Venice to Persia in 1717, the *Propaganda Fide* agreed in exchange, as requested, to commend the following matter to the king of Portugal: the monarch was asked to instruct his viceroy in Goa to reimburse the Scerimans for customs duties levied against some of their own delivered goods and in the future to no longer impose upon them anything "beyond what is customary and fair."[94] In this case, we can trace the path of the recommendation from Rome to Goa. Based on the request conveyed on the pope's behalf by the nuncio in Lisbon, John V (r. 1706–50) instructed his viceroy in Goa to reimburse the Sceriman's agent for the excess fees imposed upon them. If the Scerimans brought a complaint, the viceroy was to see that they quickly received justice.[95]

The viceroy's terse answer made clear the disdain for the Armenian merchants that had probably also constituted the background to Pietro Sceriman's complaint: If his agent made an application to him, he would show him "all possible favor." However, he knew a few Armenians in Goa who deserved the recommendations of His Holiness in neither religious nor mercantile matters.[96] When the Scerimans offered to the *Propaganda Fide* to forgive a debt of 8,283 *scudi* to benefit the missionaries in Isfahan and New Julfa in 1743, they had in mind better conditions for their trade in East Asia. In exchange, they expected the Roman Congregation to use its contacts at the court in Madrid to secure the right to load 50 *fardi* of goods tariff-free onto Spanish ships sailing from Manila to Acapulco, Mexico. Two of the Scerimans' agents would also be allowed to settle in Acapulco. The cardinals decided to support this request.[97]

The turn to Catholicism made it easier for the Scerimans to settle in the Catholic commercial centers of the Mediterranean region as well as those under Portuguese and Spanish rule in South and East Asia. It did not, however, become the point of departure for a more general union between the Armenian Church and Rome; on the contrary, it deepened the conflicts within the Armenian community. Starting in the 1690s, confessional polarization interfered with the Scerimans' position in New Julfa, which they blamed on Bishop Élie de Saint-Albert, whom they had initially supported. By leaving New Julfa forever in 1698, Gasparo Sceriman and his son Stefano avoided the increasing threats from the family's enemies within the Armenian community, who mobilized the Muslim authorities against them. In 1699, this threat forced Gasparo's brothers, Michele and Marcara, to choose temporary conversion to Islam. Under the pretense of making a pilgrimage to Mecca, Michele and Marcara left Persia shortly after converting but returned to Catholicism upon arriving in Italy.

Since the family dared not reveal the emigration plans of the two "renegades," their "apostasy" damaged its good reputation, especially among the Catholic clergy. Suddenly, doubt was cast on the signs of papal and imperial protection for the family. The friars in Isfahan reportedly made fun of the awarding of an earldom in the Kingdom of Hungary when they brought Sarat (Giacomo) and Lorenzo Sceriman the copy of the imperial patent. At the same time, the family faced urgent requests from the missionaries to honor their promises of funds for their churches despite persecution. When news of Marcara's arrival in Italy finally reached Persia, members of the family complained that their enemies could now do what they wished, and the word of the Scerimans no longer enjoyed "any credence at the courts of the grandees."[98] Family letters from the years 1704–5 give the impression that the family network now served only to get profits and capital safely out of the country. As has been suggested, this was not completely accurate, since members remaining in Persia continued to engage in the extended family's business from New Julfa into the 1740s.

The focal point was now in Venice, however, where the family strove for patrician status. When the Sceriman brothers settled in Venice in the late 1690s, they already had offices there. These did not, however, meet the need for prestige of a rich Venetian merchant family of noble estate. For that reason, Gasparo Sceriman purchased a palace on Campo di Santa Marina, where his family lived together with that of his brother Marcara as a *fraterna*, following Armenian practice. In 1727 Gasparo's son Stefano bought a palace on Rio del Gozzi in Cannaregio (Figure 14). By the end of the seventeenth century, Gasparo Sceriman had acquired a splendidly located country estate on the Riviera del Brenta in Mira, where he commissioned a villa that was completed around 1719. With the purchase of this and other landed estates on the *Terra Ferma*, the Scerimans adopted the noble lifestyle of a successful Venetian merchant family. At the same time, they married into wealthy and respected Venetian families. However, the process, begun in 1779, that would lead to their acceptance into the Venetian patriciate, was not yet complete when French troops occupied the Venetian Republic in 1797.

In Venice the family cultivated an Armenian and increasingly also a Latin confessional identity. Their Armenian identity was closely associated with the Mekhitarist monastery on the island of San Lazzaro degli Armeni, where the congregation of Uniate Armenian monks founded by Mekhitar of Sebaste in Constantinople in 1701, and approved in 1711 by Clement XI, was established in 1717 following the Benedictine Rule. Gasparo and his son Stefano Sceriman each donated an altar, with the stipulation that they would be buried there. Various other members of the family also chose the Mekhitarist church as their final resting place. Two wealthy merchants from the family who died in Bengal in the early 1760s without direct heirs left their fortunes of some half million *scudi* to the San Lazzaro monastery.[99] Other practices link the family with the Latin Church: in 1705, Basilio Sceriman received a papal dispensation allowing him to be ordained as a priest according to the Latin rite. Basilio had justified his request by stating that he was prevented from returning to Persia.[100] In 1713, the *Propaganda Fide* approved the request of a member of the family to observe the fasting periods and feast days according to the Latin calendar.[101] Stefano Sceriman, who was ultimately interred at the Mekhitarist monastery on San Lazzaro, had previously purchased a family tomb in the church of Santa Maria della Consolazione, a Latin parish church directly adjacent to the palace on Campo di Santa Marina.

The history of the Sceriman family can be read as one of the successful transfer of social and economic capital from Persia to Italy. At the same time, it illustrates the disadvantages that a merchant family could expect in Persia if their relations with the missionaries were perceived as conversion to Catholicism. These consequences arose from the fact that in both Persia and the Ottoman Empire, church communities were also the space in which Christians formed their relationships with the Muslim authorities. In particular, the churches were the framework in which they paid the taxes they owed as *ḏimmī*. If Uniate Eastern Christians left their church of origin,

Figure 14 Palazzo Sceriman on Rio del Gozzi in Cannareggio, Venice

they could accordingly be accused of wishing to avoid these obligations as "Franks," leading to more or less drastic reprisals by the Muslim authorities. Those whom the missionaries regarded as Catholics thus also generally remained connected to their churches of origin. There they participated in the rituals that mark the key moments of social existence—baptism, marriage, and burial.

Ecclesiastical authority also intervened in business dealings. Based on the previously little-studied holdings in the archives of the Holy Savior Cathedral in New Julfa, Sebouh Aslanian has explored how the Julfa Armenians secured trust and credit in their trade networks over long distances. His analysis of the merchants' correspondence shows the great extent to which commercial success depended on their reputations as honorable men. This reputation rested on respect for shared norms, as evidenced not just by business correspondence but also by letters between the episcopal see in New Julfa and the churches dependent upon it. The nonobservance of norms—in particular those underlying the *commenda* contracts—was sanctioned by informal ostracism, judgments by the merchants present on the ground, and finally by the verdicts of the *kalāntar* and the assembly of the heads of New Julfa's twenty districts, all of them representatives of the leading merchant families, plus the bishop of New Julfa. The bishop's word thus always held weight in decisions about the validity of powers of attorney, instructions in wills, or titles of ownership.[102]

For that reason, a conversion, which was experienced as a break with one's church of origin, had consequences for the entire existence of a family that extended well beyond the arena of religion. As long as both the Catholic missionaries and the Armenian ecclesiastical authorities did not draw clear confessional boundaries, the former may have discovered many potential "Catholics" among the laity, who, beyond "good correspondence" in everyday life, repeatedly turned to Catholic clerics in religious matters, making their confessions to them and receiving communion. When Catholic and Armenian clerics appeared as representatives of antagonistic confessional churches, however, families whose networks extended beyond confessional boundaries were forced to take a position. Gestures marking a preference for one church or the other acquired greater social relevance. The history of the Sceriman family shows how, under such circumstances, the diversification of social networks through the cultivation of relationships with missionaries could provoke decisions of affiliation, in both the geographical and metaphorical sense, which led to profound ruptures. Most families preferred to avoid being pushed into such a situation. This is the backdrop against which we need to understand the widespread practices of *communicatio in sacris*.

Leaving the Armenian Church "in Its Heresies"

In a 1721 letter to the *Propaganda Fide* in Rome, the Latin bishop of Isfahan, the Dominican Barnaba Fedeli di Milano, declared that the Catholic Armenians in Persia had to go to the churches of the "schismatics" if they wished to be baptized, married, or buried. If they did not do this, they faced persecutions at the hands of their priests, who wished to perform these rituals because of the stipends they earned from these services. Fedeli considered this sacramental practice to be permissible because it involved no acts with which the faithful professed allegiance to a "false sect," it resulted in no serious scandal and disruption, and no danger existed of affirming the "schismatics" in their errors. The same applied to the mere presence of Catholic Armenians at the "schismatic" mass, provided the Catholics were well informed about the errors that it contained. It was not permissible, in contrast, for Catholics to make their confession to a "schismatic" priest or to receive communion from him. In this case, there was a danger of serious scandal and disruption.[103]

In his remarks, Bishop Fedeli was responding to the questions that the *Propaganda Fide* had presented on behalf of the Holy Office to both the missionaries in the Ottoman Empire and Persia, and to those with relevant experience in these areas who were staying in Rome at the time. In the context of consultations on three *dubia* from the abbot of the Armenian monastery on San Lazzaro in Venice, the Holy Office had asked whether Catholic Armenians united with Rome were actually forced, as Abbot Mekhitar had stated, to turn to "schismatic" priests for baptism, burial, and marriage, "whether the reception of the sacraments in Catholic churches entailed grave dangers for them, whether sacramental community was necessarily confirmation of a false sect, and finally, whether it definitely caused a scandal (*scandalum*)."[104]

The findings of the unusually broad survey were intended to create the foundation for a decision by the Holy Office on how to deal with sacramental practices that implied *communicatio in sacris*. The practices of sacramental community with non-Catholics contrasted sharply with the clarity of affiliation that the early modern European confessional churches demanded of the faithful. It is thus hardly surprising that the Holy Office and the *Propaganda Fide* had disapproved of *communicatio in sacris* in a series of decisions on individual cases since the seventeenth century, although they did not issue a universal prohibition until 1729, as I show in more detail in Chapter 7. Those like Bishop Fedeli in Isfahan who justified *communicatio in sacris* referred to the bull *Ad vitanda scandala* that Martin V (Oddone Colonna, r. 1417–31) had issued in 1418. The bull limited the effects of general excommunications by stipulating that the commandment to avoid the censured persons depended upon the publication of a "special sentence explicitly mentioning them by name."[105] In the seventeenth and eighteenth centuries, this was interpreted to mean that *communicatio in sacris* with non-Uniate Eastern Christians was allowed under certain conditions, namely, when the celebrants themselves had not been condemned as "schismatics" or "heretics" by name and expressly, when no explicit profession of "schism" or "heresy" was associated with the practice, and when there was no danger of "disruption" and "scandal."[106]

The practice of *communicatio in sacris* corresponded to a religious culture that was less confessionally fixed than the Western European churches required in the wake of the Reformation. The Sceriman family also participated in such a culture, and did so even at the time around 1700, when they had shifted the focus of their commercial activities from New Julfa to Italy, where they integrated into a Catholic context. While the correspondence between two family members who had stayed in New Julfa and Gasparo Sceriman and his sons, Stefano and Basilio, in Venice expressly located the difficulties experienced by the extended family in Persia within the context of a Christian expectation of salvation, it did so without stipulating any confessional framework. As for the daughters, one of whom had just moved to her husband's home, they were expected to live "as good Christian women according to the Christian rite."[107]

Although by moving to Venice the Sceriman family had made a decision in confessional terms as well, the practice in the church its members had founded and funded in New Julfa corresponded only partially to the expectations of the aforementioned apostolic vicar and later bishop of Isfahan, Barnaba Fedeli di Milano. In 1714, based on a report by the Dominican, the *Propaganda Fide* noted that the Armenian Catholics were divided over the elimination of "abuses and errors." The Scerimans themselves, who according to Fedeli were actually "good Catholics," wanted to receive communion in part according to the rules of the Roman Church under one kind, and in part according to the old custom under both kinds.[108]

Fedeli described as "scandalous" a ceremony that was held on Maundy Thursday following the worship service in the Sceriman church, as in all Armenian churches: to honor the priesthood, the priest was carried through the church on a chair. In Poland this ceremony had been abolished when the Armenians united with Rome, and Fedeli had forbidden it in New Julfa in 1713, against the wishes of some members of the Sceriman family. If the *Propaganda Fide* prohibited it, he believed that it might be possible to abolish it altogether. The Dominican found it unseemly that the Armenian priest, after washing the feet of the people on Maundy Thursday, anointed the feet of the men and the hands of the women. He went on to object to the Armenians' eating eggs and butter on Easter Saturday, which they justified by a privilege that could not be located and whose origins were unknown.[109]

Even thornier problems arose when it came to dealing with the canon law provisions affecting marriage. It was common among Armenians in Persia to arrange marriages in early childhood. They were then performed as soon as the partners had reached a marriageable age. In contrast to other actors, Fedeli did not question the quality of these relationships as marriage before the Roman Curia. He did, however, complain that Armenian Catholics continued to insist on marrying their daughters off at a tender age, even to "schismatics." They refused to abandon this custom out of pure self-interest, despite having been granted dispensations that permitted them to ignore the canon law degrees of kinship, thus allowing for marriages among Catholic family members.[110]

As apostolic vicar and later bishop, Fedeli faced a small community of Uniate Armenians for whom sacramental community remained acceptable. Thus, the Armenians had informed Fedeli that if he abolished the anointing of women's hands on Maundy Thursday, they would simply attend the "schismatic" church instead. Under the circumstances, Fedeli was willing to compromise not only in the matter of *communicatio in sacris* but also in that of mixed marriages. He left open the possibility that such marriages be contracted, once certain preconditions were fulfilled. These included the raising of any children resulting from the union as Catholics and the delaying of betrothals until the girls had reached the age of twelve to fourteen and were already well instructed in the Catholic faith under the influence of one of the missionaries, perhaps a member of the Society of Jesus. The Armenians did not, however, accept this proposal.[111]

For the priests of the "Sceriman church" too, confessional boundaries remained strikingly permeable, and the missionaries scarcely dared to resist. Thus in 1731 the Discalced Carmelite Filippo Maria di Sant'Agostino, as episcopal vicar, told of a priest named Adeodato who had served first in the "Sceriman church" and then in a "schismatic" church but had nevertheless been allowed to return to the "Sceriman church." When his first wife died, he again turned his back on the Roman Church to enter a second marriage with the consent of the "schismatic" bishop. Bishop Fedeli nevertheless admitted him to the sacraments a third time. Thereafter Adeodato wanted to travel to Rome to receive absolution and serve as a Catholic priest again.[112]

However ambiguous such practices were, the "Sceriman church," which was founded in the 1680s during the sojourn of Élie de Saint-Albert in New Julfa, was already the result of a process of confessional disambiguation. Its character as a Catholic church was taken as a given by both the founding family and the missionaries. In the early days of the Persian missions, Armenian Christians expressed their orientation toward Catholicism only by confessing to and receiving absolution from Catholic clerics, while otherwise remaining connected with their churches of origin.

Against the background of his experiences in the 1640s and 1650s, especially his stay in New Julfa from 1652 to 1654, the Capuchin Gabriel de Chinon reflected in a report probably written around 1656 on various missionary strategies, and in the process rejected disputations with Armenian clerics because they merely engendered animosity and division. If the time was not right or people were not sufficiently capable of understanding, one sometimes had to hide the truth. Gabriel de Chinon criticized (without mentioning him by name) the Dominican Paolo Piromalli as an uncompromising and therefore failed proponent of confessional norms. In his zeal, the Dominican had announced that the vardapets of New Julfa were anathema, even in the public squares and on market days, which is why he was forced to leave the suburb in 1647. In contrast, Friar Gabriel lauded the example of another unnamed Capuchin, who learned a lesson from the Dominican's fate. (The man in question was the author himself, who was active in New Julfa from 1652 to 1654 but does not mention this in his published account.) The friar had gone to New Julfa to learn Armenian, and there he had gained the support of especially respected Armenians by engaging in harmless conversations. He had treated the Armenians not as "enemies" but as friends and servants of the faith. He had first explained to them the rejection of Nestorian Christology that Catholics and Armenians shared and had spoken as little as possible of the controversial points that, in any case, even Armenian priests did not understand properly. The Capuchin wished the Armenians to view union with Rome as a return to the practice of their forefathers rather than as conversion. Finally, he was able to open a school at the request of the wealthiest merchants. The respect he acquired as a result, among both rich and poor in New Julfa, and his avoidance of religious disputes had even won him the affection of the Armenian bishop. According to Gabriel de Chinon, these promising beginnings were disrupted because, in light of the initial successes, the Discalced Carmelites settled in New Julfa in 1652 followed by the Jesuits the next year, making the Armenian clergy feel that they were being besieged from all sides. For that reason, Gabriel de Chinon was forced to leave New Julfa after some three years of activity, along with the Jesuits and the Discalced Carmelites who were also forced to leave at that time.[113]

In 1661 when the Jesuit Aimé Chézaud, disappointed by the lack of successful conversions in Isfahan, acquired property in New Julfa instead, he proceeded in a similar manner to that chosen by Gabriel de Chinon. Chézaud brought with him the language skills needed to work among the Armenians from an earlier stay in Aleppo, where he had befriended Armenian merchants in the 1640s. In Persia he also sought the trust of influential Armenians by avoiding confessional controversies and running a school offering education that met the needs of geographically mobile and widely connected merchant families and the European diaspora. On Easter 1663, the Jesuit told his order's *assistant de France* in Rome that he was satisfied with Armenian attendance at mass. Many of them had made their confessions and taken communion. Chézaud set the bar very low for the Armenian laity to take communion: Armenians could participate in the Eucharist if they had been absolved of their sins beforehand by a Catholic priest.[114] Those who had received absolution remained connected with their original church at the same time. The implications of such a practice are made particularly clear by an episode that the Jesuit Claude-Ignace Mercier described to the *assistant de France* of his order in Rome in 1669. He described in detail how he proceeded in the case of an Armenian notable who had abandoned "heresy" after corresponding instruction. When his wife, "whom he had also made Catholic," died, he wanted Father Mercier to bury her. To avoid offending the Armenian priests, the Jesuit tried to talk the widower out of this. According to Mercier, though several Armenians were to be considered Catholics, they had left neither the Armenian priests nor their churches "except in their heresies." Since the Armenian was not convinced by his arguments, Mercier sought the Armenian bishop's consent for the burial. Because the bishop withheld his permission, the Jesuit refused the woman a Catholic funeral.[115] When the Jesuit Mercier suggested that the Armenian should not leave his priest and his church "except in their heresies," he took up the individualization of pastoral care that was associated with the Jesuits in Europe. By explicitly accepting *communicatio in sacris*, however, he also called into question the Roman Catholic Church's exclusive claim to the mediation of salvation.

Thanks to dispensing with controversial boundaries, the Jesuits managed to establish themselves long term in New Julfa. When the Venetian Ambrogio Bembo visited Isfahan in 1674, the few Armenians considered Catholic in those days preferred to attend masses said by the Jesuits in New Julfa rather than the other orders, who lived in Isfahan. In the 1680s, the Scerimans persuaded Father Jacques Villotte to reopen the school for their children and those of other respected families, which had been closed for some time. The rejection of theological controversies became the foundation for the success of this school, which was open to the sons of all those who enjoyed close social relations with the Jesuits, even if they were not Catholics. Like the Capuchin Gabriel de Chinon in the years 1652–4, the Jesuits sought to gain the trust of parents and pupils by meeting their need for better education, just as the order did in confessionally mixed communities in Central and Western Europe. Many sons of Europeans and Armenians attended the school, in which, according to Jacques Villotte, the spirit of the Society of Jesus was paramount. Apart from prayers and the fundaments of religion, pupils learned to read and write in Armenian and "Frankish" languages. Villotte instructed the older pupils in geography and the use of maps. These subjects, along with instruction in arithmetic and foreign languages, prepared the boys for their later commercial activities. Villotte taught those destined by their parents for the Indian trade Portuguese, while others learned Italian in preparation for their future duties. The games the boys played during their breaks, which allowed them to apply their knowledge of geography and Christian doctrine, may be understood as a form of Jesuit didactics in a local context, since they included question games involving calculating the local time in Peking, Venice, and Paris.[116]

The Jesuits also sought common ground with the Armenians in matters of the church calendar and the liturgy. For their church, which was newly constructed in the 1690s at the expense of the Sceriman family, they requested the pope's plenary indulgence for all those who made confession and took communion on the patron saint's name day or the following Sunday. Since the Armenians celebrated all of their holidays on Sundays, the Jesuits asked for permission to celebrate the feast days of St. Ignatius of Loyola and Francis Xavier on the following Sundays as well. Finally, they requested permission to celebrate the feast days of Gregory the Illuminator as well as the other Armenian and Persian saints who were also recognized by the Roman Church (especially the Apostles Judas Thaddeus and Bartholomew) according to both the Latin and Armenian rites.[117]

In 1699 the Jesuits received a relic of Gregory the Illuminator from Naples, which they transferred in a public procession to the church in New Julfa.

The Jesuits went farther than the other orders in asking permission to say mass not just in Armenian translation, but according to the Armenian rite. To be sure, the desire to celebrate the mass in Armenian was an old issue, which the Discalced Carmelites had already proposed to the Roman authorities unsuccessfully in 1618. In the late seventeenth and early eighteenth centuries, the Dominicans of the Congregation of Santa Sabina in Isfahan and the Discalced Carmelites took the matter up again. What they meant, however, was always a celebration of the mass according to the Latin rite translated into Armenian, such as the Dominicans practiced in Nakhchivan. In 1710–11, the *Propaganda Fide*, referring to the resolution of 1627, once again decided to reject the request, brought forward at that time by the provincial vicar of the Discalced Carmelites, for permission to celebrate parts of the mass in Armenian.[118]

The negative decisions by the *Propaganda Fide* were not directed against the use of Armenian as the language of an Armenian church united with Rome. What the *Propaganda Fide* opposed was the use of Armenian as the language of a Roman liturgy celebrated by Latin priests. The resolutions against the celebration of the mass in Armenian were part of a decision-making practice that took as a given the permissibility of the various rites but also the boundaries between the Latin and the Uniate churches. If the Jesuits wanted to take the language question a step further than the other orders, it was because since settling in New Julfa they had clearly oriented their activities toward the Armenians and, together with the Dominicans who settled in New Julfa in the 1680s, were the only missionaries to cultivate the study of the Armenian language consistently throughout their time there. The Jesuit Jacques Villotte was the only missionary in Persia to leave behind a larger body of work in Armenian.[119]

The Jesuits shared their abstention from controversies with the Armenian clergy and acceptance of *communicatio in sacris* with most of the missionaries in Isfahan and New Julfa. In Persia, locally specific particularities outweighed order-specific ones. Neither Paolo Piromalli nor Élie de Saint-Albert was representative of the missionary strategies of the Dominicans or the Discalced Carmelites in Persia. The Capuchin Gabriel de Chinon and the Jesuits instead followed an approach first developed by the Discalced Carmelites in Persia in the 1610s. Missionaries divided by membership in different orders arrived at similar approaches. Examples are the Capuchin Gabriel de Chinon and the Jesuit Aimé Chézaud, both of whom sought to gain the confidence of the Armenians. The same is true of François Pallu, bishop of Heliopolis, apostolic vicar passing through en route to East Asia, who was a guest of the Capuchins in Isfahan where he may have been influenced by conversations with Raphaël du Mans and Gabriel de Chinon. In 1662, Pallu recommended avoiding the impression that for Armenians conversion to Catholicism meant a change of religion, because this would harm their position vis-à-vis the Muslims. The converts were not to say that they were taking a new religion, but rather that they had "become better acquainted with the mysteries of the true faith, which the Armenian Church and its Holy Fathers had always believed and which the most learned among them continued to believe deep down." The *Propaganda Fide* passed Pallu's recommendations on to the missionaries, for once supporting those who preferred not to deepen the conflicts with the Armenian clergy through loud controversies.[120]

Almost Orthodox

While it remained the rule in Persia for missionaries, with exceptions like Élie de Saint-Albert, to tolerate *communicatio in sacris*, even in the early eighteenth century, Jesuits not only argued for more sympathy for persecuted Armenian Catholics, as formulated by the Dominican Fedeli and others, but also made statements that explicitly played down the differences between Armenians and the Roman Church.

A memorandum by the Jesuit Jacques Villotte, whom the Sceriman family wished to appoint as priest to their church in New Julfa in 1710 instead of a Discalced Carmelite, is illuminating in this respect. Villotte personally presented this memorandum to Pope Clement XI during an audience in 1712. In it, he poses the question of whether *communicatio in sacris* was permitted, noting that some people were absolutely opposed to it and others partially approved. The preservation or ruin of the Catholic faith and the missions "not only in Armenia but in almost the entire Orient" depended on the answer, he asserted. In his memorandum, Villotte asked for the pope's leniency in all matters affecting canon law though not divine law. Based on many years of experience, he could say that *communicatio in sacris* between Catholic and "schismatic" Armenians led to neither scandal nor disruption. If the missionaries were to take on all the tasks of conducting baptisms, weddings, and funerals, the result would be hatred and persecution from the Armenian priests. They would incite the Muslims against the Catholics, "not without the very certain ruin of the missionaries and the entire religion." For that reason, Villotte contended, one must choose the lesser of two evils and tolerate *communicatio in sacris*. Villotte argued not just in terms of the necessity of avoiding persecution, but he also maintained that the Armenian clergy administered most of the sacraments correctly.[121] Other Jesuits with experience in Persia shared this view: according to a memorandum of 1727 by Father Tadeusz Juda Krusiński, the Armenian mass, aside from a few "errors," was actually "wholly Catholic," which is why the Catholics in the Ottoman Empire attended the Armenian churches where there was no mission church.[122] Like Claude Sicard and Guillaume Dubernat in Egypt, Jacques Villotte and Tadeusz Juda Krusiński belonged to a small group of Jesuits familiar with the country, who were attacked by their rivals on the ground and in Rome because of their concessions to Eastern Christians.[123]

Much like the Jesuits Villotte and Krusiński, Mekhitar of Sebaste, abbot of the monastery of San Lazzaro degli Armeni in Venice, justified *communicatio in sacris* to the *Propaganda Fide* and the Holy Office in 1721 not only in terms of the persecution that Armenians suffered in the Ottoman Empire. The abbot also claimed that the Armenian Church, founded by Gregory the Illuminator at the time of Pope Sylvester, had "never introduced any article of faith that contradicted Catholic beliefs." Up to the present day, it preserved "the same rites, ceremonies, worship services, chants, and constitutions that [Gregory the Illuminator] had left to them with various books, which show that the Armenian Church is united with the Roman Church and subject to it." Since no "heretical" or "schismatic" rites were conducted in the Armenian Church, it did no harm to the Catholic faith if Catholics went to these churches. Rather, it was to be hoped that "schismatics" would be led to union thereby.[124] Mekhitar of Sebaste understood union with Rome, to which he had found his way under Jesuit influence, and the founding of a congregation of Armenian monks based on the

Benedictine Rule not as conversion, but as a reform of his own, Armenian Church, which largely lived within the true faith. For that reason, he rejected the establishment of a parallel Armenian Catholic hierarchy, just as he deemed *communicatio in sacris* to be permissible.[125]

Abbot Mekhitar and the Jesuits Jacques Villotte and Tadeusz Juda Krusiński argued for tolerating *communicatio in sacris* at a time when those who wished to set narrower limits on deviant local practices in varied geographical contexts—such as the controversies around the Chinese and Malabar rites—were becoming increasingly influential within the Roman Curia. In some respects, Villotte's argumentation, for example his assessment of the Armenian Church's practice of using communion wine undiluted, recalls the Jesuit position in these controversies. According to Villotte, the Armenian priests acted here not "in a schismatic spirit," but rather "based on the customs of their forefathers and habits cultivated for so many years." While others regarded the avoidance of mixing water into the wine as a symbolic reinforcement of "monophysitical" Christology, the Jesuit thus described it as a mere social custom without any deeper religious significance.[126] In the 1710s and 1720s, such modes of argumentation increasingly conflicted with the standards of the curial congregations. Under the circumstances, it is hardly surprising that in 1727 the Jesuits in Persia were still waiting in vain for the permission they had requested in the early 1690s to celebrate certain saint's days in the Armenian language and according to the Armenian rite.

*

The missionary reports repeatedly tried to estimate the number of Catholic Armenians. All observers agreed that there were not many. At the same time, it is striking how much the figures vary from one source to another. In 1662, for example, François Pallu, bishop *in partibus infidelium* of Heliopolis and apostolic vicar passing through on his way to East Asia, knew of only six Catholic Armenian family groups in New Julfa. Ten years later, another report speaks of 300 Catholics there.[127] The differences can be attributed only partly to a lack of knowledge. They also point to the difficulty of clearly identifying Armenians, beyond the small circle of families with close ties to missionaries, as "Catholic" or "schismatic."

The insistence on stricter adherence to confessional norms corresponded to a transformation within the Roman Church more generally. As in Persia, one can observe a change in missionary strategies toward Eastern Christians at the end of the seventeenth century in the Syrian provinces, for instance, in a shift toward a stronger commitment to the commandments of confessional orthodoxy. There, changes in Eastern Christian religiosity and ecclesiastical culture also corresponded to the new methods used by some missionaries.[128] The controversies surrounding the "Malabar" and "Chinese rites," which were coming to a head at that time, put up for debate the degree of adaptation to foreign systems of norms that was still permissible from the perspective of orthodoxy.[129]

Toward the end of the seventeenth century, the missionaries accordingly found themselves under increasing pressure to adapt their practice to the narrower definitions of confessional orthodoxy. By conveying an impression of confessional clarity in their correspondence, they met the expectations of the recipients—superiors of the orders and the curial congregations. At the same time, their reports still contained hints of practices of confessional ambiguity even in the administration of the sacraments, which were justified as a practice of dissimulation under conditions of persecution. Contrary to the Curia's aspiration toward confessional disambiguation, most missionaries, and not just the Jesuits, continued to be guided in their relations with Armenian clerics and laity by expectations shaped by a local religious culture in which godliness was less immediately associated with a particular confession. *Communicatio in sacris* could actually become a survival strategy in conflict situations, as the missionaries emphasized to the Curia and the superiors of their orders. Initially, however, it was an expression of a practice of "good correspondence" that also encompassed the sacramental arena, because both sides regarded each other as Christians and therefore saw nothing wrong with *communicatio in sacris*.

Although the Armenian clergy also tended to draw clearer confessional boundaries in their dealings with argumentative Catholic clerics, this was by no means a linear development. To be sure, a small community of Catholic Armenians—the "Sceriman church"—emerged in New Julfa starting in the late seventeenth century. Nevertheless, religious practice continued to be characterized by a high degree of ambiguity. While they had become less common in the late seventeenth and early eighteenth century, practices of "good correspondence" with Armenian clerics such as those the Discalced Carmelites had cultivated in the 1610s and 1620s, including within the sacramental arena, were still evident even at the time of the last Latin bishop of Isfahan, Cornelio di San Giuseppe.

Shared Christian practices were not limited to relations between Eastern Christians and Catholics. The Armenians also venerated Johann Rudolf Stadler, a Reformed clockmaker from Zurich, as a saintly figure and neomartyr. Sentenced to death in Isfahan in 1637 for killing a Muslim intruder in his house who had wanted to seduce his wife, her sister, or an enslaved woman—the accounts diverge on this point—he preferred death to the conversion to Islam that was claimed as the price of a pardon. That is why Protestant, Catholic, and Armenian Christians alike held Stadler in high esteem as a witness to faith. The Discalced Carmelites and Capuchins who visited him in prison and admonished him in vain to convert to Catholicism claimed after his execution that they could easily have attained Stadler's recognition as a martyr if only he had accepted Catholicism before his death. The grave in the Armenian cemetery in New Julfa where Armenian priests buried him at the behest of the envoy of a Protestant prince, Frederick III of Schleswig-Holstein-Gottorf (r. 1616–59), was constructed jointly by Western European Christians of various confessions. The gravestone, whose brief inscription "Here Lies Rudolf" was the sole memorial to Stadler, needed repeated repairs because it was believed to work miracles and Armenians in search of healing not only prayed there but also tended to take pieces of it home with them.[130] Unlike the approaches to confessional cooptation we find in the missionary accounts, admiration for the Reformed neomartyr Stadler was dominated by an emphasis on Christian commonality in distinction from Islam.[131]

5

As Christians among Muslims: Missionaries and European Laypeople of Different Confessions

In 1788 the last Latin bishop of Isfahan, the Discalced Carmelite Cornelio di San Giuseppe, recalled the "generous assistance of friendly and compassionate persons, especially the English and Dutch gentlemen agents and merchants," through whom divine providence had put him in a position to fulfill his duties.[1] What is remarkable about this statement is not just the choice of words and the fact that a bishop was thanking Protestants for their support but also the context in which he expressed his gratitude: in 1788, sixteen years had passed since Cornelio di San Giuseppe's return to his native Milan from the Near East. The bishop was not addressing the Protestant English and Dutchmen to curry favor, but expressing his gratitude in his testament, in which he took stock of his life as a Catholic cleric in the face of his approaching death. As I will show in this chapter, in the microcosm of the diasporas in Persia and the Persian Gulf, the conflicts that marked European societies in the confessional age were overlaid in a complex manner by local social configurations.

Cornelio di San Giuseppe had been active under precarious conditions in Persia and various trading posts in the Gulf region since 1739. He lived in Isfahan only from 1743 to 1745, as a simple member of his order. Because of the wars in Persia, after his appointment as bishop of Isfahan in 1758, like his predecessor Sebastiano di Santa Margherita, he initially preferred to perform the functions of his office from the city of Basra. Since this town belonged to the diocese of Babylon, Cornelio di San Giuseppe depended on the precarious goodwill of the local bishop. He found an alternative between 1763 and 1769, first under Dutch protection on the island of Kharg, then under the English in Bushehr. When the English closed their factory in Bushehr in 1769, he was able to persuade the *Propaganda Fide* that conditions were no longer right for him to continue as bishop of Isfahan, since he now had to live "as an exile" in Basra, where the local bishop prevented him from performing his duties.[2]

Since the seventeenth century, some missionaries, especially the Discalced Carmelites, had been cultivating close contacts with representatives of the English and Dutch East India Companies. After the Safavids were toppled in 1722, some of them followed the trading companies to the Persian Gulf. Within this region, the companies shifted their activities from the Persian ports to Basra, which was now under Ottoman rule and where the English East India Company founded a factory in 1724, followed by the VOC in 1726.

The factories in Basra enjoyed the *de iure* protection of the Ottoman capitulations, even though the local authorities had a wide scope of action. Beyond the Ottoman authorities' sphere of influence, power relations in the Gulf region were extremely fragmented. For that reason, protection was both a valuable and precarious resource there. The trading companies were among the actors able to provide a minimum of security—thanks to their business connections and relationships to local rulers as well as their armed ships and factories. Their local representatives achieved positions of power that they also used for private business, contravening the interests of the companies. VOC governor Baron Justo von Kniphausen went especially far in this regard: although his superiors in Batavia only intended to set up a trading post on Kharg Island, starting in 1753 he voluntarily expanded it into an elaborate fortress at the VOC's expense, from which he and his successors intervened in conflicts between local rulers over a good ten years, increasing their personal power in the area in the process.[3]

The ties between the Catholic clerics and Kniphausen and other representatives of the Protestant East India Companies need to be viewed against the background of Middle Eastern power relations. Cornelio di San Giuseppe described this relationship using the terminology of patrons and clients in which he could expect protection. His *Memorie concernenti alla Chiesa e diocesi di Persia* incorporate several *Memorie* about the history of the English and Dutch trading posts in Persia, because of the "great obligation" the missionaries owed the companies for their "protection and assistance."[4] The writings of Cornelio di San Giuseppe also reveal what this protection consisted of: material support, intercession with local authorities, providing travel and transport opportunities on English and Dutch ships, temporary lodgings and food in the factories, and nursing care in the case of illness.

The clergymen, for their part, offered a wide spectrum of spiritual and worldly services for European residents and travelers of various confessions. Their vow of poverty became the basis of a particular capital of trust that under some circumstances, however, brought them into conflict with the regulations of their order and the *Propaganda Fide*, which forbade them from participating in the worldly affairs of the laity. The social standing that missionaries acquired was ultimately expressed in their funerals. In 1755, Sebastiano di Santa Margherita, Cornelio di San Giuseppe's predecessor as bishop of Isfahan, was interred in the Discalced Carmelite church in Basra in the presence of the resident of the English East India Company and the English merchants as well as Catholic and "schismatic" Armenians, including their clergy. The English resident paid the funeral expenses.[5]

In the absence of clergymen from their own churches, Protestant Englishmen and Dutchmen came to appreciate Catholic clerics even as providers of Christian rituals. This is evident from the *dubia* that Cornelio di San Giuseppe intended to present to the *Propaganda Fide* for the judgment of the Holy Office. Alongside practices of "good correspondence" with non-Catholic Christians, Muslims, and Jews, which had more or less clear religious connotations,[6] the *dubia* referred mainly to the administration of the sacraments, that is, the heart of priestly activities. At the beginning of his memorandum, the Discalced Carmelite posed the question of whether a missionary could baptize a "heathen" enslaved woman who lived in concubinage with her Protestant master. The question then arose of whether the offspring of this type of extramarital relationship could be baptized. If the English or Dutch gentlemen asked for the administering of the sacrament, the missionaries could gain their favor by performing the baptism and keep them from resorting to "schismatic" priests.[7] The *dubia* had a concrete background: the better-off merchants and agents of the trading companies kept enslaved women in their houses who had to serve as maidservants and concubines.[8] The baptismal register of the Discalced Carmelites in Basra shows that they did in fact frequently baptize enslaved people and illegitimate children when asked by the English.[9]

As we have seen, Cornelio di San Giuseppe lived in Isfahan only briefly, from 1743 to 1745. His reports and his *dubia* thus refer primarily to the situation in the trading centers of the Gulf region. The Carmelite's circumstances of life there differed from those in Isfahan and New Julfa in the seventeenth century. The lack of local authorities who could have offered protection meant that transconfessional practices were embedded in relationships of protection. Conversely, in the heartland of the Safavid Empire, the focus had been on two concepts that emphasized the symmetry of reciprocal relationships: "friendship" and "good correspondence." As in relations with the Armenians, here, too, "good correspondence" meant a form of interaction in which the participants affirmed the rank-specific capital of honor with the requisite signs of mutual respect demanded in relationships between persons of high status. The term "friendship" also referred to a relationship in the context of a gift exchange economy, not a personal emotional connection. "Friends" performed material and immaterial services for one another that contributed to the longevity of the relationship.[10]

This chapter will focus on the relationships among members of the regular clergy and laypeople of European origin in Isfahan and New Julfa. I will begin with some introductory remarks on the economic activities and social practices of the European diaspora as well as the institutional contexts in which laypeople of European descent operated. Then I will explore the relationships among missionaries and the holders of episcopal jurisdiction, especially from the standpoint of membership in an order and their geographical origin. Finally, I will broaden the scope to pursue the matter of how far missionaries, despite their renunciation of the "world," were included in a practice of transconfessional "friendship" and "good correspondence" and what role the confession of the involved parties played in this. I will ask about the foundations of the social reputation they were able to acquire in this way and the meanings that their services as religious specialists, especially the administering of the sacraments, assumed under the specific local conditions.

European Laypeople in Isfahan and New Julfa

Information about the economic activities and social practices of European laypeople is scattered throughout the entire body of sources upon which this study is based. What follows will focus on two long-term Protestant residents and their descendants who maintained close relations with Catholic clerics: Jacques Rousseau and Isaac Boutet de l'Étoile. In both cases, the contacts ultimately culminated in their extended families converting to Catholicism, but, contrary to the narratives of missionary history, what will be examined here is not the end "result" but the practices of the actors in cultural contact zones. In a second subchapter, the focus shifts to the institutional conditions under which transconfessional relationships were cultivated. As we have already seen, people of European origin in the Safavid Empire were integrated into a multi-actor constellation that was politically and economically oriented primarily toward relations within Asia and defined by local standards.[11] The number of people of European descent was accordingly small in comparison, for instance, to the Indian diaspora and to the Armenians.

Economic Activities and Social Practices

The laity of European origin who traveled to Isfahan and New Julfa and stayed there for longer or shorter periods included the agents and employees of the English and Dutch East India Companies, merchants who traded on their own behalf, and artisans whose particular skills were prized at the Safavid court. Although the cited figures vary, there can be no doubt that the group of people in question was small. In 1636, the prior of the Discalced Carmelites estimated the number of the English and Dutch in Isfahan and New Julfa at ten persons each. They were joined by four or five Frenchmen and one Italian. With the exception of the representatives of the trading companies and the missionaries, beginning in 1657 all Christians were required to live in New Julfa and other suburbs. In 1662, Pierre Lambert de La Motte, bishop *in partibus infidelium* of Beirut and apostolic vicar passing through on his way to East Asia, spoke of eight or nine Roman Catholic families in all who lived in New Julfa; according to his companion François Pallu, they numbered no more than forty individuals. In 1714, the apostolic vicar, Barnaba Fedeli di Milano, estimated the number of "Franks" served by the local Jesuit, Discalced Carmelite, and Dominican churches at 100.[12]

The English and Dutch East India Companies each maintained a factory in Isfahan for their commercial transactions and as lodgings for their employees (Figure 4, p. 62). Here, too, employees supplemented their low salaries by pursuing their own business activities alongside their duties for the Company.[13] At the time of the Afghan conquest of the city in 1722, the English personnel of the East India Company in Isfahan consisted of the agent, two senior merchants or factors, a junior merchant or clerk, a chaplain, two subaltern employees, and a captain. The captain commanded several European and Armenian soldiers hired by the Company to protect the factory. In 1722, the Dutch factory had five employees of European origin. Because they had no soldiers of their own, they hired thirty Armenians *ad hoc* in light of the looming dangers. The English East India Company employed an Armenian to translate and interpret, while the VOC hired the Syrian Catholic Elias Sahid for the same purpose. According to the Dutchman Cornelis de Bruyn, in the early eighteenth century, representatives of the English and Dutch East India Companies clearly set themselves apart from those Europeans who had settled in Isfahan and New Julfa and married Armenian women: while the latter adopted the local mores and customs, East India Company men stuck to their European ways.[14] Depending on the context, the East India Companies and the Armenian merchants were rivals or partners. This both made for frequent contact and stood in the way of any very close personal relationships.

Artisans of European origin had already begun settling in Isfahan in the early seventeenth century. They served the needs of the court for products from distant lands and thus participated in the orchestration of the Safavid claim to imperial power. At the very beginning of the Carmelite mission, one of its founders had already noted that ʿAbbās I wished to receive talented clockmakers, musicians, painters, and architects at his court.[15] In fact, individual Europeans gained significant prestige in such positions under ʿAbbās I and his successors, but their numbers remained small. According to François Pallu, bishop *in partibus infidelium* of Heliopolis and apostolic vicar en route to East Asia, there were six Frenchmen residing in New Julfa in 1662: apart from Isaac Boutet de l'Étoile, who will be discussed later, there were two clockmakers, two armorers, and one engraver. Three of the six were Huguenots.[16]

The activities of Europeans left certain traces in local material culture, but these should be located within the overall context of the Safavid Empire's foreign relations, which were not determined primarily by ties with Europeans. Because of the small number of painters present at any given time, the European influence on seventeenth-century Persian painting has recently been attributed mainly to Armenian mediation (especially via the import of European prints).[17] It should be emphasized at the same time that the Safavids did not resort primarily to foreign objects of European origin in order to stage their imperial claims to power. In keeping with this circumstance, the English and Dutch India Companies did not make their greatest profits in Persia with rare commodities from Europe, but rather thanks to the intra-Asian trade, in which they participated from South Asia.[18]

Jean-Baptiste Tavernier and Jean Chardin—who for a time did business on their own behalf in the Safavid Empire, imported valuable goods from Europe, and became famous for their travel accounts—also entered these intra-Asian relations as jewel merchants.[19] While the two French Huguenots were respected members of the European diaspora, people of low social status tried their luck in Persia with all manner of petty business.

Many of these people did not go to Persia to settle permanently. Overall, a high degree of self-determined geographical mobility characterized the life of those Latin Christians who moved to Persia. Of those who never returned to their homelands, the Geneva clockmaker, jeweler, and merchant Jacques Rousseau and the Frenchman Isaac Boutet de l'Étoile and their descendants are fairly well documented and will be introduced in more detail in what follows. They were among the most respected members of the European diaspora.

The Genevan Jacques Rousseau, a cousin of the philosopher's father Isaac, died in 1753 in Isfahan, where he was buried in the Armenian cemetery (Figure 15). He had left his native city in 1699, at the age of twenty. The decision to emigrate was nothing unusual for young merchants and clockmakers from Geneva. His first destination, Constantinople, was especially popular among them, because Genevan immigrants found a receptive market there for their clocks and could earn a living maintaining and repairing them. Jacques Rousseau arrived in Constantinople at a time when the number of Genevans drawn there by the demand for the products and services they sold was on the rise. In 1694, ten of the twenty-one clockmakers and goldsmiths under French protection there came from Geneva.[20]

Figure 15 Gravestone of Jacques Rousseau in the cemetery of New Julfa: "Here lies the excellent gentleman Jacques Rousseau, clockmaker of Geneva. He lived 74 years, 48 of them in Isfahan. He died on March 29, 1753."

Some of the Calvinist Genevans who emigrated to Constantinople at a young age returned to their native city after a few years. For example, Jacques Rousseau's cousin Isaac Rousseau, also a clockmaker, moved to Constantinople after the birth of his first son in 1705, and after returning to Geneva in 1712 became the father of a second son, the future philosopher Jean-Jacques. Other Genevans settled permanently in Constantinople, where most of them earned a living as clockmakers, and others as jewelers, goldsmiths, and engravers. Unlike his cousin, Jacques Rousseau never returned to Geneva. In 1706 he traveled instead with the French envoy Pierre-Victor Michel to distant Isfahan, which attracted few Genevan clockmakers in comparison to Constantinople. There were, however, parallels in the activities of the two cousins: while Isaac maintained the clocks in the Topkapi Palace in Constantinople, Jacques Rousseau entered the service of the shah in Isfahan.

Perhaps it was precisely the almost complete absence of competitors that made it easier for Jacques Rousseau to acquire wealth and respect as a clockmaker, jeweler, and merchant. In an account of the history of Persia during this period, the Polish Jesuit

Tadeusz Juda Krusiński, who must have known the Genevan personally, mentions Rousseau as the highly reputed *chef* of Shah Sulṭān Ḥusain's clockmakers. After the ruler had tested a clock made by Rousseau, he was said to have praised the "Franks'" artisanal superiority. Rousseau managed to hold onto his position through all the chaos of the times until his death in 1753.[21]

In 1737 Jacques Rousseau married the Catholic Reine de l'Étoile in New Julfa, thereby linking himself with one of the few families of European origin that had settled permanently in Persia in the first half of the seventeenth century. The de l'Étoile family, originally Huguenots, had probably emigrated from the region of Saint-Jean d'Angély, one of the cities in Southwestern France that the Edict of Nantes had granted Protestants as a safe haven. In Isfahan, family members worked as goldsmiths and merchants. Aside from their own business enterprises, since the 1660s they had also served as agents and interpreters for the *Compagnie des Indes orientales*.[22] As goldsmiths, like Jacques Rousseau in later years, they met demand from the court. They enjoyed a good reputation within the small European diaspora. In 1652 Joan Cunaeus, an envoy of the Dutch East India Company, described Reine de l'Étoile's ancestor Isaac Boutet de l'Étoile as the "most well-regarded among the Europeans living here."[23] Isaac had married into an Armenian family in 1643; the Capuchin Valentin d'Angers agreed to perform the marriage on the condition that all of the children would be raised Catholic. In 1662 François Pallu called Isaac Boutet de l'Étoile the most important of the six Frenchmen in New Julfa. He had amassed a fortune and was a "highly honorable and obliging man."[24] Only on his deathbed in 1667 did Isaac himself also convert to Catholicism.

In their self-presentation, Isaac Boutet de l'Étoile's sons followed the expectations of the Armenian-Persian environment from which their mother came. According to Chardin, Louis, interpreter for the *Compagnie des Indes orientales*, usually dressed "à la persane."[25] When Ambrogio Bembo visited New Julfa in 1674, he found the three brothers remaining in Persia—one had moved to France—living together in the manner of an Armenian *fraterna* in a fine and comfortable house, which the Venetian described as decorated in the local way with various patterns and gold.[26]

The family's social proximity to the French Jesuits and Capuchins did not prevent their continuing close relations with Protestants and Eastern Christians whose economic and social position corresponded to the family's status. Angela, one of Isaac's daughters christened by a Catholic priest, married a non-Catholic Eastern Christian, son of the interpreter of the English East India Company, and a second daughter married the Genevan Calvinist Pierre-Didier Lagisse (1625–79). Between around 1660 and 1672, Lagisse worked as a clockmaker for the court in Isfahan. Later, after his return to Geneva, he continued to produce clocks for the Persian market. While integrating the latest innovations in mechanics, he sought to create clocks that met the aesthetic expectations of his Persian customers (Figure 16). He apparently did so with great economic success, since at his death in 1679 he left a fortune of 300,000 to 350,000 florins. The Geneva register of deaths mentions the deceased's social status as former *maître horloger du Roi de Perse*.[27] Shortly after arriving in Isfahan he had formed a company with his future father-in-law, Isaac Boutet de l'Étoile, with an equal partnership of 50 percent, for which the latter traveled to India, probably to buy gemstones.

Figure 16 Pocket watch produced by Pierre-Didier Lagisse in Geneva for the Persian market, ca. 1675 (a) face, (b) back of the movement with signature. © Patek Philippe Museum, Geneva, Inv. S-179

Reine de l'Étoile's 1737 marriage to Jacques Rousseau thus fit into a network of preexisting relationships between the de l'Étoile family and especially well-placed Protestants. As for Jacques Rousseau, the marriage may probably be regarded as a sign that the Geneva native's ties to his Protestant hometown were loosening. When Reine de l'Étoile gave birth to a son one year after the wedding, he was christened Jean-François-Xavier by the Jesuits (and not simply Jean-François like Jacques's brother in Geneva). When he was nine, Jacques Rousseau sent the boy to be educated by the Jesuits, who instructed him in Catholicism, while according to family lore Jacques himself resisted the priests' pressure to "abjure the faith of his fathers."[28]

When Jacques Rousseau died in 1753, he was one of the few European holdouts in Isfahan and New Julfa. In 1754, Jacques Rousseau's and Reine de l'Étoile's sixteen-year-old son Jean-François-Xavier saw no future for himself in Isfahan. He therefore fled to Bandar ʿAbbās and later to Basra, where he became active in trade and attracted attention because of his knowledge of the four most important languages there, Persian, Arabic, Turkish, and Armenian. In 1756 he entered the service of the *Compagnie des Indes*. Familiarity with cultural contact zones played a crucial part in the reputation and economic successes Jean-François-Xavier and his descendants built for themselves, after entering the French service from the Near East.

Institutional Conditions of "Great Freedom"

Families of European background like the de l'Étoiles and the Rousseaus achieved success in Persia under conditions that, unlike in the Ottoman Empire, were shaped by the almost total absence of corporatively organized "nations" and consular institutions. Both families lived under the jurisdiction of the local, Muslim authorities, without the protection of a consul but also without the restrictions that the *ordonnance de la marine* imposed on members of the French *nations* in the Ottoman Empire. It was only in the Ottoman city of Basra that Jacques Rousseau's son Jean-François-Xavier sought appointment as a French consul, a position he attained in 1781.

Under the Ottoman and Safavid Empires, the position of the European diasporas was defined by the legal guarantees that Christians and Jews could expect from the Muslim authorities. While they had a lower rank than Muslims, they enjoyed an autonomous legal status. This specifically included the right to practice their religion and to use existing churches and sometimes to build new ones. The right to construct new churches, however, came with certain restrictions, as the outward design of churches was to avoid disrupting Islamic public space either visually or acoustically through ringing bells. Agreements between the sultan or shah and Christian rulers or trading companies also played a role. While in the Ottoman Empire the corporative organization of merchants into "nations" under the authority of a consul predominated, under the Safavids it was the factories of the English and Dutch East India Companies and the parish-like structures of the various Catholic missions that created the institutional framework in which people of European origin gathered. It was only after 1708 that attempts began in Persia to organize a French *nation* under a consul appointed by the king on the Ottoman model. Around the same time, the French sought in a treaty with the shah to secure claims to protection over the missions. In 1720, however, the bishop of Isfahan Barnaba Fedeli di Milano still counted only two or three persons in the house of the consul, as well as a Catholic physician and the Genevan Jacques Rousseau, as part of the French "nation." An additional three Catholics of French origin lived in the factory of the English East India Company and therefore belonged to the English "nation." Fedeli regarded this as a good reason to reject the ceremonial claims made by the French consul following the rules in place in the Ottoman Empire.[29]

Since the attempts to organize a French *nation* under the authority of a consul occurred only late and ultimately failed, unlike in the Ottoman Empire, there was no secular authority in Persia that could have called for compulsory Catholicism after the revocation of the Edict of Nantes. Similarly, there were no communities of Latin Catholics in the Safavid Empire who could have created a framework of communal confessional self-discipline like the *Magnifica comunità di Pera* did in Constantinople. While the missionaries held disciplinary competencies in the field of canon law based on their *facultates*, they could not fall back on the executive power necessary to enforce them over those who called themselves Catholics.

Because of the privileges granted them by the shah, the East India Companies claimed policing and jurisdictional authority over their employees. In its trading posts in South Asia, the VOC defined itself as a Calvinist authority. The *Heren XVII* had churches and schools established there and sent out preachers, *ziekentroosters*, and schoolmasters who were supposed to work under their governors. Yet a huge gap existed between the intentions of the VOC and their actual implementation. The number of Calvinist preachers in Asia remained extremely small in comparison to the number of Catholic missionaries.³⁰ The English East India Company was supposed to maintain Church of England chaplains in its garrisons and factories. However, if we are to believe the critics, it did even less for religion than the VOC. When the East India Company began to exert political authority in India, it followed the model established by local rulers with a policy of religious patronage toward various faiths, including non-Christian ones.³¹

In Persia and on the Persian Gulf, neither the Dutch nor the English ever created an organized Protestant community comparable to the *Congrégation genevoise* in Constantinople. 'Abbās I granted both the East India Company and the VOC the right to build their own chapel when they first settled in Isfahan. Granted, this right was no longer mentioned in later versions of the VOC's privileges. This was, however, not the reason why the VOC largely dispensed with sending preachers to its trading posts in Isfahan and the Persian Gulf or why the English East India Company also only occasionally maintained its own chaplains there. Rather, the lack of pastoral care in smaller outposts corresponded to the largely commercial orientation of the East India Companies. It was therefore an exception that the Englishmen who disputed with the two Discalced Carmelites before Shah 'Abbās I in Isfahan in 1621 included the Anglican chaplain of the English East India Company. The challenges missionaries faced in their coexistence with European laypeople were thus rarely related to confessional controversies. They lay instead in the absence of a secular Christian authority to impose discipline and in the expectations placed on the missionaries, not only by Catholics, because of the social proximity within the small diasporas.

The release from control by religious authorities was discussed by various sides from contrasting viewpoints. At the very beginning of the mission to Persia, the Discalced Carmelite Juan Thadeo de San Eliseo warned that if one sent clockmakers, musicians, painters, or master builders to the court of 'Abbās I, they should be of especially steadfast faith "because of the great freedom" and frequent Muslim efforts at conversion.³² *Libertà* as a state of unmooring from values and norms was an important motif in post-Tridentine notions of the "Orient," which was portrayed as a place filled with dangers for the morals of any Christian. Religious pluralism was a particularly negative aspect of this *libertà*. The Huguenot Jean Chardin, in contrast, thought the freedom of religious practice in Persia compared favorably with the situation in his homeland, France. In addition to the English and Dutch East India Companies, there were European Protestants working as artisans in the service of the shah who were married to local women. These foreigners, he noted, served God "in their homes in their own way and with every liberty." Throughout Asia the predominant religions and above all Islam had the "reasonable, just, and pious" characteristic of forcing no one to visit the "churches of the country," allowing everyone to follow their own conscience, and doing whatever they wished in their own home "according to the principles of their own religion."³³

When Jean Chardin praised the degree of religious freedom in Persia and all of Asia in contrast to conditions under Catholic authorities in Europe, this implied no rejection of a practice of close contacts with Catholic clerics in the Safavid Empire. Release from the strictures of confessional authorities contributed to Protestants not only cultivating social relationships with Catholic clerics marked by "friendship" and "good correspondence," but also expecting some of their services as religious specialists beyond confessional designations.

Relations between missionaries and the laity of other confessions also depended on the relationships that clerics of different orders and origins maintained with one another as well as with their secular patrons. We have long known from South Asia that non-Portuguese missionaries, and the Dutch and English trading companies, sometimes enjoyed good relations with each other against the backdrop of their shared conflicts with the Portuguese clergy and its secular patrons. When the Discalced Carmelites were expelled from the *Estado da Índia* in 1709, some of them sought refuge in Bombay. In light of the multifarious conflicts with the Portuguese clerics, the East India Company pursued the exemption of Bombay from the jurisdiction of the archbishop of Goa. In 1720, it expelled the Portuguese priests and replaced them with the Discalced Carmelites of the Italian Congregation. At the same time, the transfer of ecclesiastical jurisdiction from the archbishop of Goa to the apostolic vicar general responsible for the Mughal Empire, a Discalced Carmelite, was sealed with his oath of obedience to His Majesty. The VOC took a similar approach in the South Indian city of Cochin. There the Dutch trading company also favored the Discalced Carmelites dispatched by the *Propaganda Fide*. In 1712 the pope affirmed the establishment of two new episcopal sees for Cochin and the *Sierra,* and Discalced Carmelites were appointed to both. In Bombay and Cochin, conditions were favorable for the coexistence between people of different origins and religious affiliations.[34] In what follows, we will therefore need to ask to what extent the practices of "friendship" and "good correspondence" in Persia should be viewed not just from the perspective of "Frankish" diasporas in the Near East but also as part of everyday South Asian relations shaped by intra-Catholic conflicts and context-driven transconfessional rapprochement.

Missionaries among Themselves

Although Catholic clerics shared common duties in the service of their church, other factors could become dominant in the lives of missionaries. Depending on their situation, these might include the particulars of their membership in different orders, as well as the opportunities and restraints offered by networks of men from the same region or country and their obligations toward secular rulers. The coexistence at close quarters of members of at times five different orders as well as secular priests of the *Missions étrangères de Paris* in Isfahan and New Julfa contrasted with the circumstances in most other mission territories in Asia. This is most reminiscent of the situation in Pera and Galata, where members of five orders were also active in the seventeenth century. Unlike the clerics in Isfahan and New Julfa, though, who only arrived in Persia in the context of the post-Tridentine mission, the Franciscans and Dominicans in Galata had already settled there in the thirteenth century. Conditions varied widely as to the number of Catholics living there: in Pera and Galata, the Franciscans, the Reformed Franciscans, and Dominicans looked after three Latin parishes with several hundred faithful each. Apart from "Franks" residing there temporarily, they included members of families who had been settled in Pera and Galata for generations, some of them since pre-Ottoman days.

In Constantinople, clerics cultivated close ties to secular patrons. For example, the Reformed Franciscans worked as chaplains to the head of the Venetian community and envoy of the Republic (*bailo*), while the Capuchins and Jesuits were dependent on the French Crown, as they were at the Safavid court. In Pera and Galata, high-ranking diplomats figured as secular patrons for missionaries. Conditions were different in Isfahan. Here it was the Augustinians and Capuchins themselves who took on these duties as political agents of the Portuguese and French Crowns, respectively. Only with the French legations of the early eighteenth century did developments begin to emerge in Persia that were intended to approximate those in the Ottoman Empire. Because of internal upheavals starting in the 1720s, these changes were of brief duration. By the seventeenth century, however, both in Constantinople and Isfahan, political conflicts between Catholic rulers were affecting the missions, contrary to the Christian commandment of peace.

The presence of missionaries of varying origins and orders fostered conflicts among the clerics. In some cases, the conflicts even pushed confessional boundaries into the background, for instance when Portuguese hostility forced the Discalced Carmelites to depend on the English and the Dutch. In what follows, I will begin by determining the impact that membership in an order, geographical origin, and claims to secular rights of patronage had on relationships among the missionaries. Then I will turn my attention to their relations with the holders of episcopal jurisdiction.

Affiliation with an Order, Geographical Origin, and Claims to Secular Rights of Patronage

In 1662 Pierre Lambert de La Motte, bishop of Beirut and apostolic vicar, described relations among the missionaries of the four orders then present in Isfahan as follows:

> It has been deemed inappropriate to speak in detail of the missions in Isfahan because one cannot do so without upsetting several good religious there, whose views are not wholly in keeping with Apostolic life; ... Suffice it to say, in a few words, that it is easy to see that of the four religious houses in the city there are three too many ... , because the fathers, lacking neither great human means nor the aid of the secular authorities, recognize no superiors other than those of their orders and, being of several minds, one allows what the other rejects.[35]

Coexistence between clerics of different orders and origins in one place was often burdened by conflicts. The first secretary of the *Propaganda Fide*, Francesco Ingoli, therefore argued that only the members of a single order should be sent to a given region. Later, he became more appreciative of the advantages of deploying members of several orders at the same place, because they would monitor and spur each other on.[36] In fact, a large part of knowledge in Rome was based on accounts written by rivals in local conflict situations.

Affiliation with different orders and the patronage claims of the Portuguese Crown made it likely that conflicts would arise between the Discalced Carmelites of the Italian Congregation and the Portuguese Augustinians before the former even arrived in Persia. Clement VIII accordingly enjoined the Augustinians to work with the Discalced Carmelites in unity and harmony for the cause of the faith. Yet, when they were faced with the Discalced Carmelites, the Augustinians appealed to the rights of patronage of the *Estado da Índia*.[37] "National" distinctions followed a primarily jurisdictional rather than geographical criterion: of the four Discalced Carmelites sent to Persia by Clement VIII in 1604, three came from Spain and one from Genoa, and because of these origins, they were connected with the Spanish monarchy.[38]

The French monarch's claims to the protection of the missions in Persia took shape with the settlement of French Capuchins in 1628, Jesuits in 1647, and individual priests of the *Missions étrangères de Paris* toward the end of the seventeenth century. While the Roman Curia initially welcomed the French clerics in Asia as a counterweight to the Portuguese *Padroado*, this presence soon proved to be a further challenge to papal claims to primacy. At the same time, however, the varying affiliations of French clerics—Capuchins, Jesuits, and secular priests of the *Missions étrangères*—brought French controversies and conflicts between the orders to Persia, which sometimes outweighed their shared ties to the king of France. Novel relationships emerged in which clerics, all of them under the protection of the French Crown, were divided by an extreme rivalry.

Of the three orders already present in Persia when the Jesuits arrived, it was mainly the French Capuchins who made life difficult for their recently arrived compatriots. The Capuchins allegedly used their position at court to harm the Jesuits. These conflicts recall research findings from Europe; thus, Hillard von Thiessen's conclusion, based on the example of two German cities, that Capuchins and Jesuits regarded "each other as fundamentally different types of orders" while "nevertheless competing in many areas of pastoral care," applies to the mission in Persia as well.[39]

The conflicts in Persia resulted less from the differences between the orders than from the similarity of their aims and approaches, which turned them into rivals. Both orders provided prominent participants in the disputations with Shī'a scholars, and in the 1650s and 1660s the Capuchin Gabriel de Chinon and the Jesuit Aimé Chézaud sought in similar ways to gain access to the Armenians by accepting *communicatio in sacris*. Capuchins like Valentin d'Angers as well as Jesuits like Aimé Chézaud then placed their hopes in social proximity to rich and respected Protestants, and they were prepared to sacrifice some confessional orthodoxy in the process—Valentin d'Angers by tolerating mixed marriages, Aimé Chézaud by celebrating masses in the home of a wealthy Calvinist, Isaac Boutet de l'Étoile.

While the French Jesuits found their most formidable opponents in the French Capuchins, in the 1650s and 1660s, they boasted at the same time of their good relationship with the Italian Discalced Carmelites and of the support from the "Portuguese friends" who lived in Isfahan to manage the affairs of the king of Portugal.[40] These episodes show how the lines of conflict visible in overarching contexts—in this case, those between the Jesuits and Capuchins, Rome and the French Church, and the *Padroado* and French *protection*—situationally developed their significance on the ground, but sometimes also retreated into the background. The same is true of the relationship between the Jesuits, on the one hand, and the priests of the *Missions étrangères de Paris* and the French bishops of Babylon, on the other: despite their taking opposing positions within the French controversies around Jansenism, in Persia these relationships were by no means always conflictual. Before François Sanson, one of the priests, was able to buy a house in New Julfa, he enjoyed the hospitality of the Jesuits. Since they had no church of their own, in 1692 Pidou de Saint-Olon and Martin Gaudereau celebrated mass with the Jesuits. At least for a time, their shared French origins thus brought together clerics who would have been estranged had they met at home. Matters were different for the French Jesuit Jacques Villotte. He not only opposed the efforts of the French court to unite the dioceses of Isfahan and Babylon, to which the pope could only appoint French clerics, but also criticized the settlement of priests from the *Missions étrangères* in Isfahan and New Julfa because they contested the Jesuits' parochial rights.[41] The relationships between various affiliations were thus changeable. Conflicts between the orders might divide clerics of the same geographical origin, while in other contexts regional affiliations and obligations toward a secular patron might prove at least temporarily binding, beyond the boundaries of religious orders.

Within the orders, too, geographical ties were not only important when members of the order pursued personal matters in Rome from their distant mission stations; they also shaped conditions on the ground in Persia. "Both the Portuguese and French nations care greatly for their king and the advantage of their nation. From experience, I see and have seen that religious, despite having renounced the world, are full of fervor, and this pits one nation jealously against the other," wrote the provincial vicar of the Discalced Carmelites in Shiraz in 1675, speaking of the reluctance of the Portuguese in Goa to accept friars of French origin. The Polish-born friar himself claimed to get along "with all nations."[42] In fact, the conflicts between Catholic monarchs increasingly also affected his order over the course of the seventeenth century.

In the Jesuit order as well, geographical ties played an important role, in contrast with the assertion that the Society of Jesus was "one single nation," and thus divided into provinces for purely practical reasons.[43] Conflicts between Jesuit fathers of different origins made themselves felt with particular force in Isfahan in 1657. That year the Carinthian-born Father Bernhard Diestel arrived in Isfahan bearing letters to the shah from the emperor, the kings of France and Poland, the grand duke of Tuscany, and the general of the Jesuit order. Yet, in the opinion of the French superior Alexandre de Rhodes, he put too little effort into persuading the shah to grant the mission a settlement site. Since Alexandre de Rhodes refused to allow Father Diestel to take the fourth vow of obedience to the pope, Father Diestel called the *assistant de France* in Rome a "dog," responded to warnings with "unworthy words attacking the entire *assistance de France*," and accused de Rhodes of treating him "tyrannically." Alexandre de Rhodes's complaint culminated in the accusation that Diestel had made arrangements with the VOC's dragoman to be called to the court as the sole deliverer of gifts from the king of France, for which he, de Rhodes, had done all the preparations. Diestel had promised the dragoman to ensure that the emperor appointed him as an agent at the shah's court "with a very substantial annual salary." The Dutch dragoman, a Catholic, was however "wholly devoted to the Capuchin friars" who had raised him since childhood. If we are to believe Alexandre de Rhodes's assertions, the episode points to the salience of geographical identities *within* the Society of Jesus and shows, at the same time, how these were overlaid by other attributions of identity, since the Capuchins for their part were also of French origin.[44]

While the Augustinians in Persia were perceived throughout the existence of their mission as agents of the Portuguese Crown and the viceroy of the *Estado da Índia*, the relationship between the Jesuits and the French Crown lacked a comparable jurisdictional basis. The efforts of the French Crown to bind the Society's French provinces and heighten the distinct Gallican identity of the *Assistance de France* within the order and vis-à-vis the pope, however, also affected the Jesuits in the Safavid Empire.[45] For example, in his correspondence with the *assistant de France* in Rome, Claude-Ignace Mercier, successor to Alexandre de Rhodes and Aimé Chézaud, equated the mission with the unfolding of French power in Asia. In 1673 he lauded the French conquest of São Tomé (now a district of Madras/Chennai in Southern India) as a gift of divine providence intended to show the entire world that France would revive the faith that the Apostle Thomas had once brought there.[46] The Jesuits granted the royal envoys of secular status who came to Isfahan in 1708 and 1718 the desired ceremonial in their church as ambassadors of the Most Christian King. Placing their house of worship, as a "French church," at the disposal of the envoys Pierre-Victor Michel and Ange de Gardane allowed them to contest the Capuchins' primacy as French missionaries. Meanwhile, it also helped them to gain the envoys' backing in defending the privileges of their order against the holder of episcopal jurisdiction.

Members of Religious Orders and Episcopal Authority

The institutions of the local church were marked by the interactions between secular claims to rights of patronage and attempts by the Roman Curia to enforce papal primacy. Like other mission territories, Persia remained a *de facto* realm of ecclesiastical particular law, because for many years the missionaries were not subject to a bishop or had in practice resisted episcopal authority. The intention expressed since the founding of the *Propaganda Fide*, especially by its first secretary Francesco Ingoli, of subjecting missionaries from the regular clergy to effective episcopal control only gradually began to take shape in Persia in the 1680s. In 1632, when bishops were appointed to the dioceses of Isfahan and Babylon (Baghdad), the missionaries were already being placed under the jurisdiction of these prelates. This decision remained ineffective in practice, however, because the bishop of Isfahan, the Discalced Carmelite Juan Thadeo de San Eliseo, died before he was able to take office in Persia, and the bishop of Babylon never entered his diocese. Instead, from 1638 to 1696 the French bishops of Babylon also served as apostolic vicars of the diocese of Isfahan. The missionaries, meanwhile, only saw themselves confronted with episcopal authority in the years 1640 to 1642 and then again periodically after 1682, the only periods when the bishops of Babylon actually fulfilled their residential duty and lived in Isfahan or Hamadan.

With the appointment of the Discalced Carmelite Élie de Saint-Albert as bishop of Isfahan in 1693 and his consecration in 1696, a prelate more closely allied to the

Propaganda Fide de iure replaced the French bishop of Babylon. Since the latter, however, still resided in Isfahan or Hamadan as a result of the adverse conditions in Baghdad, for a time there were two bishops living in the same diocese, or even the same city. Because of the bishops' differing origins and the diplomatic tasks with which the French Crown entrusted the bishop of Babylon, European fault lines influenced the local context. The conflicts were temporally limited because Élie de Saint-Albert only remained in Isfahan until 1699 and then traveled to Rome to seek backing for his controversial conduct of office. For the first time, the episcopal see was occupied for a longer period by a prelate resident in the city after the Discalced Carmelite's death in 1708: the Dominican Barnaba Fedeli di Milano was appointed apostolic vicar and in 1716 bishop of Isfahan. After his death in 1731, Clement XII (Lorenzo Corsini, r. 1730–40) appointed the Discalced Carmelite Filippo Maria di Sant'Agostino, who performed his duties from New Julfa from his consecration in 1736 until his death in 1749. Because of the dangerous living conditions, his two successors, the Discalced Carmelites Sebastiano di Santa Margherita (1751–5) and Cornelio di San Giuseppe (1758–97), no longer resided in Isfahan or New Julfa, but in Basra and other trading posts in the Gulf region. In 1771 Cornelio di San Giuseppe returned to Italy, leaving behind an administrator.

The only sporadic presence of a bishop or apostolic vicar enabled the missionaries to assume parochial rights over the faithful who attended their church. This corresponded to the *facultates*, which permitted them to administer all of the sacraments with the exception of ordination and confirmation in all dioceses without a bishop or apostolic vicar as well as in parishes without a parish priest. Although we cannot speak of "national churches" in the strict sense of the term, several churches *de facto* entrusted with parochial functions arose in Isfahan and Julfa and were led by clerics from different orders and geographical origins. This also applied to the orders whose constitutions excluded their members from the administration of parishes. Thus, the Jesuits based the claim that their church in New Julfa should be considered the only parish church of the "Franks" and Catholic Armenians largely on the fact that the Armenian quarter had long had no other Catholic church. In 1694, the *Propaganda Fide* rejected the Jesuit request. Nevertheless, the Jesuits continued to perform parochial functions in their church. This was confirmed by one of their opponents, the Dominican Barnaba Fedeli di Milano, who was probably unaware of the *Propaganda Fide* decision of 1694, when he stated in 1714 that he wished to begin the visitation of the missions with the Jesuits, "because their church is the only parish in Julfa."[47]

If a bishop or apostolic vicar actually wanted to assume the functions of his office, conflicts were sure to follow. This occurred for the first time when the Discalced Carmelite Bernard de Sainte-Thérèse, bishop of Babylon, arrived in Isfahan in 1640. The bishop spoke none of the local languages and had no missionary experience at all. He showed no willingness whatsoever to judge local practices according to anything but the strict confessional norms he brought from his homeland. He deployed his jurisdictional authority as bishop against anyone he regarded as not respecting these norms, rather than using the possibilities of dispensation offered by canon law. The regular clergy found their rights to act as parish priests at stake. Despite being members of the same order, the bishop's relationship with the Discalced Carmelites was by no means better than that with the Augustinians and Capuchins. One of the Discalced Carmelites complained that the bishop had called them "dastards, brutes, and rogues," and suspended them from taking confession.[48] After completely isolating himself, Bernard de Sainte-Thérèse appointed the Augustinian prior as vicar general and returned to France in 1642, after a sojourn of just two years. It would be forty years before another bishop of Babylon came to Isfahan to assume episcopal functions as apostolic vicar. François Picquet arrived in 1682. Unlike Bernard de Sainte-Thérèse, Picquet was familiar with the missions in the Ottoman Near East, although not with conditions in Persia: before his 1664 ordination as a priest, he had served as French consul in Aleppo. He, too, met with strong resistance in his attempts to subject the regular clergy to stricter episcopal authority. The missionaries insisted on their privileges and asserted that the bishop was intent on destroying the religious orders. Upon his arrival, Picquet demanded that the regular clerics present their patents to him and that they exercise their *facultates* in dependence upon him as the holder of episcopal jurisdiction.

Opposition to the bishop united members of various orders who disagreed on other matters. The Discalced Carmelite Élie de Saint-Albert regarded the bishop's claim to the right to scrutinize the *facultates* as a violation of the *bulla persica* with which Clement VIII had exempted the missionaries of his order from the jurisdiction of all prelates and ecclesiastical officeholders. In the manner of the French bishops, he said, Picquet sought to subject the regular clergy to a "heavy yoke."[49] According to the French Capuchin Raphaël du Mans, the missionaries of all orders refused to assemble regularly under Picquet's authority. Both the Discalced Carmelite and the Capuchin explained the antipathy toward Picquet in part as a response to his companions, who had been dispatched by the *Missions étrangères de Paris*. "Everywhere they went," wrote Élie de Saint-Albert, "they immediately sought to dominate the clergy" and to "subjugate" the religious.[50] Raphaël du Mans in turn lent additional weight to this allegation by placing the bishop and his companions in the Jansenist camp.[51] With this accusation, he brought into play an argument calculated to weaken the bishop's position with the *Propaganda Fide*.

The appointment of the Discalced Carmelite Élie de Saint-Albert as bishop of Isfahan occurred at the urging of the Sceriman brothers, one of the richest Armenian merchant families in New Julfa, who supported a union between the Armenian Church and Rome and, according to the future bishop, had promised to finance his position. The choice of the zealous friar corresponded to the tendency to subject the missions more strongly to the authority of Rome. To that end, the *Propaganda Fide* henceforth selected the bishop or apostolic vicar from the ranks of the Discalced Carmelites or the Dominican Congregation of Santa Sabina, both of which maintained comparatively close ties to the Curia.

Following the appointment of Élie de Saint-Albert as bishop of Isfahan, the Jesuits led the regular clergy's resistance to the restriction of their privileges. In the case of Élie de Saint-Albert, the jurisdictional conflict coincided with controversies surrounding the treatment of "schismatic" Armenians. While such controversies lost urgency under the Discalced Carmelite's successor Barnaba Fedeli di Milano, the jurisdictional conflict was further exacerbated. In 1714 Fedeli—still in his capacity as apostolic vicar—had to dispense with the visitation of the churches with which the *Propaganda Fide* had entrusted him because the Jesuits challenged his jurisdiction. In 1718 he undertook a renewed attempt to perform visitations after a decision in his favor by the *Propaganda Fide*. Yet once again he was rejected by the Jesuits. They cited the privileges of their order, while Fedeli argued that the Jesuits, too, were subject to the ordinary episcopal jurisdiction in the exercise of their parochial rights.[52]

The Jesuits found allies in the French envoys Michel and Gardane, who came to Isfahan in 1708 and 1718, respectively.[53] Like the ambassadors in Constantinople and the consuls in the Ottoman Empire, they asserted the French claim to protect the missions and Catholic Christians by cultivating relationships with the missionaries of French origin and enabling them to exercise parochial rights. The non-French religious wavered between a fundamental rejection of the French claim to protection and exploiting it pragmatically in order to play it off against local authorities and the "schismatic" Armenians. The Lombard Dominican Barnaba Fedeli di Milano evolved from an initially positive assessment of a stronger French presence as a guarantor of "peace" and "freedom" for the missionaries and Catholics more generally to harsh repudiation: in 1722 he wrote that Gardane wanted "more power than he is entitled to and does nothing for the missions."[54]

The controversies surrounding what ceremonial could be provided for the French envoy in the Jesuit church in New Julfa were emblematic of the conflicts between the privileges of orders, secular patronage claims, and episcopal jurisdiction. When the Jesuits granted the French envoys Michel and Gardane the ceremonial and thus the precedence owed to an ambassador in their church, they were seeking confirmation of their own legal claims vis-à-vis the bishop. A fierce conflict erupted in 1720, when during a pontifical office in the Jesuit church on the day of the patron, St. Joseph, to which Gardane had also been invited, Barnaba Fedeli di Milano did not pray for Louis XV (r. 1715–74) according to French ceremonial. He replaced the "Lord, save our King Louis," usual in churches under French patronage, with "Lord, save your servants," and during the *oremus* he mentioned "King Louis" but omitted the pronoun "our." While Gardane wished the Jesuit church to be regarded as a "French church," the bishop stressed that all churches were subject to *his* authority.[55] From Fedeli's perspective, what was at stake was his authority as a papal representative vis-à-vis the unjustified patronage claim of a secular ruler. Not the king of France but the pope was the "protector and superior of all missions in the world," Barnaba Fedeli emphasized. Since as bishop he was a servant of the pope, the Jesuit church must also be subject to his jurisdiction.[56]

Matters were less clear-cut in practice. Like the competencies of the curial congregations, the applicability of the privileges of orders, secular claims to patronage rights, or episcopal prerogatives was not clearly defined, but rather was affirmed *in actu* in any given case. Attempts by the bishops to assert their competency as the holders of the ordinary ecclesiastical jurisdiction in keeping with the Council of Trent were only partially successful. They elicited fierce opposition from the missionaries, who cited the privileges of their orders and their *facultates*. That the missions followed their own rules was also apparent in relations between clerics and people of different confessions.

Transconfessional "Friendship" and "Good Correspondence"

In 1672, the Jesuit Claude-Ignace Mercier stated that while in Europe he had been threatened by "heretics," in Persia these "heretics" met the fathers with "all manner of affection." Upon their arrival the "heretics" had gifted him with a cheese brought from Europe; subsequently, he had frequently received the fruits of their hunting and fishing parties. Twice, the "heretics" had invited the fathers to a banquet, and when they departed for India, one of them had even left them alms.[57] In his letter to his order's *assistant de France* in Rome, Mercier referred to specific practices of transconfessional communication between the fathers and those whom he nevertheless called "heretics," at least in his correspondence with a superior of his order. The frequent small gifts, invitations, and alms not only made everyday life easier for the clerics but also, in the gift exchange economy of the European diaspora, enacted a relationship of "friendship" and "good correspondence" on a symbolic level. With their gifts Protestants, too, acknowledged the social position of the clerics, who, based on their status as propertyless religious, were not expected to offer return gifts of equal value, but instead performed specific services of an immaterial nature. This practice of unequal gift exchange created commonalities between people who, in a Muslim environment, perceived each other as Christians despite their different confessions.

In what follows I will trace the practices of "friendship" and "good correspondence" of European Christians at various points in their lives, from their arrival from Europe and journeys between settlements in the Near East and beyond to coexistence in Isfahan and New Julfa, where a small number of European Christians shared common social spaces. The account concludes by addressing the importance of the missionaries' services as religious specialists on the ground. We will thus return to some of the questions already treated in the previous chapter about the Armenians, since the problem of *communicatio in sacris* also arose in relations with Protestants.

Help along the Way

The journey from Italy across the Mediterranean and through the Ottoman Empire took about six months if it proceeded without incident. The likelihood of a missionary spending at least part of this time in the company of non-Catholic Europeans was considerable. On their travels from the ports of Southern Europe to Isfahan, the missionaries followed the shipping and caravan routes used by merchants of varied origins. Even the sea voyage from Italy to the Levant was often made on ships sailing under Protestant flags. In 1625, for example, the Discalced Carmelite Eliseo de San Andrés, a native of Tarazona in Aragon, sailed on a Dutch ship from Genoa to Iskenderun, whence he intended to continue to Isfahan by land. Traveling in the opposite direction in 1645, a Wallonian Discalced Carmelite, whom his superiors had instructed to make the journey via India on Dutch and English ships, chose instead to take the land route via Baghdad to the Mediterranean, where he hoped to sail on a ship under either of those two flags.

While the caravan routes in the heartlands of the Safavid Empire offered a high degree of safety in the seventeenth century and thus the possibility of traveling in small groups, large stretches of the travel routes to Isfahan initially led through borderlands in which the authority of the Ottomans and Safavids was very limited and the necessity for travelers to defend themselves was all the greater. In general, the missionaries joined large trade caravans, as these took useful safety precautions.[58] In 1625, for instance, Eliseo de San Andrés found himself in the company of two French Huguenots for the dangerous overland journey from Aleppo to Isfahan.

For the voyage between India and the Persian Gulf, the Augustinians relied on the networks of the Portuguese *Estado da Índia*. At the same time, they collaborated with the secular authorities of the *Estado* in order to prevent other missionaries who were not working under the *Padroado* from traveling to India. This meant that passages on Dutch ships were all the more sought after, as a Discalced Carmelite noted in 1656 while waiting in Basra with two fellow friars for a means of traveling to Surat. The three Discalced Carmelites had to convince the Dutch that they were not intending to travel to one of the Portuguese colonies in South Asia. Then, however, the Dutch captain, who was "very affectionate" toward the friars, waived the cost of the voyage for which other passengers had to pay twenty-five *scudi* each—half of the sum allotted to a Discalced Carmelite for an entire year.[59] Other clerics used English ships.

When priests from the French *Missions étrangères de Paris* became active in Asia in the 1660s, in competition with the missionaries under the Portuguese *Padroado*, they also had to travel with English or Dutch ships. While Persia was rather insignificant as a missionary territory for the *Missions étrangères*, some French priests traveled through the Safavid Empire on their way to Southeast Asia and China because the Portuguese maritime routes were closed to them. While independence from the Portuguese, English, and Dutch, "who hold the keys to these broad seas in their hands," seemed desirable to François Pallu,[60] in practice, the lack of a French presence and the hostility of the Portuguese nonetheless made it necessary to seek the good will of the English and Dutch. François Pallu himself expected that he would be able to travel to Surat on an English vessel, like the two apostolic vicars who had preceded him. After arriving in Bandar 'Abbās he sent further advice for future missionaries to his *procureurs* in France: they must take great care to acquire letters of recommendation for the English and Dutch from consuls and merchants. There could be no doubt that the French priests would be treated well by the Dutch as long as they did not meddle in their commercial affairs.[61]

To be sure, 1664 saw the founding of the French *Compagnie des Indes Orientales*, whose commercial interests François Pallu hoped would prove useful for the *Missions étrangères*, but such hopes were only partially fulfilled, as business was not particularly successful: French ships reached Bandar 'Abbās for the first time in 1670, and by 1706 the trading company was in debt and had stopped doing business.[62]

"Good correspondence" between the missionaries and the Dutch and English encompassed not just permitting passages under financially advantageous conditions but also the provision of assistance, protection, and hospitality in the various locations along the travel route. English and Dutch merchants, representatives of trading companies, and consuls often provided assistance for missionaries on their journeys, such as organizing their passage on specific ships, helping them navigate custom duties, and providing them with board and lodging while they waited for onward connections. In his *Itinerario Orientale*, the Carmelite lay brother Francesco Maria di San Siro described how, on their way to Persia, he and his traveling companions enjoyed the protection of a non-Catholic Englishman named Prescott in Erzurum, where he performed the duties of a consul. Immediately after their arrival in the city, Prescott had visited them and presented them with a large wether. The "gentleman" was of "another religion" but nevertheless the "protector" of the traveling missionaries, the friar noted. Prescott had helped them with the Turks, invited them to stay at his home, and provided them with money for the onward journey. He had done everything that "the most pious Catholic" could have done. Later, Brother Francesco Maria traveled to India from Isfahan. When the customs officials in Bandar ʿAbbās made trouble for him upon his return from India, he turned to the director of the Dutch factory, Jacobus Hoogcamer. When the officials learned that the lay brother was under the Dutchman's protection, they immediately allowed him to be on his way.[63] On the Persian Gulf, the protection of the representatives of important trading companies was all the more valuable because, in contexts distant from the court, the amount of duty to be paid depended on both the interest of tax collectors in the continuation of trade and the entanglement of traders in local power structures.[64]

Such aid was integrated into a gift exchange economy. The religious orders also maintained settlements in unfamiliar surroundings that could prove useful for travelers. There the clerics offered a hospitable reception and assistance, especially expert advice about the country and connections with people who, because of their position locally, could make their lives easier or more difficult. As we will see in Chapter 6 in an analysis of the economy of the mission in Basra, the friars could earn urgently needed income by hosting travelers. Other potential sources of income were rents, alms and legacies from persons connected with the clerics, and payments for funerals.

While the convents in Isfahan and New Julfa were mainly important for travelers who operated outside the networks of the trading companies—such as the Huguenots Tavernier and Chardin, whose relations with various missionaries will be explored in more detail presently—the Discalced Carmelite convent in Shiraz offered welcome support not just for other travelers but also for employees of the East India Companies on their way between Isfahan and the Persian Gulf. In 1674, it was there that the Venetian traveler Ambrogio Bembo met the agent of the East India Company and other Englishmen from Bandar ʿAbbās who were traveling to Isfahan. When John Fryer, the English East India Company physician, stopped in Shiraz in 1677, he and his companions were welcomed by the Armenians and the local Discalced Carmelites, while they stayed overnight at the house of the East India Company. Together with the other Christians, the friars were invited on this occasion to a dinner at the home of the trading company's translator. At the beginning of 1678, Fryer traveled back to Bandar ʿAbbās on the Persian Gulf from Isfahan, accompanied by a Discalced Carmelite. During the subsequent return journey to Isfahan that spring, he stopped in Shiraz to offer medical treatment to the visitor of the Discalced Carmelites. He then undertook the onward journey to Isfahan in the company of a rich Armenian merchant, a Dominican, and a Discalced Carmelite.[65]

The French Calvinists Jean-Baptiste Tavernier and Jean Chardin also stayed with the Discalced Carmelites in Shiraz. Chardin, who had already enjoyed the hospitality of the local Theatines and Capuchins in Mingrelia, Gori, Tbilisi, and Tabriz, stressed that the Discalced Carmelites in Shiraz were a "great comfort" to all European travelers, whom they treated "with much humanity" regardless of confessional allegiance. This was, however, all that they could do. Although lacking neither zeal nor knowledge, they themselves would concede that they had never converted anyone to Christianity. According to Chardin, this was because of the "cult of images," which the Muslims condemned as idolatry.[66]

Soon after the settlement in Shiraz was founded, the fact that it could claim no missionary successes and served above all to house travelers had led to doubts within the order about its usefulness. In 1630, Epifanio di San Giovanni Battista argued as visitor general of the missions in Persia and India that the settlement should be abandoned. It was "superfluous and harmful," brought no benefit to the mission, and "served merely to spend endless amounts of money and offer shelter to clerics, merchants, soldiers, and the Portuguese on their way from India to Persia."[67] In 1638, the general of the order charged a new visitor general with the task of testing the state of the settlement in spiritual and secular matters as well as assessing its spiritual and material utility. In particular, he was to find out how much was spent on housing Christians traveling through and what benefits arose from this practice.[68] Such misgivings did not win out, however. The settlement in Shiraz was only closed in 1738, when, as a consequence of the decline of European trade in Persia, it had largely lost its function as a service provider for Europeans passing through and thus could no longer rely on the resulting revenues and the protection of the Dutch and English East India Companies.

Paying One's Respects

Assistance to travelers was of more than just practical utility. Indeed, it was integrated into relationships marked by mutual professions of respect between men of high status. It is striking that even religious who had taken vows of poverty and humility placed much value in noting that ships' captains afforded them those signs of respect that persons of higher rank could expect. They, too, thus adapted to worldly status hierarchies. The Jesuit Alexandre de Rhodes, who in 1646–8 used English ships for his return journey from Southeast Asia to the Persian Gulf, stressed the captains' obliging and respectful behavior toward him. On their ships, the English treated him with every courtesy that he might have wished for. These "courtesies" included not only being invited to sit at the captain's table but also being given the most honorable seat.[69]

The integration of clerics into a transconfessional exchange of signs of respect becomes most tangible in the practice of visits and return visits in Isfahan and New Julfa. Upon arrival, persons of rank within the small European diaspora, regardless of confession, could expect to receive visits from all those who would enter into social exchange with them. Accordingly, François Pallu, bishop of Heliopolis, who stopped in Isfahan in 1662 while traveling to East Asia, was visited on arrival by all of the "Franks" in town—the missionaries of the various orders as well as representatives of the English and Dutch East India Companies. He then needed several days to reciprocate these visits. When he left the city, Catholics and Protestants alike came to bid him farewell.[70] The Jesuit Jacques Villotte attributed his rapid recovery from the rigors of his journey to the "acts of kindness" he received in 1688 from the missionaries of all orders, the Frenchmen in the service of the shah, and the English and Dutch merchants, and the "acts of charity" of all the Europeans at the Persian court. As in 1688, upon his return after a longer absence in 1696, Villotte again received visits from the "Franks" and Armenians of Isfahan and New Julfa, which he returned soon after. Among the "Franks" who honored him with a visit were "Messieurs les Anglais" whom Villotte thanked during his return visit for the "good offices" their compatriots had shown him in Constantinople, Erzurum, and Tripoli.[71]

As in early modern Western Europe, the visits set strong examples of "good correspondence." The sequence and more or less speedy return of visits marked differences of rank and status, which is why they were carefully noted in diplomatic reports. Joan Cunaeus, who arrived in Isfahan in 1652 as an envoy of the VOC, received visits the very same day from the Capuchins, Augustinians, and Discalced Carmelites, but waited an entire month before responding to these tokens of respect in the company of the director of trade in Persia, Senior Merchant Dirck Sarterius. Then, however, just six days later, Cunaeus spent an entire afternoon visiting the Augustinians, who had expressly requested it. The Augustinians visited the envoy a second time in the company of the (Calvinist) Frenchman Isaac Boutet de l'Étoile, the former housekeeper to three senior merchants of the VOC, and the widow of a Dutch merchant. Cunaeus hosted all of them for lunch "in a courteous and friendly manner." Before leaving the city, Cunaeus made parting visits to all three convents. He was offered food and drink by the Discalced Carmelites "according to their means," that is, their status as regular clerics who had taken vows of poverty.[72]

Beginning around 1700, the tsar's diplomats also claimed a place in the local status hierarchy among European Christians of different confessions. The reports of the Discalced Carmelite Leandro di Santa Cecilia offer relevant insights. After receiving visits from missionaries of his own and other orders upon his arrival in Isfahan in 1737, the provincial vicar of his order took him to see the tsar's envoy, who happened to be in the city, and the Dutch factor, both of whom received him "with many signs of affection." The Russian envoy invited the bishop of Isfahan, the Discalced Carmelite Filippo Maria di Sant'Agostino, and all of the missionaries to a banquet the following Sunday. The seating plan followed a strict "hierarchy of dignity," as Leandro di Santa Cecilia observed: the envoy did the Catholic bishop the honor of sitting across from him under a baldachin. Leandro di Santa Cecilia noted that he occupied the second place at the envoy's right, and that the latter was the first to toast to the health of the pope and the bishop.[73]

If the arriving travelers were envoys in the service of European monarchs, they were in some cases greeted before or during their entry into the city by the local Europeans, who thereby participated in staging their status. Catholic clerics were also present at the reception of the envoys of non-Catholic rulers. When President Carel Constant came to Isfahan in the summer of 1644 on behalf of the VOC, he was met by laymen and clerics of various origins outside the city, where he was invited to dine in a garden. They caroused all night and the next morning accompanied the Dutchman to his lodgings in the city. Upon his return from a journey to the court in Qazwīn, Constant was again lavishly entertained in Isfahan. Among the local clergy, the Augustinians participated in the protracted banqueting, while the Discalced Carmelites and Capuchins refused to eat outside their convents on this occasion. While this removed them from social intercourse, they explained it in terms not of confession but rather of the duty to comply with their Rule, which kept their nonattendance from becoming an affront.[74]

Envoys set great store in an appropriate retinue of laity and clergy because this displayed their capital of honor. When two Jesuits encountered an "ambassadeur" of the tsar shortly before arriving in Isfahan in 1700, they greeted "this legate of a great ruler of Europe, loyal friend and Christian." The next day they acceded to the envoy's request to enter Isfahan with his retinue and accompany him to his quarters.[75] Conversely, those present during the 1699 entry into Isfahan of Pietro Paolo di San Francesco, bishop *in partibus infidelium* of Ankara, included not just the gentlemen of the East India Companies but also members of the Russian resident's retinue. The bishop, who traveled as the envoy of various Catholic rulers (including the pope), received the same signs of courtesy from the local Protestants as those that the clerics offered to non-Catholic envoys.[76]

As the examples described here show, a practice of social intercourse independent of confession had evolved over the decades. This had not always been the case. According to the testimony of the Discalced Carmelite Juan Thadeo de San Eliseo and his close associate, the Italian traveler Pietro Della Valle, in 1617 they had faced the issue of whether contact with "heretics" was permitted in the case of the English envoy Edward Connock. In those days Connock was negotiating trade privileges on behalf of his king and the East India Company at the court of Shah ʿAbbās I, thus helping to undermine the position of the Portuguese in Persia. The Discalced Carmelite and Della Valle had resolved to visit Connock and treat him amicably since any open display of discord before an "infidel" ruler would have harmed the reputation of Christians. Apart from solidarity among Christians across confessional lines in a Muslim environment and the Discalced Carmelites' underlying interest in weakening the Portuguese *Padroado*, they also made a distinction between religious and secular existence. According to Pietro Della Valle, they wanted to show the shah that they could maintain unity in civil interactions despite religious disagreements. As justification, Della Valle pointed to the solidarity between Catholics and Protestants in the Ottoman Empire, where the English and Dutch envoys did not treat the Jesuits as enemies but were, on the contrary, the first to stand up for them. Their missionary duties also made it necessary for the Discalced Carmelites to communicate with the English envoy. Juan Thadeo de San Eliseo and Pietro Della Valle accordingly visited Edward Connock on the day of his arrival, and the diplomat made a return visit with a large retinue. After that they had always coexisted "in the best friendship."[77]

While in 1617 there had still been a discussion of whether Catholics were permitted to visit the English resident Edward Connock and cultivate his "friendship," Della Valle mentions his visit together with the provincial vicar of the Discalced Carmelites, Friar Juan Thadeo, to his successor Edward Monox in March 1620 only in passing.[78] In 1620 the provincial vicar, Della Valle, and three employees of the English factory jointly sent off a Muslim ambassador, whom ʿAbbās I dispatched to Constantinople. Such practices reveal the same integration into a transconfessional and transreligious exchange of courtesies. While the Discalced Carmelite and Della Valle commended the ambassador to the Venetian *bailo* as a "friend" to all "Franks," the English used the opportunity to send post to their envoy at the Sublime Porte.[79]

Conversely, the representatives of the English and Dutch East India Companies at first met the Capuchin Pacifique de Provins and his companions with mistrust when they arrived in 1628—not because they were Catholic missionaries, but because they feared that the friars might have a royal commission to establish a French trading company that would harm their own interests. For that reason, the English and Dutch captains at first sent employees of lower rank to visit the friars and inquire into the reason for their presence. Once assured that they were "simple clerics with no interest in matters of state or commerce," the two captains visited the Capuchins twice at their lodgings. The English captain then invited them to a banquet together with the Discalced Carmelite Juan Thadeo de San Eliseo and the Augustinian prior.[80] Once the impression of rivalry in their own field of endeavor had been dispelled, there was also room for assistance in everyday local relations and those gestures of "charity" that the Capuchin Toussaint de Landerneau attributed to representatives of the English and Dutch East India Companies in 1634.[81]

In such interactions, the shared Christian identity to which Pietro Della Valle had referred in 1617 became a common European one based on a shared capital of honor and increasingly also a civilizatory disassociation from the "Orient." In this context, the numerous visits and return visits expressed close connections among Europeans of secular and clerical status, as evident, for example, in the following description by Paul Lucas, who arrived in Isfahan in early 1701 together with the Capuchin Bernard de Bourges:

> All of the Europeans are quite united with one another and with the religious, which makes for very frequent visits, which never end without drinking. For that reason, these visits have been given the name *galopiner* [probably "running from one house to the next like messenger boys"]; instead of saying "let's make a visit" one says "let's *galopiner*." And if one is at someone's house, they say, "Welcome *Messieurs les Galopins*," and then a bottle arrives at the table.[82]

The useful services discussed in the following were integrated into these everyday relationships.

Useful Services: Transporting Mail

Functioning postal services were both a precondition for and a consequence of the multi-local activities of religious orders and trading companies. We have already explored the instrumental and symbolic significance of correspondence for the missions.[83] For the trading companies, speedy postal transport was of fundamental importance when it came to information about the given market situation and the prices of commodities in various locations. When the English, Dutch, and finally French East India Companies advanced into Asia in the seventeenth century, the missionary orders already had comparatively well-functioning networks in many parts of the continent that facilitated the transport of letters and the transmission of information about events in foreign lands. Over the course of the seventeenth century, the trading companies expanded their own networks by intensifying trade and shipping and establishing new factories. The VOC, for example, increasingly entrusted the Dutch consul in Aleppo with attending to correspondence sent via that city to other destinations, while continuing to have more or less trustworthy non-Dutch "friends" manage the transport of post between Aleppo and Isfahan.[84]

Given the lack of institutionalized postal services, their efficiency remained dependent ad hoc on the personal relationships of the participants. From the perspective of the trading companies, trustworthiness was a function not of shared religious beliefs but of the absence of economic rivalry. Relative confessional proximity did nothing to change the fact that the English and Dutch East India Companies were the fiercest competitors in the Asian trade. This placed limits on any reciprocal postal services. Letters from competitors could be held back or opened and copied.

The "friends" with local knowledge whom the VOC and the English East India Company used for postal services included Catholic missionaries. Postal services across confessional boundaries depended on the relationship that the orders cultivated with the Catholic powers in Europe. The Discalced Carmelites enjoyed a better reputation among the English and the Dutch than the Portuguese Augustinians or the French Capuchins and Jesuits because they were dependent on the Roman Curia rather than on a power with political and economic interests in Asia.

As long as the trading companies maintained no permanent settlements in Basra, the possibility of using the Discalced Carmelite convent there as an address and entrusting the friars with the transport of post between Basra and Aleppo was important for both companies. In 1650, the president and council of the East India Company in Surat recommended that their superiors in England send all letters meant for transport by land from the Mediterranean to Basra to the Italian Discalced Carmelite Ignazio di Gesù, who would forward them to the intended recipients. The friar enjoyed a good reputation, was well disposed toward the English nation, and would be at the service of the Company.[85] In 1654, the agent and factors of the English East India Company in Isfahan reported that they had thanked Felice di Sant'Antonio, who had previously lived in Basra and now resided in Isfahan as provincial vicar of the Discalced Carmelites, for his good offices in Basra sending and receiving their letters, and rewarded him "with some small matter."[86] The VOC's envoy to the Safavid court, Joan Cunaeus, for his part granted the Discalced Carmelites an annual subsidy of sixty *rijksdaaler* (the equivalent of about sixty piasters or sixty *scudi*) in 1652, along with some commodities and spices for their own use in exchange for postal services in Basra.[87] By giving the trading companies the opportunity to use their correspondence networks, the missionaries were thus able to earn income that was very welcome in their generally precarious financial situation.

Sometimes members of several orders were involved in postal services. In 1652, Joan Cunaeus entrusted his mail from Shiraz to Europe to the Discalced Carmelites, who sent it to the Capuchins in Aleppo at an Arabic address. The letters from Bandar 'Abbās to the Netherlands were supposed to be dispatched by courier to Baghdad and handed to the Capuchins there, who were to forward them as quickly as possible to the Dutch consul in Aleppo.[88] The political circumstances had changed by 1672: because of the war with France, it was important to keep the letters from falling into the hands of the French Capuchins. The Capuchin Raphaël du Mans not only served the shah as a translator and interpreter but also, together with Armenian merchants, arranged for the dispatch of post and the flow of information between Western Europe and the Safavid court. The VOC suspected the friar of manipulating these services to its detriment.[89]

Situations of commercial and political rivalry did not necessarily always impede cooperation in small matters. In 1667, a VOC courier transported letters from Aleppo to Isfahan for the agents of the English and French East India Companies and the French Capuchins along with his employers' letters. In those days, the guardian of the Capuchins entrusted a VOC courier with forwarding the correspondence of the French consul in Aleppo from Isfahan to Surat. To be on the safe side, he also gave the English courier departing at the same time a note referring to the consul's correspondence. In the spring of 1668, two VOC couriers brought post from Syria to the guardian of the Capuchins as well as the English, the Discalced Carmelites, and the Jesuits.[90]

While the trading companies focused on the practical utility of the postal services, Catholic clerics occasionally wondered whether they were actually opportune and permissible. Because of the Dutch conquest of Portuguese possessions in South Asia, in the 1650s the Discalced Carmelites in Basra found themselves under particular pressure to justify the provision of postal services for the enemies of a Catholic power. On the positive side, the letters usually referred to business matters only, and the Discalced Carmelites benefited from the "great alms" of sixty piasters a year they received from the Dutch (this is the subsidy granted in 1652 by Cunaeus) and many other signs of favor, including presents and free passage for members of the order on Dutch ships between the Persian Gulf and India. The Discalced Carmelites stressed that they could also send their own post from Basra via the Dutch and English couriers.[91]

The trading companies provided services associated with the "friendship" between the parties not just by sending letters but also by transferring money. Unlike postal services, these favors were not reciprocal. In 1666, for example, the prior of the Discalced Carmelites asked the *directeur* of the VOC in Isfahan—"a Dutchman who is our friend"—to transfer 100 *zecchini di oro* (around 194 *scudi*) to the port of Tatta in India.[92] Even war between the powers was not always an obstacle to such services. In 1703, during the war of the Spanish succession, the French bishop of Babylon Louis-Marie Pidou de Saint-Olon reached an agreement with the "very honorable agent" of the English East India Company regarding the transfer of money for the *Missions étrangères* from France to Isfahan. As soon as the agent learned that the money had arrived with the English consul in Aleppo, he paid it to the bishop in Isfahan.[93]

Knowledge and Relationships

When the Venetian Ambrogio Bembo reported how he had received many pieces of news and stories from Europe and Asia during his stay in Isfahan, he emphasized the importance of the orders' information networks. The news from Europe arrived via the Capuchins, Jesuits, and other Frenchmen, and letters from laypeople containing printed accounts from France. News from the East Indies and Portugal reached the Augustinians and Discalced Carmelites. Thanks to their settlements, the Discalced Carmelites also received news from the Ottoman Empire. According to Bembo, the significance of these information networks was also recognized by Persians, many of whom visited the friars in their convents when they wanted to know what was going on in Europe. The friars then explained everything to them in Farsi, and in turn received reports about events in Persia. This knowledge then put them in a position to present themselves to other Europeans as experts on Persia.[94] Bembo's account is confirmed by the documentation of the trading companies. In 1654, thanks to the correspondence networks of the Armenians and the Discalced Carmelites, the representatives of the English East India Company in Isfahan learned of the arrival in northern Persia of the English envoy Henry Bard, Viscount Bellomont. The *Journal* of Joan Cunaeus's legation shows how communicating knowledge also helped to cultivate relationships: after receiving letters from Aleppo, a Capuchin went to see the VOC's envoy to share the news of European politics that they contained.[95]

The importance of sharing knowledge and contacts becomes particularly evident in the example of the Capuchin Raphaël du Mans, already discussed in connection with the services he performed as an interpreter and translator at court during his nearly fifty-year sojourn in Persia from 1647 to 1696. According to an account that one of his confrères penned after the Capuchin's death in 1696, Raphaël du Mans had been loved for his "good offices" by "all Europeans, Englishmen, Dutchmen and other Franks."[96] In fact, his contemporaries of various ranks and religions considered the French Capuchin to be the very epitome of a well-connected missionary and expert on the country, who was both admired and feared for it. In his *État de la Perse* the Capuchin compiled an impressive wealth of knowledge about the beliefs and customs of Persian Muslims. Many travelers lauded the richness of the friar's library. The few surviving letters show how Raphaël du Mans used his correspondence to convey information about relationships and events on the ground and in the broader Asian context to his addressees, and to acquire information in return. The Capuchin became one of the key resources in Isfahan for visitors of various confessions. The French Huguenot Jean-Baptiste Tavernier, for example, who had traveled from Aleppo to Isfahan with Raphaël du Mans in 1647, maintained close relations with the Capuchins during his later commercial trips to Persia; when he departed for India in 1665 he left the friars "good alms" in gratitude for their services as translators and for the connections at court that Friar Raphaël had arranged for his business.[97] Tavernier also repaid the Capuchins with his mercantile connections: in 1662, the Capuchin Valentin d'Angers had asked his "old and singular friend and benefactor" Tavernier to acquire for him a breviary, a new edition of the works of Thomas à Kempis, and the Latin-French dictionary by the Jesuit Philibert Monet.[98]

The jewel merchant Jean Chardin, also a French Huguenot, lodged with the Capuchins and Discalced Carmelites several times during his sojourns in Persia in the years 1666 to 1667, 1669, and 1672 to 1677. While living at the Capuchin hospice during his first stay, Friar Raphaël introduced him to a Sufi and to learned Muslims, including an astronomer who made astrolabes. He allowed Chardin and Tavernier to read his *État de la Perse* and other writings, which in this way would influence the

Enlightenment view of Persia via the two Huguenots' printed travelogues. After his final stay in Isfahan, Chardin continued to cultivate his contact through correspondence. In a text written in 1680 while on his way back to Europe, he praised the Capuchin as the source of the best information to be found in accounts by travelers of all nations.[99] When the Englishman John Fryer, a physician for the East India Company, visited Isfahan for a few weeks in 1677, like Chardin he praised the quality of the information he acquired from Raphaël du Mans. The Capuchin was "not only a holy man" with an exemplary way of life but also "discreet and learned" and "well acquainted with the country."[100] In *The Present State of Persia*, Fryer incorporated information and interpretations from the Capuchin's texts.

The Dutchman Ludwig Fabritius, who came to Isfahan twice in the 1680s as a Swedish envoy, received a friendly reception not just from Raphaël du Mans but also from other missionaries. In 1684 Fabritius commended two traveling companions who continued on to Shiraz to the care of the prior of the Discalced Carmelites there, Athanase de Sainte-Thérèse; at the same time, he asked Athanase de Sainte-Thérèse to purchase a "small barrel of the best and darkest Shiraz wine," which he wished to send to the king of Sweden.[101] Raphaël du Mans also assisted the members of the second Swedish legation (1684 to 1686). Shortly after their arrival in late March 1684 he gave them a brief introduction to the Turkish language, one of the languages of the Safavid court. Engelbert Kaempfer, secretary of the Swedish legation, formed a closer relationship with Friar Raphaël, whom he described as a "man of the highest candor and erudition." The friar maintained a correspondence with Kaempfer, the son of a Lutheran pastor, for at least two years after Kaempfer's departure in November 1685.[102] Friar Raphaël met the practical need for information of the legation secretary Kaempfer as well as the *curiositas* of the polymath. In this way, Kaempfer acquired information about how the legation's requests were received at court, but also a condensed version of the description of Persia that the Capuchin wrote specifically for him in 1684, based on his *État de la Perse*. When asked to provide a list of all the schools, mosques, and markets of Isfahan, Friar Raphaël consulted a Shi'a cleric.[103]

The respect that Raphaël du Mans enjoyed locally thus depended, as these examples show, largely on his ability to convey knowledge and broker connections. At the same time, the very services that secular travelers praised could also be cited as evidence of the rather unorthodox lives of the missionaries in Isfahan and New Julfa. For instance, the Jesuit Jacques Tilhac complained that the Capuchin Raphaël du Mans had spent more than fifty years cultivating his conversational abilities with "some gentlemen of the court and men of letters." For Tilhac, Friar Raphaël's connections with courtiers and Muslim scholars, so appreciated by secular travelers, symbolized the unobservant life not just of the Capuchin, but of the missionaries in Persia more generally.[104]

The degree of familiarity with local conditions in Isfahan that Raphaël du Mans embodied was unmatched by any European layman of the seventeenth or eighteenth centuries. Conversely, the agents and merchants of the trading companies played a significant role in brokering relationships in settings beyond the court. Having their protection was very important particularly in the port cities of the Persian Gulf, since the missionaries' connections at court counted little there, while the economic and military might of the trading companies was all the more valuable. Starting in the second half of the seventeenth century, such relationships also grew in importance in the Safavid heartland. In 1673, Ange de Saint-Joseph, prior of the convent in Isfahan, defended himself against accusations of being too friendly with the heretic laity, remarking that those in Rome needed to realize that for a number of years, the missionaries had only been tolerated in Persia because they were associated with the English and Dutch trading companies and their personnel.[105] Given the precarious security situation after the toppling of the Safavids, the protection of the trading companies became more important even in Isfahan and New Julfa. Cornelio di San Giuseppe reported of his time in Isfahan between 1743 and 1745 that the English factor had convinced Nādir Šāh to reaffirm the old privileges of the Discalced Carmelites and thereby exempt them from the annual taxes they had to pay for their house and garden.[106]

Alms, Gifts, and Loans

In the 1740s, the English factor's protection did not stop at interceding with the monarch. Apart from numerous alms, he also paid for a new habit for every missionary and the Catholic bishop each year. The Englishman also reportedly supplied the latter, a Discalced Carmelite, with bread, wine, and other items daily. Similar indications could already be found much earlier, but especially during the hard times that followed the fall of the Safavids in 1722. In the 1720s, Nicolaas Schorer, captain of the VOC factory in Isfahan, helped the destitute Jesuits with alms and invited them to dine at his home on Sundays, so that they could eat their fill at least once a week and have something other than bread, water, and pulses. In order to survive, the fathers, who were deeply in debt, had been forced to sell part of the church silver. They lacked the funds to repair their now dilapidated house in New Julfa.[107]

Referring to the gifts as alms implied that these were works of charity, provided without any expectation of material return gifts. As works of mercy, alms referred to the transcendental in the early modern period: giving alms to religious who had dedicated themselves to a life of poverty was among the good works with which Christians could, in Catholic teaching, increase their capital of grace. The reward would accordingly follow not in this world but the next.

But what did alms mean within the social practice of the European diaspora in Persia? What was the relationship of alms to other material gifts from the laity, especially loans provided at conditions that depended on the personal relationship between the parties? The sources offer no indication that Protestants in Isfahan and New Julfa adopted Tridentine notions of the efficacy of good works. For them, alms, together with other forms of material support, were primarily part of a secular gift exchange economy. This did not exclude a transcendental dimension, however. While they could not expect return gifts of similar material value from the clerics, they did expect correspondence, including services as religious specialists, as we will see in the next section.

Critics within the Catholic Church took offense at the obligation of correspondence with non-Catholics associated with the gifts. In 1712, Gratien de Galisson, coadjutor of the bishop of Babylon, ventriloquized the criticism of ʿAlī-Qulī Ǧadīd al-Islām, a former Portuguese Augustinian who had converted to Islam. According to him, ʿAlī-

Qulī Ğadīd al-Islām could not bear it that the missionaries occasionally supported the English simply because they received all the fabric for their habits from them, along with other aid and money.[108] Like the regular clergy, the priests of the *Missions étrangères*, to which Galisson himself belonged, also sought English and Dutch support. After the 1685 death in Hamadan of François Picquet, bishop of Babylon and apostolic vicar of Isfahan, François Sanson, priest of the *Missions étrangères,* traveled to the court at Isfahan to secure the protection necessary to continue the mission in Hamadan. While he enlisted the help of the French-born superiors of the Capuchins and Jesuits and two French laymen in the service of the shah for his petitions at court, when it came to the *Missions étrangères*' activities in Southeast Asia, he cultivated "friendship" with employees of the Dutch and English East India Companies.[109]

The missionaries also borrowed money from Protestants. In part, these loans were expressly associated with the "friendship" and "good correspondence" between creditors and debtors. In the late 1710s and the 1720s, loans at favorable conditions, which the Discalced Carmelites received from the English and Dutch, stood alongside alms and gifts. The best-documented relationship between debtor and creditor is that between the Dominican Barnaba Fedeli di Milano, apostolic vicar and later bishop of Isfahan, and Jacques Rousseau. The first mention of Rousseau in the Dominican's correspondence with the *Propaganda Fide* came in 1716, when he was referred to as a "Genevan merchant" in a letter. Because of a falling out with the Sceriman family, some of whose members lived in Italy, Barnaba, then apostolic vicar of the diocese of Isfahan, had to borrow 250 *scudi* from Rousseau. The *Propaganda Fide* was supposed to repay the money to his brother in Geneva, Jean-François Rousseau, out of the subsidies for the Dominican mission. In 1718, Barnaba Fedeli reported to Rome that he had turned to Jacques Rousseau again because the money for the missionaries had not arrived and they had nothing to live on. No one but the "mercante di Ginevra" wanted to lend him money. Jacques Rousseau paid the apostolic vicar an advance of 100 *scudi* on the subsidies for 1718; he gave the prior of the Dominicans, Arcangelo da Brescia, a further loan of 150 *scudi*, also against the subsidies. Barnaba Fedeli asked the *Propaganda Fide* to reimburse the money immediately upon the presentation of the bills of exchange.[110]

In the 1720s, Rousseau became the most important creditor of Barnaba Fedeli di Milano, then Catholic bishop of Isfahan. The relationship was in both their interests and also evidence of a social relationship that surpassed the purely economic: For several years beginning in 1722, the Afghan invasion of Persia interrupted the bishop's connections with the *Propaganda Fide* in Rome, which was not in a position to send subsidies to the missionaries in Persia. Jacques Rousseau for his part wanted to send part of his savings to safety in Geneva because of the many dangers of the time. He also had to find a way to pay for deliveries from Geneva. Bills of exchange to be paid to his brother Jean-François in Geneva provided Rousseau with a comparatively secure opportunity to transfer money, provided that his brother was reimbursed relatively promptly. Between 1722, the year of the Afghan siege and conquest of Isfahan, and 1731, the year of Barnaba Fedeli di Milano's death, Jacques Rousseau loaned the bishop 1,050 *scudi* in several installments; during that same period, the Dominican received just 500 *scudi* of credit from the Scerimans, who had previously been his most important creditors, against the subsidies paid out in Rome.

In early modern societies, the economic was firmly linked with the religious and the social.[111] Accordingly, the act of borrowing from non-Catholics required an explanation at least to the Curia that took account of not just material considerations but also the values and norms that viewed credit relations as part of a moral economy: as Bishop Fedeli wrote to the prefects of the *Propaganda Fide* in 1728 to justify his repeatedly borrowing from a Calvinist, "no other merchant, even a Catholic," had "favored" him with "the fine manners, the love, and the very advantageous exchange" that Jacques Rousseau had.[112] When the *Propaganda Fide* refused to pay back a bill of exchange for 300 *scudi* after the bishop's death because it had already covered all of the prelate's claims, a kinsman of the bishop, Count Gian Antonio Fedeli, stated that the congregation had to fulfill "the laws of good faith [even] to those who lived according to a different [religious] law." The dead man's "personal dignity" and trust in the "good faith" of his successors were to be preserved by paying the bill of exchange.[113]

In Persia, the loans by a Genevan clockmaker and merchant to a Catholic missionary and bishop were nothing surprising. Transconfessional credit relationships had long been important for missionaries there. When the Capuchins acquired their own house in 1628 after founding the mission, the captain of the Dutch East India Company, Nicolaas Jacobsz Overschie, advanced them the purchase price. The closeness to the missionaries confirmed by loans was part of the relationship capital that Jacques Rousseau passed down to his son Jean-François-Xavier and which he was able to take with him from New Julfa to Basra. The son went to school with the Jesuits in New Julfa, who had also borrowed money from Jacques Rousseau. After fleeing New Julfa in 1754, the young Rousseau's new beginning in Basra was facilitated by, among others, the bishop of Babylon, Emmanuel Ballyet de Saint-Albert, a "friend" of his father's.[114] In 1773 the son of a Geneva clockmaker used his connections with the Discalced Carmelites to obtain a knighthood in the order of San Giovanni in Laterano from Pope Clement XIV through the mediation of the *praepositus generalis* and the prefect of the *Propaganda Fide* as a reward for his services to the order of the Discalced Carmelites and the Catholic faith in Persia and Basra.[115] The outcome was typical of the way in which services dependent upon status related to one another in a gift exchange economy: in this case, the relational resources of the clerics and the prestige associated with the papal order corresponded to the services rendered by a merchant in the form of cheap credit and protection.

*

To summarize, "friendship" within the European diaspora did not obey a logic of equal value, but rather a duty of correspondence that the participants performed according to their own, individual possibilities in keeping with their rank. This was particularly true of relationships involving the regular clergy. Because of their vows of poverty, they could accept alms, gifts, and material benefits such as inexpensive loans or free passage on ships without being obliged to reciprocate in kind. When religious did give presents to the laity, these gifts created an obligation in the recipient not by virtue of their material value but as expressions of personal thoughtfulness. This was the case, for example, when the superiors of the Discalced Carmelites in Rome sent olives from Italy to the commandant of the VOC in Bandar ʿAbbās.[116] Because of the differences in status, gifts were only of equal value in a few areas. In Persia, the reciprocal nature of useful services was most pronounced in the field of postal transport, where ecclesiastical and commercial networks complemented one another splendidly without creating competition because of the different objectives of the actors.

To be sure, the difference in status exempted the regular clergy from the obligation to provide return gifts of equal value. It did not, however, relieve them of the duty of correspondence, which they fulfilled by means of services befitting their status. Their radical abnegation of the "world" and the attendant ideal of nonentanglement in turn influenced the "world." For example, this disregard for temporal concerns formed the basis of the trust that Protestants also placed in the postal services of the regular clergy such as the Discalced Carmelites, whom they did not view as economic competitors.

The ability to arbitrate conflicts was located at the intersection of religion and society. It rested on the reputation of leading a godly life removed from worldly concerns and thus had been exercised in Europe since the Middle Ages by the mendicant orders in particular. In Western Europe, too, we find occasional evidence of the transconfessional involvement of religious in deescalating conflicts.[117] In the following episode reported by Jean-Baptiste Tavernier, this activity nevertheless seems specific to the diaspora in its integration into a confessionally mixed sociability between laymen and clerics. The French Calvinist describes how Portuguese Augustinians and French Capuchins in Isfahan jointly resolved an affair of honor between the agent of the English East India Company and the Dutch envoy Carel Constant, who had challenged the Englishman to a duel after consuming a good deal of alcohol. During the reconciliation in the Augustinian convent, the English agent had first to drink to the Dutchman's health together with the friars. Then the Dutchman and his retinue toasted the health of the Englishman, the clerics, and the other "Franks" present. Finally, all of them spent the rest of the day at the Augustinian convent where, as a sign of renewed "good correspondence," they ate lunch and dinner together.[118]

The arbitration of the affair of honor between a Dutchman and an Englishman reveals that even non-Catholics assigned the participating Augustinians and Capuchins status-specific qualities as religious that distinguished them from the laity. The Augustinians and Capuchins succeeded in interrupting the exchange of insults by invoking the shared Christian commandments of forgiveness and reconciliation and thereby persuading the Dutchman, who believed his honor had been violated, to withdraw his challenge to a duel as a means of defending his honor. Such a success rested not just on the social esteem in which the involved religious were held. It also shows that, in the European diaspora, shared Christian values could be mobilized across confessional boundaries. This brings us to the question of the specific nature of religiosity in the diaspora.

Shared Religious Practices in the Diaspora

When Catholic clerics spent weeks or months traveling with Europeans of other confessions in an unfamiliar environment, the common ground between Christians came to outweigh confessional differences, although such differences were not forgotten altogether. The following example drives this home. The Calvinist Jean-Baptiste Tavernier met the Capuchin Raphaël du Mans, who would later put him up in Isfahan, in March 1647, on the way from Aleppo to Hamadan during his third journey to Persia. At that time, Friar Raphaël was at the beginning of his long stay in Persia. He was traveling with another Capuchin for whom Tavernier would later commission a grave with an epitaph in Surat. The two Capuchins and the Calvinist Tavernier were welcomed in the Nestorian and Armenian communities between Urfa and Mosul because they were all Christians. On one occasion, Tavernier and the Capuchins visited an Armenian church in which a vardapet was celebrating mass. After the service, the vardapet gave a tour of the church and cemetery to the travelers, whom he recognized as Christian "Franks," and showed them the grave of a saint and the pedestal of a statue of a saint, which was venerated as miraculous. On Easter Sunday, 1647, Tavernier invited the two Capuchins to a meal to mark the holiday, but, being a Protestant, he did not attend the friars' Easter mass.[119] In contrast, the travelogue of a Catholic "barber" from the margravate of Baden who passed through Persia in 1700 in the company of two Jesuit priests and two novices on their way to India noted that the non-Catholic Christians in the caravan from Isfahan to Bandar ʿAbbās also "reverently" attended the mass and sang the great litany daily with the others.[120]

The Christian mutuality that emerges in such episodes was part of the practice of "friendship" and "good correspondence" discussed in the previous subchapter. The line that Tavernier drew between the social occasion of a shared Easter meal and the sacramental act of the Easter mass was crossed in the second case. A similar situation arose when missionaries in Isfahan and New Julfa invited Christians of different confessions to their church on the occasion of a church feast. Then, too, the exchange of courtesies had a religious connotation, which the participants definitely noted, but which in Isfahan was no impediment to "amicable" interactions. In his account of the legation of Frederick III of Schleswig-Holstein-Gottorf, for example, Adam Olearius describes how in 1637 the envoys with their entire retinue, along with a Russian, an "Armenian archbishop with a number of priests," and the English merchants, were invited to celebrate the birth of the Virgin Mary by the "Catholic Spanish monks, the friars of the Augustinian order." "Among the infidels," the shared "Christian name" bridged the confessional differences that in Europe would have divided the hosts from their guests: "For although these nations may dislike each other for reasons of religion in their places in Christendom, here they nevertheless stayed together among infidels because of the Christian name and cultivated rather good friendship among one another." The Augustinians inviting the Lutheran envoys and their retinue to attend mass in their church was part of this, in clear violation of the Roman prohibition of *communicatio in sacris*. Olearius describes how they were first led to mass in the church and then invited to a banquet. They spent the rest of the day in the convent's "fine pleasure gardens" "with good conversation and jolly music." The invitation to a church festival was integrated into the practice of visits and return visits discussed in the preceding subchapter. It was followed by the invitation to a banquet by the *kalāntar* of the Armenian community of New Julfa and his brothers, in which the legation from Schleswig-Holstein participated together with the prior and an Augustinian friar who served as "senior interpreter." Finally, the envoys from Schleswig-Holstein in turn issued an invitation to a "princely banquet" on October 1, 1637: their guests were the *kalāntar* with his two brothers, the "most distinguished members of the English Company," "a number of Frenchmen," the "Spanish Augustinians," and "a number of Italian Carmelite monks."[121]

While the social dimension clearly dominated when Christian clerics and laypeople participated in Muslim feast days, when it came to Christian holidays, the church authorities worried about whether the shared practices recognized "schismatics" and "heretics" as more or less orthodox. When Bishop Bernard de Sainte-Thérèse accused the Discalced Carmelite provincial vicar of visiting the English at Christmas to wish them a good holiday, the vicar countered that the English honored the Lord's birthday, despite their "errors."

> He also accuses me of cultivating friendship with the English gentlemen and wishing them a good holiday on the day of our Lord's birth. All of this is true, and since they already honor His birth, may it please the Lord in His mercy to make them aware of the error in which they live. To maintain good correspondence with the aforementioned gentlemen is appropriate, because they could do us much harm with the king [shah] if they so desired; I am also obligated by the signs of charity [alms] that they offer us from time to time.[122]

In what follows, shared Christian practices will be explored with a focus on rituals in which the confessional churches demanded particular clarity: the Eucharist, baptism, marriage, and funerals. With the exception of burials, the Catholic Church considered these rituals to be sacraments. For that reason, it rejected, in principle, participation by non-Catholics. Boundary violations gave rise to controversies, which is why the sources are more abundant than in less sensitive areas. As in other confessionally mixed contexts, in Persia, too, the controversies arose from the fact that the rituals administered by the confessional churches all possessed both a religious and a social character. This becomes especially obvious in the consecration of a bishop, who is thereby confirmed in both his ecclesiastical office and his superior social position. Based on its social relevance, this ritual attracted a confessionally mixed audience in Isfahan. Thus in 1696, the consecration of Élie de Saint-Albert as bishop of Isfahan was attended by "all of the Europeans" at the Persian court, including Frans Castelijn as head of the VOC branch there, despite the Discalced Carmelite's reputation as a confessional agitator.[123] If the social significance of the bishop's installation in office encouraged the highest ranking representative of the VOC to attend the consecration, other rituals also posed the question of transconfessional religious content.

Celebrating Mass in Private Homes

Writing to the superiors of his order in 1660, Aimé Chézaud described the fact that he could say mass every Sunday and holiday in the house of Isaac Boutet de l'Étoile for his family and neighbors as one of the few tangible successes of the mission in Isfahan.[124] Boutet de l'Étoile was a Calvinist, but upon his marriage to an Armenian woman in 1643 he had been obliged to promise the Capuchin Valentin d'Angers, who performed the wedding, that he would raise all of their children as Catholics. He not only fulfilled this condition but maintained close relations with the Capuchins and Jesuits for the rest of his life. In 1662, the Jesuit Aimé Chézaud spoke of Isaac Boutet de l'Étoile as "one of our friends, despite being a Calvinist."[125] When the Capuchin Raphaël du Mans gave one of his sons a recommendation to the French consul in Aleppo in 1667, he referred to more than thirty years of "close friendship and correspondence" between the family and the friars. Before his death earlier that year, Boutet de l'Étoile had scarcely done anything without consulting him, and bid him, "as refuge, counsel, and true friend" in all situations, to continue, even after his demise, to bestow his "affection" upon his widow and children. He, Raphaël du Mans, had taught the two sons Louis and François the fundamentals of the faith as well as reading and writing.[126]

Boutet de l'Étoile himself converted to Catholicism on his deathbed. The Jesuit Claude-Ignace Mercier took credit for hearing the dying man's confession and administering extreme unction.[127] To be sure, various descendants of Isaac Boutet de l'Étoile married Protestants and non-Uniate Eastern Christians, seemingly calling into question the family's turn to Catholicism. One of Isaac's daughters, Angela, for example, left the Catholic faith when she married the son of the English East India Company's interpreter, a non-Catholic Eastern Christian. Later, however, while gravely ill, she made a general confession to a Discalced Carmelite. Overall, the descendants of Isaac Boutet de l'Étoile remained closely tied to the Jesuits; in the early eighteenth century they were reportedly numerous enough to fill the Jesuit church.[128] Finally, Reine de l'Étoile and her Genevan husband Jacques Rousseau also cultivated their relationship with the Jesuits, as we have seen. The Capuchins and Jesuits could thus consider the conversion of Isaac Boutet de l'Étoile's Armenian wife, their children, and eventually the paterfamilias himself a success of their mission strategy that accepted compromises in confessional orthodoxy with the aim of creating social proximity and gaining the trust of people of other faiths. This included mixed marriage, which I will discuss below, and also the Jesuit celebration of masses in a Huguenot's home.

In an effort to gain access to the houses of non-Catholic Christians, the Jesuits were not the only clerics to say mass in private homes in the Christian quarter of New Julfa. Apart from Aimé Chézaud, the Augustinians and the vicar of the bishop of Babylon also did so in the early 1660s. According to Ange de Saint-Joseph's *Pharmacopoea persica*, the respect that Friar Matteo di San Giuseppe had acquired as a physician enabled him to offer instruction in the English East India Company's house in Bandar ʿAbbās to the Indian-born servants of the English and the Dutch alongside Catholic Christians.[129] While Ange de Saint-Joseph left open the question of whether or not his fellow friar also celebrated mass in the house of the English East India Company, other accounts show that the Discalced Carmelites did so when they enjoyed the hospitality of the English or Dutch East India Company. Although these trading companies represented Protestant powers, their personnel included Catholic and non-Uniate Eastern Christians. Moreover, their houses sometimes also accommodated merchants of varying origin. In 1726, Bishop Barnaba Fedeli di Milano wrote a letter to the *Propaganda Fide* in which he reported a Discalced Carmelite who had traveled from Bandar ʿAbbās to Isfahan together with an agent of the English East India Company. Since he did not belong to the mission, the friar was not housed by his order, but instead stayed in the English factory. There he was permitted to say mass, since five or six French Catholic soldiers were also accommodated in the English house. Furthermore, he performed this service in the Dutch factory and the house of a Muslim in which Christians also lived.[130]

If we follow Bishop Barnaba Fedeli's correspondence with the *Propaganda Fide*, we find that it was mainly the Jesuits who met the demand for masses in private homes in Isfahan in the 1720s. In so doing, they violated the standards of the post-Tridentine Church in two respects: they took the sacred into the unconsecrated space of private houses and they practiced *communicatio in sacris* if non-Catholics were also present. The Dominican accordingly took such masses as an occasion to exercise his powers as bishop. When he forbade such celebrations, he combined orthodoxy in the sense intended by the post-Tridentine Church with the assertion that the missionaries were subject to his jurisdiction as the "delegate of the Holy See."[131]

Fedeli first opposed the celebration of masses in private homes in a 1720 dispute with Consul Ange de Gardane and the Jesuits, when, under threat of suspension *a divinis*, he forbade all missionaries to celebrate mass in the consul's house chapel on the holy days of the Church. In 1725, citing the Council of Trent, the bishop repeated a general prohibition on celebrating mass in the homes of the laity. Once again, he threatened clerics who did so with suspension *a divinis* and laypeople with an interdict. The Jesuits resisted these episcopal orders, as did the Discalced Carmelites. Citing the privileges of their order, the Jesuits explicitly rejected the claim to jurisdiction that the episcopal decree implied; the bishop, in their view, was usurping an authority over the Society of Jesus that belonged to the pope alone. As a result, they could not and were not obliged to obey him. The regular clergy were not the bishop's "subjects," and he should treat them not as "servants," but as "brothers and friends."[132] The Discalced Carmelites for their part pointed to the privileges granted to them for the Persian mission by Clement VIII and Paul V.[133]

The fact that the masses were celebrated in the house of a Catholic did not exclude non-Catholics from participating. Faced with the resistance of the regular clergy who rejected his authority, Bishop Fedeli presented a relevant case to the *Propaganda Fide* in 1726. In 1724 a Jesuit had begun to say mass regularly in the house of the Dutch Syrian-Catholic interpreter family Sahid, to whom the fathers were obligated because of extensive donations to furnish their church. At first, the bishop had permitted the father to do so as an exception, because he claimed that the interpreter's frail mother was also in the house. Then, however, he had learned that this was no longer the case and that the mass was being celebrated in a room that was otherwise used for gathering, eating and drinking, playing games, and sleeping. Finally, he had heard that the (Protestant) captain of the Dutch attended the masses together with numerous members of his household and "schismatic Armenians." A letter that Fedeli wrote to the Jesuit superior Father Lagarde had not stopped Lagarde from continuing to say mass at the home of the Dutch interpreters. Lagarde had celebrated mass in their house not just on All Souls' Day but also the following day after engaging in "lively conversation" with fifteen or sixteen laypeople, "schismatics" and "heretics," who had eaten, drunk, and laughed together, and then slept topsy-turvy in the same room, according to the custom of the country. The bishop asked the *Propaganda Fide* whether he should continue to tolerate this "disobedience." Should he allow even Easter communion to be administered in the houses of laymen, and not just in Catholic but also in "heretical" houses?[134]

Celebrating mass in private homes thus posed the risk that the sacraments might be desecrated in more ways than one: through administration in an inappropriate setting and also through sacramental community with non-Catholics. However, the missionaries could also understand such celebrations of the mass as opportunities to introduce "schismatics" and "heretics" to the Catholic Church. The same ambiguity surrounded the practice of mixed marriage as well.

Mixed Marriages

In 1643, the Capuchin Valentin d'Angers celebrated the marriage of Isaac Boutet de l'Étoile and an Armenian woman under the condition that all of their children would be raised in the Catholic faith. What would be justified in retrospect as part of a successful mission strategy—the deathbed conversion of the paterfamilias and his descendants' relationships with the missionaries—was, at the time of the wedding, little more than a response to the close relations among families of different confessions. At the beginning of the eighteenth century, according to the Dutchman Cornelis de Bruyn, most men of European origin in Persia were married to "schismatic" Armenian women, and the children of these marriages followed their mother's religion.[135] Missionaries of all the orders active in Isfahan were involved in the weddings: in an attempt to prevent marriages between employees and Armenian or other local Christian women not approved by the VOC, the Dutch envoy Joan Cunaeus thus turned to the Discalced Carmelites, the Capuchins, and the Augustinians alike in 1652 to elicit a formal promise to perform such marriage ceremonies only if presented with written permission from the trading company.[136]

While the VOC sought to prevent marriages with local women to stop their employees from putting down roots and to retain their undivided loyalty, from a Roman perspective mixed marriages contradicted the sacramental character of matrimony, which the post-Tridentine Church elevated to one of the touchstones of orthodoxy. In the words of John Bossy, marriage was transformed "from a social process which the Church guaranteed to an ecclesiastical process which it administered."[137] On a symbolic level, this "ecclesiasticalization" of marriage was expressed in the fact that, according to the *Rituale romanum* of 1614, it was contracted at the altar. Mixed marriages required either the conversion of the partner belonging to another confession or a dispensation. Unless these conditions were met, no Catholic priest was allowed to celebrate a marriage. By requiring the publication of the banns of marriage and their celebration in the church, which necessitated the presence of a priest, the Council of Trent's *Tametsi* decree of 1563 created the prerequisites for the invalidation of mixed marriages.[138] The decree had widespread consequences, as in Catholic territories the legal status of a marriage depended on the Church. Yet in confessionally mixed Christian communities subject to no Catholic secular authority where legally binding marriages could be concluded without the presence of a Catholic priest—the Netherlands, as well as the diasporas under Muslim rule in the Mediterranean region and in Asia—ecclesiastical actors on all levels, from the missionaries on the ground to the Curia, had to decide how far to tolerate deviations from canon law or to integrate mixed marriages into the ecclesiastical order with formal dispensations.

Because violations of matrimonial law had increasingly been treated as religious offenses since the sixteenth century, in conflict situations criticism of mixed marriages was well suited to highlight the critic's own orthodoxy, and thus to position him favorably in the eyes of higher-ranking authorities. In other cases, it was newcomers without local experience who perceived the specific local practices as "abuses." This was how the knowledge of such practices traveled from Persia to Rome in the first place, to the *Propaganda Fide*, the Holy Office, and the superiors of the orders. Since the marriage registers from Isfahan and New Julfa have not survived, historians also have to rely on these accounts.

Ten months after arriving in Persia, in 1630 the Discalced Carmelite Ignazio di Gesù wrote to the *praepositus generalis* of his order to describe the sorry state of affairs he had discovered. This included the fact that one of the three houses available to the Discalced Carmelites was inhabited by three families who were unworthy to live in a house belonging to regular clerics. Some years before, one of these families had given the Dutch captain a young woman as a "concubine." This had now happened again, since a Jacobite priest also residing in the friars' house had offered two daughters to the new captain of the VOC and another Dutchman. This had caused "much scandal" and "dishonor" again. The Discalced Carmelites had remedied the situation, however, by kicking the people out of the house. What Ignazio di Gesù described as "concubinage" would have been a perfectly legal marriage from the perspective of the participants, since the friar himself described the relationship as a "contract."[139]

When Bishop Bernard de Sainte-Thérèse settled in Isfahan in 1640 and imposed his jurisdictional authority as apostolic vicar, the norms of the post-Tridentine Church clashed with those of local society with unprecedented severity. In letters to his sister, he painted conditions in the darkest colors. All that happened in Isfahan were "evil deeds and persecution by the heretics and bad Christians of the country, who called themselves Catholics but were worse than the Mohammedans." They had come to "live according to their freedom" and the clergy allowed them to do so. If he wished to create order as bishop, they threatened him with violence and conversion to Islam. Since the limits of his jurisdictional authority were drawn too narrowly to suppress "the dreadful manners" of the "Franks," after less than one year Bernard de Sainte-Thérèse was already speaking of returning to Europe. The missionaries baptized the children of Protestants, and despite his entreaties and prohibitions did not cease to see them, visit them, eat with them, and welcome them to their convents.

When Bernard de Sainte-Thérèse complained of the "despicable and scandalous life" of Europeans in Isfahan and New Julfa, he was especially dismayed by the local practices of mixed marriage. In May 1641 he reported to his sister that he had just tried to stop the relationship between a poor French Catholic woman and a Dutchman from the VOC. Although he had threatened the girl's uncle, under whose authority she lived, with excommunication, he had not been able to prevent the Dutchman from "prostituting" the girl with her uncle's consent. "All the poor Catholic daughters" only served "these depraved Dutchmen, Englishmen, and Frenchmen."[140] Despite the wording, the relationships that the bishop sought to prevent were by no means primarily illicit. The issue, instead, was the validity and permissibility of noncanonical mixed marriages, which Catholic parents used as an opportunity to increase the economic and social capital of their families.

Bernard de Sainte-Thérèse's barely two-year tenure in Isfahan put the issue of confessional orthodoxy front and center in the conflicts between the Capuchins, Discalced Carmelites, and Augustinians. In 1657, the Capuchin Valentin d'Angers, who as mentioned above had already celebrated the marriage of Boutet de l'Étoile, was compelled to defend himself before the *Propaganda Fide* against the Augustinians' accusation that he had presided over the wedding between a Catholic woman and a French Protestant, after the latter had assured him in writing that their children would be raised as Catholics. In his own defense, the Capuchin cited the case of a couple who, when the bishop of Babylon refused them permission to marry, had married in the Jacobite church instead; as revenge for the affront, the Protestant husband had forbidden his Catholic wife to practice her religion. If mixed marriages were allowed, Protestant men would permit their wives to continue to live as Catholics and have their children instructed by the friars.[141] The *Propaganda Fide* nevertheless reaffirmed the ban on mixed marriages. Valentin d'Angers was not giving up, though, and once again addressed the *Propaganda Fide*. He did not simply justify his own practice of allowing mixed marriages but also accused the Augustinians who had reported him of themselves agreeing to the marriage between a Catholic woman and a Dutchman. In this case, he stressed, the Augustinians had even failed to obtain a promise from the groom that he would permit his wife to retain her faith and raise the children as Catholics.[142]

One cannot, in fact, infer from the Augustinian allegations against which the Capuchin had to defend himself that they themselves refrained from officiating at mixed marriages. As part of the local practice of "friendship" and "good correspondence," mixed marriages enjoyed a high degree of social acceptance on the ground. The missionaries could not escape the expectations that the European laity of different confessions derived from social intercourse with them. Accordingly, the celebration of mixed marriages was only called into question in specific situations by individual missionaries. While those who defended the local matrimonial practices were unlikely to prevail in Rome, there was every indication that this had only a minor impact on local practices. Turning marriage into a sacrament did nothing to change the fact that a ritual that so strongly influenced everyday life and the social status of individuals retained secular dimensions even when it was administered by the Church.

Baptisms and Godparenthood

The ritual of baptism also had a dual religious and social character that revealed itself in the question of godparenthood. This combined religious obligation in the presence of the Church with the creation and intensification of social relationships between godparents and the baptizands and their parents, as well as among the *compatres*. In this area, too, the Council of Trent formulated rules that had a profound impact on society: on the one hand, by adhering to the notion that baptismal sponsorships, contrary to Protestant criticisms, created spiritual kinship and thus legally relevant impediments to marriage, and on the other by limiting the number of sponsors to two persons of different sexes. The Council Fathers considered the search for wealthy and respected *compatres*—that is, for worldly advantages rather than divine grace—to be an abuse. For that reason, they sought to transform godparenthood into a relationship in which persons close to the baptizand and of similar social rank assumed responsibility for their religious education vis-à-vis the Church. Case studies in European contexts, however, have shown that the restriction to two baptismal sponsors had the opposite effect in practice; it led to parents being more attentive than previously to filling this role with respected persons of high social status. These persons in turn represented and cemented their superior social position by accepting sponsorships.[143]

Godparenthood thus retained a dual ecclesiastical and profane character. While sponsorship, as part of the sacrament of baptism, was an essentially religious institution for the various confessional churches, for the laity, concern for the family's economic and social capital stood alongside the religious function of godparenthood. When Catholics and non-Catholics lived in "good correspondence" at close quarters, this necessarily affected the choice of godparents. Moreover, in Persia, as in other diasporas in which Protestants had no pastor of their own, Protestants had their children christened by Catholic missionaries. When Protestants expected missionaries as religious specialists to perform a Christian ritual on their children, this further defied the authority of the confessional churches.[144]

The Capuchin Valentin d'Angers, for instance, defended not only mixed marriages but also a local baptismal practice that did not draw the boundaries between Catholics and Protestants as sharply as the post-Tridentine Church demanded. In the face of the prohibitions imposed by Bishop Bernard de Sainte-Thérèse, in 1641 Valentin d'Angers formulated two *dubia,* which, however, could only be met with a negative response in Rome. First, he wanted to know whether a Catholic woman who had married an unbeliever could receive the sacraments. Second, he asked whether "heretics" could serve as godparents for the baptism of Catholic children or, conversely, whether Catholics were allowed to sponsor "heretical" children. According to Friar Valentin, many "heretics" in Isfahan lived on good terms with Catholics, without any antipathy arising between them for religious reasons. When they had children, they asked Catholics to serve as godparents, and Catholics did the same. Because of the bishop of Babylon's ban, a Catholic had recently had his son christened in the Armenian church. In the future, Catholics as well as Protestants, who before the episcopal prohibition had brought their children to the Catholic church for baptism, would follow his example. Valentin d'Angers asserted that it seemed to him and all people with knowledge of the country and the methods of successful mission that the previous "favor" should be preserved. The Protestants appreciated the education and instruction of their sons by the missionaries; there was not the same antipathy between them as existed in Europe. In his zeal, the bishop of Babylon failed to consider what was appropriate for conditions in the country. Instead, his passionate and wrathful behavior aroused the aversion of everyone he met.[145]

The *Propaganda Fide* was not prepared to entertain such considerations. In the matters of both the participation of women married to "unbelievers" in the sacraments and the question of godparenthood, it pointed to earlier negative decisions. In 1658, the Congregation again deliberated on a letter from the Capuchin Valentin d'Angers, in which he described the disadvantages that arose when mixed marriages were forbidden and Protestants were not allowed to stand as godparents: most of them were powerful men by virtue of their positions in the service of the shah or their commercial activities; if they were excluded from the honor of godparenthood, they could do much to harm the mission. Once again, the *Propaganda Fide* rejected both mixed marriages and non-Catholic baptismal sponsors.[146]

The refusal to baptize a child could be the cause of enmity and annoyance, as the Discalced Carmelite Corneille de Saint-Cyprien explained to a member of his order's *Definitorium*. For example, the Discalced Carmelites had not wished to christen the child of a Dutchman in Bandar ʿAbbās: while they knew him to be a crypto-Catholic, they (erroneously) assumed he would choose "heretics" as godparents. According to the Discalced Carmelite, the Dutchman responded fiercely, and pointed out that in secular matters, the friars were quick "to receive courtesy and grace," but in spiritual matters they shunned "any inconvenience." Judging by the friar's account, the Dutchman experienced the refusal to baptize his child as a violation of the unwritten rules of the gift exchange economy into which the missionaries were integrated. The allegation also needs to be viewed against the backdrop of competition between the orders. In light of the refusal of the Discalced Carmelites, the Dutchman turned to an Augustinian, who immediately traveled from Bandar-i Kung to Bandar ʿAbbās to perform the christening. According to Corneille de Saint-Cyprien, the Capuchins for their part declared that in such a case they would even have hurried over from Isfahan by donkey.[147]

With regard to the intensification of useful relationships, nothing seemed more normal in Persia than to designate leading representatives of the trading companies as godparents, even though they were not Catholic. Accepting godparenthood affirmed a patron's transconfessional obligation toward a client or between "friends." The social norm of entanglement, however, conflicted with the ecclesiastical norm, for which baptismal sponsorship was a component of a sacramental act in which persons of other confessions could have no part. A way out was offered by a practice that Cornelio di San Giuseppe described in the *Centuria decima*, which he wrote around 1790 based on his memories of the time of his sojourn in Isfahan from 1743 to 1745. In those days, the Protestant resident of the VOC had offered to act as godfather to one of the sons of his interpreter from the Syrian-Catholic Sahid family. With regard to the Discalced Carmelite's negative decision based on the confessional difference, the interpreter reminded him of the great obligation of the missions and the missionaries toward the Dutchman. The resident of the VOC had always favored them with his protection, organizing the release of imprisoned Christians and paying the mission's debts out of his own pocket. Cornelio di San Giuseppe saw reason and promised the interpreter the requested "grace." On the day of the christening, the resident and his retinue came at the appointed time to the Discalced Carmelite church, where Friar Cornelio greeted him "with the shows of respect owed to his rank." Friar Cornelio had arrived at the following arrangement so that the baptism might do justice both to church ritual and the social requirements: he accorded the resident—as the sponsor in the "world"—the honorable role of carrying a large and richly adorned candle during the entire ceremony, while at the precise moment of the act of baptism the baby was handed to the priest by another man—the sponsor in the eyes of the Church. This allowed them to keep up the social appearance of godparenthood: the resident thanked the Discalced Carmelite for the honor he had done him and after the christening wished to present him with "a goodly number of gold coins." Cornelio di San Giuseppe refused to accept them, however, because, as he explained to the resident, the Church forbade him from accepting money to administer the sacraments. In the belief that he had really become the godfather, on various occasions the resident later did a number of good deeds for the church, the mission, and still more for the family of the interpreter.[148] With his actions, Friar Cornelio drew a dividing line between the sacramental and social dimensions of baptism not foreseen by the *Rituale romanum*. The success of this distinction depended, however, on the fact that the non-church actors did not recognize it.

A papal decision of 1763 on a series of *dubia* that the *Propaganda Fide* had presented to the Holy Office because of a letter from the prefect of the mission in Tripoli (present-day Libya) is reminiscent of Cornelio di San Giuseppe's actions. The matter in question was whether it was permissible to baptize the children of "heretics," whether this could be done in the private home of the English consul, and whether a "heretical" godparent could be admitted to the ceremony together with the Catholic godparent. The prefect had written that for three years, the English consul had had his children christened according to the Latin rather than the Greek rite. To this end, he had summoned the prefect along with the other missionaries to his house, where an altar was set up and the ceremony performed according to the Roman rite. He always had both a Protestant and a second, Catholic, godparent. This had now occurred three times in the presence of Catholic and Protestant consuls. The Protestant consuls also came to the mission church if the Catholics invited them to christenings. If the prefect believed his conduct to be proper, the Holy Office soon informed him of his error: reading his report had occasioned some bitterness. The issue was clear for the Holy Office and Pope Clement XIII (Carlo Rezzonico, r. 1758–69): while the presence of Protestants who attended Catholic worship services and christenings of their own accord could be tolerated, Catholics must not invite the "heretics," so as not to contribute to *communicatio in sacris*, which contravened the spirit and laws of the Church. Catholic clerics were not to baptize the children of Protestant parents as long as those parents were responsible for their education. "Heretics" were forbidden to be godparents to Catholics since they could not ensure that the baptizand would be raised in the Catholic faith. This doctrinaire explanation, however, was followed by a remarkable concession: if the missionary could not prevent the involvement of a "heretic," he must at least declare that the Catholic alone would assume the role of godparent and that the "heretic" was merely attending the baptism as a witness. The baptismal register must then mention only the Catholic sponsor.[149]

Despite the clear rejection of practices that implied *communicatio in sacris*, the papal decision, based on statements from the *consultores* and cardinals, expresses a certain sympathy for the specific situation in which missionaries could find themselves when it came to baptism. While they were obliged to reject Protestants as godparents pursuant to the *Rituale romanum*, allowing them as witnesses opened up the possibility of reconciling the affirmation of an ecclesiastical norm with the local requirements of "good correspondence."

The *dubia* referred to baptismal practices that were widespread well beyond Tripoli, and not only with regard to godparenthood. On the question of whether it was permissible to baptize the children of Protestants, the Holy Office clung to a position that it had already formulated in other contexts: a baptism should only be performed when the baptizand was sure to be raised in the Catholic faith or was obviously dying. This position contradicted the demand for religious rituals with which Protestants presented Catholic priests in Persia. As in the Maghreb, when they asked the missionaries to christen their children, they expected the ritual to be performed not in the church but in their own homes.

Based on the probabilist moral theology of their brother Paul Laymann, in the 1720s the Jesuits in Isfahan wished to do a favor for the captain of the VOC factory, Nicolaas Schorer, and other Dutchmen by baptizing children in their homes. This could be understood as returning a favor, since the Dutch had helped them survive during the difficult years after the fall of the Safavids. Bishop Barnaba Fedeli di Milano, in contrast, presented himself as a defender of Tridentine sacramental practice. In a 1726 letter to the prefect of the *Propaganda Fide* he asked whether he should permit baptisms to be performed without any necessity in the homes of the laity—not just Catholics but also "heretics."[150]

In 1727, the bishop claimed that many years prior to his arrival, as a favor to the Dutch, a missionary had baptized a child in their house. If we read the Dominican's letters more closely, however, they suggest a more ambiguous practice during his own tenure as well, in which he even participated to some degree. In two instances he did not forbid the baptisms, but merely admonished the missionaries to perform the christenings in their church rather than the parents' home. In one case, the Protestant captain of the VOC was allowed to serve as godfather at the baptism of the child of Catholic parents; in the second, the baptizand was the son of the captain and his "schismatic concubine." Bishop Fedeli claimed to have subsequently made a closer study of the pope's "best doctrine" and on this basis to have prohibited further christenings of the children of Protestant parents except in cases of impending death. The Dutchmen involved ultimately had their children baptized by an Armenian priest.[151] As unwilling as they were to dispense with the Christian ritual of baptism, its providers were thus to a certain degree interchangeable across confessional lines. Contrary to what Bishop Fedeli's remarks might at first suggest, transconfessional baptismal practices lived on.

Caring for the Dying and Funerals

The presence of people of other confessions at funerals could also give rise to controversy: in confessionally mixed communities in Western and Central Europe, many disputes arose around the matter of burials in cemeteries whose ground was hallowed from a Catholic standpoint and was thought to be desecrated if "heretics" were interred there. Protestants who attended Catholic burials were criticized by their own church authorities because the priests used the sacramentals of their church (especially holy water). Funerals, however, had an especially marked dual character, as contemporaries also understood. They were at once rituals of honor and occasions on which people, regardless of their religious affiliation, felt a particular need for the sacred. Burial itself was not a sacrament for the Catholic Church. While the church ceremony was combined with a mass, the funeral processions and interments were primarily rituals of honor. The participants paid their "last respects" to the deceased as people of a certain status and not so much as members of a particular confessional church. That is why in the confessionally mixed societies of Western and Central Europe people of different confessions also often participated in funerals. A revered Catholic patrician, a Catholic nobleman, or even officeholders from a monastery were not merely Catholics but also men of rank, who deserved the corresponding signs of respect.[152]

From the viewpoint of missionaries in Persia and other mission territories, the transconfessional composition of the mourners upon the death of a brother was a particular sign of the esteem in which the deceased missionaries were held.[153] The descriptions of burials express a discourse of honor that located the orders and their members within a worldly status hierarchy.[154] If even people of other confessions honored a member of an order by participating in his funeral, this was consummate proof of the reputation that he had acquired during his lifetime. This reputation was attributed in turn to the deceased's religious mission, which transformed the deplorable *communicatio in sacris* at the funeral mass and the acceptance of secular signs of respect that were problematic for the regular clergy into a religious triumph.

As Nicolas Standaert has shown for the Jesuits in China, such funerals sometimes required significant adaptations of the usual church rituals. This was especially true when the emperor paid the funeral expenses of Jesuits who had acquired prestige at court.[155] In the case of missionaries in Isfahan and New Julfa, it was mainly the attendance of numerous non-Catholics at funeral masses that needed justification in light of the prohibition of *communicatio in sacris*. According to a report by Aimé Chézaud, after the death of his fellow Jesuit Alexandre de Rhodes, clerics of the other orders, French, Portuguese, and English laymen, and a few Armenians followed the funeral cortège from the house of the Jesuits in Isfahan to the Christian cemetery in New Julfa. There, and one week later in the Jesuit chapel, the Augustinian prior celebrated as apostolic vicar. Most Armenians regarded it as an honor that the father, whom according to Chézaud they considered a saint, was interred near their own graves. Ever since the funeral, many indigenous Christians, even priests and vardapets, had come to pray at his grave and ask the deceased Jesuit for his intercession.[156]

When Aimé Chézaud, the founder and first superior of the Jesuit mission in New Julfa, died in September 1664, his funeral mass, according to Father Mercier, was attended not just by Catholic clerics but also by many Armenian priests, three or four Armenian vardapets, and an envoy from the tsar with his retinue. Mercier also noted that a group of Armenian priests headed the funeral procession to the Christian cemetery of New Julfa, while the "heretical French," together with the English and Dutch, numerous Armenian notables, and the envoy of the tsar, accompanied the cortège on horseback. One of the most powerful Armenians of New Julfa had wanted to inter the priest in his own family plot as the "father of his nation," but he, Mercier, had preferred to bury him together with other clerics in the Catholic section of the cemetery. Several Muslims had even paid their respects to the priest when he was laid out in the Jesuits' house, offering their condolences to his companion.[157]

Raphaël du Mans's funeral in 1696 in the small Capuchin church was attended not just by the Catholic clerics of Isfahan and New Julfa but also by the *kalāntar*, many Armenian notables, and two representatives of the English East India Company. One of the two surviving friars reported that "all of the Europeans, English, Dutch, and other Franks," as well as the Armenians and Muslims, had loved Friar Raphaël and now missed him.[158]

As we have seen, critics within the Church accused Raphaël du Mans of doing too little for the mission and focusing on cultivating worldly relationships instead. The criteria of rule observance and confessional conformity, however, obscure our view of his diaspora-specific pastoral achievements. Writing from Bandar ʿAbbās, the Lutheran pastor's son Kaempfer commended himself to the "prayers" and "favor" of Raphaël du Mans.[159] John Fryer, a physician in the service of the English East India Company, praised not only Friar Raphaël's knowledge of the country and contacts at court but also his practice of caring for the dying: in contrast to most other clerics, "he is no intruder on men's principles, when about to depart this life, as most of them are, but recommends them to God with their own conscience."[160] In this way, the friar met a demand for Christian rituals that, in the absence of a Protestant pastor, transcended strictly confessional frameworks. At the same time, caring for the dying offered the missionaries a final opportunity to convert Protestants, as the Jesuit Claude-Ignace Mercier managed to do in the case of Isaac Boutet de l'Étoile.

When the missionaries reported their participation in the funerals of non-Catholics, they were anxious to note that they had not undertaken any religious acts in the process. The Discalced Carmelites expressly referred to the funeral's nature as a ritual of honor in 1663 when they requested the *Propaganda Fide*'s permission to continue to accompany deceased Protestants to the cemetery without performing any ecclesiastical acts "for the sake of honor," in response to the protection they had received.[161] As in other, similar cases, the *Propaganda Fide* preferred not to issue a decision, so as neither to approve the practice explicitly nor to run the risk of a negative decision being ignored.[162]

Was it actually true, however, that the missionaries, with their various forms of participation in Protestant funerals, were meeting a purely secular obligation and not also a demand for the sacred? In 1696, the English asked the Jesuits in New Julfa to lay out the body of a captain in their house until he could be buried. In a report published in Paris in 1730, Father Jacques Villotte (or the compiler of his account) insisted that the fathers had assented because it was a "purely civil act" and there had never been any question of "cultivating community with the Englishmen in prayer or a religious ceremony." The argument took up the same distinctions that the Jesuits used to justify their practices of accommodation in China and South India during the controversies over rites. As accurate as it may have been that the English were not concerned with the Catholic sacrament of the mass for the dead, they may well have regarded the Jesuits' house as a place removed from the sphere of the mundane in a broader sense, which they therefore preferred to the house of their interpreter, although it would have offered quite a prestigious setting.[163]

*

To summarize the most important findings on relations between missionaries and the European laity of different confessions: Contacts with persons of other faiths were the very essence of missionary activity. At the same time, in conflict situations between or within the orders they were liable to be instrumentalized against those who cultivated them. In actual practice, the lines of transition between the conversion of persons of other faiths and the undesirable cultivation of shared religious practices remained fluid. The exceptional situation of a diaspora in which, as a rule, only the Catholic clergy could satisfy the demand for European Christian rituals influenced the reinterpretation and reshaping of ecclesiastical practices. The relationships between missionaries and non-Catholic European Christians reveal that even those who were supposed to enforce confessional forms of religiosity on the ground often cultivated practices that did not conform to ecclesiastical norms. Catholics were linked to Protestants not only by shared origins or languages but also by participation in a gift exchange economy. The relationships involved were described using terms such as "friendship" and "good correspondence." Aside from the duty to show respect in a status-appropriate manner, the practices associated with these relationships consisted of obligatory gifts and return gifts appropriate to one's rank. While both clerics and the employees of the trading companies could be expected, depending on the situation, to use their local connections for the benefit of a "friend," because of their vows of poverty the regular clergy brought no gifts of material value into the relationships—olives from Italy, for example, were a small personal token, not a commodity measured in monetary terms. Offering alms or loans under favorable conditions was a matter for merchants. For their part, in some cases, at least, they expected Catholic clerics to meet their demand for religious rituals that were not covered by a pastor of their own church. Under these conditions, Catholic priests also performed status-specific services for people of other confessions, upon which their social reputation depended, and which could not be separated from their position as religious specialists.

The scattered accounts of diverse origins yield the image of a system of social exchange whose expectations the clerics could scarcely escape even when they violated the norms of their order and church. In the Latin diasporas, depending on the situation, even missionaries often looked upon Protestants more as fellow Christians than as "heretics." This encouraged many missionaries to agree to requests for religious services, within certain boundaries. For example, they performed baptisms despite knowing that the children would not be raised as Catholics, tolerated the presence of Protestants at masses in private homes, or lent a sacred dimension to the funerals of Protestants.

Finally, we need to ask to what extent we can draw conclusions about longer-term developments and how these findings might be integrated into a more general history of transconfessional practices. One might be tempted to interpret the controversies between Bishop Fedeli and the Jesuits in the 1720s, for instance, as an indicator of the stricter enforcement of confessional norms, similar to what Bernard Heyberger has demonstrated for the Catholic missions in Syria and to what our documentation suggests for relations with the Armenians. The statements and practices of the last Latin bishop of Isfahan, Cornelio di San Giuseppe, however, show that we cannot speak of a linear development. The specific local circumstances, but also the individual orientations of the persons involved, meant that transformations in the overall context of the Catholic Church had only fragmentary impacts on the ground.

As in relations with the Armenians, the *Propaganda Fide*, the Holy Office, and the superiors of the orders also drew clear boundaries in principle in dealing with Protestants, as we have seen in their positions on mixed marriages or the admissibility of non-Catholics as baptismal sponsors. The missionaries were left with no doubt about the desirability of confessional conformity. This was in turn reflected in the formulations missionaries chose in their correspondence with the Curia and the superiors of their orders. At the same time, the admission of Protestants as baptismal witnesses, for example, shows that the Holy Office was also not completely out of touch with local requirements. Changes in the treatment of mixed marriages during the pontificate of Benedict XIV, which will be addressed in Chapter 7, suggest similar conclusions.

The findings presented here point to a history of transconfessional practices that assumed specific characteristics in the diasporas in the Near East and South Asia, but which in part could also be found in early modern Western and Central Europe. The Persian findings need first to be located within a Near Eastern and South Asian context, but the current state of research makes this difficult. Despite a lively interest in the transgression of religious boundaries in the Muslim lands of the Mediterranean region and the Near East, scholars have paid little attention thus far to relations between European Christians of different confessions.[164] A recent essay addresses the conversion of Protestants to Catholicism in the Syro-Palestinian region.[165] The rather rare conversions that the Franciscans effected and documented in the Holy Land fit a model familiar to Europeans. My findings, however, demonstrate that the phenomenon of confessional ambiguity was much more widespread and highly typical of diasporas in the Near Eastern context.

Thus, in the case of the Boutet de l'Étoile and Rousseau families, the turn to Catholicism was the result of a long process, which ultimately created no clarity. Doubts about the quality of the conversions in the Boutet de l'Étoile family are evident, for example, in the report by the Frenchman Poullet, who visited Isfahan in 1659. He stated that Boutet de l'Étoile's wife, children, and some relatives practiced Catholicism because it stood between the Armenians and Calvinism.[166] Regardless of the fact that Jean-François-Xavier Rousseau was made a knight of San Giovanni in Laterano in 1773 by Clement XIV for his services to the order of the Discalced Carmelites and the Catholic faith in Persia and Basra, the son of the Geneva clockmaker and merchant Jacques Rousseau himself continued to live on the confessional borderlines. In 1761 he married an Armenian in the Discalced Carmelite church in Basra. When she died just two years later, she was interred in the courtyard of the mission there. The Discalced Carmelite who made the entry in the burial register claimed that it had only been noticed three or four days after her death that the assumption that she had converted to Catholicism upon her marriage was incorrect, and that in reality she had died "in the principles of her heretical religion." For that reason, the friars had stopped any further prayers for the deceased woman.[167] Although Rousseau continued to cultivate relations with Rome after 1773 and occasionally made use of them, for instance to effect a dispensation, he knew that it was not the clarity of his affiliation but his deep knowledge of how to navigate liminal cultural spaces that constituted an essential element of his reputation and economic success. He accordingly cultivated his relationships with Calvinist kin in Geneva along with his connections with the Catholic missionaries and the authorities in Rome. In 1773, the year in which Jean-François-Xavier was made a knight of a papal order, his Calvinist cousin Théodore Rousseau intervened on his behalf with the French king's resident in Geneva, Pierre-Michel Hennin. Hennin was to make representations to the naval ministry so that Jean-François-Xavier could be appointed to succeed the late consul in Basra, which actually occurred in 1781.[168]

Other studies have already shown that inner-European affiliations declined in social relevance when Christians of European origin met in a foreign environment such as the European factories on the Persian Gulf and the Indian Ocean, but they address the issue of confession only in passing.[169] In the territories that belonged in the stricter sense to the VOC, too, the mission of implementing confessional norms—in this instance those of a Calvinist authority—contrasted with boundary violations in everyday life. Hendrik Adriaan van Reede tot Drakenstein, who became known for his anti-Catholic measures in the service of the VOC in Cochin and Ceylon, counted the Discalced Carmelite Matteo di San Giuseppe among his most important collaborators in the preparation of the *Hortus malabaricus* for publication beginning in 1678. Similarly, the implementation of Calvinist morals remained far removed from the aspirations of the Reformed Church, even in Batavia and the larger VOC settlements in South Asia. The adoption of illegitimate children from relationships with local women, for example, seemed to make up for deviations from strict Calvinist sexual morality.[170]

In Western Europe, too, alongside territories in which most people belonged to a single confession, there were also many regions for whose inhabitants multiconfessionalism was an everyday experience. Coexistence there was by no means continuously dominated by sharp and violent attempts to separate people into groups of various confessional denominations. We should think here of pragmatic forms of tolerating those of other faiths (not in the sense of tolerance as the conscious acceptance of religious pluralism) on the one hand, and religious practices that, to the dismay of the religious authorities, were not universally conditioned by confession, on the other. Between the rare instances of formalized biconfessionalism with a shared use of the parish church (*simultaneum*) and the restriction of subjects of a different faith to *devotio domestica*, there were many practices that allowed people of different confessions to practice their religion and coexist peacefully.[171] In Europe, too, the view that all Christians, whether Catholic or Protestant, could achieve salvation as long as they led a godly life stood in the way of the clear separation into "good" and "evil." People of different confessions shared some common interests, values, and loyalties. While they all regarded heresy as despicable, they could retain ties to one another as neighbors, relatives, and members of the same community or entity.[172] Even confessional agitators might except people of other faiths whom they knew personally from the animosity they felt for their church.[173] Accordingly, recent studies in cultural history have emphasized the existence of transconfessional spaces even in early modern Western and Central Europe. They use the term "transconfessional" to refer to forms of religious culture shaped by the "pluralism" of "beliefs and practices" that were "often only partially congruent with the profile of a confession or religion clearly defined by the authorities."[174]

Nevertheless, we should not lose sight of the fact that the authorities of the different confessional churches in seventeenth-century Europe proceeded quite successfully against the practices of transconfessionalism and confessional indifference. The increasingly narrow definition of orthodoxy in the wake of the Protestant Reformation and Catholic reform drastically reduced the willingness to tolerate divergent doctrines and practices. Any confessionally charged public act could provoke disputes and sometimes violent clashes.[175] Almost everywhere in early modern Europe, confessional boundary violations and conversions had severe effects for a person's position in society. Even in the United Provinces, those Christians who did not profess the Calvinist faith were merely tolerated and their religious practices banished from public space; people paid a high price for their adherence to Catholicism in the form of legal and social discrimination.[176]

In conclusion, against this backdrop we need to emphasize once again the extent and specific character of shared religious practice in the diasporas under non-Christian and especially Muslim authorities. In a Muslim environment, what Christians shared was frequently more important than what divided them. The fact that the Persian and Ottoman authorities primarily perceived and treated Western European Christians of different confessions as "Franks" and not as Catholics or Protestants will have played an important role here. The transconfessional commonalities that grew out of social proximity can then be explained by a shared Christian separation from the Muslim surroundings when it came to defending material interests or a pan-Christian capital of honor, or to preventing conversions to Islam. The religious common ground as "Frankish" Christians ultimately formed the basis for a self-identification as "Europeans." For example, Dutchmen and Poles took the side of a Portuguese man in an affair of honor with a Muslim "to avenge the affront done to a European."[177] In this way, "Europe" confronted "the Orient." Yet it was only in the late eighteenth century, in the guise of *Rousseau de Perse* during his sojourn in France and in his correspondence, that Jacques Rousseau's son Jean-François-Xavier presented himself as a specialist in relations with that part of the world, which was now deemed less civilized than Europe.

In the context that concerns us here, however, Christian mutuality was at least as important as shared European origins, as the episodes of transconfessional solidarity in the face of the danger of falling away from the faith and converting to Islam illustrate. This also included Eastern Christians. Thus, for example, according to his own account, the Catholic Armenian Petros Bedik owed his ability to resist the temptation to convert to Islam to the advice of the Capuchin Raphaël du Mans and an English agent, as well as to God's help.[178] Assistance with efforts to prevent Christians of various geographical origins from converting to Islam was part of the protection offered by the agents and merchants of the Protestant trading companies for which Cornelio di San Giuseppe expressed gratitude in his last will and testament. In his *Memorie cronologiche che puonno servire a meglio sovvenirmi de varii altri incidenti di mia vita*, the Discalced Carmelite recounted how in 1746, "with God's help and the support of the English," Portuguese sailors who had been living in Bushehr without pay for six months and in some cases had converted to Islam as a result were able to travel to India hidden on English ships. When the VOC lost its trading post on Kharg Island, the bishop and the English resident in Bushehr jointly negotiated an opportunity to leave the island for a trading company clerk's New Julfa-born widow. The bishop raised the funds for a dowry intended to allow her to marry again, in part because of the "generosity of the English." Instead of traveling to Surat to be with her family, however, the woman remained in Muscat, where a Discalced Carmelite presided over her marriage to the Calvinist VOC agent, as Cornelio di San Giuseppe, now writing from a confessional viewpoint, noted with dismay.[179]

Beyond the cooperation between Catholic clerics and agents of the English East India Company as fellow Christians, such episodes also illustrate the connection between mobility and the liberation of the individual from confessional obligations. The chronicler of the Discalced Carmelites in Basra complained bitterly in 1720 about the Catholics who arrived in the Near East as merchants, driven by the search for rare objects, the observation of foreign lands, or a "wanton desire for travel," and once there gave themselves over to a sinful way of life, resisting the obligations of church laws.[180] In the case of young Genevan clockmakers in Constantinople, the fact that the decision to migrate offered young, often still unmarried men freedoms they could not

Figure 17 Gravestone of Jean Malom in the cemetery of New Julfa: "Here lies Jean Malom, French by nation, Roman by religion and physician by profession. He died at the age of 40 [years] in the year of Our Lord 1646."

have found at home also gave the strict Calvinist *Compagnie des pasteurs* in their native city cause for concern. It lamented their insufficient piety and dissolute way of life, by which the pastors referred to mixed marriages with the daughters of Eastern Christian families, as well as extramarital relationships.[181] The almost total absence of Protestant preachers and chaplains in Persia and at the trading posts of the VOC and the English East India Company in the Persian Gulf led to an asymmetry in the rallying force of the Catholic and the Protestant churches. Thus it is striking that, unlike the gravestones of many Catholics (Figure 17), those of the Protestants in the cemetery of New Julfa do not refer to the deceased person's confession. In the context explored here, there is nothing to confirm the thesis that the rituals of the Church of England became an important marker of identification for the merchants and employees of the East India Company. The church officials who could have performed these rituals with any regularity were simply lacking.[182]

While confessional affiliations retreated into the background in Persia or the Persian Gulf, we should recall the practices explored in the two preceding chapters, which were cultivated in relationships between the missionaries and their Muslim or Armenian environment and demonstrated the recognition of the missionaries as men of God. The dominant understanding of the sacred, which did not exclude confessional attributions, did not necessarily assign godliness to a specific confession. Dividing lines or commonalities defined interactions depending on the situation. The fact that Protestants used the services of missionaries as religious specialists in certain situations is especially illuminating here. Thus, in the absence of pastors of their own confession, Protestant employees of the VOC and the East India Company turned either to priests of the Eastern churches or Catholic clerics for certain religious rituals, primarily baptism. This demand for Christian rituals and the expectations that the regular clergy, with their lives removed from the "world," also elicited among non-Catholics brought the missionaries into conflict not just with the confessional orthodoxy demanded by the post-Tridentine Church but also with the observance of the Rule demanded by their own orders.

6

Local Interconnections and Observance: The Missionaries in Conflict with the Norms of Their Order

Members of religious orders vowed to organize their everyday lives in accordance with the observances stipulated by their communities. They gained social prestige from adhering to the rules of a life in seclusion from the "world," and this informed their relationships with the laity of different confessions. According to the Calvinist Jean Chardin, the missionaries could operate in Persia wearing their own habits because their unworldly, godly way of life was also pleasing to Muslims.[1] John Fryer, who arrived in Isfahan in 1677 as a physician in the service of the English East India Company, also attributed the widespread respect for the friars to their specific way of life according to the required vow of poverty. For that reason, they gained "a reputation and reverence" from the ruler and his subjects. Following the shah's example, his subjects also often sent the clerics "meat, bread and other provisions for their sustenance" and paid them "a respect equal to their own devote[e]s."[2]

The *Propaganda Fide* painted a less flattering picture than the two Protestant authors. In a memorandum presented to the Congregation in 1625, its first secretary, Francesco Ingoli, mentions two main obstacles to successful missionary work: first, the discord between bishops and regular clergy and between the monastic orders and the Jesuits; second, the greed of many missionaries, whose sole aim was to accumulate wealth and bring it back to Europe. Ingoli accused the superiors of the orders of shunting the worst members off to India.[3] In his *Relazione delle Quattro Parti del Mondo*, written during the years 1629–31, he went even further in his criticism of the missionaries' way of life. According to him, those sent to the East Indies, in particular, usually aspired to return to Europe as rich men. They hoped to bring gold, silver, jewels, commodities, and valuable objects to Europe for themselves or their kinsmen, as gifts for friends, ecclesiastical and secular lords, or as a means to step on the path to ecclesiastical or court office.[4]

The scathing criticism of the lives of the regular clergy and the unwillingness or inability of their superiors to rectify the situation legitimized the efforts of the *Propaganda Fide* to impose a normative frame of reference for all orders. Later memoranda gave the impression that scarcely anything had changed in decades: Cardinal Giuseppe Renato Imperiali was still lamenting the same state of affairs in 1707. By leading an immoral life, seeking personal advantage, and engaging in trade, missionaries hindered the mission instead of furthering it. Like the authors of previous reports, Imperiali claimed that missionaries resisted the authority of the *Propaganda Fide* and ignored its decrees and instructions.[5] Discussions in the Congregation could mobilize mistrust of the regular clergy and the superiors at any time. Arguing that what made a good Christian was not the habit he wore, and the claim that explanations by the procurators of the orders were "always full of falsehood and deceit," Cardinal Vitaliano Borromeo even stated in 1783 that he preferred an Armenian priest as administrator of the church in Isfahan to a Dominican or a Discalced Carmelite.[6]

The fact that the *Propaganda Fide* continued to depend on the orders' personnel resources in the eighteenth century and gained direct control over the clerics' everyday lives only in exceptional cases contributed to the persistence of the antiorder discourse. The fact that missionaries needed to be possessed of *facultates* issued by the Congregation was more indicative of a symbolic than a practical subjection to the authority of the *Propaganda Fide*. It did not lead to the curial congregations establishing an information-based personnel administration such as that realized to some degree within the Society of Jesus. As a distant Roman administrative body whose legitimacy was questioned by the regular clergy, the *Propaganda Fide* could only enforce the formal adherence to a series of procedural rules, while religious owed their internalized obedience to the superiors of their orders.[7] Reports to the *Propaganda Fide* followed fixed forms and were accordingly stereotypical, unless particular circumstances, notably conflicts on the ground, caused individual missionaries to present their concerns to the Congregation. Accusations of deficient observance, orthodoxy, and orthopraxy served primarily to discredit opponents. In 1648, for example, the *Propaganda Fide* had to deal with the allegations traded by the Augustinian José do Rosário and the Capuchin Valentin d'Angers: the Capuchin countered the Augustinian's accusation that he offered generous dispensations from the requirement to fast by alleging that the latter administered the sacraments to Christian women married to Muslims and had turned his convent into a "house of amusement and parties."[8] It was allegations like these that gave the *Propaganda Fide* occasion to demand confessional orthodoxy and observance. Only under such conditions could the Congregation intervene directly in the everyday lives of missionaries for once.

A history of the missionaries' adaptive efforts therefore needs to view them first and foremost as members of the regular clergy. In so doing, we need to recall once again the uneven preservation of the archives of the different orders, which conditions the extent to which we can adopt an order-centered approach. While existing scholarship on other mission territories has focused one-sidedly on the Jesuits, in Persia the Discalced Carmelites come to the fore, while the practices of missionaries with other affiliations can be considered only selectively through the surviving records. The focus is thus on members of an order whose constitution, unlike that of the Jesuits, did not offer the option of outward accommodation. This makes the question of how those who were involved met the challenges of working in an unfamiliar environment all the more fascinating.

The Discalced Carmelites: Unsuited to Mission?

When Clement VIII sent Discalced Carmelites to Persia in 1604, the order's recently founded Italian congregation faced several problems. Given the small number of members, they found it difficult to locate the necessary personnel for such a mission. More importantly still, the papal decision meant a fundamental reorientation for a contemplative order, whose institutional structures and rules envisaged a life of seclusion behind convent walls, not missionary work. It is therefore not surprising that the question of whether missionary activities were compatible with the Rule was hotly debated for several decades in the Italian Congregation of the Discalced Carmelites, with the leadership of the order reaching different conclusions depending on the composition of the *Definitorium generale* and the General Chapter. Via the channels explored in Chapter 1, especially correspondence, visitations, and participation in the General Chapters, the discussions among missionaries on the ground informed decisions by the leadership of the order, which in turn became points of reference that guided actions in Persia.[9]

Immediately before the order's first missionaries were dispatched to Persia, Juan de Jesús María wrote a *Tractatus quo asseruntur missiones* (Treatise in defense of the missions). In this treatise, written at the instigation of the Italian Congregation's commissioner general, Pedro de la Madre de Dios, Juan de Jesús María argued that, regardless of the commandment of strict observance, the friars must also attend to the dissemination of the faith. Mission was not merely permitted to them; if they wished to follow the spirit of Teresa of Ávila, whom they revered as their foundress, it was their duty to accept the missionary mandate.[10] In light of continued criticism from Spain in particular, Juan de Jesús María would go on to cite this argument repeatedly until his death in 1615. It also found its way into the preface of the constitutions passed by the first General Chapter of the Italian Congregation in 1605.[11] Aside from the Persian mission, the General Chapter of 1605 wished to establish two other missions over the following three years. All nine participants in the General Chapter offered to work in the mission themselves. The General Chapter then entrusted Juan de Jesús María with the task of compiling an *Instructio Missionum* outlining the rules to be obeyed in the mission.[12] Because of still-smoldering controversies, the reference to Teresa of Ávila as the reformer of an order oriented toward *contemplatio* and *actio* alike, which had been included in the preface to the first constitutions of 1605, was left out of the printed version of 1606, but reinserted in 1611 after Juan de Jesús María was appointed *praepositus generalis*.[13]

The mission manual *De procuranda salute omnium gentium* (On how to bring about the salvation of all peoples) by the Discalced Carmelite Tomás de Jesús, which appeared in 1613 and was widely disseminated beyond the order, may be located on the same controversial terrain.[14] The author had already published a programmatic work in 1610 assigning the special task of spreading the faith throughout the world to the regular clergy, above all the mendicant orders. In his view, the favors and privileges the popes granted these orders derived from this mandate.[15]

Over the course of the seventeenth century, whenever Discalced Carmelites wrote and published works about their order's missions in the Near East and Asia, they more or less explicitly addressed the question of whether mission actually corresponded to their order's vocation. In this regard, the *Itinerarium orientale* of the French Carmelite Philippe de la Très Sainte Trinité, first published in Latin in 1649 and later translated into French and Italian, departed decidedly from the accounts by Jesuits and members of other orders whose origins themselves gave them a strong orientation toward preaching and mission. As provincial of his native province, definitor, and finally general, Friar Philippe held positions of great influence within the order's hierarchy when he argued on behalf of the Discalced Carmelite's orientation toward mission. Although the main vocation of the Discalced Carmelites was contemplation, the "works of the active life" also particularly comprised those that affected the spiritual well-being of one's fellows, following in the footsteps of the prophet Elijah as the order's founder and St. Teresa of Ávila as its "restorer." Based on a sketch of the history of the order's missions, Philippe de la Très Sainte Trinité showed the degree to which the missionary spirit was in keeping with the vocation of the Discalced Carmelites. The author devoted special attention to the martyrdom of two members of the order in Sumatra in 1638.[16]

Martyrdom was the highest degree of church service, which justified the order's privileges at a time when they were being questioned by the Curia. At the same time, the Discalced Carmelites had to defend their *nobilitas* against other, older orders. For that reason, Philippe de la Très Sainte Trinité published his *Theologia carmelitana* (Carmelite theology) in 1665, in which he defended the "old nobility" of the order against its opponents and "imitators."[17] Mission also played a key role in the *Historia Generalis Fratrum Discalceatorum Ordinis* (General history of the order of the Discalced Carmelite friars) by Isidore de Saint-Joseph and Pierre de Saint-André, which was published at the instigation of Philippe de la Très Sainte Trinité when he served as general of the order. In this work, the controversy over the suitability of mission for the Discalced Carmelites was portrayed as a dispute that ended when Pope Clement VIII decided to dispatch them to Persia. In this reading, the privileges granted to the missionaries were derived from Christ's mission to the apostles and legitimated thereby.[18]

The publications printed under Philippe de la Très Sainte Trinité's name or inspired by him took positions in disputes conducted within his own order, with rival orders, and between the order and the Roman Curia. These disputes concerned the compatibility of contemplation and mission, "nobility" and rank among the orders, and the continued existence of privileges that ensured exemption from the ordinary ecclesiastical jurisdiction in many situations, but particularly in the mission setting.

Since their dispatch to Persia and in connection with the founding of the *Propaganda Fide*, the Discalced Carmelites of the Italian Congregation were seen as regular clerics who bowed more than others to the expectations of the Curia. Because of the controversies within the order, the *Propaganda Fide* at times nevertheless gained the impression that they were seeking to withdraw from mission in favor of the *vita contemplativa*. Francesco Ingoli accordingly felt compelled in 1631 to describe missionary activity to the General Chapter of the Discalced Carmelites as especially godly in comparison to "the tranquility of the purely contemplative life."[19]

Ingoli intervened in this way in disputes that led to the superiors of the order imposing restrictive measures on the everyday lives of missionaries on the ground that contradicted the demands of missionary activities. The contradictory instructions given to visitors in the 1620s and 1630s by the *Definitorium* and the *praepositi generales* reflected these tensions within the order. In 1630, the *Definitorium* instructed the visitor general, Epifanio di San Giovanni Battista, to place strict observance above the needs of the mission. The definitors formulated a number of prescriptions and prohibitions committing the friars to a purely contemplative life. The friars were to leave the convent as infrequently as possible, avoid contact with the laity, and never intervene in secular affairs.[20]

The instructions that the *praepositus generalis*, Paolo Simone di Gesù Maria, gave visitors in 1624 and 1634 were quite different. He sought to solve practical problems and expand the scope of missionary activity. In 1624, the general of the order, himself one of the first missionaries dispatched to Persia in 1604, instructed the visitor to check that his predecessor's *ordinationes* were being respected but also encouraged him not to formulate any additional instructions unless it was urgently necessary. He was instead to endeavor to render them less burdensome.[21] After his reelection as *praepositus generalis*, at the General Chapter of 1632, Paolo Simone di Gesù Maria brought about a clarification in support of the order's missionary orientation, as demanded by the secretary of the *Propaganda Fide*, Francesco Ingoli. The instruction, which Friar Paolo Simone gave the visitor traveling to Persia in 1634, reaffirmed the orientation toward the needs of the mission set out in 1624.[22]

The instructions of 1624 and 1634 on the one hand and 1630 on the other marked out the poles of opinion between which the Discalced Carmelites operated in Persia. The questions suggested here will be explored further later in this chapter. What consequences did the contradictory prescriptions have in social practice, that is, how was action in the world combined with contemplation? How did actors behave on the ground if they found it difficult to shape their lives in accordance with specific requirements, all the while knowing that there were disagreements about the orientation of their order within the General Chapter and the *Definitorium*? Given the limited opportunities to impose norms from above, did the changing and contradictory requirements create a greater scope of action that subaltern actors could use?

Local Social Integration and Observance

The question of the proper relationship between *actio* and contemplation was posed not just in the context of foreign missions, and not for the first time in the sixteenth and seventeenth centuries. European expansion and the emergence of competing confessional churches in the wake of the Counter-Reformation and Catholic reform made it more urgent, however. *Missio* in the sense of spreading the faith among non-Christians and intensifying the faith among Christians demanded a new type of clergy, ready and able to vouch for their church in the "world"; in practice, this mainly meant the regular clergy. At the same time, challenged by Reformation critiques, which homed in on the contradictions between norms and lived practice, the reformers of religious orders fought against the secularization of their communities. For that reason, the question of the relationship between *actio* and contemplation was closely associated with the problem of rule observance. In the wake of reform efforts, religious were measured against their adherence to the Rule within the orders, while the enforcement of rule observance also legitimized interventions by the Roman Curia that violated their privileges and were intended to strengthen papal primacy.

The question of maintaining discipline presents itself with particular acuity in the case of foreign missions. Contemporaries were already convinced that missionaries all over the world faced expectations that could not be reconciled with the norms of their orders. The orders arrived at different responses to these challenges. In the constitutions of the Jesuit order, Ignatius of Loyola defined the outward adaptation of clothing, food, sleep schedules, and "other necessary or useful things in life" to place, time, and persons while remaining oriented to the values and objectives of the order as the rule of life for members. The constitutions thus did not specify a habit for the order, but only stipulated that the clothing be in keeping with the members' vow of poverty.[23] Accordingly, the Jesuits in the Near East dressed like the clerics of the Eastern churches, and those in China like Confucian scholars. When traveling in the Near East they often adopted the garb of Armenian merchants, which gave them the appearance of Christians but not Europeans.

The Discalced Carmelites, in contrast, initially followed the same strict regulations on their habit and food in the mission territory as they did in the Catholic regions of Western Europe. Their constitutions stipulated that they must live in the convent community and that other ways of life were mere temporary exceptions. Following the example of the Apostles, the friars were always to travel in pairs.[24]

The life of Carmelite missionaries continued to be marked by contradictions between the rules of strict observance and those of the social contexts in which they operated. This tension will be explored first in the following settings: at the court of a Muslim ruler, in the use of signs of social distinction, and in the practices of "friendship" and "good correspondence" with the laity. A separate subchapter will then examine the extent of the involvement of the Discalced Carmelites' Persian missions in the local economy. After all, missionaries who could not depend on financing from Europe and were thus left to their own devices found that their inevitable secular business dealings brought them into conflict with the norms of their order and the Roman Curia. Finally, the chapter will explore the justification strategies used by a Discalced Carmelite, Ange de Saint-Joseph, whom we have already encountered as a personality skilled in languages and knowledgeable about Persia. The way in which he and other missionaries constructed the normative horizon of their own enterprise in opposition to that of Catholic Europe takes us to the question of the processes of cultural relativization that emerged not just from contact with local practices of religiosity but also from the experiences and adaptations of the regular clergy in everyday life.

Courtiers Not Missionaries?

Competing norms had already been laid out in 1604 in Pope Clement VIII's dispatch of the Discalced Carmelites to Persia: the friars were not only tasked with effecting the conversion of Muslims and "schismatics," but were also expected to explore the possibilities of an anti-Ottoman alliance between the Catholic courts and the Safavids on the pope's behalf. Clement VIII expected the Discalced Carmelites to conceal their aim of spreading the Gospel. They were instead supposed to say that His Holiness had sent them to congratulate the king of Persia on his many victories over the common enemy, the Turks, and to suggest an alliance between the Christian monarchs and the shah.[25] This papal commission contrasted sharply with the order's ideals of nonentanglement and retreat from the "world." The pope demanded something of the Discalced Carmelites that the *Propaganda Fide* would later categorically prohibit the missionaries from doing. The *Propaganda Fide* came to require that missionaries not merely avoid any active intervention in political matters but also make no mention of affairs of state in their correspondence with the Congregation. These instructions were frequently repeated, for instance, in the aforementioned memorandum by Cardinal Giuseppe Renato Imperiali in 1707, which forbade the missionaries from intervening in political affairs on pain of "very severe penalties."[26]

The *Propaganda Fide* thereby confirmed regulations that the regular clergy had already been expected to obey before 1622 based on the norms of their own orders. Clement VIII's commission to the Discalced Carmelites contradicted this: when they were received in Persia in 1607 as envoys from the pope, they found it difficult to resist practices of social contact that clashed with the strict rules of a reformed mendicant order. According to the account by Paolo Simone di Gesù Maria, in the northern Persian city of Ardabil they at first insisted on staying at an inn. Although they carried letters for the shah, they were not ambassadors but "poor friars." They did, however, yield to the urgings of the governor, who accommodated them in a house specially laid out with carpets and invited them to a lavish banquet, as dictated by his duties when hosting foreign envoys. Because of the contrast with his order's vows of poverty, Friar Paolo Simone had to justify his behavior and that of his fellow friars in the report he sent to Rome, noting that they had only acted under protest. While his description showed that he and his companions were received as envoys after all, the friar also insisted that the Discalced Carmelites acquired more respect in this situation precisely because of their order's renunciation of the "world."

As ambassadors, they received gifts that could not be equated with the alms of the faithful, which essentially constituted the livelihood of members of the mendicant orders. With the refusal to accept the gifts, however, the friars contradicted the norms regulating social relations on the ground. The Discalced Carmelites had already encountered this problem during their journey in 1607. Citing the rules of their order, which allowed them to accept only what they strictly needed to live, they refused the gift of five horses and 100 *zecchini* (about 194 *scudi*) in cash offered to them for their onward journey by the ḫān of Šamāḫi. This refusal was followed by attempts at mediation. Finally, the friars signed a paper in which they explained the reasons for their refusal, thereby clearing the ḫān from the suspicion that he had neglected his duties of hospitality.[27]

After their arrival at the court of the shah, the Discalced Carmelites had to negotiate a path between the varied expectations of them. Paolo Simone di Gesù Maria emphasized that in 1607–8 he and his fellow friars had accepted neither gifts nor money beyond food for themselves. Although the strict observance of their order's vow of poverty could create trust, in other cases adaptation to the demands of court life proved inevitable. Since court society in Persia—as in Europe—required physical presence, individual friars had to travel in the shah's retinue and relinquish convent life for longer periods if they were to fulfill their political duties. Those friars sent to cultivate contacts at court were subject to accusations by their confreres that they did not take seclusion, and the norms of their order more generally, as seriously as they should. As early as 1609, Juan Thadeo de San Eliseo reported that his brothers disapproved greatly of his intention to follow the shah's army.[28] In 1616 this criticism was reflected in a resolution by the order's *Definitorium* requiring the friars to avoid this practice whenever possible.[29]

Yet presence at court and in the shah's retinue served not just to discharge diplomatic duties but also to pursue the interests of the mission. In 1618 Juan Thadeo de San Eliseo followed the shah to northern Persia until his fellow friars in Isfahan demanded that he return to the convent. He firmly rejected the admonitions of the superiors of the order in Rome to lead a contemplative life, avoid conversing with the laity, and refuse to see the ruler. This ran counter to the intentions of the pope, who had instructed the Discalced Carmelites to care for not just their own spiritual well-being but also that of their fellows. If the people saw that the ruler favored the Discalced Carmelites, the friars would attain "good credit" among his subjects. The shah appreciated frequent visits and being courted. Because of their dependence on the shah's favor, the Discalced Carmelites found themselves in a situation similar to that of his Muslim and Christian subjects, who also needed to cultivate a presence at court. According to Juan Thadeo, if they failed to do so, they would ultimately be compelled to regain the shah's favor with splendid gifts.[30]

The French Capuchins, who were dispatched to the Ottoman Empire and Persia at the instigation of Cardinal Richelieu's *éminence grise*, Friar Joseph de Paris, found themselves in a similar situation to that of the Discalced Carmelites. In an account on the origins of the convent in Isfahan, the founder, Pacifique de Provins, after falling out with his influential fellow brother, portrayed his actions as those of a friar devoted to exclusively religious aims who preferred not to be regarded as a royal envoy. For that reason, he claimed, in 1628 he had refused to live in a house, complete with servants, which the shah had offered to him; instead, he had lodged in a caravanserai, together with his donkey. It was improper for a member of his order to accept shows of honor fitting only for an ambassador. He had wanted everyone to recognize in him the spirit of his order; for that reason, he had asked the shah "to leave him [to live] in the ordinary exercises of his vocation as a Capuchin, which are discomfort, pain, suffering, humility, poverty, and contempt."[31]

Although the hopes of an anti-Ottoman alliance had already been dashed in the early period of the Persian mission, thus rendering the most important diplomatic mission with which Clement VIII had tasked "his" Discalced Carmelites irrelevant, they and other religious present in Isfahan retained their role as intermediaries at court until the toppling of the Safavid dynasty in 1722 and in some cases beyond that. The normative conflicts their roles entailed are documented especially well for two Capuchins, Raphaël du Mans and Felice Maria da Sellano. As a translator and interpreter serving the shah, Friar Raphaël participated in forms of court sociability that ran counter to his status as a member of a mendicant order: lavish consumption of food and alcohol, dance performances, music, and song.³² For the Jesuit Jacques Tilhac, he and Felice Maria da Sellano, who traveled to the Safavid court in 1700 as a papal envoy, were frightening examples of the transformation of mendicant friars into courtiers and noblemen as a result of their presence at court.³³ Felice Maria da Sellano himself excused the fact that he had presented himself as the pope's "ambassador" upon arrival in Yerevan with his mission to help the poor Catholics in the Safavid Empire. For the sake of the legation's honor, he had been forced to ignore his vocation as a Capuchin and exchange his habit for a gold and silver garment and acquire a retinue of twenty-five persons.³⁴

Contested Signs of Social Distinction

Presence at court was associated with adaptation to courtly norms of behavior. Given the conflicts between the orders, the unfriendly comments by the Jesuit Jacques Tilhac about the two Capuchins may not be surprising. This notwithstanding, other sources also confirm that some missionaries strove for a social status in the "world" that they had supposedly rejected by taking their vows. This included adopting signs of social distinction that contradicted the friars' vocation as members of the regular clergy: for example, in the name of "honor," Discalced Carmelites rode through the city on horseback instead of contenting themselves with donkeys or, better yet, accepting the effort of long walks. Similarly, some friars carried weapons to elevate their status and dressed in a manner that deviated from the order's habit, for example, by not going barefoot in sandals, which gave the order its name, or by wearing comparatively costly fabrics. Other controversial status symbols were the purchase of enslaved people or the hiring of paid domestic servants. Because of frequently repeated criticisms and prohibitions throughout the time of the missions' existence, and given the social demands of life on the ground, it seems likely that the regulations were often ignored.

In the constitutions of the Discalced Carmelites, strict unworldliness—the rejection of the material goods and status symbols of social rank—was expressed among other things in the principle that all friars, regardless of office, should always travel on foot. When unable to do so, they should travel in a modest manner appropriate to the custom of the country. Beginning in 1605, the constitutions stipulated that the use of a coach or a sedan chair—a symbol of high status—within a city had to be a "necessity" and required the permission of the superior. In the version printed in 1631, the *praepositus generalis,* definitors and provincials were expressly forbidden to allow themselves to be carried around in a sedan chair without "urgent necessity."³⁵

Among the Discalced Carmelites in Persia, the use of horses appears to have been an emblematic sign of distinction in public space. The very first arrivals already saw themselves confronted with the offer of horses to travel to an audience with the shah. According to a 1609 account, they explained that, in keeping with their vow of poverty, they would prefer to walk like poor folks to the shah's country residence. In contrast to this ostentatious reference to the vow of poverty, the same account mentions how on another occasion the Discalced Carmelites rode on horseback, albeit barefoot, to the great square in the town center in the expectation of meeting the shah there.³⁶

In the early years, however, there were already demands from within their own circles to use mules rather than horses and to keep only one of them in their own stable. If the shah presented the Discalced Carmelites with a horse, they were required to sell it immediately. Another friar stated that, at the risk of being mocked, it was better for the Discalced Carmelites to go on foot and not always appear as papal ambassadors. The *Definitorium* took up such demands in 1616: the friars must not ride through Isfahan on horseback unless a superior of the order gave them a dispensation from the prohibition based on grave necessity; they must not keep any horses in their house.[37]

Express mentions of the use of horses and the regular repetition of prohibitions into the eighteenth century show that the instructions conflicted with the demands of life on the ground in Persia. The Italian traveler Pietro Della Valle noted in his diary not just riding out to a "delightful country house" with an Augustinian and a Dominican in 1617 but also going on outings on horseback with the Discalced Carmelite Juan Thadeo de San Eliseo.[38] When García de Silva y Figueroa, ambassador of Philip III, entered Isfahan in 1618, the Augustinians and Discalced Carmelites also belonged to his retinue of mounted Europeans.

In light of these circumstances, Vicente de San Francisco, who had already criticized the use of horses when he was a simple friar, noted in 1621, now as a visitor general, that it was not in keeping with the order's vow of poverty to ride through the city astride a horse "except in cases of grave necessity." According to his *ordinationes*, the superior must decide upon any exceptions in consultation with the three senior friars. Only one mule could be kept in the convent.[39] The repeated confirmation of the prohibition on riding horses through the streets of Isfahan, Shiraz, and other cities not just in the instructions but also in the visitors' *ordinationes* can be viewed as an indicator of repeated violations. Thus in 1669, the visitor general, Francesco di Gesù, ordered the provincial vicar to sell the horse belonging to the convent in Shiraz without further ado. In 1678, the *Definitorium generale* complained that only a few friars were observing the prohibition.[40]

Doing without horses was not simply a rejection of convenience but also a symbolic renunciation of the "world" and its specific categories of rank and honor. The regular clergy's surroundings, however, could perceive this as a sign of deficient respect. Accordingly, when Bishop Bernard de Sainte-Thérèse entered Isfahan in 1640, Discalced Carmelites openly rode horses as signs of social distinction. The provincial vicar, the prior, and three other friars rode one mile on horseback to meet the prelate, accompanied by the Augustinians, other clerics and a large number of Christians. The Discalced Carmelites had to borrow the necessary horses from the agent of the English East India Company.[41]

Aside from owning and riding horses and the friars' manner of dress, criticism focused on bearing arms and keeping servants, practices that, contradicting the vow of poverty, marked claims to social rank in the "world." Friars who rode through the streets of Isfahan on horseback, wore costly garments very different from their habit while traveling, and rode out carrying pistols, curved sabers, and other weapons argued that they did so to acquire "honor" for themselves and the order, as a visitor noted in 1677. Weapons not worn for the sake of security were symbols of a status incompatible with that of the regular clergy. The visitor juxtaposed this with the virtue and modesty that even the "barbarians" and European "heretics" valued.[42]

Keeping servants raised several controversial issues: If the expense exceeded the minimum necessary for the settlement to function, its quality as a status symbol prevailed. If the servants were laypeople, this crossed the line between the convent and the "world" and in many cases also that of orthodoxy, since in Persia servants could also be non-Catholic Christians or Muslims. If domestic labor was not taken on by lay brothers (*donati*) from the order, which was considered desirable, it could be performed in various ways: by paid servants, by young boys receiving instruction while living at the convent, and by enslaved people.

Critics demanded less a complete ban on the employment of laypeople than a restriction to the actual minimum necessary for everyday life. In 1613, Friar Vicente de San Francisco deemed two lay servants per settlement to be adequate.[43] As visitor general, in 1621 he ordered that the sons of Christians who were receiving instruction in the Christian religion and "good manners" at the convent should not live there but should go home again every day. Only two boys from Catholic Armenian families from the archdiocese of Nakhchivan were accepted as acolytes and permitted to live in the convent. They were not supposed to serve the religious, however, or be used for errands outside the house, but were to devote all of their time to studying.[44] That this *ordinatio* was not implemented is evident from a letter that the provincial vicar sent the *praepositus generalis* in 1630: several Armenian lads were learning Italian and receiving religious instruction from the friars. The vicar claimed that the boys were nearly always with the friars, performed housekeeping tasks, ate in the refectory, and indeed sometimes slept at the convent and therefore witnessed the order's most secret business. All this could prove severely disadvantageous for convent discipline.[45] The instructions for missionaries in Persia and the Orient that had already been issued by the *Definitorium generale* at the beginning of the same year addressed this unfortunate state of affairs: the friars were permitted to offer instruction on Christian teachings to the sons of Christians and non-Christians, but the pupils were to eat and sleep at home.[46]

In the same instructions, the *Definitorium generale* also stipulated that household chores were to be performed wherever possible by lay brothers of the order rather than by laypeople. It was up to the superiors of the order to implement this statement of intent by dispatching lay brothers. In fact, this occurred only sporadically. Instead, the settlements in Persia continued to employ servants of secular estate even after 1630. The Discalced Carmelite convents in Isfahan and later in New Julfa each had a room for a live-in servant.

The sources also provide repeated evidence that some of these servants were Muslims. When the Discalced Carmelites argued with their bishop in 1641, they did so in the presence of the convent's servants and three Muslims who also worked in the house. In 1719, the friars had a Muslim gardener whose terminally ill little daughter they christened Maria Teresa. In the 1740s, Bishop Filippo Maria di Sant'Agostino employed a Muslim in Isfahan and was said to be very satisfied with his loyalty and attentiveness. The man was unmarried; the fact that he contracted a temporary marriage during each Ramadan as permitted by Shi'a Islam led to astonished queries from Friar Cornelio di San Giuseppe, but proved no impediment to his continued employment at the convent.[47]

Slaveholding was particularly controversial. In 1645, Denis de la Couronne d'Épines demonstrated his strictly observant perspective when he expounded on his decision to cease employing servants or slaves in the convent in Isfahan. In the past, he stated, the friars had always kept one or several servants or slaves for domestic chores. They had deemed this necessary, but now they had already managed well without them for eight months. This was better "for poverty and our peace [of mind]." This renunciation was possible thanks to two *donati*, who, unlike the lay brothers of Portuguese origin, did not consider the "humble services" to be "beneath their dignity."[48]

Reactions to a ban on the purchase of slaves that Francesco di Gesù issued in 1669 show that this renunciation was only temporary. The visitor general's decision deprived the convents of their best servants, a friar from Isfahan explained in a letter to the *praepositus generalis*. No one served the houses better than the slaves trained there. Other servants, Muslims or Armenians, betrayed them, gave bad service, and stole things.[49] Ange de Saint-Joseph offered especially eloquent disagreement from Shiraz. He, too, explained that Muslims and Eastern Christians provided poor service when compared to slaves. The ban on slaveholding also violated the spirit of the mission, since those enslaved were "schismatic" or "pagan" boys whom the missionaries were raising as Catholics. In Shiraz the Discalced Carmelites held two Black slaves, who had previously been "heathens" but now were "good servants and good Christians." In Isfahan the friars kept an enslaved Georgian who "served like an angel" and had become a good Catholic. In Basra, in turn, the friars had reared a servant "of pagan birth," who had been freed several years before upon attaining his majority and now lived so perfectly in the faith and in European customs that he was "among the coryphaei of the best neophytes." The purchase and training of slaves was thus a way of performing mission especially suited to local conditions. The best thing a rich man who wished to "make friends in Heaven" could do was to grant the missionaries a large sum of money so that they might acquire and instruct "pagan," "infidel," and "schismatic" slaves. How, then, could one forbid the clerics from "buying souls" who served Christ and "bodies that served the order" and instead subject the friars to "other Oriental servants"? Friar Ange therefore called upon the *Definitorium* to lift the visitor's ban—unsuccessfully, it appears from the documents.[50]

When Ange de Saint-Joseph defended slavery, he was justifying a practice common in the missions of various orders in Asia, Africa, and America.[51] While slavery was subject to extensive restrictions in Western Europe, the Church regarded the enslavement of "heathens" overseas as permissible under certain conditions, for instance when they were captured in a "just war" or when "savages" living in a state of nature refused to convert to Christianity. The most controversial issue was how to treat enslaved people who converted to Christianity or Christian prisoners acquired from "infidels."[52] The conflicts over ownership of enslaved people by the Discalced Carmelites in Persia focused not on whether it was permissible as such, but rather on whether it was compatible with a mendicant order's vow of poverty. When a visitor forbade the order to buy slaves, he argued against a practice that not only provided the order with labor power but also increased the status of those who owned them.

Thus far, we have addressed the signs of social distinction in the lives of the Discalced Carmelites. Given the uneven nature of the sources, it is difficult to compare them with the lifestyles of the other orders present in Persia. If we follow contemporary travel accounts, including those written by Protestants, only the convent of the Portuguese Augustinians differed fundamentally from that of the Discalced Carmelites because of its artful and lavish furnishings. According to the Englishman John Fryer, the friars walked "humbly about the streets and markets, discalceated, and in their distinct habits, none of them mounting an horse." Only the Augustinian prior dressed according to his status as Portuguese resident and lived "in a splendid palace, with noble walks and gardens."[53] The Venetian Ambrogio Bembo reported that the Augustinian rode through the city on horseback, preceded by a servant who cleared the way for him through the crowds.[54] When the Augustinians arrived in Isfahan in 1602, they received a house from ʿAbbās I that had previously been used to accommodate foreign envoys. The construction and furnishing of the settlement, which was referred to as the "royal convent," matched the political functions that the Portuguese Crown and its viceroys in Goa had assigned the Augustinians in Isfahan at the height of Portugal's influence in South Asia. Jean Chardin described the convent as a "royal palace" with numerous gardens and gilded and painted rooms large enough to host 100 people. According to Chardin, by the late 1660s and 1670s most of the rooms stood empty because only three or four clerics lived there with seven or eight servants. He had heard that the house of the Augustinians had previously been adorned with gold brocade and that the inhabitants had lived quite lavishly. Visitors had always been welcome and were served excellent meals.[55]

In contrast to Jean Chardin, who never stayed with the Augustinians, two Italian travelers who visited them in 1674 and 1694, respectively, offer no indication that they were living less extravagantly. According to Bembo, the church was painted in many colors and gold in the Persian manner; the Venetian saw richly decorated objects from China in the sacristy. Bembo praised the guest apartments, which were furnished in the Italian style with very good beds. In a corridor with a fine view of the garden he found a table with many sweets on Venetian glass plates. In the absence of lay brothers, the Augustinians were served by Armenian Christians who, Bembo noted, labored like beasts, and kept everything perfectly clean and tidy.[56] Giovanni Battista Gemelli Careri similarly described how the Augustinians put him up during his 1694 visit in their most beautiful rooms, painted in the local style in blue and gold, with a view of a lovely garden. According to Gemelli Careri, the Augustinians ate the most refined dishes prepared for them by a Portuguese cook; they kept twelve servants—three "Moors," two Arabs, three Armenians, and four Indians.[57]

The elaborate furnishings and large staff of servants recall the lifestyle of the Indo-Portuguese elites. The diverse origins and religions of the servants document the integration of the Augustinians into a sociocultural context and an economy that were both local and shaped by relations with South Asia. Initially, the Augustinians had a close relationship with the Portuguese Crown and the viceroy of the *Estado da Índia*, which financed the mission in the context of the *Padroado*. Yet once Portuguese power in Asia began to decline, the Augustinians in Isfahan appear to have been successful in providing for themselves. However, this achievement came at the price of extensive accommodation, which in the late seventeenth century even culminated in the conversion of two friars to Islam, as discussed in Chapter 3. In 1685—even before the sensational conversions—the viceroy of the *Estado da Índia* had already noted that he had no doubts that the convent in Isfahan had once been much revered. At present, however, the Augustinians in Isfahan as well as Bandar-i Kung, Bengal, and Mombasa were scarcely interested in anything but "amassing wealth, buying carpets, and engaging in similar business enterprises."[58]

If we are to believe Ambrogio Bembo, the settlements of the Discalced Carmelites, Capuchins, and Jesuits differed markedly from the Augustinian convent. Bembo described the Capuchin convent as comfortable but plain, in keeping with the order's Rule. He further noted that the Jesuits in New Julfa also possessed a good house with a garden, but lived in great poverty because they depended on the modest sums—he mentions ninety *reales* (ninety *scudi*) per annum—that they received from France; the superior had accordingly served him ordinary fruits and vinegary wine. The criticisms formulated within the Discalced Carmelite order concerning the ownership and use of horses, the carrying of weapons, changes to the habit, the employment of servants, and the purchase of enslaved people must be viewed in the context of their modest overall economic circumstances. The frame of reference of those who criticized such signs of social distinction as incompatible with the way of life of members of a mendicant order was the extremely strict normative order that emerged from the reform of the Carmelites in the sixteenth century in Europe.

The descriptions by the Protestants Jean Chardin and John Fryer cited above probably came closer to how members of the orders were perceived in local society than the criticisms of visitors and superiors. This impression is confirmed by Ambrogio Bembo, who describes how the Augustinians tried to persuade him to stay with them instead of the Discalced Carmelites because their convent was more comfortable and the Rule they followed less strict. Bembo regretted that the vicar of the Discalced Carmelites rarely graced his table with his presence because of the order's rules on fasting.[59] If the Discalced Carmelites in particular enjoyed respect beyond the narrow confines of a tiny Catholic community, it was a result not least of their reputation for having renounced the "world," despite all the deviations from strict observance that met with criticism from within the order.

"Friendship" and "Good Correspondence" with Laypeople

The practices of "friendship" and "good correspondence" that the Discalced Carmelites shared with the laity of various confessions were a mark of the respect they had attained in the local community. Such forms of sociability led to ceaseless controversies, as we shall see. That a Discalced Carmelite should not converse with laypeople and if he did, only for their spiritual well-being, was one of the central principles of life in the order.[60] The ideal of the Discalced Carmelite order was a life devoted to prayer in the seclusion of the friars' cells, far removed from the "world."[61] The constitutions admonished the brothers not to leave the cloister if at all possible, and regulated the conditions for doing so extremely restrictively. Through their activities, the officeholders made it possible for the other friars to remain cloistered. At the same time, they were also warned to restrict any business that took them outside the house to one or two days a week. All Discalced Carmelites were admonished, on pain of severe punishment, to accept food or drink outside of their house only rarely, only in cases of serious necessity, and with the express permission of their superior. Laymen were not to be housed in the convent unless they had performed some particular service for the Congregation. Similarly, they were only to be invited very occasionally to meals in the refectory. Visitors, no matter their status, were never to be served meat, which the Discalced Carmelites were not allowed to consume except in cases of illness.[62]

Soon after the mission was founded in Isfahan, differences over practices that integrated the friars into intense secular social contacts, contrary to the requirements of a contemplative life in seclusion from the world, emerged among members of the order. Given that one of the friars, Vicente de San Francisco, called for restrictions in a letter to the *praepositus generalis* as early as 1613, we can draw conclusions about the friars' social contacts. These included visits to the homes of Muslims and above all Armenians, who according to their customs offered guests food and drink, as well as return visits by Armenians, whom the friars were required to offer food and drink in turn. In his capacity as visitor in 1621, the same friar had the opportunity to impose strict limits on his fellow friars' social contacts. The Discalced Carmelites were to leave their convent rarely, and the prior was to see to it that business outside the house was dealt with by a third party rather than a friar. Visitors—which meant mainly Armenians and Muslims—must not be offered food. The Discalced Carmelites for their part were to accept neither food nor drink when they visited the homes of Armenians or Muslims. Laypeople should only rarely be invited to the refectory, and by no means should the friars host Muslims, "pagans," or other "infidels" there. Hosting strangers overnight could disrupt the tranquility necessary for prayer and other spiritual exercises. Here, too, Friar Vicente de San Francisco had more to say: he forbade the friars to host clerics of other orders and laypeople at the convent for longer than three to five days. Only one of the missionaries chosen by the superior was to be allowed to speak to the guests.[63] Such rules found their way into the 1630 instructions for the missionaries in Persia and the Orient: if the missionaries could not avoid offering temporary lodging to a cleric of another order or a layman until he found other accommodations, the superior of the house was to delegate a "prudent and edifying cleric" to chaperone the guest.[64]

Such regulations restricted the convents' function as hostelries. They thus contrasted sharply with the practices of "friendship" and "good correspondence," which the missionaries could scarcely resist, and deprived the friars of urgently needed income. As in other situations, the practice of dispensation offered a possibility to adapt to local social realities while at the same time affirming the order's norms in all their severity. Granting the competence to dispense members from the application of individual stipulations of the *ordinationes* and the instructions of 1630 to the convents' *discreti*, that is, to especially respected friars, turned the discipline from above into a *de facto* self-discipline by local actors.

The practices of "good correspondence" came to the attention of the superiors above all when tensions disrupted concord on the ground and individual members of the order positioned themselves as especially rule-abiding individuals. In such cases, accusations could even be directed at a visitor. For example, in 1669 the provincial vicar and prior of the convent of Isfahan wrote that the visitor, Francesco di Gesù, had allowed a layman in Shiraz to invite other laypeople to a banquet at the refectory of the Discalced Carmelites where meat was served. They met at the order's house for more than two hours every evening with the secular guests. This complaint was directed against a visitor who demanded strict observance, but who according to all accounts did not honor it himself. For it was further reported that, during his stay in Bandar ʿAbbās, the visitor had ridden out on horseback twice, which was incompatible with the "humility of a regular cleric and the credibility of the reform order."[65]

A visitation report of 1677 shows how tense the conflict over the compatibility of contemplation and mission remained within the order. The visitor noted at the time that occasions for leaving the convent were actually rare; it sufficed for them to go to New Julfa once a week. It was completely unsuitable for a Discalced Carmelite to eat and drink with laypeople outside the house and participate in large banquets. He also disapproved of the fact that the Discalced Carmelites in Persia did not maintain a shared household. The superiors of the convents lived apart and in quite lavish circumstances. Many of them sought the friendship of laymen to gain better supplies; the priors kept many gifts for themselves instead of sharing them with the other friars. As a consequence, some of them traveled like knights and others like beggars, and they incurred many needless expenses during their travels.[66] Following the visitation, in 1678 the *Definitorium* forbade the missionaries, including the superiors, to attend public banquets. In cases of disobedience, the provincial vicar was to impose fifteen days of spiritual exercises on simple clerics, while superiors were to be deprived of their offices.[67]

The visitor's 1677 *ordinatio* picked up where the 1630 instructions for the missionaries in Persia had left off. The *Definitorium generale* had issued them at a time when those opposed to missionary *actio* had gained the upper hand. In 1683, when the *Definitorium generale* summarized the guidelines set down over the years in new instructions, it attempted to reconcile the discipline of a predominantly contemplative order with the requirements of mission. These included the express obligation to be available to the Armenians and all others for whose salvation the missionaries were responsible by treating them kindly and visiting them frequently in their homes. Thus, what had previously been tolerated only as an exception was now defined as a missionary duty.[68]

The instructions of 1683 dispensed with defining the conditions under which missionaries could leave the house in detail. It was only in a later version that the *Definitorium* required the missionaries to obtain their superior's permission if they wished to leave the house, even if they were called to hear confession. The superiors were to see to it that their subordinates did not spend unnecessary time in the homes of laypeople but would instead make themselves useful in the convent. Alongside this fundamental commitment to life in the convent, however, new stipulations were added that obliged friars to work outside the convent as well: the missionaries were to make sure that the "flock of Christ was not carried off by wolves" and that "new sheep were added daily to this flock." They were expressly instructed to travel to neighboring towns as well to preach the word of God and administer the sacraments—with the written permission of the provincial vicar, now called a prefect—even beyond a distance of thirty Italian miles.⁶⁹

All this notwithstanding, in 1684 the visitor, Agnello dell'Immacolata Concezione, criticized the Discalced Carmelite Élie de Saint-Albert, who had moved to New Julfa in 1679 and combined confessional clarity with close social relations with the Armenian laity there, particularly the Sceriman family. He accused Élie de Saint-Albert, prior of the convent of Isfahan between 1682 and 1686, of violating the order's vow of poverty with his practice of dining, drinking, and staying overnight in the houses of laypeople in the Armenian quarter, even though this enabled him to give a religious address after the meal.⁷⁰ Like the visits of Élie de Saint-Albert in New Julfa, the return visits of the Armenians became the focus of criticism: a friar, Fortunato di Gesù Maria, asked the superiors of the order to allow him to return to Europe so that he might live "according to his condition as a reformed Carmelite." The house in Isfahan was "more an inn for the [prior's] secular friends" than a convent.⁷¹ While the visitor, Agnello dell'Immacolata Concezione, censured Friar Fortunato for his deficient observance of the Rule, he also accused the prior of having turned the convent into a "caravanserai for Armenians," who tethered their horses outside the monks' cells and disturbed their tranquility.⁷²

The Discalced Carmelites were not the only order where tensions arose between those who insisted on the literal observance of the Rule and those who, citing their knowledge of the country, justified deviations from it as inevitable. In 1700, the Jesuit Jacques Tilhac also explained his request for permission to return to his province in terms of the dangers that the unavoidable integration into transconfessional sociability posed to his spiritual well-being. No missionary could consistently avoid the obligation to visit other Europeans. During the visits, the guests ate and drank heavily, as was the local custom. And then there were the banquets held by the missionaries themselves on the occasion of order or church feast days or for legations. These visits and gatherings were said to maintain brotherly love, but the missionary's true brotherly love— the love of God and the concern for spiritual welfare—could scarcely be cultivated in this manner. Long experience showed, he noted, that visits and gatherings soon ruined "the entire inner spirit of a religious."⁷³ Such practices were the result of the increasing integration of missionaries into local social contexts. The extent and impact of this integration is nowhere more apparent than in the economic activities of the convent. These will be the focus of the following subchapter.

All-Too-Worldly Business

The surviving archives of the *Propaganda Fide* suggest that subsidies from Europe constituted the greater part of mission financing. Soon after the Congregation's founding in 1622, the records show subsidies for the Discalced Carmelites and, after they settled in New Julfa in the 1680s, also for the Dominicans of the Roman congregation of Santa Sabina. The Augustinians, Capuchins, and Jesuits received financial support from Portugal and the *Estado da Índia*, France, and Poland, but the amounts are unknown. To the extent that we do have quantitative evidence, the economic impact of subsidies from Europe on the everyday life of the missions was minimal. In Basra, where two surviving account books allow quantitative insights into the convent economy, transfers from Italy made up just 2.4 percent of the Discalced Carmelites' income between 1719 and 1753.[74] There is scant evidence that the proportions were significantly different in the heartland of the Safavid Empire than in the port city on the Persian Gulf, which had become part of the Ottoman Empire at the time the account books were kept. Until now, the history of early modern Catholic missions has addressed economic issues only partially and mostly with respect to the Society of Jesus.[75] In what follows, I will briefly sketch the normative framework laid down by the Discalced Carmelite order and secondarily by the Roman Curia. Then I will elucidate the practice of Roman subsidies. Ultimately, the question of the real economy of the settlements in Persia is largely unknown territory.[76] Although Basra was never under Safavid dominion, the mission in this town will be included alongside Isfahan and New Julfa for two reasons: First, from the order's perspective, the mission there remained organizationally part of the Persian mission, even after the Ottomans captured the city. Second, the surviving account books are exceptional in that they span several decades, which makes it possible to offer solid quantitative evidence about the origins of the convent's revenues. On this basis, we can pose the question anew of the significance of subsidies in relations between missionaries on the ground, on the one hand, and their superiors and the *Propaganda Fide*, on the other.

Roman Norms

Viewed from Rome, matters were clear: the position that missionaries should not involve themselves in the affairs of the laity and should refrain from participating in trade and financial dealings is a common thread running through the texts with which the superiors of the orders and the *Propaganda Fide* intervened in the everyday life of the missions. As a consequence of the radical abnegation of the "world" demanded by the Teresian reform, the Discalced Carmelites in particular were supposed to remain aloof from secular business. In his *ordinationes* of 1621, the visitor general, Vicente de San Francisco, reminded the friars that the constitutions forbade any involvement in credit and commercial transactions with the laity.[77] In the instructions of 1630 for the missions in Persia and the Orient, the *Definitorium generale* recalled the prohibition in the order's constitutions on doing business with laypeople. Similarly, the missionaries were not to lend money to merchants or other persons.[78] In 1644, the General Chapter reaffirmed the prohibition on secular business dealings; the superiors would be suspended from their offices for six months, and simple clerics would lose their seat and vote in the chapter for one year, if they served as the representatives, agents, or administrators of persons outside the order or participated in brokering marriages.[79] In 1683, the *Definitorium* confirmed the ban in the instructions for the missionaries in the East on intervening "in the business of laypeople." Unlike in 1630, the convents and other settlements were now allowed to invest money at interest in urgent cases, provided they had the consent of the chapter of the convents or of all the clerics in the other settlements, as well as written permission from the provincial vicar. The provincial vicar for his part was now even obliged to invest all the alms that the conventuals received from Goa at a profit, and to distribute the interest to the settlements according to their needs.[80]

What was new about the instructions of 1683 was that the order's *Definitorium generale* now also referred to the constitutions of the *Propaganda Fide*. As we know, the first secretary of the Congregation, Francesco Ingoli, had identified the greed of many missionaries as one of the main impediments to successful missionary activities. He particularly had in mind the material and symbolic profits the missionaries gained from brokering objects from foreign lands. In the seventeenth and eighteenth centuries, such criticisms defined the normative framework set out by the Curia. I will mention just a few milestones here. In 1633, when Urban VIII, at the instigation of the *Propaganda Fide*, issued the papal bull *Ex debito pastoralis officii* removing the missionary territories in Asia that were not directly under Portuguese rule from subjection to the *Padroado*, he simultaneously forbade any direct or indirect involvement by the regular clerics active there in profit-oriented trade or financial dealings, on pain of excommunication and other penalties. The *Propaganda Fide* repeated this prohibition in the 1659 instructions for the apostolic vicars. In the constitution *Sollicitudo pastoralis officii* of 1669, Pope Clement IX (Giulio Rospigliosi, r. 1667–9) declared that the material hardship of the missions was no reason to ignore the prohibition. Not only would the missionaries who flouted the ban themselves face excommunication, but so, too, would the superiors who did not pursue the violations. In an extensive account of the sad state of affairs in the missions in 1707, Cardinal Giuseppe Renato Imperiali once again accused the regular clergy of seeking personal advantage and engaging in trade. The rules that the *Propaganda Fide* then instituted reminded missionaries once more of the relevant prohibitions, especially the papal constitution of 1669: "And still less should you involve yourselves in business with the laity, whether Catholic or infidel, or conduct [business dealings] with others that are the specific province of laymen and merchants."[81] In summary, both the order and the Roman Curia subjected secular business to extensive restrictions. At the same time, the frequent reiteration of the prohibitions can be taken as an indication that they were not being followed.

The Subsidies from Rome

Observing the requirements of the order and the Curia would have presupposed sufficient subsidies or financing through alms and endowments. Before we attempt to gain insights into the local economy of the Discalced Carmelites' Persian missions, we must therefore first introduce the practice of subsidy payments. Francesco Cimino, Baron of Cacurri, met one of the future missionaries to Persia, Juan Thadeo de San Eliseo, as a penitent in Naples. In 1608, he bequeathed 3,000 Neapolitan ducats or 2,250 Roman *scudi* annually for the maintenance of a Discalced Carmelite missionary seminary. His nephew and heir, Paolo Cimino, was supposed to pay this sum from the revenues of the property he had inherited. In fact, only part of the quite substantial legacy ever went to the Discalced Carmelites. Since the heir refused to honor his obligation, a protracted trial ensued. The legal case ended in 1622 with a settlement, on the basis of which the missionary seminary had to make do with a capital of 21,103

Neapolitan ducats (15,827 Roman *scudi*). This sum consisted of the proceeds of various taxes on goods in the Kingdom of Naples, which were contingent on political and economic circumstances and, therefore, were not forthcoming for many years.[82] The funds from the Baron of Cacurri's endowment were not supplemented by other legacies, which might have compensated for these losses.

In 1617, the *Definitorium generale* resolved to use the endowment to pay each missionary in Persia fifty *scudi* for his travel expenses, and an additional fifty *scudi* per year for his upkeep.[83] The sum of fifty *scudi* per annum set a standard that the *Propaganda Fide* would also follow in years to come. In the eighteenth century, it paid subsidies at the same level to the Dominicans of the Roman congregation of Santa Sabina, who had lived in New Julfa since the 1680s. As bishops, the Dominican Barnaba Fedeli di Milano and his Discalced Carmelite successors all received 200 *scudi* yearly from the *Propaganda Fide*.

The sum of fifty Roman *scudi* per missionary roughly corresponded to the per capita expenditures for food, clothing, and medical care of a mendicant in Italy in the mid-seventeenth century.[84] Given the modest way of life expected of the friars, this must have seemed appropriate from the Italian perspective of the superiors of the Discalced Carmelite order or a curial congregation. No allowances were made, however, for differences in living expenses or losses from transfer and exchange rates. A far more serious problem was that the earmarked sums only arrived in Persia partially and after great delays. In the thirty-five years between 1719 and 1753, the Discalced Carmelites in Basra received a mere eleven money transfers from Rome. Using the various channels available to them, the missionaries therefore repeatedly pressed for more reliable financing. This had already been the aim of Juan Thadeo de San Eliseo's 1619 suggestion to the *Definitorium* that payments be transferred two years in advance, to allow the clerics in Persia reserves for one year in case of emergency. It made no sense, he noted, to keep 500 *scudi* in reserve in Italy; instead, the money should be transferred to Persia.[85] The *Definitorium generale* responded to the requests in 1620 with a resolution to send 500 *scudi* to Persia every year out of the revenues from Baron of Cacurri's legacy. Since the transfers continued to arrive irregularly, in 1624 the friars in Isfahan decided to send their prior, Próspero del Espíritu Santo, to Rome. They were forced to go into debt to cover their running costs. They recommended sending one or two friars to France to beg for alms there. Princes and republics were to be asked to take over the protection of the settlements in Persia.[86] The *Propaganda Fide* acted as the protector of the Persian missions for the first time in 1625 by providing the sum of 500 *scudi* to pay off debts that the prior of the Discalced Carmelites had incurred when purchasing a house for the settlement in Shiraz. Further concessions followed. In 1629, for example, the Congregation promised six Discalced Carmelites dispatched to Persia that it would cover travel expenses of 400 *scudi* in all. These were quite substantial sums given the modest financing of the *Propaganda Fide* itself.[87] They brought only momentary relief, however, and did not lead to permanent funding for the Persian missions by the curial congregation.

Thus, beginning in the 1620s the friars could occasionally benefit from the fact that the *Propaganda Fide* used financial concessions to affirm its right to run the missions, while the superiors of the order also continued to consider this their purview. This notwithstanding, the precarious situation on the ground remained essentially unchanged. To make matters worse, in 1655 Alexander VII transferred the right of disposal over the order's own revenues intended for the missions to the *Propaganda Fide*. This occasioned new worries among the missionaries. Now they had to enlist their superiors and the procurator general to move a notoriously unapproachable curial congregation that was known for making life hard for petitioners.

Eventually, the *Definitorium generale* of the Discalced Carmelites saw itself forced in 1695 to consider the question of the subsidies. In consultation with the *Propaganda Fide*, it resolved to limit financial support for the missions in the Near East to those in Tripoli, Aleppo, Basra, Shiraz, and Isfahan. Two priests were to live in each of these places with a subsidy of fifty *scudi* per year each. The settlements could keep the income from masses and alms for themselves. This decision went hand in hand with efforts by superiors of the order to gain insights into the missions' finances. Representatives of the missions were supposed to account to the General Chapter for the subsidies received and the income and expenditures of the settlements more generally.[88]

Still, in the years that followed subsidies continued to arrive only partially and with delays. The missionaries in Persia complained to the *Propaganda Fide* about this situation at regular intervals. The replies to the missionaries' grievances reveal the *Propaganda Fide*'s tendency to leverage shared jurisdiction to blame the superiors of the orders both for the state of affairs and for offering no remedy for the situation. When the *Propaganda Fide* called upon the procurator general of the Discalced Carmelites to offer his opinion in 1701, he pointed out that the responsible *syndicus* had transferred the subsidies, albeit to Bishop Élie de Saint-Albert. He was supposed to send them on, even though he was staying in Rome at the time. In 1707, in response to renewed grievances from the Discalced Carmelites, the secretary of the *Propaganda Fide* noted that the subsidies were not paid out by the Congregation itself but came from the revenues of the *Seminario di San Pancrazio*. The Dominicans in Isfahan received a similar notification that same year, after also writing to the *Propaganda Fide* about the absence of their subsidies: the prior of Santa Sabina in Rome, not the Congregation, was responsible for transferring the annual subsidies of fifty *scudi* per missionary.[89] Such notices were formally correct but must have fed the topos of the "Roman slowness" that the missionaries associated with the curial congregation. At the same time, in conjunction with the material constraints, they contributed to the justification of practices that contradicted the demands of strict observance. In 1721, the provincial vicar in Isfahan frankly described to the *Definitorium generale* what the friars had resorted to doing in the absence of annual payments: borrowing from non-Christian Indians and Protestant Englishmen, making and selling wine, and currying favor with the English in Bandar ʿAbbās with the aim of receiving money and gifts—all practices that the provincial vicar had to know were frowned upon in Rome.[90]

Local Economies

The local convent economies bore only a very distant resemblance to the prescriptions of the orders and the Curia. The boundaries to the world of the laity that the orders and the Roman Curia had drawn were bound to crumble in the face of the material constraints that arose from insufficient financing from Europe. The missions in Persia were no exceptions in this regard, as will be explored below based on the scholarship on Jesuit missions in South and East Asia.

Two account books have survived for the Discalced Carmelite settlement in Basra which offer insights into the local convent economy, one for the years 1674 to 1727, and another for the period from 1728 to 1772.[91] Such account books cannot, however, simply be taken as a reflection of the real economy, as is evident from a comment that the vicar responsible for the accounts appended at the end of his entries for 1718: Anyone who found the expenditures for the last two months too high, he noted, should be aware that he had only just now begun to record everything. Previously, he had not registered one third of the expenses. With these words the vicar departed, for reasons we can no longer reconstruct, from a bookkeeping practice that up to that point had made the account book less a reflection of the actual economy of the convent than of what the friar who kept the books wished to commit to paper. Yet, contrary to the friar's claim, the obfuscation was intended more to conceal certain revenues than the (in any case nonitemized) expenditures, whose numbers were "fiddled" in proportion to the undocumented income. Up to 1718, the Discalced Carmelites in Basra only recorded their income from priestly activities (especially alms for masses), the subsidies from Rome, rental income, and gifts from grateful guests. From December 1718 on, they recorded additional revenues, which we can assume, based on the vicar's comment, had previously already played an important role: for the first time, in December 1718, the account book lists an income of 278 'abbāsī "ex industria"; under the same rubric, 705 'abbāsī are mentioned in July 1719, 500 in January 1720, 600 in July 1720, 350 in December 1720, 400 in April 1721, 1,300 in July 1722, and so forth. Beginning in 1724, these revenues "ex industria" were supplemented by substantial income from the sale of rosewater, which was produced in the city's environs. Because of Basra's importance as a trade hub and the friars' close relationships with the mercantile milieu, which represented their most important spiritual clientele, we can assume that "ex industria" also referred to the sale of goods. If we are to believe the account of a Scottish captain and merchant, the friars engaged in a profitable trade in arrack that they distilled from dates and sold to Christians, Jews, Muslims, and "pagans."[92]

The analysis of the records for the years 1719 to 1753 impressively documents the extent of the mission's economic autonomy: as already mentioned, during this period only 2.4 percent of revenues came from the subsidies, which arrived in Basra from Europe at very irregular intervals. While the settlement managed to survive despite the lack of funds from Europe, this was due to the friars' success in building a modest but independent convent economy. In 1747, the account book recorded the repayment of a loan for the renovation of the church, noting that the settlement was now debt-free. The account book shows that the Discalced Carmelites in fact regularly achieved a modest surplus. They relied on the provision of services that were in demand in the port city by Europeans passing through and Eastern Christians of various confessions. In the process, they benefited from the fact that Basra was integrated into the trade networks connecting the Indian Ocean and the Persian Gulf with Aleppo and the Mediterranean by land. Between the 1720s and early 1770s, the city grew into a booming transit port. English, Dutch, and French merchants became more important in the city's long-distance trade. At the same time, Basra became a place of refuge for Armenian merchants from New Julfa.[93]

The Discalced Carmelite settlement in Basra was primarily a hostelry, where the friars offered the growing number of Christian merchants in the city lodgings and spiritual services. Occasionally, the tenants included a rare Muslim among the many Europeans and Eastern Christians. Ambrogio Bembo reports that the Discalced Carmelites met him at the harbor with a boat in 1673 and took him to their house. The friars had been informed of the Venetian's impending arrival in a letter from the English consul in Aleppo. They offered their guest more than just a place to sleep: at the convent Bembo met other Europeans staying in Basra—a Frenchman and the VOC agent—in whose company he explored the environs of the city with their many canals. The superior of the Discalced Carmelites looked after the interests of the French and English in the city, and, because the customs formalities preceding the Venetian's departure for India dragged on, he also intervened on his behalf with the customs official.[94] Merchants and travelers looked to the Discalced Carmelites for the latest information on local procedures. In 1669, representatives of the *Compagnie des Indes orientales* who lodged in the friars' house negotiated the conditions for doing business with local authorities using the vicar as an intermediary and then received local merchants there.[95]

Around 1670, the Discalced Carmelites rented out a house as well as the rooms of a caravanserai adjacent to the convent. Over the years, they invested the surplus income in the purchase of further properties. During the period from 1719 to 1753, 41 percent of the convent's revenues came from rents on several houses and the rooms in the caravanserai, and occasionally from letting rooms in the convent itself. A further 33.6 percent of income came from alms and legacies, which the Discalced Carmelites received mainly from people who had once lodged with them; 6.2 percent consisted of payments for burials in the convent's courtyard and church. The friars also used their connections in the mercantile milieu to engage in their own business, which provided 16.5 percent of revenues in the period from 1719 to 1753. For a time, they specialized in the trade of rosewater: throughout this period, 8.1 percent of total revenues came from this activity, and in the years 1734 to 1738 nearly 23 percent.

If we are to believe the account books' figures on income from the sale of goods, there was a significant shift over the period studied here from such commerce to services for European and Eastern Christian merchants. In 1719, when the vicar decided to switch to a more complete mode of bookkeeping, the proportion of documented revenues from commodity sales soared from zero to 41.6 percent. After 1740, such sales largely disappear from the account book, which only mentions the occasional sale of goods that the friars had probably acquired as donations. The fact that the Discalced Carmelites acquired additional properties to rent to travelers during the same period might indicate that they specialized as service providers for merchants and mariners. It is also possible, however, that the trade activities that so patently violated the Rule were simply erased from the account books as they had been up to 1718.

The fact that the close social relations with the European trading companies and involvement in commercial dealings are documented for the 1750s in the papers of Cornelio di San Giuseppe is possible evidence of deliberate omission. For foreign merchants without local connections in Basra, the friar seemed to be a trustworthy contact for their local business. In the absence of an agent and consul, he facilitated the transactions of the *Compagnie des Indes* and the French consulate in Basra. The reward for his efforts contributed to the Discalced Carmelites' involvement in other commercial dealings: in recognition of the friar's services to the *Compagnie des Indes* and the French *nation*, the trading company sold the settlement of his order in Basra a barrel of Madeira wine annually at a reduced price starting in 1752, which the missionaries partly consumed themselves and partly resold at a profit.[96]

Unfortunately, the state of the sources for the finances of the Discalced Carmelite settlements in Isfahan, New Julfa, and Shiraz is far poorer. There, as in Basra, the friars also had various potential solutions for their financial hardships. These turned them into actors in the local economies but also distanced them to some extent from the norms of their order: aside from the hope of alms and endowments appropriate for a mendicant order, here, too, they had the option of active participation in secular business.

Income from masses and alms represented the two elements of independent financing that could be reconciled with the order's constitutions. Immediately after they arrived in Isfahan in 1607, however, the Discalced Carmelites had already been forced to concede that Persia offered little in this regard. Juan Thadeo de San Eliseo informed the *Definitorium* in 1619 that it would be frowned upon if they asked Muslims or local Christians for alms; begging would harm the missionaries' reputation. There were few "Franks" in Persia, and most of them were merchants more interested in making money than giving it to others.[97] Although conflicts with the Portuguese *Padroado* were likely to result in problems, the Discalced Carmelites sought the consent of the archbishop of Goa and the viceroy of the *Estado da Índia* to establish settlements in Goa and Hormuz. When they were finally able to found the convent in Goa around 1620, it was the hopes of alms and endowments from the wealthy Indian city that moved the superiors of the order to approve the friars' unauthorized actions.

The alms from India did, in fact, substantially help to alleviate the financial hardships of missionaries in Persia. In 1649, the procurator of the Persian missions reported to the General Chapter that most of the revenues for the missions in Persia came from India in the form of alms and payment for masses; another part came from Rome. During hard times, friars or lay brothers were repeatedly sent to India from Persia. The alms that the lay brother Francesco Maria di San Siro brought back to Persia in 1701 were said to suffice to repay the missions' large debts.[98]

There were limits, however, to the financing available from the *Estado da Índia*. These had to do with the weakening of Portugal's position in South Asia and with the conflicts over relations with the Portuguese *Padroado*, which led to the expulsion of the Discalced Carmelites from Goa in 1709. Starting in the 1650s, the consequences of the advance of the Dutch into South Asia for Portuguese trade, and thus for alms and gifts to ecclesiastical institutions, were cause for concern among the Discalced Carmelites. The Portuguese had not donated for a single mass lately, one of the Discalced Carmelites in Basra lamented in 1655. He used this fact to justify the transconfessional relations discussed in Chapter 5, to which the friars owed the payments they received from the Dutch.[99]

Since alms from Catholics were often associated with the obligation to read masses, the small number of priests available to perform these duties meant that the settlements in Isfahan, Shiraz, and Basra soon ran up against practical obstacles. In 1678, the visitor general mentioned a debt of 11,000 masses, which the friars would not have time to celebrate even in three years. The previous year, the order's procurator general in Rome had brokered an additional 800 masses. While they thanked him, they also let it be known that the Persian missions could not accept any more alms of this kind; they were now fully dependent on the aid of God and the superiors of the order.[100] Since the latter reached out only sporadically, in economic matters the missionaries had no choice but to engage in the local world of the laity.

Parallel to their efforts to acquire funding from India, the Discalced Carmelites in Isfahan had also been trying to tap into local resources since the 1610s. Two concessions from ʿAbbās I created the preconditions for economic autonomy: Like the Augustinians before them, the Discalced Carmelites were offered a house free of charge by the shah in 1609. It stood in a large garden and offered room for workshops and stables for horses. The friars kept this property until they gave up the mission in the 1750s. Thanks to Friar Juan Thadeo's connections at court, the Discalced Carmelites also acquired a piece of land outside the city for their use.

The two plots of land formed the basis of a modest convent economy. As in Basra, the Discalced Carmelites in Isfahan offered hospitality. While the sources required to quantify their economic significance are lacking, travel accounts reveal that the friars set up their house to receive travelers as guests. Ambrogio Bembo was assigned several rooms with his own kitchen in the convent courtyard, while at the same time a separate house served as an inn. According to Bembo, Europeans were constantly staying there; during his own sojourn one of the guests was the "heretical Frenchman" Jean Chardin, together with Antoine Raisin of Lyon, both of them jewel merchants.[101]

The friars kept chickens in the convent garden and grew vegetables, fruit, cereals, and pulses. The trees provided some of the firewood needed for the convent. The copious water supply from an underground canal (*qanāt*) and three wells facilitated agriculture. While the monks consumed most of the produce from the convent garden themselves, Prior Juan Thadeo de San Eliseo wanted to use the plot of land outside the city not just as a Catholic cemetery but also as a vineyard. In 1616 he reported to a fellow friar then in Rome that he had had a wall built around the piece of land thanks to a loan guaranteed by two rich Armenian merchants from New Julfa. The planting of 25,000 grape vines, which he mentions in the same report, shows that the prior aimed to produce several thousand liters of wine annually, which far exceeded the convent's own needs. However, the commercial sale of the wine, which was in high demand in the capital, especially at court, gave rise to criticism from fellow friars and the superiors of the order.[102]

The initiator of the wine production defended himself in 1619 by arguing that the main use of the land was as a burial place for Catholic Christians. He had not violated the vow of poverty, since the constitutions stipulated that the Discalced Carmelites could maintain suitable places for observance and gardens to grow their own food. Unlike the letter of 1616 to a fellow friar from his own convent, the 1619 letter to the *praepositus generalis* no longer mentions 25,000 grapevines, but only "four meager vines."¹⁰³ This last bit must be rhetoric, since the *Definitorium generale* felt compelled in 1630 to instruct the missionaries in Isfahan to use the plot of land referred to as a cemetery for that purpose alone and not to plant anything there.¹⁰⁴ Nevertheless, the Discalced Carmelites, with the help of their servants, subsequently pressed wine, and not only for their own consumption. According to a memorandum written by an unknown friar probably around 1670, their servants sold wine and brandy, which caused a "scandal" and led to the missionaries being regarded as taverners. For that reason, the friars were to make wine only for their own use; however, they were currently producing double the amount by claiming that was what they needed.¹⁰⁵ How extensive the production of wine and brandy actually was must remain open, given the lack of additional sources. When the author of the memorandum spoke of a "scandal," he may have been referring to criticisms concerning either the flouting of observance or the sale of alcohol to Muslims, which was frowned upon by the Muslim religious authorities.

Indications that the Discalced Carmelites were making wine are not only found in Isfahan, however. In 1721 the provincial vicar reported that because no funding had arrived from Rome, the friars in Shiraz had borrowed money and produced a large quantity of wine, which they sold to the French consul and the Portuguese agent. Thanks to the proceeds from the trade in the Shiraz wine, which was in high demand and was also exported to India via the ports on the Persian Gulf, they secured a living for themselves and were able to repair their dilapidated settlement.¹⁰⁶

The sale of their own wine and brandy was not the only way in which the Discalced Carmelites participated in trade. The relationships they entered into in India with an eye to the acquisition of alms and endowments also had a commercial dimension. While accepting alms corresponded to the constitutions of a mendicant order, the resulting flow of money gave occasion to economic practices that took the missionaries into the economic world of the laity and that recall the criticism of missionaries' acquisitiveness that the secretary of the *Propaganda Fide*, Francesco Ingoli, had voiced. The utility of alms could be maximized if they were used to buy goods that could be sold for a profit in Persia. This was precisely what the *praepositus generalis* himself had in mind when he instructed the visitor general in 1624 to buy easily transportable goods with the alms he received in Goa.¹⁰⁷ When he returned to Persia from a sojourn in Goa in the 1630s, Dimas della Croce brought with him 4,000 piasters (the equivalent of 4,000 *scudi*) not just in cash but also in the form of ambergris and diamonds, which could be sold at a profit in Persia.¹⁰⁸

Individual members of the order used their extensive connections to acquire valuable or rare items from distant lands, whether for their own use or for that of the convent. It is not always easy to determine with certainty how truthful such accounts were; skepticism is warranted, for example, in the case of a visitor general who had complained of numerous violations of the Rule being accused by one of his targets of himself having traveled to India with costly Persian rugs, clearly in order to sell them there for a profit.¹⁰⁹ The effects of an ecclesiastical visitor who died in Basra included not just twenty piasters (the equivalent of twenty *scudi*) belonging to the mission and an additional one hundred *zecchini in oro* (ca. 194 *scudi*) but also bezoar stones, several pearl rings, and many other *curiosità*.¹¹⁰ In one of his *centurie*, Cornelio di San

Giuseppe mocked a fellow friar who, after fourteen years in Basra, wanted to travel to Rome with two camels, in the hope of acquiring "honor" for his order with the foreign beasts, like the Jesuits who returned in Chinese or Japanese dress.[111] Conversely, there are a few cases of friars seeking to use their connections with Rome to pave the way for profitable small business enterprises. For example, in 1655 Barnaba di San Carlo asked one of the superiors of the order to send him ten small clocks from Rome, which he could sell in Basra at five times the price.[112]

Such business was closely associated with the "friendship" and "good correspondence" with merchants of various confessions discussed in Chapter 5. The friar who criticized the selling of wine and brandy probably around 1670 lamented not just the practice of bringing alms from Goa in the form of commodities; he also claimed that merchants dispatched goods under the Discalced Carmelite name, which were then sold in the order's houses. The friars were therefore considered to be merchants, which greatly damaged their reputation.[113] There is evidence that relationships with the merchants whom the Discalced Carmelites hosted in their houses occasionally led to commercial transactions. As prior of the convent in Isfahan, for instance, Ange de Saint-Joseph purchased a few clocks from a Catholic French merchant who found himself in difficulties; he later sold them at a profit, mainly to the shah's clockmaker.[114]

The missions' interest-earning business was also tied to their connections in the mercantile milieu. While we have only selective figures on the volume of credit, they reveal that, at least sometimes, the Discalced Carmelites possessed liquid funds that they did not immediately need and thus sought to invest at a profit. If the 1683 instructions of the *Definitorium generale*, unlike those of 1630, allowed the convents to invest money at interest, the superiors were adapting the normative framework to widespread practice. Although the business of credit raised controversial questions, especially regarding the compatibility of the frequently high interest rates with the canonical prohibition on usury[115] and the permissibility of credit relations with non-Catholics, even before 1683 the superiors of the order were repeatedly informed with surprising candor about the financial advantages of investments in this or that location and across religious lines. In 1653, the Discalced Carmelite Felice di Sant'Antonio in Basra spoke in favor of investing the mission's money with the Dutch at an annual interest rate of 12 percent, which he himself had done on several occasions.[116] The vicar of Basra, Barnaba di San Carlo, made a similar argument in his correspondence with one of the definitors. He, too, highlighted the advantages of investing the money from the Persian missions in Basra and Baghdad instead of Isfahan. While in Isfahan one could not obtain more than 6 percent interest per annum, in Baghdad one could earn up to 24 percent and in Basra at least 12 percent.[117]

The friar's statements appear plausible against the background of local financial history, although the details cannot be corroborated.[118] If the information seems to reflect a knowledge of the credit markets born of experience, the outcome of the credit transactions shows that both friars failed to recognize the risks lurking behind the high interest rates. Critics focused on this rather than the permissibility of interest-yielding business, as the following examples show. During his tenure as provincial vicar in the years 1654–62, Felice di Sant'Antonio placed the Persian missions' money in investments that promised high interest rates. In the process, he lost large sums of money several times. The consequences were all the more serious because in 1656 the *Definitorium generale* had authorized him as provincial vicar to manage the income from all the settlements. The allegations of his fellow friars focused on his high-handed behavior as provincial vicar and later prior of the convent of Isfahan (1671–5), his neglect of investment risks, and his credit relationships with Muslims and "pagans" (probably members of the Hindu and Jain communities). In 1657, the prior of the convent of Isfahan accused the provincial vicar of having taken it upon himself to instruct the procurator of the convent to withdraw ten *tumān* (the equivalent of 150 *scudi*) secretly from the merchant with whom the convent's money was invested without telling the prior and the friars. The provincial vicar had then invested this money, with an additional fifteen *tumān* (225 *scudi*) from Goa, with another merchant whose name was known only to himself and the procurator.[119]

Perhaps to counter these allegations, the provincial vicar in turn accused the friars in Isfahan of lending the Jesuits 300 *scudi* in his absence. Now the Jesuits were writing to Europe and asking for alms so they could repay the sum. The poor (the Discalced Carmelites) would then be considered rich and the rich (the Jesuits) poor.[120] The controversies continued when Felice di Sant'Antonio was no longer provincial vicar, but prior of the convent in Isfahan. In 1671, Ange de Saint-Joseph accused him of having good intentions but no ability to run a mission. He was a spendthrift and extremely inept at secular business. He had loaned money to "certain *Banias*" and Muslims, although well aware of the prohibition on lending to the latter. Financial losses had occurred in several cases.[121] Friar Ange had already urged him in 1669 to make investments that promised only "modest profit" but also entailed a lower risk of losing everything. In his view, the *Definitorium* should only allow interest-bearing investments if the creditors were the French *Compagnie des Indes orientales* or "other Christians of similar credit." The superiors of the convents should only be permitted to invest limited sums with Muslims, and only with the consent of the prior or vicar and the other friars.[122] In 1675 Ange de Saint-Joseph reported that the Discalced Carmelites in Isfahan had invested 300 *tumān* (the equivalent of 4,500 *scudi*) with two "Gentiles" two years previously and in the current year 100 *tumān* (1,500 *scudi*) with another "pagan." In both cases, the capital was lost, which caused the friar to lament the lack of diversification of the investments. The friar argued that no more than fifty *tumān* (750 *scudi*) should be invested at the same time in the same location.[123]

The conflicts surrounding the credit transactions cast a spotlight on the missionaries' economic relationships with laypeople of different confessions and religions. Apart from Christians and Muslims, the correspondence of the Discalced Carmelites also alludes to Indian "pagans," who were not considered a target group of the Persian mission and are thus otherwise rarely mentioned. Indians—"pagans" and Muslims alike—did indeed play a central role in the commercial and financial networks between Persia, the Persian Gulf, and South Asia. When the missionaries turned to them, they were following the lead of European and Armenian merchants. It is unclear whether this had to do with the fact that members of the Hindu and Jain communities were not bound by the restrictions on charging interest that Christians and Muslims faced. In any case, the correspondence of the Discalced Carmelites reveals no religion-specific practices in the treatment of high-interest loans; the friars did not consider religious reservations about charging interest to be a notable impediment.

In the same context, the missionaries offered services based on the capital of trust that they enjoyed as a result of the renunciation of worldly interests that others attributed to them. These services ranged from dispatching letters to accepting deposits and exercising powers of attorney. While the first was never questioned, the prohibition on intervening in the business of the laity applied specifically to the exercise of powers of attorney. This implied not just activities repugnant to the clerical estate but also financial risks that could adversely affect church assets.

The exercise of powers of attorney was accordingly usually shrouded in a mantle of secrecy. As a rule, it only appears in the sources when serious problems arose. For example, in the 1670s the Discalced Carmelites faced a good deal of inconvenience because they had invested money with "pagans" and Muslims on behalf of Smikan Gioerida [Ǧuwairī], one of the sisters of the late wife of Pietro Della Valle. The "pagan" agent of the Dutch East India Company owed the Discalced Carmelites 400 *tumān* (the equivalent of 6,000 *scudi*), and a Muslim owed them one hundred *tumān* (1500 *scudi*). Smikan Gioerida therefore tried to demand the return of capital from an endowment she had set up in 1666 to benefit the Discalced Carmelites in order to recoup some of her money.[124] This capital amounted to 200 *tumān* (3,000 *scudi*). The revenues were intended to support the mission in Shiraz. In exchange, the Discalced Carmelites were to say a daily mass for the soul of the donor and her relatives in perpetuity. In 1667, Friar Dionisio di Gesù in Shiraz also promised to instruct the donor's nephews and to see to her assets and her grave.[125]

Such an obligation violated the strict prohibition on involvement in the business of the laity and on accepting powers of attorney from them. In 1669, the visitor general, Francesco di Gesù, criticized the repeated disregard by the superiors of the convents in Persia for the ban enshrined in the constitutions and called upon the friars and their superiors to adhere to these regulations in the future.[126] The potential risks of exercising powers of attorney had not yet emerged in 1669. Several friars therefore contested the visitor's *ordinatio*. They argued that it called into question the endowment for the settlement in Shiraz, since it was tied to their exercise of the donor's power of attorney. According to one of the friars, exercising the power of attorney was limited to collecting the proceeds from the merchants with whom Smikan had invested her money and entering the sums into the books. If the "very Catholic and honorable house" of Gioerida could no longer count on the support of the Discalced Carmelites, it would place itself in the hands of the Dutch, since Smikan's nephew, whom the friars were to educate, had a Dutch father.[127] The exercise of the power of attorney was thus also legitimized by a defense of the lines between Western Christian orthodoxy and "heresy," which in reality were anything but clearly drawn. Another friar, Ange de Saint-Joseph, justified the practice of attending to the business of laypeople as "tutors" or "procurators" by referring to the specific local circumstances. The few Christians on the ground did not simply request the services of the missionaries as an expression of Christian care but also claimed them as a right because they had nobody else to turn to. In the missions, what was true of the spiritual realm also applied to the worldly one; one could not exist without the other.[128]

In 1675, when it became apparent that the Discalced Carmelites' finances and reputation would sustain losses as a result of their dealings in worldly business affairs, Ange de Saint-Joseph changed course and asked the *praepositus generalis* to order the missionaries to return the power of attorney that Smikan Gioerida had granted them. In 1677, the visitor general, Giovanni Battista di San Giuseppe, took the occasion to remind the friars of the ban on involvement in the business of the laity. The following year, Ange de Saint-Joseph also had to justify himself to the visitor general, Giovanni Battista di San Giuseppe. As prior of the convent in Isfahan, he in turn was accused of having caused losses to the detriment of the mission and Smikan Gioerida's power of attorney. Contrary to his previous statements, the friar now claimed that the "pagans" with whom the money was invested had enjoyed the "greatest credit." According to him, the friars had also invested funds from the mission and Smikan Gioerida with two Armenians and one Muslim merchant.[129]

Friar Ange had apparently done the very thing he had warned others against, namely, concentrating large sums of money on individual persons instead of diversifying the investments and thus the risks. In any case, it was such allegations made by fellow friars that instigated the visitor general's efforts to clear up the problems. Unlike his predecessors, the friar had invested the entirety of the mission's capital and Smikan Gioerida's money with a single Indian merchant, who had ultimately gone bankrupt. Ignoring the warnings of his fellow friars, he had lost all of the Persian mission's money, some 4,000 *scudi*, and the friars were now totally dependent upon the subsidies from Rome.[130] In fact, the entirety of the money from the endowment set up in 1666 was exhausted ten years later. Part of the capital was lost as a result of misguided investment decisions, while the friars spent another part on construction work and other necessities.

It is impossible to determine how gravely these losses actually affected the Discalced Carmelites' Persian missions because the indications in the sources remain sporadic throughout. In connection with the bankruptcy of the *Compagnie des Indes orientales* in 1706, at any rate, there is mention once again of a larger loss, a capital of more than 7,000 rupees (or some 3,500 *scudi*) invested with the *Compagnie*.[131] This information confirms two things: it shows that the Discalced Carmelites in Persia were able to amass funds that surpassed by many times the subsidies from Italy, and it illustrates once again the financial risks to which the missions were subject.

How the Capuchins, Augustinians, and Dominicans in Persia supplemented their subsidies from Europe must remain an open question, given the lack of relevant sources. We know a bit more about the Jesuits. They had an endowment of 15,000 *livres tournois* (approximately 5,000 *scudi*), which the queen of Poland had placed at their disposal when they founded the mission in Isfahan. Since the mission was connected with the Jesuit province of Lyon, this capital was invested in France in 1654. The responsible procurator was instructed to transfer the proceeds to Persia annually. As the first superior of the mission in Isfahan saw it (and never tired of emphasizing in his correspondence with the general of the order between 1656 and his death in 1660), the capital should be transferred to Persia because of delayed and partial payments from France and the possibility of higher yields there—more than 10 percent per annum as opposed to 4 percent. The general of the order finally saw the light in 1658 and ordered the transfer of an initial 6,000 *livres tournois* (2,000 *scudi*) to Persia. Since this solution was undermined in France, however, the money was unavailable in Isfahan as starting capital for a local mission economy. The fathers remained dependent on the irregular and partial transfers of revenues from their endowment and insecure local payments.[132]

The highly fragmentary documentary record hints at additional, sometimes less orthodox sources of income, suggesting the outlines of a local economy reminiscent of that of the Discalced Carmelites: sales of produce from the settlement's garden, commercial transactions, and investments of money. To alleviate the poverty of the Jesuits in Persia, goods were sent to Goa for sale, Alexandre de Rhodes wrote in 1659.[133] Until they moved to New Julfa in 1661, the fathers in Isfahan faced demands for wine from their Muslim neighbors. The settlement in New Julfa that the order acquired in 1661 included a poultry farm and a garden attached to a canal with vineyards, fruit trees, and areas for sowing, some of whose produce was intended for sale (Figure 18). Like the Discalced Carmelites, the superior of the Jesuits invested money with a merchant. He was soon reminded that investing money at high interest rates could be risky, when the debtor left Isfahan in 1661 without repaying his debts.[134] Among the Jesuits, too, religious boundaries did not curb cooperation with merchants and financiers: in 1666, the superior, Father Mercier, recommended avoiding the Portuguese and entrusting money transfers to China to "our banias," since they would undertake the task "without risk" and "for a moderate exchange fee."[135]

The findings on the Discalced Carmelites and Jesuits in Persia presented here are in keeping with the picture of mainly local mission economies that has been drawn for the Jesuits in other parts of Asia. The poverty of the Jesuits in Persia, who were largely left to their own devices, contrasted sharply, however, with the prosperity or even wealth of their settlements in other regions of the world. The image of the Society of Jesus as a globally integrated enterprise breaks down in the light of such information.[136] At the same time, our findings confirm how important the embedding of individual settlements in translocal relationship networks was for their survival. Scholarship on Japan, China, India, and Brazil shows the Jesuits engaging in many worldly forms of capital creation, including landownership, the trade in gold, silver, precious stones, and silk, and loaning money at high interest rates.[137]

Social proximity to laypeople active in trade thus did not help just the Discalced Carmelites in Persia to improve the financial situation of their settlements. In the various parts of Asia, insufficient financing from Europe forced missionaries to engage with the world of the laity in economic matters. Financing from Europe was probably only a decisive support at the beginning of the missions. If they were to survive, the missionaries had to use this "starting capital" to tap into local sources of income. In this way, the settlements in Persia made themselves independent of the sporadic subsidies to such a degree that their practical significance was only very minor. Like the analysis of the account books of the Basra mission, the controversies surrounding the Discalced Carmelites' investment behavior and the figures mentioned in this context show that the missionaries had access to funds that surpassed the remuneration from Italy many times over. The funds from Rome nevertheless remained a central topic in correspondence with the superiors of the order and the *Propaganda Fide*, especially

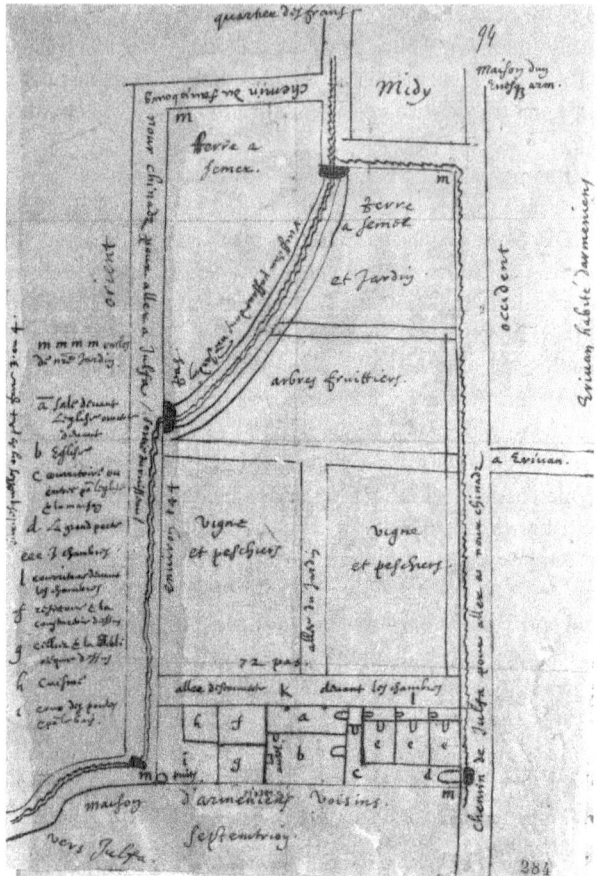

Figure 18 Map of the Jesuit settlement in New Julfa, n.d. (ARSI, Gallia, 97 III, doc. 94, fol. 284r). © ARSI

where the Discalced Carmelites were concerned. This was due to the symbolic significance of the subsidies as signs that the superiors and the Curia cared about the well-being of the missions.

The absence of subsidies from Italy helped to justify practices that rubbed up against the observance demanded of the missionaries. The friars did not always attempt to hide from their superiors the financial ties and transactions that could be held against them from the standpoint of strict observance. Instead, they described this form of financing as an inevitable result of the lack of outside support. Given the chronic underfunding of the missions, what could have been more logical for the missionaries than to avail themselves of the services of merchants for the (permissible) transfer of subsidies and alms from Europe or India? And why should they not have used these same connections to borrow money or to invest what they did not immediately need at high interest rates? Granted, this begged the question of whether this could be reconciled with the canonical prohibition on usury. However, given the prevailing material constraints, such violations had no consequences even when word of them reached the Holy Office. In 1709, the *Propaganda Fide* presented reports to the Holy Office alleging that some missionaries in Persia had loaned money to merchants at interest and had even claimed that this was permissible. By instructing the bishop of Isfahan not merely to admonish the culprits but to formally establish the legal circumstances of the matter, the Holy Office affirmed the universal application of the canonical norm, without, however, pursuing the enforcement of this decree from the *Propaganda Fide*.[138] Both the normative universalism and its qualification in practice were characteristic of the tension in which missionaries all over the world operated. Although superiors and curial congregations tended to deny the legitimacy of local normative contexts, in practice they were often forced to retreat before them.

The Mission as a World Turned Upside Down: Justification Strategies and Cultural Relativization

In the mission context, clerics with a mandate from their church became actors whose lives were increasingly oriented toward local frames of reference. This becomes apparent in their efforts to attain social prestige in Persia, in their economic behavior, and their actions as religious specialists. The less the constitutions of an order accounted for the specific conditions of missionary work, the graver were the normative conflicts and the necessity to seek justifications for deviations from the observance of the Rule. When Discalced Carmelites were sent to Persia and other missions outside Europe, this need for justification also extended to everyday practices of outward accommodation that were already explicitly planned for in the Jesuit constitutions, given that order's specific missionary orientation. The friars usually countered allegations of deficient observance with the argument of cultural difference, which made behaviors that seemed to deviate from established norms appear necessary. By appealing to their local knowledge, they could challenge both the applicability of higher normative orders and the authority of distant decision-makers and instead demand autonomy of action for themselves. Just as it was difficult for a medical doctor to recognize illnesses and their causes from a distance and properly treat them, the Discalced Carmelite Juan Thadeo de San Eliseo wrote in 1624, the *definitores* in Rome were in no position to remedy individual cases that demanded presence in Persia.[139] Proceeding from such reflections, I will show in what follows how Ange de Saint-Joseph, a Discalced Carmelite familiar with Persia, constructed the mission as a counter-world to Catholic Europe. He did so in the context of conflicts within the order but also in contact with the European republic of letters, in order to justify the conduct of which he stood accused. The example illustrates the processes of cultural relativization resulting from the normative conflicts analyzed in this chapter and takes us to a wider problem which I shall treat in Chapter 7: the role of missionary experiences in the transformational processes of the European Enlightenment.

Ange de Saint-Joseph, whom we have already encountered several times, was an ambivalent figure: On the one hand, in both Persia and later in the Netherlands, he repeatedly confronted allegations that he did not take the requirements of observance seriously enough. On the other, he attained respect within his order and beyond for his language skills and local knowledge. In his correspondence and published works he presented himself as a knowledgeable and active missionary rather than a member of an order primarily dedicated to a contemplative way of life. During his stay in Persia, he cultivated contacts with European travelers and scholars. Those who benefited from his hospitality and knowledge in Isfahan included the Calvinist Jean Chardin. From Basra, Ange de Saint-Joseph and another Discalced Carmelite corresponded with Robert Huntington, the learned chaplain of the *Levant Company* in Aleppo and future provost of Trinity College Dublin and Anglican bishop of Raphoe. This scholarly correspondence across confessional lines focused on the religion and writings of a religious community little known in Western Europe, the Mandaeans.[140]

When Ange de Saint-Joseph returned to Rome in 1678, the visitor general, Giovanni Battista di San Giuseppe, recommended him to the order's procurator general because of his outstanding knowledge of languages. Clerics and laypeople alike agreed that they had never seen anyone who could speak Persian better than Friar Ange. He also had a good command of Arabic and Turkish. In Rome the friar wished to meet the *praepositus generalis* and ask whether he could publish his Persian–Italian dictionary (a work later expanded into the quadrilingual *Gazophylacium*) with the support of the *Propaganda Fide*. According to the visitor general, publishing this work would greatly benefit the missionaries who were learning Persian and would bring honor to the order.[141] In 1680–1, however, the *Propaganda Fide* denied Ange de Saint-Joseph the requested permission to publish as well as funding to travel to Paris, where he had hoped to print the dictionary. The meeting minutes shed no light on the precise reasons for this refusal.[142] Did the Discalced Carmelite lack the effective protection needed to overcome the sluggish bureaucratic routines of the *Propaganda Fide*? Or did the *Propaganda Fide* not appreciate the manner in which he repeatedly cited his knowledge of Persia to justify deviations from observance of the Rule?

Whatever the case, in 1681 he published his Latin translation of the pharmacology text by Muzaffar b. Muḥammad al-Ḥusaini aš-Šifāʾī mentioned in Chapter 3 in Paris, but his *Gazophylacium linguae Persarum*, which he expanded into a Persian-Italian-Latin-French dictionary, appeared only in 1683 in Amsterdam, a city under Calvinist authorities. Although contemporaries disagreed on the quality of Friar Ange's philological work, there can be no doubt about the breadth of his knowledge, which extended well beyond theology. In his published works he sought to share this knowledge with a wide circle of readers: missionaries, linguists, theologians, merchants, and other interested parties. The *approbationes & facultates* printed on the first pages of his dictionary in 1683 also give evidence of his entanglement across confessional boundaries. The book had been endorsed by various members of the regular clergy, the French ambassador in Constantinople, and François Pétis de la Croix, son of the *secrétaire-interprète du Roi pour les langues arabe et turque* and pupil of the Capuchin Raphaël du Mans as well as the author during his sojourn in Isfahan. But we also find three commendations from Protestants. These included the approbation to print addressed to the States General, with which the Calvinist Jean Chardin expressed his gratitude for the author's good offices during his stay in Isfahan.[143]

In Persia (as later in the Netherlands), Ange de Saint-Joseph had both admirers and enemies. His surviving correspondence and his published works reveal a personality who did not shy away from controversy. In 1670, he became prior of the convent in Isfahan. Since the only participants in the election were the candidate himself and one other friar, the other missionaries questioned its validity. While in 1674 the *Definitorium generale* affirmed in principle the canonical validity of an election involving just two voters, it also instructed the visitor general to examine the legitimacy of Friar Ange's election in particular and, if appropriate, to appoint a new prior.[144] Ange de Saint-Joseph had to relinquish the office of prior in the course of the visitation. Yet this ultimately had less to do with the form of his election than with the misgivings among a segment of his fellow friars concerning his conduct of office. In a 1675 letter to the *praepositus generalis*, the provincial vicar described him as "absolutely unsuited to the missions." He was so "carried away by the vanity of his self-esteem" that he was still defending his failings in spiritual and secular matters as wise and proper. He had already reported to the general of the order the punishments the friar deserved.[145] For his part, in 1675–6 Ange de Saint-Joseph defended himself in several letters to the *praepositus generalis*, arguing against being tested by a visitor with no knowledge of the country.

The animosities among the missionaries on the ground followed the smoldering conflicts about whether missionary activities could be reconciled with an orientation toward a contemplative life in seclusion from the "world." Ever since his election as prior in 1670, Ange de Saint-Joseph had accordingly combined criticism of the strict enforcement of norms unsuited to conditions in Persia with a reproof of the selection of clerics; he argued that the selection process must pay greater attention to clerics' education and knowledge of local languages, given the frequent contacts with Muslim scholars there. In 1670 he criticized a newly arrived Polish friar as "an extravagant saint and zealot without wisdom" who shocked everyone. Ange de Saint-Joseph suggested that the *definitor* (and later *praepositus generalis*) whom he contacted about this should ensure that "mainly Frenchmen and not such capricious and opinionated bigots" were dispatched to Persia.[146] According to Ange de Saint-Joseph, the new arrivals, who could not help but live in seclusion, used the pretext of observance to harass all those, like himself, who knew the local customs and language and thus often had to leave the house on behalf of the mission and other matters. While he had proselytized in New Julfa and handled the convent's business with Muslims, his successor as prior had left the convent just twice between January and September 1675.[147]

In several years of correspondence with the *definitor* and later *praepositus generalis* Jean Chrysostome de Saint-Paul, whom he had already known before joining the order, Ange de Saint-Joseph wrote of many aspects of life in Persia for which he believed that strict observance and mission were incompatible. In this correspondence, in which he portrayed Persia as a counter-world to Catholic Europe, the problems became crystalized in questions of dress. Unlike the constitutions of the Society of Jesus, those of the Discalced Carmelites contained strict rules about dress that were oriented toward life in a European convent. The application of these rules in the mission confronted the friars with various problems, either because the norms contradicted the expectations of their surroundings or because the prescribed fabrics were unavailable.

The superiors of the order were largely unwilling to allow the friars to adapt their habit to local conditions. In 1671 and 1674, the General Chapter ordered that missionaries in the East must under no circumstances alter their habit. After a visitor complained in 1677 that while traveling the friars in Persia wore not the order's habit but various types of costly Persian attire, the *Definitorium* confirmed the strict dress code allowing for very few variations. In the cities, it forbade any change to the habit, especially the wearing of Persian head coverings or cloaks; while traveling, the friars could, when required out of consideration for the Muslim population, wear a simple Persian cloak in the same gray as the order's habit.[148]

Ange de Saint-Joseph had gone further in his demands. In his view, outward accommodation as well as education and knowledge of local languages were the keys to acceptance and respect on the ground. "All of the universal principles of conscience, politics, domestic economy, and observance" represented in the books could not be applied so easily in Persia, he wrote in a 1672 letter to Jean Chrysostome de Saint-Paul, then still *definitor* of the order. In Persia, Christians and other non-Muslims were viewed as unclean. Clerics were only accepted if they were known to be learned and well-bred persons. "Poverty, simple dress, bare feet, and other things deemed useful for edification in Christian lands," were instead the "object of scandal and dismay" in Persia. According to Ange de Saint-Joseph, the missionaries gained authority not based on their poverty and penitential exercises, but rather from being able, after years of practice, to dispute the most varied branches of knowledge "with the most sophisticated men in the world."[149]

The reformed Carmelites in Persia found themselves in a special quandary because of the eponymous commandment to appear "discalced," that is, barefoot in sandals. In 1675—against the background of his abovementioned dismissal as prior by the visitor—Ange de Saint-Joseph therefore advised Jean Chrysostome de Saint-Paul, then *praepositus generalis* of the order, to limit the strict enforcement of this part of the order's constitutions to the convent. He justified deviating from the Rule outside the convent by referring to papal privileges that gave the missionaries the freedom to dress according to local requirements. Since the houses and churches were laid out with carpets, one could not appear there with naked, dirty feet without attracting the outrage of all those present. Thus far, all of the Discalced Carmelites in Persia had covered their feet in socks and black slippers, which had gained the express approval of an earlier visitor possessed of the requisite local knowledge. This practice had nevertheless been criticized during the most recent visitation. As to their clothing, they had to use better cloth to go before a judge or another respected person than that intended for their habit. Overall, he noted, there were substantial deviations from the constitutions in Persia, but these could be excused by local circumstances.[150] Against the backdrop of the attacks against him, Ange de Saint-Joseph repeatedly returned to this problem in his correspondence with the *praepositus generalis*. The rules on dress could not be applied on the ground and would mean dispensing with any kind of mission.

Ange de Saint-Joseph's correspondence shows how, in relations between missionaries and their superiors, local knowledge could offer the basis for the self-empowerment of subaltern actors and with it for challenging established authority.

The Discalced Carmelite used the foreignness of local conditions to defend various deviations from his order's constitutions. When he qualified those norms of everyday life that were considered especially godly from a European standpoint, his willingness to accept the local culture's equal status, especially in the field of scholarship, except in matters relating to religion, becomes apparent. Ange de Saint-Joseph was among the most vocal of the missionaries in Persia, but his case stands for a more general problem. The heightened preoccupation with foreign cultures in the mission context resulted in a broadening of perspectives that was not what the church authorities had had in mind. The experiences of the regular clergy led to unintended processes of cultural relativizing, from forms of everyday life that contrasted with the demanded observance to practices of religiosity that brought them too close to "heretics" and "schismatics" or could be regarded as reversions to "idolatry." To what degree did the Catholic missions unwittingly help to create the foundations for the transformation processes of the European Enlightenment, and how did the curial congregations and the pope handle such challenges within their own decision-making practices?

7

Undesirable Outcomes: From Mission to Enlightenment?

In the seventeenth century, the missions played a central role in efforts by both the Catholic Church and secular rulers to "mark out religious and confessional boundaries, defend them when necessary and, where possible, shift them to their own advantage."[1] They embodied the post-Tridentine *Ecclesia triumphans*. For the Roman Catholic Church, the "gains" in the foreign missions compensated for the "losses" suffered in Europe as a result of the Protestant Reformations. By canonizing figures such as Ignatius of Loyola, Francis Xavier, Charles Borromeo, and Philip Neri, the papacy propagated an ideal image of saints whose endeavors were directed toward defending and spreading the Catholic faith. These saintly images informed the concrete expectations placed on the clergy, which these canonized men had belonged to in life. Even an order like the Discalced Carmelites with origins in the contemplative life could not escape these expectations. Conflicts with the norms of the order were one of the unintended challenges with which the missions confronted the post-Tridentine confessional church. The demands of everyday life on the ground relativized the certainties associated with the regular clergy's way of life.

The diverse new local forms of church life emerging in missionary areas outside Europe also ran counter to the drive toward strict adherence to the requirements of the post-Tridentine Church in matters of ritual and doctrine. Viewed from a global perspective, post-Tridentine Catholicism was characterized in equal measure by processes of standardization and pluralization. In the mission territories in the Americas, Asia, and Africa, conversion to Catholicism rarely meant a complete rejection of earlier beliefs and practices. As priests of the newly established churches, missionaries from Europe thus partook in or at least had to tolerate hybrid practices. Even in many parts of the Americas, where mission is widely regarded as an undertaking imposed from the outside that destroyed local cultures, missionaries and Indigenous people entered into an (unequal) exchange to which the latter contributed elements of their own precolonial cultures.[2] When missionaries learned foreign languages and communicated the practices and teachings of their church in these idioms, they also adapted to the corresponding normative systems. Such practices of accommodation could occasion more or less conflict with the confessional orthodoxy expected of them, as the countless *dubia* sent from the mission territories to the *Propaganda Fide* and the Holy Office illustrate. Some of these *dubia* were settled within the narrow confines of the congregations and their communication with the missionaries. Others were deliberately forgotten—often with the involvement of the Curia. Still others led to controversies that escaped the control of the ecclesiastical authorities. Through these controversies, the integration of the missionaries into local contexts had repercussions for the Church as a whole and its place within European society.

Contrary to the Church's efforts to keep the laity out of theological debates,[3] the controversies were increasingly fought out by clerics and laypeople in speech and writing in newly emerging public spaces. In this respect, the debates over missionary practices were linked to theological controversies that originated in Europe, such as those surrounding Jansenism or probabilism. All of them were part of a transformation process that Martin Gierl has referred to, in the Pietist setting, as a "reform of scholarly communication."[4] In a Catholic context, this meant that the authority of the theologically trained members of the republic of letters asserted itself alongside the monarchical authority that the papacy claimed for itself.[5] Even the members of the Roman congregations were part of communication networks that extended beyond the realm of curial secrecy, and they sometimes presented their standpoints to a wider public in published form.[6]

What was at stake was not "merely" the magisterium of the Church. Europeans now confronted foreign alternatives to their own understanding of the world, which also challenged the "natural connection between sociation and Christianity," thereby altering the conditions in which Christianity as such was constituted.[7] The missions in America and Asia had led to the discovery of a plethora of doctrines and rituals that Europeans described in comparison to those of "pagan" antiquity, knowledge of which Humanism and the Renaissance had promoted. Although the missionary reports were still rooted in the distinction between "true" and "false" teachings, they nevertheless contributed to the awakening of a novel learned interest in religion as a social phenomenon, which became a topic of comparative scholarship starting in the second half of the seventeenth century.[8] Only now was it conceivable to exclude the question of truth when describing the religious rituals of "all the peoples of the world," as the compiler Jean Frédéric Bernard did together with the illustrator Bernard Picart in the seven-volume *Cérémonies et coutumes religieuses de tous les peuples du monde*, published in Amsterdam between 1723 and 1737.[9]

Montesquieu's *Lettres persanes*, published in 1721, illustrate the consequences of observing and describing diverse societal conditions outside Europe in an especially effective literary form. Inspired by the works of Jean Chardin and Jean-Baptiste Tavernier, who had cultivated close contacts with Catholic missionaries in Isfahan and received information from them about Persia and its people, Montesquieu made Persia a point of reference for a critique of society that not only targeted monarchical "despotism," but also, despite the author's reticence, did not spare the Church and religion. The author employed the literary fiction of the epistolary novel to contrast various systems of norms and values and emphasize the situational validity of modes of argumentation and practices. To that end, he portrayed "his" Persians as representatives of a culture that allowed them to relate to others as equals in their host country, France, and to pass rational judgments on their experiences there. Beyond the individual criticisms of such issues as religious intolerance or the abuse of clerical power expressed by his characters, Montesquieu turned Islam and Christianity into topics of investigation that were guided by the "spirit of the laws" and thus were subject to comparison. That the Persia of the *Lettres persanes* had little in common with the contemporary realities in that country did nothing to diminish the text's impact. Against the backdrop of an increasingly radical Enlightenment critique of the Church, the Sacred Congregation of the Index banned the work in 1762, forty years after its first publication. At that point it already existed in more than forty French editions and had been extraordinarily widely disseminated in German, English, and Dutch translation, so that its inclusion in the index of prohibited books could not stop its spread even in the Papal States.[10]

Starting in the latter half of the seventeenth century, the reception of missionary knowledge about non-Christian societies in China and South India became an especially important point of departure for cultural relativizing processes.[11] The Jesuits used the concept of adiaphora in their efforts to justify their extensive adaptation to local society in order to declare everything outside the one, unalterable reality of divine revelation in the Gospels to be superfluous. With their extensive publishing activities, they spread the knowledge they had gained in the missions beyond the ecclesiastical context and across confessional boundaries to the European republic of letters, with controversies heightening the impact. In the 1930s, Paul Hazard had already cited this relativizing of certainties that emerged from such confrontations with foreign cultures as an important factor in the "crisis of the European mind" around 1700. He referred in particular to China, with good reason: nowhere else were the repercussions of the missionary confrontation with a non-Christian culture so far-reaching. To be sure, the Jesuits classified their observations on the specific sociocultural and religious circumstances within the established ecclesiastical framework of a figurist method that took up Old Testament and Greco-Roman references. Yet, proceeding from the reception of their reports by the seventeenth-century French skeptics, China appeared as a non-Christian counter-world that not merely offered the example of an (at least) equal culture but also featured its own morality, which was not rooted in religion.[12] In connection with the description of the *literati* as a meritocracy devoted to the common good, such notions formed the religious and social basis of a "cognitive shock" for European societies organized into estates.[13]

Together with the Jesuits in China, Roberto de' Nobili, who was active in South India in the early half of the seventeenth century, played a central role in the emergence of an anthropology of religion, which initially distinguished various non-Christian religions, and ultimately the Christian faith and social ethics, from each other. By thinking of the civil and religious spheres as separate realms with their own norms, Roberto de Nobili and his fellow Jesuits in East Asia could justify their submission to the political and societal order of a different religion.[14] This was a more general phenomenon related to the constraints of missions under non-Christian rule. Jesuit missionaries in India and China were not the only ones to justify such distinctions, which in Europe had begun to challenge the connection between confession and political rule since the religious peace regimes of the sixteenth century.[15] The missionaries adopted the same approach in Persia when they came to terms with the Muslim authorities to secure a similar scope of action to that which the religious peace agreements in Europe had afforded

Christians of a different confession. In Persia, the distinction between religious and civil acts affected the treatment of non-Catholic Christians. Acts that took place in the gray area of the sacred were justified by their unambiguous location in the "world." For example, the Jesuit Jacques Villotte claimed that laying out the body of a non-Catholic Englishman in the Jesuits' house was a "purely secular action." The Discalced Carmelites argued similarly to defend their participation in Protestant burials.[16]

In what follows, we will explore the question of how the Roman Curia reacted to the unintended and undesirable expansions of missionary experiences from a perspective that reaches beyond Persia to focus on the most important mission territories in Asia. Starting with the observation that the decisions on *communicatio in sacris* and on the Chinese and Malabar rites followed a similar chronology, we will first compare the curial positions in these matters and argue that they were all reflective of a boom in doctrinal disambiguation. Like the controversies in the Chinese and South Indian missions, the question of *communicatio in sacris* in Persia was transformed, over the course of the seventeenth century, from an internal problem of the orders to an affair in which the jurisdiction of the curial congregations came to the fore. These reflections are based on the assumption that those who sought to limit the plural forms of adaptation were by no means interested in the mission churches alone but were also reacting to processes of change that, proceeding from experiences of alterity, called into question the conditions that had constituted Christianity up to that point. The second subchapter will inquire into the reasons for the curial practice of avoiding decision-making in matters in which the Church's truth claim was at stake. Finally, attention will shift to the ways in which the Curia responded to situations in which the relevance of competing normative orders could no longer be denied.

Doctrinal Disambiguation

Communicatio in sacris was practiced for as long as the Persian missions existed, as this book has already shown in the case of relations between the missionaries and Armenians and Protestants. *Communicatio* with non-Uniate Eastern Christians nevertheless appeared with greater intensity in the discussions of the *Propaganda Fide* and the Holy Office at certain times. According to observations by Cesare Santus, the number of cases treated rose sharply for the first time in the 1630s, in the wake of the founding of the *Propaganda Fide*. The reason for this temporary increase may be that at the time, the newly established Congregation was demanding competencies to examine the *dubia* from the missions, in competition with the Holy Office. Once these competencies were decided in favor of the Holy Office, the curial interest in *communicatio in sacris* returned to a low level and only began to rise permanently starting in the 1660s. It attained unusual levels during the pontificates of Clement XI (1700–1721) and Benedict XIV (1740–58)—in striking parallel to the controversies around the Chinese and Malabar rites. It thus makes sense to inquire into the connections between the marked intensification of discussions on practices of accommodation in the various mission territories in Asia. Like the temporal distribution of the cases considered, the geographical spread does not merely reflect practices on the ground but also the attention the curial congregations paid to them at a given moment. In the case of the Chinese—and to a lesser extent the Malabar—rites, the congregations responded to the fact that the controversies were increasingly being fought out before a European audience, and even developed a dynamic of their own beyond confessional boundaries. In the case of *communicatio in sacris*, however, the density of communication networks and geographical proximity to the heartlands of Latin Christendom played a decisive role. Conditions in the Ottoman Empire were accordingly in the foreground of discussions in the curial congregations. Persia and the territories in the Caucasus bordering the Ottoman Empire, in contrast, made up only 10 percent of the cases mentioned by Cesare Santus.[17]

Scholars have variously pointed out that it was only in the late seventeenth or even the first half of the eighteenth century that the Eastern churches distanced themselves with increasing clarity from the Roman Catholic Church.[18] Up to that point—and in some cases later as well—a practice of accommodation to local practices, including the toleration of *communicatio in sacris*, dominated among missionaries as well. The superiors of the orders and the Roman Curia, in contrast, had adopted a clear position against *communicatio in sacris* far earlier in a series of individual decisions in the first half of the seventeenth century. Based on old ideas about "schismatics" and "heretics," they distanced themselves from the Eastern churches, in sharp contrast to their far more positive assessment of non-Christian cultures in South and East Asia. This more positive view was rooted in the notion that people with no previous knowledge of Christian revelation could participate in a fundamental insight into the existence of a single God because of the "natural light." The Eastern Christians, in contrast, had separated from Rome and closed their eyes to the truth revealed to them since the time of the Apostles. While one could tolerate deviations in matters of rites and canon law by Uniate Christians, *communicatio in sacris* with non-Uniate Christians plainly contradicted the Catholic Church's view of itself as the one true Christian Church.

Since the beginning of the Discalced Carmelites' Persian mission, there was, accordingly, no dearth of admonitions from on high that left no doubt about the illicit nature of *communicatio in sacris*. As early as 1608, the *praepositus generalis*, Fernando de Santa María, reminded his order's missionaries in Persia that, as they knew, *communicatio* with "schismatics" was not allowed, except in conversation. Against the background of the rules of observance specific to the order, the *praepositus* went further in this regard than the Holy Office and the *Propaganda Fide* would do later: he even wished to restrict the practices of "good correspondence." In his view, the missionaries should not visit the "schismatic" prelates and, where there was no hope of conversion, they must not cultivate any contact with them.[19]

In its connection with the issue of observance, Fernando de Santa María's instruction also took a position in debates within the order. Within the context of the reorientation toward mission, other members of the order were emphasizing the necessity of reaching out to the "infidels." In his *Instructio Missionum*, written on behalf of the General Chapter in 1605, Juan de Jesús María had recommended adopting "a gentle and effective approach to the infidels" to "open the door to the Catholic faith." In this case, one could trust in the impact of the arguments according to the "light of nature." As far as the Christian faith permitted it, the missionaries were to strive for concord and confidential relations with all peoples. When religion was mentioned, they were to point out "errors" and at the same time maintain their affection for the persons concerned.[20]

The 1613 *De procuranda salute omnium gentium* (On how to bring about the salvation of all peoples) by Tomás de Jesús, which served as the most important missionary manual for the Discalced Carmelites, even contained an explicit defense of *communicatio in sacris*. Tomás de Jesús, who had gained insights into the practice of confessionally mixed communities in the Netherlands, also noted that "heretics" were to be strictly avoided, while proceeding to follow the usual interpretations of the bull *Ad vitanda scandala*. The author used these to justify not just "civil transactions" with "heretics," but also *communicatio in sacris* as well as mixed marriages when the Catholic partners professed their faith and the children were raised as Catholics. According to Tomás de Jesús, in confessionally mixed communities Catholics could receive the sacraments from "heretical" priests and bishops, provided the clerics had not been personally excommunicated, the Catholics suffered no disadvantages, the "legitimate ecclesiastical form" was maintained in administering the sacraments, and the celebrants were actually priests or bishops, there was no evidence of "heretical depravity," and the person receiving the sacraments was in no danger of errors of faith.[21]

Such advice conflicted with the restrictive position that the *praepositus generalis* had reiterated in 1608. The fact that from 1622 onward this work was among the books that the *Propaganda Fide* would send along with the missionaries—including those of other orders—shows at the same time that Tomás de Jesús remained within the confines of what the highest levels of the Church deemed suitable for missionary activities "by gentle means and full of charity," as the Congregation demanded in its early years.[22] In apparent contradiction to this policy, in 1621 a visitor chided the missionaries in Persia: Pope Paul V, he averred, had been outraged by the suggestion that some Discalced Carmelites should be allowed to celebrate mass in "schismatic" churches.[23] In its instructions of 1630 for the missionaries, the *Definitorium generale* similarly linked strict observance with the prohibition on the friars' engaging in *communicatio in sacris*. Once again, it recalled the papal ban on celebrating mass in the churches of the "schismatics." The missionaries more generally were not to communicate with the "schismatics" while the sacraments were being administered, for instance by attending their masses in priestly garb. This was reserved solely for Catholics of a different rite.[24] These internal instructions did not regulate the practice of the laity because visitations and instructions alike served primarily to improve the lives of members of the order.

In the course of the seventeenth century, the jurisdiction of the Holy Office came to the fore in matters of *communicatio in sacris*. There was competition into the 1630s and in some points beyond from the *Propaganda Fide* following its founding in 1622. In responding to *dubia*, which mainly came to Rome from the Ottoman Empire, the curial congregations made a series of individual decisions with which they were already explicitly condemning many forms of *communicatio in sacris*, which the Curia would still be dealing with in the eighteenth century.

Although certain decisions by the Holy Office and the *Propaganda Fide* left some scope in everyday life, they never explicitly expressed approval of *communicatio in sacris*, but rather always contained formulations that combined concessions in individual cases with unmistakable restrictions. For example, in 1671 the Holy Office limited the permission to have children baptized by "schismatic" priests to extreme emergencies, giving preference to a Catholic layperson over a "schismatic" priest. Only occasionally did the Holy Office and the *Propaganda Fide* show a willingness to relativize the "schismatic" or "heretical" character of the non-Uniate Eastern churches, although the missionaries themselves frequently did so. Despite a ban by the *Propaganda Fide*, in 1638 its secretary, Francesco Ingoli, allowed the converts in Aleppo to continue to attend their usual churches as long as the rite contained no "heresy," and no "heretics" were venerated as saints. In 1639, the Holy Office permitted Catholic Greeks to receive ordination as priests by "tolerated [*sic*] excommunicated schismatic bishops," bishops, that is, who, pursuant to Martin V's bull *Ad vitanda scandala*, had not been personally excommunicated.[25]

Strictly limited concessions did nothing to change the increasing tendency in the jurisprudence of the curial congregations over the course of the seventeenth century to forbid *communicatio in sacris*, at least when formulated as a *dubium* that explicitly posed the question of church doctrine. When those who nevertheless practiced *communicatio in sacris* with non-Uniate Eastern Christians sought a canonical legitimation, they needed, as illustrated above, to refer to a bull of the early fifteenth century and first reinterpret it to address the questions at hand, since the 1418 bull *Ad vitanda scandala* did not refer to *communicatio in sacris* with non-Uniate Eastern Christians. The contemporary jurisprudence of the curial congregations, in contrast, yielded only implicit room for tolerating deviating practices but by no means explicit approval of them. In this case, subaltern actors thus operated not within the normative order of the post-Tridentine Church but within its gaps. The practice of *communicatio in sacris* was only truly disrupted, however, when local conflicts led to intervention by outside actors.

The more the knowledge of the curial congregations' negative stance reached the mission territories, the stronger the tendency became to couch local conflicts in the categories of confessional orthodoxy in communications with Rome. In the Persian missions, too, the promotions of confessional agitators to church dignities showed the protagonists how they had to present themselves in order to gain favor at the Curia.[26] The controversies surrounding such decisions in turn meant that the flow of information became denser and deviations were increasingly noticed in Rome, which contributed to the spectacular intensification of curial regulatory activity during the pontificates of Clement XI (1700–1721) and Benedict XIV (1740–58).

In response to various *dubia* from the missionaries in Isfahan and New Julfa, in 1709 the Holy Office again issued a number of prohibitions on different forms of *communicatio*: baptisms and marriage ceremonies by "schismatic and heretical priests"; mixed marriages; the ordination of a Catholic priest by a "schismatic bishop"; communion in the "schismatic church." The Holy Office ordered that the prohibitions be announced in decrees that left no room for interpretation; the phrases used were "it is not allowed" and "it is in no way allowed."[27]

Yet these were still only individual decisions on requests from specific mission territories. Although such decisions may have served as precedents for further action by the Holy Office, they did not yet create an obligation to take direct measures beyond the individual case to which they referred. It was not until twenty years later, in 1729, that the *Propaganda Fide* issued a general ban on all types of *communicatio in sacris* with "schismatics" and "heretics" in the form of an instruction for the missionaries in the Ottoman Empire and Persia. This decision followed long debates within and between the curial congregations.[28] The *Propaganda Fide* further hammered the ban home by rooting it not in canon but in natural and divine law, from which even the pope himself could not offer dispensation. The instruction ended with directions not to make *communicatio* a topic of dispute among missionaries. In opposition to widespread practices of fluid boundaries, the *Propaganda Fide* formulated unmistakably clear guidelines and removed them from theological debate by referring to the papal magisterium. The likelihood of transgression was accepted as a given and regulated by means of instructions to confessors on how to deal with sinners.[29] In the decades that followed, the instruction of 1729 remained an important point of reference for the decision-making practice of the *Propaganda Fide* and the Holy Office. It promoted the systematization of curial decision-making which, while it continued to proceed from individual cases, was shaped more by the principle of a general prohibition on *communicatio in sacris*. The establishment of parallel hierarchies united with Rome in the various Eastern churches in the Ottoman Empire also contributed to doctrinal disambiguation: by confirming Abraham Petros I as patriarch of Cilicia in 1742, Benedict XIV created an independent Armenian Catholic parallel hierarchy separate from the jurisdiction of the catholicos.[30]

The decisions against the Chinese and Malabar rites were made at the same time as the confessional clarifications in relations with the Eastern churches. In the deliberations of the curial congregations, the dossiers were treated side by side despite the distances between the mission territories. This created close cross-references between the decisions on practices in China and South India, and *communicatio in sacris* with non-Uniate Eastern Christians. In the bull *Ex quo singulari* of 1742, Benedict XIV brought about a clarification at the highest level of the most spectacular missionary controversy—that over the Chinese rites—followed in 1744 by a similar decision against the Malabar rites. The pope thereby confirmed the will, based on his ultimate decision-making authority, to end the controversies and enforce the most uniform ritual practice possible.[31]

Word of the practices that were curbed by the two decisions had reached Rome an entire century earlier, and the curial congregations had been discussing them repeatedly ever since. The debate concerned forms of accommodation that opponents criticized as backsliding into "idolatry" and "superstition." The Chinese rites controversy revolved around the methods that Jesuits in China had used since the time of Matteo Ricci in their attempts to reconcile Christianity and Confucianism. Ricci had famously adopted the dress and manner of Confucian scholars, appropriated their erudition, and sought at the same time to win their favor by communicating the achievements of European scholarship.[32] The Jesuit missionaries to China who followed in Ricci's wake saw in the Confucian classics the "natural light" of a monotheistic knowledge of God, which prepared the Chinese to receive the Christian message. The Jesuits elicited criticism within the Church because they tolerated Confucian ancestor worship and rituals in honor of Confucius, among other things, arguing that they were "civil," not religious, practices.

Roberto de' Nobili, who had been working in South India since 1606, made claims similar to those of Matteo Ricci and later Jesuit missionaries to China. Nobili adopted the Brahman way of life there, which he described as that of respectable scholars rather than priests. He saw in their writings, the Vedas, the "natural light" of divine truth, which he was supposed to proclaim in India. In his understanding of the history of salvation, the humanist-educated Nobili viewed the "philosophy" of the Brahmans, as Matteo Ricci and his successors did the teachings of Confucius, as similar to the apparent equivalents in Greek and Roman antiquity that had become established components of Christian knowledge culture. The customs of the Brahmans, which his opponents attacked as "a sorry heathen mess," were civil acts. Nobili thus understood them as expressions not of religious affiliation but of a social system that corresponded to natural law in the sense described by Thomas Aquinas, which could therefore also be brought into line with the Christian message.[33]

The first opposition to the positions of Ricci or Nobili came from within the ranks of the Jesuits themselves. Criticism of Nobili's conduct was expressed by Portuguese Jesuits, who also regarded the Italian priest of noble birth as a threat to their own position and the Portuguese *Padroado*. Since he had made enemies on the ground, Nobili sought support at the highest levels in Rome: in 1623, Pope Gregory XV initially allowed Nobili's methods, until a final decision based on more extensive information could be made. At first, Nobili's methods served as a model for the *Propaganda Fide*. In his *Relazione delle Quattro Parti del Mondo* written between 1629 and 1631, the Congregation's first secretary, Francesco Ingoli, adopted Nobili's description of the Brahmans as the "philosophers and sages" of ancient India; the Brahman thread (*upavita*), which Nobili's opponents objected to as a religious symbol, was a sign of noble status or at most a "slight superstition," but no obstacle to the true faith once they received good Christian instruction.[34]

In the case of the Chinese rites, it took longer for the controversies initially fought out among the Jesuits on the ground to come before the curial congregations. This only occurred when Spanish Franciscans and Dominicans were dispatched to China from the Philippines. In 1645, the *Propaganda Fide* granted a claim on all points that had been brought forward by a Dominican. Henceforth, in the competition with other orders, the forms of accommodation practiced in China since Matteo Ricci were increasingly associated with the Society of Jesus. When the *Propaganda Fide*'s decree became known in China in 1650, the Jesuit Martino Martini left for Rome, where he arrived in 1655. During his sojourn in Rome, his order invested heavily in a number of publications that shed a positive light on the achievements of the Jesuits as China experts and missionaries. These efforts bore fruit in 1656: after consulting with the Holy Office, Pope Alexander VII followed the Jesuit Martini, who had described ancestor worship as an expression of the respect of descendants for their forefathers and who had denied the religious nature of the veneration of Confucius.[35]

The papal decision of 1656 did not end the conflict. Rather, the two decisions of 1645 and 1656 represented the points of reference for a controversy that continued to smolder and was exacerbated by the arrival in China of priests from the French

Missions étrangères in the 1690s. The conflicts over the practices now known as "Chinese rites" were fought out with growing intensity on various levels: between the missionaries in China, in their communications with the Roman Curia, at the Curia, and in the theological faculties in Europe, but also beyond confessional boundaries in the European republic of letters and among a broader public. At the Roman Curia, the critics increasingly gained the upper hand beginning around 1700, in striking parallel to the intensification of interest in *communicatio in sacris* and to some extent under the aegis of the same theological advisors.[36] After seven years of consultation with the Holy Office, Clement XI decided to ban the Chinese rites in his 1704 decree *Cum Deus optimus*. In 1715 he confirmed his decision in the bull *Ex illa die* and threatened violators with excommunication.

The decisions that the curial congregations and the popes made in the first half of the eighteenth century in obvious parallel to the Chinese and Malabar rites and the issue of *communicatio in sacris* with non-Uniate Eastern Christians were about far more than practices in distant mission territories. Since the first verdict of 1645 against the "Chinese rites," the *Propaganda Fide*'s decision-making practice suggests fears that the practices used to deal with non-Christian societies in Asia might lead to a relativizing of Christian faith and morality. The Congregation and its secretary, Francesco Ingoli, opposed the "Chinese rites" at that time, although they had adopted Nobili's comparable actions in South India as their own program in the 1620s. Ingoli now invoked the danger that two Christianities might emerge in China, one following the regulations of the Roman Church, and the other reflecting the taste of the missionaries, who could be seriously wrong.[37]

In the same context, there was a growing awareness of the potential unintended consequences of missionaries' dealing with Islam. For that reason, the *Propaganda Fide* banned the dissemination of a revised version of the Arabic translation of Filippo Guadagnoli's *Considerationes ad Mahomettanos* (Considerations for the Mohammedans) in 1649, despite the fact that it had just printed an edition of 500 copies in its own printing shop. The decision must have been all the more surprising for the author of the book, which had been in the works since the 1620s and was closely associated with the activities of the *Propaganda Fide* in those years. In the context of the controversies with the Discalced Carmelites and Pietro Della Valle in Isfahan, Shi'a scholars had sent a treatise to Pope Urban VIII. In this text, one such scholar, Sayyid Aḥmad ʿAlawī, refuted the *Truth-Showing Mirror* that the Jesuit Jerónimo Javier de Ezpeleta y Goñi had written in the Persian language in India. The *Propaganda Fide* took the scholars' purported announcement that a persuasive response to the treatise would cause them to convert to Christianity seriously enough to entrust a "congregation of most learned theologians" with the task.[38] The first to compose a response on behalf of the *Propaganda Fide* was Bonaventura Malvasia. After his work failed to meet the expectations of the Congregation, Filippo Guadagnoli took over; his work appeared in Latin in 1631 under the title *Apologia pro Christiana Religione* (Apology of the Christian religion), followed by an Arabic version in 1637 (Figure 19).[39]

The *Propaganda Fide* banned the dissemination of the revised Arabic version in 1649 because of a newly added chapter in which Guadagnoli sought to demonstrate that the Quran, "in those points in which it tells the truth, does not contradict the

Figure 19 Title page of the Arabic translation of Filippo Guadagnoli's *Pro Christiana Religione Responsio* (Answer in favor of the Christian religion), printed in 1637

Gospels." In Guadagnoli's effort to win Muslim readers over to Christianity based on common aspects of faith and to refute Islam using the Quran, his critics believed that he had overemphasized the commonalities between the Quran and the Bible. They accused the author of not expressly stating that the Quran was absolutely wrong. If a Muslim considered the author's statements to be true, he would, according to one of the censors, be confirmed in his belief that the Quran was a "good, God-given book."[40]

Because Guadagnoli refused to accept the ban, the *Propaganda Fide* ended up presenting the book to the Holy Office for scrutiny. However, the Holy Office then recommended publication of the work in 1652 with only a slight amendment—an expanded title. The Holy Office had found nothing contrary to doctrine or good morals and also praised the "great utility" of the work for Muslims and missionaries.[41] The differences between the two congregations recall the opposing decisions of 1645 and 1656 on the "Chinese rites." Such divergent views not only provided leeway for subaltern actors but also helped to make the way missionaries handled cultural diversity a topic of hot debate beyond the Curia.

The banning of Guadagnoli's work illustrates the consequences that the *Propaganda Fide* feared would arise from a comparative treatment of foreign religions. As a result, even Islam was no longer regarded in every respect as the work of the Devil, and Muhammad was rehabilitated as a "legislator."[42] The *Propaganda Fide* itself played a key role in communicating "Orientalist" knowledge. The efforts to unite the Eastern churches with Rome meant that more Christians from the Near East brought their specific experiences of dealing with Muslims to Rome. The *Collegio dei Maroniti* founded in 1584 had created an institutional framework for such forms of exchange and knowledge transfer.[43] The Maronite scholar Abraham Ecchellensis (1605–64) had also traveled to Rome in this context, and his input as an expert contributed to the *Propaganda Fide*'s decision to oppose the dissemination of Guadagnoli's work "based on the duty of his office and out of pure zeal for the Catholic religion," as Ecchellensis noted.[44] The Maronite himself had already run up against similar ecclesiastical censorship, because in his efforts to show the continuity of Arab culture since antiquity he had also discovered in the works of Muslim authors evidence of a morality that called upon believers to seek a knowledge of God in their studies and to live a godly life. In Ecchellensis's *Semita Sapientiae sive ad scientias comparandas methodus* (The path to wisdom, or method to acquire the sciences), published in Paris in 1646, the Oratorian Richard Simon (1638–1712) would later find evidence that one should appreciate the Muslim religion for all "that it contains of good, notably with regard to morality." In his efforts to gain the respect of the European republic of letters for Arab culture, including Muslim culture, Ecchellensis contributed, as Bernard Heyberger has shown, to the desacralized worldview of *libertinage érudit*, although he himself rejected the *libertin* relativization of Christian faith and morality.[45]

By placing obstacles in the way of Ecchellensis and banning the dissemination of the 1649 edition of Filippo Guadagnoli's *Considerationes ad Mahomettanos*, the *Propaganda Fide* also implicitly rejected the missionaries' practice in Persia of entering into discussions with Muslims, which were rooted in commonalities not only in a shared cultural background (such as Greek philosophy) but also in common beliefs. To be sure, all participants saw disputations ideally ending with the conversion of those of the other faith. At the same time, the debates were integrated into social contexts in which even Catholic clerics could reach the conclusion that not everything about the other faith was bad. It was in this spirit that even the last Latin bishop of Isfahan, Cornelio di San Giuseppe, wrote in his *Centurie* in the 1760s that apart from the "freedom of the flesh"—the alleged permissiveness in sexual matters—the Quran contained "many very good precepts" that were in line with the Gospels and thereby not merely with natural but also with divine law.[46]

By adopting a clearer stance than ever in opposing the Chinese rites and *communicatio in sacris*, in the first half of the eighteenth century the Roman Curia sought to halt the relativizing processes that issued from the spread of missionary knowledge and the attendant debates. The *Propaganda Fide*'s first decision against the Chinese rites (1645) and the prohibition on disseminating the work of Filippo Guadagnoli (1649) had coincided with changes in the relationship between theology, philosophy, and science that Jonathan I. Israel has called the starting point of the radical Enlightenment. When the opponents of extensive missionary accommodation increasingly gained the upper hand at the Roman Curia around 1700, they discussed the threats they perceived alongside those associated with competition from the churches that emerged from the Reformation in Europe. By the 1740s, the time of Benedict XIV's final decisions against the Chinese and Malabar rites, the efforts to reconcile the old and the new in theological categories could be considered as having failed.[47] Herein, too, lay the difficulty in the case of missionary controversies. These debates attracted a surprising amount of attention given the tiny number of directly affected Catholics in the mission territories because they were no longer expressed using the conventional categories of schism, heresy, and idolatry, which allowed for their containment. Instead, the very status of Christianity within society was put up for negotiation. The opponents of the Society of Jesus in the Chinese rites controversy clearly named such consequences: for instance, as deliberations of the Holy Office were under way, the Dominican cardinal Aloisio Maria Lucini criticized the practice of the Society, which, he claimed, defended superstition in China and true doctrine in Europe, thus setting an example for those who lived in Europe without religion. By proscribing the Chinese rites as a reversion to idolatry and superstition, Benedict XIV also opposed the notion of a morality separate from religion.[48]

The clarifications in the controversies over the rites and on the matter of *communicatio in sacris* occurred in Rome, while enforcement on the ground remained uncertain. And not only this: if we focus not just on the papal final decisions, but equally on the long phases of ambiguity that preceded them, the decision-making processes in the Curia itself appear in a different light. The deliberations of the curial congregations did not ignore realities on the ground. Especially at the Holy Office, staff were aware of the consequences of the nonenforceability of curial decisions. Particularly in the mission arena, cardinals and popes thus sought to avoid decisions as much as possible if their enforcement could be expected to cause serious problems and potential damage. The following section will address these specific practices of decision avoidance.

Truth Claims and Limits to Norm Enforcement: The Practice of Avoiding Decisions

"We know where the thorny affair of the Chinese rites led, and that is enough." Thus spoke a *consultor* of the Holy Office, Father Lorenzo Ganganelli, the future Pope Clement XIV (1769–74) in 1757. The decisions condemning the participation of Christians in Confucian rituals threatened the very existence of the churches in China sponsored by the Jesuits. Lorenzo Ganganelli had this outcome in mind when he used the aforementioned words to take a position on the treatment of mixed marriages and *communicatio in sacris* in the Near East. Ganganelli and two other *consultores* did not question the proscription of these practices as such. Instead, they turned against the draft of a decree with which the *Propaganda Fide* sought to subject *communicatio in sacris* and mixed marriages to the jurisdiction of the episcopate as *casus reservati* and punish the participation of clerics in the celebration of mixed marriages with suspension *ipso facto* from the priesthood. As most missionaries did, the *consultores* referred to Martin V's bull and the potential serious consequences for the Catholics in the Ottoman Empire.[49] The *consultores* thus refused to penalize what were essentially undisputed norms by imposing mandatory punishments that would have placed a heavy burden on relations with missionaries and the laity and excluded the fallible instead of reintegrating them into the Church through penance. They convinced the Holy Office to pay no further attention to the dossier. The matter ended with no decision. Such a result was not at all unusual, but instead constituted a fixed component of the decision-making practice of the curial congregation, which was frequently expressed in an established Latin phrase: "nihil esse respondendum" (nothing is to be answered). The highest decision-makers used this practice to respond to the discrepancy between the universal scope of their truth claims rooted in the history of salvation and divine and natural law and the limited opportunities to enforce them. Such considerations increased the tendency—rooted in their dependence on competing noble factions and foreign courts—of cardinals and popes to avoid controversial decisions and instead, with an eye to reason of state and their careers, to favor refined modes of conduct calculated to increase their relational capital.[50]

Neither in Persia nor in the Ottoman Empire could the Curia effectively prevent *communicatio in sacris*. The continued existence of the small Uniate communities could be secured only at the cost of compromises that ran counter to efforts toward restriction to a single confession and to the enforcement of orthodox confessional behavior. The culture of confessional ambiguity that had still dominated missionaries' reports to the Curia and their superiors in the first decades of the seventeenth century gave way only partially to sharper distinctions on the ground between "Catholics" and "schismatics" or "heretics." These increasingly rigid outlines had been demanded by Rome and were a major factor in the narrative spin that missionaries gave their "success stories." The curial congregations were well aware of this, since the curial information system was comparatively efficient for the early modern period, despite all the limitations explored in this study. Thus, a survey conducted in 1720 at the behest of the Holy Office impressively demonstrated how widespread the practices of *communicatio in sacris* remained in the Ottoman Empire and Persia. The survey showed that, despite the many individual prohibitions, many missionaries continued to justify *communicatio in sacris*, expressly citing Martin V's bull of 1418. At the same time, it revealed disagreements between missionaries on the ground. The *relatio* prepared at the Holy Office that summarized these findings offered a nuanced picture of the practices, which became the basis of subsequent decision-making processes within the Congregation.[51] The care with which the Holy Office used intelligence gathered locally distinguished it from early modern secular authorities, which often ignored painstakingly gathered information relevant for governance.[52] Nevertheless, this could not resolve the conflict between the ban on sacramental community with non-Catholics, on the one hand, and actual practice on the ground, on the other. Rather, the Holy Office sought to limit the potential damage to the Church's truth claims from the nonenforcement of norms.

It is worth noting that the Holy Office repeatedly came into conflict with the *Propaganda Fide*, which had fewer misgivings in this regard. When the latter announced a general ban on *communicatio in sacris* with the instruction of 1729 and forbade the missionaries to make this question the subject of disputes, it expressly opposed previous decisions by the Holy Office. According to the *ristretto* that prepared for the consultations of the particular congregation installed by the *Propaganda Fide*, these decisions led to each missionary expressing his own opinion and to Catholics no longer knowing whom they should believe, which caused "grave scandal and consternation." The *Propaganda Fide* thus justified its expansion into an area that actually fell under the jurisdiction of the Holy Office by portraying itself as the better guardian of true church doctrine.[53]

Thus far, the majority of cardinals at the Holy Office and the pope had in fact shied away from a general ban on *communicatio in sacris*. By 1708, consultor of the Holy Office Giovanni Damasceno Bragaldi had already suggested issuing general instructions in order to stop missionaries from engaging in what he saw as a mistaken and forbidden practice. While Clement XI approved all of the consultor's recommended decisions on individual *dubia* concerning *communicatio* in 1709, he refrained from proclaiming general instructions and a general decision regarding the jurisdictional authority of the bishops of the non-Uniate Eastern churches. There was to be no scrutiny of these matters.[54]

The Holy Office and the pope exercised the same reticence in the dossier that led to the commissioning of the abovementioned survey in 1720. The starting point had been the 1718 observations of Mekhitar, abbot of San Lazzaro degli Armeni in Venice, according to which the Armenians were compelled to turn to "schismatic" priests for baptisms, burials, and marriages. In 1718–19, a majority of the cardinals and the pope did not follow the argument of the *consultores* favoring a general ban on *communicatio in sacris*. Instead, they recommended that missionaries "consult doctors [of theology] and righteous, learned clerics with long experience in those missions" and at the same time "refrain from all acts that contain a profession of a false sect as well as all occasions of scandal and subversion."[55] This was an ambiguous statement that delegated the decision to the missionaries, while also recalling Martin V's bull *Ad vitanda scandala* and its interpretations. This was also how the missionaries understood the decision. Abbot Mekhitar and two of his monks reportedly even wrote to the Ottoman Empire that the Catholics could now freely enter the churches of the "schismatics." For that reason, the cardinals of the Holy Office admonished the abbot in November 1720 not to abuse the resolution of 1719. Once again, the cardinals nevertheless did not follow the urging of a majority of the *consultores* to expressly declare *communicatio in sacris* generally impermissible. Before deciding, the *Propaganda Fide* had to request more precise information about the practices and their inevitability from missionaries on the ground and those in Rome.[56] This was the starting point for the broad-based survey that formed the basis of further consultations starting in 1722.

Even after 1729, the Holy Office remained more hesitant than the *Propaganda Fide* to condemn practices that it well knew to be still widespread. The general prohibition that the *Propaganda Fide* issued in 1729 in the form of an instruction was not a formal decree that might have expressly posed the question of orthodoxy. The statements by Ganganelli and the two additional *consultores* who were entrusted in 1757 with examining the *Propaganda Fide*'s draft decree, as well as the Holy Office's non-treatment of the dossier, went even further in that direction.

In an environment where confessional distinctions were drawn extremely sharply, the Holy Office thus maintained more reticence when judging local practices on the matter of *communicatio in sacris*, which was so fundamental to relations with the Eastern Christians. This ran counter to the otherwise-observable process of an increasing disambiguation of church regulations. The negative opinion of the *consultores* in 1757 may have been influenced by the fact that one of their number, Giuseppe Simone Assemani, had himself been born a Maronite Catholic in the Ottoman Empire and, after studying at the *Collegio dei Maroniti* in Rome, had made a career at the Curia and gained influence with his reputation as an expert on the Eastern churches.[57] Assemani was indeed especially firm in his opposition to the suggestions of the *Propaganda Fide*. According to him, the permissibility of *communicatio in sacris* could not be defined independent of the specific case, the persons involved, or the circumstances.[58]

Assemani was the only one of the three *consultores* to write an *osservazione particolare* in addition to the *osservazione generale*. It amended individual passages of the *Propaganda Fide*'s draft decree and further illuminated his position. Instead of writing "rites intrinsically sullied by errors," Assemani suggested the phrase "rites usually sullied by errors." Citing the *Congregazione per la correzione dei libri degli Orientali* that had emerged from the *Propaganda Fide*, he supported the view that the Greek rite was free of errors with respect to the administration of the sacraments. The same could also be said of the sacraments of the Armenians, Syrians, and Copts. Mixed marriages were forbidden not by divine law but merely by canon law, which was also why the pope could bestow dispensations. Since there were cases in which *communicatio* was permissible based on Martin V's bull or for some other reason, the text of the decree should also take this into account. For that reason, Assemani recommended expanding the text to contain the following wording, formatted here in italics:

> There are all too clear arguments to decide that such community cannot be permitted in *almost* any instance, because for the actual circumstances, those reasons that forbid it *either by canon or* by divine and natural law *nearly always* apply completely or at least partially.

Instead of making *communicatio in sacris* a *casus reservatus* and suspending priests who participated in celebrating mixed marriages *ipso facto* from the administration of the sacraments, Assemani preferred to admonish the bishops and confessors to impose "the most grave, salvific penances" upon the sinners.[59]

Assemani's personal influence alone, however, is not sufficient to explain the Holy Office's greater reluctance in comparison to the *Propaganda Fide*. We also need to consider the specific status of the decisions of the Holy Office whose definitions of church teachings were universally binding. While the Holy Office no longer dealt with the dossier after the *consultores*' negative verdict, in other cases it deliberately decided not to respond to inquiries. "Nihil esse respondendum" had become a common phrase when the Holy Office faced *dubia* in which a deep chasm opened between the principles of the post-Tridentine Church, from which the congregation preferred not to retreat, and the constraints of local conditions.[60] With this phrase, the refusal to make a decision became a component of a formalized procedure that was particularly typical of the curial congregations. The ideal-typical characteristics of such a procedure included an ultimate decision, in this case "nihil esse respondendum."

Those who turned to the Congregation with a *dubium* experienced the effects of this phrase—which was not itself communicated to them—as a nonresponse, akin to the incomplete treatment of a dossier. Both practices suggest that the Curia was well aware of the limits of enforceability in matters where "proper" doctrine was at stake. They could come into play by turns in the same matter. This will be illustrated in several cases that follow.

In 1699, the Capuchins in Persia and Georgia presented a fourteen-point list of *dubia* to the *Propaganda Fide* concerning various aspects of religious practice among Catholic Armenians. While the *dubia* also referred to different fasting requirements and holiday customs, it was the practices of *communicatio in sacris* that raised truly controversial questions: Were Catholic Armenians permitted to go to the Armenian church if they rejected the errors in the mass and prayers there? How should a Catholic Armenian behave given that he had to confess to his priest and receive communion before marriage and could not turn to the missionaries for the wedding ceremony either? Was it permissible for a woman who had secretly converted to come to confession and communion just four or five times a year in a Catholic church, while she otherwise attended the Armenian church with her family? Further "doubts" concerned the priests: Must a Catholic Armenian priest add water to the communion wine? It was scarcely possible for him to do so since the Armenian mass was always celebrated in the presence of all priests. Was he allowed to pronounce the names of Dioscorus and Ioannes Ozinellus in the canon, whom the Roman Church had condemned as heretics? These two *dubia* implicitly addressed the question of whether Catholic and "schismatic" Armenian priests could celebrate the mass together. How integrated Catholic Armenian priests remained—at least at times—into their non-Uniate community is also illustrated by the question of whether they were allowed to hear confessions from non-Uniate Armenians.

The *dubia* referred expressly to differences between missionaries: while some were of the opinion that terminally ill Catholic Armenians were forbidden to confess to a "schismatic" priest even when no Catholic priest was available, others were more lenient. The missionaries were equally at odds with each other on the matter of whether Catholic Armenians could confess to a Catholic priest and then take communion in the Armenian church.[61]

The *Propaganda Fide* forwarded the *dubia* to the Holy Office for its consideration. The *consultor* charged with assessing them, Giovanni Damasceno Bragaldi, responded negatively to all *dubia* concerning *communicatio in sacris*: It was not permissible to perform the outward actions and disagree with the errors only inwardly. One must not incur eternal punishment in order to avert temporal harm![62] The Holy Office, however, preferred not to address the Capuchins' awkward *dubia*.[63] It was not until 1709 that the cardinals and Pope Clement XI arrived at a verdict, once again based on an opinion by Bragaldi, grounded in a similar list of *dubia* from the missionaries in Isfahan and New Julfa. The pope simultaneously rejected the idea to decree a general ban on *communicatio in sacris*, as discussed above.

One of the *dubia* of 1699 concerning Catholics confessing to "schismatic" priests when they had no access to a Catholic cleric continued to be the subject of decision avoidance by the Holy Office and the pope after 1709. The arguments referred to the fact that the Council of Trent had left open the possibility that priests not approved by the Church could give absolution *ad articulum mortis*. While the Council had thereby confirmed the practice according to which no reservation existed in cases of mortal danger, and any (Catholic) priest could absolve the penitents of their sins, the *dubia* from Persia and the Ottoman Empire were concerned with something else: the authority of "schismatic priests" to give absolution. For that reason, any response would have had implications for the validity of the ordination of non-Uniate priests. Not providing an answer thus appeared to be the appropriate course. While the *dubium*, limited to the confessions of the terminally ill, remained unanswered in 1699, together with all the other *dubia*, a *dubium* of 1704—this time submitted by a Capuchin in Constantinople—was decided by Clement XI who, after hearing the views of the cardinals of the Holy Office, used the phrase "nihil esse respondendum." With the request to "consult the theologians," the pope made the decision the responsibility of the missionaries.[64] The Holy Office again had to address a similar query from a Discalced Carmelite in the Levant in 1718. Although the *dubium* now referred to missionaries and laypeople who were not in mortal danger but had long had no access to a Catholic confessor, the opinions of the *consultores* and the decision of the pope once again revealed the effort to avoid being pinned down. Seven of the twelve *consultores* believed that the practice should be declared illicit but that this answer should be formulated not as a decree but as a less-binding simple instruction. Three *consultores* did not wish to respond to the *dubium* and, as in 1704, preferred to delegate the decision to the missionaries with the call to consult the theological authorities. Two *consultores* noted that Catholics could not confess their sins to "schismatics" but stated that the missionaries should consult the theological authorities "in the case of necessity and impending death." Here, too, after hearing the cardinals, Clement XI ultimately decided "nihil esse respondendum."[65]

In the 1710s, as apostolic vicar of the diocese of Isfahan, the Dominican Barnaba Fedeli reported to the *Propaganda Fide* on a number of "abuses" by Catholic Armenians in New Julfa. They all referred to the Sceriman family, which exercised patronage over the Catholic Armenian church in New Julfa. In this case, too, most *dubia* took the prescribed route from the *Propaganda Fide* to the Holy Office. On the issue of communion under both kinds, the *consultores* joined the opinion of Father Giovanni Damasceno Bragaldi, who considered it to be tolerable as long as it was not an expression of "heresy" and "error."[66] In the case of the Easter customs that Fedeli found objectionable, the *Propaganda Fide* and the Holy Office (to the extent that the *Propaganda Fide* consulted it) also withheld judgment. As to the anointing of men's feet and women's hands on Maundy Thursday, the custom of carrying the priest through the church on a chair after worship, and the habit of eating eggs and butter after mass on Easter Saturday, in 1715 the *Propaganda Fide* suggested explaining the reasons for abolishing these practices to persons "of the highest authority and esteem." Should this prove unsuccessful, the apostolic vicar should clarify whether a pastoral letter from the Congregation would be helpful. In any case, he must always proceed "prudently and cautiously" to prevent the Armenians from falling back into "schism." Four years later, the *Propaganda Fide* gave permission to eat eggs and dairy products after mass on Easter Saturday.[67] For its part, the Holy Office preferred not to comment on this custom: "Nihil esse respondendum."[68]

The *dubia* of Barnaba Fedeli concerning marriageable age and mixed marriages between Catholic Armenians and "schismatics" presented far thornier questions than these practices, which from a Roman viewpoint had to be considered "old abuses" rather than dogmatic "errors." The *dubia* concerning the sacrament of marriage touched on the core of the post-Tridentine confessional church's self-image. In this concrete case, however, the *dubia* referred to the Sceriman family, upon whom the continued existence of the Catholic Armenian community in New Julfa depended. This prompted a cautious approach. It was common among the Armenians of New Julfa to arrange marriages in early childhood. The marriages were then consummated after the couple had reached puberty. From the perspective of missionaries and the curial congregations, the legal status of the arrangement of marriages between children remained unclear, just as opinions diverged about whether the resolutions of the Council of Trent applied to the Catholic Armenians in New Julfa. In his letter of 1713 to the *Propaganda Fide*, Barnaba Fedeli therefore spoke of "sponsali, e matrimonii" and "sponsali, o matrimonii" (betrothals and/or marriages), and it is only the minutes of the Congregation's meeting that speak unambiguously of marriages. The *Propaganda Fide* objected above all to the fact that the little girls were given in marriage to "schismatics" and refused to compromise with the Armenians on this point. Instead, it presented the *dubia* to the Holy Office for its opinion. There, in 1714, the dossier only got as far as the *consultores*, who referred to the mixed marriages as illicit and refused to allow them even with conditions. Rather, the apostolic vicar was to prevent them as much as possible. The cardinals provided no decision, and the matter therefore remained legally unresolved. Instead, the *Propaganda Fide* asked a member of the Sceriman family who was living as a merchant in Italy to admonish his relatives in Persia to obey the ecclesiastical requirements; in the meantime, the missionaries should proceed with "charity" and "caution" to avoid "scandal" and "discord." While the treatment of the Scerimans was characterized by respect for the family's position, the Congregation called upon the apostolic vicar to name the missionary who had purportedly reinforced the family's mistaken idea that the Church permitted mixed marriages between little girls and schismatics.[69] In a later, similar, case in 1719, the cardinals of the Holy Office confirmed the cautious approach to Catholic Armenians. The *Propaganda Fide* had requested their opinion on a *dubium* that once again had been presented by Barnaba Fedeli. He wished to know how he should proceed in the case of a girl, now aged sixteen, who refused to consummate her marriage to a "schismatic" to whom she had been betrothed as a child, and who lent weight to her request for permission to marry someone else by threatening to convert to Islam otherwise. Once again, the decision was "nihil esse respondendum."[70]

Finally, we will explore a case before the Holy Office that reveals the importance that the person most affected, Gregorio Agdollo of New Julfa, accorded relations with the powerful kinship network of the Scerimans. In this case, which might have led to the serious charge of *bigamia simultanea*, the Armenian temporarily used the impressive name of Sceriman in addition to his own.[71] Moreover, the case illustrates the individual leeway that the normative gaps between the Roman and the Armenian Church could yield.

Gregorio Agdollo is not an unknown figure in the history of the Armenian diasporas in Italy. In later life, he showed notable skill in cultivating personal relationships and navigating between different normative orders. He served as a middleman in commercial and financial matters, as well as art purchases, for Elector Frederick August II of Saxony (r. 1733–63; King August III of Poland, r. 1734–63), who appointed him resident in Florence in 1740 and—despite a sensational bankruptcy—*chargé d'affaires* in Venice in 1750.[72] The case that concerns us here in 1736–7 revolved around the validity of the marriage that Gregorio Agdollo had contracted in New Julfa in 1727 with the nine-year-old Anna Agigahn when he himself was sixteen. At the time, Gregorio was about to travel to Europe, where he planned to engage in trade. His mother, who headed the household as a widow, made her consent to this undertaking dependent on his marriage with the girl. Based on a papal *facultas*, Bishop Barnaba Fedeli issued a dispensation for the marriage within the prohibited degrees of kinship on the condition that the newlyweds live together only after they had both reached the prescribed age of marriage.[73]

In 1732, Gregorio Agdollo settled in Florence as a merchant. There he fell in love with his landlord's daughter, a certain Gaspara Parigi. The connection he had entered into in New Julfa in 1727 now stood in the way of his marriage to Gaspara, with whom he fathered a child. For that reason, in 1736 Gregorio sought a declaration from the Holy Office that the relationship he had contracted in 1727, which he now referred to as a betrothal, was not a valid marriage. He alleged that his consent had occurred under duress and had only been given verbally. Since he could not offer written proof of his unwed status because of resistance from his relatives in New Julfa to the marriage with Gaspara, he requested that the Holy Office allow him to provide an oath instead. The outcome of the case depended on whether or not Gregorio could persuade the Holy Office that the alliance of 1727 should be judged according to the Tridentine rules and would thus be considered a betrothal that could be dissolved rather than a valid marriage. It was in this spirit that Gregorio compiled the dossier he presented to the Holy Office: an Armenian priest had prepared a declaration for him stating that the Catholic Armenians of New Julfa had accepted the Council of Trent and therefore only regarded the "marriages" contracted in childhood as valid when both the man and woman had attained the minimum age stipulated by the council decrees.

On June 27, 1736, the cardinals decided to put the case to the *consultores*. They adopted Gregorio's wording, asking the *consultores* not about the validity of a "marriage" (*matrimonium*), but rather of a betrothal (*sponsalia*) sealed by the presentation of a ring. On July 4, 1736, the cardinals decided to ask the bishop of Isfahan whether he regarded the relationship in question as "a marriage or a betrothal" and whether it still existed. Just two weeks later, however, they overturned this decision by allowing Gregorio to take an oath attesting to his unmarried status. Gregorio then married Gaspara in Florence.

This was not the end of the case before the Holy Office, however. In late August 1736, the Florentine inquisitor forwarded a letter to the Holy Office that the Discalced Carmelite Filippo Maria di Sant'Agostino, now bishop of Isfahan, had written to him. According to the bishop, Gregorio had spontaneously ratified his "marriage" in letters to him and Anna Agigahn in 1731, and it must therefore be considered valid. According to this argument, Gregorio must be viewed as a bigamist because of his marriage in Florence to Gaspara Parigi. This additional information meant that the Holy Office had to reopen the case. The Florentine inquisitor was charged with questioning

Gregorio about the statements made by the bishop of Isfahan; the bishop was to send extracts from the baptismal and matrimonial registers, copies of the episcopal dispensation, and Gregorio's letters of 1731 to Rome along with additional papers. While Gregorio confirmed his previous testimony to the vicar general of the Holy Office in Florence, the bishop of Isfahan answered that the requested documents were no longer available; the baptismal and marriage registers in New Julfa, in particular, had been destroyed to make it more difficult to prove kinship when converts to Islam made claims to family property. Instead, the bishop sent copies of letters written in 1734 in which Gregorio had expressed his hope of soon returning to Persia and being with Anna.

All this notwithstanding, the relation of the dossier in the Holy Office archives ends with a vote according to which the letters attributed to Gregorio contained no ratification of the contract that would have turned the "betrothal" into a "marriage." Apparently, though, no formal verdict was ever issued in Gregorio's favor. The Holy Office likewise never tried Gregorio for *bigamia simultanea*, which would have been necessary had the alliance of 1727 been interpreted as a marriage. Was this because, once again, the most important Uniate family in New Julfa, the Scerimans, appeared to be directly affected, but the Holy Office shied away from defining the Tridentine formal obligation as a precondition for the validity of the marriage of a Catholic Armenian from New Julfa? A formal decision in this sense would have had consequences well beyond the individual case. All of these factors may have contributed to the failure to issue a decision, along with the fact that the correspondence with the bishop of Isfahan had uncovered a number of irregularities in the missionaries' and bishops' conduct of office, including the deliberate destruction of baptismal and marriage registers or the fact that the episcopal dispensations could not be located. The winner was Gregorio Agdollo, who succeeded in convincing the Holy Office to assess his situation from the viewpoint of Tridentine marriage law, thus providing him with a means to extract himself from a tricky situation that would not have been available to him from the Armenian perspective, represented in this case by the Latin bishop of Isfahan.

Focusing on the practices of decision avoidance takes us to a field of research that we can only touch on here: the procedures of curial decision-making. In order to do so, we need to pay attention not just to the content of the decisions but also to the forms in which they were communicated. Both the Holy Office and the *Propaganda Fide* often preferred to communicate guidelines for action not as decrees but in the less binding form of instructions. In 1635, the *Propaganda Fide* noted, presumably at the instigation of Francesco Ingoli, that it was inopportune to tie their hands with decisions described as decrees; instructions were easier to alter where necessary.[74] With the same intentions, Clement X ordered in 1671 that the *Propaganda Fide* be supplied with the Holy Office's responses to the *dubia* without any mention of the date when they had been discussed. He had the secretary of the *Propaganda Fide* instructed to send all decisions to the missionaries as *instructiones* rather than *definitiones*.[75] The *Propaganda Fide* thereupon resolved to pass on the responses to the *dubia* from the Holy Office and the Congregation of the Council as *monita* or *institutiones* and not as *decreta*.[76] Instructions, *monita*, and *institutiones* were not merely simpler to revise than decrees; while the effect was legally and symbolically less binding, the consequences of the expected nonobservance were also less far-reaching, for the laypeople and clerics who violated them but also for the Church's truth claims.

The curial congregations had recourse to a wide spectrum of practices to react to such challenges: from disregarding awkward dossiers to the formalized practice of avoiding decisions—"nihil esse respondendum"—and the adjustment of the level of obligation attributed to the verdicts that were issued. During deliberations over a response to the *dubia* concerning the Chinese rites between 1643 and 1645, the *Propaganda Fide* and the Holy Office discussed not only the jurisdiction and content but also the various modes of response, as we see from the positions taken by Francesco Ingoli. The options were to offer no answer, as preferred by the Holy Office;[77] to communicate the answers in the binding form of a papal brief, combined with the threat of excommunication *latae sententiae* against violators, as the mendicants demanded; or, finally, to issue a theological opinion, which the missionaries would be expected to adhere to until such time as they received a different order from the Holy See. Ingoli himself once again preferred the last method, which allowed for the changing of decisions when they proved unenforceable. The missionaries were thus to be provided with clear specifications so that they did not put off potential converts with contradictory statements and practices. At the same time, Ingoli sought to maintain scope for the integration of Catholic diversity.[78]

Ideally, the authority of the papal prince was more absolute than the authority of any other ruler. In matters of faith, the papacy combined "the mode of the bureaucrats" with "the spiritual mode" to produce "decisions that effectively merged the claim to truth with an obliging commitment to that truth," as Birgit Emich has shown. This combination was intended to give the religious-theological decisions "the highest possible degree of legitimacy."[79] Yet, contrary to the superficial impression fed by the quite limited number of controversial decisions—from the trial of Galileo to the decisions in the rites controversies—the Roman Curia in the early modern period was anything but enthusiastic about making decisions.[80] Its members were all too aware of the diversity of inner-Catholic positions, their connections with powerful ecclesiastical and secular actors, and the limits of their own capacity for enforcement outside the Papal States. Even in the eighteenth century, the extent of doctrinal disambiguation remained limited by a practice of avoiding decisions.

Normative Orders outside the Church

The integration of missionaries into local contexts of action throughout the world did not just lead to pluralization within the Church but also fostered the emergence of classification systems alongside those of the Roman Church. While Gregorio Agdollo played Tridentine marital law off against the norms of his Armenian environment in New Julfa, thereby fending off the danger of bigamy charges, the controversies surrounding *communicatio in sacris* and the Chinese and Malabar rites were about far more than just an individual's situational use of differing canon law norms. While *communicatio in sacris* implicitly challenged the Roman Church's claim to be the only

Church of Christ, the experiences of the missionaries in China and India and the ensuing controversies helped to undermine the notion that there was no alternative to Christianity.

From the period around 1700 onward, the Roman Curia adopted increasingly restrictive positions on *communicatio in sacris* as well as the Chinese and Malabar rites, because the Church in Catholic Europe, including Italy, had to face the fact that the lines between the sacred and the "world" were being redrawn and were shifting to its detriment—in the realm of knowledge as well as in the relationship between secular and ecclesiastical jurisdiction.[81] As rulers of the Papal States, the popes had been weakened both economically and politically.[82] At the same time, for better or worse, the Roman Curia had to adapt to the growing societal relevance of competing normative orders. These circumstances led to the apparent contradictions in papal policy, especially during the pontificate of Benedict XIV. The settlement of controversial questions led to a sharpening of confessional lines but also to a willingness to recognize secularized normative orders, at least implicitly, alongside the Church. The restrictive reinterpretation of Martin V's bull *Ad vitanda scandala*, which the Holy Office gleaned in 1753 from the remarks of Benedict XIV in his *De Synodo dioecesana libri tredecim* (Thirteen books on the diocesan synod), for example, points in this direction: In contrast to the interpretation common up to that point, the Congregation no longer concluded from the bull that *communicatio in sacris* was permissible under certain circumstances. Instead, it only applied the bull to transactions in "purely profane and civil matters," which were allowed in light of the "miserable conditions of our times."[83]

The willingness to recognize competing normative orders under certain circumstances and at the same time to sharpen confessional boundaries revealed itself especially impressively in the treatment of mixed marriages. The *Tametsi* decree issued by the Council of Trent proceeded from a shared ecclesiastical and secular normative order in matters of matrimony, but the *Declaratio benedictina* of 1741 was based on the insight that the two frameworks could diverge under certain circumstances while each retained its own legal validity. It was no coincidence that Benedict XIV's declaration initially referred to the United Provinces of the Netherlands. As early as the seventeenth century, the Catholic Church there faced a situation in which mixed marriages were not only widely tolerated, but the possibility of civil marriage before a secular magistrate created procedures that even deprived religious confession of its legal relevance in this matter. The Holy Office initially responded by creating possibilities for the retroactive canonical validation of such marriages, while at the same time recalling their illicit nature by linking their validation to penitential obligations.[84] In this way, it met the demands of the local environment without fundamentally departing from the formal obligation set out by the Council of Trent. The *Declaratio benedictina* of 1741 took a different approach: in it, Benedict XIV limited the Tridentine formal obligation to purely Catholic marriages and recognized the legal validity of the mixed marriages contracted in the United Provinces that disregarded the Council's provisions. At the same time, the pope confirmed the notion that such liaisons were illicit because of the sacramental nature of matrimony, which is why the ecclesiastical punishments reserved for them were to be imposed. Preventing mixed marriages wherever possible and reintegrating repentant sinners into the church community after the appropriate penance were the confessors' tasks.[85]

The *Declaratio benedictina* of 1741 influenced the practice of curial decision-making well beyond its original scope of application in the Netherlands, for example on *dubia* from the Ottoman Empire and Persia. In his 1754 instructions for the apostolic vicar in Constantinople, Benedict XIV affirmed the validity of the mixed marriages contracted there between Catholics and "schismatics" or "heretics." Only the validity of marriages between Latin Catholics depended on the observance of the Council's resolutions because the custom of holding these weddings before a Catholic priest amounted to the publication of the decrees.[86] Just how far curial decision-making practices adjusted to the existence of legal systems beyond canon law is evident from the vote of the Dominican Serafino Maria Maccarinelli, commissary of the Holy Office. In 1768 he cited the *Declaratio* of 1741 and the instructions of 1754 to confirm the validity of a marriage between a Catholic woman and a Protestant man that a Protestant pastor had performed in Pera. He argued that wherever Catholics, "heretics," and "schismatics" lived together and enjoyed the freedom to practice their religion, "two societies, a Catholic and a schismatic or heretical one," coexisted and "governed themselves according to their own laws and customs." For Maccarinelli, legal validity did not mean that the Church regarded the Catholic woman's mixed marriage as "licit": the woman must be instructed on "the graveness of her offense" and must be allowed to take communion again only "after performing suitable, salutary penances."[87] Nine of the twelve *consultores* agreed with Maccarinelli's verdict; the remaining three preferred to maintain the invalidity of the marriage contracted before a Protestant pastor. Pope Clement XIII, for his part, followed the majority of the *consultores*.[88] The *Declaratio benedictina* was thus also enforced *de facto* in Constantinople, although no formal expansion of the scope of validity ensued, so as not to further promote mixed marriages. In the years 1773 to 1775, the Holy Office adopted the same approach to the few remaining Armenian Catholics in New Julfa. The Holy Office and the papacy chose not to bestow the *facultas* to issue dispensations for mixed marriages between Armenian Catholics and "heretics" upon the Armenian Catholic priest there, which would have been tantamount to declaring such relationships not merely legally valid but also licit in the eyes of the Church. Instead, the Congregation and the pope preferred to point to the 1754 instructions for the apostolic vicar of Constantinople and thus, in substance if not in form, to the *Declaratio Benedictina*.[89]

How did the decisions in the controversies over the rites and the question of *communicatio in sacris* on the one hand, and the *Declaratio Benedictina* on the other, fit with the image of Benedict XIV as a prince of the Church whose governing practice was said to correspond more closely than that of any pope before or since to the ideas of the Catholic Enlightenment? We know that Prospero Lorenzo Lambertini devoted himself as archbishop of Bologna and as pope to reforming the clergy and the liturgy in keeping with the Council of Trent. By signing concordats with the kings of Sardinia-Piedmont, Naples, Portugal, and Spain, he endeavored, in light of new practices of statehood, to attain a modus vivendi in areas where temporal and ecclesiastical jurisdiction clashed.[90] As ruler of the Papal States, Benedict XIV sought recognition from his subjects as a promoter of good order and administration. He corresponded widely within the European republic of letters, whose expectations he met by, for example, acknowledging the insights of Copernicus and Galileo. As Mario Rosa has emphasized, such rapprochements occurred "within a consolidated hierarchy of values and orientations," which Benedict XIV defended by condemning Freemasonry, Montesquieu's *Esprit des Lois,* and Voltaire's entire oeuvre and also, crucially, through the final decisions in the controversies over the Chinese and Malabar rites and the disambiguation on the question of *communicatio in sacris.* The limits he drew to the toleration of those of other faiths by Catholic authorities were correspondingly narrow.[91]

When the same pope sought in his final decision to end the rites controversies, confirmed the condemnation of *communicatio in sacris,* and at the same time recognized the legal validity of mixed marriages under certain conditions, he asserted the Church's teaching authority in a core area of religion in the face of multiple threats. His disambiguation in areas where the magisterium was challenged, like his openness to the Catholic Enlightenment, marked him as a conservative reformer, who in this way picked up where his predecessors in the late seventeenth and early eighteenth centuries had left off. Like them, Benedict XIV aimed to assert the place of the Roman Catholic Church in a changing world. Thus, at the beginning of his pontificate, he stated that his duty was to "steer the regrettably agitated ship of St. Peter into calm waters."[92] Moreover, as archbishop of Bologna and as pope, he sought to make church institutions perform more efficiently by reforming procedures and the selection of personnel. Limited concessions in matters such as heliocentrism were intended to defuse conflicts over the findings of scientific research.[93] The reform of the Holy Office and the Roman Index instigated by Benedict XIV, with the objective of rationalizing and standardizing bureaucratic procedures, like the selective reception of Enlightenment knowledge practices, was meant to strengthen papal primacy and the authority of the Holy See in matters of doctrine and church discipline. The revision of the Index aimed not to give authors more scope, but to improve the reputation of ecclesiastical censorship.[94] Like this reform, the attempt to end the rites controversies by a final papal decision was directed not just at the content but also at strengthening the Church's claim to infallibility, which suffered when issues of doctrine were fought out by clerics *and* laypeople in the public space, as had increasingly been the case.

The efforts to reform the Church, following the example of the Council of Trent, to strengthen the papal magisterium and produce the greatest clarity, were also a response to the challenges posed by the pluralization of ecclesiastical practice in the mission context. Given the diversity of social and cultural contexts in which actors dependent on the Curia were active, however, the papal claim to ultimate decision-making authority created unwanted and ultimately uncontrollable dynamics that became counterforces to confessional reductionism. Procedures that promoted the authoritative establishment of doctrine and church discipline themselves contributed to the arrival in Rome, in the form of *dubia,* of countless questions of everyday life in the Church alongside the familiar controversies. These *dubia* also demonstrated the difficulties of dealing with cultural diversity. Hard-to-implement decisions fanned the controversies and unwittingly also the processes of relativizing ecclesiastical certainties. The practices of avoiding decisions on the sensitive matter of *communicatio in sacris* show that such dynamics were recognized at the highest levels. At no time did the conflicts manifest themselves more plainly than during the pontificate of Benedict XIV: while the pope enjoyed great prestige in the republic of letters because of his personal erudition and his role as protector of the sciences, especially in his capacity as archbishop of Bologna, in the missions he drew tighter boundaries around the permissible than his predecessors ever had. In the process, Benedict XIV did something his predecessors had preferred to avoid: he made unambiguous decisions on controversial matters. This effort at removing ambiguity contrasted with the culture of compromise that, because of the cardinals' and popes' dependence on competing factions of nobles and foreign powers, had characterized the Roman court up to that point. In its way, this effort corresponded to the new importance of rational and reasonable argumentation that distinguished the Enlightenment. To the degree that papal decisions affected non-European actors and their practices, they also corresponded to the universal "civilizing mission" of the European Enlightenment.

To be sure, by acknowledging legal systems beyond canon law in the *Declaratio benedictina*, the pope adjusted to the existence of realms alongside the religious sphere that, as a consequence of secularization processes, were increasingly beyond the reach of the Church. The *Declaratio*, however, was not merely a concession to the practical requirements of confessionally mixed contexts and the conditions created by processes of societal transformation. It also aimed to bind individual religiosity more closely to the Roman Church and to promote the internalization of its norms through confession and penance. The objective of "Romanizing" Catholic religiosity thus went hand in hand with the acknowledgment of the laws of "profane and civil society."

Conclusion

In the early seventeenth century, Augustinians from Goa and Discalced Carmelites from Rome arrived in Isfahan in quick succession and settled there with lofty expectations of an anti-Ottoman alliance between Catholic powers and the shah and of the conversion of Persian Muslims. Measured against the expectations that occasioned their dispatch, the Persian missions soon proved quite unsuccessful. In fact, neither did an alliance against the Turks ensue nor did a larger number of Armenians, let alone Muslims, convert to Catholicism. The missionaries were also spared martyrdom, since they enjoyed a high degree of security in Persia before the decline and fall of the Safavid dynasty threatened law and order for Christians and Muslims alike. It is thus probably no surprise that the confessionally tinged historiography on Catholic missions has devoted little attention to the Persian missions.

Indeed, religious superiors and the congregations of the Roman Curia would have been none too pleased by certain of the "success stories" related here. For missionaries defined their social roles on the ground according to specific local normative expectations and thereby gained renown—also, but not only—as religious specialists. Mission, by no means only in Persia, thus led away from the confessional model of the *Ecclesia triumphans* of the Counter-Reformation. It is in the unintended consequences of the missions that their significance for European cultural history lies, as Chapter 7 shows.

As Catholic priests, missionaries in Persia lived in an environment where the relevance of religious boundaries depended to an unusual degree on the specific local circumstances, at least from a Western European perspective. In Persia, Catholic clerics were party to relationships of "friendship" and "good correspondence" with Christians of various confessions as well as Muslims. Apparently, they frequently lived up to the expectations of their interlocutors. Thousands of "baptisms" of terminally ill children suggest that the missionaries were able to meet Muslim parents' expectations of a cure for their offspring not just because of their medical knowledge but also by dint of their reputation as men of God.

In their interactions with Protestants, confessional conflicts were overlaid by Christian commonalities in a Muslim environment. The houses of the missionary orders, especially of the Discalced Carmelites and Capuchins, became favored places of refuge for European travelers of various walks of life and confessions who found accommodation, sociability, advice, and comfort in the most diverse situations, as well as medical care, when necessary. Missionaries who had been in Persia for a long time offered travelers information as well as their services as translators and interpreters, all while helping to put them in touch with people of diverse rank and religion. Acting as hosts was part of the "friendship" and "good correspondence" that members of the orders cultivated with representatives of the Dutch and English East India Companies. For their part, the Dutch and the English reciprocated the hospitality they found with the Discalced Carmelites in Shiraz, for example, by housing missionaries in their outposts on the Persian Gulf and offering them protection in their dealings with local officials or transportation services on the ships traveling between the Gulf and India. A mutually beneficial cooperation developed in the dispatch, transportation, and forwarding of letters.

The signs of esteem that the missionaries experienced in their relations with European laypeople of various confessions also applied to the qualities attributed to them by virtue of their clerical status: their rejection of the "world" bolstered faith in their work not only as authorized representatives and brokers but also as religious specialists. As such, the religious conveyed a particular closeness to God and, therefore, also met the needs of non-Catholics for Christian rituals, for instance when they christened the children of Protestant parents.

After the arrival of the Augustinians and Discalced Carmelites in the early seventeenth century, relations with the Armenian clergy were also initially marked by "friendship" and "good correspondence," which included sacramental community (*communicatio in sacris*) between clerics of the two churches. To be sure, this study largely confirms Bernard Heyberger's finding for the Syrian provinces of the Ottoman Empire of a growing polarization between different Christian communities, Eastern and Latin Christians in particular, starting in the late seventeenth century. In relations with the Armenian clergy, however, confessional boundaries were not always paramount even in the eighteenth century, contradicting the claims of those who cited threats of persecution to justify the *communicatio in sacris* of Armenian Catholics with "schismatics" and "heretics." As demonstrated, for example, by the *dubia* of the last Latin bishop of Isfahan, Cornelio di San Giuseppe, *communicatio in sacris* continued to be not just a strategy used by Uniate Eastern Christians to protect themselves from persecution but also a means of integrating missionaries into local contexts, which could still include "friendship" and "good correspondence" with clerics of non-Uniate Eastern churches.

The positive image that Protestant authors painted of the way of life of Catholic clerics in Persia against the background of transconfessional "good correspondence" contrasted sharply with the criticism of missionaries worldwide which the Congregation for the Propagation of the Faith had formulated from its inception in 1622. Missionaries who inserted themselves all too successfully into local systems of reference did not meet the expectations placed upon them as confessional multipliers. The resulting suspicions targeted both missionaries and the superiors of their orders. To justify its demand that missionaries be integrated into its own networks, the newly formed *Propaganda Fide* accused the superiors of ignoring violations of the Rule. In light of the increasingly evident diversity of the world, Rome was to become *the* central hub of missionary knowledge.

In the late Middle Ages and increasingly from the sixteenth century onward, the Roman Church and the Papal States became models for the early modern state. Their features included the papal claim to *plenitudo potestatis*, the resulting efforts to centralize decision-making in the Curia, and the expansion of its bureaucracy. Within these long-term developments, the establishment of the *Propaganda Fide* in 1622 signaled the unity of the missions in various regions of the world and affirmed the Roman Church's claim to universal truth. However, the assertion of responsibility for the world based on the history of salvation and divine and natural law contrasted with the narrow limits on an effective enforcement of norms, which have become evident in studies that focus on the local churches. Early modern ecclesiastical and secular institutions were both often unable to enforce their decisions, not least because of their strong internal diversity. This plurality of norms and practices became visible even where religious like the Discalced Carmelites, with their comparatively close relationship to the papacy, became active in mission. Such a conclusion bolsters research findings that have exposed notions of a unified Tridentine Catholicism as nineteenth-century constructs and turned their attention to forms of Christianity anchored in local ways of life in Europe as well.

Like those of secular rulers, the Roman Curia's relationships with the periphery were structured by personal connections and therefore followed similar dynamics. Thus, for example, relations between Clement VIII and the Discalced Carmelites of the Italian congregation, whom the pope dispatched for "his" mission to Persia, can be compared to the patron–client relations between a secular prince and a secular body. The reorganization of mission administration with the founding of the Congregation for the Propagation of the Faith in 1622 had parallels with the methods secular rulers used to intensify their reach on the periphery by instituting patron–client ties with institutions that followed a more bureaucratic rationale. Like the institutions of secular monarchies, the *Propaganda Fide* frequently relied on personal connections to enforce its authority. Similarly, petitioners saw themselves compelled to seek out close relationships with decision-makers in Rome if they wished to achieve anything there. Personal connection shaped the practice of decision-making. While in some cases it facilitated the enforcement of decisions, in others it led to the breaching of institutional logics. The *ad hoc* consideration of each case by the curial congregations allowed for deviations on all levels from the requirements of strict confessional rules. This can be seen, albeit in a different way, in the cultivation of "good correspondence" with non-Catholics on the local level as well as in decisions by the curial congregations concerning relations with members of the Sceriman family.

Roman congregations were subject to the same limitations as early modern secular central authorities. They faced similar difficulties in adapting decisions to local conditions and enforcing them effectively due to the dearth of adequate information. In the early modern period, "centralization" in the ecclesiastical realm, as well, depended on whether subordinate actors used the new institutions. As long as the actors on the ground did not reach out to the curial congregations, it was rather unlikely that the congregations could intervene effectively. This applied in particular to missions in far-off countries. For their decision-making, the curial congregations depended on the reports written by missionaries abroad. The enormous distances and scant administrative resources gave wide latitude to the missionaries of all orders, even on key questions of orthodoxy and orthopraxy such as the Chinese rites or *communicatio in sacris*, as long as local rivals did not appeal to the Curia. The curial congregations intervened above all when people on the ground apprised them of irregularities, couching local conflicts in the language of the post-Tridentine Church.

In the sphere of influence of the Iberian powers in Asia, rights of patronage and the privileges of religious orders set narrow limits on attempts at intervention by the papacy. Outside the missionary settlements and colonial territories, in turn, the absence of Catholic authorities meant that there was little possibility of taking coercive action to enforce curial decisions. This applied both to those Catholic Eastern Christians in Persia or the Ottoman Empire who relapsed into "schism" or "heresy" and to missionaries who were not prepared to submit to the demands of their superiors or the *Propaganda Fide*. Under these circumstances, the efficacy of decisions by the curial congregations depended upon the willingness of those who had been rebuked to recognize the Church's authority as defined by the Curia. That is, they needed to be profoundly convinced that there was no salvation for them outside the Roman Church and that they therefore had no choice but to repent and submit to the penances imposed upon them. This, however, was precisely the problem: the practice of *communicatio in sacris*, which was still widespread in the eighteenth century despite repeated unambiguous statements by the Holy Office and the *Propaganda Fide*, was evidence of forms of Christian religiosity that resisted strict definition and contradicted the self-image of the confessional church.

While the forms of interaction between the periphery and center show many similarities in the secular and ecclesiastical contexts, the content of the exchanges differed markedly. Whereas tax payments or the levying of troops were negotiated in more or less clearly asymmetrical relations between a prince and the representatives of the estates, and all manner of compromises could be reached, the Church's claim to represent the sole truth was not open to negotiation. In practice, however, its enforcement was subject to similarly narrow limits, which demanded specific responses from the Curia: the practices that limited damage to the claim of primacy inherent in the Roman understanding of the vicariate of Christ included tacit papal toleration or even explicit confirmation of the particular law of local churches, the issuing of dispensations, and the practice of *nihil esse respondendum* (nothing is to be answered). The avoidance of making decisions was a specific response to the impossibility of implementing those decisions that actually urgently needed to be made based on what was regarded as true church doctrine.

The diasporas in Persia cannot be viewed simply as microcosms of European conflicts. The reality was more complex and ambiguous: French Capuchins saw their Protestant compatriots not just as "heretics" but also as fellow Frenchmen who deserved hospitality. Intra-Catholic lines of conflict were also redefined, for example when, unlike in their native France, Jesuits and the priests of the *Missions étrangères de Paris* in Isfahan sometimes maintained good relations with each other. The practices of missionaries abroad can be only partly explained by their participation in the order-specific cultures to which they were subject: clerics like the Dominican Paolo Piromalli or the Discalced Carmelite Élie de Saint-Albert, who tried to enforce narrow confessional norms, acted as individuals and not as representatives of their orders. Piromalli's overzealousness did not seem to contemporaries to be typical of the Dominicans in the Safavid Empire overall, nor were the Discalced Carmelites usually known for a marked penchant for confessional controversy. Instead, in early seventeenth-century Persia, the Discalced Carmelites, much like the Jesuit Roberto de' Nobili in South India, stood for that mission "by gentle means" which the *Propaganda Fide* also initially demanded after its founding in 1622. Following the departure of Élie de Saint-Albert, the Discalced Carmelites in Isfahan and New Julfa sought to renew their "good correspondence" with the Armenian clergy.

Not only Jesuits but also members of other orders, especially the Discalced Carmelites, set the boundaries of what was permissible in relations with non-Catholics along the fundamental line between a "civil" and a religious sphere. In many cases they were prepared to tolerate transgressions of these boundaries and sometimes even to overstep them themselves. It is also striking that authors of Persian travel accounts who did not belong to an order rarely noted differences between the ways of life of the clerics. The sole exception was the lavish lifestyle of the Augustinians, which was, however, attributed to the prior's role as an agent of the king of Portugal and his viceroy in Goa. The Dutch and the English favored the Discalced Carmelites to expedite their letters not because of the order's culture but rather because of its lack of ties to economic and political rivals, which distinguished them from clerics from Portugal and France.

A study of the Persian missions can therefore serve as a corrective to notions that have emerged from scholars' one-sided orientation toward the missions of the Society of Jesus. Discalced Carmelites, Capuchins, and Dominicans in Persia arrived at practices of adaptation quite similar to those commonly attributed to the Jesuits. However, as the discussion of observance has shown, this does not mean that the situation of members of the individual orders and their relations with their superiors were not also influenced by the specific requirements of their orders. Thus, while they adapted to local expectations, the Discalced Carmelites had to tolerate difficult conflicts within their order that arose from the contrast between missionary activities and the demands of strict observance. In their correspondence with superiors and their dealings with the visitors who were dispatched periodically, members of the order represented their own conduct and that of their opponents within the order from the standpoint of these rigid norms. While some of them demanded strict observance of the Rule without regard to the cultural environment, others justified the necessity of accommodation in dress and way of life by constructing the mission as a counterworld to Catholic Europe.

The Jesuits had it easier in this respect, since their order's basic texts prepared them for missionary activities by allowing them wider latitude. As regards both the different social roles played by priests and their treatment of *communicatio in sacris*, the parallels across orders may be understood all the more as indicators of the extent to which they were integrated into local contexts. Viewed from this perspective, accommodation was a pragmatic response to local expectations that was shared by members of various orders. In the missionary controversies that caused a sensation in Europe, the fronts did indeed sometimes run along the lines of membership in an order. As local actors, though, the religious had fewer differences with one another than we might expect based on the scholarly literature that has emphasized these controversies, and especially the role of the Jesuits. The call for a decentering approach to the early modern Catholic Church is therefore all the more justified.[1]

An approach that focuses on the history of religious orders is especially well suited to foregrounding the internal diversity of the Church that continued to mark post-Tridentine Catholicism. This characteristic was particularly evident in the missions. In the lives of missionaries, the Roman Curia and the leadership of the orders did not always possess the power to set norms that they claimed for themselves. To be sure, in seventeenth- and eighteenth-century Persia, instances of missionaries converting to Islam were limited to the two Augustinians mentioned in this study. The fact that the Christian creed as such was scarcely ever questioned does not mean, however, that the religious never challenged the Roman Curia as a norm-setting authority. Although Clement VIII dispatched the Discalced Carmelites to Persia because of their proximity to the papacy, the Discalced Carmelites, too—and even more so the Portuguese Augustinians and the French Capuchins and Jesuits—acted primarily as members of an order and not on instructions from the pope or the *Propaganda Fide*. Aside from individual obligatory interactions (especially the issuing of the *facultates*), their contact with the *Propaganda Fide* was situational: it was sought above all when they were trying to use the congregation's offer of protection in conflicts with members of other orders or rivals within their own order.

Apart from such situations, the Discalced Carmelites, too, clearly prioritized duties to their own order. While their order was one of those that fairly regularly answered to the *Propaganda Fide*, correspondence with their superiors was incomparably more important to the friars. Additional channels of communication within the order included the visitations and occasionally the participation of representatives of even distant missions in the General Chapter in Rome. It is thus precisely the relative closeness of the Italian congregation of Discalced Carmelites to the papacy that shows the extent to which the mission remained the preserve of the orders in the seventeenth and eighteenth centuries. The enduring image of a unified Tridentine Catholicism thus reveals itself to be quite far removed from historical reality. The overwhelming scholarly reliance on the archival sources of the *Propaganda Fide*—the research on the Jesuit missions constitutes a notable exception in this regard—has contributed to this view of Catholicism, which this book seeks to challenge.

In the early modern period, the limits of obedience in the ecclesiastical and secular realm emerged from a social logic of gift exchange economies. Behind powerless petitioners' criticisms of their treatment by Rome lay the view that the Roman Curia was abandoning the duties associated with gift exchange between a powerful patron and his clients. In a mendicant order like the Discalced Carmelites, interventions by the pope and the *Propaganda Fide* fed resentments against the wealth of the Roman court, which did not spare the pope. The conviction that the order's strict vow of poverty made its members better able to fulfill the duties of a Christian life than the "rich pope" and his court is very evident here. The challenges, privations, and perils of their lives nourished the missionaries' self-confidence vis-à-vis the Roman Curia. As we know, the Discalced Carmelites, like the Capuchins and the Jesuits, were members of a reformed order that emerged in the sixteenth century from critiques of the official church. The resistance associated with their early history, which brought the orders' founders a fair share of trouble, including accusations of heresy,[2] plainly continued in the reactions of the Discalced Carmelites to their stronger subordination to the *Propaganda Fide* in the 1650s. At the time, this resistance was not limited to linking their duty of obedience to the preservation of the ancient law of their order, but it also contrasted their own orientation toward the divine commandments with the papacy's claim to a responsibility for the world, justified by the history of salvation and divine and natural law.

Precisely because its point of reference was in the transcendental realm, the obedience of the religious, while in theory unconditional, was at the same time subordinate to their duty toward God. The extent and at the same time limits of the duty of obedience rooted in the individual conscience of a Christian have been explored thus far primarily for the Society of Jesus. But were they actually specific to the culture of the Jesuit order?[3] In light of the findings of this study, the extent and limits of the duty of obedience seem to have been a characteristic of the culture of early modern orders more generally, although they could assume order-specific traits.[4] While the Discalced Carmelites contrasted the usefulness of the mission with strict observance of the Rule or a prohibition on *communicatio in sacris*, in their own way they also derived an individual latitude of action from their duty to God. Their transgressions in aspects of religious practice also suggest that, despite their confessional socialization, they did indeed feel that serving God and the Church as an institution were not always one and the same.

There were great obstacles to integrating the missionaries dispersed throughout the world into shared normative systems of reference, not just in their relationship with the Roman Curia but also within the orders. To be sure, the varying constitutions of the orders meant that, given the missionaries' integration into local sociocultural systems, the issue of observing the Rule presented itself in specific ways in each of them. What the superiors of the orders had in common was their bewilderment at the fact that the clerics they dispatched became actors whose lives were in many respects oriented toward local systems of reference—in their economic behavior, the ways in which they gained respect in the local context, and their handling of church rituals. The image of the missions was correspondingly ambivalent. They variously represented the triumph of the Roman Church over the Protestant competition and sites of danger to the observance of the Rule and thus to the salvation of order members.

Such ambivalences influenced the form and content of communication within the orders. Up until now, scholars have mainly studied the conditions and practices of the Society of Jesus. The literature has shown how the Jesuit order sought to counteract the growing autonomy of its members scattered across the globe. The Jesuits did so both by establishing a bureaucratized system of correspondence and knowledge management and by cultivating practices intended to encourage members to internalize the norms that guided their actions. In so doing, the order's superiors hoped that the individual Jesuits, when left to their own devices, would make the correct decisions without precise instructions from their superiors. Focusing on the example of the Discalced Carmelites, this study has identified such practices both across and within orders. To the extent that they existed across orders, they should be understood as epoch-specific responses to the problems of governance from afar that arose with particular acuteness in foreign missions. Differences from the Society of Jesus are evident less in the practices as such than in the degree to which the practices were systematized, formalized, and standardized. Thus, correspondence was quite dense among the Discalced Carmelites, too; similarly, there was no lack of agreement about the necessity of appropriate information. What was missing from the transfer of information was the formalization and regularity that distinguished Jesuit practice from other comparable examples, such as the *Propaganda Fide*.[5]

While in the Society of Jesus the *ius scribendi* was limited to officeholders and integrated into channels that followed the hierarchy of office, the Discalced Carmelites expressly postulated not merely the right but also the duty of each missionary to report to his superiors on the state of the missions without involving any intermediate officeholders. Such a precept was in line with the governance of the order by the entire community, as promoted by the Teresian reform of the Carmelites in the tradition of the mendicant orders as an expression of the vow of poverty and the rejection of worldly symbols of distinctions of rank. The effects proved contradictory when it came to the leadership of the missions: while it helped to keep the superiors of the order abreast of events on the ground, it also weakened the authority of the local and intermediate officeholders (priors and provincial vicars) and fueled conflicts between the missionaries.

While the centrality of Rome as a norm-setting authority in everyday missionary life was challenged, this was not merely because of the conditions of communication between missionaries, superiors, and the Roman Curia. The circumstances under which people of European origin made contact with Asian societies in the seventeenth century were also crucial: these relationships were still far removed from the asymmetry of nineteenth-century colonial settings. For the Safavid Empire, political and economic interrelationships in the Asian context were far more important than those with Southern and Western Europe. The Portuguese joined in these relationships with South Asia along with the English, Dutch, and French East India Companies when they developed contacts with the Safavid Empire from India. Aside from religion, seventeenth-century clerics and laypeople from Europe frequently regarded the cultures of the great Asian empires as equal to their own. This fostered a willingness to relativize the norms of their societies of origin not just for pragmatic reasons. When they made contact with the courts of Asian rulers, clerics and laypeople submitted to the local ceremonial practices with which local rulers enacted their own centrality.

Missionaries themselves became part of non-European centers when they placed themselves at the service of rulers who viewed Rome not as the fulcrum of the world but at most as that of a remote European periphery. This applied to court Jesuits in Beijing as well as to the Discalced Carmelite Juan Thadeo de San Eliseo and the Capuchin Raphaël du Mans in Isfahan. The papacy's claim to enforce a universally valid truth and the global orientation of the orders active as missionaries contrasted with integration in the places of mission, which turned missionaries into local actors. This last point was also demonstrated here through an analysis of mission economies, which showed not just the extremely small proportion of financing that came from Europe but also the local interrelationships that replaced this flow of money. The missionaries met local needs with their services in matters both secular and religious.

At the same time, their relations with Armenian merchants and Indian financiers as well as the East India Companies reveal the missionaries' dependencies on other actors in early modern globalization processes, which from the sixteenth century onward led to closer relations between various parts of the world. As translocal actors, the missionaries also remained bound to the normative horizons of their societies of origin, much as the agents and merchants of the East India Companies remained answerable to their own superiors.

The repercussions for the Catholic Church and European societies more generally of the experiences of alterity and the practices in the various missionary contexts were out of proportion to the minuscule number of clerics of mainly low rank who participated directly in interactions with the great Asian empires. Beginning around 1700, decision-makers at the Roman Curia became increasingly aware of the scope of the challenges that arose from the experience of cultural diversity, the attendant variety of social roles played by the missionaries, and the publicly conducted controversies on these issues. This led, during the pontificates of Clement XI (1700–1721), Benedict XIII (1724–30), and Benedict XIV (1740–58), to a marked, strikingly parallel intensification of discussions about the practices of *communicatio in sacris* and the Chinese and Malabar rites. In all these cases, the tendency to tighten the boundaries of the permissible won out. Thus in 1729, for the first time, the *Propaganda Fide* issued a general prohibition on *communicatio in sacris* rather than simply making another individual, situational decision, while in 1742 and 1744 Benedict XIV sought to end the controversies surrounding the Chinese and Malabar rites with a final papal decision.

Even at the highest level, there was no dearth of voices warning against the negative effects of such decisions. In 1757, referring to the consequences of Benedict XIV's decision in the "thorny matter of the Chinese Rites," Lorenzo Ganganelli, then a *consultor* of the Holy Office and future Pope Clement XIV, spoke out against imposing compulsory tough sanctions in combination with the prohibition on *communicatio in sacris*, which might lead to the exclusion of the fallible from the community of the Church. In fact, the authoritative disambiguation of church doctrine exacerbated conflicts with the practice of the faithful, giving rise to new controversies.

Despite engagement with the Protestant Reformations and the resulting confessional polarization, early modern Catholicism still offered room for a broad spectrum of doctrinal opinions and practices in the seventeenth century, as long as they were not expressly associated with Protestantism. The variety of missionary practices that have been explored here was therefore not simply a function of the limits of rule from afar but also had a counterpart in the diversity of early modern European Catholicisms. This diversity was represented by, among others, the various reformed orders that had been founded since the sixteenth century, which also sent their members to Persia.

Beginning around 1700, however, the Roman Curia, faced with novel threats to its authority, increasingly defined the boundaries of orthodoxy in a way that excluded ever broader circles. Among these were Uniate Eastern Christians, who, however close they may have been to Catholic missionaries, remained in sacramental community with their "schismatic" or "heretical" church of origin. Also excluded were Chinese Christians, who continued to cultivate the customs of their Confucian-influenced social milieu, as well as, for example, Western European Catholics who as "Jansenists" were accused by their opponents of being too close to Protestant "heresy" because of their orientation toward the theology of the Church Father Augustine. The processes of doctrinal disambiguation and exclusion associated with the emergence of competing confessional churches since the sixteenth century thus continued and deepened. Starting around 1700, by making clear-cut decisions on controversial matters, the Roman Curia participated in its own way in the processes of disambiguation that characterized the culture of the Enlightenment. In the course of secularization, these processes culminated in the Catholic Church's withdrawal into a core area of religion separated from "profane and civil society." It was during this process that the nineteenth-century papacy would attain a degree of power over the Church that makes it difficult for us even today to recognize the diversity of early modern Catholicisms.

Notes

Introduction

1. Jean Chardin, *Voyages du chevalier Chardin, en Perse, et autres lieux de l'Orient*, ed. Louis-Mathieu Langlès, 10 vols. (Paris, 1811), vol. 7, 438. On Chardin's life and works, see John Emerson, "Chardin, Sir John," in *Encyclopaedia Iranica* online. Article published Dec. 15, 1991; last updated Oct. 13, 2011. http://www.iranicaonline.org/articles/chardin-sir-john. Translator's note: the existing English translations of Chardin's *Travels in Persia* are incomplete. For that reason, in this and other footnotes, reference is made only to the French edition of 1811.
2. Thomas Bauer's reflections on the tolerance for ambiguity within premodern Islamicate societies, which he contrasts with the Western "separate path" of removing ambiguity as far as possible, correspond to Chardin's perceptions. See Thomas Bauer, *A Culture of Ambiguity: An Alternative History of Islam* (New York: Columbia University Press, 2021), 260, 268–74. Translator's note: the term "confessional church" is used throughout this book to translate the concept of the *Konfessionskirche*, which is well established in the German historiography on confessionalization to express the specific quality of early modern confession-based churches.
3. On Jesuit missionaries in Asia, see, for example, Ines G. Županov, *Disputed Mission: Jesuit Experiments and Brahmanical Knowledge in Seventeenth-Century India* (New Delhi: OUP, 1999), and the same author's *Missionary Tropics: The Catholic Frontier in India (16th–17th Centuries)* (Ann Arbor: University of Michigan Press, 2005); Ronnie Po-chia Hsia, *A Jesuit in the Forbidden City: Matteo Ricci 1552–1610* (Oxford: OUP, 2010); Nicolas Standaert, *The Interweaving of Rituals: Funerals in the Cultural Exchange between China and Europe* (Seattle: University of Washington Press, 2008); and Nadine Amsler, *Jesuits and Matriarchs: Domestic Worship in Early Modern China* (Seattle: University of Washington Press, 2018). On Jesuit missionaries as global actors, see Luke Clossey, *Salvation and Globalization in the Early Jesuit Missions* (Cambridge: CUP, 2008). On the history of the Society of Jesus see, most recently, Markus Friedrich, *The Jesuits: A History* (Princeton: Princeton University Press, 2022), and Ines G. Županov, ed., *The Oxford Handbook of the Jesuits* (New York: OUP, 2019).
4. Contrary to most microhistorical accounts that narrowly focus on a single person, family, village, or event, the book combines microhistory and a wider interpretative framework seeking to offer "a global history on a small scale" of Catholicism in the seventeenth and eighteenth centuries. Cf. Francesca Trivellato, *The Familiarity of Strangers: The Sephardic Diaspora, Livorno, and Cross-Cultural Trade in the Early Modern Period* (New Haven: Yale University Press, 2009), 7, and the same author's "Is There a Future for Italian Microhistory in the Age of Global History?" *California Italian Studies* 2 (2011), https://escholarship.org/uc/item/0z94n9hq. Thick description of local settings and their relationships with other contexts of

action aims to uncover the dynamic interactions between the actors' everyday lives, social structures, and historical processes. On this, see the contributions in Bernard Lepetit, ed., *Les formes de l'expérience: Une autre histoire sociale* (Paris: Albin Michel, 1995), and Jacques Revel, ed., *Jeux d'échelles: La micro-analyse à l'expérience* (Paris: Gallimard/Éditions du Seuil, 1996). In his seminal work on a Piemontese exorcist, Giovanni Levi asserted that microhistorical analysis seeks to reveal "the instability of individual preferences, institutional entities, and social hierarchies and values." Levi, *Inheriting Power: The Story of an Exorcist* (Chicago: University of Chicago Press, 1988), xviii. The present study therefore does not accept as a given that those who sent the missionaries were always the determining norm-giving authorities in their lives on the ground. Instead, it will consider this as *one* possible hypothesis among others. Cf. John-Paul Ghobrial, "The Secret Life of Elias of Babylon and the Uses of Global Microhistory," *Past and Present* 222 (Feb. 2014): 51–93, and Ghobrial, ed., *Global History and Microhistory* (Oxford: OUP, 2019).

5 See Hubert Wolf, "Trient und 'tridentinisch' im Katholizismus des 19. Jahrhunderts," in *Das Konzil von Trient und die katholische Konfessionskultur (1563–2013)*, ed. Peter Walter and Günther Wassilowsky (Münster: Aschendorff, 2016), 67–82. In his monumental work on Baroque Catholicism, Peter Hersche emphasizes the diversity of early modern Catholicisms. Hersche, *Muße und Verschwendung: Europäische Gesellschaft und Kultur im Barockzeitalter*, 2 vols. (Freiburg im Br.: Herder, 2006), esp. vol. 1, 112–52. On European "local Catholicisms," see the pioneering studies of William A. Christian, *Local Religion in Sixteenth-Century Spain* (Princeton: Princeton University Press, 1981), and Marc R. Forster, *The Counter-Reformation in the Villages: Religion and Reform in the Bishopric of Speyer, 1560–1720* (Ithaca: Cornell University Press, 1992). On Jesuits and Capuchins as brokers between the church hierarchy and local society in the European context, see, for example, Jennifer D. Selwyn, *A Paradise Inhabited by Devils: The Jesuits' Civilizing Mission in Early Modern Naples* (Aldershot: Ashgate, 2004); Daniel Sidler, *Heiligkeit aushandeln: Katholische Reform und lokale Glaubenspraxis in der Eidgenossenschaft* (Frankfurt a. M.: Campus, 2017), esp. 288–355; Dominic Sieber, *Jesuitische Missionierung, priesterliche Liebe, sakramentale Magie: Volkskulturen in Luzern 1563 bis 1614* (Basel: Schwabe, 2005); and Hillard von Thiessen, *Die Kapuziner zwischen Konfessionalisierung und Alltagskultur: Vergleichende Fallstudie am Beispiel Freiburgs und Hildesheims 1599–1750* (Freiburg im Br.: Rombach, 2002).

6 On the intertwined global and local worlds of a Chinese Christian, cf. Dominic Sachsenmaier, *Global Entanglements of a Man Who Never Travelled: A Seventeenth-Century Chinese Christian and His Conflicted Worlds* (New York: Columbia University Press, 2018), esp. 9–11, 151–68.

7 On this, see Hillard von Thiessen, *Das Zeitalter der Ambiguität: Vom Umgang mit Werten und Normen in der Frühen Neuzeit* (Cologne: Böhlau, 2021), esp. 321–64.

8 On the two "souls" of the papal prince, see Paolo Prodi, *Il sovrano pontefice: Un corpo e due anime; La monarchia papale nella prima età moderna* (Bologna: Il Mulino, 1982). On the interactions between institution building and the development of interpersonal networks at the papal court, see Wolfgang Reinhard, *Paul V. Borghese (1605–1621): Mikropolitische Papstgeschichte* (Stuttgart: Anton Hiersemann, 2009); Birgit Emich, *Bürokratie und Nepotismus unter Paul V. (1605–1621)* (Stuttgart: Anton Hiersemann, 2001); and Gianvittorio Signorotto and Maria Antonietta Visceglia, eds., *Court and Politics in Papal Rome, 1492–1700* (Cambridge: CUP, 2002). Based on the study of conclave reform, Wassilowsky demonstrates that the call for a strict

orientation toward the common good stood in opposition to the ethos of patronage. Günther Wassilowsky, *Die Konklavereform Gregors XV. (1621/22): Wertekonflikte, symbolische Inszenierung und Verfahrenswandel im posttridentinischen Papsttum* (Stuttgart: Anton Hiersemann, 2010).

9   Cf. Christian Windler, "Early Modern Composite Catholicism from a Global Perspective: Catholic Missionaries and the English East India Company," in *Pathways through Early Modern Christianities*, ed. Andreea Badea, Bruno Boute, and Birgit Emich (Cologne: Böhlau, 2023).

10 On the "totalitarian tendencies" of the Safavids, see Roger Savory, *Iran under the Safavids* (Cambridge: CUP, 1980), esp. 27–49.

11 On this, see esp. Rudi Matthee, *Persia in Crisis: Safavid Decline and the Fall of Isfahan* (London: I. B. Tauris, 2012), 10, 27–31, 146–7, 173–8, 254; Andrew J. Newman, *Safavid Iran: Rebirth of a Persian Empire* (London: I. B. Tauris, 2006), 9, 45–6, 71–2.

12 Colin P. Mitchell, *The Practice of Politics in Safavid Iran: Power, Religion and Rhetoric* (London: I. B. Tauris, 2009), 3–4, 12, 176–99, 202; Sholeh A. Quinn, *Historical Writing during the Reign of Shah 'Abbas: Ideology, Imitation, and Legitimacy in Safavid Chronicles* (Salt Lake City: University of Utah Press, 2000), 44–6, 52–3, 86–91, 127–43.

13 Here we follow Dipesh Chakrabarty, *Provincializing Europe: Postcolonial Thought and Historical Difference* (Princeton: Princeton University Press, 2000), esp. chap. 1 "Postcoloniality and the Artifice of History," 27–46.

14 Jürgen Osterhammel, *Unfabling the East: The Enlightenment's Encounter with Asia* (Princeton: Princeton University Press, 2018), 489.

15 See Sonja Brentjes, "The Interests of the Republic of Letters in the Middle East," *Science in Context* 12 (1999): 435–68, 450–4, and "Pride and Prejudice: The Invention of a 'Historiography of Science' in the Ottoman and Safavid Empires by European Travellers and Writers in the Sixteenth and Seventeenth Centuries," in her *Travellers from Europe in the Ottoman and Safavid Empires, 16th–17th Centuries* (Aldershot: Ashgate, 2010). On the comparisons between the Ottomans and the "less barbarian" Muslim rulers in the historiography of Italian humanism, see Margaret Meserve, *Empires of Islam in Renaissance Historical Thought* (Cambridge, MA: Harvard University Press, 2008). On the Safavid Empire as a "mirror" for France, see Susan Mokhberi, *The Persian Mirror: Reflections of the Safavid Empire in Early Modern France* (Oxford: OUP, 2019).

16 See, for example, Sanjay Subrahmanyam, *Explorations in Connected History: From the Tagus to the Ganges* (New Delhi: OUP, 2004), and *Explorations in Connected History: Mughals and Franks* (New Delhi: OUP, 2005). Cf. David Veevers, *The Origins of the British Empire in Asia, 1600–1750* (Cambridge: CUP, 2020).

17 On India, see Guido van Meersbergen, *Ethnography and Encounter: The Dutch and English in Seventeenth Century South Asia* (Leiden: Brill, 2021), 140–97, and the same author's "'Intirely the Kings Vassalls': East India Company Gifting Practices and Anglo-Mughal Political Exchange (c. 1670–1720)," *Diplomatica: A Journal of Diplomacy and Society* 2 (2020): 270–90. On China, see John E. Wills, *Embassies and Illusions: Dutch and Portuguese Envoys to Kang'si, 1666–1687* (Cambridge, MA: Harvard University Asia Center, 1984). On Japan, see Adam Clulow, *The Company and the Shogun: The Dutch Encounter with Tokugawa Japan* (New York: Columbia University Press, 2016). Situations like that in Ceylon, where in the sixteenth century the Portuguese managed to convince local rulers to recognize their suzerainty and by the end of the century asserted territorial sovereignty over the island, were the

exception rather than the rule in Asia. See Zoltán Biedermann, *(Dis)connected Empires: Imperial Portugal, Sri Lankan Diplomacy, and the Making of a Habsburg Conquest in Asia* (Oxford: OUP, 2018); Alan Strathern, *Kingship and Conversion in Sixteenth-Century Sri Lanka: Portuguese Imperialism in a Buddhist Land* (Cambridge: CUP, 2007).

18 See Adriano Prosperi, "L'Europa cristiana e il mondo: Alle origini dell'idea di missione," *Dimensioni e problemi della ricerca storica* 2 (1992): 189–220.

19 Members of religious orders accordingly began writing the histories of the missions of their communities. Interestingly, the first three volumes of the *Istoria della Compagnia di Giesù* by Daniello Bartoli published in Italian in 1653, 1660, and 1663 were concerned with the history of the Jesuit missions in Asia. On Daniello Bartoli, see Simon Ditchfield, "Baroque around the Clock: Daniello Bartoli SJ (1608–1685) and the Uses of Global History," *Transactions of the Royal Historical Society* 31 (2021): 49–73. Other orders that played a less prominent role tried to emulate the Jesuits' self-promotion. In their *Historia Generalis Fratrum Discalceatorum Ordinis* published in 1668 and 1671, Isidore de Saint-Joseph and Pierre de Saint-André treated the missions as an important dimension of the general history of the Italian congregation of the Discalced Carmelites.

20 In the Netherlands, to be sure, calls to promote Calvinist mission in the sphere of influence and power of the East and West India Companies had already been heard in the seventeenth century. See Jos Gommans and Ineke Loots, "Arguing with the Heathens: The Further Reformation and the Ethnohistory of Johannes Hoornbeeck (1617–1666)," *Itinerario* 39 (2015): 45–68. The active conversion of people of other faiths, however, conflicted not just with the commercial interests of the WIC and VOC but also with the Calvinist doctrine of grace, with its emphasis on predestination. Despite recent calls for a reevaluation of Protestant missionary efforts (see Ulinka Rublack, *Protestant Empires: Globalizing the Reformations* [Cambridge: CUP, 2020]), the success of Dutch missions in the seventeenth century was limited. On early English missionary activities among the Eastern Christians, see, most recently, Simon Mills, *A Commerce of Knowledge: Trade, Religion, and Scholarship between England and the Ottoman Empire, c.1600–1760* (Oxford: OUP, 2020), 203–76.

21 See, for example, Liam Matthew Brockey, *The Visitor: André Palmeiro and the Jesuits in Asia* (Cambridge, MA: The Belknap Press of Harvard University Press, 2014); Steven E. Turley, *Franciscan Spirituality and Mission in New Spain, 1524–1599: Conflict Beneath the Sycamore Tree (Luke 19:1–10)* (Aldershot: Ashgate, 2014).

22 Cf. Liam Matthew Brockey, *Journey to the East: The Jesuit Mission to China, 1579–1724* (Cambridge, MA: The Belknap Press of Harvard University Press, 2007), 204–12, and Simon Ditchfield, "Decentering the Catholic Reformation: Papacy and Peoples in the Early Modern World," *Archiv für Reformationsgeschichte* 101 (2010): 186–208.

23 See the contributions in Charlotte de Castelnau-L'Estoile, Marie-Lucie Copete, Aliocha Maldavsky, and Ines G. Županov, eds., *Missions d'évangélisation et circulation des savoirs, XVIe–XVIIIe siècle* (Madrid: Casa de Velázquez, 2011). On Catholic Orientalism and the discovery of the Eastern churches, see Alastair Hamilton, *The Copts and the West: The European Discovery of the Egyptian Church* (Oxford: OUP, 2006). On the accumulation of knowledge by the religious in the context of the Portuguese *Estado da Índia*, see Ángela Barreto Xavier and Ines G. Županov, *Catholic Orientalism: Portuguese Empire, Indian Knowledge (16th–18th*

Centuries) (New Delhi: OUP, 2015), 113-241; Joan-Pau Rubiés, *Travel and Ethnology in the Renaissance: South India through European Eyes, 1250-1625* (Cambridge: CUP, 2000), 308-48.

24 For an example from relations with the Maghreb in the eighteenth century, see Christian Windler, *La diplomatie comme expérience de l'Autre: Consuls français au Maghreb (1700-1840)* (Geneva: Librairie Droz, 2002), esp. 347-52. On the cross-cultural trade relations of the Sephardic Jews in Livorno, see Trivellato, *The Familiarity of Strangers*.

25 Paul Hazard, *The European Mind (1680-1715)* (London: Hollis & Carter, 1953), 23. Cf. Jonathan I. Israel, *Enlightenment Contested: Philosophy, Modernity, and the Emancipation of Man 1670-1752* (Oxford: OUP, 2006), 640-62. Guy G. Stroumsa's observations on the discovery of religion as an object of a new science build on Paul Hazard's work. See Stroumsa, *A New Science: The Discovery of Religion in the Age of Reason* (Cambridge, MA: Harvard University Press, 2010).

26 Erik Zürcher, "The Jesuit Mission in Fujian in Late Ming Times: Levels of Response," in *Development and Decline of Fukien Province in the 17th and 18th Centuries*, ed. Eduard B. Vermeer (Leiden: Brill, 1990); Sachsenmaier, *Global Entanglements*; and Nicolas Standaert, *The Interweaving of Rituals,* and *Chinese Voices in the Rites Controversy: Travelling Books, Community Networks, Intercultural Arguments* (Rome: Institutum Historicum Societatis Iesu, 2012).

27 Henrietta Harrison, *The Missionary's Curse and Other Tales from a Chinese Catholic Village* (Berkeley: University of California Press, 2013); Eugenio Menegon, *Ancestors, Virgins, and Friars: Christianity as a Local Religion in Late Imperial China* (Cambridge, MA: Harvard University Press, 2009).

28 Amsler, *Jesuits and Matriarchs*.

29 Ronnie Po-chia Hsia, "Translating Christianity: Counter-Reformation Europe and the Catholic Mission in China, 1580-1780," in *Conversion: Old Worlds and New*, ed. Kenneth Mills and Anthony Grafton (Rochester: University of Rochester Press, 2003), 94. On the place of the profane sciences in the Jesuit missions, see Florence C. Hsia, *Sojourners in a Strange Land: Jesuits and Their Scientific Mission in Late Imperial China* (Chicago: University of Chicago Press, 2009).

30 Županov, *Missionary Tropics*, 24-8, 269-70. See also Margherita Trento, *Writing Tamil Catholicism: Literature, Persuasion and Devotion in the Eighteenth Century* (Leiden: Brill, 2022).

31 Bernard Heyberger, *Les Chrétiens du Proche-Orient au temps de la Réforme catholique* (Rome: École française de Rome, 1994), 381-549. On new forms of female piety, see Heyberger, *Hindiyya, Mystic and Criminal, 1720-1798: A Political and Religious Crisis in Lebanon* (Cambridge: James Clarke, 2013).

32 The Catholic Church used the terms *communicatio in sacris* or *communicatio in divinis* to refer to the violation of boundaries in the sacramental realm between Christians of different confessions, for instance, when a Catholic received the sacraments from a "schismatic" or "heretical" priest or a Catholic priest gave the sacraments to a "schismatic" or a "heretic." On *communicatio in sacris*, see Christian Windler, "Ambiguous Belongings: How Catholic Missionaries in Persia and the Roman Curia Dealt with *Communicatio in Sacris*," in *A Companion to Early Modern Catholic Global Missions*, ed. Ronnie Po-chia Hsia (Leiden: Brill, 2018); Cesare Santus, *Trasgressioni necessarie: Communicatio in sacris, coesistenza e conflitti tra le communità cristiane orientali (Levante e Impero ottomano, XVII-XVIII secolo)* (Rome: École française de Rome, 2019).

33 Ines G. Županov and Pierre Antoine Fabre, "The Rites Controversies in the Early Modern World: An Introduction," in *The Rites Controversies in the Early Modern World*, ed. Županov and Fabre (Leiden: Brill, 2018), 20.
34 On the missionaries' reception in Safavid Persia, see Rudi Matthee, "Safavid Iran and the Christian Missionary Experience: Between Tolerance and Refutation," *Mélanges de l'Institut dominicain d'études orientales* 35 (2020): 65–100. For an overview from the perspective of mission history, see Wilhelm de Vries, "Die Propaganda und die Christen im Nahen asiatischen und afrikanischen Osten," in *Sacrae Congregationis de Propaganda Fide Memoria Rerum, 1622–1972*, ed. Josef Metzler, vol. I/1: *1622–1700* (Rome: Herder, 1971); Josef Metzler, "Nicht erfüllte Hoffnungen in Persien" in ibid.; and Ambrosius Eszer, "Missionen im Halbrund der zwischen Schwarzem Meer, Kaspisee und Persischem Golf: Krim, Kaukasien, Georgien und Persien," in *Sacrae Congregationis de Propaganda Fide Memoria Rerum, 1622–1972*, ed. Metzler, vol. II: *1700–1815* (Rome: Herder, 1973).
35 On the global entanglements of the Armenian merchant families of New Julfa, see Sebouh David Aslanian, *From the Indian Ocean to the Mediterranean: The Global Trade Networks of Armenian Merchants from New Julfa* (Berkeley: University of California Press, 2011).
36 On the missions of the Discalced Carmelites, see [Herbert Chick], *A Chronicle of the Carmelites in Persia and the Papal Mission of the XVIIth and XVIIIth Centuries*, 2 vols. (London: Eyre & Spottiswoode, 1939; repr.: London: I. B. Tauris, 2012); on the Augustinians, see John M. Flannery, *The Mission of the Portuguese Augustinians to Persia and Beyond (1602–1747)* (Leiden: Brill, 2013). Carlos Alonso and Roberto Gulbenkian have published numerous articles including editions of manuscript sources. They will be cited in the notes where relevant.
37 On the reorganization of the papal government under Clement VIII, see Maria Teresa Fattori, *Clemente VIII e il Sacro Collegio, 1592–1605: Meccanismi istituzionali e accentramento di governo* (Stuttgart: Anton Hiersemann, 2004). From the perspective of relations between the Curia and the European peripheries of early modern Catholicism, see Tadgh Ó hAnnracháin, *Catholic Europe, 1592–1648: Centre and Peripheries* (Oxford: OUP, 2015), esp. 1–28.
38 Apart from conclave reform, the establishment of the Congregation for the Propagation of the Faith (referred to here as the *Propaganda Fide*), which will be discussed in more detail in Chapter 1, was the most important reform undertaken during the brief pontificate of Gregory XV. Both undertakings had failed under Clement VIII, because of Spanish resistance, among other factors. On conclave reform, see Wassilowsky, *Die Konklavereform*. See also Miles Pattenden, *Electing the Pope in Early Modern Italy, 1450–1700* (Oxford: OUP, 2017), 90–7.
39 Cf. Opher Mansour, "Picturing Global Conversion: Art and Diplomacy at the Court of Paul V (1605–1621)," *Journal of Early Modern History* 17 (2013): 525–59.
40 On the Capuchin mission, see Francis Richard, *Raphaël du Mans, missionnaire en Perse au XVIIe siècle*, vol. 1: *Biographie. Correspondance*, vol. 2: *Estats et Mémoire* (Paris: L'Harmattan, 1995); on the Jesuits, see Rudi Matthee, "Poverty and Perseverance: The Jesuit Mission of Isfahan and Shamakhi in Late Safavid Iran," *Al-Qanṭara* 36 (2015): 463–501; on the activities of the Dominicans in Persia, see Ambrosius Eszer, "Sebastianus Knab O.P., Erzbischof von Naxijevan (1682–1690): Neue Forschungen zu seinem Leben," *Archivum Fratrum Praedicatorum* 43 (1973): 215–86, and "Barnaba Fedeli di Milano O.P. (1663–1731): Das Schicksal eines Missionars und Bischofs im Sturm der Zeiten," *Archivum Fratrum Praedicatorum* 44 (1974): 179–262.

41 The present study does not address the presence of Catholic clerics in the Caucasus. The missions there were only distantly related to those in the core area of the Safavid Empire and the Persian Gulf.
42 In 1671, only twenty-seven Discalced Carmelites of the Italian congregation were involved in the missions in the Ottoman Empire, Persia, and other regions of Asia. The congregation counted 3,051 members at the time, 1,778 of whom were priests. Missionaries thus represented 0.9 percent of total members and 1.5 percent of priests. Figures for the missionaries come from Heyberger, *Les Chrétiens du Proche-Orient*, 293. For the number of members of the order, see Antonio Fortes, *Acta capituli generalis O.C.D. Congregationis S. Eliae*, vol. 1: *1605–1641*, vol. 2: *1644–1698*, vol. 3: *1701–1797* (Rome: Teresianum, 1990–2), vol. 2, 356–57.
43 Unfortunately, the state of the sources for the Persian missions is quite uneven. Compared to the rich holdings of the archives of the *Curia generalizia* of the Discalced Carmelites in Rome, the internal documents are extremely fragmentary for the Jesuits and wholly or nearly absent for the Augustinians, Capuchins, and Dominicans. This archival situation prevents a systematic comparison of the practices of the various orders.
44 Only parts of the convent libraries have been preserved. They are currently inaccessible. See Dominique Carnoy-Torabi, "A biblioteca esquecida dos missionários de Ispaão/The Forgotten Library of the Isfahan Missionaries," *Oriente: Revista quadrimestral da Fundação Oriente* 19 (2008): 94–105.
45 On the spiritual dimensions of the Jesuits' correspondences as a reflection on their own mission, see Jean-Claude Laborie, *Mangeurs d'hommes et mangeurs d'âmes: Une correspondance missionnaire au XVIe; La lettre jésuite du Brésil, 1549–1568* (Paris: H. Champion, 2003); Charlotte de Castelnau-L'Estoile, *Les ouvriers d'une vigne stérile: Les jésuites et la conversion des Indiens au Brésil, 1580–1620* (Lisbon: Fundação Calouste Gulbenkian, 2000).
46 Such questions take up Thomas Bauer's reflections on the "culture of ambiguity" in the premodern societies of the Near East influenced by Sunni Islam (see n. 2).

Chapter 1

1 Prodi, *Il sovrano pontefice*.
2 Cf. Windler, "Early Modern Composite Catholicism."
3 Reinhard, *Paul V. Borghese*. Cf. Emich, *Bürokratie und Nepotismus*; Signorotto and Visceglia, eds., *Court and Politics*; and Wassilowsky, *Die Konklavereform*. From a European and comparative perspective, see Thiessen, *Das Zeitalter der Ambiguität*.
4 Renata Ago, *Carriere e clientele nella Roma barocca* (Rome: Laterza, 1990), esp. 157–8, 176–80, and "Hegemony over the Social Scene and Zealous Popes (1676–1700)," in *Court and Politics*, ed. Signorotto and Visceglia.
5 On the election of the pope, see Pattenden, *Electing the Pope*; Maria Antonietta Visceglia, *Morte e elezione del papa: Norme, riti e conflitti; L'Età moderna* (Rome: Viella, 2013); and Wassilowsky, *Die Konklavereform*.
6 Birgit Emich, *Territoriale Integration in der Frühen Neuzeit: Ferrara und der Kirchenstaat* (Cologne: Böhlau, 2005); Nicole Reinhardt, *Macht und Ohnmacht der Verflechtung: Rom und Bologna unter Paul V.; Studien zur frühneuzeitlichen Mikropolitik im Kirchenstaat* (Tübingen: Bibliotheca academica Verlag, 2000);

Hillard von Thiessen, *Diplomatie und Patronage: Die spanisch-römischen Beziehungen 1605–1621 in akteurszentrierter Perspektive* (Epfendorf: Bibliotheca Academica, 2010).

7 See Antonio Menniti Ippolito, *1664. Un anno della Chiesa universale: Saggio sull'italianità del papato in età moderna* (Rome: Viella, 2011). On the Papal States, see Irene Fosi, *Papal Justice: Subjects and Courts in the Papal State, 1500–1750* (Washington, DC: Catholic University of America Press, 2011).

8 Silvano Giordano, *Domenico di Gesù Maria, Ruzola (1559–1630): Un carmelitano scalzo tra politica e riforma nella chiesa posttridentina* (Rome: Teresianum, 1991), 95–8; Anastasio Roggero, *Genova e gli inizi della riforma teresiana Italia (1584–1597)* (Rome: Teresianum, 1984).

9 Cf., referring to the Jesuit order, Markus Friedrich, *Der lange Arm Roms? Globale Verwaltung und Kommunikation im Jesuitenorden 1540–1773* (Frankfurt am Main: Campus, 2011).

10 On the concept, see André Holenstein, "Introduction: Empowering Interactions. Looking at Statebuilding from Below," in *Empowering Interactions: Political Cultures and the Emergence of the State in Europe 1300–1900*, ed. Wim Blockmans, A. Holenstein, and Jon Mathieu (Farnham: Ashgate, 2009).

11 See, among others, Katherine Aron-Beller and Christopher Black, eds., *The Roman Inquisition: Centre versus Peripheries* (Leiden: Brill, 2018); Maurice A. Finocchiaro, *On Trial for Reason: Science, Religion, and Culture in the Galileo Affair* (Oxford: OUP, 2019); Massimo Firpo, *La presa di potere dell'Inquisizione romana, 1550–1553* (Bari: Laterza, 2014); Thomas F. Mayer, *The Roman Inquisition: A Papal Bureaucracy and Its Laws in the Age of Galileo* (Philadelphia: University of Pennsylvania Press, 2013), *The Roman Inquisition on the Stage of Italy, c. 1590–1640* (Philadelphia: University of Pennsylvania Press, 2014), and *The Roman Inquisition: Trying Galileo* (Philadelphia: University of Pennsylvania Press, 2015); Charles H. Parker and Gretchen Starr-LeBeau, eds., *Judging Faith, Punishing Sin: Inquisitions and Consistories in the Early Modern World* (Cambridge: CUP, 2017); and Adriano Prosperi, *Tribunali della coscienza: Inquisitori, confessori, missionari* (Turin: Giulio Einaudi, 1996). For an overview of the Holy Office's activities as a court of the Inquisition, see Christopher F. Black, *The Italian Inquisition* (New Haven: Yale University Press, 2009).

12 A fundamental work is "Administrer les sacrements en Europe et au nouveau monde: La Curie romaine et les *dubia circa sacramenta*," *Mélanges de l'École française de Rome: Italie et Méditerranée* 121/1 (2009): 5–217. Cf. Santus, *Trasgressioni necessarie*, and Windler, "Ambiguous Belongings."

13 On the origins and founding of the *Propaganda Fide*, see Josef Metzler, "Wegbereiter und Vorläufer der Kongregation: Vorschläge und erste Gründungsversuche einer römischen Missionszentrale," and "Foundation of the Congregation 'de Propaganda Fide' by Gregory XV," in *Sacrae Congregationis de Propaganda Fide Memoria Rerum*, ed. Metzler, vol. I/1.

14 Wassilowsky, *Die Konklavereform*, 169 (quotation), 224, 227–8, 236–7, 247, 282.

15 Nearly every study of Catholic mission in the early modern period incorporates documents from the *Propaganda Fide*. From the perspective of the history of the curial bureaucracy, the *Propaganda Fide* has been studied above all by Giovanni Pizzorusso, most recently in his *Governare le missioni, conoscere il mondo nel XVII secolo: La Congregazione Pontificia de Propaganda Fide* (Viterbo: Edizioni Sette Città, 2018).

16 Thus far, only Giovanni Pizzorusso has offered initial insights into the finances of the *Propaganda Fide*. See his "Lo 'Stato temporale' della Congregazione 'de Propaganda Fide' nel Seicento," in Ad ultimos usque terrarum terminos in fide propaganda: *Roma fra promozione e difesa della fede in età moderna*, ed. Massimiliano Ghilardi, Gaetano Sabatini, Matteo Sanfilippo, and Donatella Strangio (Viterbo: Edizioni Sette Città, 2014), 51–66. The following remarks are based on my own analysis of the *bilanci* that survive in the series *SC. Stato temporale* in the archives of the *Propaganda Fide* (vols. 2–16). For a more detailed analysis, see the tables in the original German edition (Christian Windler, *Missionare in Persien: Kulturelle Diversität und Normenkonkurrenz im globalen Katholizismus [17.–18. Jahrhundert]* [Cologne: Böhlau, 2018], 42–3, 46–9). Unfortunately, the important studies by Wolfgang Reinhard (*Papstfinanz und Nepotismus unter Paul V. [1605–1621]: Studien und Quellen zur Struktur und zu quantitativen Aspekten des päpstlichen Herrschaftssystems*, 2 vols. [Stuttgart: Anton Hiersemann, 1974]) and Volker Reinhardt (*Kardinal Scipione Borghese [1605–1633]: Vermögen, Finanzen und sozialer Aufstieg eines Papstnepoten* [Tübingen: Max Niemeyer, 1984]) did not lead to a more intensive treatment of the papal finances beyond the first decades of the seventeenth century. No comparable studies exist for the period that interests us here.
17 Reinhardt, *Kardinal Scipione Borghese*, 549.
18 Ibid., 96–7.
19 Germano Maifreda, *The Business of the Inquisition in the Early Modern Era* (London: Routledge, 2017), 25.
20 Reinhard, *Papstfinanz und Nepotismus*, vol. 1, 53–101.
21 Antonio Menniti Ippolito, *Il tramonto della Curia nepotista: Papi, nipoti e burocrazia curiale tra XVI e XVII secolo* (Rome: Viella, 1999), 90–3.
22 On the court of Versailles, see Daniel Dessert, *Argent, pouvoir et société au Grand Siècle* (Paris: Fayard, 1984), 416.
23 Pizzorusso, "Lo 'Stato temporale'," 54–7.
24 See Chapter 6, "All-Too-Worldly Business."
25 See "Administrer les sacrements."
26 Josef Metzler, "Controversia tra Propaganda e S. Uffizio circa una commissione teologica (1622–1658)," *Pontificiae Universitatis Urbanianae Annales* (1968–9): 47–62, and "Orientation, programme et premières décisions (1622–1649)," in *Sacrae Congregationis de Propaganda Fide Memoria Rerum*, ed. Metzler, vol. I/1.
27 See Chapter 7, "Doctrinal Disambiguation."
28 Francesco Ingoli, *Relatione delle Quattro Parti del Mondo (1629–1631)*, ed. Fabio Tosi (Rome: Urbaniana University Press, 1999), 153–7, 164.
29 On this, see Roland Jacques, *De Castro Marim à Faïfo: Naissance et développement du padroado portugais d'Orient des origines à 1659* (Lisbon: Fundação Calouste Gulbenkian, 1999), 18–26, 35–101. On the close relations between the clergy and the Crown in the context of conflicts with the papacy, see Giuseppe Marcocci, "Conscience and Empire: Politics and Moral Theology in the Early Modern Portuguese World," *Journal of Early Modern History* 18 (2014): 473–94.
30 On this, from the perspective of relations with China, see Antonella Romano, *Impressions de Chine: L'Europe et l'englobement du monde (XVIe–XVIIe siècle)* (Paris: Fayard, 2016), 289–305.
31 Dominique Deslandres, *Croire et faire croire: Les missions françaises au XVIIe siècle (1600–1650)* (Paris: Fayard, 2003), esp. 32–40. On Joseph de Paris, see Benoist Pierre, *Le père Joseph: L'éminence grise de Richelieu* (Paris: Perrin, 2007).

32 Khanbaba Bayani, *Les relations de l'Iran avec l'Europe occidentale à l'époque safavide (Portugal, Espagne, Angleterre, Hollande et France) (avec documents inédits)* (Paris: Les Presses modernes, 1937), 188–9. On the Ottoman Empire, see Heyberger, *Les Chrétiens du Proche-Orient*, 241–71.

33 On relations between the *Propaganda Fide* and the regular clergy, see Giovanni Pizzorusso, "La Congregazione 'de Propaganda Fide' e gli ordini religiosi: conflittualità nel mondo delle missioni del XVII secolo," in *Cheiron* 43-4 (2005): 197–240, and "Le pape rouge et le pape noir: Aux origines des conflits entre la Congrégation 'de Propaganda fide' et la Compagnie de Jésus au XVIIe siècle," in *Les antijésuites: Discours, figures et lieux de l'antijésuitisme à l'époque moderne*, ed. Pierre-Antoine Fabre and Catherine Maire (Rennes: PUR, 2010).

34 A collection of the order's privileges had already been published in 1617. *Privilegia Fratrum Discalceatorum [...]* (Rome, 1617).

35 *Congregazione particolare*, Sept. 4, 1657 (APF, Acta, vol. 26, 355–402, esp. 374–9, 390–1).

36 See Chapter 6, "The Discalced Carmelites: Unsuited to Mission."

37 Friedrich, *Der lange Arm Roms?*, 46–62, 295–321.

38 See Thiessen, *Die Kapuziner*, 466–7.

39 See Michela Catto, *La Compagnia divisa: Il dissenso nell'ordine gesuitico tra '500 e '600* (Brescia: Editrice Morcelliana, 2009).

40 Hartmut Lehmann, *Das Zeitalter des Absolutismus: Gottesgnadentum und Kriegsnot* (Stuttgart: Kohlhammer, 1980), 53.

41 Friedrich, *Der lange Arm Roms?*, 229 (quotation), 322–7.

42 Ibid., 334–40.

43 Pierre-Antoine Fabre, "Introduction," in *Ignace de Loyola: Écrits*, ed. Maurice Giuliani (Paris: Desclée de Brouwer, 1991), 390–1.

44 See Silvia Mostaccio, *Early Modern Jesuits between Obedience and Conscience during the Generalate of Claudio Acquaviva (1581–1615)* (Farnham: Ashgate, 2014).

45 See, among others, Gillian T.W. Ahlgren, *Teresa of Avila and the Politics of Sanctity* (Ithaca: Cornell University Press, 1996); Jodi Bilinkoff, *The Avila of Saint Teresa: Religious Reform in a Sixteenth-Century City* (Ithaca: Cornell University Press, 1989); Alison Weber, *Teresa of Avila and the Rhetoric of Femininity* (Princeton: Princeton University Press, 1990).

46 Giordano, *Domenico di Gesù Maria*, and Roggero, *Genova e gli inizi*.

47 Gilles Sinicropi, *"D'oraison et d'action:" Les Carmes déchaux en France aux XVIIe et XVIIIe siècles* (Saint-Étienne: Publications de l'Université de Saint-Étienne, 2013).

48 Starting in the thirteenth century, the Order of Preachers (Dominicans) had provided the model for such a constitution. See David A. Knowles, *From Pachomius to Ignatius: A Study of the Constitutional History of the Religious Orders* (Oxford: Clarendon Press, 1966), 51–3.

49 On the governance of the Jesuits, see Friedrich, *Der lange Arm Roms?*, esp. 45–55, quotation: 48.

50 Flavio Rurale, *Monaci, frati, chierici: Gli ordini religiosi in età moderna* (Rome: Carocci editore, 2008), 130–44.

51 General Chapter, May 6, 1743. Fortes, *Acta capituli*, vol. 3, 470–1.

52 Ninon Maillard, *Réforme religieuse et droit: La traduction juridique et structurelle du retour à l'observance; Le cas des Dominicains de France, 1629–1660* (Paris: Les Éditions du Cerf, 2015), 43–4, 46–9, 77–8, 96).

53 *Definitorium generale*, Dec. 19, 1703. Antonio Fortes, *Acta definitorii generalis O.C.D. Congregationis S. Eliae*, vol. 1: *1605–1658*, vol. 2: *1658–1710*, vol. 3: *1710–1766* (Rome: Teresianum, 1985, 1986, 1988) vol. 2, 534–5.

54 General Chapter, June 4, 1620. Fortes, *Acta capituli*, vol. 1, 119.
55 General Chapter, Apr. 30 and May 4, 1638. Ibid., vol. 1, 347–8, 355.
56 *Definitorium generale,* Nov. 21, 1689. Fortes, *Acta definitorii*, vol. 2, 311.
57 Denis de la Couronne d'Épines to Isidoro di San Nicolò, Isfahan, July 18, 1657 (AGOCD, 237/c/34).
58 Denis de la Couronne d'Épines to [Isidore de Saint-Dominique], Isfahan, Oct. 22, 1657 (AGOCD, 237/c/38).
59 Denis de la Couronne d'Épines to Isidore de Saint-Joseph, Isfahan, Feb. 22, 1657 (AGOCD, 237/c/32).
60 *Definitorium generale,* Nov. 19, 1658. Fortes, *Acta definitorii*, vol. 2, 8.
61 *Definitorium generale,* June 16, 1620. Fortes, *Acta definitorii,* vol. 1, 66.
62 Instruttione per gli nostri padri […] che si manda d'ordine del definitorio generale del 1630 a 6 di Jenaro, signed by Fernando de Santa María (AGOCD, 289/e/1).
63 Fortes, *Acta definitorii*, vol. 3, 711.
64 There are no case studies of the Discalced Carmelite visitation practice. On the practice of the Society of Jesus, see Brockey, *The Visitor*.
65 Ingoli, *Quattro Parti del Mondo*, 166.
66 Memoria al nostro Padre Visitatore generale […], n.p., n.d. [1621] (AGOCD, 236/a/17).
67 Felice di Sant'Antonio to Isidore de Saint-Joseph, Basra, Dec. 20, 1661 (AGOCD, 241/k/19).
68 Girolamo di Gesù Maria to Jean Chrysostome de Saint-Paul, Shiraz, Aug. 31 and Sept. 3, 1675 (AGOCD, 238/q/2 and 5) and to Emmanuele di Gesù Maria, Shiraz, Aug. 31, 1675 (AGOCD, 238/q/3).
69 See Chapter 6, "Local Social Integration and Observance" and "All-Too-Worldly Business."
70 Jürgen Schlumbohm, "Gesetze, die nicht durchgesetzt werden: Ein Strukturmerkmal des frühneuzeitlichen Staates?," *Geschichte und Gesellschaft* 23 (1997): 647–63.
71 On the spiritual exercises, see John W. O'Malley, *The First Jesuits* (Cambridge, MA: Harvard University Press, 1993), 37–50.
72 Wolfgang Reinhard, "Gegenreformation als Modernisierung? Prolegomena zu einer Theorie des konfessionellen Zeitalters," *Archiv für Reformationsgeschichte* 68 (1977): 226–51, esp. 240.
73 On the parallels between the spiritual exercises of the Jesuits and the Discalced Carmelites, see Christian Belin, *La conversation intérieure: La méditation en France au XVIIe siècle* (Paris: H. Champion, 2002), 99.
74 Pedro de la Madre de Dios, Instruttione di quello che hanno da fare li padri et fratelli che vanno a Persia, n.d. [1604] (AGOCD, 281/e/44).
75 J. Michelle Molina, *To Overcome Oneself: The Jesuit Ethic and Spirit of Global Expansion, 1520–1767* (Berkeley: University of California Press, 2013). Cf. Moshe Sluhovsky, *Becoming a New Self: Practices of Belief in Early Modern Catholicism* (Chicago: University of Chicago Press, 2017), esp. 67–95.
76 Belin, *La conversation intérieure*, 84–98.
77 Mostaccio, *Early Modern Jesuits between Obedience and Conscience*. See also Fernanda Alfieri and Claudio Ferlan, eds., *Avventure dell'obbedienza nella Compagnia di Gesù: Teorie e prassi fra XVI e XIX secolo* (Bologna: Il Mulino, 2012).
78 See Chapter 6, "The Mission as a World Turned Upside Down: Justification Strategies and Cultural Relativization."
79 On this topic, taking the example of the political relationships maintained by the kings of Prussia, see Nadir Weber, *Lokale Interessen und große Strategie: Das*

Fürstentum Neuchâtel und die politischen Beziehungen der Könige von Preußen (1707-1806) (Cologne: Böhlau, 2015), 189–202.

80 Friedrich, *Der lange Arm Roms?*, 80–112, 340–78, 388–9, quotation: 341. On correspondence as reflection upon one's own mission and as a means of cultivating relationships among members of the Society scattered across the globe, see Laborie, *Mangeurs d'hommes*.

81 Especially Isidore de Saint-Joseph and Pierre de Saint-André, *Historia Generalis Fratrum Discalceatorum [...]*, vol. 1 (Rome, 1668), 359–73; vol. 2 (Rome, 1671), 32–71, 134–90, 350–92, 615–44, 673–84, 691–707, 782–96.

82 Friedrich, *Der lange Arm Roms?*, 231 (quotation), 251–8.

83 Pedro de la Madre de Dios, Instruttione [...], n.d. [1604] (AGOCD, 281//45).

84 [Ordinationes], by Vicente de San Francisco, Isfahan, Sept. 22, 1621 (AGOCD, 235/l/1 and 236/a/14).

85 See Friedrich, *Der lange Arm Roms?*, 49–50, 101 (quotation)–6.

86 See Chapter 5, "Useful Services: Transporting Mail."

87 See Aimé Chézaud to Claude Boucher, Isfahan, Jan. 22, 1662 (ARSI, Gallia, 97 II, doc. 112, fol. 323r).

88 René J. Barendse, "The Long Road to Livorno: The Overland Messenger Services of the Dutch East India Company in the Seventeenth Century," *Itinerario* 12 (1988): 25–43, 29.

89 Felice di Sant'Antonio to the *Definitorium generale*, Shiraz, Aug. 1 and Oct. 8, 1670, Jan. 2 and Apr. 10, 1671 (AGOCD, 238/p/9, 10, 12, 14 and 15).

90 Letters from Alexandre de Rhodes to Goswinus Nickel, Isfahan, 1656–60 (ARSI, Gallia, 103 I and II).

91 Felice di Sant'Antonio to [Jacopo di Santa Teresa] and the *Definitorium generale*, Isfahan, Feb. 15, 1655 (AGOCD, 237/i/14).

92 Felice di Sant'Antonio to [Gioachino] di Gesù Maria, Isfahan, Mar. 25, 1655 (AGOCD, 237/i/16).

93 Chézaud to the *assistant de France*, Isfahan, Dec. 16, 1661 (ARSI, Gallia, 97 II, doc. 111, fol. 321r).

94 Ange de Saint-Joseph to [Philippe de la Très Sainte Trinité], Isfahan, Mar. 20, 1671 (AGOCD, 236/i/14).

95 According to Ange de Saint-Joseph, the lack of correspondence harmed the reputation of the Discalced Carmelites among the members of other orders (Ange de Saint-Joseph to Jean Chrysostome de Saint-Paul, Isfahan, Feb. 26, 1671 [AGOCD, 236/i/7]). See Gary Schneider, *The Culture of Epistolarity: Vernacular Letters and Letter Writing in Early Modern England, 1500–1700* (Newark: University of Delaware Press, 2005), 56–9, 61–5, 84–91, on the importance of continuity and reciprocity in correspondence.

96 Works on inner-European diplomatic practice in particular have recently underlined the importance of letters as means of cultivating relationships and embodying symbolic capital. See Corina Bastian, *Verhandeln in Briefen: Frauen in der höfischen Diplomatie des frühen 18. Jahrhunderts* (Cologne: Böhlau, 2013), 177–340; Tilman Haug, *Ungleiche Außenbeziehungen und grenzüberschreitende Patronage: Die französische Krone und die geistlichen Kurfürsten (1648–1679)* (Cologne: Böhlau, 2015), 248–81; and Weber, *Lokale Interessen und große Strategie*, esp. 217–18.

97 In the seventeenth and eighteenth centuries, three quarters of French Discalced Carmelites also gave up their baptismal names. Sinicropi, *"D'oraison et d'action,"* 115–33.

98 Adriano Prosperi, *La vocazione: Storie di gesuiti tra Cinquecento e Seicento* (Turin: Giulio Einaudi, 2016), 106–241. Cf. Barbara B. Diefendorf, "Give Us Back Our Children: Patriarchal Authority and Parental Consent to Religious Vocations in Early Counter-Reformation France," *The Journal of Modern History* 68 (1996): 265–307.

99 Samuel Weber, "Pining for Stability: The Borromeo Family and the Crisis of the Spanish Monarchy, 1610-1680" (PhD thesis, University of Bern and Durham University, 2019), 300–301.

100 Aliocha Maldavsky, "Les familles du missionnaire: Une histoire sociale des horizons missionnaires milanais au début du XVIIe siècle," in *Milano, l'Ambrosiana e la conoscenza dei nuovi mondi (secoli XVII–XVIII)*, ed. Michela Catto and Gianvittorio Signorotto (Milan: Biblioteca Ambrosiana, 2015), 149–53.

101 *Instructiones Fratrum Discalceatorum [...]* (Rome, 1630), 6.

102 General Chapter, Apr. 20, 1644. Fortes, *Acta capituli*, vol. 2, 10–11.

103 General Chapter, June 6, 1623. Fortes, *Acta capituli*, vol. 1, 194. Petitioners regarded members of the regular clergy who were staying in or traveling to Rome as inexpensive and, thanks to their orders' networks, as well-established intermediaries. See Sidler, *Heiligkeit aushandeln*, esp. 428–39.

104 Since some clerics, well aware of their meager earnings, strove after offices within the orders "per mezzo di patrocini e favore di personaggi," Pope Innocent XI (Benedetto Odescalchi, r. 1676–89) declared the beneficiaries of such practices to be incapable *ipso facto* of holding the office in question and other offices. See the letter from [Secretary of State Alderano] Cibo to the General Chapter, Rome, Apr. 27, 1680, reproduced in Fortes, *Acta capituli*, vol. 2, 442–4.

105 See Chapter 3, "Diplomatic Assignments."

106 Gratien de Galisson to Jacques-Charles de Brisacier, Isfahan, May 13, 1712 (MEP, vol. 354, 437–48).

107 *Congregazione generale*, Aug. 8, 1757 (APF, Acta, vol. 127, fol. 323r/v).

108 Cornelio di San Giuseppe, Memorie cronologiche che puonno servire a meglio sovvenirmi de varii altri incidenti di mia vita, n.p., n.d. (BA, & 211 sup., 168, 186, 188-9, 191-2, 208).

109 Mattheo de la Cruz to Fernando de Santa María, Isfahan, Mar. 30, 1630 (AGOCD, 238/a/2).

110 Juan Thadeo de San Eliseo to Paolo Simone di Gesù Maria, Isfahan, Oct. 27, 1621 (AGOCD, 233/d/4).

111 Fortunato di Gesù Maria to Carolus Felix a Sancta Teresia, Isfahan, Oct. 20, 1678 and Mar. 20, 1679 (AGOCD, 237/k/1 and 2).

112 Fortunato di Gesù Maria to [Bernardo Maria di Gesù], Isfahan, Apr. 28 and Sept. 28, 1682 (AGOCD, 237/k/4 and 6); id. to Martial de Saint-Paulin, Isfahan, Apr. 28 and Sept. 28, 1682 (AGOCD, 237/k/5 and 7).

113 Fortunato di Gesù Maria to Bernardo Maria di Gesù, Isfahan, Feb. 20, 1684 (AGOCD, 237/k/8).

114 Fortunato di Gesù Maria to Bernardo Maria di Gesù, Isfahan, June 10, 1684 (AGOCD, 237/k/9).

115 Fortunato di Gesù Maria to Bernardo Maria di Gesù, Isfahan, June 26, 1684 (AGOCD, 237/k/10).

116 See Schneider, *The Culture of Epistolarity*, 28–37; Christian Windler, "Städte am Hof: Burgundische Deputierte und Agenten in Madrid und Versailles (16.–18. Jahrhundert)," *Zeitschrift für Historische Forschung* 30 (2003): 207–50, 229–34.

117 Casimir Joseph de Sainte-Thérèse to Isidore de Saint-Joseph, Basra, Dec. 16, 1656, and Jan. 17, 1657 (AGOCD, 241/h/1 and 2).
118 Barnaba di San Carlo to Isidore de Saint-Joseph, Basra, Apr. 5, 1654, May 27, 1654, and Jan. 15, 1655 (AGOCD, 241/f/9–11).
119 Windler, *La diplomatie*, 170–7.
120 Felice di Sant'Antonio to Jean Chrysostome de Saint-Paul, Shiraz, Jan. 31, 1673 (AGOCD, 238/p/18 and 19).
121 Pedro de la Madre de Dios, Instruttione […], n.d. [1604] (AGOCD, 281/e/45).
122 François Picquet to Étienne Pallu, Hamadan, May 7, 1685 (MEP, vol. 351, 115).
123 *Congregazione generale*, June 30, 1664 (APF, Acta, vol. 33, fol. 106v–07r). The Jesuits tried where possible to avoid correspondence with the *Propaganda Fide*. See Giovanni Pizzorusso, "La Congrégation de Propaganda fide à Rome: Centre d'accumulation et de production de 'savoirs missionnaires' (XVIIe–début XIXe siècle)," in *Missions d'évangélisation*, ed. Castelnau-L'Estoile, Copete, Maldavsky, and Županov, 216, 236–67, and "La Congregazione 'de Propaganda Fide.'"
124 General Chapter, June 14, 1623. Fortes, *Acta capituli*, vol. 1, 219.
125 *Definitorium generale*, Sept. 28, 1629. Fortes, *Acta definitorii*, vol. 1, 171.
126 After just one year, Alexander VII moved away from excluding his kinsmen, as this called into question the foundations of his power and the governability of the Church and the Papal States. Marie-Luise Rodén, *Church Politics in Seventeenth-Century Rome: Cardinal Decio Azzolino, Queen Christina of Sweden, and the* Squadrone Volante (Stockholm: Almqvist & Wiksell International, 2000), 133–44; see also Francesco Benigno, "Ripensare il nepotismo papale nel Seicento," *Società* 12 (2006): 93–113; and Menniti Ippolito, *Il tramonto*, 50–7, 80–9.
127 [Chick], *Chronicle*, vol. 2, 763–4.
128 Marcella Campanelli, *Geografia conventuale in Italia nel XVII secolo: Soppressioni e reintegrazioni innocenziane* (Rome: Edizioni di storia e letteratura, 2016), esp. 2–3, 82–4. See also Emanuele Boaga, *La soppressione innocenziana dei piccoli conventi in Italia* (Rome: Edizioni di storia e letteratura, 1971), 72–3, 84–5, 88–100, 103–5. According to Boaga, 1,513 convents were closed.
129 Riflessioni sopra il Breve di Alessandro VII […], n.d. [probably 1655] (AGOCD, 223/a/3–4).
130 Barnaba di San Carlo to [Isidore de Saint-Joseph ?], Basra, July 20, 1656 (AGOCD, 241/f/16).
131 Felice di Sant'Antonio to the *Definitorium generale*, Shiraz, Oct. 21, 1656 (AGOCD, 237/i/23).
132 Casimir Joseph de Sainte-Thérèse to Isidore de Saint-Joseph, Basra, Dec. 16, 1656 (AGOCD, 241/h/1).
133 The extent of the critique had not escaped the attention of the ecclesiastical authorities in Castile. This at least partially explains the proceedings that the Inquisition opened against Teresa of Ávila. On this, see Ahlgren, *Teresa of Avila*, 26–34, 40–66, 114–44.
134 Barnaba di San Carlo to [Isidore de Saint-Joseph ?], Basra, June 14, 1658 (AGOCD, 241/f/3).
135 Barnaba di San Carlo to [Isidore de Saint-Joseph], Basra, Feb. 25, 1658 (AGOCD, 241/f/2).
136 In 1752, we still find mentions of monies belonging to the order's "missioni particolari." *Congregazione generale*, Jan. 31, 1752 (APF, Acta, vol. 122, fol. 10r/v).
137 General Chapter, Apr. 29, 1665. Fortes, *Acta capituli*, vol. 2, 311.

138 *Acta Definitorii nostri Generalis super correctiones nostrarum Constitutionum* (Rome, 1740), reproduced in Fortes, *Acta definitorii*, vol. 3, 785–852, 834.
139 Instructiones pro missionibus orientalibus, 1683 (AGOCD, Acta Definitorii Generalis ab anno 1676 usque ad annum 1687, vol. 6, 243–51).
140 Instructiones conditae a Definitorio nostro generali die 30 Julii anni 1683, confirmatae ab eodem Definitorio die 20 10^{bris} an. 1719 [...] (AGOCD, 289/e/1).
141 Istruttione generale, n.d. (APF, Istruzioni diverse, 1639–1648, fol. 163v).
142 Denis de la Couronne d'Épines to [Ingoli], Shiraz, Feb. 16, 1640 (APF, SOCG, vol. 209, fol. 68r/v; vol. 120, fol. 292r/v).
143 Felice di Sant'Antonio to Gioachino di Gesù Maria, Basra, Oct. 10, 1655 (AGOCD, 241/k/17).
144 Cornelio di San Giuseppe, Memorie cronologiche [...], n.p., n.d. (BA, & 211 sup.); Miscellanea d'alcune historiette piacevoli e risposte pronte in diverse Centurie divise e raccolte per puro divertimento e passatempo da F. C[ornelio] di S. Giuseppe Carmelitano Scalzo, n.p., n.d. (BA, L 13 suss.).
145 See Chapter 5, "As Christians among Muslims: Missionaries and European Laypeople of Different Confessions."
146 Miscellanea d'alcune historiette [...] raccolte [...] da F. C[ornelio] di S. Giuseppe Carmelitano Scalzo, n.p., n.d. (BA, L 13 suss., fol. 31r/v).
147 Ibid., fol. 252v–3r.
148 Cornelio di San Giuseppe to Mario Marefoschi, Bushehr, Oct. 15, 1767 (APF, SC. Mesopotamia e Persia. Caldei e Latini, vol. 7, fol. 466r).
149 Cornelio di San Giuseppe, Memorie cronologiche [...], n.p., n.d. (BA, & 211 sup., 167–8).
150 Ibid., 172–5, quotation: 174.
151 Note written by Stefano Borgia on the letter sent to him by Cornelio di San Giuseppe, Milan, Apr. 9, 1776 (APF, SC. Mesopotamia e Persia. Caldei e Latini, vol. 8, fol. 540v).
152 Secretariat of State to Borgia, Jan. 21, 1777 (APF, SC. Mesopotamia e Persia. Caldei e Latini, vol. 8, fol. 621r).
153 Cornelio di San Giuseppe to Leonardo Antonelli, Milan, July 23, 1788 (APF, SC. Mesopotamia e Persia. Caldei e Latini, vol. 10, fol. 180r).
154 Županov, *Disputed Mission*, 71.

Chapter 2

1 Rudi Matthee, "The Safavids under Western Eyes: Seventeenth-Century European Travelers to Iran," *Journal of Early Modern History* 13 (2009): 137–71, esp. 137–8. Cf. Zoltán Biedermann, "Mapping the Backyard of an Empire: Portuguese Cartographies of the Persian Littoral during the Safavid Period," in *Portugal, the Persian Gulf and Safavid Persia*, ed. R. Matthee and Jorge Flores (Louvain: Peeters, 2011).
2 On relations between the Roman Curia and the court of ʿAbbās I, see Angelo Michele Piemontese, "I due ambasciatori di Persia ricevuti da Papa Paolo V al Quirinale," in *Miscellanea Bibliothecae Apostolicae Vaticanae* 12 (2005): 357–425, and *La Persia istoriata in Roma* (Vatican City: Biblioteca Apostolica Vaticana, 2014). On relations between the Luso-Hispanic empire and the court of ʿAbbās I, see Luis Gil Fernández, *El imperio luso-español y la Persia safávida*, 2 vols. (Madrid: Fundación Universitaria Española, 2006, 2009).

3   The breves are reproduced in [Chick], *Chronicle*, vol. 2, 1272–4, 1297.
4   On the Shirley brothers, see Gil Fernández, *El imperio luso-español*, vol. 1, 79–253, vol. 2, 76–9, 121–69, 359–421; Niels Steensgaard, *The Asian Trade Revolution: The East India Companies and the Decline of the Caravan Trade* (Chicago: University of Chicago Press, 1974), 211–304; and Sanjay Subrahmanyam, *Three Ways to Be Alien: Travails & Encounters in the Early Modern World* (Waltham, MA: Brandeis University Press, 2011), 88–132.
5   Flannery, *The Mission*, 73–8.
6   [Chick], *Chronicle*, vol. 2, 1029–39.
7   Holden Furber, *Rival Empires of Trade in the Orient 1600–1800* (Minneapolis: University of Minnesota Press, 1976), 103–24, 203–7; Laurence Lockhart, *The Fall of the Safavi Dynasty and the Afghan Occupation of Persia* (Cambridge: CUP, 1958), 360–407, 426–72; and Peter Rietbergen, "Upon a Silk Thread? Relations between the Safavid Court of Persia and the Dutch East Indies Company, 1623–1722," in *Hof en Handel: Aziatische Vorsten en de VOC 1620–1720*, ed. Elsbeth Locher-Scholten and P. Rietbergen (Leiden: KITLV Uitgeverij, 2004).
8   Charles Ralph Boxer, "Anglo-Portuguese Rivalry in the Persian Gulf, 1615–1635," in *Chapters in Anglo-Portuguese Relations*, ed. Edgar Prestage (Watford: Voss & Michael, 1935), 46–129.
9   Willem Floor, *The Persian Gulf: A Political and Economic History of Five Port Cities, 1500–1730* (Washington, DC: Mage, 2006), 237–47, 250–322.
10 See, for example, Steensgard, *The Asian Trade Revolution*. For an overview of the more recent literature, see Rudi Matthee, "The Safavid Economy as Part of the World Economy," in *Iran and the World in the Safavid Age*, ed. Willem Floor and Edmund Herzig (London: I. B. Tauris, 2012).
11 Aslanian, *From the Indian Ocean*; Bhaswati Bhattacharya, "Armenian-European Relationship in India, 1500–1800: No Armenian Foundation for European Empire?," *Journal of Economic and Social History of the Orient* 48 (2005): 277–322; and Peter Good, *The East India Company in Persia: Trade and Cultural Exchange in the Eighteenth Century* (London: I. B. Tauris, 2022), 127–42, 149–51.
12 Ambrosio Bembo, *Il viaggio in Asia (1671–1675) nei manoscritti di Minneapolis e di Bergamo*, ed. Antonio Invernizzi (Alessandria: Edizioni dell'Orso, 2012), 366, 379. Translator's note: Because the English translation published by the University of California Press takes into account only one of the existing manuscript versions of the text, this and other footnotes refer solely to Invernizzi's Italian edition. On the Indian commercial and financial diaspora in Persia, see Stephen Frederic Dale, *Indian Merchants and Eurasian Trade, 1600–1750* (Cambridge: CUP, 1994), esp. 57, 67, 124–6; Scott C. Levi, "India XIII. Indo-Iranian Commercial Relations," in *Encyclopaedia Iranica* online. Article published Dec. 15, 2004; last updated Mar. 27, 2012. http://www.iranicaonline.org/articles/india-xiii-indo-iranian-commercial-relations, and "India XXX. Indian Merchants in Central Asia and Iran," in *Encyclopaedia Iranica* online. Article published Dec. 15, 2004; last updated Mar. 27, 2012. http://www.iranicaonline.org/articles/india-xxx-indian-merchants-in-central-asia-and-iran.
13 Rietbergen, "Upon a Silk Thread?," 173–6.
14 On relations with the Ottomans, Mongols, and Uzbeks, see Barat Dahmardeh, "The Shaybanid Uzbeks, Moghuls and Safavids in Eastern Iran," in *Iran and the World*, ed. Floor and Herzig; Sanjay Subrahmanyam, "An Infernal Triangle: The Contest between Mughals, Safavids and Portuguese, 1590–1605," in ibid.; and Ernest Tucker,

"From Rhetoric of War to Realities of Peace: The Evolution of Ottoman-Iranian Diplomacy through the Safavid Era," in ibid.
15 Sussan Babaie, *Isfahan and Its Palaces: Statecraft, Shi'ism and the Architecture of Conviviality in Early Modern Iran* (Edinburgh: Edinburgh University Press, 2008), 192–4.
16 Relazione della Persia [...], Isfahan, May 23, 1665 (Biblioteca Nazionale Centrale, Florence, Panciatichiano 219, 142–3, 152–3).
17 The conflict over honor continued in Delhi, where Aurangzēb had the horses his envoy had brought back as gifts from the shah publicly butchered. Riazul Islam, *Indo-Persian Relations: A Study of the Political and Diplomatic Relations between the Mughul Empire and Iran* (Teheran: Iranian Culture Foundation, 1970), 127–30.
18 Iskandar Bēg Munšī, *History of 'Abbas the Great (Tārīḵ-e 'Ālamārā-ye 'Abbāsī)*, trans. Roger M. Savory, 3 vols. (vols. 1 and 2, Boulder: Westview Press, 1978; vol. 3, New York: Bibliotheca Persica, 1986), vol. 2, 1305–7. The Latin original of the breve is reproduced in [Chick], *Chronicle*, vol. 2, 1294.
19 Savory, *Iran under the Safavids*, esp. 27–49.
20 Matthee, *Persia in Crisis*, 10, 173–7; Newman, *Rebirth of a Persian Empire*, 9.
21 See Masashi Haneda, *Le Châh et les Qizilbāš: Le système militaire safavide* (Berlin: Klaus Schwarz, 1987).
22 Rula Jurdi Abisaab, *Converting Persia: Religion and Power in the Safavid Empire* (London: I. B. Tauris, 2004), 7–52.
23 Sussan Babaie, Kathryn Babayan, Ina Baghdiantz McCabe, and Massumeh Farhad, eds., *Slaves of the Shah: New Elites of Safavid Iran* (London: I. B. Tauris, 2004), esp. 20–79; Ina Baghdiantz McCabe, *The Shah's Silk for Europe's Silver: The Eurasian Trade of the Julfa Armenians in Safavid Iran and India (1530–1750)* (Atlanta: Scholars Press, 1999), 115–70.
24 On the Georgian *ġulām*, see Hirotake Maeda, "Against All Odds: The Safavids and the Georgians," in *The Safavid World*, ed. Rudi Matthee (London: Routledge, 2021).
25 See Matthee, *Persia in Crisis*, 27–31, 146–7, 177–8, 254; Newman, *Rebirth of a Persian Empire*, 45–6, 71–2.
26 Mitchell, *The Practice of Politics*, 3–4, 12, 176–97, 199, 202. The orientation toward plural legitimatory references is also observable in historiography under 'Abbās I. The legendary reference to Timur played an especially important role in the construction of an imperial discourse, which 'Abbās I deployed in his rivalry with the Mughals. See Quinn, *Historical Writing*, 44–6, 52–3, 86–91, 127–43. A plurality of references also characterized the legitimation of rule in other Asian dynasties and was particularly marked in the case of the Qing emperors in China, who staged themselves as Confucians and protectors of Tibetan Buddhism while at the same time continuing to cultivate the shamanistic rituals of the Manchus. See Evelyn S. Rawski, *The Last Emperors: A Social History of Qing Imperial Institutions* (Berkeley: University of California Press, 1998), 195–294.
27 Babaie, *Isfahan and Its Palaces*; Kathryn Babayan, *Mystics, Monarchs, and Messiahs: Cultural Landscapes of Early Modern Iran* (Cambridge, MA: Harvard University Press, 2002), 356–64.
28 Aslanian, *From the Indian Ocean*, 30–43; Edmund M. Herzig, "The Armenian Merchants of New Julfa, Isfahan: A Study in Pre-Modern Asian Trade" (PhD thesis, University of Oxford, 1991), 46–67.
29 Of the more recent studies, see in particular, Aslanian, *From the Indian Ocean*.

30 Herzig, "The Armenian Merchants," 90-2; Rudi Matthee, "Christians in Safavid Iran: Hospitality and Harassment," *Studies on Persianate Societies* 3 (2005): 3-43, 22-3.
31 Matthee, *Persia in Crisis,* 181.
32 Baghdiantz McCabe, *The Shah's Silk,* 180-98; Matthee, *Persia in Crisis,* 182-93, 220; and Vera B. Moreen, *Iranian Jewry's Hour of Peril and Heroism: A Study of Bābāi Ibn Lutf's Chronicle (1617-1662)* (New York: Columbia University Press, 1987), 62-79.
33 Tijana Krstič, *Contested Conversions to Islam: Narratives of Religious Change in the Early Modern Ottoman Empire* (Stanford: Stanford University Press, 2011), esp. 15-16, 165-74.
34 Herzig, "The Armenian Merchants," 105-8, 269-70. On Nādir Šāh, see Michael Axworthy, *The Sword of Persia: Nader Shah from Tribal Warrior to Conquering Tyrant* (London: I. B. Tauris, 2006); Ernest Tucker, *Nadir Shah's Quest for Legitimacy in Post-Safavid Iran* (Gainesville: University Press of Florida, 2006). On the conflicts that followed the murder of Nādir Šāh, see John R. Perry, *Karim Khan Zand: A History of Iran, 1747-1779* (Chicago: University of Chicago Press, 1979).
35 Vazken S. Ghougassian, *The Emergence of the Armenian Diocese of New Julfa in the Seventeenth Century* (Atlanta: Scholars Press, 1998), 84-5, 92-4, 105-22.
36 Kéram Kévonian, "Marchands arméniens au XVIIe siècle: À propos d'un livre arménien publié à Amsterdam en 1699," *Cahiers du monde russe et soviétique* 16 (1975): 199-244, 199-206, 218-24.
37 John Carswell, *New Julfa: The Armenian Churches and Other Buildings* (Oxford: Clarendon, 1968), 10, 65-8, 81, 86, plates vi-viii, 70, 72-3, 75, 79-80.
38 Amy S. Landau, "*Farangī-Sāzī* at Isfahan: The Court Painter Muḥammad Zamān, the Armenians of New Julfa and Shāh Sulaymān (1666-1694)," (PhD thesis, Oxford University, 2009), esp. 50-1, 202-9, 222-6, 245-51, and "European Religious Iconography in Safavid Iran: Decoration and Patronage of *Meydani* Bet'ghehem (Bethlehem of the Maydan)," in *Iran and the World,* ed. Floor and Herzig; A. S. Landau and Theo Maarten Van Lint, "Armenian Merchant Patronage of New Julfa's Sacred Spaces," in *Sacred Precincts: The Religious Architecture of Non-Muslim Communities across the Islamic World,* ed. Mohammad Gharipour (Leiden: Brill, 2015); and Sâyeh Laporte-Eftekharian, "Transmission et métamorphose de modèles iconographiques occidentaux, principalement flamands, dans les églises de la Nouvelle-Djoulfa (Ispahan)," *Revue belge d'archéologie et d'histoire de l'art* 73 (2004): 63-80. On the dissemination of Western modes of representation in the Syrian provinces, see Bernard Heyberger, "De l'image religieuse à l'image profane? L'essor de l'image chez les Chrétiens de Syrie et du Liban (XVIIe-XIXe siècle)," in *La multiplication des images en pays d'Islam: De l'estampe à la télévision (17e-21e siècle),* ed. B. Heyberger and Silvia Naef (Würzburg: Ergon, 2003).
39 Aslanian, *From the Indian Ocean,* 144-64, 166-201; Herzig, "The Armenian Merchants," 156-82.
40 Aslanian, *From the Indian Ocean,* 121-44, 164-5, 202-14; Herzig, "The Armenian Merchants," 105-8, 213-26, 269-70.
41 Rudi Matthee, *The Politics of Trade in Safavid Iran: Silk for Silver, 1600-1730* (Cambridge: CUP, 1999), 192-202, 218-23; Stefan Troebst, "Isfahan—Moskau—Amsterdam: Zur Entstehungsgeschichte des moskauischen Transitprivilegs für die Armenische Handelskompanie in Persien (1666-1676)," *Jahrbücher für die Geschichte Osteuropas* 41 (1993): 179-209.
42 Sebouh David Aslanian, "Julfan Merchants and European East India Companies: Overland Trade, Protection Costs, and the Limits of Collective Self-Representation

in Early Modern Safavid Iran," in *Mapping Safavid Iran*, ed. Nobuaki Kondo (Fuchu, Tokyo: Research Institute for Languages and Cultures of Asia and Africa, 2015), 197–205; Bhattacharya, "Armenian-European Relationship"; Ronald W. Ferrier, "The Armenians and the East India Company in Persia in the Seventeenth and Early Eighteenth Centuries," *Economic History Review* 26 (1973): 38–62.

43   See Chapter 4, "Trade Networks, Mobility, and Confessional Affiliation: The Sceriman Family."
44   Reproduced in [Chick], *Chronicle*, vol. 2, 1276–7.
45   Felix de Jesus, Primeira Parte da Chronica […], dated Goa, Jan. 15, 1606, in Arnulf Hartmann, O.S.A., "The Augustinians in Golden Goa, According to a Manuscript by Felix of Jesus, O.S.A.," *Analecta Augustiniana* 30 (1967): 5–147, 90 (quotation)–97.
46   Marianna Shreve Simpson, "The Morgan Bible and the Giving of Religious Gifts between Iran and Europe/Europe and Iran during the Reign of Shah ʿAbbas I," in *Between the Picture and the World: Manuscript Studies from the Index of Christian Art*, ed. Colum Hourihane (Princeton: Index of Christian Art, in association with Penn State University Press, 2005). On the Arabic editions of the Gospels and Euclid's *Elements*, see Dennis Halft, "The Arabic Vulgate in Safavid Persia: Arabic Printing of the Gospels, Catholic Missionaries, and the Rise of Shīʿī Anti-Christian Polemics," (PhD thesis, Freie Universität Berlin, 2016), 44–66, 70–1.
47   Juan Thadeo de San Eliseo, Relación breve de las cosas pertenecientes al Rey de Persia y sus costumbres, 1609 (AGOCD, 237/m/1 and 3).
48   Relatione del P. Benigno di S. Michele sul suo viaggio in Persia, Isfahan, Aug. 10, 1609 (AGOCD, 234/e/^{bis}, fol. 27v).
49   [Chick], *Chronicle*, vol. 1, 259–66.
50   Gregorio Orsini, Relatio undecima de fidei propagatione in Persarum Regno […], 1626 (APF, SOCG, vol. 209, fol. 8r/v).
51   Istruttione per li due vescovi […], approved by the *Propaganda Fide* on Nov. 8, 1632 (APF, Istruzioni diverse, 1623–38, fol. 181r/v).
52   Parere del Signore Pietro Della Valle […], treated in the *Congregazione generale* of Nov. 22, 1632 (APF, SOCG, vol. 209, fol. 232r–3v).
53   Felix de Jesus, Primeira Parte da Chronica, 98–9, 108.
54   Cf. Bauer, *A Culture of Ambiguity*.

Chapter 3

1   José de Acosta, *De procuranda Indorum Salute*, ed. Luciano Pereña Vicente, V. Abril, C. Baciero, A. García, D. Ramos, J. Barrientos, and F. Maseda, 2 vols. (1588; Madrid: CSIC, 1984, 1987), vol. 1, 60–3.
2   This contrasts sharply with methods used in the Caribbean or Brazil, as well as with the stance toward the rural populations and urban lower classes in Europe. On the Kingdom of Naples, see Selwyn, *A Paradise Inhabited by Devils*.
3   Relatione del P. Benigno di S. Michele sul suo viaggio in Persia, Isfahan, Aug. 10, 1609 (AGOCD, 234/e/^{bis}, fol. 38v, cf. 39r).
4   Philippe de la Très Sainte Trinité, *Itinerarium Orientale […]* (Lyon, 1649), 82–3.
5   Pacifique de Provins, *Le voyage de Perse et Brève relation du voyage des Îles de l'Amérique*, ed. Godefroy de Paris and Hilaire de Wingene (1631 and 1646; Assisi: Collegio S. Lorenzo da Brindisi, 1939), 254–5.

6   Alexandre de Rhodes, "Les divers voyages et missions [...]," in his *Divers voyages et missions [...]* (Paris, 1653), 55–6.
7   On this from the perspective of the Habsburg monarchy, see Carina L. Johnson, *Cultural Hierarchy in Sixteenth-Century Europe: The Ottomans and Mexicans* (Cambridge: CUP, 2011).
8   Brentjes, "The Interests," 450–4, and "Pride and Prejudice."
9   Meserve, *Empires of Islam*, esp. 218–19.
10 Relation du voyage de Perse, par M. [Jean] de Montheron, n.p., n.d. (Montpellier, Bibliothèque interuniversitaire. Section Médecine, H 100, fol. 35r, cf. 46v–7r, 51v–3v, 58r).
11 According to Rudi Matthee, "From Splendour and Admiration to Ruin and Condescension: Western Travellers to Iran from the Safavids to the Qajars," *Iran* 54 (2016): 3–22.
12 Raphaël du Mans, État de la Perse, 1660, reproduced in Richard, *Raphaël du Mans*, vol. 2, 1–199, esp. 9 and 198.
13 When Montesquieu associated the concept of "Oriental despotism" with Persia, he was adopting Chardin's analysis of those elements that supported his construction of this type of rule. See Osterhammel, *Unfabling the East*, 346–51.
14 [Jean-Antoine du Cerceau and Tadeusz Juda Krusiński], *Histoire de la dernière Révolution de Perse*, 2 vols. (Paris, 1728; 1st ed. The Hague, 1728).
15 Osterhammel, *Unfabling the East*, 272–9. See also Olivier Bonnerot, *La Perse dans la littérature et la pensée françaises au XVIIIe siècle: De l'image au mythe* (Paris: H. Champion, 1988), 46–51, 53–4, 61–2, 64, 215–16, 223–5.
16 *Congregazione generale*, Aug. 22, 1769 (APF, Acta, vol. 139, fol. 311r).
17 Babaie, *Isfahan and Its Palaces*, esp. 1–2, 7–8, 10–11, 65–9, 99–103, 143–9, 224–66. For a comparison between palace architecture among the Ottomans, Safavids, and Mughals, see Gülru Necipoğlu "Framing the Gaze in Ottoman, Safavid and Mughal Palaces," *Ars Orientalis* 23 (1993): 303–42.
18 The correspondence is reproduced in Carlos Alonso, "Cartas del P. Melchor de los Ángeles, OSA, y otros documentos sobre su actividad en Persia (1610–1619)," *Analecta Augustiniana* 44 (1981): 249–98, and the same author's "Novísimo florilegio documental sobre los Agustinos en Persia (1608–1622)," *Analecta Augustiniana* 50 (1987): 47–119.
19 See García de Silva y Figueroa, *Comentarios de la Embaxada al Rey Xa Abbas de Persia (1614–1624)*, parts 1 and 2, ed. Rui Manuel Loureiro, Ana Cristina Costa Gomes, and Vasco Resende (Lisbon: Centro de História de Além-Mar, 2011); R. M. Loureiro and V. Resende, eds., *Estudos sobre Don García de Silva y Figueroa e os "Comentarios" da Embaixada à Pérsia (1614–1624)* (Lisbon: Centro de História de Além-Mar, 2011); Gil Fernández, *El imperio luso-español*, vol. 2, 241–358; and Joan Pau Rubiés, "Political Rationality and Cultural Distance in the European Embassies to Shah Abbas I," *Journal of Early Modern History* 20 (2016): 351–89.
20 Belchior dos Anjos to Juan de Ciriza, Isfahan, Jan. 18, 1618, reproduced in Alonso, "Cartas del P. Melchor de los Ángeles," 292–3.
21 René J. Barendse, *The Arabian Seas: The Indian Ocean World of the Seventeenth Century* (Armonk, NY: M. E. Sharpe, 2002), 46–7; Floor, *The Persian Gulf*, 429–76.
22 Jean Aubin, *L'ambassade de Gregório Pereira Fidalgo à la cour de Châh Soltân-Hosseyn, 1696–1697* (Lisbon: Comité national portugais pour la célébration du 2500e anniversaire de la fondation de la monarchie en Perse, 1971), esp. 14–25, 77, 79.
23 Instrucção que ha de seguir o Dr Gregorio Pereira Fidalgo [...], signed by [Pedro António de Noronha de Albuquerque], Conde de Vila Verde, Goa, Mar. 20, 1696,

reproduced in *Collecção de tratados e concertos de pazes que o Estado da Índia Portugueza fez com os Reis e Senhores com quem teve relações nas partes da Asia e Africa Oriental [...]*, ed. Julio Firmino and Judice Biker (Lisbon, 1884), vol. 4, 246–83, esp. 247–8, 251, 269, 281 (quotation).

24 Peter II to Noronha de Albuquerque, Conde de Vila Verde, Lisbon, Jan. 26 and Mar. 22, 1697 (DAAG, 70: Monções, vol. 61, fol. 195r, 255r/v).

25 See the subchapter "From Social Proximity to Conversion to Islam."

26 Rodrigo da Costa to John V, Goa, Dec. 31, 1709, reproduced in *Arquivo Português Oriental*, I: *Historia política, diplomática e militar*, ed. A. B. de Bragança Pereira, vol. 3, part 2: *1709–1719* (Bastorá: Tipografia Rangel, 1940), 21.

27 Luís Carlos Inácio Xavier de Meneses, Conde da Ericeira, to John V, Goa, Jan. 15, 1719, reproduced in *Arquivo Português Oriental*, I, vol. 3, part 2, 366.

28 Georges Goyau, *Un précurseur: François Picquet, consul de Louis XIV en Alep et évêque de Babylone* (Paris: Paul Geuthner, 1942), 283–4, 287–94, 297, 299, 301–2, 305–8.

29 Lockhart, *The Fall of the Safavi Dynasty*, 437–72. On relations between the French and Persian courts at the time of Louis XIV, see Mokhberi, *The Persian Mirror*, 44–63.

30 Extraits des lettres écrites au S^r [Pierre-Victor] Michel [...], 1708 (MAE, Correspondance politique. Perse, vol. 2, fol. 18r–21r).

31 Mémoire du Sr Michel sur son voyage de Perse, n.p., n.d. (BNF, Mss. fr. 7200, 119–22, 134–5); Ange de Gardane, Sieur de Sainte-Croix, to ?, Isfahan, June 10, 1721 (MAE, Correspondance politique. Perse, vol. 6, fol. 66v–7r).

32 Christina Brauner, *Kompanien, Könige und* caboceers: *Interkulturelle Diplomatie an Gold- und Sklavenküste im 17. und 18. Jahrhundert* (Cologne: Böhlau, 2015), 214–25, 559 (quotation)–60.

33 Rapport door ons ondergeschrevene gedaen aan den wel edele heere Joan van Leene [...], signed by Jan Bonstoe and Frans Castelijn, Isfahan, Nov. 20, 1690 (NA, VOC 1459, fol. 1028r; VOC 1476, fol. 599r).

34 On this, see Bastian, *Verhandeln in Briefen*, 274–81, 429; Eva Kathrin Dade, *Madame de Pompadour: Die Mätresse und die Diplomatie* (Cologne: Böhlau, 2010), 228–42.

35 Juan Thadeo de San Eliseo, Relación breve [...], 1609 (AGOCD, 237/m/1).

36 Halft, "The Arabic Vulgate," 44–66, 70–1, 76, 81–2.

37 Della Valle to Mario Schipano, Isfahan, Aug. 24 and Oct. 21, 1619, Apr. 4, 1620, Sept. 24, 1621, in P. Della Valle, *Viaggi [...], Parte seconda: La Persia*, 2 vols. (Rome, 1658), vol. 2, 23, 49–50, 62–3, 65, 72–4, 109–10, 239–40.

38 Richard, *Raphaël du Mans*, vol. 1, 62–8.

39 Relazione della Persia [...], Isfahan, May 23, 1665 (Biblioteca Nazionale Centrale, Firenze, Panciatichiano 219, 150–1).

40 Richard, *Raphaël du Mans*, vol. 1, 68–74.

41 Ibid., 94–6.

42 Engelbert Kaempfer, *Amoenitatum Exoticarum Politico-Physico-Medicarum Fasciculi V [...]* (Lemgo, 1712), 232–3, 237.

43 Rudi Matthee, "Negotiating across Cultures: The Dutch Van Leene Mission to the Iranian Court of Šāh Sulaymān, 1689–1692," *Eurasian Studies* 3 (2004): 35–63, 50–63.

44 Notulen [...] van de principale en voornaemste saecken en belangen van d'edele Compagnie in de ambassade aan't hoff van den koning van Persia, 1690 (NA, VOC 1476, fol. 376–95, 378r/v, 382r–3r, 389v).

45 Babayan, *Mystics, Monarchs, and Messiahs*, 356, 405–6.

46 Abisaab, *Converting Persia*, 56, 71–2.

47 Henry Corbin, *L'École d'Isfahan: L'École shaykhie; Le Douzième Imâm* (Paris: Gallimard, 1972), 7–201.
48 *Abisaab, Converting Persia*, 121–38; *Babayan, Mystics, Monarchs, and Messiahs*, 407–8, 410–12, 471–2, 484–5; Leonard Lewisohn, "Sufism and the School of Iṣfahān: *Taṣawwuf* and *ʿirfān* in Late Safavid Iran (ʿAbd al-Razzāq Lāhījī and Fayḍ-i Kāshānī on the Relation of *taṣawwuf, hikmat* and *ʿirfān*)," in *The Heritage of Sufism*, vol. 3: *Late Classical Persianate Sufism (1501–1750): The Safavid and Mughal Period*, ed. L. Lewisohn and David Morgan (Oxford: Oneworld, 1999); and Andrew J. Newman, "Clerical Perceptions of Sufi Practices in Late Seventeenth-Century Persia: Arguments over the Permissibility of Singing (*Ghinā*)," in ibid.
49 Relatione della prima audienza […], 1621 (APF, SC. Mesopotamia e Persia. Caldei e Latini, vol. 1, fol. 33r–9v, 34v–9v).
50 On debates about free will within Shi'ism, see Daniel Gimaret, "Free Will, I. In Twelver Shiʿism, II. In Isma'ili Shiʿism," in *Encyclopaedia Iranica* online. Article published Dec. 15, 2000; last updated Jan. 31, 2012. http://www.iranicaonline.org/articles/free-will-.
51 On this, see Muzaffar Alam and Sanjay Subrahmanyam, "Catholics and Muslims in the Court of Jahangir (1608–1611)," in their *Writing the Mughal World: Studies on Culture and Politics* (New York: Columbia University Press, 2011).
52 See Hugues Didier, "Muslim Heterodoxy, Persian Murtaddun and Jesuit Missionaries at the Court of King Akbar (1580–1605)," *The Heythrop Journal* 49 (2008): 898–939.
53 Gauvin Alexander Bailey, "'The Truth-Showing Mirror': Jesuit Catechism and the Arts in Mughal India," in *The Jesuits: Cultures, Sciences, and the Arts, 1540–1773*, ed. John W. O'Malley, G. A. Bailey, Steven J. Harris, and T. Frank Kennedy (Toronto: University of Toronto Press, 1999).
54 Juan Thadeo de San Eliseo to [Fernando de Santa María ?], n.p., n.d. [probably Aug. 1608] (AGOCD, 236/a).
55 Juan Thadeo de San Eliseo to [Fernando de Santa María], Isfahan, Feb. 12, 1616 (AGOCD, 237/m/8).
56 Juan Thadeo de San Eliseo to Benigno di San Michele, Isfahan, Mar. 26, 1616 (AGOCD, 237/m/9).
57 Nota delli libri portati di Persia […], n.p., n.d. (APF, SOCG, vol. 209, fol. 355r/v).
58 Della Valle, [Diario di viaggio], 1614–26 (here Aug. 28, 1617) (BAV, Ottob. lat. 3382, fol. 1r–260r, 77v–8v). On Della Valle's contacts with scholars in Lār who had shared astronomical interests on the subject, including the question of heliocentrism, see Avner Ben-Zaken, *Cross-Cultural Scientific Exchanges in the Eastern Mediterranean, 1560–1660* (Baltimore: Johns Hopkins University Press, 2010), 46–75.
59 Felice di Sant'Antonio to the General Chapter, Rome, Oct. 15, 1649 (AGOCD, 261/m/1).
60 Ange de Saint-Joseph, Gazophylacium linguae Persarum […] (Amsterdam, 1684), reproduced in Michel Bastiaensen, *Souvenirs de la Perse safavide et autres lieux d'Orient [1664–1678] en version persane et européenne* (Brussels: Éditions de l'Université de Bruxelles, 1985), 38–41, 120–1.
61 On this work, see the section "Priesthood, Medicine, and Miraculous Healing."
62 Ange de Saint-Joseph to [Jean Chrysostome de Saint-Paul], [Isfahan], addendum of Jan. 18, 1676 to a letter begun on an earlier date (AGOCD, 236/b/20).
63 See, for example, Brockey, *Journey to the East*, 15–16, 34–5, 46–8, 52, 58–60, 75–8, 257–8, 284–94, 410–11; Hsia, *Sojourners in a Strange Land*.

64 Jean-Baptiste Tavernier, *Les six voyages [...] qu'il a faits en Turquie, en Perse, et aux Indes [...]* (Paris, 1676), vol. 1, 465, 482. On the instruments constructed by Friar Raphaël, see David A. King, *World-Maps for Finding the Direction and Distance to Mecca: Innovation and Tradition in Islamic Science* (Leiden: Brill, 1999), 312–17.

65 Raphaël du Mans to Kaempfer, Isfahan, Sept. 19, 1685, reproduced in Engelbert Kaempfer, *Briefe, 1683-1715*, ed. Detlef Haberland (Munich: Iudicium, 2001), 218–19.

66 [Nicolas Frizon and Jacques Villotte], *Voyages d'un missionnaire de la Compagnie de Jésus en Turquie, en Perse, en Arménie, en Arabie, et en Barbarie* (Paris, 1730), 442–6.

67 Juan Thadeo de San Eliseo to [Fernando de Santa María ?], n.p., n.d. [probably Aug. 1608] (AGOCD, 236/a/2).

68 Próspero del Espíritu Santo to Mathías de San Francisco, Isfahan, Dec. 2, 1621; and to Paolo Simone di Gesù Maria, Isfahan, Sept. 23, 1623 (AGOCD, 238/d/9, 10 and 21), reproduced in *Próspero del Espíritu Santo (1583-1653): Relaciones y cartas*, ed. Zubizarreta (Rome: Teresianum, 2006), 489, 535–56.

69 Cf. Corbin, *L'École d'Isfahan*, 54–122; Reza Pourjavady and Sabine Schmidtke, "An Eastern Renaissance? Greek Philosophy under the Safavids (16th–18th Centuries AD)," *Intellectual History of the Islamicate World* 3 (2015): 248–90; Sajjad H. Rizvi, *Mullā Ṣadrā Shīrāzī: His Life and Works and the Sources for Safavid Philosophy* (Oxford: OUP, 2007); and Mathieu Terrier, "La représentation de la sagesse grecque comme discours et mode de vie chez les philosophes šīʿites de l'Iran safavide (XIᵉ/XVIIᵉ siècles)," *Studia graeco-arabica* 5 (2015): 299–320.

70 António de Gouveia, *Jornada [...]* (Coimbra, 1606), fol. 147r.

71 Babayan, *Mystics, Monarchs, and Messiahs*, 439–48. On the coffeehouses as sites of free conversation, see Chardin, *Voyages*, vol. 4, 67–9.

72 The works by Muslim and Christian authors that emerged from the debates on religion, each seeking to refute the arguments of the other side, provide written evidence of these discussions. See Dennis Halft, "A Newly Discovered Persian Treatise on Biblical 'Proofs' of Muḥammad's Prophethood (ca. 1702) by a Missionary Convert to Šīʿī Islam," *Mélanges de l'Institut dominicain d'études orientales* 35 (2020): 137–60, and "The Arabic Vulgate"; Francis Richard, "Catholicisme et Islam chiite au 'Grand Siècle': Autour de quelques documents concernant les Missions catholiques en Perse au XVIIᵉ siècle," *Euntes docete* 33 (1980): 339–403; and Alberto Tiburcio, *Muslim-Christian Polemics in Safavid Iran* (Edinburgh: Edinburgh University Press, 2020). On missionaries' contacts with Sunni Muslims in the Syrian provinces of the Ottoman Empire, see Bernard Heyberger, "Polemic Dialogues between Christians and Muslims in the Seventeenth Century," *Journal of the Economic and Social History of the Orient* 55 (2012): 281–302. For an overview, see the contributions in David Thomas and John Chesworth, eds., *Ottoman and Safavid Empires (1600-1700)* (Leiden: Brill, 2017).

73 Della Valle to Schipano, Isfahan, Apr. 22 and May 5, 1619, in Della Valle, *Viaggi*, Parte seconda: *La Persia*, vol. 1, 345.

74 Della Valle to Schipano, Isfahan, Sept. 24, 1621, in Della Valle, *Viaggi*, Parte seconda: *La Persia*, vol. 2, 253–4.

75 On Mīr Dāmād and Aḥmad ʿAlawī, see Corbin, *L'École d'Isfahan*, 9–53; Halft, "The Arabic Vulgate," 98–142.

76 On the content of the response, see Halft, "The Arabic Vulgate," 126–33.

77 See Hava Lazarus-Yafeh, *Intertwined Worlds: Medieval Islam and Bible Criticism* (Princeton: Princeton University Press, 1992), 50–74.

78 Gabriel de Paris to the *Propaganda Fide*, Isfahan, Mar. 6, 1635 (APF, SOCG, vol. 135, fol. 502r).
79 Richard, "Catholicisme et Islam chiite," 345–8.
80 Ibid., 383–95.
81 Redempto de la Cruz, Relación de algunas cosas hechas en la Persia [...], 1617 (AGOCD, 234/d, fol. 7v).
82 Chézaud to the *assistant de France*, Isfahan, Dec. 16, 1661 (ARSI, Gallia, 97 II, doc. 111, fol. 320r).
83 According to Thomas Bauer, writing about societies shaped by Sunni Islam. Bauer, *A Culture of Ambiguity*, 130–7.
84 Instruttione per gli nostri padri [...] che si manda d'ordine del definitorio generale del 1630 a 6 di Jenaro, signed by Fernando de Santa María (AGOCD, 289/e/1).
85 Pedro dos Santos, Breve relatione delli servitii [...], n.d. [1640], reproduced in Carlos Alonso, "Stato delle missioni agostiniane nelle Indie orientali secondo una relazione inedita del 1640," *Analecta Augustiniana* 25 (1962): 290–325, 321–2.
86 Richard, *Raphaël du Mans*, vol. 1, 33–4.
87 Faustino di San Carlo to the *Definitorium generale*, Isfahan, May 26, 1721 (AGOCD, 238/g/9).
88 Brentjes, "The Interests," 457–60.
89 Raphaël du Mans to Kaempfer, [Isfahan], Sept. 19 and Oct. 8, 1685, reproduced in Kaempfer, *Briefe*, 218–19, 230–1.
90 Description des présents [...], n.p., n.d. (ARSI, Gallia, 97 II, doc. 102, fol. 299r–303v).
91 Kaempfer to Johan Bergenhielm, Šamāḫi, Apr. 12 and 22, 1684, and to Georg Weijer, Isfahan, Oct. 1, 1685, reproduced in Kaempfer, *Briefe*, 167, 226–8.
92 Miscellanea d'alcune historiette [...] raccolte [...] da F. C[ornelio] di S. Giuseppe Carmelitano Scalzo. Centuria quinta, n.p. [Bushehr], n.d. [probably 1767] (BA, L 13 suss., fol. 99v).
93 Belchior dos Anjos, Relação das cousas da cristandade [...], n.p., n.d. [1605], reproduced in Roberto Gulbenkian, *L'ambassade en Perse de Luis Pereira de Lacerda et des Pères Portugais de l'Ordre de Saint-Augustin, Belchior dos Anjos et Guilherme de Santo Agostinho* (Lisbon: Comité national portugais pour la célébration du 2500[e] anniversaire de la fondation de la monarchie en Perse, 1972), 81, 143.
94 Paolo Simone di Gesù Maria, Descrizione di Persia, n.p., n.d. (AGOCD, 234/b/2).
95 Franz Caspar Schillinger, *Persianische und Ost-Indianische Reis [...]* (Nuremberg, 1707), 241–2.
96 Cornelio di San Giuseppe, Memorie concernenti alla Chiesa e diocesi di Persia, n.p., n.d. (BA, H 136 suss., fol. 177r).
97 Paolo Simone di Gesù Maria, Descrizione di Persia, n.p., n.d. (AGOCD, 234/b/2).
98 See Frederick William Hasluck, *Christianity and Islam under the Sultans*, 2 vols. (Oxford: Clarendon Press, 1929), vol. 1, 63–74. For reflections on the various forms of convergence, see Benjamin Z. Kedar, "Convergences of Oriental Christian, Muslim, and Frankish Worshippers: The Case of Saydnaya," in De Sion exibit lex et verbum domini de Hierusalem: *Essays on Medieval Law, Liturgy, and Literature in Honour of Ammon Linder*, ed. Yitzhak Hen (Turnhout: Brepols, 2001); Dorothea Weltecke, "Multireligiöse Loca Sancta und die mächtigen Heiligen der Christen," *Der Islam: Zeitschrift für Geschichte und Kultur des islamischen Orients* 88 (2011): 73–95.
99 Della Valle to Schipano, Isfahan, Apr. 4, 1620, in Della Valle, *Viaggi*, Parte seconda: La Persia, vol. 2, 101–4.

100 Próspero del Espíritu Santo to Fernando de Santa María, Isfahan, Sept. 29, 1621 (AGOCD, 238/d), reproduced in Próspero del Espíritu Santo, *Relaciones y cartas*, 476.
101 Bembo, *Il viaggio in Asia*, 383.
102 Chardin, *Voyages*, vol. 3, 409, vol. 4, 440–1.
103 See Laurence Moulinier-Brogi, "Un aspect particulier de la médecine des religieux après le XIIe siècle: L'attrait pour l'astrologie médicale," in *Médecine et religion: Compétitions, collaborations, conflits (XIIe–XXe siècles)*, ed. Maria Pia Donato, Luc Berlivet, Sara Cabibbo, Raimondo Michetti, and Marilyn Nicoud (Rome: École française de Rome, 2013).
104 In France, the authorities and population expected the Discalced Carmelites to provide medical remedies and minister to the sick. Sinicropi, "D'oraison et d'action," 273–84. On the Jesuits in Europe and the foreign missions, cf. Sabine Anagnostou, *Missionspharmazie: Konzepte, Praxis, Organisation und wissenschaftliche Ausstrahlung* (Stuttgart: Franz Steiner, 2011), 89–115.
105 Elisa Andretta, *Roma medica: Anatomie d'un système médical au XVIe siècle* (Rome: École française de Rome, 2011).
106 On the connection between medicine and the Jesuit mission in India, see Županov, *Missionary Tropics*, 195–231, and "Conversion, Illness and Possession: Catholic Missionary Healing in Early Modern South Asia," in *Divins remèdes: Médecine et religion en Asie du Sud*, ed. I.G. Županov and Caterina Guenzi (Paris: Éditions de l'EHESS, 2008).
107 Della Valle to Francesco Crescenzi, Isfahan, Dec. 29, 1618 (BAV, Ottob. lat. 3383, fol. 77v).
108 Miscellanea d'alcune historiette [...] raccolte [...] da F. C[ornelio] di S. Giuseppe Carmelitano Scalzo. Centuria ottava, n.p. [probably Bushehr], n.d. [probably 1767] (BA, L 13 suss., fol. 120r).
109 Chardin, *Voyages*, vol. 4, 75–6.
110 Ange de Saint-Joseph, *Pharmacopoea persica ex idiomate persico in Latinum conversa [...]* (Paris, 1681), 5, 7, 35–7.
111 Ibid., 11–25.
112 This is consistent with findings on the Italian and French context. See, for example, David Gentilcore, *Healers and Healing in Early Modern Italy* (Manchester: Manchester University Press, 1998), esp. 1–28 and 203–10; Albrecht Burkardt, *Les clients des saints: Maladie et quête du miracle à travers les procès de canonisation de la première moitié du XVIIe siècle en France* (Rome: École française de Rome, 2004).
113 Ange de Saint-Joseph, *Pharmacopoea persica*, 8–10.
114 Ange de Saint-Joseph, *Gazophylacium linguae Persarum*, reproduced in Bastiaensen, *Souvenirs de la Perse safavide*, 164–5.
115 From the seventeenth century on, when the Church was considering canonizations, virtually the only miracles recognized as such were the cures that physicians could not explain according to their scientific knowledge. See Lorraine Daston, "Marvelous Facts and Miraculous Evidence in Early Modern Europe," in *Superstition and Magic in Early Modern Europe: A Reader*, ed. Helen L. Parish (London: Bloomsbury Academic, 2015), esp. 124–5; Jacalyn Duffin, *Medical Miracles: Doctors, Saints, and Healing in the Modern World* (New York: OUP, 2009), esp. 15–35, 71–111; Gianna Pomata, "Malpighi and the Holy Body: Medical Experts and Miraculous Evidence in Seventeenth-Century Italy," *Renaissance Studies* 21 (2007): 568–86; and Fernando Vidal, "Miracles, Science and Testimony in Post-Tridentine Saint-Making," *Science in Context* 20 (2007): 481–508.

116 Thiessen, *Die Kapuziner*, 330. Cf. Gentilcore, *Healers and Healing*, 156–202. On the diversity of local practices of holiness, see Sidler, *Heiligkeit aushandeln*.
117 Thiessen, *Die Kapuziner*, 320–63, quotations: 321, 330. Protestants, in turn, used the accounts of "false" and "invented" miracles to stamp the Catholic Church as a "false" church. Helen L. Parish, "'Lying Histories Fayning False Miracles': Magic, Miracles and Medieval History in Reformation Polemic," in *Superstition and Magic*, ed. Parish.
118 Cf. Alexandra Walsham, "Miracles and the Counter-Reformation Mission to England," *The Historical Journal* 46 (2003): 779–815, and "In Sickness and in Health: Medicine and Inter-Confessional Relations in Post-Reformation England," in *Living with Religious Diversity in Early-Modern Europe*, ed. C. Scott Dixon, Dagmar Freist, and Mark Greengrass (Farnham: Ashgate, 2009).
119 On the clericalization of exorcism in the sixteenth and early seventeenth centuries, see Brian P. Levack, *The Devil Within: Possession & Exorcism in the Christian West* (New Haven: Yale University Press, 2013), 85–93; Moshe Sluhovsky, *Believe Not Every Spirit: Possession, Mysticism & Discernment in Early Modern Catholicism* (Chicago: University of Chicago Press, 2007), 61–93.
120 On the translation to Isfahan of two relics of Teresa of Ávila, see José de Jesús María to Juan Thadeo de San Eliseo, Madrid, Mar. 12, 1618 (AGOCD, 233/d/18).
121 Miscellanea d'alcune historiette [...] raccolte [...] da F. C[ornelio] di S. Giuseppe Carmelitano Scalzo. Centuria quinta, n.p. [Bushehr], n.d. [probably 1767], fol. 102v–3v.
122 Ibid., fol. 103v–4r.
123 Pedro dos Santos, Breve relatione delli servitii [...], n.d. [1640], reproduced in Alonso, "Stato delle missioni," 308–9.
124 On the Syrian provinces, see Heyberger, *Les Chrétiens du Proche-Orient*, 321, 351–3.
125 Ignazio di Gesù to Paolo Simone di Gesù Maria, Shiraz, Nov. 30, 1634 (AGOCD, 238/r/1).
126 Denis de la Couronne d'Épines, Relatione dell'administratione del Santo Battesimo [...] fatta nel 1650; Relatione d'alcune cose [...], n.p., n.d. [1650] (AGOCD, 235/d/1 and 2).
127 Briève relation des missions [...], faite en l'année 1656, par le R. Père Alexandre de Saint-Sylvestre, Carme déchaussé, reproduced in Antoine Rabbath, *Documents inédits pour servir à l'histoire du christianisme en Orient (XVIe–XIXe siècle)*, vol. 1 (in 3 fascicles) (Paris: A. Picard & fils, Leipzig: Otto Harrassowitz, and London: Luzac, 1905-7), 432–43, 438–40.
128 Relatione delle missioni [...], fatta dal Padre Valerio di S. Giuseppe [...], Rome, Mar. 26, 1671 (APF, SC. Mesopotamia e Persia. Caldei e Latini, vol. 1, fol. 252r–73v, 263v–4r).
129 De Rhodes to Pierre Le Cazre, Isfahan, Feb. 16, 1657 (ARSI, Gallia, 97 I, doc. 103, fol. 305r/v).
130 Gabriel de Chinon, *Relations nouvelles du Levant [...]* (Lyon, 1671), 174–5.
131 Dominicus a Sancto Nicolao to Isidore de Saint-Joseph, Isfahan, Jan. 17, 1649 (AGOCD, 237/g/1). On Piromalli, see Chapter 4, "Confessional Agitators with Rome's Approval."
132 Relatione dell'administratione del Santo Battesimo [...] fatta nel 1650; Stefano di Gesù to ?, Isfahan, Nov. 18, 1650 (AGOCD, 235/d/1 and 2).
133 *Feria IV*, Oct. 1, 1659 (ACDF, SO, Dubia circa Baptismum, vol. 1: 1618–98, XXVII, fol. 530r–1v).
134 *Feria IV*, Mar. 22, 1683 (ACDF, SO, Dubia circa Baptismum, vol. 1: 1618–98, XXII, fol. 421r, 422r, 492r). On the formula "nihil esse respondendum," see

Chapter 7, "Truth Claims and Limits to Norm Enforcement: The Practice of Avoiding Decisions."

135 Chardin, *Voyages*, vol. 7, 438.
136 [Frizon and Villotte], *Voyages d'un missionnaire*, 179.
137 Miscellanea d'alcune historiette [...] raccolte [...] da F. C[ornelio] di S. Giuseppe Carmelitano Scalzo. Centuria quinta, n.p. [Bushehr], n.d. [1767] (BA, L 13 suss., fol. 104v).
138 Ibid., fol. 105v–6v.
139 See Ata Anzali, *"Mysticism" in Iran: The Safavid Roots of a Modern Concept* (Columbia: University of South Carolina Press, 2017), esp. 24–116; Newman, "Clerical Perceptions."
140 This was the tenor of the disdainful account in Raphaël du Mans's 1660 *État de la Perse*, reproduced in Richard, *Raphaël du Mans*, vol. 2, 169–70.
141 Tiburcio, *Muslim-Christian Polemics*, 24–9.
142 Louis-Marie Pidou de Saint-Olon to his brother [François Pidou], seigneur de Saint-Olon, Isfahan, Oct. 25, 1697, reproduced in Carlos Alonso, "El convento agustiniano de Ispahan durante el período 1690–1702," *Analecta Augustiniana* 57 (1983): 141–84. On the writings of the convert, see Tiburcio, *Muslim-Christian Polemics*, cf. Halft, "A Newly Discovered Persian Treatise."
143 António do Desterro to [Nicola Serani], Isfahan, Dec. 21, 1699, reproduced in Alonso, "El convento agustiniano de Ispahan," 175.
144 Noronha de Albuquerque, Conde de Vila Verde, to Peter II, Goa, Dec. 28, 1697 (DAAG, 70: Monções, vol. 61, fol. 196r).
145 Consultations of the *Conselho do Estado* on Jan. 14, 1702, reproduced in *Assentos do Conselho do Estado*, vol. 5: *1696–1750*, ed. Panduronga S.S. Pissurlencar (Bastorá: Tipografía Rangel, 1957), 130.
146 Galisson to Brisacier, Isfahan, Feb. 3, and Feb. 24, 1712 (MEP, vol. 354, 397–8, 400–402).
147 Galisson to Brisacier, Isfahan, June 2, 1712 (MEP, vol. 354, 455bis).
148 Galisson to Brisacier, Isfahan, May 24 and June 1, 1712 (MEP, vol. 354, 451, 494).
149 Informacione do convento de Santo Agostino em a cidade de Aspan pera o Rev[mo] e dignissimo Padre Geral de toda la Ordem Agustiniana, 1700, reproduced in Alonso, "El convento agustiniano de Ispahan," 178–80.
150 Chardin, *Voyages*, vol. 6, 155–6.
151 Hsia, "Translating Christianity," 94.
152 Gregorio Orsini, De statu Christianae Religionis [...], 1626, reproduced in Ambrosius Eszer, "Der Bericht des Gregorio Orsini O.P. über die Länder des Nahen und Mittleren Ostens," *Archivum Fratrum Praedicatorum* 44 (1974): 305–97, 342–3.
153 Heyberger, *Les Chrétiens du Proche-Orient*, 155–60.
154 Cf. Bernard Heyberger, "Peuples 'sans loi, sans foi, ni prêtre': Druzes et nusayrîs de Syrie redécouverts par les missionnaires catholiques (XVIIe–XVIIIe siècles)," in *L'Islam des marges: Mission chrétienne et espaces périphériques du monde musulman, XVIe–XXe siècles*, ed. B. Heyberger and Rémy Madinier (Paris: Éditions Karthala/IISMM, 2011).
155 Maurus Reinkowski has spoken in this connection of "metadoxy" as a state of pre-dogmatic ambiguity. Reinkowski, "Keine Kryptoreligion, aber doch kryptoreligiös: Zur Frage einer realen Existenz von Kryptojuden und Kryptochristen im islamisch geprägten Mittelmeerraum und Nahen Osten," in *Konfessionelle Ambiguität: Uneindeutigkeit und Verstellung als religiöse Praxis in der Frühen Neuzeit*, ed. Andreas Pietsch and Barbara Stollberg-Rilinger (Gütersloh: Gütersloher Verlagshaus, 2013),

esp. 79–80. See also Molly Greene, *A Shared World: Christians and Muslims in the Early-Modern Mediterranean* (Princeton: Princeton University Press, 2000); Lucette Valensi, "Inter-Communal Relations and Changes in Religious Affiliation in the Middle East (17th to 19th Centuries)," *Comparative Studies in Society and History* 39 (1997): 251–69.
156 Bauer, *A Culture of Ambiguity*, 13–14, cf. 268–74.
157 On the connections between the formation of confessional identities and the negative depictions of the Ottomans, cf. Johnson, *Cultural Hierarchy*.

Chapter 4

1 Antoine Arnauld, *La perpétuité de la foi de l'Église catholique touchant l'Eucharistie […]*, vol. 3 (Paris: 1674), 776–83, quotation: 778. On the preoccupation with the Eastern churches in the context of the controversies between Catholics and Protestants, see Aurélien Girard, "Le christianisme oriental (XVIIe–XVIIIe siècles): Essor de l'orientalisme catholique en Europe et construction des identités confessionnelles au Proche-Orient" (doctoral thesis, EPHE, Paris, 2011), 62–83; Alastair Hamilton, "From East to West: Jansenists, Orientalists, and the Eucharistic Controversy," in *How the West Was Won: Essays on Literary Imagination, the Canon, and the Christian Middle Ages for Burcht Pranger*, ed. Willemien Otten, Arjo Vanderjagt, and Hent de Vries (Leiden: Brill, 2010); Rémi Snoeks, *L'argument de la tradition dans la controverse eucharistique entre catholiques et réformés français au XVIIe siècle* (Louvain: Publications universitaires de Louvain and Gembloux: Éditions J. Duculot, 1951), 205–6, 223–5, 269–78, 286–90, 346–8, 357–62, 374–82.
2 See Bernard Heyberger, "Monachisme oriental, catholicisme et érudition (XVIIe–XXe siècles)," in *Monachismes d'Orient: Images, échanges, influences; Hommage à Antoine Guillaumont*, ed. Florence Jullien and Marie-Joseph Pierre (Turnhout: Brepols, 2011).
3 On the Armenian Church's rejection of the Council of Chalcedon, see Nina Garsoïan, *L'Église arménienne et le grand schisme d'Orient* (Louvain: Peeters, 1999), esp. 401–9.
4 Peter Halfter, *Das Papsttum und die Armenier im Frühen und Hohen Mittelalter: Von den ersten Kontakten bis zur Fixierung der Kirchenunion im Jahre 1198* (Cologne: Böhlau, 1996), 68–84, 122–43, 164–70, 177–81, 221–32, 297–303, 307–30. For the Latin historiography of the twelfth to fourteenth century, the fact that the Armenians were non-Chalcedonians played a lesser role than differences in liturgical practice. See Anna-Dorothee van den Brincken, *Die "Nationes Christianorum orientalium" im Verständnis der lateinischen Historiographie von der Mitte des 12. bis in die zweite Hälfte des 14. Jahrhunderts* (Cologne: Böhlau, 1974), 181–210.
5 Jean Richard, *La Papauté et les missions d'Orient au Moyen Âge (XIIIe–XVe siècles)* (Rome: École française de Rome, 1977), 167–225. Cf. Marcus Antonius van den Oudenrijn, "Uniteurs et Dominicains d'Arménie," *Oriens Christianus* 40 (1956): 94–112; 42 (1958): 110–33; 43 (1959): 110–19; 45 (1961): 95–108; 46 (1962): 99–116.
6 On the Council of Florence and the Armenians, see Joseph Gill, *The Council of Florence* (Cambridge: CUP, 1959), 305–10.
7 Heyberger, *Les Chrétiens du Proche-Orient*, 235–9; Wilhelm de Vries, *Rom und die Patriarchate des Ostens* (Freiburg im Br.: Karl Alber, 1963), 226–32.
8 Maria Teresa Fattori, *Benedetto XIV e Trento: Tradurre il Concilio nel Settecento* (Stuttgart: Anton Hiersemann, 2015), 203–29.

9   Belchior dos Anjos, Relação das cousas da cristandade [...], n.p., n.d. [1605], reproduced in Gulbenkian, *L'ambassade en Perse*, 83–5, 145–6.
10 Ibid., 84, 93–4, 145, 150–1.
11 Roberto B. Gulbenkian, "Relações religiosas entre os Arménios e os Agostinhos portugueses na Pérsia no século XVII," *Anais da Academia Portuguesa da História*, n.s., 37 (1989): 303–52, 314.
12 Paolo Simone di Gesù Maria, Relatione di Persia, n.p., n.d. (AGOCD, 234/b/1).
13 Juan Thadeo de San Eliseo to [Fernando de Santa María ?], n.p., n.d. [probably Aug. 1608] (AGOCD, 236/a/2).
14 Pacifique de Provins, *Le voyage de Perse*, 225–44, 226.
15 Juan Thadeo de San Eliseo to [Fernando de Santa María ?], n.p., n.d. [probably Aug. 1608] (AGOCD, 236/a/2).
16 Heyberger, *Les Chrétiens du Proche-Orient*, 139–40.
17 Juan Thadeo de San Eliseo to Benigno di San Michele, Isfahan, Mar. 26, 1616 (AGOCD, 237/m/9). On Ḫwāğa Safar, see Herzig, "The Armenian Merchants," 84–5, 97, 207–8.
18 Della Valle, [Diario di viaggio], May 26 and Oct. 19, 1617 (BAV, Ottob. lat. 3382, fol. 1r–260r, 74v–5r, 80r/v).
19 Dimas della Croce to Benigno di San Michele, Isfahan, Dec. 31, 1618 (AGOCD, 237/b/2).
20 Juan Thadeo de San Eliseo to [Domingo de Jesús María], Isfahan, Jan. 3, 1619 (AGOCD, 237/m/14 and 15).
21 Della Valle to Schipano, Baghdad, Dec. 23, 1616, in Della Valle, *Viaggi [...], Parte prima: La Turchia* (Rome, 1650), 744, 746. On Maani Gioerida [Ǧuwairī] and her family, see John Gurney, "Della Valle, Pietro," in *Encyclopaedia Iranica* online. Article published Dec. 15, 1994; last updated Nov. 21, 2011. http://www.iranicaonline.org/articles/della-valle.
22 Della Valle to Schipano, Isfahan, Apr. 22 and May 8, 1619, in Della Valle, *Viaggi*, Parte seconda: *La Persia*, vol. 1, 466–72.
23 [Ordinationes], by Vicente de San Francisco, Isfahan, Sept. 22, 1621 (AGOCD, 235/l/1 and 236/a/14).
24 Instruttione per gli nostri padri [...] che si manda d'ordine del definitorio generale del 1630 a 6 di Jenaro, signed by Fernando de Santa María (AGOCD, 289/e/1).
25 On Vardapet Moses, see Ghougassian, *The Emergence of the Armenian Diocese*, 87–9.
26 Próspero del Espíritu Santo, Compendio [...] dall'anno 1621 fino a questo presente 1624, reproduced in Próspero del Espíritu Santo, *Relaciones y cartas*, 92–102.
27 Eugenio di San Benedetto to the *Propaganda Fide*, Relatione delle missioni de' Carmelitani scalzi [...], n.p., n.d. [probably 1627] (AGOCD, 234/k/1).
28 Dimas della Croce to [?], Isfahan, July 20, 1631 (AGOCD, 237/b/41).
29 Discorso del Segretario intorno alla missione di Persia [...], 1625 (APF, SOCG, vol. 209, fol. 45v).
30 Dimas della Croce to Ludovico Ludovisi, Isfahan, Nov. 25, 1629 (APF, SOCG, vol. 73, fol. 239r/v).
31 Istruttione per li due vescovi [...], approved by the Congregation on Nov. 8, 1623 (APF, Istruzioni diverse, 1623–38, fol. 181v).
32 Robert Stodart, *The Journal of Robert Stodart: Being an Account of His Experiences as a Member of Sir Dodmore Cotton's Mission in Persia in 1628–29*, ed. E. Denison Ross (London: Luzac, 1935), 70.

33 Juan Thadeo de San Eliseo, Sommario della lettera del Patriarcha Moyse […], n.p., n.d. (AGOCD, 236/a/8); Interpretatio epistolae lingua armena scriptae Summo Pontifici a Moise Archiepiscopo, a Cacciatur episcopo, et ab Aristaches vartapiet, n.p., n.d. (AGOCD, 236/a/25).
34 Dimas della Croce to [Antonio Barberini], Isfahan, May 11, 1638 (APF, SOCG, vol. 118, fol. 160v).
35 Dubia missionariorum Persiae cum responsionibus secretarii Ingoli, n.d. [1643] (APF, SOCG, vol. 209, fol. 77r/v).
36 Jan. 28, 1637 (ACDF, Dubia circa baptismum, vol. 1: 1618–98, fol. 177r–84v).
37 Copia della lettera de' vescovi di Giulfa in Persia, New Julfa, Oct. 13, 1698 (APF, SC. Armeni, vol. 4, 555r/v, 558r–9r). In referring to themselves as "dottori e vescovi," the three vardapets followed a widespread European terminology. The "diletto, e fedele Signor Agha" was probably Paron Agha di Matus, who rose in Italy from *commenda* agent to a position as a rich merchant in his own right. In 1698 he played a leading role in the Armenian community of Livorno. That same year he was granted several papal honorary titles. Sebouh David Aslanian, "The Early Arrival of Print in Safavid Iran: New Light on the First Armenian Printing Press in New Julfa, Isfahan (1636–1650, 1686–1693)," *Handes Amsorya* 128 (2014): 381–468, 428–31, 434–9, 447–8.
38 Copia della lettera de' vescovi di Giulfa in Persia, New Julfa, Oct. 13, 1698 (APF, SC. Armeni, vol. 4, 558r/v).
39 On the various Eastern churches in the Syrian region from this perspective, see Heyberger, *Les Chrétiens du Proche-Orient*, 381–549.
40 Gulbenkian, "Relações religiosas," 315–21, and "Deux lettres surprenantes du Catholicos arménien David IV à Philippe III d'Espagne, II de Portugal, 1612–1614," in his *Estudos Históricos*, vol. 1: *Relações entre Portugal, Arménia e Médio Oriente* (Lisbon: Academia Portuguesa da História, 1995), 311–18, 327.
41 On these events in Lviv and Rome, see Gregorio Petrowicz, *L'unione degli Armeni di Polonia con la Santa Sede (1626–1686)* (Rome: Pontificium Institutum Orientalium Studiorum, 1950), 60–78, 206–13.
42 *Congregazione particolare,* Jan. 30, 1635 (APF, Acta, vol. 10, fol. 181v–4r; APF, SOCG, vol. 291, fol. 146r–51v).
43 Ambrosius Eszer, "Paolo-Angelo Cittadini O.P. (O. Cart.): Neue Forschungen zu seinem Leben und zur Geschichte des Erzbistums Naxijevan," *Archivum Fratrum Praedicatorum* 39 (1969): 336–423.
44 Relatione degl'errori della chiesa Armena fatta da fra Paolo Pyromallo […], n.d. [dealt with by the *Propaganda Fide* on June 22, 1637] (APF, SOCG, vol. 293, fol. 4r).
45 Paolo Piromalli to Ingoli, Isfahan, Mar. 9, 1647 (APF, SOCG, vol. 65, fol. 331v).
46 Valentin d'Angers to Ingoli, Isfahan, Sept. 4, 1647 (APF, SOCG, vol. 65, fol. 332r).
47 *Congregazione generale,* Jan. 19, 1644 (APF, Acta, vol. 16, fol. 11v–12r).
48 Denis de la Couronne d'Épines to Isidore de Saint-Joseph, Isfahan, Apr. 8, 1656 (AGOCD, 237/c/25).
49 Carlo Longo, *Silvestro Bendici: Un missionario calabrese del secolo XVII* (Rome: Istituto Storico Domenicano, 1998), 118, 129–52.
50 Francesco Maria di San Siro, Vita Venerabilis Patris Eliae a S. Alberto […], n.p., n.d. (AGOCD, 320/e).
51 Professio orthodoxa Reverendissimi Domini Michaelis Magistri et Episcopi Julpaensis […], n.p. [New Julfa], n.d. [1689] (AGOCD, 237/h/7).
52 Élie de Saint-Albert to the *Propaganda Fide,* Isfahan, May 20, 1689 (AGOCD, 237/h/6).

53 *Feria II*, Mar. 2, 1705; *Feria V*, May 14, 1705 (ACDF, SO, St.St., QQ 2 f, XXV, fol. 363r–4r).
54 De Vries, *Rom und die Patriarchate*, 226–32.
55 Élie de Saint-Albert to the *Propaganda Fide*, Isfahan, Aug. 21, 1684 (APF, SOCG, vol. 497, fol. 325r).
56 Élie de Saint-Albert to Francesco Barberini, n.p., n.d. [1696 or later] (MEP, vol. 353, 385–6).
57 Relatione della persecutione de' missionarii, et delli cattolici di Giulfa in Persia […] scritta dal loro superiore P. F. Elia di S. Alberto, n.p. [Isfahan], n.d. [1694] (AGOCD, 280/a/f).
58 *Congregazioni generali*, Mar. 15 and Apr. 26, 1706, and Aug. 22, 1707 (APF, Acta, vol. 76, fol. 67v–8r, 104v; vol. 77, fol. 274r/v).
59 Agnello dell'Immacolata Concezione to the *praepositus generalis* and the *definitores generales*, Shiraz, Oct. 26, 1684 (AGOCD, 238/k/1).
60 Relatione della persecutione de' missionarii, et delli cattolici di Giulfa […] scritta dal loro superiore P. F. Elia di S. Alberto, n.p. [Isfahan], n.d. [1694] (AGOCD, 280/a/f).
61 Basile de Saint-Charles to Carlo Agostino Fabroni, Isfahan, Feb. 2, 1700 (APF, SOCG, vol. 538, fol. 409r).
62 *Congregazioni generali*, Feb. 6 and 28, 1708 (APF, Acta, vol. 78, fol. 94v, 143v).
63 Arakʿel of Tabriz, *Book of History (Arakʿel Dawrizhetsʿi, Girkʿ patmutʿeantsʿ)*, ed. and trans. George A. Bournoutian (Costa Mesa: Mazda, 2010), 309–10, 316–18.
64 Aslanian, "The Early Arrival of Print," 402–22, and "Port Cities and Printers: Reflections on Early Modern Global Armenian Print Culture," *Book History* 17 (2014): 51–93, esp. 64–71.
65 Blaise de Nantes to Léonard de Paris, Isfahan, Feb. 25, 1640 (BNF, n.a.f. 10220, 432–3).
66 Ghougassian, *The Emergence of the Armenian Diocese*, 98, 100, 169–72.
67 Balthasar de Santa Maria to [Gioachino di Gesù Maria], Isfahan, Aug. 9, 1653 (AGOCD, 236/k/7).
68 Ghougassian, *The Emergence of the Armenian Diocese*, 142–3.
69 Aslanian, "The Early Arrival of Print," 422–48, 451–68. The Armenian printing shop in Constantinople equally received a boost from the controversies with the Catholic missionaries at around the same time, as did the one in Isfahan. See Raymond H. Kévorkian, "Le livre imprimé en milieu arménien ottoman aux XVIe–XVIIIe siècles," *Revue des mondes musulmans et de la Méditerranée* 87–8 (1999): 173–85.
70 Ghougassian, *The Emergence of the Armenian Diocese*, 106–11.
71 *Congregazioni generali*, Aug. 17, 1662 (APF, Acta, vol. 31, fol. 183r–4r), Jan. 23, 1663 (ibid., vol. 32, fol. 6v–9v).
72 [Frizon and Villotte], *Voyages d'un missionnaire*, 245–6.
73 Ghougassian, *The Emergence of the Armenian Diocese*, 121–2, 149–56.
74 Pierre d'Issoudun to [Giuseppe Sacripanti], Tabriz, June 30, 1707 (APF, SC. Mesopotamia e Persia. Caldei e Latini, vol. 2, fol. 513r–14r).
75 Louis-Marie Pidou de Saint-Olon to the *Propaganda Fide*, Hamadan, Oct. 23, 1711 (APF, SOCG, vol. 587, fol. 28r/v).
76 Galisson to Jérôme Phélypeaux, comte de Pontchartrain, n.p. [Isfahan], n.d. [1712] (MEP, vol. 354, 419).
77 Barnaba Fedeli di Milano to Sacripanti, Isfahan, Feb. 22, 1722 (APF, SC. Mesopotamia e Persia. Caldei e Latini, vol. 3, fol. 530r).

78 Fedeli di Milano to Vincenzo Petra, New Julfa, Nov. 17, 1727 (APF, SC. Mesopotamia e Persia. Caldei e Latini, vol. 3, 546r/v).
79 Filippo Maria di Sant'Agostino to Petra, Isfahan, Nov. 4, 1740 (APF, SOCG, vol. 708, fol. 165r–6v).
80 *Congregazione generale,* July 4, 1746 (APF, Acta, vol. 116, fol. 169r/v).
81 Cornelio di San Giuseppe, Memorie cronologiche […], n.p., n.d. (BA, & 211 sup., 115–16).
82 Cornelio di San Giuseppe, Minuta d'alcuni dubii […], n.p., n.d. (BA, H 136 suss., fol. 355v, 356r, 358r).
83 Dello Stato presente della Persia e di quelle Missioni. Relatione presentata alla S. Congregazione di Propaganda da Mr Cornelio di San Giuseppe […], 1772 (APF, Miscellanee varie, vol. 1, fol. 272v, 277v–8r).
84 Balthasar de Santa Maria to [Gioachino di Gesù Maria], Isfahan, Aug. 9, 1653 (AGOCD, 236/k/7).
85 Pietro Paolo di San Francesco to the *Propaganda Fide*, Bandar ʿAbbās, Apr. 1, 1700 (APF, SOCG, vol. 541, fol. 17v).
86 Joseph-Marie de Jésus to Sacripanti, Isfahan, Feb. 28, 1712 (APF, SOCG, vol. 587, fol. 134r).
87 On the Armenian merchants from New Julfa in Venice and Livorno, see Aslanian, *From the Indian Ocean*, 70–5, 150; Claudia Bonardi, "Gli Sceriman di Venezia da mercanti a possidenti," in *Ad limina Italiae/Ar druns Italioy: In viaggio per l'Italia con mercanti e monaci armeni,* ed. Boghos Levon Zekiyan (Padua: Editoriale Programma, 1996); Edmund Herzig, "Venice and the Julfa Armenian Merchants," in *Gli Armeni e Venezia: Dagli Sceriman a Mechitar; Il momento culminante di una consuetudine millenaria,* ed. Boghos Levon Zekiyan and Aldo Ferrari (Venice: Istituto veneto di Scienze, Lettere ed Arti, 2004); Evelyn Korsch, "The Sherimans and Cross-Cultural Trade in Gems: The Armenian Diaspora in Venice and Its Trading Networks in the First Half of the Eighteenth Century," in *Commercial Networks and European Cities, 1400–1800,* ed. Andrea Caracausi and Christof Jeggle (London: Pickering & Chatto, 2014).
88 Cf. Heyberger, *Les Chrétiens du Proche-Orient*, 408–23.
89 *Congregazioni generali,* June 23, July 28, and Aug. 26, 1692 (APF, Acta, vol. 62, fol. 136v, 150v–1r, 168r–9r, 173r).
90 Aslanian, *From the Indian Ocean*, 157, 163–4.
91 [Chick], *Chronicle,* vol. 1, 485–6, 649–54, 658, 679, 711.
92 The bull is reproduced in Donald Maxwell White, *Zaccaria Seriman (1709–1784) and the Viaggi di Enrico Wanton: A Contribution to the Study of Enlightenment in Italy* (Manchester: Manchester University Press, 1961), 14.
93 *Congregazione generale,* Dec. 15, 1670 (APF, Acta, vol. 40, fol. 278r).
94 *Congregazione generale,* Nov. 15, 1717 (APF, Acta, vol. 87, fol. 380v–1r).
95 *Congregazioni generali,* Jan. 22, June 12, and Aug. 6, 1714 (APF, Acta, vol. 84, fol. 90r/v, 345v–6r, 471r/v).
96 Meneses, conde da Ericeira, to John V, Goa, Jan. 10, 1719 (DAAG, 93: Monções, vol. 84B, fol. 277r).
97 *Congregazione generale,* Dec. 9, 1743 (APF, Acta, vol. 113, fol. 440v–2r).
98 Lorenzo and Sarat (Giacomo) Sceriman to the "Illustrissimi Signori Patroni" [probably Marcara and Gasparo Sceriman], Stefano and Basilio Sceriman in Venice, Lviv, May 8, 1704 (ASPD, Sceriman, not inventoried, no. 10, fol. 6r/v).
99 Sebouh David Aslanian, "Reader Response and the Circulation of Mkhitʻarist Books across the Armenian Communities of the Early Modern Indian Ocean," *Journal of the Society for Armenian Studies* 22 (2013): 31–70, 56–8.

100 *Feria IV*, Dec. 16, 1705 (ACDF, SO, Dispensationes variae, vol. 8, fol. 323v).
101 *Congregazione generale*, Nov. 13, 1713 (APF, Acta, vol. 83, fol. 624r/v).
102 Aslanian, *From the Indian Ocean*, 166–201.
103 Fedeli di Milano to Sacripanti, Isfahan, June 29, 1721 (ACDF, SO, St.St., M 3 a, xiv, fol. 290r).
104 This is how it is summarized in de Vries, *Rom und die Patriarchate*, 383.
105 Christian Jaser, *Ecclesia maledicens: Rituelle und zeremonielle Exkommunikationsformen im Mittelalter* (Tübingen: Mohr Siebeck, 2013), 370–3, quotation: 371.
106 On the history of the early modern reception of the bull with regard to the question of *communicatio in sacris*, see Santus, *Trasgressioni necessarie*, 169–96.
107 Lorenzo and Sarat (Giacomo) Sceriman to Gasparo, Stefano, and Basilio Sceriman in Venice, Isfahan, Apr. 15, 1701 (ASPD, Sceriman, not inventoried, no. 10, fol. 228r/v).
108 *Congregazione generale*, Jan. 22, 1714 (APF, Acta, vol. 84, fol. 90r/v, 92r/v).
109 *Congregazioni generali*, Nov. 13, 1713, and July 9, 1715 (APF, Acta, vol. 83, fol. 624r/v, vol. 85, fol. 383v–4v).
110 *Congregazioni generali*, Jan. 22, June 12, and Aug. 6, 1714 (APF, Acta, vol. 84, fol. 90r/v, 345v–6r, 471r/v).
111 Fedeli di Milano to Sacripanti, New Julfa, June 21, 1713 (APF, SC. Mesopotamia e Persia. Caldei e Latini, vol. 3, fol. 418r–19v).
112 *Congregazione generale*, May 5, 1732 (APF, Acta, vol. 102, fol. 247v–8r).
113 Gabriel de Chinon, *Relations nouvelles*, 306–36.
114 Chézaud to Claude Boucher, Isfahan, Mar. 25, 1663 (ARSI, Gallia, 97 II, doc. 115, fol. 328r).
115 Claude-Ignace Mercier to Claude Boucher, Isfahan, Jan. 16, 1669 (ARSI, Gallia, 97 II, doc. 125, fol. 345v–7r, quotation: 345v–6r).
116 [Frizon and Villotte], *Voyages d'un missionnaire*, 168, 419–20, 424–7.
117 Jean Boucher to Tirso González, Isfahan, Oct. 18, 1692 (ARSI, Gallia, 97 I, fol. 375v, 379r).
118 *Congregazioni generali*, Aug. 18, 1710 (APF, Acta, vol. 80, fol. 365r) and Jan. 12, 1711 (ibid., vol. 81, fol. 43r–4r).
119 *Congregazione generale*, Dec. 2, 1709 (APF, Acta, vol. 79, fol. 516r/v); memorandum by Jacques Villotte, n.p., n.d. (ARSI, Fondo Gesuitico, 720 II, no. 9).
120 *Congregazione generale*, Mar. 18, 1664 (APF, Acta, vol. 33, fol. 58r [quotation]–59r).
121 Circa missiones Armeniae quaeritur an possint Armeni Catholici, in Sacris communicare cum Armenis Haereticis, memorandum by Villotte, presented to Pope Clement XI, 1712 (ACDF, SO, St.St., UV 54, XXIX, fol. n.n.).
122 [Tadeusz Juda Krusiński], Informatio de missionibus persicis, n.p., n.d. [1727] (ARSI, Fondo Gesuitico, 720 II, no. 9).
123 On Sicard and Dubernat, see Hamilton, *The Copts and the West*, 85–7, 91, 159–62.
124 Informatione alla Sagra Congregatione del S. Uffitio fatta dal Pad. Mechitar Pietro […] circa la questione […] se sia lecito alli Cattolici di andare nelle Chiese delli Scismatici […], n.p., n.d. [1721] (ACDF, SO, St.St., M 3 a, xiv, fol. 338r–52v, 338v–42r).
125 John Whooley, "The Mekhitarists: Religion, Culture and Ecumenism in Armenian-Catholic Relations," in *Eastern Christianity: Studies in Modern History, Religion and Politics*, ed. Anthony O'Mahony (London: Melisende, 2004). On the position of Mekhitar and the Mekhitarists on the matter of *communicatio in sacris*, see Santus, *Trasgressioni necessarie*, esp. 386–97, 410–12, 421–7.

126 Circa missiones Armeniae quaeritur [...], memorandum by Villotte, presented to Pope Clement XI, 1712 (ACDF, SO, St.St., UV 54, xxix, fol. n.n.).
127 Richard, *Raphaël du Mans*, vol. 1, 54, 82.
128 Heyberger, *Les Chrétiens du Proche-Orient*, esp. 381-549. On the intensifying conflicts between Latin and Greek Christians, see Kallystos Timothy Ware, "Orthodox and Catholics in the Seventeenth Century: Schism or Intercommunion?" in *Schism, Heresy and Religious Protest*, ed. Derek Baker (Cambridge: CUP, 1972). According to him, the schism only began to affect everyday religious life in the second quarter of the eighteenth century.
129 See Chapter 7, "Doctrinal Disambiguation."
130 Chardin, *Voyages*, vol. 8, 116-17; Gabriel de Chinon, *Relations nouvelles*, 158-62; Adam Olearius, *Vermehrte Newe Beschreibung der Muscowitischen und Persischen Reyse [...]* (Schleswig, 1656), 520-4; Tavernier, *Les six voyages*, vol. 1, 540-8.
131 Similar findings emerge with regard to the treatment of orthodox neomartyrs in the Ottoman Empire. Krstič, *Contested Conversions*, 121-42.

Chapter 5

1   Vita e Memorie Cronologiche di Monsig^r Fra Cornelio Reina [...], "ordinate dal suo segretario p. Cesario di S. Antonio," Milan, July 30, 1797 (BA, P 181 sup., 163-4).
2   Cornelio di San Giuseppe, Memorie concernenti alla Chiesa e diocesi di Persia, n.p., n.d. (BA, H 136 suss., 119-20).
3   René J. Barendse, *The Arabian Seas 1700-1763*, 4 vols. (Leiden: Brill, 2009), vol. 1: *The Western Indian Ocean in the Eighteenth Century*, 221-73, vol. 4: *Europe in Asia, 1621-3*, 1634-6. Cf. Willem Floor, "The Dutch on Khark Island: A Commercial Mishap," *International Journal of Middle East Studies* 24 (1992): 441-60; Perry, *Karim Khan Zand*, 150-66; Thomas M. Ricks, *Notables, Merchants, and Shaykhs of Southern Iran and Its Ports: Politics and Trade of the Persian Gulf Region, AD 1728-1789* (Piscataway: Gorgias Press, 2012).
4   Cornelio di San Giuseppe, Memorie concernenti alla Chiesa e diocesi di Persia, n.p., n.d. (BA, H 136 suss., 93).
5   Cornelio di San Giuseppe, Memorie cronologiche [...], n.p., n.d. (BA, & 211 sup., 34).
6   For example, the participation of the Catholic laity or even missionaries in the banquet that the English consuls gave every year on the anniversary of Henry VIII's break with Rome and the establishment of the Church of England with himself as its head.
7   Cornelio di San Giuseppe, Minuta d'alcuni dubii [...], n.p., n.d. (BA, H 136 suss., fol. 353r, 359r).
8   See Barendse, *Arabian Seas 1700-1763*, vol. 3: *Men and Merchandise*, 1216-17. On the VOC trading posts in Southeast and South Asia, see Ulbe Bosma and Remco Raben, *Being "Dutch" in the Indies: A History of Creolisation and Empire, 1500-1920* (Singapore: NUS Press, and Athens, Ohio: Ohio University Press, 2008), 26-46; Carla van Wamelen, *Family Life onder de VOC: Een handelscompagnie in huwelijks- en gezinszaken* (Hilversum: Uitgeverij Verloren, 2014), esp. 367-97.
9   [Index baptizatorum], 1755-1843 (AGOCD, 484/a).
10 On the connection of the semantics of "friendship" and "good correspondence" in early modern foreign relations, see Weber, *Lokale Interessen und große Strategie*, 243-6.

11 See Chapter 2, "The European Powers in the Safavid System of Imperial Rule."
12 Jacopo di Santa Teresa to Della Valle, Isfahan, June 30, 1636 and Aug. 31, 1639 (AAV, Archivio Della Valle-Del Bufalo, 53, fol. 11v, 62r); Extrait d'un journal de Monseigneur [Pierre Lambert de La Motte] l'évêque de Béryte […], 1662 (ARSI, Gallia, 97 I, doc. 114, fol. 326r); François Pallu, Journal, [1662] (BNF, Mss. fr. 25063, 4007); *Congregazione generale*, Aug. 27, 1714 (APF, Acta, vol. 84, fol. 745v-6r).
13 Recent scholarship has underlined the significance of employees trading on their own account not just for themselves but also for the trading companies. See Chris Nierstrasz, "In the Shadow of the Companies: Empires of Trade in the Orient and Informal Entrepreneurship," in *Beyond Empires: Global, Self-Organizing, Cross-Imperial Networks, 1500–1800*, ed. Amelia Polónia and Cátia Antunes (Leiden: Brill, 2016).
14 De Bruyn, *Voyages*, vol. 1, 238–9.
15 Juan Thadeo de San Eliseo to [Fernando de Santa María ?], n.p., n.d. [probably Aug. 1608] (AGOCD, 236/a/2).
16 Pallu, Journal, [1662] (BNF, Mss. fr. 25063, 4007). On the presence of Dutch painters in the Safavid Empire, see Willem Floor, "Dutch Painters in Iran during the First Half of the 17th Century," *Persica* 8 (1979): 145–61; Amy S. Landau, "*Farangī-Sāzī* at Isfahan," 39–41, 115–18; Carolin Stolte, *Philip Angel's Deex-Autaers: Vaiṣṇava Mythology from Manuscript to Book Market in the Context of the Dutch East India Company, c. 1600–1672* (New Delhi: Manohar, 2012), 55–66. On the activities of clockmakers, see Willem Floor, "Clocks," in *Encyclopaedia Iranica* online. Article published Dec. 15, 1992; last updated Oct. 21, 2011. http://www.iranicaonline.org/articles/clocks-pers.
17 See Landau, "*Farangī-Sāzī* at Isfahan," 199–218; "Reconfiguring the Northern European Print to Depict Sacred History at the Persian Court," in *Mediating Netherlandish Art and Material Culture in Asia*, ed. Thomas DaCosta Kaufmann and Michael North (Amsterdam: Amsterdam University Press, 2014).
18 Rietbergen, "Upon a Silk Thread?" 173–6.
19 Kim Siebenhüner, *Die Spur der Juwelen: Materielle Kultur und transkontinentale Verbindungen in der Frühen Neuzeit* (Cologne: Böhlau, 2017), 65–6, 197–224.
20 On the Genevan clockmakers in Constantinople, see Antony Babel, *Histoire corporative de l'horlogerie, de l'orfèvrerie et des industries annexes* (Geneva: A. Jullien, George et Cie., 1916), 516–29.
21 [Du Cerceau and Krusiński], *Histoire de la dernière Révolution*, vol. 1, 128–9.
22 On the De l'Étoile family and their relations with the *Compagnie des Indes orientales*, see Anne Kroell, "Alexandre de Lestoille, dernier agent de la Compagnie royale des Indes en Perse," *Moyen Orient & Océan Indien* 1 (1984): 65–72; Richard, *Raphaël du Mans*, vol. 1, 203–4, 206–7.
23 Cornelis Speelman, *Journal der Reis van den Gezant der O.I. Compagnie Joan Cunaeus naar Perzië in 1651–1652 door Cornelis Speelman*, ed. Albertus Hotz (Amsterdam: Johannes Müller, 1908), 207.
24 Pallu, Journal, [1662] (BNF, Mss. fr. 25063, 4007).
25 Chardin, *Voyages*, vol. 3, 100.
26 Bembo, *Il viaggio in Asia*, 392.
27 Bouda Etemad, "Un horloger genevois à la cour de Perse au XVIIe siècle," *Revue du Vieux Genève* 15 (1985): 9–11.
28 Antoine-Isaac Silvestre de Sacy, Notice historique sur J. F. Rousseau consul général de France à Bagdad, n.p., n.d. [between 1808 and 1814] (MAE, Personnel, 1ère série nominative. Volumes reliés, vol. 61, fol. 188r–202v, 191r).

29 Fedeli di Milano to Sacripanti, New Julfa, Nov. 2, 1720 (APF, SOCG, vol. 634, fol. 358r).
30 Gerrit Jan Schutte, ed., *Het indisch Sion: De Gereformeerde kerk onder de Verenigte Oost-Indische Compagnie* (Hilversum: Uitgeverij Verloren, 2002); Van Wamelen, *Family Life*, 128–72.
31 Penelope Carson, *The East India Company and Religion, 1698–1858* (Woodbridge: Boydell Press, 2012), 7–17; Windler, "Early Modern Composite Catholicism." The appointment of chaplains for the factories of the Levant Company in Aleppo, Smyrna, and Constantinople also needs to be compared with the incomparably denser presence of Catholic clerics in even rather unimportant commercial centers in the Ottoman Empire. See Alison Games, *The Web of Empire: English Cosmopolitans in an Age of Expansion, 1560–1660* (Oxford: OUP, 2008), 223, 232.
32 Juan Thadeo de San Eliseo to [Fernando de Santa María ?], n.p., n.d. [probably Aug. 1608] (AGOCD, 236/a/2).
33 Chardin, *Voyages*, vol. 6, 163.
34 Jos Gommans, "South Asian Cosmopolitanism and the Dutch Microcosmos in Seventeenth-Century Cochin (Kerala)," in *Exploring the Dutch Empire: Agents, Networks and Institutions, 1600–2000*, ed. Catia Antunes and Jos Gommans (London: Bloomsbury Academic, 2015); Windler, "Early Modern Composite Catholicism."
35 Extrait d'un journal de Monseigneur [Pierre Lambert de La Motte] l'évêque de Béryte [...], 1662 (ARSI, Gallia, 97 I, doc. 114, fol. 326r).
36 Josef Metzler, "Francesco Ingoli, der erste Sekretär der Kongregation (1578–1649)," in *Sacrae Congregationis de Propaganda Fide Memoria Rerum*, ed. Metzler, vol. I/1.
37 Flannery, *The Mission*, 185–95.
38 On "Portuguese," "Englishmen," and "Dutchmen" in the port cities of the Persian Gulf and the Indian Ocean, see Barendse, *Arabian Seas 1700–1763*, vol. 2: *Kings, Gangsters and Companies*, esp. 505–95.
39 Thiessen, *Die Kapuziner*, 45.
40 Alexandre de Rhodes attributed his success in purchasing a house to this support (de Rhodes to Nickel, Isfahan, Sept. 23, 1657 [ARSI, Gallia, 103 II, fol. 227v]).
41 Villotte to Sacripanti, Rome, Sept. 15, 1710 (APF, SOCG, vol. 573, fol. 346r-8v).
42 Girolamo di Gesù Maria to Jean Chrysostome de Saint-Paul, Shiraz, Aug. 31, 1675 (AGOCD, 238/q/2).
43 Friedrich, *Der lange Arm Roms?*, 391, 403–22, 425–9.
44 De Rhodes to Nickel, Isfahan, Mar. 5, 1657 (ARSI, Gallia, 103 II, fol. 223r-4r, quotation: 223v).
45 On relations between the French Crown and the Society of Jesus and the split in the order along the lines of provinces and assistances on the central moral theological issue of the proper handling of the *opiniones probabiles*, see Jean-Pascal Gay, *Jesuit Civil Wars: Theology, Politics and Government under Tirso González (1687–1705)* (Farnham: Ashgate, 2012), 13–77, 157–96.
46 Mercier to Claude Boucher, Isfahan, Jan. 12, 1673 (ARSI, Gallia, 97 II, doc.128, fol. 353r-4r).
47 *Congregazioni generali*, May 4, 1694, and Dec. 17, 1714 (APF, Acta, vol. 64, fol. 68r/v, vol. 84, fol. 745v).
48 ? to [Paolo Simone di Gesù Maria], Isfahan, May 25, 1641 (AGOCD, 236/a/48).
49 Élie de Saint-Albert to [Charles de Saint-Bruno], Isfahan, July 14, 1683 (AGOCD, 237/h/1).

50 Élie de Saint-Albert to Onorio dell'Assunta, Isfahan, July 24, 1689 (AGOCD, 237/h/8).
51 Raphaël du Mans to Urbain de Paris, Isfahan, July 30, 1683, reproduced in Richard, *Raphaël du Mans*, vol. 1, 275–86.
52 Fedeli di Milano to [Sacripanti], Isfahan, Nov. 24, 1718 (APF, SC. Mesopotamia e Persia. Caldei e Latini, vol. 3, fol. 430v–1r).
53 Cf. Chapter 3, "Diplomatic Assignments."
54 Fedeli di Milano to Sacripanti, Isfahan, Jan. 10, 1722 (APF, SC. Mesopotamia e Persia. Caldei e Latini, vol. 3, fol. 518v).
55 Gardane to ?, Isfahan, June 20, 1720 (MAE, Correspondance politique. Perse, vol. 5, fol. 289v–90v).
56 Fedeli di Milano to Sacripanti, [New Julfa or Isfahan], May 25, 1720 (APF, SOCG, vol. 634, fol. 349r).
57 Mercier to Claude Boucher, Isfahan, Feb. 28, 1672 (ARSI, Gallia, 97 II, doc. 127, fol. 350r).
58 Steensgaard, *The Asian Trade Revolution*, 60–3, 68–9, 74.
59 Vincenzo Maria di Santa Caterina to Isidore de Saint-Dominique, Basra, Sept. 10, 1656 (AGOCD, 242/a/14).
60 Pallu, Additions aux Instructions […], Isfahan, Sept. 10, 1662, reproduced in François Pallu, *Lettres de Monseigneur Pallu écrites de 1654 à 1684*, ed. Adrien Launay and Frédéric Mantienne (Paris: Les Indes savantes, 2008), 34.
61 Pallu to his *procureurs*, Gombroon [Bandar 'Abbās], Nov. 26, 1662, reproduced in Pallu, *Lettres*, 42–4.
62 Furber, *Rival Empires of Trade*, 103–24, 203–7.
63 Francesco Maria di San Siro, Itinerario Orientale […], Vienna 1706 and Milan 1713 (BAV, Borg. lat. 317, 75, 529–30). The Discalced Carmelite was probably speaking of Alexander Prescott, who worked for the Levant Company.
64 See Steensgaard, *The Asian Trade Revolution*, 64–7.
65 John Fryer, *A New Account of East India and Persia Being Nine Years Travels, 1672–1681*, ed. William Crooke (London: Hakluyt Society, 1912), vol. 2, 209, 320, 344, 346.
66 Chardin, *Voyages*, vol. 8, 447, cf. 459.
67 Epifanio di San Giovanni Battista to [Fernando de Santa María ?], Goa, Mar. 21, 1630 (AGOCD, 261/l/4).
68 Instruttione per il Visitatore Generale [Carlo di Gesù Maria] […], 1638 (AGOCD, 284/g/2).
69 De Rhodes, *Les divers voyages et missions*, 44, 51.
70 Louis Baudiment, *François Pallu, principal fondateur de la Société des Missions étrangères* (Paris: Gabriel Beauchesne et ses fils, 1934), 124, 128.
71 [Frizon and Villotte], *Voyages d'un missionnaire*, 131, 416–17.
72 Speelman, *Journal der Reis*, 138, 180, 194, 294, 309–10, 316.
73 Leandro di Santa Cecilia, *Persia ovvero secondo viaggio […] dell'Oriente […]* (Rome, 1757), 182–3.
74 Jean-Baptiste Tavernier, "Histoire de la conduite des Hollandais en Asie," in his *Recueil de plusieurs relations et traités singuliers et curieux […]* (Paris, 1679), 110–11, 116–21.
75 Schillinger, *Persianische und Ost-Indianische Reis*, 180–1.
76 Élie de Saint-Albert to [Carlo Barberini ?], Isfahan, June 12, 1699 (APF, SC. Mesopotamia e Persia. Caldei e Latini, vol. 2, fol. 266r).

77 Della Valle to Schipano, Isfahan, Dec. 18, 1617, in Della Valle, *Viaggi*, Parte seconda: *La Persia*, vol. 1, 133–6.
78 Della Valle to Schipano, Isfahan, Apr. 4, 1620, in Della Valle, *Viaggi*, Parte seconda: *La Persia*, vol. 2, 111.
79 Della Valle to Schipano, Isfahan, June 20, 1620, in Della Valle, *Viaggi*, Parte seconda: *La Persia*, vol. 2, 124–5.
80 Pacifique de Provins, *Le voyage de Perse*, 226 (quotation), 228.
81 Toussaint de Landerneau to Raphaël de Nantes, Isfahan, Apr. 4, 1634 (BNF, n.a.f. 10220, 194).
82 Paul Lucas, *Voyage du Sieur Paul Lucas au Levant: juin 1699–juillet 1703*, ed. Henri Duranton (1704; Saint-Étienne: Publications de l'Université de Saint-Étienne, 1998), 161.
83 See Chapter 1, "Maintaining Proximity from a Distance."
84 Barendse, "The Long Road to Livorno," 25–7, 30–2.
85 Thomas Merry, George Tash, Edward Pearce and George Oxenden to their superiors, Surat, Jan. 25, 1650, William Foster, *The English Factories in India, 1646–1650: A Calendar of Documents in the India Office* (Oxford: Clarendon Press, 1914), 281.
86 Agent and factors in Isfahan to the president and council in Surat, Isfahan, Sept. 1, 1654, W. Foster, *The English Factories in India, 1651–1654: A Calendar of Documents in the India Office* (Oxford: Clarendon Press, 1915), 287.
87 Barendse, "The Long Road to Livorno," 34.
88 Speelman, *Journal der Reis*, 334; Instructie waar nae den oppercoopman Jacob Willemszoon […], signed by Joan Cunaeus, Isfahan, June 14, 1652 (NA, VOC 1188, fol. 361r–4v, 362r).
89 Francois de Hase, Adolf Willingk, Paulus Vaans, and Nicolaas Bitsert to Joan Maatsuyker and his councilors, Gombroon [Bandar ʿAbbās], Sept. 19, 1672 (NA, VOC 1295, fol. 404r).
90 Raphaël du Mans to François Baron, Isfahan, Oct. 18 and Nov. 27, 1667, Apr. 23, 1668, reproduced in Richard, *Raphaël du Mans*, vol. 1, 206, 213, 223, 228–9.
91 Felice di Sant'Antonio to Isidore de Saint-Joseph, Isfahan, May 12, 1655 (AGOCD, 237/i/18).
92 Felice di Sant'Antonio to Carolus Felix a Sancta Teresia, Naples, Jan. 11, 1677 (AGOCD, 481/c/9).
93 Pidou de Saint-Olon to the *directeurs* of the *Séminaire des Mission étrangères*, Isfahan, Aug. 16, 1703 (MEP, vol. 351, 468).
94 Bembo, *Il viaggio in Asia*, 362–3.
95 Speelman, *Journal der Reis*, 314.
96 Séraphin d'Orléans to the guardian of the Capuchins in Le Mans, May 1, 1696, cited in Richard, *Raphaël du Mans*, vol. 1, 7.
97 Martial de Thorigné, Relation de ce qui s'est passé dans les missions du Levant l'an 1665, Isfahan 1665, reproduced in Richard, *Raphaël du Mans*, vol. 1, 156.
98 Valentin d'Angers to Tavernier, Isfahan, Dec. 6, 1662, reproduced in Richard, *Raphaël du Mans*, vol. 1, 137–42, quotation: 141.
99 Richard, *Raphaël du Mans*, vol. 1, 74–6, 98–101.
100 Fryer, *A New Account*, vol. 2, 246–7.
101 Ludwig Fabritius to Athanase de Sainte-Thérèse, n.p. [Isfahan or New Djulfa], n.d. [after Sept. 30, 1684], reproduced in Kaempfer, *Briefe*, 201–2.
102 Richard, *Raphaël du Mans*, vol. 1, 118–21, quotation: 120.
103 See the correspondence between Kaempfer and the Capuchin, reproduced in Kaempfer, *Briefe*, 196–7, 203–12, 218–19, 230–1, 245–6, 250–2, 260–4, 299–300, 318–20.

104 Memorandum by Jacques Tilhac, enclosure to his letter to Tirso González, Isfahan, Dec. 27, 1700 (ARSI, Gallia, 97 II, fol. 395r).
105 Ange de Saint-Joseph to Jean Chrysostome de Saint-Paul, Isfahan, Jan. 3, 1673 (AGOCD, 236/i/23).
106 Cornelio di San Giuseppe, Memorie concernenti alla Chiesa e diocesi di Persia, n.p., n.d. (BA, H 136 suss., 97–8).
107 [Tadeusz Juda Krusiński], Informatio de missionibus persicis, n.p., n.d. [1727] (ARSI, Fondo Gesuitico, 720 II, no. 9).
108 Galisson to Brisacier, Isfahan, June 2, 1712 (MEP, vol. 354, 455bis).
109 François Sanson to the *directeurs* of the *Séminaire des Missions étrangères,* Isfahan, Jan. 10, 1686 (MEP, vol. 351, 175).
110 Fedeli di Milano to Sacripanti, New Julfa, July 11, 1716, and Isfahan, Apr. 28, 1718 (APF, SOCG, vol. 608, fol. 487r/v, vol. 617, fol. 204r/v).
111 See Laurence Fontaine, *The Moral Economy: Poverty, Credit and Trust in Early Modern Europe* (Cambridge: CUP, 2014).
112 Fedeli di Milano to Petra, New Julfa, Oct. 6, 1728 (APF, SC. Mesopotamia e Persia. Caldei e Latini, vol. 3, 554r).
113 Gian Antonio Fedeli to Petra, Milan, Apr. 23 and June 9, 1732 (APF, SC. Mesopotamia e Persia. Caldei e Latini, vol. 4, fol. 550r, 564r, 565r).
114 Mémoire du Sr Jean François Rousseau [...], 1773 (AN, AE B^I 197, fol. 179r).
115 Jean-François-Xavier Rousseau to Giuseppe Maria Castelli, Basra, June 10, 1773 (APF, SC. Mesopotamia e Persia. Caldei e Latini, vol. 8, fol. 227r/v); and to [Eusebio di Santa Maria], Basra, June 10, 1773 (ibid., fol. 229r–30r).
116 Dionisio di Gesù to [Philippe de la Très Sainte Trinité?], Bandar ʿAbbās, Dec. 22, 1668 (AGOCD, 237/d/7).
117 See Thiessen, *Die Kapuziner*, 276–85.
118 Tavernier, "Histoire de la conduite des Hollandais," 121–2, 127–9.
119 Tavernier, *Les six voyages*, vol. 1, 162, 168, 172, 179.
120 Schillinger, *Persianische und Ost-Indianische Reis*, 273.
121 Olearius, *Vermehrte Newe Beschreibung*, 513–16, 518.
122 Domenico di Christo to [Filippo di San Jacopo], Shiraz, Apr. 11, 1641 (AGOCD, 238/i/7).
123 Gregório Pereira Fidalgo da Silveira, Relação da jornada que fez o doutor Gregório Pereira Fidalgo [...], Bandar-i Kung, Oct. 25, 1697, reproduced in Aubin, *L'ambassade de Gregório Pereira Fidalgo*, 64–5.
124 Chézaud to Le Cazre, Isfahan, Oct. 21, 1660 (ARSI, Gallia, 97 II, doc. 108, fol. 315r).
125 Chézaud to Claude Boucher, Isfahan, May 20, 1662, addition of June 20, 1662 (ARSI, Gallia, 97 II, doc. 113, fol. 325r).
126 Raphaël du Mans to Baron, Isfahan, Oct. 18, 1667, reproduced in Richard, *Raphaël du Mans*, vol. 1, 206–7.
127 Mercier to Baron, Isfahan, Nov. 7, 1667 (MEP, vol. 350, 264–5).
128 Pidou de Saint-Olon to the *directeurs* of the *Séminaire des Mission étrangères*, Hamadan, May 25, 1705 (MEP, vol. 351, 486).
129 Ange de Saint-Joseph, *Pharmacopoea persica*, 10.
130 Fedeli di Milano to Sacripanti, New Julfa, May 2, 1726 (APF, SC. Mesopotamia e Persia. Caldei e Latini, vol. 3, 537r, 550r).
131 Copia della risposta fatta da Monsignore Barnaba [Fedeli di Milano] vescovo d'Haspan [...] (AGOCD, 236/b/7).
132 Exhibitio privilegiorum missionariorum regularium, signed by Jean Martial Lagarde, Tadeusz Juda Krusiński, and Arnolphe François Duhan, New Julfa, Apr. 23, 1725 (AGOCD, 243/c/2).

133 Filippo Maria di Sant'Agostino to Fedeli di Milano, New Julfa, Apr. 19, 1725 (AGOCD, 238/u/1a and 1b).
134 Fedeli di Milano to Sacripanti, New Julfa, May 2, 1726 (APF, SC. Mesopotamia e Persia. Caldei e Latini, vol. 3, 550r–2r).
135 De Bruyn, *Voyages*, vol. 1, 238–9.
136 Speelman, *Journal der Reis*, 294, 316, 318.
137 John Bossy, *Christianity in the West, 1400–1700* (Oxford: OUP, 1985), 25.
138 Jean Gaudemet, *Le mariage en Occident: Les mœurs et le droit* (Paris: Les Éditions du Cerf, 1987), 290–4.
139 Ignazio di Gesù to [Fernando de Santa María ?], Isfahan, June 12, 1630 (AGOCD, 237/l/3).
140 Bernard de Sainte-Thérèse to Anne Duval, Isfahan, Sept. 9, 1641, reproduced in Léon Mirot, "Lettres écrites de Perse et de Syrie par le Révérend Père Bernard de Sainte-Thérèse, évêque de Babylone," *Bulletin de la Société scientifique de Clameci*, 3e série, 8 (1932): 125–65, 151–3.
141 Valentin d'Angers to the *Propaganda Fide*, Isfahan, Sept. 27, 1657 (APF, SOCG, vol. 238, fol. 56r/v).
142 *Congregazione generale*, Aug. 22, 1661 (APF, Acta, vol. 30, fol. 142v).
143 The discussion here follows Guido Alfani, *Fathers and Godfathers: Spiritual Kinship in Early-Modern Italy* (Farnham: Ashgate, 2009); G. Alfani and Vincent Gourdon, "Spiritual Kinship and Godparenthood: An Introduction," in *Spiritual Kinship in Europe, 1500–1900*, ed. G. Alfani and V. Gourdon (Basingstoke: Palgrave Macmillan, 2012), 10–25.
144 On Tunis, see Windler, *La diplomatie*, 116–20.
145 Valentin d'Angers to [Antonio Barberini,] Isfahan, n.d. [1641] (APF, SOCG, vol. 121, fol. 145r/v).
146 Valentin d'Angers to the *Propaganda Fide*, Isfahan, Sept. 27, 1657 (APF, SOCG, vol. 238, fol. 56r/v); *Congregazione generale*, Aug. 6, 1658 (APF, Acta, vol. 27, fol. 217v–18r).
147 Corneille de Saint-Cyprien to Isidore de Saint-Joseph, Isfahan, Jan. 10, 1656 (AGOCD, 237/a/4).
148 Miscellanea d'alcune historiette [...] raccolte [...] da F. C[ornelio] di S. Giuseppe Carmelitano Scalzo. Centuria decima, e ultima, n.p. [Milan ?], n.d. [probably around 1790] (BA, L 13 suss., fol. 244r/v).
149 ACDF, SO, Dubia circa Baptismum, vol. 4: 1760–6, IX, fol. 380r–423v.
150 Fedeli di Milano to Sacripanti, New Julfa, May 2, 1726 (APF, SC. Mesopotamia e Persia. Caldei e Latini, vol. 3, 539v, 552r).
151 Fedeli di Milano to [Petra], New Julfa, May 4, 1727 (APF, SC. Mesopotamia e Persia. Caldei e Latini, vol. 3, 543r–4r).
152 Benjamin J. Kaplan, *Divided by Faith: Religious Conflict and the Practice of Toleration in Early Modern Europe* (Cambridge, MA: The Belknap Press of Harvard University Press, 2007), 94–6; Craig M. Koslofsky, *The Reformation of the Dead: Death and Ritual in Early Modern Germany, 1450–1700* (Basingstoke: Macmillan, 2000), esp. 100, 104–7.
153 In the Syrian region, too, there were reports of funeral processions for missionaries in which the clergy of the different churches participated. See Heyberger, *Les Chrétiens du Proche-Orient*, 61.
154 This was not specific to the mission churches. The Capuchins in Freiburg and Hildesheim, for example, also sought to promote the honor of their order in the "world." See Thiessen, *Die Kapuziner*, 308–12.

155 Standaert, *The Interweaving of Rituals*, 184–206.
156 Chézaud to ?, Isfahan, Nov. 11, 1660, reproduced in Rabbath, *Documents inédits*, 299–307, 306.
157 Mercier to Nicolas de Sainte-Geneviève, New Julfa, Jan. 25, 1665, reproduced in Rabbath, *Documents inédits*, 87–93, 90–1.
158 Jean-Baptiste de Montmoreau to John Gladman, Isfahan, Apr. 10, 1696, and Séraphin d'Orléans to the guardian of the Capuchins in Le Mans, May 1, 1696, quoted in Richard, *Raphaël du Mans*, vol. 1, 7 (quotation)–8.
159 Kaempfer to Raphaël du Mans, [Bandar ʿAbbās, autumn 1687], reproduced in Kaempfer, *Briefe*, 263–4.
160 Fryer, *A New Account*, vol. 2, 247.
161 [Baldassarre di Santa Caterina di Siena] to the *Propaganda Fide*, n.p., n.d. (APF, SOCG, vol. 239, fol. 185r–6v).
162 *Congregazione generale*, Sept. 4, 1663 (APF, Acta, vol. 32, fol. 211v).
163 [Frizon and Villotte], *Voyages d'un missionnaire*, 418–19.
164 On Tunis, see Windler, *La diplomatie*, 111–20. On relations between French Protestants and Capuchins in Persia, see Nicolas Fornerod, "Une alliance française? Missionnaires capucins et voyageurs réformés à la cour safavide," *Dix-septième siècle* 278 (2018): 25–48. On the Holy Office's handling of transconfessional practices in the Ottoman Empire, see Felicita Tramontana, "An Unusual Setting: Interactions between Protestants and Catholics in the Ottoman Empire," in *Religious Minorities and Majorities in Early Modern Europe: Confessional Boundaries and Contested Identities*, ed. Simon Burton, Michał Choptiany, and Piotr Wilczek (Göttingen: Vandenhoeck & Ruprecht, 2019). On Dutch protection of the Franciscan missions in Constantinople and Smyrna as well as the island of Chios, see Johan van Droffelaar, "'Flemish Fathers' in the Levant: Dutch Protection of Three Franciscan Missions in the 17th and 18th Centuries," in *Eastward Bound: Dutch Ventures and Adventures in the Middle East*, ed. Geert Jan van Gelder and Ed de Moor (Amsterdam: Rodopi, 1994).
165 Felicita Tramontana, "Protestants' Conversions to Catholicism in the Syro-Palestinian Region (17th Century)," *Zeitschrift für Historische Forschung* 41 (2014): 401–22.
166 [Nicolas] Poullet, *Nouvelles relations du Levant [...] Seconde partie* (Paris, 1668), 274.
167 [Index defunctorum], 1755–1816, entry of Feb. 27, 1763 (no. 67) (AGOCD, 484/c).
168 Théodore Rousseau to Pierre-Michel Hennin, Geneva, Nov. 26, 1773 (Bibliothèque de l'Institut de France, Ms. 1275: Papiers et correspondance de Pierre-Michel Hennin, vol. 56, fol. 194r–5r).
169 On the European "nations" in the Persian Gulf and the Indian Ocean, see Barendse, *The Arabian Seas*, esp. 87–125.
170 Bosma and Raben, *Being "Dutch,"* 26–46.
171 Kaplan, *Divided by Faith*, 172–234.
172 See Christine Kooi, *Calvinists and Catholics during Holland's Golden Age: Heretics and Idolaters* (Cambridge: CUP, 2012), 175–214.
173 Kaplan, *Divided by Faith*, 261–3; Judith Pollmann, *Religious Choice in the Dutch Republic: The Reformation of Arnoldus Buchelius (1565–1641)* (Manchester: Manchester University Press, 1999).
174 Kim Siebenhüner, "Glaubenswechsel in der Frühen Neuzeit," *Zeitschrift für Historische Forschung* 34 (2007): 243–72, 270–2. For an overview of the scholarship on the question of ambiguity and indifference in the confessional age, see Andreas Pietsch and Barbara Stollberg-Rilinger, eds., *Konfessionelle*

Ambiguität: Uneindeutigkeit und Verstellung als religiöse Praxis in der Frühen Neuzeit (Gütersloh: Gütersloher Verlagshaus, 2013).

175 Kaplan, *Divided by Faith*, 73–98; Keith P. Luria, *Sacred Boundaries: Religious Coexistence and Conflict in Early Modern France* (Washington, DC: Catholic University of America Press, 2005).

176 On the Catholic minority in the Netherlands, see Bertrand Forclaz, *Catholiques au défi de la Réforme: La coexistence confessionnelle à Utrecht au XVIIe siècle* (Paris: H. Champion, 2014); Kooi, *Calvinists and Catholics*; and Charles H. Parker, *Faith on the Margins: Catholics and Catholicism in the Dutch Golden Age* (Cambridge, MA: Harvard University Press, 2008). The living conditions of the Catholic minority in England were far more difficult than those of their coreligionists in the Netherlands. See Michael Questier, *Catholicism and Community in Early Modern England: Politics, Aristocratic Patronage and Religion, c. 1550–1640* (Cambridge: CUP, 2006); Alexandra Walsham, *Charitable Hatred: Tolerance and Intolerance in England, 1500–1740* (Manchester: Manchester University Press, 2006), and *Catholic Reformation in Protestant Britain* (Farnham: Ashgate, 2014).

177 [Frizon and Villotte], *Voyages d'un missionnaire*, 160–1.

178 Pedros Bedik, *Cehil Sutun, seu explicatio utriusque celeberrimi, ac pretiosissimi theatri quadraginta columnarum in Perside Orientis [...]* (Vienna, 1678), 315, English translation: Colette Ouahes and Willem Floor, eds., *A Man of Two Worlds: Pedros Bedik in Iran, 1670–1675* (Washington, DC: Mage, 2014), 348.

179 Cornelio di San Giuseppe, Memorie cronologiche [...], n.p., n.d. (BA, & 211 sup., 19–20, 97–8).

180 Hermann Gollancz, ed., *Chronicle of Events between the Years 1623 and 1733 Relating to the Settlement of the Order of Carmelites in Mesopotamia (Bassora) [...]* (London: OUP and Humphrey Milford, Publisher to the University, 1927), 262–5, 580–3.

181 See, for example, the protocol of the *Compagnie des pasteurs*, Dec. 3, 1652, reproduced in André Archinard and Théophile Heyer, "Genève et Constantinople: 1592–1732," *Bulletin de la Société de l'histoire du protestantisme français* 10 (1861): 233–58, 235.

182 If, because of its lack of internal cohesion, English Protestantism overall did not appear to act as "a uniform and consistent arm of conquest" (Games, *The Web of Empire*, 252), its role as a marker of identity postulated by Alison Games also needs to be called into question from the geographical perspective chosen here (ibid., esp. 222–3, 252–3).

Chapter 6

1 Chardin, *Voyages*, vol. 7, 438.
2 Fryer, *A New Account*, vol. 2, 246.
3 Metzler, "Orientation, programme et premières décisions," 160–1.
4 Ingoli, *Quattro Parti del Mondo*, 164–7, 277.
5 *Congregazione generale*, Oct. 3, 1707 (APF, Acta, vol. 77, fol. 379r–87r).
6 *Congregazione generale*, Dec. 1, 1783 (APF, Acta, vol. 153, fol. 510r, 514r).
7 See Chapter 1, "Internalized Discipline and Self-Empowerment."
8 Valentin d'Angers to the *Propaganda Fide*, Isfahan, Sept. 4, 1647 (APF, SOCG, vol. 65, fol. 333r).

9   On the relationship between contemplation and *actio* in a European context, see Sinicropi, *"D'oraison et d'action."*
10 Juan de Jesús María, Tractatus quo asseruntur missiones […], reproduced in his *Scritti missionari*, ed. and trans. Giovanni Strina (Brussels: Éditions Soumillion, 1994), 165–81, 174.
11 *Constitutiones Carmelitarum Discalceatorum Congregationis S. Eliae anno 1605 latae*, ed. Giovanni Marco Strina (Genoa: Tipo-Litografia Opera SS. Vergine di Pompei, 1968), 32–3, chap. 17, 103.
12 Juan de Jesús María, Instructio Missionum, reproduced in his *Scritti missionari*, 193–272.
13 *Regula primitiva et Constitutiones Fratrum Discalceatorum Congregationis S. Eliae Ordinis B. Virginis Mariae de Monte Carmelo* (Rome, 1611), part 1, 12.
14 Tomás de Jesús, *De procuranda salute omnium gentium […]* (Antwerp, 1613).
15 Tomás de Jesús, *Stimulus missionum, sive de propaganda a religiosis per universum orbem fide […]* (Rome, 1610).
16 Philippe de la Très Sainte Trinité, *Itinerarium Orientale*, 1–6, 309–84.
17 Philippe de la Très Sainte Trinité, *Theologia carmelitana, sive Apologia scholastica religionis carmelitanae pro tuenda suae nobilitatis antiquitate […]* (Rome, 1665).
18 Isidore de Saint-Joseph and Pierre de Saint-André, *Historia Generalis Fratrum Discalceatorum […]*, vol. 1, 362–5, 369–73.
19 Metzler, "Francesco Ingoli," 210.
20 Instruttione per gli nostri padri […] che si manda d'ordine del definitorio generale del 1630 a 6 di Jenaro, signed by Fernando de Santa María (AGOCD, 289/e/1).
21 Instructions for Eugenio di San Benedetto, n.d. [1624] (AGOCD, 261/d/1 and 2).
22 Instructions for Jacopo di Santa Teresa, n.d. [1634] (AGOCD, 236/a/45).
23 *Sancti Ignatii de Loyola Constitutiones Societatis Jesu*, vol. 3: *Textus latinus* (Rome: Typis Pontificiae Universitatis Gregorianae, 1938), 186–7.
24 As already stipulated in the *Primae Constitutiones Congregationis Sancti Eliae O.C.D. anno 1599 a Card. P. Pinelli, auctoritate Apostolica approbatae*, ed. Valentino di Santa Maria (Rome: apud Curiam Generalem, 1973), part 1, chap. 14, 62–3.
25 Paolo Simone di Gesù Maria, Relatione dell'ambasciata […], n.p., n.d. (AGOCD, 234/a/1).
26 *Congregazione generale*, Oct. 3, 1707 (APF, Acta, vol. 77, fol. 379r–90v, quotation: 387v–8r).
27 Paolo Simone di Gesù Maria, Relatione di Persia, n.p., n.d. (AGOCD, 234/b/1).
28 Juan Thadeo de San Eliseo to Vicente de San Francisco, Isfahan, May 14, 1609 (AGOCD, 237/m/4).
29 *Definitorium generale*, Jan. 4, 1616. Fortes, *Acta definitorii*, vol. 1, 30, 42.
30 Juan Thadeo de San Eliseo to [Domingo de Jesús María], Isfahan, Jan. 3, 1619 (AGOCD, 237/m/13).
31 Pacifique de Provins, *Le voyage de Perse*, 232.
32 See, for example, the description in André Daulier Deslandes, *Les beautés de la Perse: Relation d'un voyage en Perse de 1663 à 1666*, ed. Françoise de Valence (1673; Paris: Maisonneuve et Larose, 2003), 49–51; André Daulier Deslandes to his brother, Isfahan, Feb. 15, 1665, post scriptum, reproduced in ibid., 98–100.
33 Memorandum by Tilhac, enclosed with his letter to Tirso González, Isfahan, Dec. 27, 1700 (ARSI, Gallia, 97 II, fol. 395r).
34 Felice Maria da Sellano to the *Propaganda Fide*, Tabriz, Sept. 22, 1700 (APF, SC. Mesopotamia e Persia. Caldei e Latini, vol. 2, fol. 378r/v).

35 *Constitutiones Fratrum Discalceatorum Congregationis S. Eliae Ordinis Beatissimae Virginia Mariae de Monte Carmelo* (Rome, 1631), part 1, chap. 13, 50–1.
36 Relatione del P. Benigno di S. Michele sul suo viaggio in Persia, Isfahan, Aug. 10, 1609 (AGOCD, 234/e/bis, fol. 25r, 33r–4v, 35v–6r, 37r).
37 *Definitorium generale,* Jan. 4, 1616. Fortes, *Acta definitorii,* vol. 1, 30.
38 Della Valle, [Diario di viaggio], 1614–26 (here Mar. 5 and Oct. 19, 1617) (BAV, Ottob. lat. 3382, fol. 1r–260r, 71r, 74v–5r, 80r/v).
39 [Ordinationes], by Vicente de San Francisco, Isfahan, Sept. 22, 1621 (AGOCD, 235/l/1 and 236/a/14).
40 *Definitorium generale,* June 27, 1678. Fortes, *Acta definitorii,* vol. 2, 181.
41 Bernard de Sainte-Thérèse to Bernard de Saint-Joseph, Isfahan, July 8, 1640 (MEP, vol. 352, 25).
42 Giovanni Battista di San Giuseppe to the *Definitorium generale,* Isfahan, Sept. 9, 1677 (AGOCD, 236/m/5).
43 Vicente de San Francisco to Juan de Jesús María, Hormuz, June 3, 1613 (AGOCD, 239/b/5. See also [Chick], *Chronicle,* vol. 1, 201).
44 [Ordinationes], by Vicente de San Francisco, Isfahan, Sept. 22, 1621 (AGOCD, 235/l/1 and 236/a/14).
45 Ignazio di Gesù to [Fernando de Santa María], Isfahan, June 12 and Aug. 2, 1630 (AGOCD, 237/l/3 and 4).
46 Instruttione per gli nostri padri […] che si manda d'ordine del definitorio generale del 1630 a 6 di Jenaro, signed by Fernando de Santa María (AGOCD, 289/e/1).
47 Miscellanea d'alcune historiette […] raccolte […] da F. C[ornelio] di S. Giuseppe Carmelitano Scalzo. Centuria decima, e ultima, n.p. [Milan ?], n.d. [ca. 1790] (BA, L 13 suss., fol. 258r/v).
48 Denis de la Couronne d'Épines to [Eugenio di San Benedetto], Isfahan, May 8, 1645 (AGOCD, 237/c/2).
49 Girolamo di Gesù Maria to Philippe de la Très Sainte Trinité, Isfahan, July 31, 1669 (AGOCD, 237/n/1).
50 Ange de Saint-Joseph to Jean Chrysostome de Saint-Paul, Shiraz, June 1, 1669 (AGOCD, 238/l/2).
51 In Asia, the Jesuits also kept enslaved people as house servants, and in Brazil they relied on the labor of enslaved Blacks to cultivate their plantations. Dauril Alden, *The Making of an Enterprise: The Society of Jesus in Portugal, Its Empire, and Beyond, 1540–1750* (Stanford: Stanford University Press, 1996), 506–27; Carlos Alberto de Moura Ribeiro Zeron, *Ligne de foi: La Compagnie de Jésus et l'esclavage dans le processus de formation de la société coloniale en Amérique portugaise (XVIe–XVIIe siècles)* (Paris: H. Champion, 2009).
52 On the Roman Church's positions on the slavery question, see Maria Teresa Fattori, "'Licere—Non licere': La legittimità della schiavitù nelle decisioni della Sede apostolica romana tra XVII e XIX secolo," *Rivista storica italiana* 132 (2020): 393–436; Richard Gray, "The Papacy and the Atlantic Slave Trade: Lourenço da Silva, the Capuchins and the Decisions of the Holy Office," *Past & Present* 115 (1987): 52–68. On the practice of slavery in Rome, see Marina Caffiero, *Gli schiavi del papa: Conversioni e libertà dei musulmani a Roma in età moderna* (Brescia: Morcelliana, 2022).
53 Fryer, *A New Account,* vol. 2, 247.
54 Bembo, *Il viaggio in Asia,* 362.
55 Chardin, *Voyages,* vol. 8, 10, 12–13.

56 Bembo, *Il viaggio in Asia*, 369.
57 Giovanni Francesco Gemelli Careri, *Giro del mondo [...]. Nuova edizione [...]. Tomo secondo [...]* (Venice, 1719), 60.
58 Francisco de Távora to Peter II, Goa, Jan. 20, 1685 (DAAG, 56: Monções, vol. 49, fol. 230r).
59 Bembo, *Il viaggio in Asia*, 360, 362, 369, 391.
60 *Constitutiones Fratrum Discalceatorum [...]*, 1631, prologus, 15.
61 In Europe, the "holy deserts" served as retreats into solitude. See Trevor Johnson, "Gardening for God: Carmelite Deserts and the Sacralisation of Natural Space in Counter-Reformation Spain," in *Sacred Space in Early Modern Europe*, ed. Will Coster and Andrew Spicer (Cambridge: CUP, 2005); Sinicropi, *"D'oraison et d'action,"* 247–68. No such retreats were established in the Persian missions.
62 *Primae Constitutiones Congregationis Sancti Eliae [...]*, 1599, part 1, chap. 10 and 14; part 2, chap. 8, 56, 61–3, 74; *Constitutiones Carmelitarum Discalceatorum [...]*, 1605, part 1, chap. 9 and 13; part 2, chap. 8, 49, 53–6, 69; *Regula primitiva et Constitutiones Fratrum Discalceatorum [...]*, 1611, part 1, chap. 9, 13 and 14, 31–2, 38–42, 53; *Constitutiones Fratrum Discalceatorum [...]*, 1631, part 1, chap. 9, 13 and 19, 38, 45–52, 64.
63 [Ordinationes], by Vicente de San Francisco, Isfahan, Sept. 22, 1621 (AGOCD, 235/l/1 and 236/a/14).
64 Instruttione per gli nostri padri [...] che si manda d'ordine del definitorio generale del 1630 a 6 di Jenaro, signed by Fernando de Santa María (AGOCD, 289/e/1).
65 Dionisio di Gesù to [Philippe de la Très Sainte Trinité ?], Bandar 'Abbās, Feb. 15, 1669 (AGOCD, 237/d/8).
66 Giovanni Battista di San Giuseppe to the *definitores generales*, Isfahan, Sept. 9, 1677 (AGOCD, 236/m/5).
67 *Definitorium generale*, June 27, 1678. Fortes, *Acta definitorii*, vol. 2, 181.
68 Instructiones pro missionibus orientalibus, 1683 (AGOCD, Acta Definitorii Generalis ab anno 1676 usque ad annum 1687, vol. 6, 243–4).
69 Instructiones conditae a Definitorio nostro generali die 30 Julii anni 1683, confirmatae ab eodem Definitorio die 20 10^{bris} an. 1719 (AGOCD, 289/e/1).
70 Agnello dell'Immacolata Concezione to the *praepositus generalis* and the *definitores generales*, Shiraz, Oct. 26, 1684 (AGOCD, 238/k/1 and 2).
71 Fortunato di Gesù Maria to Bernardo Maria di Gesù, Isfahan, June 10, 1684 (AGOCD, 237/k/9).
72 Agnello dell'Immacolata Concezione to the *praepositus generalis* and the *definitores generales*, Shiraz, Oct. 26, 1684 (AGOCD, 238/k/1).
73 Memorandum by Tilhac, enclosed with his letter to Tirso González, Isfahan, Dec. 27, 1700 (ARSI, Gallia, 97 II, fol. 394r–5v).
74 Liber accepti et expensi [...], 1674–1727 (AGOCD, 483/f); [Liber computum], 1728–72 (AGOCD, 484/e).
75 See the review of the literature thus far in Frederik Vermote, "Finances of the Missions," in *A Companion to Early Modern Catholic Global Missions*, ed. Hsia, and the contributions in Hélène Vu Thanh and Ines G. Županov, eds., *Trade and Finance in Global Missions (16th–18th Centuries)* (Leiden: Brill, 2021).
76 Herbert Chick offers important insights into the practice of the Roman subsidy payments but does not inquire into alternative sources of financing ([Chick], *Chronicle*, vol. 2, 757–72).
77 [Ordinationes], by Vicente de San Francisco, Isfahan, Sept. 22, 1621 (AGOCD, 235/l/1 and 236/a/14).

78 Instruttione per gli nostri padri [...] che si manda d'ordine del definitorio generale del 1630 a 6 di Jenaro, signed by Fernando de Santa María (AGOCD, 289/e/1).
79 General Chapter, Apr. 20 and 23, 1644. Fortes, *Acta capituli*, vol. 2, 11, 28. The regulation was subsequently confirmed by all General Chapters.
80 Instructiones pro missionibus orientalibus, 1683 (AGOCD, Acta Definitorii Generalis ab anno 1676 usque ad annum 1687, vol. 6, 243, 250).
81 Regulae ac Decreta [...] ab episcopis, vicariis apostolicis caeterisque missionariis observanda, n.d. (APF, SC Missioni. Miscellanee vol. 2, fol. 376v [quotation]–7r).
82 [Chick], *Chronicle*, vol. 2, 757–8, 920.
83 *Definitorium generale*, Nov. 8, 1617. Fortes, *Acta definitorii*, vol. 1, 30, 47. The *Definitorium* later raised the travel expenses allotted for missionaries in Persia to 100 scudi.
84 See Boaga, *La soppressione innocenziana*, 56.
85 Juan Thadeo de San Eliseo to [Domingo de Jesús María], Isfahan, Jan. 3, 1619 (AGOCD, 237/m/13).
86 Juan Thadeo de San Eliseo, Balthasar de Santa Maria, and Domenico di Santa Maria to the *praepositus generalis* and the *definitores generales*, Isfahan, Aug. 24, 1624 (AGOCD, 233/d/16).
87 *Congregazioni generali*, Sept. 5, 1625, and Jan. 30, 1629 (APF, Acta, vol. 3, fol. 258v, and vol. 6, fol. 212v).
88 *Definitorium generale*, Nov. 21/22, 1695. Fortes, *Acta definitorii*, vol. 2, 399.
89 *Congregazioni generali*, Mar. 28 and Aug. 22, 1707 (APF, Acta, vol. 77, fol. 89r/v, 274v–5r).
90 Faustino di San Carlo to the *Definitorium generale*, Isfahan, May 26, 1721 (AGOCD, 238/g/9).
91 Liber accepti et expensi [...], 1674–1727 (AGOCD, 483/f); [Liber computum], 1728–72 (AGOCD, 484/e). For details of the analysis, see the table in the original German edition of this volume, Windler, *Missionare in Persien*, 553–4.
92 Alexander Hamilton, *A New Account of the East Indies [...]* (Edinburgh, 1727), vol. 1, 84–6.
93 Thabit A. J. Abdullah, *Merchants, Mamluks, and Murder: The Political Economy of Trade in Eighteenth-Century Basra* (Albany: SUNY Press, 2001), 45–82; Barendse, *Arabian Seas 1700–1763*, vol. 1, 221–40.
94 Bembo, *Il viaggio in Asia*, 109–10, 113–15.
95 Barthélémy Carré, Premier voyage de Mr Carré en Orient, reproduced in his *Le courrier du Roi en Orient: Relations de deux voyages en Perse et en Inde, 1668–1674*, ed. Dirk van der Cruysse (Paris: Fayard, 2005), 113–16.
96 Cornelio di San Giuseppe, Memorie cronologiche [...], n.p., n.d. (BA, & 211 sup., 25, 27).
97 Juan Thadeo de San Eliseo to [Domingo de Jesús María], Isfahan, Jan. 3, 1619 (AGOCD, 237/m/13).
98 Felice di Sant'Antonio to the General Chapter, Rome, Oct. 15, 1649 (AGOCD, 261/m/1); [Chick], *Chronicle*, vol. 2, 893, 1229.
99 Casimir Joseph de Sainte-Thérèse to Isidore de Saint-Joseph, Basra, Nov. 29, 1655 (AGOCD, 241/h/5).
100 Giovanni Battista di San Giuseppe to Carolus Felix a Sancta Teresia, Basra, Mar. 21, 1678 (AGOCD, 242/a/22).
101 Bembo, *Il viaggio in Asia*, 360–1.

102 Juan Thadeo de San Eliseo to Benigno di San Michele, Isfahan, Mar. 26, 1616 (AGOCD, 237/m/9). On the consumption of wine in the Safavid Empire, see Rudi Matthee, *The Pursuit of Pleasure: Drugs and Stimulants in Iranian History, 1500–1900* (Princeton: Princeton University Press, 2005), 43–68.
103 Juan Thadeo de San Eliseo to [Domingo de Jesús María], Isfahan, Jan. 3, 1619 (AGOCD, 237/m/14 and 15).
104 Instruttione per gli nostri padri […] che si manda d'ordine del definitorio generale del 1630 a 6 di Jenaro, signed by Fernando de Santa María (AGOCD, 289/e/1).
105 Memoria delle cose che devo rappresentare alli nostri signori definitori per le missioni, n.p., n.d. [ca. 1670] (AGOCD, 243/b/3).
106 Faustino di San Carlo to the *Definitorium generale*, Isfahan, May 26, 1721 (AGOCD, 238/g/9).
107 Instructions by Paolo Simone di Gesù Maria, *praepositus generalis*, for Eugenio di San Benedetto, n.d. [1624] (AGOCD, 261/d/1 and 2).
108 Giovanni Stefano di Santa Teresa to the *Definitorium generale*, Goa, Sept. 15, 1639 (AGOCD, 261/g/1 and 2).
109 Amedeo della Santissima Trinità to [Bernardo Maria di Gesù], Shiraz, Mar. 31, 1685 (AGOCD, 238/i/6).
110 Felice di Sant'Antonio to the *Definitorium generale*, Shiraz, Apr. 10, 1671 (AGOCD, 238/p/14 and 15).
111 Miscellanea d'alcune historiette […] raccolte […] da F. C[ornelio] di S. Giuseppe Carmelitano Scalzo. Centuria seconda, n.p., n.d. (BA, L 13 suss., fol. 124r/v).
112 Barnaba di San Carlo to [Isidore de Saint-Joseph ?], Basra, Jan. 15, 1655 (AGOCD, 241/f/11).
113 Memoria delle cose che devo rappresentare alli nostri signori definitori per le missioni, n.p., n.d. [ca. 1670] (AGOCD, 243/b/3).
114 Responses by Ange de Saint-Joseph to nine questions posed to him by the visitor general, Giovanni Battista di San Giuseppe, Basra, Mar. 7, 1678 (AGOCD, 241/d/7).
115 The most interesting thing in this connection is the fact that the people lending money for interest in Persia were members of the regular clergy. In 1645, the *Propaganda Fide* decided that missionaries in China should not make excessive difficulties for their penitents—laypeople and not clerics—because of interest transactions. On the jurisprudence of the *Propaganda Fide* and the Holy Office, see Paola Vismara, *Oltre l'usura: La Chiesa moderna e il prestito a interesse* (Soveria Mannelli: Rubbettino Editore, 2004), 253–368.
116 Felice di Sant'Antonio to Isidore de Saint-Joseph, Basra, Feb. 6, 1653 (AGOCD, 241/k/2).
117 Barnaba di San Carlo to [Isidore de Saint-Joseph ?], Basra, Nov. 30, 1655 (AGOCD, 241/f/13).
118 Edmund Herzig has found the same range of 6 to 24 percent interest in credit transactions among the Armenian merchants of New Julfa. Herzig, "The Armenian Merchants," 240–2.
119 Denis de la Couronne d'Épines to [Isidore de Saint-Dominique], Isfahan, Jan. 3, 1657 (AGOCD, 237/c/31).
120 Felice di Sant'Antonio to Isidore de Saint-Dominique, Shiraz, Dec. 26, 1657 (AGOCD, 238/p/2).
121 Ange de Saint-Joseph to Valerio di San Giuseppe, Isfahan, Apr. 27, 1671 (AGOCD, 236/i/16).

122 Ange de Saint-Joseph to the *Definitorium generale*, Isfahan, June 5, 1669 (AGOCD, 238/l/7). That the friar misconstrued the creditworthiness of the French East India Company need not be discussed in detail here. On this topic, see page 248 as well as Furber, *Rival Empires of Trade*, 103–24, 203–7.
123 Ange de Saint-Joseph to [Jean Chrysostome de Saint-Paul], Isfahan, Dec. 22, 1675 (AGOCD, 236/b/18).
124 Ange de Saint-Joseph to [Jean Chrysostome de Saint-Paul], Isfahan, Sept. 1, 1675 (AGOCD, 236/i/27).
125 Deed of donation, Shiraz, May 22, 1666 (AGOCD, 238/h/2); declaration of commitment, Shiraz, Mar. 27, 1667 (AGOCD, 238/h/2).
126 [Ordinationes], by Francesco di Gesù, Bandar ʿAbbās, Jan. 28, 1669 (AGOCD, 235/h/18; 236/a/52; 237/d/13).
127 Girolamo di Gesù Maria to Philippe de la Très Sainte Trinité, Isfahan, July 31, 1669 (AGOCD, 237/n/1).
128 Ange de Saint-Joseph to the *Definitorium generale*, Isfahan, June 5, 1669 (AGOCD, 238/l/7).
129 Replies of Ange de Saint-Joseph to nine questions posed to him by the visitor general, Giovanni Battista di San Giuseppe, Basra, Mar. 7, 1678 (AGOCD, 241/d/7).
130 Girolamo di Gesù Maria to Jean Chrysostome de Saint-Paul, Basra, Aug. 30, 1673 (AGOCD, 241/l/7).
131 Faustino di San Carlo to [Philippe-Thérèse de Sainte-Anne], [Isfahan], n.d. [1719] (AGOCD, 242/b/13).
132 Numerous letters from de Rhodes to Nickel, Isfahan 1656–60 (ARSI, Gallia, 103 I and II).
133 De Rhodes to Nickel, Isfahan, May 30, 1659 (ARSI, Gallia, 103 II, fol. 271r).
134 Chézaud to the *assistant de France*, Isfahan, Dec. 16, 1661 (ARSI, Gallia, 97 II, doc. 111, fol. 320v).
135 Mercier to Claude Boucher, Isfahan, Sept. 9, 1666 (ARSI, Gallia, 97 II, doc. 121, fol. 336r).
136 See Vermote, "Finances of the Missions," 375–8, 387–9. On the Society of Jesus as a global enterprise, see Alden, *The Making of an Enterprise*.
137 On Japan, See Charles Ralph Boxer, *The Christian Century in Japan, 1549–1650* (Berkeley: University of California Press, 1951), 91–121; Mihoko Oka, *The Namban Trade: Merchants and Missionaries in 16th and 17th Century Japan* (Leiden: Brill, 2021); and Hélène Vu Thanh, *Devenir japonais: La mission jésuite au Japon (1549–1614)* (Paris: Presses de l'Université Paris-Sorbonne, 2016), 46–51, 157–9. On China and India, see Noël Golvers, *François de Rougemont, S.J., Missionary in Ch'ang-shu (Chiang-nan): A Study of the Account Book (1674–1676) and the Eulogium* (Louvain: Leuven University Press, 1999), 553–630; Julia Lederle, *Mission und Ökonomie der Jesuiten in Indien: Intermediäres Handeln am Beispiel der Malabar-Provinz im 18. Jahrhundert* (Wiesbaden: Harrassowitz, 2009), esp. 178–251; and Frederik Vermote, "The Role of Urban Real Estate in Jesuit Finances and Networks between Europe and China, 1612–1778" (PhD thesis, University of British Columbia, 2012).
138 Relatio; *Feria V*, Nov. 28, 1709 (ACDF, SO, St.St., M 3 a, fol. 69v–70v, 147v).
139 Juan Thadeo de San Eliseo to Paolo Simone di Gesù Maria, Isfahan, Aug. 31, 1624 (AGOCD, 237/m/22).
140 Robert Huntington, *D. Roberti Huntingtoni, episcopi rapotensis, epistolae [...]* (London, 1704), xx–xxi, 37–44, 82–7. On Huntington's scholarly cooperation with Discalced Carmelites, see Mills, *A Commerce of Knowledge*, 117–23.

141 Giovanni Battista di San Giuseppe to Carolus Felix a Sancta Teresia, Basra, Mar. 21, 1678 (AGOCD, 242/a/22).
142 *Congregazioni generali*, Jan. 15, 1680 (APF, Acta, vol. 50, fol. 6r/v) and Sept. 2, 1681 (APF, Acta, vol. 51, fol. 256r).
143 Ange de Saint-Joseph, *Gazophylacium linguae Persarum*, first unnumbered pages.
144 *Definitorium generale*, May 7, 1674. Fortes, *Acta definitorii*, vol. 2, 144.
145 Girolamo di Gesù Maria to Jean Chrysostome de Saint-Paul, Shiraz, Aug. 31, 1675 (AGOCD, 238/q/2 and 3).
146 Ange de Saint-Joseph to Jean Chrysostome de Saint-Paul, Isfahan, Sept. 1, 1670 (AGOCD, 236/i/4).
147 Ange de Saint-Joseph to [Jean Chrysostome de Saint-Paul], Isfahan, Sept. 8 and Dec. 22, 1675 (AGOCD, 236/b/18 and 19).
148 *Definitorium generale*, June 27, 1678. Fortes, *Acta definitorii*, vol. 2, 181.
149 Ange de Saint-Joseph to Jean Chrysostome de Saint-Paul, Isfahan, Oct. 1, 1672 (AGOCD, 236/i/19 and 20).
150 Ange de Saint-Joseph to [Jean Chrysostome de Saint-Paul], Isfahan, Sept. 1 (AGOCD, 236/i/27), Sept. 8 and Dec. 22, 1675 (AGOCD, 236/b/18 and 19).

Chapter 7

1 Siebenhüner, "Glaubenswechsel," 251.
2 On the Andes region, see, for example, Peter Gose, *Invaders as Ancestors: On the Intercultural Making and Unmaking of Spanish Colonialism in the Andes* (Toronto: University of Toronto Press, 2008). On Nouvelle France, see Allan Greer, *Mohawk Saint: Catherine Tekakwitha and the Jesuits* (New York: OUP, 2005).
3 See, for example, Gigliola Fragnito, *Proibito capire: La Chiesa e il volgare nella prima età moderna* (Bologna: Il Mulino, 2005).
4 Martin Gierl, *Pietismus und Aufklärung: Theologische Polemik und die Kommunikationsreform der Wissenschaft am Ende des 17. Jahrhunderts* (Göttingen: Vandenhoeck & Ruprecht, 1997).
5 Jean-Pascal Gay, "Lettres de controverse: Religion, publication et espace public en France au XVIIe siècle," *Annales: Histoire, Sciences Sociales* 68 (2013): 7–41, 37–8. Cf. the same author's *Morales en conflit: Théologie et polémique au Grand Siècle (1640–1700)* (Paris: Les Éditions du Cerf, 2011) and *Jesuit Civil Wars*, 294–300.
6 Maria Pia Donato, "Reorder and Restore: Benedict XIV, the Index, and the Holy Office," in *Benedict XIV and the Enlightenment: Art, Science, and Spirituality*, ed. Rebecca Messbarger, Christopher M. S. Johns, and Philip Gavitt (Toronto: University of Toronto Press, 2016), 231–2.
7 Rudolf Schlögl, *Religion and Society at the Dawn of Modern Europe: Christianity Transformed, 1750–1850* (London: Bloomsbury Academic, 2020), 205 (quotation)–7.
8 Paul Hazard had already described the basic characteristics of these transformations in the 1930s. Hazard, *The European Mind*. On the discovery of religion as the subject of a new academic field, see Stroumsa, *A New Science*. On the Chinese and Malabar rites controversies as part of global transformation processes, see Županov and Fabre, eds., *The Rites Controversies*.
9 See Lynn Hunt, Margaret C. Jacob, and Wijnand Mijnhardt, *The Book That Changed Europe: Picart & Bernard's Religious Ceremonies of the World* (Cambridge, MA: The Belknap Press of Harvard University Press, 2010).

10 See Laurence Macé, "Les *Lettres persanes* devant l'Index: Une censure 'posthume;" in *Montesquieu en 2005*, ed. Catherine Volpilhac-Auger (Oxford: Voltaire Foundation, 2005). On the ways French travelers, authors, and diplomatic envoys described and reinvented Safavid Iran, see Mokhberi, *The Persian Mirror*. On the Enlightenment's Persia, cf. Bonnerot, *La Perse,* and Cyrus Masroori, Whitney Mannies, and John Christian Laursen, eds., *Persia and the Enlightenment* (Liverpool: Liverpool University Press, 2021).

11 In the seventeenth century, European knowledge of China was based almost exclusively on the reports of Catholic missionaries. See Romano, *Impressions de Chine*. The sources of European knowledge about South India were more varied, but here, too, missionaries played a central role especially in the description of religious practices. Joan-Pau Rubiés, "From Christian Apologetics to Deism: Libertine Readings of Hinduism, 1650–1730," in *God in the Enlightenment*, ed. William J. Bulman and Robert G. Ingram (Oxford: OUP, 2016).

12 Hazard, *The European Mind,* esp. 20–4. See also Virgile Pinot, *La Chine et la formation de l'esprit philosophique en France (1640–1715)* (Paris: Paul Geuthner, 1932), 187–430, and Israel, *Enlightenment Contested*, 640–62. On the issue of atheism in the Chinese rites controversy, see Michela Catto, "Atheism: A Word Travelling To and Fro between Europe and China," in *The Rites Controversies*, ed. Županov and Fabre.

13 On the image of the *literati* as a meritocracy, see Osterhammel, *Unfabling the East*, 404 (quotation)–408.

14 Ines G. Županov, "Le repli du religieux: Les missionnaires jésuites du XVIIe siècle entre la théologie chrétienne et une éthique païenne," *Annales: Histoire, Sciences Sociales* 51 (1996): 1201–23. See also the same author's *Missionary Tropics*, 14, 267–70, and Barreto Xavier and Županov, *Catholic Orientalism*, 119, 121–2, 145–57.

15 On this, see, for example, Olivier Christin, *La paix de religion: L'autonomisation de la raison politique au XVIe siècle* (Paris: Éditions du Seuil, 1997).

16 See Chapter 5, "Caring for the Dying and Funerals."

17 Santus, *Trasgressioni necessarie*, 17–21.

18 Ibid., 121, 227–39, 287–96, 309–427, 436–41.

19 Fernando de Santa María to the Discalced Carmelites in Persia, Rome, Oct. 18, 1608 (AGOCD, 236/a/5).

20 Juan de Jesús María, Instructio Missionum, reproduced in his *Scritti missionari*, 193–272, 200, 217.

21 Tomás de Jesús, *De procuranda salute,* 551–6 (quotation).

22 Ingoli, Litterae Encyclicae Sacrae Congregationis de Propaganda Fide ad omnes nuntios apostolicos, Rome, Jan. 15, 1622, reproduced in *Collectanea S. Congregationis de Propaganda fide seu decreta instructiones rescripta pro apostolicis missionibus*, vol. 1: *Ann. 1622–1866* (Rome: Ex typographia polyglotta S.C. de Propaganda fide, 1907), 1–2 (quotation). On the bull *Ad vitanda scandala*, see Chapter 4, "Leaving the Armenian Church 'in Its Heresies."

23 [Ordinationes], by Vicente de San Francisco, Isfahan, Sept. 22, 1621 (AGOCD, 235/l/1 and 236/a/14).

24 Instruttione per gli nostri padri […] che si manda d'ordine del definitorio generale del 1630 a 6 di Jenaro, signed by Fernando de Santa María (AGOCD, 289/e/1).

25 De Vries, *Rom und die Patriarchate*, 379–82.

26 On this, see Chapter 4, "Confessional Agitators with Rome's Approval."

27 Relatio; *Feria V,* Nov. 14 and 21, 1709 (ACDF, SO, St.St., M 3 a, X, fol. 68r–70v, 147v).

28 Santus, *Trasgressioni necessarie*, 177–96.

29 Istruzione per l'Oriente sopra la Communicazione in divinis de' Cattolici co' Scismatici, ed Eretici [...], July 5, 1729, signed by Petra, reproduced in *Sacrorum Conciliorum nova et amplissima collectio [...]*, vol. 46: *Synodi Melchitarum, 1716–1902* (Paris: expensis Huberti Welter, 1911), c. 99–103.
30 Charles A. Frazee, *Catholics and Sultans: The Church and the Ottoman Empire, 1453–1923* (Cambridge: CUP, 1983), 185–9, 202; Heyberger, *Les Chrétiens du Proche-Orient*, 399.
31 The controversies surrounding the "Chinese rites" have long been a focus of scholarship on the Jesuit missions in China. See Nicolas Standaert, "The Rites Controversy," in *Handbook of Christianity in China*, vol. 1: *1635–1800*, ed. N. Standaert (Leiden: Brill, 2001), and *Chinese Voices*. On the origins of the disputes over the "Malabar rites," see Županov, *Disputed Mission*. On the later developments, see Édouard René Hambye, *Christianity in India*, vol. 3: *The Eighteenth Century* (Bangalore: The Church History Association of India, 1997), 211–37. Cf. Paolo Aranha, "Sacramenti o *saṃskārāḥ*? L'illusione dell'*accommodatio* nella controversia dei riti malabarici," *Cristianesimo nella storia* 31 (2010): 621–46.
32 Brockey, *Journey to the East*, 43–63; Hsia, *A Jesuit in the Forbidden City*.
33 Županov, *Disputed Mission*, 24–7, 35, 46–7, 58–9, 97–101, 119, 121. See also the same author's "Le repli du religieux," and Joan-Pau Rubiés, "The Concept of Cultural Dialogue and the Jesuit Method of Accommodation: Between Idolatry and Civilization," *Archivum Historicum Societatis Iesu* 74 (2005): 237–80, 257.
34 Ingoli, *Quattro Parti del Mondo*, 125.
35 See Severino Vareschi, "Heiliges Offizium gegen *Propaganda*? Das Dekret des Jahres 1656 in der Ritenfrage und die Rolle Martino Martinis," in *Martino Martini S.J. (1614–61) und die Chinamission im 17. Jahrhundert*, ed. Roman Malek and Arnold Zingerle (Nettetal: Steyler, 2000).
36 Santus, *Trasgressioni necessarie*, 177, 179–80.
37 Ingoli to [Angelo Giori], Aug. 3, 1643 (APF, SOCG, vol. 36, fol. 1r/v).
38 *Congregazione generale*, July 21, 1625 (APF, Acta, vol. 3, fol. 243v–4r).
39 Bonaventura *Malvasia, Dilucidatio Speculi verum monstrantis [...]* (Rome, 1628); Filippo *Guadagnoli, Apologia pro Christiana Religione [...]* (Rome, 1631), and *Pro christiana religione responsio ad obiectiones Ahmed filii Zin Alabedin, Persae Asphahensis [...]* (Rome, 1637).
40 Filippo Guadagnoli, *Considerationes ad Mahomettanos, cum responsione ad obiectiones Ahmed filii Zin Alabedin, Persae Asphahanensis [...]* (Rome, 1649). Cf. Giovanni Pizzorusso, "Filippo Guadagnoli, i Caraccciolini et lo studio delle lingue orientali e della controversia con l'Islam a Roma nel XVII secolo," *Studi medievali e moderni: Arte, letteratura, storia* 14 (2010): 245–78, 266–73.
41 Giovanni Battista Giattini, Athanasius Kircher, Bartolomeo da Pettorano, Antonio dall'Aquila and Ludovico Marracci to the Holy Office, Sept. 3, 1652 (ACDF, SO, Censura librorum 1641–54, no. 25, fol. 565r).
42 The learned libertine Gabriel Naudé had already published his *Apologie pour tous les grands personnages qui ont été faussement soupçonnés de magie* in Paris in 1625, in which he (as Thomas Hobbes would in his 1651 *Leviathan*) counted Muhammad among the "most refined and cunning legislators" who had claimed a divine origin for their laws with regard to their efficacy (49–50). On the importance of Islam in the European Enlightenment, see Israel, *Enlightenment Contested*, 615–39.
43 On seventeenth-century Roman Orientalism, see Girard, "Le christianisme oriental," esp. 254–345; Bernard Heyberger, "Chrétiens orientaux dans l'Europe catholique (XVIIe–XVIIIe siècles)," in *Hommes de l'entre-deux: Parcours individuels et portraits*

de groupes sur la frontière de la Méditerranée, XVIe–XXe siècle, ed. B. Heyberger and Chantal Verdeil (Paris: Les Indes Savantes, 2009). On the role of the *Propaganda Fide*, see Pizzorusso, "Filippo Guadagnoli," and the same author's "Les écoles de langue arabe et le milieu orientaliste autour de la Congrégation *de Propaganda fide* au temps d'Abraham Ecchellensis," in *Orientalisme, science et controverse: Abraham Ecchellensis (1605–1664)*, ed. B. Heyberger (Turnhout: Brepols, 2010).

44 Abraham Ecchellensis to the *Propaganda Fide*, n.p., n.d. [1649] (APF, CP, vol. 6, fol. 721r, 726v).
45 Bernard Heyberger, "L'Islam et les Arabes chez un érudit maronite au service de l'Église catholique (Abraham Ecchellensis)," *Al-Qanṭara* 31 (2010): 481–512, 491–5, 497, and Heyberger, ed., *Orientalisme, science et controverse*.
46 Miscellanea d'alcune historiette […] raccolte […] da F. C[ornelio] di S. Giuseppe Carmelitano Scalzo. Centuria seconda, n.p. [probably Bushehr], n.d. (BA, L 13 suss., fol. 94v).
47 See, with no reference to the decisions in the rites controversies, Israel, *Enlightenment Contested*, 65.
48 Michela Catto, "Superstizione, monoteismo e unità della Chiesa: Benedetto XIV e la condanna dei riti cinesi (1742)," in *Storia, medicina e diritto nei trattati di Prospero Lambertini Benedetto XIV*, ed. Maria Teresa Fattori (Rome: Edizioni di storia e letteratura, 2013), 97–108, 104–5, 108.
49 Osservazione generale […], signed by Giuseppe [Simone] Assemani, n.d. [1757]; vote by Lorenzo Ganganelli, n.d. [1757]; Riflessioni […], signed by Giuseppe Maria Castelli, n.d. [1757] (ACDF, SO, St.St., M 3 b, XV, fol. 790r–4v, 800r–805v [quotation], 808r–37v).
50 According to Ago, *Carriere e clientele*, esp. 158.
51 Relatio, n.d. (ACDF, SO, St.St., M 3 a, XIV, fol. 390r–405v).
52 Arndt Brendecke, *The Empirical Empire: Spanish Colonial Rule and the Politics of Knowledge* (Berlin: De Gruyter Oldenbourg, 2016), esp. 252–78.
53 Ristretto per la Congregazione Particolare […] de' Greci Melchiti, written by Carlo Uslenghi, discussed by the *Congregazioni particolari* of Mar. 15 and 31, Apr. 5 and 26, May 3 and 12, and July 5, 1729, reproduced in *Sacrorum Conciliorum nova et amplissima collectio*, vol. 46, c. 1–88, c. 22–3.
54 Santus, *Trasgressioni necessarie*, 177–80.
55 *Feria V*, Jan. 12, 1719 (ACDF, SO, St.St., M 3 a, XIV, fol. 202v). Cf. de Vries, *Rom und die Patriarchate*, 383.
56 *Feria II*, Oct. 21, 1720; *Feria V*, Nov. 7, 1720 (ACDF, SO, St.St., M 3 a, XIV, fol. 214v, 220v).
57 On Assemani, see Heyberger, "Chrétiens orientaux dans l'Europe catholique," 63–4, 85–7; Nasser Gemayel, *Les échanges culturels entre les Maronites et l'Europe: Du Collège Maronite de Rome (1584) au Collège de ʿAyn Warqa (1789)*, 2 vols. (Beirut: Imprimerie Gemayel, 1984), vol. 2, 420–33.
58 Osservazione generale […], signed by Assemani, n.d. [1757] (ACDF, SO, St.St., M 3 b, XV, fol. 790r–4v).
59 Osservazione particolare […], signed by Assemani, n.d. [1757] (ACDF, SO, St.St., M 3 b, XV, fol. 795r–6v).
60 The phrase was used in this or similar forms by other curial congregations as well. On the *Propaganda Fide*, see Bernard Heyberger, "'Pro nunc nihil est respondendum'. Recherche d'information et prise de décision à la Propagande: L'exemple du Levant (XVIIIe siècle)," *Mélanges de l'École française de Rome: Italie et Méditerranée* 109/2

(1997): 539–54. The author focuses on the Congregation's uncertainty about the appropriateness of the information it had received as an explanation for the "non-answer." The documentation of the Holy Office, in contrast, suggests that the main reason for this practice was the fear that making unenforceable decisions would undermine the Church's authority. Precisely because the Congregation believed it possessed appropriate knowledge, it decided to dispense with a reply.

61 Dubbi proposti da PP. Cappuccini Missionarii [...], n.d. [1699] (ACDF, SO, St.St., UV 20, fol. 221r–31v).
62 Resolutio by Giovanni Damasceno Bragaldi, n.d. [1699] (ACDF, SO, St.St., UV 20, fol. 224r–31r).
63 Dubbi proposti da PP. Cappuccini Missionarii [...], n.d. [1699] (ACDF, SO, St.St., OO 5 h, fol. n.n.).
64 Resolutio by Bragaldi, n.d. [1704]; *Feria V*, Aug. 7, 1704 (ACDF, SO, St.St., UV 19, fol. 230r, 244v).
65 *Feria II*, July 4, 1718; *Feria V*, July 14, 1718 (ACDF, SO, Dubia circa Poenitentiam, 1625–1770, XVIII, fol. 97r, 99r, 104v).
66 *Feria II*, Apr. 23, 1714; vote by Bragaldi, n.d. (ACDF, SO, Dubia circa matrimonium, vol. 1: 1603–1722, XXXX, fol. 426r/v, 438r–41v).
67 *Congregazioni generali*, July 9, 1715 (APF, Acta, vol. 85, fol. 384v–5r) and Sept. 25, 1719 (APF, Acta, vol. 89, fol. 381r/v).
68 Dubbi proposti da Mons. Barnaba Fedeli [...], n.d.; *Feria IV*, Nov. 15, 1719 (ACDF, SO, Dubia diversa, 1708–30, XV, fol. 334r, 336v).
69 Articolo di lettera del P. Barnaba [Fedeli] di Milano [...] [to the *Propaganda Fide*], [Isfahan], May 30 and June 21, 1713 (ACDF, SO, Dubia circa matrimonium, vol. 1: 1603–1722, XXXX, fol. 428r–9r, 431r–2r); *Congregazione generale*, June 12, 1714 (APF, Acta, vol. 84, fol. 345v–6r, 347r [quotation]).
70 Dubbi proposti da Mons. Barnaba Fedeli [...], n.d.; *Feria II*, Nov. 13, 1719; *Feria IV*, Nov. 15, 1719 (ACDF, SO, Dubia diversa, 1708–30, XV, fol. 334r, 336v).
71 In 1733, when he showed his appreciation to the Discalced Carmelite nuns in Florence by gifting them with a relic of the true cross and the silver reliquary that went with it, he even called himself Count Gregorio Agdollo Sceriman. See Ildefonso di San Luigi, *Vita della Ven. Serva di Dio Suor Maria Agnese di Gesù Carmelitana Scalza [...]* (Florence, 1762), 127. In his business undertakings in Florence, in contrast, Agdollo dispensed with the name Sceriman. See, for example, ASFI, Libri di commercio e di famiglia, 10–13.
72 On Agdollo's activities as a middleman in the service of Saxony-Poland, see Evelyn Korsch, "Meriten und Machenschaften des Gregorio Agdollo: Ein Armenier im Dienste Sachsens," *Ars Mercaturae: Jahrbuch für internationale Handelsgeschichte* 3 (2017): 107–38.
73 My observations are based on a study of the following Holy Office dossier: Armeno Catholico, qui matrimonium in Patria invitus contraxerat cum Puella Novennii, datur facultas nubendi alteri Puellae, cum qua rem habuerat sub spe futuri matrimonii, 1736-7 (ACDF, SO, St.St., QQ 2 g, XXXII, fol. 307r–93v).
74 *Congregazione generale*, Aug. 21, 1635 (APF, Acta, vol. 10, fol. 294v).
75 Decretum SS^{mi} DD. Clementis X circa modum, quo haec S. Congregatio transmittere debeat [...] responsiones ad dubia [...], 1671 (ACDF, SO, Dubia diversa, 1669–1707, XVIII, fol. 160r, 161r; Dubia circa matrimonia 1603–1722, XVII, fol. 836r, 839r, 840v).
76 *Congregazione generale*, Oct. 6, 1671 (APF, Acta, vol. 41, fol. 308v).

77 Ingoli to [Giori], Aug. 3,1643 (APF, SOCG, vol. 36, fol. 1r [quotation]/v).
78 Parere del segretario Francesco Ingoli, n.d. (APF, SOCG, vol. 192, fol. 181r/v); memorandum to Pope Innocent X from Ingoli, Oct. 22, 1644 (APF, CP, vol. 4, fol. 142r-3r).
79 Birgit Emich, "The Production of Truth in the Manufacture of Saints: Procedures, Credibility and Patronage in Early Modern Processes of Canonization," in *Making Truth in Early Modern Catholicism*, ed. Andreea Badea, Bruno Boute, Marco Cavarzere, and Steven Vanden Broecke (Amsterdam: Amsterdam University Press, 2021), esp. 167, 185.
80 On the decision-making practice of the Sacred Congregation of Rites in processes of beatification and canonization, see Sidler, *Heiligkeit aushandeln*, 465-8, 476-8.
81 Claudio Donati, "La Chiesa di Roma tra antico regime e riforme settecentesche (1675-1760)," in *La Chiesa e il potere politico dal Medioevo all'età contemporanea*, ed. Giorgio Chittolini and Giovanni Miccoli (Turin: Giulio Einaudi, 1986), 735-8.
82 See Mario Caravale and Alberto Caracciolo, *Lo Stato pontificio da Martino V a Pio IX* (Turin: UTET, 1978), 449-75.
83 Decision by the Holy Office, May 10, 1753, reproduced in Raphaël de Martinis, *Iuris Pontificii de Propaganda Fide pars secunda [...]* (Rome: ex Typographia polyglotta, 1909), part 2, 326, no. 591.
84 Forclaz, *Catholiques au défi de la Réforme*, 287-92.
85 Gaudemet, *Le mariage*, 305. On the *Declaratio benedictina* as a tool to maintain the doctrinal authority of the Church in spite of its limited enforcement capability, see Cecilia Cristellon, "Choosing Information, Selecting Truth: The Roman Congregations, the Benedictine Declaration, and the Establishment of Religious Pluralism," in *Making Truth*, ed. Badea, Boute, Cavarzere, and Vanden Broecke.
86 Instructions from Benedict XIV for the apostolic vicar of Constantinople, Nov. 30, 1754 (ACDF, SO, Dubia circa matrimonium, vol. 8: 1768-70, VIII, fol. n.n.).
87 Vote by Serafino Maria Maccarinelli, n.d. [1768] (ACDF, SO, Dubia circa matrimonium, vol. 8: 1768-70, VIII, fol. n.n.).
88 *Feria II*, Jan. 25, 1768; *Feria V*, Apr. 14, 1768 (ACDF, SO, Dubia circa matrimonium, vol. 8: 1768-70, VIII, fol. n.n.).
89 *Feria II*, June 28, 1773; audience Clement XIV, n.d.; *Feria II*, May 16, 1774; *Feria V*, June 9, 1774, and May 23, 1775 (ACDF, SO, Dubia circa matrimonium, vol. 10: 1773-80, III, fol. n.n.).
90 Fattori, *Benedetto XIV e Trento*.
91 Mario Rosa, "The Catholic *Aufklärung* in Italy," in *A Companion to the Catholic Enlightenment in Europe*, ed. Ulrich L. Lehner and Michael O'Neill Printy (Leiden: Brill, 2010), 224-9, quotation: 227. See also Messbarger, Johns, and Gavitt, eds., *Benedict XIV*; U. L. Lehner, *The Catholic Enlightenment: The Forgotten History of a Global Movement* (Oxford: OUP, 2016), 67-71.
92 Benedict XIV to the Cathedral Chapter of Bologna, Apr. 8, 1741, quoted in Fattori, *Benedetto XIV e Trento*, 26.
93 See Maurice A. Finocchiaro, "Benedict XIV and the Galileo Affair: Liberalization or Carelessness?," in *Benedict XIV*, ed. Messbarger, Johns, and Gavitt, 206-26.
94 On the reform of the Holy Office and the Congregation of the Index, see Patrizia Delpiano, "La riorganizzazione della censura libraria," in *Storia, medicina e diritto*, ed. Fattori; Donato, "Reorder and Restore"; Maria Teresa Fattori, "Lambertini's Treatises and the Cultural Project of Benedict XIV: Two Sides of the Same Policy," in *Benedict XIV*, ed. Messbarger, Johns, and Gavitt; and Hubert Wolf and Bernward Schmidt, *Benedikt XIV. und die Reform des Buchzensurverfahrens: Zur Geschichte und Rezeption von "Sollicita ac provida"* (Paderborn: Ferdinand Schöningh, 2011).

Conclusion

1   See Ditchfield, "Decentering the Catholic Reformation."
2   On Ignatius of Loyola, see Stefania Pastore, "Unwise Paths: Ignatius Loyola and the Years of Alcalá de Henares," in *A Companion to Ignatius of Loyola: Life, Writings, Spirituality, Influence*, ed. Robert Aleksander Maryks (Leiden: Brill, 2014); Sabina Pavone, "A Saint under Trial: Ignatius of Loyola between Alcalá and Rome," in ibid. On Teresa of Ávila, see the literature cited in n. 133, p. 306.
3   According to Mostaccio, *Between Obedience and Conscience*.
4   The practices of resistance rooted in the orientation of one's own life toward God were limited neither to mission nor to the male branches of an order. On the resistance of French nuns to the papal bull *Unigenitus*, see Françoise de Noirfontaine, "Les carmélites dans la résistance à l'*Unigenitus*," in *Carmes et carmélites en France du XVIIe siècle à nos jours: Actes du colloque de Lyon (Sept. 25-26, 1997)*, ed. Bernard Hours (Paris: Les Éditions du Cerf, 2001).
5   Friedrich, *Der lange Arm Roms?*, 111–12.

Sources and Bibliography

1   For a detailed listing of all the holdings consulted, see Windler, *Missionare in Persien*, 649–55.
2   For the complete titles and a detailed listing of all the printed sources consulted, see Windler, *Missionare in Persien*, 655–67.
3   This bibliography contains only the titles quoted in the footnotes. For a complete list of all the research literature consulted for this project up to 2018, see Windler, *Missionare in Persien*, 667–727.

Sources and Bibliography

Manuscript Sources[1]

Évora, Biblioteca Pública: *Coleção Patrimonial*
Florence, Archivio di Stato: *Libri di commercio e di famiglia*
Florence, Biblioteca Nazionale Centrale: *Manoscritti e Rari*
Goa, Directorate of Archives and Archeology: *Monções do Reino; Livros dos Reis Vizinhos; Regimentos*
Lausanne, Bibliothèque Cantonale et Universitaire: *Manuscrits*
Lisbon, Biblioteca da Academia das Ciências: *Manuscritos*
Lisbon, Biblioteca Nacional: *Manuscritos*
London, British Library: *India Office Records*
Milan, Archivio di Stato: *Fondo di religione*
Milan, Biblioteca Ambrosiana: *Manoscritti*
Montpellier, Bibliothèque interuniversitaire. Section Médecine: *Manuscrits*
Padua, Archivio di Stato: *Archivio Sceriman*
Paris, Archives des Missions étrangères de Paris: *Séminaire; Perse*
Paris (La Courneuve), Archives du Ministère des Affaires étrangères: *Correspondance politique. Perse; Personnel*
Paris, Archives Nationales de France: *Marine, fonds "Affaires étrangères"*
Paris, Bibliothèque de l'Institut de France: *Manuscrits*
Paris, Bibliothèque Nationale de France: *Manuscrits*
Rome, Archivio Apostolico Vaticano: *Archivio della Valle-del Bufalo; Missioni*
Rome, Archivio Storico *de Propaganda fide*: *Acta; CP; Fondo Vienna; Greci Melchiti. CP; Istruzioni diverse; Lettere; Miscellanee varie; SC. Armeni; SC. Missioni. Miscellanee; SC. Mesopotamia e Persia; SC. Stato temporale; SOCG*
Rome, Archivum Congregationis pro Doctrina Fidei: *Index, Diari; Index, Prot.; SO, Censura librorum; SO, Decreta; SO, Dispensationes variae; SO, Dubia circa baptismum; SO, Dubia circa confirmationem, extremam unctionem et olea sacra; SO, Dubia circa matrimonium; SO, Dubia circa poenitentiam; SO, Dubia diversa; SO, St.St.*
Rome, Archivum Generale Augustinianum
Rome, Archivum Generale Ordinis Carmelitarum Discalceatorum
Rome, Archivum Romanum Societatis Iesu
Rome, Biblioteca Apostolica Vaticana: *Manoscritti*
Rome, Biblioteca Nazionale Centrale: *Manoscritti*
The Hague, Nationaal Archief: *Archief van de Verenigde Oost-Indische Compagnie (VOC)*

Printed Sources[2]

Acosta, José de. *De procuranda Indorum Salute*. Salamanca, 1588. Edited by Luciano Pereña Vicente, V. Abril, C. Baciero, A. García, D. Ramos, J. Barrientos, and F. Maseda. Corpus Hispanorum de Pace 23 and 24. 2 vols. Madrid: CSIC, 1984, 1987.

Ange de Saint-Joseph. *Gazophylacium linguae Persarum [...]*. Amsterdam, 1684. Abridged French translation in Michel Bastiaensen, *Souvenirs de la Perse safavide et autres lieux d'Orient [1664–1678] en version persane et européenne*. Travaux de la Faculté de Philosophie et Lettres 93. Brussels: Éditions de l'Université de Bruxelles, 1985.

Ange de Saint-Joseph. *Pharmacopoea persica ex idiomate persico in Latinum conversa [...]*. Paris, 1681.

Arak'el of Tabriz, *Book of History (Arak'el Dawrizhets'i, Girk' patmut'eants')*. Introduction and annotated translation from the critical text by George A. Bournoutian. Costa Mesa: Mazda, 2010.

Arnauld, Antoine. *La perpétuité de la foi de l'Église catholique touchant l'Eucharistie [...]*. Vol. 3. Paris, 1674.

Arquivo Português Oriental, I: *Historia política, diplomática e militar*. Vol. 3, part 1: *1700–1708*, part 2: *1709–1719*, part 3: *1720–1726*, part 4: *1727–1736*. Edited by A. B. de Bragança Pereira. Bastorá: Tipografia Rangel, 1939–40.

Assentos do Conselho do Estado. Vol. 5: *1696–1750*. Edited by Panduronga S.S. Pissurlencar. Bastorá: Tipografía Rangel, 1957.

Bedik, Petros. *Cehil Sutun, seu explicatio utriusque celeberrimi, ac pretiosissimi theatri quadraginta columnarum in Perside Orientis [...]*. Vienna, 1678. English translation in *A Man of Two Worlds: Pedros Bedik in Iran, 1670–1675*. Edited by Colette Ouahes and Willem Floor. Washington, DC: Mage, 2014.

Bembo, Ambrogio. *Il viaggio in Asia (1671–1675) nei manoscritti di Minneapolis e di Bergamo*. Edited by Antonio Invernizzi. Alessandria: Edizioni dell'Orso, 2012. English translation: *The Travels and Journal of Ambrosio Bembo*. Translated by Clara Bargellini; edited by Anthony Welch. Berkeley: University of California Press, 2007.

Carré, Barthélémy. *Le courrier du Roi en Orient: Relations de deux voyages en Perse et en Inde, 1668–1674*. Edited by Dirk van der Cruysse. Paris: Fayard, 2005.

Chardin, Jean. *Voyages du chevalier Chardin, en Perse, et autres lieux de l'Orient*. Edited by Louis-Mathieu Langlès. 10 vols. Paris, 1811.

Chronica Bassorensis Missionis Carmelitarum Discalceatorum annis 1733–1778 ab auctoribus anonymis conscripta. Edited by P. Ambrosio a Sancta Teresia. Rome: apud Curiam Generalitiam, 1934.

Collecção de tratados e concertos de pazes que o Estado da Índia Portugueza fez com os Reis e Senhores com quem teve relações nas partes da Asia e Africa Oriental [...]. Edited by Julio Firmino Judice Biker. Vol. 4. Lisbon: Imprensa Nacional, 1884.

Collectanea S. Congregationis de Propaganda fide seu decreta instructiones rescripta pro apostolicis missionibus. Vol. 1: *Ann. 1622–1866*. Rome: Ex typographia polyglotta S.C. de Propaganda fide, 1907.

Constitutiones Carmelitarum Discalceatorum Congregationis S. Eliae anno 1605 latae. Edited by Giovanni Marco Strina. Genoa: Tipo-Litografia Opera SS. Vergine di Pompei, 1968.

Constitutiones Fratrum Discalceatorum Congregationis S. Eliae Ordinis Beatissimae Virginia Mariae de Monte Carmelo. Rome, 1631.

Daulier Deslandes, André. *Les beautés de la Perse: Relation d'un voyage en Perse de 1663 à 1666*. Paris, 1673. Edited by Françoise de Valence. Paris: Maisonneuve et Larose, 2003.

De Bruyn, Cornelis. *Voyages de Corneille le Brun par la Moscovie, en Perse, et aux Indes orientales*. 2 vols. Amsterdam, 1718.

Della Valle, Pietro. *Viaggi [...] Parte prima: La Turchia*. Rome, 1650.

Della Valle, Pietro. *Viaggi [...]. Parte seconda: La Persia*. 2 vols. Rome, 1658.

[Du Cerceau, Jean-Antoine and Tadeusz Juda Krusiński]. *Histoire de la dernière Révolution de Perse*. 2 vols. Paris, 1728. First edn. The Hague, 1728.
Felix de Jesus. Primeira Parte da Chronica e Relação do Principio que teve a Comgregação da Ordem de S. Augustinho nas Indias Orientais [...], dated Goa, Jan. 15, 1606, in Arnulf Hartmann. "The Augustinians in Golden Goa, According to a Manuscript by Felix of Jesus, O.S.A." *Analecta Augustiniana* 30 (1967): 5–147.
Fortes, Antonio. *Acta capituli generalis O.C.D. Congregationis S. Eliae*. Vol. 1: *1605–41*, vol. 2: *1644–98*, vol. 3: *1701–97*. Monumenta Historica Carmeli Teresiani 11, 13 and 14. Rome: Teresianum, 1990–2.
Fortes, Antonio. *Acta definitorii generalis O.C.D. Congregationis S. Eliae*. Vol. 1: *1605–58*, vol. 2: *1658–710*, vol. 3: *1710–66*. Monumenta Historica Carmeli Teresiani: Subsidia 3–5. Rome: Teresianum, 1985, 1986, 1988.
Foster, William. *The English Factories in India, 1646–1650: A Calendar of Documents in the India Office*. Oxford: Clarendon Press, 1914.
Foster, William. *The English Factories in India, 1651–1654: A Calendar of Documents in the India Office*. Oxford: Clarendon Press, 1915.
[Frizon, Nicolas and Jacques Villotte]. *Voyages d'un missionnaire de la Compagnie de Jésus en Turquie, en Perse, en Arménie, en Arabie, et en Barbarie*. Paris, 1730.
Fryer, John. *A New Account of East India and Persia Being Nine Years Travels, 1672–1681*. Edited by William Crooke. Vols. 2 and 3. London: Hakluyt Society, 1912, 1915.
Gabriel de Chinon. *Relations nouvelles du Levant [...]*. Lyon, 1671.
Gemelli Careri, Giovanni Francesco. *Giro del mondo del Dottor D. Gio. Francesco Gemelli Careri. Nuova edizione [...]. Tomo secondo contenente le cose piú ragguardevoli vedute nella Persia*. Venice, 1719.
Gollancz, Hermann, ed. *Chronicle of Events between the Years 1623 and 1733 Relating to the Settlement of the Order of Carmelites in Mesopotamia (Bassora): A Contribution to the History of Christian Missions in the East, Written by Agathangelus of St. Theresa and Others. Now Edited for the First Time with Translation and Notes from a Unique (Autograph) Ms. in the Possession of the Author*. London: OUP and Humphrey Milford, Publisher to the University, 1927.
Gouveia, António de. *Jornada do Arcebispo de Goa Dom Frey Aleixo de Menezes Primaz da Índia Oriental, religioso da Ordem de S. Agostinho [...]*. Coimbra, 1606.
Guadagnoli, Filippo. *Apologia pro Christiana Religione [...]*. Rome, 1631.
Guadagnoli, Filippo. *Considerationes ad Mahomettanos, cum responsione ad obiectiones Ahmed filii Zin Alabedin, Persae Asphahanensis [...]*. Rome, 1649.
Guadagnoli, Filippo. *Pro christiana religione responsio ad obiectiones Ahmed filii Zin Alabedin, Persae Asphahensis [...]*. Rome, 1637.
Hamilton, Alexander. *A New Account of the East Indies [...]*. Vol. 1. Edinburgh, 1727.
Huntington, Robert. *D. Roberti Huntingtoni, episcopi rapotensis, epistolae [...]*. London, 1704.
Ildefonso di San Luigi. *Vita della Ven. Serva di Dio Suor Maria Agnese di Gesù Carmelitana Scalza [...]*. Florence, 1762.
Ingoli, Francesco, *Relatione delle Quattro Parti del Mondo (1629–1631)*. Edited by Fabio Tosi. Rome: Urbaniana University Press, 1999.
Instructiones Fratrum Discalceatorum [...]. Rome, 1630.
Isidore de Saint-Joseph and Pierre de Saint-André. *Historia Generalis Fratrum Discalceatorum Ordinis [...]*. 2 vols. Rome, 1668, 1671.
Iskandar Bēg Munšī. *History of ʿAbbas the Great (Tārīḵ-e ʿĀlamārā-ye ʿAbbāsī)*. Translated by Roger M. Savory. 3 vols. Vols. 1 and 2, Boulder: Westview Press, 1978. Vol. 3, Persian Heritage Series 28. New York: Bibliotheca Persica, 1986.

Juan de Jesús María. *Scritti missionari*. Edited and translated by Giovanni Strina. Collana Ioannes a Iesu Maria 10. Brussels: Éditions Soumillion, 1994.

Kaempfer, Engelbert. *Amoenitatum Exoticarum Politico-Physico-Medicarum Fasciculi V [...]*. Lemgo, 1712.

Kaempfer, Engelbert. *Briefe, 1683–1715*. Edited by Detlef Haberland. Engelbert Kaempfer, Werke: Kritische Ausgabe in Einzelbänden 2. Munich: Iudicium, 2001.

Leandro di Santa Cecilia. *Persia ovvero secondo viaggio [...] dell'Oriente [...]*. Rome, 1757.

Lucas, Paul, *Voyage du Sieur Paul Lucas au Levant: juin 1699–juillet 1703*. Paris, 1704. Edited by Henri Duranton. Saint-Étienne: Publications de l'Université de Saint-Étienne, 1998.

Malvasia, Bonaventura. *Dilucidatio Speculi verum monstrantis [...]*. Rome, 1628.

Martinis, Raphaël de. *Iuris Pontificii de Propaganda Fide pars secunda [...]*. Rome: ex Typographia polyglotta, 1909.

Mirot, Léon. "Lettres écrites de Perse et de Syrie par le Révérend Père Bernard de Sainte-Thérèse, évêque de Babylone." *Bulletin de la Société scientifique de Clamecy*, 3e série, 8 (1932): 125–65.

Naudé, Gabriel. *Apologie pour tous les grands personnages qui ont été faussement soupçonnés de magie*. Paris, 1625.

Olearius, Adam. *Vermehrte Newe Beschreibung der Muscowitischen und Persischen Reyse [...]*. Schleswig, 1656.

Pacifique de Provins. *Le voyage de Perse et Brève relation du voyage des Îles de l'Amérique*. Paris, 1631 and 1646. Edited by P. Godefroy de Paris and P. Hilaire de Wingene. Bibliotheca Seraphico-Capuccina, Sectio historica 3 and 4. Assisi: Collegio S. Lorenzo da Brindisi, 1939.

Pallu, François, *Lettres de Monseigneur Pallu écrites de 1654 à 1684*. Edited by Adrien Launay and Frédéric Mantienne. Paris: Les Indes savantes, 2008.

Philippe de la Très Sainte Trinité. *Historia V.P. Dominici a Iesu Maria Discalceatorum Ordinis Beatissimae Virginis Mariae de Monte Carmelo Congregationis S. Eliae Praepositi Generalis [...]*. Lyon, 1659.

Philippe de la Très Sainte Trinité. *Itinerarium Orientale [...]*. Lyon, 1649.

Philippe de la Très Sainte Trinité. *Theologia carmelitana, sive Apologia scholastica religionis carmelitanae pro tuenda suae nobilitatis antiquitate [...]*, Rome, 1665.

Poullet, [Nicolas]. *Nouvelles relations du Levant [...] Seconde partie*. Paris, 1668.

Primae Constitutiones Congregationis Sancti Eliae O.C.D. anno 1599 a Card. P. Pinelli, auctoritate Apostolica approbatae. Edited by Valentino di Santa Maria. Rome: apud Curiam Generalem, 1973.

Privilegia Fratrum Discalceatorum [...]. Rome, 1617.

Próspero del Espíritu Santo. *Próspero del Espíritu Santo (1583–1653): Relaciones y cartas*. Edited by Víctor Zubizarreta. Monumenta Historica Carmeli Teresiani 23. Rome: Teresianum, 2006.

Rabbath, Antoine, *Documents inédits pour servir à l'histoire du christianisme en Orient (XVIe–XIXe siècle)*. Vol. 1 (in 3 fascicles). Paris: A. Picard & fils, Leipzig: Otto Harrassovitz, and London: Luzac, 1905–7.

Regula primitiva et Constitutiones Fratrum Discalceatorum Congregationis S. Eliae Ordinis B. Virginis Mariae de Monte Carmelo. Rome, 1611.

Rhodes, Alexandre de. "Les divers voyages et missions du père Alexandre de Rhodes. Troisième partie." In his *Divers voyages et missions [...]*. Paris, 1653.

Sacrorum Conciliorum nova et amplissima collectio [...]. Vol. 46: *Synodi Melchitarum, 1716–1902*. Paris: expensis Huberti Welter, 1911.

Sancti Ignatii de Loyola Constitutiones Societatis Jesu. Vol. 3: *Textus latinus*. Monumenta ignatiana ex autographis vel ex antiquioribus exemplis collecta, 3rd series, Monumenta Historica Societatis Jesu 65. Rome: Typis Pontificiae Universitatis Gregorianae, 1938.

Schillinger, Franz Caspar. *Persianische und Ost-Indianische Reis [...]*. Nuremberg, 1707.

Silva y Figueroa, García de. *Comentarios de la Embaxada al Rey Xa Abbas de Persia (1614–1624)*. Parts 1 and 2. Edited by Rui Manuel Loureiro, Ana Cristina Costa Gomes, and Vasco Resende. Estudos & Documentos 9. Lisbon: Centro de História de Além-Mar, 2011.

Speelman, Cornelis. *Journal der Reis van den Gezant der O.I. Compagnie Joan Cunaeus naar Perzië in 1651–1652 door Cornelis Speelman*. Edited by Albertus Hotz. Werken uitgegeven door het Historisch Genootschap (gevestigd te Utrecht), 3rd series, 26. Amsterdam: Johannes Müller, 1908.

Stodart, Robert. *The Journal of Robert Stodart: Being an Account of His Experiences as a Member of Sir Dodmore Cotton's Mission in Persia in 1628–29*. Introduction and Notes by Sir E. Denison Ross. London: Luzac, 1935.

Tavernier, Jean-Baptiste. "Histoire de la conduite des Hollandais en Asie." In J.-B. Tavernier. *Recueil de plusieurs relations et traités singuliers et curieux [...]*. Paris, 1679.

Tavernier, Jean-Baptiste. *Les six voyages de Jean-Baptiste Tavernier, [...] qu'il a faits en Turquie, en Perse, et aux Indes [...]*. Vol. 1. Paris, 1676.

Tomás de Jesús. *De procuranda salute omnium gentium [...]*. Antwerp, 1613.

Tomás de Jesús. *Stimulus missionum, sive de propaganda a religiosis per universum orbem fide [...]*. Rome, 1610.

Villotte, Jacques. *Dictionarium Novum Latino-Armenum ex praecipuis Armeniae linguae scriptoribus concinnatum [...]*. Rome, 1714.

Secondary Literature[3]

Abdullah, Thabit A. J. *Merchants, Mamluks, and Murder: The Political Economy of Trade in Eighteenth-Century Basra*. Albany: SUNY Press, 2001.

Abisaab, Rula Jurdi. *Converting Persia: Religion and Power in the Safavid Empire*. London: I. B. Tauris, 2004.

"Administrer les sacrements en Europe et au Nouveau Monde: La Curie romaine et les dubia circa sacramenta." *Mélanges de l'École française de Rome: Italie et Méditerranée* 121/1 (2009): 5–217.

Ago, Renata. *Carriere e clientele nella Roma barocca*. Rome: Laterza, 1990.

Ago, Renata. "Hegemony over the Social Scene and Zealous Popes (1676–1700)." In *Court and Politics in Papal Rome, 1492–1700*, edited by Gianvittorio Signorotto and Maria Antonietta Visceglia, 229–46. Cambridge: CUP, 2002.

Ahlgren, Gillian T. W. *Teresa of Avila and the Politics of Sanctity*. Ithaca: Cornell University Press, 1996.

Alam, Muzaffar and Sanjay Subrahmanyam. "Catholics and Muslims in the Court of Jahangir (1608–1611)." In their *Writing the Mughal World: Studies on Culture and Politics*, 249–310. New York: Columbia University Press, 2011.

Alden, Dauril. *The Making of an Enterprise: The Society of Jesus in Portugal, Its Empire, and Beyond, 1540–1750*. Stanford: Stanford University Press, 1996.

Alfani, Guido. *Fathers and Godfathers: Spiritual Kinship in Early-Modern Italy*. Farnham: Ashgate, 2009.

Alfani, Guido and Vincent Gourdon. "Spiritual Kinship and Godparenthood: An Introduction." In *Spiritual Kinship in Europe, 1500–1900*, edited by Guido Alfani and Vincent Gourdon. Basingstoke: Palgrave Macmillan, 2012, 1–43.

Alfieri, Fernanda and Claudio Ferlan, eds. *Avventure dell'obbedienza nella Compagnia di Gesù: Teorie e prassi fra XVI e XIX secolo*. Bologna: Il Mulino, 2012.

Alonso, Carlos. "Cartas del P. Melchor de los Ángeles, OSA, y otros documentos sobre su actividad en Persia (1610–1619)." *Analecta Augustiniana* 44 (1981): 249–98.

Alonso, Carlos. "El convento agustiniano de Ispahan durante el período 1690–1702." *Archivo Agustiniano* 57 (1983): 141–84.

Alonso, Carlos. "Novísimo florilegio documental sobre los Agustinos en Persia (1608–1622)." *Analecta Augustiniana* 50 (1987): 47–119.

Alonso, Carlos. "Stato delle missioni agostiniane nelle Indie orientali secondo una relazione inedita del 1640." *Analecta Augustiniana* 25 (1962): 290–325.

Amsler, Nadine. *Jesuits and Matriarchs: Domestic Worship in Early Modern China*. Seattle: University of Washington Press, 2018.

Anagnostou, Sabine. *Missionspharmazie: Konzepte, Praxis, Organisation und wissenschaftliche Ausstrahlung*. Sudhoffs Archiv: Zeitschrift für Wissenschaftsgeschichte; Beihefte 60. Stuttgart: Franz Steiner Verlag, 2011.

Andretta, Elisa. *Roma medica: Anatomie d'un système médical au XVIe siècle*. Collection de l'École française de Rome 448. Rome: École française de Rome, 2011.

Anzali, Ata. *"Mysticism" in Iran: The Safavid Roots of a Modern Concept*. Columbia: University of South Carolina Press, 2017.

Aranha, Paolo. "Sacramenti o *saṃskārāḥ*? L'illusione dell'*accommodatio* nella controversia dei riti malabarici." *Cristianesimo nella storia* 31 (2010): 621–46.

Archinard, André and Théophile Heyer. "Genève et Constantinople: 1592–1732." *Bulletin de la Société de l'histoire du protestantisme français* 10 (1861): 233–58.

Aron-Beller, Katherine and Christopher Black, eds. *The Roman Inquisition: Centre versus Peripheries*. Catholic Christendom, 1300–1700. Leiden: Brill, 2018.

Aslanian, Sebouh David. "The Early Arrival of Print in Safavid Iran: New Light on the First Armenian Printing Press in New Julfa, Isfahan (1636–1650, 1686–1693)." *Handes Amsorya* 128 (2014): 381–468.

Aslanian, Sebouh David. *From the Indian Ocean to the Mediterranean: The Global Trade Networks of Armenian Merchants from New Julfa*. Berkeley: University of California Press, 2011.

Aslanian, Sebouh David. "Julfan Merchants and European East India Companies: Overland Trade, Protection Costs, and the Limits of Collective Self-Representation in Early Modern Safavid Iran." In *Mapping Safavid Iran*, edited by Nobuaki Kondo, 189–222. Studia Culturae Islamicae 105. Fuchu, Tokyo: Research Institute for Languages and Cultures of Asia and Africa, 2015.

Aslanian, Sebouh David. "Port Cities and Printers: Reflections on Early Modern Global Armenian Print Culture." *Book History* 17 (2014): 51–93.

Aslanian, Sebouh David. "Reader Response and the Circulation of Mkhit'arist Books across the Armenian Communities of the Early Modern Indian Ocean." *Journal of the Society for Armenian Studies* 22 (2013): 31–70.

Aubin, Jean. *L'ambassade de Gregório Pereira Fidalgo à la cour de Châh Soltân-Hosseyn, 1696–1697*. Lisbon: Comité national portugais pour la célébration du 2500e anniversaire de la fondation de la monarchie en Perse, 1971.

Axworthy, Michael. *The Sword of Persia: Nader Shah from Tribal Warrior to Conquering Tyrant*. London: I. B. Tauris, 2006.

Babaie, Sussan. *Isfahan and Its Palaces: Statecraft, Shi'ism and the Architecture of Conviviality in Early Modern Iran.* Edinburgh: Edinburgh University Press, 2008.

Babaie, Sussan, Kathryn Babayan, Ina Baghdiantz Mccabe, and Massumeh Farhad. *Slaves of the Shah: New Elites of Safavid Iran.* London: I. B. Tauris, 2004.

Babayan, Kathryn. *Mystics, Monarchs, and Messiahs: Cultural Landscapes of Early Modern Iran.* Cambridge, MA: Harvard University Press, 2002.

Babel, Antony. *Histoire corporative de l'horlogerie, de l'orfèvrerie et des industries annexes.* Mémoires et documents, publiés par la Société d'histoire et d'archéologie de Genève 33. Geneva: A. Jullien, George et Cie., 1916.

Baghdiantz McCabe, Ina. *The Shah's Silk for Europe's Silver: The Eurasian Trade of the Julfa Armenians in Safavid Iran and India (1530–1750).* Atlanta: Scholars Press, 1999.

Bailey, Gauvin Alexander. "'The Truth-Showing Mirror': Jesuit Catechism and the Arts in Mughal India." In *The Jesuits: Cultures, Sciences, and the Arts, 1540–1773*, edited by John W. O'Malley, Gauvin Alexander Bailey, Steven J. Harris, and T. Frank Kennedy, 380–401. Toronto: University of Toronto Press, 1999.

Barendse, René J. *Arabian Seas 1700–1763.* Vol. 1: *The Western Indian Ocean in the Eighteenth Century*, vol. 2: *Kings, Gangsters and Companies*, vol. 3: *Men and Merchandise*, vol. 4: *Europe in Asia*. European Expansion and Indigenous Response 3/1–4. Leiden: Brill, 2009.

Barendse, René J. *The Arabian Seas: The Indian Ocean World of the Seventeenth Century.* Armonk, NY: M. E. Sharpe, 2002.

Barendse, René J. "The Long Road to Livorno: The Overland Messenger Services of the Dutch East India Company in the Seventeenth Century." *Itinerario* 12 (1988): 25–43.

Barreto Xavier, Ángela and Ines G. Županov. *Catholic Orientalism: Portuguese Empire, Indian Knowledge (16th–18th Centuries).* New Delhi: OUP, 2015.

Bastian, Corina, *Verhandeln in Briefen: Frauen in der höfischen Diplomatie des frühen 18. Jahrhunderts.* Externa: Geschichte der Außenbeziehungen in neuen Perspektiven 4. Cologne: Böhlau, 2013.

Baudiment, Louis. *François Pallu, principal fondateur de la Société des Missions étrangères.* Paris: Gabriel Beauchesne et ses fils, 1934.

Bauer, Thomas. *A Culture of Ambiguity: An Alternative History of Islam.* Translated by Hinrich Biesterfeldt and Tricia Tunstall. New York: Columbia University Press, 2021.

Bayani, Khanbaba. *Les relations de l'Iran avec l'Europe occidentale à l'époque safavide (Portugal, Espagne, Angleterre, Hollande et France) (avec documents inédits).* Paris: Les Presses modernes, 1937.

Belin, Christian. *La conversation intérieure: La méditation en France au XVIIe siècle.* Paris: H. Champion, 2002.

Benigno, Francesco. "Ripensare il nepotismo papale nel Seicento." *Società* 12 (2006): 93–113.

Ben-Zaken, Avner. *Cross-Cultural Scientific Exchanges in the Eastern Mediterranean, 1560–1660.* Baltimore: The Johns Hopkins University Press, 2010.

Bhattacharya, Bhaswati. "Armenian-European Relationship in India, 1500–1800: No Armenian Foundation for European Empire?" *Journal of Economic and Social History of the Orient* 48 (2005): 277–322.

Biedermann, Zoltán. *(Dis)connected Empires: Imperial Portugal, Sri Lankan Diplomacy, and the Making of a Habsburg Conquest in Asia.* Oxford: OUP, 2018.

Biedermann, Zoltán. "Mapping the Backyard of an Empire: Portuguese Cartographies of the Persian Littoral during the Safavid Period." In *Portugal, the Persian Gulf and Safavid Persia*, edited by Rudi Matthee and Jorge Flores, 51–78. Louvain: Peeters, 2011.

Bilinkoff, Jodi. *The Avila of Saint Teresa: Religious Reform in a Sixteenth-Century City.* Ithaca: Cornell University Press, 1989.
Black, Christopher F. *The Italian Inquisition.* New Haven: Yale University Press, 2009.
Boaga, Emanuele. *La soppressione innocenziana dei piccoli conventi in Italia.* Rome: Edizioni di storia e letteratura, 1971.
Bonardi, Claudia. "Gli Sceriman di Venezia da mercanti a possidenti." In *Ad limina Italiae/ Ar druns Italioy: In viaggio per l'Italia con mercanti e monaci Armeni*, edited by Boghos Levon Zekiyan, 229–50. Eurasiatica: Quaderni del Dipartimento di Studi Eurasiatici. Università degli Studi Ca' Foscari di Venezia 37; Armeniaca italica 1. Padua: Editoriale Programma, 1996.
Bonnerot, Olivier. *La Perse dans la littérature et la pensée françaises au XVIIIe siècle: De l'image au mythe.* Paris: H. Champion, 1988.
Bosma, Ulbe and Remco Raben. *Being "Dutch" in the Indies: A History of Creolisation and Empire, 1500–1920.* Singapore: NUS Press, and Athens: Ohio University Press, 2008.
Bossy, John. *Christianity in the West, 1400–1700.* Oxford: OUP, 1985.
Boxer, Charles Ralph. "Anglo-Portuguese Rivalry in the Persian Gulf, 1615–1635." In *Chapters in Anglo-Portuguese Relations*, edited by Edgar Prestage, 46–129. Watford: Voss & Michael, 1935. Reprinted in the same author's *Portuguese Conquest and Commerce in Southern Asia, 1500–1750.* London: Variorum, 1985.
Boxer, Charles Ralph. *The Christian Century in Japan, 1549–1650.* Berkeley: University of California Press, 1951.
Boxer, Charles Ralph. *The Portuguese Seaborne Empire: 1415–1825.* New York: Alfred A. Knopf, 1975.
Brauner, Christina. *Kompanien, Könige und* caboceers: *Interkulturelle Diplomatie an Gold- und Sklavenküste im 17. und 18. Jahrhundert.* Externa: Geschichte der Außenbeziehungen in neuen Perspektiven 8. Cologne: Böhlau, 2015.
Brendecke, Arndt. *The Empirical Empire: Spanish Colonial Rule and the Politics of Knowledge.* Translated by Jeremiah Riemer. Berlin: De Gruyter Oldenbourg, 2016.
Brentjes, Sonja. "The Interests of the Republic of Letters in the Middle East." *Science in Context* 12 (1999): 435–68.
Brentjes, Sonja. "Pride and Prejudice: The Invention of a 'Historiography of Science' in the Ottoman and Safavid Empires by European Travellers and Writers in the Sixteenth and Seventeenth Centuries." In her *Travellers from Europe in the Ottoman and Safavid Empires, 16th–17th Centuries*, text VI, 229–54. Aldershot: Ashgate, 2010.
Brincken, Anna-Dorothee v. den. *Die "Nationes Christianorum orientalium" im Verständnis der lateinischen Historiographie von der Mitte des 12. bis in die zweite Hälfte des 14. Jahrhunderts.* Kölner Historische Abhandlungen 22. Cologne: Böhlau, 1973.
Brockey, Liam Matthew. *Journey to the East: The Jesuit Mission to China, 1579–1724.* Cambridge, MA: The Belknap Press of Harvard University Press, 2007.
Brockey, Liam Matthew. *The Visitor: André Palmeiro and the Jesuits in Asia.* Cambridge, MA: The Belknap Press of Harvard University Press, 2014.
Burkardt, Albrecht. *Les clients des saints: Maladie et quête du miracle à travers les procès de canonisation de la première moitié du XVIIe siècle en France.* Collection de l'École française de Rome 338. Rome: École française de Rome, 2004.
Caffiero, Marina. *Gli schiavi del papa: Conversioni e libertà dei musulmani a Roma in età moderna.* Brescia: Morcelliana, 2022.
Campanelli, Marcella. *Geografia conventuale in Italia nel XVII secolo: Soppressioni e reintegrazioni innocenziane.* Rome: Edizioni di storia e letteratura, 2016.

Caravale, Mario and Alberto Caracciolo. *Lo Stato pontificio da Martino V a Pio IX*. Storia d'Italia, 14. Turin: UTET, 1978.

Carnoy-Torabi, Dominique. "A biblioteca esquecida dos missionários de Ispaão/The Forgotten Library of the Isfahan Missionaries." *Oriente: Revista quadrimestral da Fundação Oriente* 19 (2008): 94–105.

Carson, Penelope. *The East India Company and Religion, 1698–1858*. Woodbridge: The Boydell Press, 2012.

Carswell, John. *New Julfa: The Armenian Churches and Other Buildings*. Oxford: Clarendon, 1968.

Castelnau-L'Estoile, Charlotte de. *Les ouvriers d'une vigne sterile: Les jésuites et la conversion des Indiens au Brésil, 1580–1620*. Lisbon: Fundação Calouste Gulbenkian, 2000.

Castelnau-L'Estoile, Charlotte de, Marie-Lucie Copete, Aliocha Maldavsky, and Ines G. Županov, eds. *Missions d'évangélisation et circulation des savoirs, XVIe–XVIIIe siècle*. Collection de la Casa de Velázquez 120. Madrid: Casa de Velázquez, 2011.

Catto, Michela. "Atheism: A Word Travelling To and Fro between Europe and China." In *The Rites Controversies in the Early Modern World*, edited by Ines G. Županov and Pierre Antoine Fabre, 68–88. Studies in Christian Mission 53. Leiden: Brill, 2018.

Catto, Michela. *La Compagnia divisa: Il dissenso nell'ordine gesuitico tra '500 e '600*. Brescia: Morcelliana, 2009.

Catto, Michela. "Superstizione, monoteismo e unità della Chiesa: Benedetto XIV e la condanna dei riti cinesi (1742)." In *Storia, medicina e diritto nei trattati di Prospero Lambertini Benedetto XIV*, edited by Maria Teresa Fattori, 97–108. Rome: Edizioni di storia e letteratura, 2013.

Chakrabarty, Dipesh. *Provincializing Europe: Postcolonial Thought and Historical Difference*. Princeton: Princeton University Press, 2000.

[Chick, Herbert]. *A Chronicle of the Carmelites in Persia and the Papal Mission of the XVIIth and XVIIIth Centuries*. 2 vols. London: Eyre & Spottiswoode, 1939. Reprint: London: I. B. Tauris, 2012.

Christian, William A. *Local Religion in Sixteenth-Century Spain*. Princeton: Princeton University Press, 1981.

Christin, Olivier. *La paix de religion: L'autonomisation de la raison politique au XVIe siècle*. Paris: Éditions du Seuil, 1997.

Clossey, Luke. *Salvation and Globalization in the Early Jesuit Missions*. Cambridge: CUP, 2008.

Clulow, Adam. *The Company and the Shogun: The Dutch Encounter with Tokugawa Japan*. New York: Columbia University Press, 2016.

Corbin, Henry. *L'École d'Isfahan: L'École shaykhie; Le Douzième Imâm. En Islam iranien: Aspects spirituels et philosophiques 4*. Paris: Gallimard, 1972.

Cristellon, Cecilia. "Choosing Information, Selecting Truth: The Roman Congregations, the Benedictine Declaration, and the Establishment of Religious Pluralism." In *Making Truth in Early Modern Catholicism*, edited by Andreea Badea, Bruno Boute, Marco Cavarzere, and Steven Vanden Broecke, 279–303. Scientiae Studies 1. Amsterdam: Amsterdam University Press, 2021.

Dade, Eva Kathrin. *Madame de Pompadour: Die Mätresse und die Diplomatie*. Externa: Geschichte der Außenbeziehungen in neuen Perspektiven 2. Cologne: Böhlau, 2010.

Dahmardeh, Barat. "The Shaybanid Uzbeks, Moghuls and Safavids in Eastern Iran." In *Iran and the World in the Safavid Age*, edited by Willem Floor and Edmund Herzig, 131–48. London: I. B. Tauris, 2012.

Dale, Stephen Frederic. *Indian Merchants and Eurasian Trade, 1600–1750*. Cambridge: CUP, 1994.

Daston, Lorraine. "Marvelous Facts and Miraculous Evidence in Early Modern Europe." In *Superstition and Magic in Early Modern Europe: A Reader*, edited by Helen L. Parish, 108–31. London: Bloomsbury Academic, 2015.

Delpiano, Patrizia. "La riorganizzazione della censura libraria." In *Storia, medicina e diritto nei trattati di Prospero Lambertini Benedetto XIV*, edited by Maria Teresa Fattori, 109–24. Rome: Edizioni di storia e letteratura, 2013.

Deslandres, Dominique. *Croire et faire croire: Les missions françaises au XVIIe siècle (1600–1650)*. Paris: Fayard, 2003.

Dessert, Daniel. *Argent, pouvoir et société au Grand Siècle*. Paris: Fayard, 1984.

Didier, Hugues. "Muslim Heterodoxy, Persian Murtaddun and Jesuit Missionaries at the Court of King Akbar (1580–1605)." *The Heythrop Journal* 49 (2008): 898–939.

Diefendorf, Barbara B. "Give Us Back Our Children: Patriarchal Authority and Parental Consent to Religious Vocations in Early Counter-Reformation France." *The Journal of Modern History* 68 (1996): 265–307.

Ditchfield, Simon. "Baroque around the Clock: Daniello Bartoli SJ (1608–1685) and the Uses of Global History." *Transactions of the Royal Historical Society* 31 (2021): 49–73.

Ditchfield, Simon. "Decentering the Catholic Reformation: Papacy and Peoples in the Early Modern World." *Archiv für Reformationsgeschichte* 101 (2010): 186–208.

Donati, Claudio. "La Chiesa di Roma tra antico regime e riforme settecentesche (1675–1760)." In *La Chiesa e il potere politico dal Medioevo all'età contemporanea*, edited by Giorgio Chittolini and Giovanni Miccoli, 719–66. Storia d'Italia: Annali 9. Turin: Giulio Einaudi, 1986.

Donato, Maria Pia. "Reorder and Restore: Benedict XIV, the Index, and the Holy Office." In *Benedict XIV and the Enlightenment: Art, Science, and Spirituality*, edited by Rebecca Messbarger, Christopher M. S. Johns, and Philip Gavitt, 227–52. Toronto: University of Toronto Press, 2016.

Duffin, Jacalyn. *Medical Miracles: Doctors, Saints, and Healing in the Modern World*. New York: OUP, 2009.

Emerson, John. "Chardin, Sir John." In *Encyclopaedia Iranica* online. Article published Dec. 15, 1991; last updated Oct. 13, 2011, http://www.iranicaonline.org/articles/chardin-sir-john.

Emich, Birgit. *Bürokratie und Nepotismus unter Paul V. (1605–1621)*. Päpste und Papsttum 30. Stuttgart: Anton Hiersemann, 2001.

Emich, Birgit. "The Production of Truth in the Manufacture of Saints: Procedures, Credibility, and Patronage in Early Modern Processes of Canonization." In *Making Truth in Early Modern Catholicism*, edited by Andreea Badea, Bruno Boute, Marco Cavarzere, and Steven Vanden Broecke, 165–90. Scientiae Studies 1. Amsterdam: Amsterdam University Press, 2021.

Emich, Birgit. *Territoriale Integration in der Frühen Neuzeit: Ferrara und der Kirchenstaat*. Cologne: Böhlau, 2005.

Eszer, Ambrosius. "Barnaba Fedeli di Milano O.P. (1663–1731): Das Schicksal eines Missionars und Bischofs im Sturm der Zeiten." *Archivum Fratrum Praedicatorum* 44 (1974): 179–262.

Eszer, Ambrosius. "Der Bericht des Gregorio Orsini O.P. über die Länder des Nahen und Mittleren Ostens." *Archivum Fratrum Praedicatorum* 44 (1974): 305–97.

Eszer, Ambrosius. "Missionen im Halbrund der Länder zwischen Schwarzem Meer, Kaspisee und Persischem Golf: Krim, Kaukasien, Georgien und Persien." In *Sacrae*

Congregationis de Propaganda Fide Memoria Rerum, 1622–1972, edited by Josef Metzler. Vol. II: *1700–1815*, 421–62. Rome: Herder, 1973.

Eszer, Ambrosius. "Paolo-Angelo Cittadini O.P. (O. Cart.): Neue Forschungen zu seinem Leben und zur Geschichte des Erzbistums Naxijevan." *Archivum Fratrum Praedicatorum* 39 (1969): 336–423.

Eszer, Ambrosius. "Sebastianus Knab O.P., Erzbischof von Naxijevan (1682–1690): Neue Forschungen zu seinem Leben." *Archivum Fratrum Praedicatorum* 43 (1973): 215–86.

Etemad, Bouda. "Un horloger genevois à la cour de Perse au XVIIe siècle." *Revue du Vieux Genève* 15 (1985): 9–11.

Fabre, Pierre-Antoine. "Introduction." In *Ignace de Loyola: Écrits*, edited by Maurice Giuliani, 385–91. Paris: Desclée de Brouwer, 1991.

Fabre, Pierre-Antoine and Bernard Vincent, eds. *Missions religieuses modernes: "Notre lieu est le monde."* Collection de l'École française de Rome 376. Rome: École française de Rome, 2007.

Fattori, Maria Teresa. *Benedetto XIV e Trento: Tradurre il Concilio nel Settecento*. Päpste und Papsttum 44. Stuttgart: Anton Hiersemann, 2015.

Fattori, Maria Teresa. *Clemente VIII e il Sacro Collegio, 1592–1605: Meccanismi istituzionali e accentramento di governo*. Päpste und Papsttum 33. Stuttgart: Anton Hiersemann, 2004.

Fattori, Maria Teresa. "Lambertini's Treatises and the Cultural Project of Benedict XIV: Two Sides of the Same Policy." In *Benedict XIV and the Enlightenment: Art, Science, and Spirituality*, edited by Rebecca Messbarger, Christopher M.S. Johns, and Philip Gavitt, 255–75. Toronto: University of Toronto Press, 2016.

Fattori, Maria Teresa. "'Licere—Non licere': La legittimità della schiavitù nelle decisioni della Sede apostolica romana tra XVII e XIX secolo." *Rivista storica italiana* 132 (2020): 393–436.

Ferrier, Ronald W. "The Armenians and the East India Company in Persia in the Seventeenth and Early Eighteenth Centuries." *Economic History Review* 26 (1973): 38–62.

Finocchiaro, Maurice A. "Benedict XIV and the Galileo Affair: Liberalization or Carelessness?" In *Benedict XIV and the Enlightenment: Art, Science, and Spirituality*, edited by Rebecca Messbarger, Christopher M.S. Johns, and Philip Gavitt, 206–26. Toronto: University of Toronto Press, 2016.

Finocchiaro, Maurice A. *On Trial for Reason: Science, Religion, and Culture in the Galileo Affair*. Oxford: OUP, 2019.

Firpo, Massimo. *La presa di potere dell'Inquisizione romana, 1550–1553*. Bari: Laterza, 2014.

Flannery, John M. *The Mission of the Portuguese Augustinians to Persia and Beyond (1602–1747)*. Studies in Christian Missions 43. Leiden: Brill, 2013.

Floor, Willem. "Clocks." In *Encyclopaedia Iranica* online. Article published Dec. 15, 1992; last updated Oct. 21, 2011, http://www.iranicaonline.org/articles/clocks-pers.

Floor, Willem. "Dutch Painters in Iran during the First Half of the 17th Century." *Persica* 8 (1979): 145–61.

Floor, Willem. "The Dutch on Khark Island: A Commercial Mishap." *International Journal of Middle East Studies* 24 (1992): 441–60.

Floor, Willem. *The Economy of Safavid Persia*. Iran—Turan, 1. Wiesbaden: Reichert, 2000.

Floor, Willem. *The Persian Gulf: A Political and Economic History of Five Port Cities, 1500–1730*. Washington, DC: Mage, 2006.

Fontaine, Laurence. *The Moral Economy: Poverty, Credit and Trust in Early Modern Europe*. Translated by Anne C. Tedeschi. Cambridge: CUP, 2014.
Forclaz, Bertrand. *Catholiques au défi de la Réforme: La coexistence confessionnelle à Utrecht au XVIIe siècle*. Paris: H. Champion, 2014.
Fornerod, Nicolas. "Une alliance française? Missionnaires capucins et voyageurs réformés à la cour safavide." *Dix-septième siècle* 278 (2018): 25–48.
Forrestal, Alison and Seán Alexander Smith, eds. *The Frontiers of Mission: Perspectives on Early Modern Missionary Catholicism*. Leiden: Brill, 2016.
Forster, Marc R. *The Counter-Reformation in the Villages: Religion and Reform in the Bishopric of Speyer, 1560–1720*. Ithaca: Cornell University Press, 1992.
Fosi, Irene. *Papal Justice: Subjects and Courts in the Papal State, 1500–1750*. Washington, DC: Catholic University of America Press, 2011.
Fragnito, Gigliola. *Proibito capire: La Chiesa e il volgare nella prima età moderna*. Bologna: Il Mulino, 2005.
Frazee, Charles A. *Catholics and Sultans: The Church and the Ottoman Empire, 1453–1923*. Cambridge: CUP, 1983.
Friedrich, Markus. *Der lange Arm Roms? Globale Verwaltung und Kommunikation im Jesuitenorden 1540–1773*. Frankfurt am Main: Campus, 2011.
Friedrich, Markus. *The Jesuits: A History*. Translated by John Noël Dillon. Princeton: Princeton University Press, 2022.
Furber, Holden. *Rival Empires of Trade in the Orient 1600–1800*. Minneapolis, University of Minnesota Press, 1976.
Games, Alison. *The Web of Empire: English Cosmopolitans in an Age of Expansion, 1560–1660*. Oxford: OUP, 2008.
Garsoïan, Nina. *L'Église arménienne et le grand schisme d'Orient*. Corpus scriptorum Christianorum Orientalium 574; Subsidia 100. Louvain: Peeters, 1999.
Gaudemet, Jean. *Le mariage en Occident: Les mœurs et le droit*. Paris: Les Éditions du Cerf, 1987.
Gay, Jean-Pascal. *Jesuit Civil Wars: Theology, Politics and Government under Tirso González (1687–1705)*. Farnham: Ashgate, 2012.
Gay, Jean-Pascal. "Lettres de controverse: Religion, publication et espace public en France au XVIIe siècle." *Annales: Histoire, Sciences Sociales* 68 (2013): 7–41.
Gay, Jean-Pascal. *Morales en conflit: Théologie et polémique au Grand Siècle (1640–1700)*. Paris: Les Éditions du Cerf, 2011.
Gemayel, Nasser. *Les échanges culturels entre les Maronites et l'Europe: Du Collège Maronite de Rome (1584) au Collège de ʿAyn Warqa (1789)*. 2 vols. Beirut: Gemayel, 1984.
Gentilcore, David. *Healers and Healing in Early Modern Italy*. Manchester: Manchester University Press, 1998.
Ghobrial, John-Paul, ed. *Global History and Microhistory*. Past & Present: Supplement 14. Oxford: OUP, 2019.
Ghobrial, John-Paul. "The Secret Life of Elias of Babylon and the Uses of Global Microhistory." *Past & Present* 222 (Feb. 2014): 51–93.
Ghougassian, Vazken S. *The Emergence of the Armenian Diocese of New Julfa in the Seventeenth Century*. Atlanta: Scholars Press, 1998.
Gierl, Martin. *Pietismus und Aufklärung: Theologische Polemik und die Kommunikationsreform der Wissenschaft am Ende des 17. Jahrhunderts*. Veröffentlichungen des Max-Planck-Instituts für Geschichte 127. Göttingen: Vandenhoeck & Ruprecht, 1997.

Gil Fernández, Luis. *El imperio luso-español y la Persia safávida*. Vol. 1: *1582–1605*, vol. 2: *1606–1622*. Madrid: Fundación Universitaria Española, 2006, 2009.

Gill, Joseph. *The Council of Florence*. Cambridge: CUP, 1959.

Gimaret, Daniel. "Free Will. I. In Twelver Shiʿism, II. In Ismaʾili Shiʿism." In *Encyclopaedia Iranica* online. Article published Dec. 15, 2000; last updated Jan. 31, 2012, http://www.iranicaonline.org/articles/free-will-.

Giordano, Silvano. *Domenico di Gesù Maria, Ruzola (1559–1630): Un carmelitano scalzo tra politica e riforma nella chiesa posttridentina*. Institutum Historicum Teresianum: Studia 6. Rome: Teresianum, 1991.

Girard, Aurélien. "Le christianisme oriental (XVIIe–XVIIIe siècles): Essor de l'orientalisme catholique en Europe et construction des identités confessionnelles au Proche-Orient." PhD thesis, École Pratique des Hautes Études, Paris, 2011.

Golvers, Noël. *François de Rougemont, S.J., Missionary in Ch'ang-shu (Chiang-nan): A Study of the Account Book (1674–1676) and the Eulogium*. Louvain: Leuven University Press, 1999.

Gommans, Jos. "South Asian Cosmopolitanism and the Dutch Microcosmos in Seventeenth-Century Cochin (Kerala)." In *Exploring the Dutch Empire: Agents, Networks and Institutions, 1600–2000*, edited by Catia Antunes and Jos Gommans, 3–25. London: Bloomsbury Academic, 2015.

Gommans, Jos and Ineke Loots. "Arguing with the Heathens: The Further Reformation and the Ethnohistory of Johannes Hoornbeeck (1617–1666)." *Itinerario* 39 (2015): 45–68.

Good, Peter. *The East India Company in Persia: Trade and Cultural Exchange in the Eighteenth Century*. London: I. B. Tauris, 2022.

Gose, Peter. *Invaders as Ancestors: On the Intercultural Making and Unmaking of Spanish Colonialism in the Andes*. Toronto: University of Toronto Press, 2008.

Goyau, Georges. *Un précurseur: François Picquet, consul de Louis XIV en Alep et évêque de Babylone*. Institut français de Damas: Bibliothèque orientale 2. Paris: Paul Geuthner, 1942.

Gray, Richard. "The Papacy and the Atlantic Slave Trade: Lourenço da Silva, the Capuchins and the Decisions of the Holy Office." *Past & Present* 115 (1987): 52–68.

Greene, Molly. *A Shared World: Christians and Muslims in the Early-Modern Mediterranean*. Princeton: Princeton University Press, 2000.

Greer, Allan. *Mohawk Saint: Catherine Tekakwitha and the Jesuits*. New York: OUP, 2005.

Gulbenkian, Roberto B. "Deux lettres surprenantes du Catholicos arménien David IV à Philippe III d'Espagne, II de Portugal, 1612–1614." In his *Estudos Históricos*. Vol. 1: *Relações entre Portugal, Arménia e Médio Oriente*, 301–56. Lisbon: Academia Portuguesa da História, 1995.

Gulbenkian, Roberto B. *L'ambassade en Perse de Luis Pereira de Lacerda et des Pères Portugais de l'Ordre de Saint-Augustin, Belchior dos Anjos et Guilherme de Santo Agostinho*. Lisbon: Comité national portugais pour la célébration du 2500e anniversaire de la fondation de la monarchie en Perse, 1972.

Gulbenkian, Roberto B. "Relações religiosas entre os Arménios e os Agostinhos portugueses na Pérsia no século XVII." *Anais da Academia Portuguesa da História*, n.s., 37 (1989): 303–52. Reprinted in the same author's *Estudos Históricos*. Vol. 1: *Relações entre Portugal, Arménia e Médio Oriente*, 211–53. Lisbon: Academia Portuguesa da História, 1995.

Gurney, John. "Della Valle, Pietro." In *Encyclopaedia Iranica* online. Article published Dec. 15, 1994; last updated Nov. 21, 2011, http://www.iranicaonline.org/articles/della-valle.

Halft, Dennis. "The Arabic Vulgate in Safavid Persia: Arabic Printing of the Gospels, Catholic Missionaries, and the Rise of Shīʿī Anti-Christian Polemics." PhD dissertation, Freie Universität Berlin, 2016.

Halft, Dennis. "A Newly Discovered Persian Treatise on Biblical 'Proofs' of Muḥammad's Prophethood (ca. 1702) by a Missionary Convert to Šīʿī Islam." *Mélanges de l'Institut dominicain d'études orientales* 35 (2020): 137–60.

Halft, Dennis. "Schiitische Polemik gegen das Christentum im safavidischen Iran des 11./17. Jhdts: Sayyid Aḥmad ʿAlawīs *Lawāmiʿ-i rabbānī dar radd-i šubha-yi naṣrānī*." In *Contacts and Controversies between Muslims, Jews and Christians in the Ottoman Empire and Pre-Modern Iran*, edited by Camilla Adang and Sabine Schmidtke, 273–334. Istanbuler Texte und Studien 21. Würzburg: Ergon, 2010.

Halfter, Peter. *Das Papsttum und die Armenier im Frühen und Hohen Mittelalter: Von den ersten Kontakten bis zur Fixierung der Kirchenunion im Jahre 1198*. Forschungen zur Kaiser-und Papstgeschichte des Mittelalters: Beihefte zu J. F. Böhmer, Regesta Imperii 15. Cologne: Böhlau, 1996.

Hambye, Édouard René. *History of Christianity in India*. Vol. 3: *The Eighteenth Century*. Bangalore: The Church History Association of India, 1997.

Hamilton, Alastair. *The Copts and the West: The European Discovery of the Egyptian Church*. Oxford: OUP, 2006.

Hamilton, Alastair. "From East to West: Jansenists, Orientalists, and the Eucharistic Controversy." In *How the West Was Won: Essays on Literary Imagination, the Canon, and the Christian Middle Ages for Burcht Pranger*, edited by Willemien Otten, Arjo Vanderjagt, and Hent de Vries, 83–100. Leiden: Brill, 2010.

Haneda, Masashi. *Le Chāh et les Qizilbāš: Le système militaire safavide*. Islamkundliche Untersuchungen 119. Berlin: Klaus Schwarz, 1987.

Harrison, Henrietta. *The Missionary's Curse and Other Tales from a Chinese Catholic Village*. Berkeley: University of California Press, 2013.

Hartmann, Arnulf. "The Augustinians in Golden Goa, According to a Manuscript by Felix of Jesus, O.S.A." *Analecta Augustiniana* 30 (1967): 5–147.

Hasluck, Frederick William. *Christianity and Islam under the Sultans*. 2 vols. Oxford: Clarendon Press, 1929.

Haug, Tilman. *Ungleiche Außenbeziehungen und grenzüberschreitende Patronage: Die französische Krone und die geistlichen Kurfürsten (1648–1679)*. Externa: Geschichte der Außenbeziehungen in neuen Perspektiven 6. Cologne: Böhlau, 2015.

Hazard, Paul. *The European Mind (1680–1715)*. Translated by J. Lewis May. London: Hollis & Carter, 1953.

Hersche, Peter. *Muße und Verschwendung. Europäische Gesellschaft und Kultur im Barockzeitalter*. 2 vols. Freiburg im Br.: Herder, 2006.

Herzig, Edmund M. "The Armenian Merchants of New Julfa, Isfahan: A Study in Pre-Modern Asian Trade." PhD thesis, University of Oxford, 1991.

Herzig, Edmund M. "Venice and the Julfa Armenian Merchants." In *Gli Armeni e Venezia: Dagli Sceriman a Mechitar; Il momento culminante di una consuetudine millenaria*, edited by Boghos Levon Zekiyan and Aldo Ferrari, 141–64. Venice: Istituto veneto di Scienze, Lettere ed Arti, 2004.

Heyberger, Bernard. "Chrétiens orientaux dans l'Europe catholique (XVIIe–XVIIIe siècles)." In *Hommes de l'entre-deux: Parcours individuels et portraits de groupes sur la frontière de la Méditerranée, XVIe–XXe siècle*, edited by Bernard Heyberger and Chantal Verdeil, 61–93. Paris: Les Indes Savantes, 2009.

Heyberger, Bernard. "De l'image religieuse à l'image profane? L'essor de l'image chez les Chrétiens de Syrie et du Liban (XVIIe–XIXe siècle)." In *La multiplication des images* en pays d'Islam: De l'estampe à la télévision (17ᵉ–21ᵉ siècle). Actes du colloque "Images: fonctions et langages. L'incursion de l'image moderne dans l'Orient musulman et sa périphérie." Istanbul, Université du Bosphore (Boğaziçi Üniversitesi), 25–27 mars 1999, edited by Bernard Heyberger and Silvia Naef, 31–56. Istanbuler Texte und Studien 2. Würzburg: Ergon, 2003.

Heyberger, Bernard. *Hindiyya, Mystic and Criminal, 1720–1798: A Political and Religious Crisis in Lebanon*. Translated by Renée Champion. Cambridge: James Clarke, 2013.

Heyberger, Bernard. *Les Chrétiens du Proche-Orient au temps de la Réforme catholique*. Bibliothèque des Écoles françaises d'Athènes et de Rome 284. Rome: École française de Rome, 1994.

Heyberger, Bernard. "L'Islam et les Arabes chez un érudit maronite au service de l'Église catholique (Abraham Ecchellensis)." *Al-Qanṭara* 31 (2010): 481–512.

Heyberger, Bernard. "Monachisme oriental, catholicisme et érudition (XVIIᵉ–XXᵉ siècles)." In *Monachismes d'Orient: Images, échanges, influences: Hommage à Antoine Guillaumont*, edited by Florence Jullien and Marie-Joseph Pierre, 165–83. Bibliothèque de l'École des Hautes Études: Sciences religieuses 148. Turnhout: Brepols, 2011.

Heyberger, Bernard. *Orientalisme, science et controverse: Abraham Ecchellensis (1605–1664)*. Bibliothèque de l'École des Hautes Études: Sciences religieuses 143. Turnhout: Brepols, 2010.

Heyberger, Bernard. "Peuples 'sans loi, sans foi, ni prêtre': Druzes et nusayrîs de Syrie redécouverts par les missionnaires catholiques (XVIIᵉ–XVIIIᵉ siècles)." In *L'Islam des marges: Mission chrétienne et espaces périphériques du monde musulman, XVIᵉ–XXᵉ siècles*, edited by Bernard Heyberger and Rémy Madinier, 45–80. Paris: Éditions Karthala/IISMM, 2011.

Heyberger, Bernard. "Polemic Dialogues between Christians and Muslims in the Seventeenth Century." *Journal of the Economic and Social History of the Orient* 55 (2012): 281–302.

Heyberger, Bernard. "'Pro nunc nihil est respondendum'. Recherche d'information et prise de décision à la Propagande: L'exemple du Levant (XVIIIᵉ siècle)." *Mélanges de l'École française de Rome: Italie et Méditerranée* 109/2 (1997): 539–54.

Holenstein, André. "Introduction: Empowering Interactions. Looking at Statebuilding from Below." In *Empowering Interactions: Political Cultures and the Emergence of the State in Europe 1300–1900*, edited by Wim Blockmans, André Holenstein, and Jon Mathieu, 1–31. Farnham: Ashgate, 2009.

Hsia, Florence C. *Sojourners in a Strange Land: Jesuits and Their Scientific Mission in Late Imperial China*. Chicago: University of Chicago Press, 2009.

Hsia, Ronnie Po-chia, ed. *A Companion to Early Modern Catholic Global Missions*. Brill's Companions to the Christian Tradition 80. Leiden: Brill, 2018.

Hsia, Ronnie Po-chia. *A Jesuit in the Forbidden City: Matteo Ricci 1552–1610*. Oxford: OUP, 2010.

Hsia, Ronnie Po-chia. "Translating Christianity: Counter-Reformation Europe and the Catholic Mission in China, 1580–1780." In *Conversion: Old Worlds and New*, edited by Kenneth Mills and Anthony Grafton, 87–108. Rochester: University of Rochester Press, 2003.

Hsia, Ronnie Po-chia. *The World of Catholic Renewal 1540–1770*. Cambridge: CUP, 1998.

Hunt, Lynn, Margaret C. Jacob, and Wijnand Mijnhardt. *The Book That Changed Europe: Picart & Bernard's Religious Ceremonies of the World*. Cambridge, MA: The Belknap Press of Harvard University Press, 2010.

Islam, Riazul. *Indo-Persian Relations: A Study of the Political and Diplomatic Relations between the Mughul Empire and Iran*. Sources of the History and Geography of Iran 32. Teheran: Iranian Culture Foundation, 1970.
Israel, Jonathan I. *Enlightenment Contested: Philosophy, Modernity, and the Emancipation of Man 1670-1752*. Oxford: OUP, 2006.
Jackson, Peter and Laurence Lockhart, eds. *The Timurid and Safavid Periods*. The Cambridge History of Iran 6. Cambridge: CUP, 1986.
Jacques, Roland. *De Castro Marim à Faïfo: Naissance et développement du padroado portugais d'Orient des origines à 1659*. Lisbon: Fundação Calouste Gulbenkian, 1999.
Jaser, Christian. *Ecclesia maledicens: Rituelle und zeremonielle Exkommunikationsformen im Mittelalter*. Spätmittelalter, Humanismus, Reformation/Studies in the Late Middle Ages, Humanism and the Reformation 75. Tübingen: Mohr Siebeck, 2013.
Johnson, Carina L. *Cultural Hierarchy in Sixteenth-Century Europe: The Ottomans and Mexicans*. Cambridge: CUP, 2011.
Johnson, Trevor. "Gardening for God: Carmelite Deserts and the Sacralisation of Natural Space in Counter-Reformation Spain." In *Sacred Space in Early Modern Europe*, edited by Will Coster and Andrew Spicer, 193-210. Cambridge: CUP, 2005.
Kaplan, Benjamin J. *Divided by Faith: Religious Conflict and the Practice of Toleration in Early Modern Europe*. Cambridge, MA: The Belknap Press of Harvard University Press, 2007.
Kedar, Benjamin Z. "Convergences of Oriental Christian, Muslim, and Frankish Worshippers: The Case of Saydnaya." In De Sion exibit lex et verbum domini de Hierusalem: *Essays on Medieval Law, Liturgy, and Literature in Honour of Ammon Linder*, edited by Yitzhak Hen, 59-69. Cultural Encounters in Late Antiquity and the Middle Ages 1. Turnhout: Brepols, 2001.
Kévonian, Kéram. "Marchands arméniens au XVIIe siècle: À propos d'un livre arménien publié à Amsterdam en 1699." *Cahiers du monde russe et soviétique* 16 (1975): 199-244.
Kévorkian, Raymond H. "Le livre imprimé en milieu arménien ottoman aux XVIe-XVIIIe siècles." *Revue des mondes musulmans et de la Méditerranée* 87-8 (1999): 173-85.
King, David A. *World-Maps for Finding the Direction and Distance to Mecca: Innovation and Tradition in Islamic Science*. Islamic Philosophy, Theology and Science 36. Leiden: Brill, 1999.
Knowles, David. *From Pachomius to Ignatius: A Study of the Constitutional History of the Religious Orders*. Oxford: Clarendon Press, 1966.
Kooi, Christine. *Calvinists and Catholics during Holland's Golden Age: Heretics and Idolaters*. Cambridge: CUP, 2012.
Korsch, Evelyn. "Meriten und Machenschaften des Gregorio Agdollo: Ein Armenier im Dienste Sachsens." *Ars Mercaturae: Jahrbuch für internationale Handelsgeschichte* 3 (2017): 107-38.
Korsch, Evelyn. "The Sherimans and Cross-Cultural Trade in Gems: The Armenian Diaspora in Venice and Its Trading Networks in the First Half of the Eighteenth Century." In *Commercial Networks and European Cities, 1400-1800*, edited by Andrea Caracausi and Christof Jeggle, 223-39. London: Pickering & Chatto, 2014.
Koslofsky, Craig M. *The Reformation of the Dead: Death and Ritual in Early Modern Germany, 1450-1700*. Basingstoke: Macmillan, 2000.
Kroell, Anne. "Alexandre de Lestoille, dernier agent de la Compagnie royale des Indes en Perse." *Moyen Orient & Océan Indien* 1 (1984): 65-72.
Krstič, Tijana. *Contested Conversions to Islam: Narratives of Religious Change in the Early Modern Ottoman Empire*. Stanford, Stanford University Press, 2011.

Laborie, Jean-Claude. *Mangeurs d'hommes et mangeurs d'âmes: Une correspondance missionaire au XVI*; *La lettre jésuite du Brésil, 1549–1568*. Paris: H. Champion, 2003.

Landau, Amy S. "European Religious Iconography in Safavid Iran: Decoration and Patronage of *Meydani* Bet'ghehem (Bethlehem of the Maydan)." In *Iran and the World in the Safavid Age*, edited by Willem Floor and Edmund Herzig, 425–46. London: I. B. Tauris and Iran Heritage Foundation, 2012.

Landau, Amy S. "*Farangī-Sāzī* at Isfahan: The Court Painter Muḥammad Zamān, the Armenians of New Julfa and Shāh Sulaymān (1666–1694)." PhD thesis, University of Oxford, 2009.

Landau, Amy S. "Reconfiguring the Northern European Print to Depict Sacred History at the Persian Court." In *Mediating Netherlandish Art and Material Culture in Asia*, edited by Thomas DaCosta Kaufmann and Michael North, 65–82. Amsterdam: Amsterdam University Press, 2014.

Landau, Amy S. and Theo Maarten Van Lint. "Armenian Merchant Patronage of New Julfa's Sacred Spaces." In *Sacred Precincts: The Religious Architecture of Non-Muslim Communities across the Islamic World*, edited by Mohammad Gharipour, 308–33. Arts and Archaeology of the Islamic World, 3. Leiden: Brill, 2015.

Laporte-Eftekharian, Sâyeh. "Transmission et métamorphose de modèles iconographiques occidentaux, principalement flamands, dans les églises de la Nouvelle-Djoulfa (Ispahan)." *Revue belge d'archéologie et d'histoire de l'art* 73 (2004): 63–80.

Lazarus-Yafeh, Hava. *Intertwined Worlds: Medieval Islam and Bible Criticism*. Princeton: Princeton University Press, 1992.

Lederle, Julia. *Mission und Ökonomie der Jesuiten in Indien: Intermediäres Handeln am Beispiel der Malabar-Provinz im 18. Jahrhundert*. Studien zur Außereuropäischen Christentumsgeschichte: Asien, Afrika, Lateinamerika 14. Wiesbaden: Harrassowitz, 2009.

Lehmann, Hartmut. *Das Zeitalter des Absolutismus: Gottesgnadentum und Kriegsnot*. Stuttgart: Kohlhammer, 1980.

Lehner, Ulrich L. *The Catholic Enlightenment: The Forgotten History of a Global Movement*. Oxford: OUP, 2016.

Lepetit, Bernard, ed. *Les formes de l'expérience: Une autre histoire sociale*. Paris: Albin Michel, 1995.

Levack, Brian P. *The Devil Within: Possession & Exorcism in the Christian West*. New Haven: Yale University Press, 2013.

Levi, Giovanni. *Inheriting Power: The Story of an Exorcist*. Translated by Lydia G. Cochrane. Chicago: University of Chicago Press, 1988.

Levi, Scott C. "India XIII. Indo-Iranian Commercial Relations." In *Encyclopaedia Iranica* online. Article published Dec. 15, 2004; last updated Mar. 27, 2012, http://www.iranicaonline.org/articles/india-xiii-indo-iranian-commercial-relations.

Levi, Scott C. "India XXX. Indian Merchants in Central Asia and Iran." In *Encyclopaedia Iranica* online. Article published Dec. 15, 2004; last updated Mar. 27, 2012, http://www.iranicaonline.org/articles/india-xxx-indian-merchants-in-central-asia-and-iran.

Lewisohn, Leonard. "Sufism and the School of Iṣfahān: *Taṣawwuf* and *'irfān* in Late Safavid Iran ('Abd al-Razzāq Lāhījī and Fayḍ-i Kāshānī on the Relation of *taṣawwuf, hikmat* and *'irfān*)." In *The Heritage of Sufism*. Vol. 3: *Late Classical Persianate Sufism (1501–1750): The Safavid and Mughal Period*, edited by L. Lewisohn and David Morgan, 63–134. Oxford: Oneworld, 1999.

Lockhart, Laurence. *The Fall of the Safavi Dynasty and the Afghan Occupation of Persia*. Cambridge: CUP, 1958.

Longo, Carlo. *Silvestro Bendici: Un missionario calabrese del secolo XVII*. Institutum Historicum Fratrum Praedicatorum, Romae: Dissertationes Historicae 24. Rome: Istituto Storico Domenicano, 1998.

Loureiro, Rui Manuel and Vasco Resende, eds. *Estudos sobre Don García de Silva y Figueroa e os "Comentarios" da Embaixada à Pérsia (1614–1624)*. Estudos & Documentos 9. Lisbon: Centro de História de Além-Mar, 2011.

Luria, Keith P. *Sacred Boundaries: Religious Coexistence and Conflict in Early Modern France*. Washington, DC: Catholic University of America Press, 2005.

Macé, Laurence. "Les *Lettres persanes* devant l'Index: Une censure 'posthume.'" In *Montesquieu en 2005*, edited by Catherine Volpilhac-Auger, 48–59. Oxford: Voltaire Foundation, 2005.

Maeda, Hirotake. "Against all Odds: The Safavids and the Georgians." In *The Safavid World*, edited by Rudi Matthee, 125–43. London: Routledge, 2021.

Maifreda, Germano. *The Business of the Inquisition in the Early Modern Era*. London: Routledge, 2017.

Maillard, Ninon. *Réforme religieuse et droit: La traduction juridique et structurelle du retour à l'observance; Le cas des Dominicains de France, 1629–1660*. Paris: Les Éditions du Cerf, 2015.

Maldavsky, Aliocha. "Les familles du missionnaire: Une histoire sociale des horizons missionnaires milanais au début du XVIIe siècle." In *Milano, l'Ambrosiana e la conoscenza dei nuovi mondi (secoli XVII–XVIII)*, edited by Michela Catto and Gianvittorio Signorotto, 125–60. Studia Borromaica 28. Milan: Biblioteca Ambrosiana, 2015.

Mansour, Opher. "Picturing Global Conversion: Art and Diplomacy at the Court of Paul V (1605–1621)." *Journal of Early Modern History* 17 (2013): 525–59.

Marcocci, Giuseppe. "Conscience and Empire: Politics and Moral Theology in the Early Modern Portuguese World." *Journal of Early Modern History* 18 (2014): 473–94.

Masroori, Cyrus, Whitney Mannies, and John Christian Laursen, eds. *Persia and the Enlightenment*. Oxford University Studies in the Enlightenment. Liverpool: Liverpool University Press, 2021.

Matthee, Rudi. "Christians in Safavid Iran: Hospitality and Harassment." *Studies on Persianate Societies* 3 (2005): 3–43.

Matthee, Rudi. "From Splendour and Admiration to Ruin and Condescension: Western Travellers to Iran from the Safavids to the Qajars." *Iran* 54 (2016): 3–22.

Matthee, Rudi. "Negotiating across Cultures: The Dutch Van Leene Mission to the Iranian Court of Šāh Sulaymān, 1689–1692." *Eurasian Studies* 3 (2004): 35–63.

Matthee, Rudi. *Persia in Crisis: Safavid Decline and the Fall of Isfahan*. London: I. B. Tauris, 2012.

Matthee, Rudi. *The Politics of Trade in Safavid Iran: Silk for Silver, 1600–1730*. Cambridge: CUP, 1999.

Matthee, Rudi. "Poverty and Perseverance: The Jesuit Mission of Isfahan and Shamakhi in Late Safavid Iran." *Al-Qanṭara* 36 (2015): 463–501.

Matthee, Rudi. *The Pursuit of Pleasure: Drugs and Stimulants in Iranian History, 1500–1900*. Princeton: Princeton University Press, 2005.

Matthee, Rudi. "The Safavid Economy as Part of the World Economy." In *Iran and the World in the Safavid Age*, edited by Willem Floor and Edmund Herzig, 31–47. London: I. B. Tauris, 2012.

Matthee, Rudi. "Safavid Iran and the Christian Missionary Experience: Between Tolerance and Refutation." *Mélanges de l'Institut dominicain d'études orientales* 35 (2020): 65–100.

Matthee, Rudi, ed. *The Safavid World*. London: Routledge, 2021.
Matthee, Rudi. "The Safavids under Western Eyes: Seventeenth-Century European Travelers to Iran." *Journal of Early Modern History* 13 (2009): 137-71.
Mayer, Thomas F. *The Roman Inquisition: A Papal Bureaucracy and Its Laws in the Age of Galileo*. Philadelphia: University of Pennsylvania Press, 2013.
Mayer, Thomas F. *The Roman Inquisition on the Stage of Italy, c. 1590-1640*. Philadelphia: University of Pennsylvania Press, 2014.
Mayer, Thomas F. *The Roman Inquisition: Trying Galileo*. Philadelphia: University of Pennsylvania Press, 2015.
Menegon, Eugenio. *Ancestors, Virgins, and Friars: Christianity as a Local Religion in Late Imperial China*. Cambridge, MA: Harvard University Press, 2009.
Menniti Ippolito, Antonio. *Il tramonto della Curia nepotista: Papi, nipoti e burocrazia curiale tra XVI e XVII secolo*. La corte dei papi 5. Rome: Viella, 1999.
Menniti Ippolito, Antonio. *1664. Un anno della Chiesa universale: Saggio sull'italianità del papato in età moderna*. Rome: Viella, 2011.
Meserve, Margaret. *Empires of Islam in Renaissance Historical Thought*. Cambridge, MA: Harvard University Press, 2008.
Messbarger, Rebecca, Christopher M. S. Johns, and Philip Gavitt, eds. *Benedict XIV and the Enlightenment: Art, Science, and Spirituality*. Toronto: University of Toronto Press, 2016.
Metzler, Josef. "Controversia tra Propaganda e S. Uffizio circa una commissione teologica (1622-1658)." *Pontificiae Universitatis Urbanianae Annales* (1968-9): 47-62.
Metzler, Josef. "Die Kongregation im Zeitalter der Aufklärung: Struktur, Missionspläne und Maßnahmen allgemeiner Art (1700-1795)." In *Sacrae Congregationis de Propaganda Fide Memoria Rerum, 1622-1972*, edited by Josef Metzler. Vol. II: *1700-1815*, 23-83. Rome: Herder, 1973.
Metzler, Josef. "Die Kongregation in der zweiten Hälfte des 17. Jahrhunderts." In *Sacrae Congregationis de Propaganda Fide Memoria Rerum, 1622-1972*, edited by Josef Metzler. Vol. I/1: *1622-1700*, 244-305. Rome: Herder, 1971.
Metzler, Josef. "Foundation of the Congregation 'de Propaganda Fide' by Gregory XV." In *Sacrae Congregationis de Propaganda Fide Memoria Rerum, 1622-1972*, edited by Josef Metzler. Vol. I/1: *1622-1700*, 79-111. Rome: Herder, 1971.
Metzler, Josef. "Francesco Ingoli, der erste Sekretär der Kongregation (1578-1649)." In *Sacrae Congregationis de Propaganda Fide Memoria Rerum, 1622-1972*, edited by Josef Metzler. Vol. I/1: *1622-1700*, 197-243. Rome: Herder, 1971.
Metzler, Josef. "Nicht erfüllte Hoffnungen in Persien." In *Sacrae Congregationis de Propaganda Fide Memoria Rerum, 1622-1972*, edited by Josef Metzler. Vol. I/1: *1622-1700*, 680-704. Rome: Herder, 1971.
Metzler, Josef. "Orientation, programme et premières décisions (1622-1649)." In *Sacrae Congregationis de Propaganda Fide Memoria Rerum, 1622-1972*, edited by Josef Metzler. Vol. I/1: *1622-1700*, 146-96. Rome: Herder, 1971.
Metzler, Josef. "Wegbereiter und Vorläufer der Kongregation: Vorschläge und erste Gründungsversuche einer römischen Missionszentrale." In *Sacrae Congregationis de Propaganda Fide Memoria Rerum, 1622-1972*, edited by Josef Metzler. Vol. I/1: *1622-1700*, 38-78. Rome: Herder, 1971.
Mills, Simon. *A Commerce of Knowledge: Trade, Religion, and Scholarship between England and the Ottoman Empire, c. 1600-1760*. Oxford: OUP, 2020.
Mitchell, Colin P. *The Practice of Politics in Safavid Iran: Power, Religion and Rhetoric* London: I. B. Tauris, 2009.

Mokhberi, Susan. *The Persian Mirror: Reflections of the Safavid Empire in Early Modern France*. Oxford: OUP, 2019.

Molina, J. Michelle. *To Overcome Oneself: The Jesuit Ethic and Spirit of Global Expansion, 1520–1767*. Berkeley: University of California Press, 2013.

Moreen, Vera Basch. *Iranian Jewry's Hour of Peril and Heroism: A Study of Bābāi Ibn Luṭf's Chronicle (1617–1662)*. New York: Columbia University Press, 1987.

Mostaccio, Silvia. *Early Modern Jesuits between Obedience and Conscience during the Generalate of Claudio Acquaviva (1581–1615)*. Farnham: Ashgate, 2014.

Moulinier-Brogi, Laurence. "Un aspect particulier de la médecine des religieux après le XIIe siècle: L'attrait pour l'astrologie médicale." In *Médecine et religion: Compétitions, collaborations, conflits (XIIe–XXe siècles)*, edited by Maria Pia Donato, Luc Berlivet, Sara Cabibbo, Raimondo Michetti, and Marilyn Nicoud, 59–86. Collection de l'École française de Rome 476. Rome: École française de Rome, 2013.

Necipoğlu, Gülru. "Framing the Gaze in Ottoman, Safavid and Mughal Palaces." *Ars Orientalis* 23 (1993): 303–42.

Nersessian, Vrej Nerses. "Armenian Christianity." In *The Blackwell Companion to Eastern Christianity*, edited by Ken Parry, 23–46. Malden: Blackwell, 2007.

Newman, Andrew J. "Clerical Perceptions of Sufi Practices in Late Seventeenth-Century Persia: Arguments over the Permissibility of Singing (*Ghinā*)." In *The Heritage of Sufism*. Vol. 3: *Late Classical Persianate Sufism (1501–1750): The Safavid and Mughal Period*, edited by Leonard Lewisohn and David Morgan, 135–64. Oxford: Oneworld, 1999.

Newman, Andrew J. *Safavid Iran: Rebirth of a Persian Empire*. London: I. B. Tauris, 2006.

Nierstrasz, Chris. "In the Shadow of the Companies: Empires of Trade in the Orient and Informal Entrepreneurship." In *Beyond Empires: Global, Self-Organizing, Cross-Imperial Networks, 1500–1800*, edited by Amelia Polónia and Cátia Antunes, 188–211. European Expansion and Indigenous Response 21. Leiden: Brill, 2016.

Noirfontaine, Françoise de. "Les carmélites dans la résistance à l'*Unigenitus*." In *Carmes et carmélites en France du XVIIe siècle à nos jours: Actes du colloque de Lyon (Sept. 25–26, 1997)*, edited by Bernard Hours, 378–403. Paris: Les Éditions du Cerf, 2001.

Ó hAnnracháin, Tadgh. *Catholic Europe, 1592–1648: Centre and Peripheries*. Oxford: OUP, 2015.

Oka, Mihoko. *The Namban Trade: Merchants and Missionaries in 16th and 17th Century Japan*. European Expansion and Indigenous Response 34. Leiden: Brill, 2021.

O'Malley, John W. *The First Jesuits*. Cambridge, MA: Harvard University Press, 1993.

Osterhammel, Jürgen. *Unfabling the East: The Enlightenment's Encounter with Asia*. Translated by Robert Savage. Princeton: Princeton University Press, 2018.

Parish, Helen L. "'Lying Histories Fayning False Miracles': Magic, Miracles and Medieval History in Reformation Polemic." In *Superstition and Magic in Early Modern Europe: A Reader*, edited by Helen L. Parish, 100–107. London: Bloomsbury Academic, 2015.

Parker, Charles H. *Faith on the Margins: Catholics and Catholicism in the Dutch Golden Age*. Cambridge, MA: Harvard University Press, 2008.

Parker, Charles H. and Gretchen Starr-LeBeau, eds. *Judging Faith, Punishing Sin: Inquisitions and Consistories in the Early Modern World*. Cambridge: CUP, 2017.

Pastore, Stefania. "Unwise Paths: Ignatius Loyola and the Years of Alcalá de Henares." In *A Companion to Ignatius of Loyola: Life, Writings, Spirituality, Influence*, edited by Robert Aleksander Maryks, 25–44. Brill's Companions to the Christian Tradition 52. Leiden: Brill, 2014.

Pattenden, Miles. *Electing the Pope in Early Modern Italy, 1450–1700*. Oxford: OUP, 2017.
Pavone, Sabina. "A Saint under Trial: Ignatius of Loyola between Alcalá and Rome." In *A Companion to Ignatius of Loyola: Life, Writings, Spirituality, Influence*, edited by Robert Aleksander Maryks, 45–65. Brill's Companions to the Christian Tradition 52. Leiden: Brill, 2014.
Perry, John R. *Karim Khan Zand: A History of Iran, 1747–1779*. Chicago: University of Chicago Press, 1979.
Petrowicz, Gregorio. *L'unione degli Armeni di Polonia con la Santa Sede (1626–1686)*. Orientalia Christiana Analecta 135. Rome: Pontificium Institutum Orientalium Studiorum, 1950.
Piemontese, Angelo Michele. "I due ambasciatori di Persia ricevuti da Papa Paolo V al Quirinale." *Miscellanea Bibliothecae Apostolicae Vaticanae* 12 (2005): 357–425.
Piemontese, Angelo Michele. *La Persia istoriata in Roma*. Studi e testi 480. Vatican City: Biblioteca Apostolica Vaticana, 2014.
Pierre, Benoist. *Le père Joseph: L'éminence grise de Richelieu*. Paris: Perrin, 2007.
Pietsch, Andreas and Barbara Stollberg-Rilinger, eds. *Konfessionelle Ambiguität: Uneindeutigkeit und Verstellung als religiöse Praxis in der Frühen Neuzeit*. Schriften des Vereins für Reformationsgeschichte 214. Gütersloh: Gütersloher Verlagshaus, 2013.
Pinot, Virgile. *La Chine et la formation de l'esprit philosophique en France (1640–1715)*. Paris: Paul Geuthner, 1932.
Pizzorusso, Giovanni. "Filippo Guadagnoli, i Caracciolini et lo studio delle lingue orientali e della controversia con l'Islam a Roma nel XVII secolo." *Studi medievali e moderni: Arte, letteratura, storia* 14 (2010): 245–78.
Pizzorusso, Giovanni. *Governare le missioni, conoscere il mondo nel XVII secolo: La Congregazione Pontificia de Propaganda Fide*. Studi di storia delle istituzioni ecclesiastiche 6. Viterbo: Edizioni Sette Città, 2018.
Pizzorusso, Giovanni. "La Congrégation de Propaganda fide à Rome: Centre d'accumulation et de production de 'savoirs missionnaires' (XVIIe–début XIXe siècle)." In *Missions d'évangélisation et circulation des savoirs, XVIe–XVIIIe siècle*, edited by Charlotte de Castelnau-l'Estoile, Marie-Lucie Copete, Aliocha Maldavsky, and Ines G. Županov, 25–40. Collection de la Casa de Velázquez 120. Madrid: Casa de Velázquez, 2011.
Pizzorusso, Giovanni. "La Congregazione 'de Propaganda Fide' e gli ordini religiosi: conflittualità nel mondo delle missioni del XVII secolo." *Cheiron* 43–4 (2005): 197–240.
Pizzorusso, Giovanni. "Le pape rouge et le pape noir: Aux origines des conflits entre la Congrégation 'de Propaganda fide' et la Compagnie de Jésus au XVIIe siècle." In *Les antijésuites: Discours, figures et lieux de l'antijésuitisme à l'époque moderne*, edited by Pierre-Antoine Fabre and Catherine Maire, 539–61. Rennes: PUR, 2010.
Pizzorusso, Giovanni. "Les écoles de langue arabe et le milieu orientaliste autour de la Congrégation *de Propaganda fide* au temps d'Abraham Ecchellensis." In *Orientalisme, science et controverse: Abraham Ecchellensis (1605–1664)*, edited by Bernard Heyberger, 59–80. Bibliothèque de l'École des Hautes Études: Sciences religieuses 143. Turnhout: Brepols, 2010.
Pizzorusso, Giovanni. "Lo 'Stato temporale' della Congregazione 'de Propaganda Fide' nel Seicento." In Ad ultimos usque terrarum terminos in fide propaganda: *Roma fra promozione e difesa della fede in età moderna*, edited by Massimiliano Ghilardi, Gaetano Sabatini, Matteo Sanfilippo, and Donatella Strangio, 51–66. Studi di storia delle istituzioni ecclesiastiche 5. Viterbo: Edizioni Sette Città, 2014.
Pollmann, Judith. *Religious Choice in the Dutch Republic: The Reformation of Arnoldus Buchelius (1565–1641)*. Manchester: Manchester University Press, 1999.

Pomata, Gianna. "Malpighi and the Holy Body: Medical Experts and Miraculous Evidence in Seventeenth-Century Italy." *Renaissance Studies* 21 (2007): 568–86.
Pourjavady, Reza and Sabine Schmidtke. "An Eastern Renaissance? Greek Philosophy under the Safavids (16th–18th Centuries AD)." *Intellectual History of the Islamicate World* 3 (2015): 248–90.
Prodi, Paolo. *Il sovrano pontefice: Un corpo e due anime; La monarchia papale nella prima età moderna*. Bologna: Il Mulino, 1982.
Prosperi, Adriano. *La vocazione: Storie di gesuiti tra Cinquecento e Seicento*. Turin: Giulio Einaudi, 2016.
Prosperi, Adriano. "L'Europa cristiana e il mondo: Alle origini dell'idea di missione." *Dimensioni e problemi della ricerca storica* 2 (1992): 189–220.
Prosperi, Adriano. *Tribunali della coscienza: Inquisitori, confessori, missionari*. Turin: Giulio Einaudi, 1996.
Questier, Michael. *Catholicism and Community in Early Modern England: Politics, Aristocratic Patronage and Religion, c. 1550–1640*. Cambridge: CUP, 2006.
Quinn, Sholeh A. *Historical Writing during the Reign of Shah ʿAbbas: Ideology, Imitation, and Legitimacy in Safavid Chronicles*. Salt Lake City: University of Utah Press, 2000.
Rawski, Evelyn S. *The Last Emperors: A Social History of Qing Imperial Institutions*. Berkeley: University of California Press, 1998.
Reinhard, Wolfgang. "Gegenreformation als Modernisierung? Prolegomena zu einer Theorie des konfessionellen Zeitalters." *Archiv für Reformationsgeschichte* 68 (1977): 226–51.
Reinhard, Wolfgang. *Papstfinanz und Nepotismus unter Paul V. (1605–1621): Studien und Quellen zur Struktur und zu quantitativen Aspekten des päpstlichen Herrschaftssystems*. 2 vols. Päpste und Papsttum 6/I and II. Stuttgart: Anton Hiersemann, 1974.
Reinhard, Wolfgang. *Paul V. Borghese (1605–1621): Mikropolitische Papstgeschichte*. Päpste und Papsttum 37. Stuttgart: Anton Hiersemann, 2009.
Reinhardt, Nicole. *Macht und Ohnmacht der Verflechtung: Rom und Bologna unter Paul V.; Studien zur frühneuzeitlichen Mikropolitik im Kirchenstaat*. Frühneuzeit-Forschungen 8. Tübingen: Bibliotheca academica Verlag, 2000.
Reinhardt, Volker. *Kardinal Scipione Borghese (1605–1633): Vermögen, Finanzen und sozialer Aufstieg eines Papstnepoten*. Bibliothek des Deutschen Historischen Instituts in Rom 58. Tübingen: Max Niemeyer, 1984.
Reinkowski, Maurus. "Keine Kryptoreligion, aber doch kryptoreligiös: Zur Frage einer realen Existenz von Kryptojuden und Kryptochristen im islamisch geprägten Mittelmeerraum und Nahen Osten." In *Konfessionelle Ambiguität: Uneindeutigkeit und Verstellung als religiöse Praxis in der Frühen Neuzeit*, edited by Andreas Pietsch and Barbara Stollberg-Rilinger, 75–98. Schriften des Vereins für Reformationsgeschichte 214. Gütersloh: Gütersloher Verlagshaus, 2013.
Revel, Jacques, ed. *Jeux d'échelles: La micro-analyse à l'expérience*. Paris: Gallimard/ Éditions du Seuil, 1996.
Richard, Francis. "Catholicisme et Islam chiite au 'Grand Siècle': Autour de quelques documents concernant les Missions catholiques en Perse au XVIIe siècle." *Euntes docete* 33 (1980): 339–403.
Richard, Francis. *Raphaël du Mans, missionnaire en Perse au XVIIe siècle*. Vol. 1: *Biographie. Correspondance*, vol. 2: *Estats et Mémoire*. Moyen Orient & Océan Indien XVIe–XIXe s. 9/1 and 2. Paris: L'Harmattan, 1995.
Richard, Francis. "Un Augustin portugais renégat, apologiste de l'Islam chiite au début du XVIIIe siècle." *Moyen Orient & Océan Indien, XVIe–XIXe* s. 1 (1984): 73–85.

Richard, Jean. *La Papauté et les missions d'Orient au Moyen Âge (XIIIe–XVe siècles)*. Collection de l'École française de Rome 33. Rome: École française de Rome, 1977.

Ricks, Thomas M. *Notables, Merchants, and Shaykhs of Southern Iran and Its Ports: Politics and Trade of the Persian Gulf Region, AD 1728–1789*. Piscataway: Gorgias Press, 2012.

Rietbergen, Peter. "Upon a Silk Thread? Relations between the Safavid Court of Persia and the Dutch East Indies Company, 1623–1722." In *Hof en Handel: Aziatische Vorsten en de VOC 1620–1720*, edited by Elsbeth Locher-Scholten and Peter Rietbergen, 159–82. Verhandelingen van het Koninklijk Instituut voor Taal-, Land- en Volkenkunde 223. Leiden: KITLV Uitgeverij, 2004.

Rizvi, Sajjad H. *Mullā Ṣadrā Shīrāzī: His Life and Works and the Sources for Safavid Philosophy*. Oxford: OUP, 2007.

Rodén, Marie-Luise. *Church Politics in Seventeenth-Century Rome: Cardinal Decio Azzolino, Queen Christina of Sweden, and the* Squadrone Volante. Acta Universitatis Stockholmensis/Stockholm Studies in History 60. Stockholm: Almqvist & Wiksell International, 2000.

Roggero, Anastasio. *Genova e gli inizi della riforma teresiana in Italia (1584–1597)*. Institutum Historicum Teresianum: Studia 3. Rome: Teresianum, 1984.

Romano, Antonella. *Impressions de Chine: L'Europe et l'englobement du monde (XVIe–XVIIe siècle)*. Paris: Fayard, 2016.

Rosa, Mario. "The Catholic *Aufklärung* in Italy." In *A Companion to the Catholic Enlightenment in Europe*, edited by Ulrich L. Lehner and Michael O'Neill Printy, 215–50. Brill's Companions to the Christian Tradition 20. Leiden: Brill, 2010.

Rubiés, Joan-Pau. "The Concept of Cultural Dialogue and the Jesuit Method of Accommodation: Between Idolatry and Civilization." *Archivum Historicum Societatis Iesu* 74 (2005): 237–80.

Rubiés, Joan-Pau. "From Christian Apologetics to Deism: Libertine Readings of Hinduism, 1650–1730." In *God in the Enlightenment*, edited by William J. Bulman and Robert G. Ingram, 107–35. Oxford: OUP, 2016.

Rubiés, Joan-Pau. "Political Rationality and Cultural Distance in the European Embassies to Shah Abbas I." *Journal of Early Modern History* 20 (2016): 351–89.

Rubiés, Joan-Pau. *Travel and Ethnology in the Renaissance: South India through European Eyes, 1250–1625*. Cambridge: CUP, 2000.

Rublack, Ulinka, ed. *Protestant Empires: Globalizing the Reformations*. Cambridge, CUP, 2020.

Rurale, Flavio. *Monaci, frati, chierici: Gli ordini religiosi in età moderna*. Rome: Carocci editore, 2008.

Sachsenmaier, Dominic. *Global Entanglements of a Man Who Never Travelled: A Seventeenth-Century Chinese Christian and His Conflicted Worlds*. New York: Columbia University Press, 2018.

Santus, Cesare. *Trasgressioni necessarie*: Communicatio in sacris, *coesistenza e conflitti tra le communità cristiane orientali (Levante e Impero ottomano, XVII–XVIII secolo)*. Bibliothèque des Écoles françaises d'Athènes et de Rome 383. Rome: École française de Rome, 2019.

Savory, Roger. *Iran under the Safavids*. Cambridge: CUP, 1980.

Schlögl, Rudolf. *Religion and Society at the Dawn of Modern Europe: Christianity Transformed, 1750–1850*. Translated by Helen Imhoff. London: Bloomsbury Academic, 2020.

Schlumbohm, Jürgen. "Gesetze, die nicht durchgesetzt werden: Ein Strukturmerkmal des frühneuzeitlichen Staates?" *Geschichte und Gesellschaft* 23 (1997): 647–63.

Schneider, Gary, *The Culture of Epistolarity: Vernacular Letters and Letter Writing in Early Modern England, 1500–1700*. Newark: University of Delaware Press, 2005.
Schutte, Gerrit Jan, ed. *Het indisch Sion: De Gereformeerde kerk onder de Verenigte Oost-Indische Compagnie*. Hilversum: Uitgeverij Verloren, 2002.
Selwyn, Jennifer D. *A Paradise Inhabited by Devils: The Jesuits' Civilizing Mission in Early Modern Naples*. Aldershot, Ashgate, 2004.
Shapiro, Henry R. "Falling Out of Love with the Franks: The Life and Writings of an Armenian Catholic Diplomat in the Service of Late Safavid Persia." *Iranian Studies* 54 (2021): 573–603.
Sidler, Daniel. *Heiligkeit aushandeln: Katholische Reform und lokale Glaubenspraxis in der Eidgenossenschaft*. Campus Historische Studien 75. Frankfurt am Main: Campus, 2017.
Siebenhüner, Kim. *Die Spur der Juwelen: Materielle Kultur und transkontinentale Verbindungen in der Frühen Neuzeit*. Ding Materialität Geschichte 3. Cologne: Böhlau, 2017.
Siebenhüner, Kim. "Glaubenswechsel in der Frühen Neuzeit." *Zeitschrift für Historische Forschung* 34 (2007): 243–72.
Sieber, Dominic. *Jesuitische Missionierung, priesterliche Liebe, sakramentale Magie: Volkskulturen in Luzern 1563 bis 1614*. Luzerner Historische Veröffentlichungen 40. Basel: Schwabe, 2005.
Signorotto, Gianvittorio and Maria Antonietta Visceglia, eds. *Court and Politics in Papal Rome, 1492–1700*. Cambridge: CUP, 2002.
Simpson, Marianna Shreve. "The Morgan Bible and the Giving of Religious Gifts between Iran and Europe/Europe and Iran during the Reign of Shah ʿAbbas I." In *Between the Picture and the World: Manuscript Studies from the Index of Christian Art*, edited by Colum Hourihane, 141–50. Princeton: Index of Christian Art, in association with Penn State University Press, 2005.
Sinicropi, Gilles. *"D'oraison et d'action:" Les Carmes déchaux en France aux XVIIe et XVIIIe siècles*. Saint-Étienne: Publications de l'Université de Saint-Étienne, 2013.
Sluhovsky, Moshe. *Becoming a New Self: Practices of Belief in Early Modern Catholicism*. Chicago: University of Chicago Press, 2017.
Sluhovsky, Moshe. *Believe Not Every Spirit: Possession, Mysticism & Discernment in Early Modern Catholicism*. Chicago: University of Chicago Press, 2007.
Snoeks, Rémi. *L'argument de la tradition dans la controverse eucharistique entre catholiques et réformés français au XVIIe siècle*. Universitas Catholica Lovaniensis: Dissertationes ad gradum magistri in Facultate Theologica vel in Facultate Iuris Canonici consequendum conscriptae, Series II, 44. Louvain: Publications universitaires de Louvain, and Gembloux: Éditions J. Duculot, 1951.
Standaert, Nicolas. *Chinese Voices in the Rites Controversy: Travelling Books, Community Networks, Intercultural Arguments*. Bibliotheca Instituti Historici S.I. 75. Rome: Institutum Historicum Societatis Iesu, 2012.
Standaert, Nicolas. *The Interweaving of Rituals: Funerals in the Cultural Exchange between China and Europe*. Seattle: University of Washington Press, 2008.
Standaert, Nicolas. "The Rites Controversy." In *Handbook of Christianity in China*. Vol. 1: *635–1800*, edited by Nicolas Standaert, 680–8. Leiden: Brill, 2001.
Steensgaard, Niels. *The Asian Trade Revolution of the Seventeenth Century: The East India Companies and the Decline of the Caravan Trade*. Chicago: University of Chicago Press, 1974.

Stolte, Carolin. *Philip Angel's Deex-Autaers: Vaiṣṇava Mythology from Manuscript to Book Market in the Context of the Dutch East India Company, c. 1600–1672*. Dutch Sources on South Asia c. 1600–1825 5. New Delhi: Manohar, 2012.

Strathern, Alan. *Kingship and Conversion in Sixteenth-Century Sri Lanka: Portuguese Imperialism in a Buddhist Land*. Cambridge: CUP, 2007.

Stroumsa, Guy G. *A New Science: The Discovery of Religion in the Age of Reason*. Cambridge, MA: Harvard University Press, 2010.

Subrahmanyam, Sanjay. *Explorations in Connected History: From the Tagus to the Ganges*. New Delhi: OUP, 2004.

Subrahmanyam, Sanjay. *Explorations in Connected History: Mughals and Franks*. New Delhi: OUP, 2005.

Subrahmanyam, Sanjay. "An Infernal Triangle: The Contest between Mughals, Safavids and Portuguese, 1590–1605." In *Iran and the World in the Safavid Age*, edited by Willem Floor and Edmund Herzig, 103–30. London: I. B. Tauris, 2012.

Subrahmanyam, Sanjay. *The Portuguese Empire in Asia, 1500–1700: A Political and Economic History*, 2nd edn. Chichester: Wiley-Blackwell, 2012.

Subrahmanyam, Sanjay. *Three Ways to Be Alien: Travails & Encounters in the Early Modern World*. Waltham, MA: Brandeis University Press, 2011.

Terrier, Mathieu. "La représentation de la sagesse grecque comme discours et mode de vie chez les philosophes šīʿites de l'Iran safavide (XIe/XVIIe siècles)." *Studia graeco-arabica* 5 (2015): 299–320.

Thiessen, Hillard von. *Das Zeitalter der Ambiguität: Vom Umgang mit Werten und Normen in der Frühen Neuzeit*. Cologne: Böhlau, 2021.

Thiessen, Hillard von. *Die Kapuziner zwischen Konfessionalisierung und Alltagskultur: Vergleichende Fallstudie am Beispiel Freiburgs und Hildesheims 1599–1750*. Historiae 13. Freiburg im Br.: Rombach, 2002.

Thiessen, Hillard von. *Diplomatie und Patronage: Die spanisch-römischen Beziehungen 1605–1621 in akteurszentrierter Perspektive*. Frühneuzeit-Forschungen 16. Epfendorf: Bibliotheca Academica, 2010.

Thomas, David and John Chesworth, eds. *Ottoman and Safavid Empires (1600–1700)*. Christian-Muslim Relations: A Bibliographical History 10. Leiden: Brill, 2017.

Tiburcio, Alberto. *Muslim-Christian Polemics in Safavid Iran*. Edinburgh: Edinburgh University Press, 2020.

Tramontana, Felicita. "Protestants' Conversions to Catholicism in the Syro-Palestinian Region (17th Century)." *Zeitschrift für Historische Forschung* 41 (2014): 401–22.

Tramontana, Felicita. "An Unusual Setting: Interactions between Protestants and Catholics in the Ottoman Empire." In *Religious Minorities and Majorities in Early Modern Europe: Confessional Boundaries and Contested Identities*, edited by Simon Burton, Michał Choptiany, and Piotr Wilczek, 189–211. Refo500 Academic Studies Series 53. Göttingen: Vandenhoeck & Ruprecht, 2019.

Trento, Margherita. *Writing Tamil Catholicism: Literature, Persuasion and Devotion in the Eighteenth Century*. Philological Encounters Monographs 3. Leiden: Brill, 2022.

Trivellato, Francesca. *The Familiarity of Strangers: The Sephardic Diaspora, Livorno, and Cross-Cultural Trade in the Early Modern Period*. New Haven: Yale University Press, 2009.

Trivellato, Francesca. "Is There a Future for Italian Microhistory in the Age of Global History?" *California Italian Studies* 2 (2011). https://escholarship.org/uc/item/0z94n9hq.

Troebst, Stefan. "Isfahan—Moskau—Amsterdam: Zur Entstehungsgeschichte des moskauischen Transitprivilegs für die Armenische Handelskompanie in Persien (1666–1676)." *Jahrbücher für die Geschichte Osteuropas* 41 (1993): 179–209.
Tucker, Ernest. "From Rhetoric of War to Realities of Peace: The Evolution of Ottoman-Iranian Diplomacy through the Safavid Era." In *Iran and the World in the Safavid Age*, edited by Willem Floor and Edmund Herzig, 81–9. London: I. B. Tauris, 2012.
Tucker, Ernest. "Nāder Shāh." In *Encyclopaedia Iranica* online. Article published Aug. 15, 2006; last updated Aug. 15, 2006, http://www.iranicaonline.org/articles/nader-shah.
Tucker, Ernest. *Nadir Shah's Quest for Legitimacy in Post-Safavid Iran*. Gainesville: University Press of Florida, 2006.
Turley, Steven E. *Franciscan Spirituality and Mission in New Spain, 1524–1599: Conflict Beneath the Sycamore Tree (Luke 19:1–10)*. Aldershot: Ashgate, 2014.
Valensi, Lucette. "Inter-Communal Relations and Changes in Religious Affiliation in the Middle East (17th to 19th Centuries)." *Comparative Studies in Society and History* 39 (1997): 251–69.
Van den Oudenrijn, Marcus Antonius. "Uniteurs et Dominicains d'Arménie." *Oriens Christianus* 40 (1956): 94–112; 42 (1958): 110–33; 43 (1959): 110–19; 45 (1961): 95–108; and 46 (1962): 99–116.
Van Droffelaar, Johan. "'Flemish Fathers' in the Levant: Dutch Protection of Three Franciscan Missions in the 17th and 18th Centuries." In *Eastward Bound: Dutch Ventures and Adventures in the Middle East*, edited by Geert Jan van Gelder and Ed de Moor, 81–113. Amsterdam: Rodopi, 1994.
Van Meersbergen, Guido. *Ethnography and Encounter: The Dutch and English in Seventeenth Century South Asia*. European Expansion and Indigenous Response 35. Leiden: Brill, 2022.
Van Meersbergen, Guido. "'Intirely the Kings Vassalls': East India Company Gifting Practices and Anglo-Mughal Political Exchange (c. 1670–1720)." *Diplomatica: A Journal of Diplomacy and Society* 2 (2020): 270–90.
Van Wamelen, Carla. *Family Life onder de VOC: Een handelscompagnie in huwelijks- en gezinszaken*. Hilversum: Uitgeverij Verloren, 2014.
Vareschi, Severino. "Heiliges Offizium gegen *Propaganda*? Das Dekret des Jahres 1656 in der Ritenfrage und die Rolle Martino Martinis." In *Martino Martini S.J. (1614–1661) und die Chinamission im 17. Jahrhundert*, edited by Roman Malek and Arnold Zingerle, 65–91. Nettetal: Steyler, 2000.
Veevers, David. *The Origins of the British Empire in Asia, 1600–1750*. Cambridge: CUP, 2020.
Vermote, Frederik. "Finances of the Missions." In *A Companion to Early Modern Catholic Global Missions*, edited by Ronnie Po-chia Hsia, 367–400. Brill's Companions to the Christian Tradition 80. Leiden: Brill, 2018.
Vermote, Frederik. "The Role of Urban Real Estate in Jesuit Finances and Networks between Europe and China, 1612–1778." PhD thesis, University of British Columbia, 2012.
Vidal, Fernando. "Miracles, Science and Testimony in Post-Tridentine Saint-Making." *Science in Context* 20 (2007): 481–508.
Visceglia, Maria Antonietta. *Morte e elezione del papa: Norme, riti e conflitti; L'Età moderna*. Rome: Viella, 2013.
Vismara, Paola. *Oltre l'usura: La Chiesa moderna e il prestito a interesse*. Soveria Mannelli: Rubbettino Editore, 2004.

Vries, Wilhelm de. "Die Propaganda und die Christen im Nahen asiatischen und afrikanischen Osten." In *Sacrae Congregationis de Propaganda Fide Memoria Rerum, 1622-1972*, edited by Josef Metzler. Vol. I/1: *1622-1700*, 561-605. Rome: Herder, 1971.

Vries, Wilhelm de. *Rom und die Patriarchate des Ostens*. Orbis academicus: Problemgeschichten der Wissenschaft in Dokumenten und Darstellungen III/4. Freiburg im Br.: Karl Alber, 1963.

Vu Thanh, Hélène. *Devenir japonais: La mission jésuite au Japon (1549-1614)*. Paris: Presses de l'Université Paris-Sorbonne, 2016.

Vu Thanh, Hélène and Ines G. Županov, eds. *Trade and Finance in Global Missions (16th-18th Centuries)*. Studies in Christian Mission 57. Leiden: Brill, 2021.

Walsham, Alexandra. *Catholic Reformation in Protestant Britain*. Farnham: Ashgate, 2014.

Walsham, Alexandra. *Charitable Hatred: Tolerance and Intolerance in England, 1500-1740*. Manchester: Manchester University Press, 2006.

Walsham, Alexandra. "In Sickness and in Health: Medicine and Inter-Confessional Relations in Post-Reformation England." In *Living with Religious Diversity in Early-Modern Europe*, edited by C. Scott Dixon, Dagmar Freist, and Mark Greengrass, 161-81. Farnham: Ashgate, 2009.

Walsham, Alexandra. "Miracles and the Counter-Reformation Mission to England." *The Historical Journal* 46 (2003): 779-815.

Ware, Kallystos Timothy. "Orthodox and Catholics in the Seventeenth Century: Schism or Intercommunion?" In *Schism, Heresy and Religious Protest*, edited by Derek Baker, 259-76. Cambridge: CUP, 1972.

Wassilowsky, Günther. *Die Konklavereform Gregors XV. (1621/22): Wertekonflikte, symbolische Inszenierung und Verfahrenswandel im posttridentinischen Papsttum*. Päpste und Papsttum 38. Stuttgart: Anton Hiersemann, 2010.

Weber, Alison. *Teresa of Avila and the Rhetoric of Femininity*. Princeton: Princeton University Press, 1990.

Weber, Nadir. *Lokale Interessen und große Strategie: Das Fürstentum Neuchâtel und die politischen Beziehungen der Könige von Preußen (1707-1806)*. Externa: Geschichte der Außenbeziehungen in neuen Perspektiven 7. Cologne: Böhlau, 2015.

Weber, Samuel. "Pining for Stability: The Borromeo Family and the Crisis of the Spanish Monarchy, 1610-1680." PhD thesis, University of Bern and Durham University, 2019.

Weltecke, Dorothea. "Multireligiöse Loca Sancta und die mächtigen Heiligen der Christen." *Der Islam: Zeitschrift für Geschichte und Kultur des islamischen Orients* 88 (2011): 73-95.

White, Donald Maxwell. *Zaccaria Seriman (1709-1784) and the* Viaggi di Enrico Wanton: *A Contribution to the Study of Enlightenment in Italy*. Manchester: Manchester University Press, 1961.

Whooley, John. "The Mekhitarists: Religion, Culture and Ecumenism in Armenian-Catholic Relations." In *Eastern Christianity: Studies in Modern History, Religion and Politics*, edited by Anthony O'Mahony, 452-89. London: Melisende, 2004.

Wills, John E. *Embassies and Illusions: Dutch and Portuguese Envoys to Kang'si, 1666-1687*. Harvard East Asian Monographs 113. Cambridge, MA: Harvard University Asia Center, 1984.

Windler, Christian. "Ambiguous Belongings: How Catholic Missionaries in Persia and the Roman Curia Dealt with *Communicatio in Sacris*." In *A Companion to Early Modern Catholic Global Missions*, edited by Ronnie Po-chia Hsia, 205-34. Brill's Companions to the Christian Tradition 80. Leiden: Brill, 2018.

Windler, Christian. "Early Modern Composite Catholicism from a Global Perspective: Catholic Missionaries and the English East India Company." In *Pathways through Early Modern Christianities*, edited by Andreea Badea, Bruno Boute, and Birgit Emich, 57–85. Cultures of Christianity: New Approaches to Early Modern History 1. Cologne: Böhlau, 2023.

Windler, Christian. *La diplomatie comme expérience de l'Autre: Consuls français au Maghreb (1700–1840)*. Geneva: Librairie Droz, 2002.

Windler, Christian. *Missionare in Persien: Kulturelle Diversität und Normenkonkurrenz im globalen Katholizismus (17.–18. Jahrhundert)*. Externa: Geschichte der Außenbeziehungen in neuen Perspektiven 12. Cologne: Böhlau, 2018.

Windler, Christian. "Städte am Hof: Burgundische Deputierte und Agenten in Madrid und Versailles (16.–18. Jahrhundert)." *Zeitschrift für Historische Forschung* 30 (2003): 207–50.

Wolf, Hubert. "Trient und 'tridentinisch' im Katholizismus des 19. Jahrhunderts." In *Das Konzil von Trient und die katholische Konfessionskultur (1563–2013): Wissenschaftliches Symposium aus Anlass des 450. Jahrestages des Abschlusses des Konzils von Trient, Freiburg i. Br. 18.–21. September 2013*, edited by Peter Walter and Günther Wassilowsky, 67–82. Reformationsgeschichtliche Studien und Texte 163. Münster: Aschendorff, 2016.

Wolf, Hubert and Bernward Schmidt. *Benedikt XIV. und die Reform des Buchzensurverfahrens: Zur Geschichte und Rezeption von "Sollicita ac provida."* Römische Inquisition und Indexkongregation 13. Paderborn: Ferdinand Schöningh, 2011.

Zeron, Carlos Alberto de Moura Ribeiro. *Ligne de foi: La Compagnie de Jésus et l'esclavage dans le processus de formation de la société coloniale en Amérique portugaise (XVIe–XVIIe siècles)*. Paris: H. Champion, 2009.

Županov, Ines G. "Conversion, Illness and Possession: Catholic Missionary Healing in Early Modern South Asia." In *Divins remèdes: Médecine et religion en Asie du Sud*, edited by Ines G. Županov and Caterina Guenzi, 263–300. Collection Puruṣārtha 27. Paris: Éditions de l'EHESS, 2008.

Županov, Ines G. *Disputed Mission: Jesuit Experiments and Brahmanical Knowledge in Seventeenth-Century India*. New Delhi: OUP, 1999.

Županov, Ines G. "Le repli du religieux: Les missionnaires jésuites du XVIIe siècle entre la théologie chrétienne et une éthique païenne." *Annales: Histoire, Sciences Sociales* 51 (1996): 1201–23.

Županov, Ines G. *Missionary Tropics: The Catholic Frontier in India (16th–17th Centuries)*. Ann Arbor: University of Michigan Press, 2005.

Županov, Ines G., ed. *The Oxford Handbook of the Jesuits*. New York: OUP, 2019.

Županov, Ines G. and Pierre Antoine Fabre, eds. *The Rites Controversies in the Early Modern World*. Studies in Christian Mission 53. Leiden: Brill, 2018.

Županov, Ines G. and Pierre Antoine Fabre. "The Rites Controversies in the Early Modern World: An Introduction." In *The Rites Controversies in the Early Modern World*, edited by Ines G. Županov and Pierre Antoine Fabre, 1–26. Studies in Christian Mission 53. Leiden: Brill, 2018.

Zürcher, Erik. "The Jesuit Mission in Fujian in Late Ming Times: Levels of Response." In *Development and Decline of Fukien Province in the 17th and 18th Centuries*, edited by Eduard B. Vermeer, 417–57. Leiden: Brill, 1990.

Index

Aaron, Armenian bishop of Erzurum 147
ʿAbbās I, shah of Persia (1588–1629) 3, 10, 59–63, 65–71, 74–9, 81–2, 85, 89–95, 99–100, 176; image of a philo-Christian ruler 75–8
ʿAbbās II, shah of Persia (r. 1642–66) 63–5, 92–3
Abraham Petros I, Armenian Catholic patriarch of Cilicia 141, 264
absolute rule 13, 26, 31–2, 57, 278, 285
Accademia dei Virtuosi 15
accommodation, by members of different religious orders 150–1, 157–64, 253–5, 286–8; Jesuits 26–7, 251, 259, 264
account books, manipulation of 240–2
Acosta, José de, SJ, *De procuranda Indorum Salute* 79
adiaphora, Jesuit use of 259
Agdollo, Gregorio 275–7, 345
Agha di Matus, Paron 134–5, 322
Agnello dell'Immacolata Concezione OCD (Carlo di Giorgi) 143, 235
Aḥmad ʿAlawī, Sayyid 100–101, 266
Akbar, Mughal emperor (r. 1556–1605) 95
Albani, Giovanni Francesco, *see* Clement XI (Giovanni Francesco Albani, pope 1700–1721)
Alberizzi, Mario, secretary of the *Propaganda Fide* 25
Albertus Magnus OP 145
Aldobrandini, Cinzio Passeri, *see* Passeri Aldobrandini, Cinzio, cardinal (1593–1610)
Aldobrandini, Ippolito, *see* Clement VIII (Ippolito Aldobrandini, pope 1592–1605)
Aldobrandini, Pietro, cardinal (1593–1621) 6, 47
Aleppo 53, 160, 183, 186, 192–4, 200, 202, 239–41, 252, 263

Alessandro di San Silvestro OCD (Francesco Montalbano) 113–14
Alexander I, catholicos of Etchmiadzin (r. 1705–14) 147
Alexander VI (Rodrigo Borgia, pope 1492–1503) 21
Alexander VII (Fabio Chigi, pope 1655–67) 17, 20, 29, 47–9, 51, 55, 139, 239, 265, 306
Alexander VIII (Pietro Vito Ottoboni, pope 1689–91) 141
ʿAlī-Qulī Ġadīd al-Islām, *see* António de Jesus OSA, alias ʿAlī-Qulī Ġadīd al-Islām
Allāhwerdi Ḫān, governor of Fars province 99
Altieri, Emilio, *see* Clement X (Emilio Altieri, pope 1670–76)
ambiguity, tolerance for 1–2, 10–11, 78, 110, 120–1, 165, 214, 218, 269–70, 282
ancient law, respect for 23–4
Ange de Saint-Joseph OCD (Joseph Labrosse) 35, 41–2, 97, 196, 230, 245–8, 251–5; correspondence with Robert Huntington 252; *Gazophylacium linguae Persarum* 97, 252; *Pharmacopoea persica* 109, 202, 252; relations with Jean Chardin 109, 252
Antoniano, Federico, *see* Giovanni Battista di San Giuseppe OCD (Federico Antoniano)
António de Jesus OSA, alias ʿAlī-Qulī Ġadīd al-Islām, conversion to Islam 116–19; role as intermediary 86, 117–18; criticism of Christianity 117, 196–7
António do Desterro OSA (António da Rocha de Oliveira) 86, 117–18
Arcangelo da Brescia OP 197

Ardabil 128, 225
Aristotle 99, 145
Armenian Catholic Church, communion under both kinds 158; Easter customs 158–9, 274. *See also* Mekhitar of Sebaste; Mekhitarists; Sceriman family, Catholic church in New Julfa
Armenian Church, changes of affiliation of clerics 159. *See also* catholicos of the Armenian Church
Armenians, and English East India Company 63, 152; and missionaries 123–65; confessional disambiguation 144–50; deportation from Julfa on the Arax 68; merchants as global actors 70–4, 151–7; Nakhchivan 125, 137–9, 162, 229; New Julfa 68–9, 70–4; Poland-Lithuania 136–8, 141. *See also* Sceriman family
Arnauld, Antoine, *La perpétuité de la foi de l'Église catholique touchant l'Eucharistie* 123
Assemani, Giuseppe Simone 272
Athanase de Sainte-Thérèse OCD 195
Aubron, Antoine, *see* Basile de Saint-Charles OCD (Antoine Aubron)
Augustinians, and Armenians 127–8, 136; and *Propaganda fide* 48; as agents of the king of Portugal 21–2, 81, 83–8, 178–9, 231–2; arbitration in an affair of honor 199; diplomatic assignments to 84–8; economy of the convent 18, 231–2, 235; first contacts with Armenians 127–8; food 189–90, 231; help by a mullah 104; housing 61, 231–2; in Basra 7; in Isfahan 6–7, 21–2, 61, 70, 84–8, 103–4, 106, 116–19, 189–90, 199–202, 204, 206, 231–2; invitation of a Lutheran legation to a church festival 200–201; lay servants 231; mass in private homes 202; mixed marriage 204, 206; Muslims visiting the Augustinians' church 106; opening of missions in Asia to 23; reception at the Safavid court 75; use of horses 228, 231. *See also* António de Jesus OSA, alias ʿAlī-Qulī Ğadīd al-Islām

Avetik, Ḥwāğa 72
Azevedo, Balthasar de, *see* Balthasar de Santa Maria OCD (Balthasar de Azevedo)

Babylon [Baghdad], French bishop of 7, 22–3, 48, 87, 105, 117, 143, 147, 180–3, 193, 196–8, 206–7
Baes, Liévin de, *see* Isidore de Saint-Joseph OCD (Liévin de Baes)
Baghdad 185, 192. *See also* Babylon [Baghdad], French bishop of
Ballyet, Jean-Claude, *see* Emmanuel de Saint-Albert OCD (Jean-Claude Ballyet)
Balthasar de Santa Maria OCD (Balthasar de Azevedo) 145
Bamhago, Chérubin, *see* Chérubin de Sainte-Thérèse OCD (Chérubin Bamhago)
Bandar ʿAbbās 61–3, 110, 174, 186–7, 192, 198, 200, 202, 208, 212, 232, 234, 239
Bandar-i Kung 85–6, 88, 208
baptism, decisions of the Holy Office 114–15; of children of Protestants 173, 206–10; of enslaved people 168–9; of Muslims *in articulo mortis* 110, 112–15, 120, 283
Barberini, Antonio Jr., cardinal (1628–71), prefect of the *Propaganda Fide* 134
Barberini, Antonio Sr., cardinal (1624–46) 17
Barberini, Maffeo, *see* Urban VIII (Maffeo Barberini, pope 1623–44)
Bard, Henry, 1st Viscount Bellomont 194
Barnaba di San Carlo OCD (Francesco Bertarello) 46, 50, 245
Bartoli, Daniello, SJ 296
Basile de Saint-Charles OCD (Antoine Aubron) 87, 143
Basra 7, 31–2, 46, 50, 53, 153, 167–9, 174–5, 182, 186–7, 192–3, 198, 214–15, 217, 230, 236, 238–45, 252
Bauer, Thomas 121, 293, 299
Bedik, Petros 216
Belchior dos Anjos OSA (Belchior Soares) 85, 106, 127–8
Bembo, Ambrogio 63, 107, 109, 161, 173, 187, 193–4, 231–2, 241, 243
Bendici, Silvestro, OP 139

Benedict XIII (Pietro Francesco Orsini, pope 1724–30) 11, 291
Benedict XIV (Prospero Lorenzo Lambertini, pope 1740–58), and the Eastern churches 126, 141, 264; and the Enlightenment 280–2, 292; *De Synodo dioecesana libri tredecim* 279; decision-making practices under 11, 260, 263–4, 281–2, 291–2; *Declaratio benedictina* 279, 282; governance of the Discalced Carmelites 29
Benigno di San Michele OCD (Orazio Romanini de Sanctis) 79
Bernal, Carlo, *see* Bernardo Maria di Gesù OCD (Carlo Bernal)
Bernard de Bourges OFM Cap 191
Bernard de Sainte-Thérèse OCD (Jean Duval) 82, 182–3, 201, 205–7, 228
Bernard, Jean Frédéric, *Cérémonies et coutumes religieuses de tous les peuples du monde* 258
Bernardo Maria di Gesù OCD (Carlo Bernal) 45
Bernini, Gian Lorenzo 17
Bertarello, Francesco, *see* Barnaba di San Carlo OCD (Francesco Bertarello)
bigamia simultanea 275–7
Bisignano 139
Blaise de Nantes OFM Cap 144
Bock, Christian, *see* Dominicus a Sancto Nicolao OCD (Christian Bock)
Bologna 53
Bombay (Mumbai) 177
Boncompagni, Ugo, *see* Gregory XIII (Ugo Boncompagni, pope 1572–85)
Borghese, Camillo, *see* Paul V (Camillo Borghese, pope 1605–21)
Borghese, Maria Virginia 17
Borghese, Scipione, cardinal (1605–33), finances 16
Borgia, Rodrigo, *see* Alexander VI (Rodrigo Borgia, pope 1492–1503)
Borgia, Stefano, secretary of the *Propaganda Fide* 55
Borromeo family 42–3
Borromeo, Carlo, cardinal (1560–84) 257
Borromeo, Vitaliano, cardinal (1766–93) 220
Borromini, Francesco 17

Bossy, John 204
Botero, Giovanni, SJ 82
Boutet de l'Étoile family 214
Boutet de l'Étoile, Angela 173, 202
Boutet de l'Étoile, François 202
Boutet de l'Étoile, Isaac 169, 171–4, 179, 189, 201–2, 204, 212
Boutet de l'Étoile, Louis 173, 202
Boutet de l'Étoile, Reine 173–4, 202
Bragaldi, Giovanni Damasceno, OFM Conv 271, 273–4
Braschi, Giovanni Angelo, *see* Pius VI (Giovanni Angelo Braschi, pope 1775–99)
Brauner, Christina 88
Bushehr 53–4, 83, 111, 167, 216–7

Cacurri, Francesco Cimino, baron of, *see* Cimino, Francesco, baron of Cacurri
Capuchins, and Cardinal Richelieu 22; and Johann Rudolf Stadler 165; and *Propaganda fide* 22, 48; and the Jesuits 41, 178–9, 181, 226–7; arbitration in an affair of honor 199; as agents of the king of France 86–7, 90; baptism of Muslims *in articulo mortis* 113–15; disputations with Shi'a scholars 101, 104, 179; first contacts with Armenians 128–9; food 190, 232; funding 18; hosting lay-people 1, 194; habit 226–7; housing 198, 226, 232; in Isfahan 1, 7, 22, 70, 86–7, 101, 104, 113–14, 138, 179, 191–5, 198–9, 206, 226–7, 232; in New Julfa 128–9, 143, 145; in Tabriz 7, 147; mixed marriage 173, 201–2, 204, 206–8; presence at the local court 90–1. *See also* Raphaël du Mans OFM Cap (Jacques Dutertre)
Casimir Joseph de Sainte-Thérèse OCD (Jean Renauldin) 46
Castelli, Giuseppe Maria, cardinal (1759–80), prefect of the *Propaganda Fide* 55
Catholicism, composite and polycentric structure of 2, 13–14, 57, 288, 291–2
catholicos of the Armenian Church 71, 74; conflicts with the bishop of New Julfa 146–7, 149; relations with the papacy 135–6, 146–7; union with Rome 125

Caucasus 66. *See also* Julfa on the Arax
Cesario di Sant'Antonio OCD (Cesareo Crespi) 44
Chakrabarty, Dipesh, *Provincializing Europe* 3, 290, 295
Chardin, Jean 1, 7, 9, 72, 82–3, 107, 109, 115, 119–21, 171, 173, 176, 187–8, 194–5, 219, 231–2, 243, 252, 258, 293, 312
Chérubin de Sainte-Thérèse OCD (Chérubin Bamhago) 43
Chézaud, Aimé, SJ 42, 44, 101–2, 104, 145, 160, 162, 179, 202-2, 211–12
Chigi, Fabio, *see* Alexander VII (Fabio Chigi, pope 1655–67)
China, missions to 4–5
Chinese rites controversies, *see* Controversies, Chinese rites
Christology, Armenian and Latin, 124, 127, 149, 160, 164
church buildings in Persia, furnishings 106; Muslims visiting Christian 106–7
Cimino, Francesco, baron of Cacurri, bequest for the missions of the Discalced Carmelites 48, 237–8
Cimino, Paolo 237
Ciołek-Drzewicki, Jan, *see* Girolamo di Gesù Maria OCD (Jan Ciołek-Drzewicki)
Cittadini, Paolo-Angelo, OP 137
Clement IX (Giulio Rospigliosi, pope 1667–9) 237
Clement VIII (Ippolito Aldobrandini, pope 1592–1605) 6, 14, 17, 23–5, 30, 60, 75, 89, 123, 179, 203, 221–2, 224–6, 285, 288
Clement X (Emilio Altieri, pope 1670-6) 277
Clement XI (Giovanni Francesco Albani, pope 1700–1721) 11, 152, 163, 260, 263, 266, 271, 273–4, 291
Clement XIII (Carlo Rezzonico, pope 1758–69) 209, 280
Clement XIV (Lorenzo Ganganelli, pope 1769–74) 55, 269, 271, 291
clockmakers 171, 176; from Geneva 171–4, 197–8, 217; from Zurich 165
Cochin 177, 215
Collegio dei Maroniti 268, 272

Colonna family 54
Colonna, Oddone, *see* Martin V (Oddone Colonna, pope 1417–31)
communicatio in sacris 5, 10–11, 128–34, 139, 149–50, 157–64, 168–9, 179, 199–218, 260–4, 266–74, 279, 281–2, 284, 286, 291–2; bull *Ad vitanda scandala* 158, 263, 269–72, 279; Holy Office and *Propaganda fide* 270–4; Jesuit justification of 160–1, 163–4; Mekhitar of Sebaste's justification of 163–4, 271
communion under both kinds 158
Compagnie des Indes (orientales), *see* East India Company, French
competing norms 2–3, 219–55, 278–82
Condulmer, Gabriele, *see* Eugene IV (Gabriele Condulmer, pope 1431–47)
confessionalization 69–70, 121. *See also* disambiguation, doctrinal
Connock, Edward 190
Constant, Carel 189–90, 199
Constantine VI, Armenian catholicos of Sis (1430–39) 125
Constantinople 82, 146, 153, 155, 171–2, 175–8, 184, 189–91, 217–18, 274, 280
consular institutions, French, absence in Persia 174–5; attempts to set up 87, 175
controversies, and the emergence of the public sphere 257–8, 261, 266, 269, 291–2; Chinese rites 5–6, 259, 264–6, 268–9, 278–9, 281, 291–2; Malabar rites 5, 259, 264–6, 268–9
conversion, lack of successful 6–7; of Armenians 141–2; of missionaries to Islam 86, 116–19, 288; of Protestants to Catholicism 173–4, 202, 212, 214–15; vain hopes to convert Muslims 6, 74–8, 103, 119
Corbin, Henry, "Isfahan School" 92, 99–100
Corneille de Saint-Cyprien OCD (Martin Piérart) 208
Cornelio di San Giuseppe OCD (Carlo Amatore Adeodato Reina) 44, 52–6, 70, 83, 167–9, 182, 213, 229–30, 241–2, 284; *Centurie* 53–4, 105, 111–12, 115–16, 196, 208–9, 244–5, 268; *Memorie concernenti alla Chiesa e diocesi di*

Persia 168; *Memorie cronologiche* 53–6, 149–50, 216–17; relations with the Roman Curia 53–6
correspondence, as a means to cultivate personal relationships 39, 42–7, 57; delays 41–2; instrumental and symbolic functions 38–42; *ius scribendi* 40, 290; mail delivery 40–1, 191–3, 284, 287; multi-stranded nature of 40; risk of loss 41
Costa, Francisco, SJ 75
Cottalorda, Giovanni Agostino, *see* Leandro di Santa Cecilia OCD (Giovanni Agostino Cottalorda)
councils, of Chalcedon 124–5, 132–3, 146–7; of Clermont 108; of Florence 125, 132; of Nicaea 133, 135; of Trent 23, 94, 110, 125–6, 203–4, 273–7, 279, 281
Cramoisy, [first name unknown], *see* Gabriel de Paris OFM Cap ([first name unknown] Cramoisy)
Crema, Cipriano, *see* Fortunato di Gesù Maria OCD (Cipriano Crema)
Crespi, Cesareo, *see* Cesario di Sant'Antonio OCD (Cesareo Crespi)
Cunaeus, Joan 173, 189, 192–4, 204
Cunto, Giuseppe de, *see* Felice di Sant'Antonio OCD (Giuseppe de Cunto)

David IV, catholicos of Etchmiadzin (1590–1629) 128, 135–6
David of Julfa, Armenian bishop of New Julfa (1652–83) 145–6
de Bruyn, Cornelis 170, 204
decision-making practices in the Roman Curia, decision avoidance 11, 269–78, 281–2, 286; formalization of procedures 15, 278; "nihil esse respondendum" 115, 270, 272–5, 278, 286, 334–5
Della Valle, Pietro 77, 96, 100–101, 103, 107, 109, 129, 190–1, 228, 266, 314; marriage to Maani Gioerida [Ǧuwairī] 130
Denis de la Couronne d'Épines OCD (Denis Grignard) 32, 52, 110, 113–14, 139, 230

dervishes, as role models for missionaries 1, 115–16, 120; relations with missionaries 115–16, 120, 194
despotism 82–3, 148, 312
Diestel, Bernhard, SJ 180–1
Dimas della Croce OCD (Giacomo Tonelli) 129, 132, 139, 244
Dionisio di Gesù OCD (Władysław Miliński) 247
Dioscorus (d. 454), patriarch of Alexandria 125, 146, 273
diplomatic envoys in Persia 84–8, 184, 189–90, 224–7; advantages of regular clerics as 85, 87–8; laypeople 87, 184; Russian 189–90
disambiguation, doctrinal 5, 121, 125, 134–50, 164–5, 260–9, 281–2, 291–2
Discalced Carmelites, acceptance of gifts 225; alms from India 242; and Johann Rudolf Stadler 165; and *Propaganda fide* 47–57; and the papacy 14, 23–5, 49–50, 52–7; and the Sceriman family 111–12, 140–3, 152, 159, 163, 183, 235; baptism of Muslims *in articulo mortis* 113–15; bequest of the Baron of Cacurri 48, 237–8; carrying weapons 228–9, 232; community-based forms of governance 27–9, 31–3, 290; contemplation and action 36–7, 221–4, 253; criticism of Roman court society 49–50, 52–7, 288–9; dealings with Indian financiers 246–8, 291; disputations with Protestants 93–5; disputations with Shi'a scholars 254; dysfunctional institutions 25–38; economy of the convents 32, 34, 48–51, 54–6, 235–51; election and appointment of priors 31–3; exercise of powers of attorney 247–8; food 190, 232–5; General Chapter 27–31; gift-giving practices 46, 198–9, 213; governance 25–38; habit, 219–20, 224, 227–8, 253–4; hosting clerics and laypeople 1, 233–5, 241, 243, 283–4; housing 61, 243; internal debates concerning the orientation toward missionary activities 221–3, 253; internalized discipline 27, 35–8; in Bandar ʿAbbās 110, 187, 198, 202,

208, 239; in Basra 7, 31–2, 46, 50, 53, 167–9, 174, 182, 186–7, 192–3, 198, 214, 217, 230, 236, 238–45, 249, 252; in Bushehr 53–4, 83, 111, 167, 216–17; in Goa 30–3, 236–7, 242, 244–6; in Isfahan 1, 7, 31–3, 52–3, 61, 70, 79, 84, 88–96, 106, 109, 113–14, 182–3, 242–8; in New Julfa 6–7, 70, 111–12, 116, 129–35, 139–45, 182; in Shiraz 7, 31–2, 99, 180, 187–8, 192, 195, 228, 230, 234, 238–9, 242–4, 247, 284; inward prayer 36–7; kinship ties within the order 43–4; lay brothers 229–30; lay servants 228–32; mass in Armenian 129; mass in private homes 202–3; mixed marriage 130, 204, 214, 262; *nobilitas* of the order 222; observance 11, 36, 38, 219–55, 287; on Kharg Island 53, 167; participation in financial dealings 236–7, 245–8, 250–1; participation in trade affairs 43, 236–7, 240–5; patron-client relations within the order 44–6; personal relationships within the order 43–7; presence at the local court 88–90, 92–5, 224–7; provincial vicars 31–2; regional allegiances within the order 44–6; relations with families of origin 42–4, 46–7; rules for written correspondence 39–40, 290; scant personnel resources 25; *Seminario di San Pancrazio* 53, 140, 239; slaveholding 227, 229–30, 232; social interactions outside the convent 232–5; social interactions with Armenians 129–30, 132, 233–5; tendencies toward monarchical forms of governance 27–9, 31–3; use of horses 227–8, 232, 234; visitations 33–5, 223, 228–9; visits to Armenians and Muslims 233–5; wine production and trade 243–4, 249
disputations, with Protestants 93–5; with Shi'a scholars 81, 92–5, 99–102, 120, 179, 254, 268
distinction between religious and secular spheres 190, 208–9, 212, 259–60, 265, 287

Domingo de Jesús María OCD (Domingo Ruzola) 77
Dominicans, and Jacques Rousseau 197–8; and the papacy 23, 48; and the *Propaganda fide* 239; and the Sceriman family 143, 158–9, 197, 274–5; in Isfahan 64–5, 90; in New Julfa 6–7, 70, 143, 170, 170; mass in Armenian 162; in Nakhchivan 125, 137–9, 162; tendencies toward monarchical forms of governance 29; use of horses 228
Dominicus a Sancto Nicolao OCD (Christian Bock) 114
Du Jardin, François, *see* Pierre de la Mère de Dieu OCD (François Du Jardin)
Dubernat, Guillaume, SJ 163
Dutertre, Jacques, *see* Raphaël du Mans OFM Cap (Jacques Dutertre)
Duval, Jean, *see* Bernard de Sainte-Thérèse OCD (Jean Duval)

East India Companies, postal services 41, 191–3
East India Company, Dutch 61–3, 91, 290–1; extramarital relations with enslaved women 168–9; in Isfahan 170, 173, 180–1, 188–91; in the Persian Gulf 167–9, 186–8, 195–6; regulation of marriages 204; postal services 41; religious policies 175–7, 215
East India Company, English 61–3, 133, 290–1; extramarital relations with enslaved women 168–9; in Isfahan 170, 173, 188–91; in the Persian Gulf 167–9, 186–8, 195–6; religious policies 175–7
East India Company, French 22, 62, 90–1, 173–4, 186, 242, 246, 248, 290–1
Eastern Christians, topos of ignorance 129–31
Eastern churches, and Protestants 123; union with Rome 123–6, 132–4, 136–8, 141–2, 151–7, 163–4
Ecchellensis, Abraham 268
Élie de Saint-Albert OCD (Laurent Mouton) 45, 134–5, 139–45, 150, 154, 159, 163, 181–3, 201, 235, 239, 286–7
Elijah, prophet 116, 222
Eliseo de San Andrés OCD (Andrés García de Montoja) 185–6

Emich, Birgit 278
Emmanuel de Saint-Albert OCD (Jean-Claude Ballyet) 198
empowering interactions 14, 52, 56–7
Enlightenment, Catholic 280–2; radical 268. *See also* Mission and the Enlightenment
Epifanio di San Giovanni Battista OCD (Giovanni Battista Soccioli) 188, 223
Erzurum 187
Esprit, Julien, *see* Philippe de la Très Sainte Trinité OCD (Julien Esprit)
Estado da Índia, viceroy 59, 84–6, 117, 154, 231–2, 242, 287
Etchmiadzin 71, 125, 135, 146–7
Euclid 75, 98–9
Eugene IV (Gabriele Condulmer, pope 1431–47) 125
Eugenio di San Benedetto OCD (Luigi del Monte)
Europeans in early modern Asia, subordinate position 3, 290. *See also* Safavid court, ceremonial of embassies from Christian rulers
exorcism 111, 131
Ezpeleta y Goñi, Jerónimo Javier de, SJ, *Truth-Showing Mirror* 19, 95, 100–103, 266

Fabritius, Ludwig 91, 195
Farnese, Alessandro, *see* Paul III (Alessandro Farnese, pope 1534–49)
Fedeli di Milano, Barnaba, OP (Giovanni Battista Fedeli) 148, 157–9, 163, 170, 175, 182–4, 197–8, 202–3, 210, 213, 238, 274–5
Fedeli, Gian Antonio 198
Fedeli, Giovanni Battista, *see* Fedeli di Milano, Barnaba, OP (Giovanni Battista Fedeli)
Felice di Sant'Antonio OCD (Giuseppe de Cunto) 32, 34, 41, 47, 49, 52, 96–7, 145, 192, 245–6
Felice Maria da Sellano OFM Cap 226–7
Felix de Jesus OSA 75, 78
Ferdinand II, grand duke of Tuscany (r. 1621–70) 64–5
Fernando de Santa María OCD (Fernando Martínez) 261

Filippo Maria di Sant'Agostino OCD (Camillo Apollonio Malachisi) 148, 159, 182, 189, 229–30, 276–7
Foglia, Pietro, *see* Matteo di San Giuseppe OCD (Pietro Foglia)
Fortunato di Gesù Maria OCD (Cipriano Crema) 45, 235
France, king of, as protector of the missions 22–3, 147, 175, 184
Francesco di Gesù OCD (Martino Rivarola) 228, 230, 234
Francesco Maria di San Siro OCD (Antonio Gorla) 140–2, 187, 242
Francis Xavier SJ (Francisco de Jassu y Javier) 257
Fratres Unitores 125, 137
Frederick August II, elector of Saxony (r. 1733–63), as August III also king of Poland (r. 1734–63) 276
Frederick III, duke of Schleswig-Holstein-Gottorf (r. 1616–59) 165, 200
Friedrich, Markus 26, 39–40
friendship, definition 169, 198
"friendship" and "good correspondence" between missionaries and Armenians 4, 128–35, 149–50; between missionaries and Protestants 4, 168–9, 185–99, 213, 284; between regular clerics and laypeople 232–5
Fryer, John 187, 195, 212, 219, 231–2
funerals, as rituals of honor 210–12

Gabriel de Chinon OFM Cap 114, 145, 160, 162, 179
Gabriel de Paris OFM Cap ([first name unknown] Cramoisy) 101, 128–9
Galisson, Gratien de 117–18, 147, 196–7
Gambart, Juan, *see* Vicente de San Francisco OCD (Juan Gambart)
Games, Alison 334
Ganganelli, Lorenzo, OFM Conv (Giovanni Vincenzo Antonio Ganganelli), *see* Clement XIV (Lorenzo Ganganelli, pope 1769–74)
Garaizabal, Martín, *see* Próspero del Espíritu Santo OCD (Martín Garaizabal)

García de Montoja, Andrés, *see* Eliseo de San Andrés OCD (Andrés García de Montoja)
Gardane, Ange de, Sieur de Sainte-Croix 87–8, 181, 184, 203
Gasparini, Gaspare 146
Gaudereau, Martin 180
Gemelli Careri, Giovanni Francesco 231
Geneva 171–5, 197–8, 214–15
Genoa 25, 185
Ghislieri, Antonio Michele, *see* Pius V (Antonio Michele Ghislieri, pope 1566–72)
Ghougassian, Vazken S. 144–5
Giacinto di Santa Teresa OCD (Vittorio Francesco Piacentini) 43–4
Gierl, Martin 258
gift exchange economy 42, 46, 169, 185–8, 196–8, 208, 213, 288
Gioerida [Ġuwairī], Laali 130
Gioerida [Ġuwairī], Maani, marriage to Pietro della Valle 130
Gioerida [Ġuwairī], Smikan 247–8
Giorgi, Carlo di, *see* Agnello dell'Immacolata Concezione OCD (Carlo di Giorgi)
Giovanni Battista di San Giuseppe OCD (Federico Antoniano) 248, 252
Girolamo di Gesù Maria OCD (Jan Ciołek-Drzewicki) 35
Goa 21, 30–3, 75, 81, 84–5, 117, 154, 177, 180, 231, 236–7, 242, 244–6, 249; archbishop of 75, 85, 177, 242
godparents, Protestant, at Catholic baptisms 207–10
"good correspondence," definition 169; between missionaries and Muslims 103–5, 118–19. *See also* "friendship" and "good correspondence"
Gori 188
Gorla, Antonio, *see* Francesco Maria di San Siro OCD (Antonio Gorla)
Gouveia [also Gouvea], António de, OSA 75, 78, 99
Gregory IX (Ugo/Ugolino di Segni, pope 1227–41) 108
Gregory XIII (Ugo Boncompagni, pope 1572–85) 108

Gregory XV (Alessandro Ludovisi, pope 1621–23) 7, 15, 17–19, 265
Gregory the Illuminator 124, 127–8, 133–4, 161–3; relics brought to Persia by the Jesuits 162
Grignard, Denis, *see* Denis de la Couronne d'Épines OCD (Denis Grignard)
Guadagnoli, Filippo, CRM, *Considerationes ad Mahomettanos* 266–8
Guilherme de Santo Agostinho OSA 127–8
ġulām 66–7

Hamadan 7, 22, 181–2, 197, 200
Hazard, Paul, "crisis of the European mind" 5, 259, 297, 341
heliocentrism 105, 281
Hennin, Pierre-Michel 215
Herodotus 82
Hersche, Peter 294
Heyberger, Bernard 5, 120, 129, 152, 213, 268, 284, 344–5
Hobbes, Thomas 343
Holy Office, establishment 15; *facultates* of the missionaries 19–20, 23–5, 220; treatment of *dubia* 9, 15, 19–20, 114–15, 157–8, 209, 257–8, 260–4, 266, 268–9, 279
Hoogcamer, Jacobus 187
Hormuz 59, 61; Persian reconquest of 63, 84–5, 94
Humāyūn, Mughal emperor (r. 1530–40, 1555–6) 64
Huntington, Robert, correspondence with Ange de Saint-Joseph OCD (Joseph Labrosse) 252
Ḥusain Qulī Mīrzā 96
Ḫwāǧa Avetik, *see* Avetik, Ḫwāǧa
Ḫwāǧa Nazar, *see* Nazar, Ḫwāǧa, *kalāntar* of New Julfa
Ḫwāǧa Safar, *see* Safar, Ḫwāǧa, *kalāntar* of New Julfa
Ḫwāǧa Sarhat, *see* Sarhat, Ḫwāǧa

Ignatius of Loyola SJ 36, 161, 224, 257
Ignazio di Gesù OCD (Carlo Leonelli) 192, 205

Imperiali, Giuseppe Renato, cardinal (1690–37) 219–20, 225, 237
India, *see* Bombay; Cochin; Goa; São Tomé (Madras); South India
Ingoli, Francesco, secretary of the *Propaganda Fide* 15, 52, 77, 132–4, 178, 181, 222–3, 237, 244, 263, 266, 277–8; *Relazione delle Quattro Parti del Mondo* 20–2, 33, 219, 265
Innocent X (Giovanni Battista Pamphilj, pope 1644–55) 49, 60
Innocent XI (Benedetto Odescalchi, pope 1676–89) 115, 305
Innocent XII (Antonio Pignatelli, pope 1691–1700) 143, 153
internalized discipline in Catholic orders and individualization processes 37–8
Ioannes Ozinellus 273
Ireland 18
Isfahan, artisans of European origin 171; *Čihil Sutūn* 63–4; clockmakers 165, 171–4, 176; European laypeople 169–77; jewel merchants 171; Latin bishop 22–3, 70, 77, 133; *Maidān-i Naqš-i Ǧahān* 67, 79–81, 84. *See also* Augustinians in Isfahan; Capuchins in Isfahan; Discalced Carmelites in Isfahan; Dominicans in Isfahan; Jesuits in Isfahan; *Missions étrangères de Paris* in Isfahan
"Isfahan School" 92, 99–100
Isidore de Saint-Joseph OCD (Liévin de Baes) 46; *Historia Generalis Fratrum Discalceatorum Ordinis* 222, 296
Iskandar Bēg Munšī 65
Iskenderun 185
Ismāʿīl I, shah of Persia (r. 1501–24) 66–7
Israel, Jonathan I. 268–9
Italo-Greci 139

Jacob IV, catholicos of Etchmiadzin (1655–80) 146
Jahāngīr, Mughal Emperor (r. 1605–27) 95
Jansenism 180, 183
Jassu y Javier, Francisco de, *see* Francis Xavier SJ (Francisco de Jassu y Javier)
Jean Chrysostome de Saint-Paul OCD (Étienne Ribitol) 253–4
Jerónimo da Cruz OSA 75, 112

Jesuits, adaptation to the Armenian church calendar 161; and *Propaganda fide* 22, 24–5, 48; and the bishop of Isfahan 183–4; and the Capuchins 41, 178–9, 181, 226–7; and the French Crown 43, 87, 179, 181, 328; and the Rousseau family 174, 198, 202; and the Sceriman family 152, 159, 163; at the Mughal court 95; baptism of Muslims *in articulo mortis* 113–15; celebration of the feast day of Gregory the Illuminator 161; contemplation in action 36; dealings with Indian financiers 249; disputations with Shiʿa scholars 101–2, 179; food 196, 224; funding 18, 235; funerals of Jesuits 211–12; governance 26–9; habit 224, 264; housing 196, 232, 249; in China 97; in Isfahan 7, 41, 79, 101–2, 179–81, 248–9; in New Julfa 6–7, 70, 98, 102, 106, 140, 143, 145, 150, 152, 160–4, 174, 181–2, 184, 196, 198, 203–4, 212, 232, 249–50; internalized discipline 35–8; *litterae annuae* 39; local economy of the missions 246, 248–50; mail delivery 41; mass in Armenian 162, 164; mass in private homes 201–4; monarchical constitution 26, 28–9; participation in financial dealings 248–9; participation in trade affairs 249; personal networks 26; relations with families of origin 42; relic of Gregory the Illuminator brought to New Julfa 162; rules for written correspondence 39–40; school in New Julfa 160–1; spiritual exercises 36–8
John V, king of Portugal (r. 1706–50) 154
José do Rosário OSA 138, 220
Joseph de Paris OFM Cap (François Le Clerc du Tremblay) 22, 226
Juan de Jesús María OCD (Juan de San Pedro), *Instructio Missionum* 221, 261–2; *Tractatus quo asseruntur missiones* 221
Juan de la Cruz OCD (Juan de Yepes Álvarez) 25
Juan Thadeo de San Eliseo OCD (Juan Roldán y Ibañez) 44, 75–7, 89–96, 99, 103, 123, 128–9, 133, 139, 181, 190–1, 226, 228, 237–8, 242–4, 251, 290

Judas Thaddaeus, apostle 123
Julfa on the Arax 60, 68, 127–8, 152

Kaempfer, Engelbert 9, 91, 105, 195, 212
Khachatur, Armenian bishop of New Julfa (1623–46) 128–9, 132–3, 137, 144
Kharg Island 53, 167–8, 216–17
Knab, Sebastian, OP 7
Kniphausen, Justo Baron von 168
Krstič, Tijana 69
Krusiński, Tadeusz Juda, SJ 109, 163–4; *Histoire de la dernière Révolution de Perse* 83, 172–3

L'Escale, René de, *see* Pacifique de Provins OFMCap (René de l'Escale)
Labrosse, Joseph, *see* Ange de Saint-Joseph OCD (Joseph Labrosse)
Ladislaus IV, king of Poland (r. 1632–48) 136
Lagar y Baylo, Pedro, *see* Redempto de la Cruz OCD (Pedro Lagar y Baylo)
Lagarde, Jean Martial, SJ 203
Lagisse, Pierre-Didier 173–4
Lambert de la Motte, Pierre 170, 178
Lambertini, Prospero Lorenzo, *see* Benedict XIV (Prospero Lorenzo Lambertini, pope 1740–58)
Landriano, Giuseppe, *see* Valerio di San Giuseppe OCD (Giuseppe Landriano)
language, Arabic and Persian lessons for missionaries 103–4; use of local language by missionaries 103, 131
Laymann, Paul, SJ 210
Le Clerc du Tremblay, François, *see* Joseph de Paris OFM Cap (François Le Clerc du Tremblay)
Le Peultre, Élisabeth 22
Leandro di Santa Cecilia OCD (Giovanni Agostino Cottalorda) 189
Lehmann, Hartmut 26
Leo I, pope (440–61) 125, 146–7
Leonelli, Carlo, *see* Ignazio di Gesù OCD (Carlo Leonelli)
Leopold I, emperor of the Holy Roman Empire (1658–1705) 153
Levi, Giovanni 294
light of nature 261, 264
local Christianities 5, 8

local knowledge and self-empowerment 251–5
Louis IX, king of France (r. 1226–70) 76
Louis XIII, king of France and Navarre (r. 1610–43) 7
Louis XIV, king of France and Navarre (r. 1643–1715) 7, 87, 153; gifts to the shah 105
Louis XV, king of France and Navarre (r. 1715–74) 184
Lucini, Aloisio (Luigi) Maria, OP, cardinal (1743–45) 269
Ludovisi, Alessandro, *see* Gregory XV (Alessandro Ludovisi, pope 1621–3)
Ludovisi, Ludovico, cardinal (1621–32), prefect of the *Propaganda Fide* 15
Lviv 136–8, 144

Maccarinelli, Serafino Maria, OP 280
Maciejowski, Bernard, cardinal (1603–8) 76
Madras (Chennai), *see* São Tomé (Madras)
magical practices 107, 110–12
Malabar rites controversies, *see* controversies, Malabar rites
Malachisi, Camillo Apollonio, *see* Filippo Maria di Sant'Agostino OCD (Camillo Apollonio Malachisi)
Malvasia, Bonaventura, OFM Conv 266
Manuel da Madre de Deus OSA (Manuel Soares) 100
Manuel de Santa Maria OSA 88; conversion to Islam 116–17
marriage, Armenians 159, 275–7
marriage, mixed 173, 201–2, 204–8, 214, 262–3, 269, 272–3, 275; Armenian measures against mixed marriage 145–6; *Declaratio benedictina* 279–80, 282; Genevan *Compagnie des pasteurs* against mixed marriage 217–18; Pietro Della Valle to Maani Gioerida [Ğuwairī] 130; *Tametsi* decree 204, 279; valid, but "illicit" 280
Martin V (Oddone Colonna, pope 1417–31) *see communicatio in sacris*, bull *Ad vitanda scandala*
Martínez, Fernando, *see* Fernando de Santa María OCD (Fernando Martínez)

Martini, Martino, SJ 265
mass in private homes 201-4
mathematics and natural sciences, missionaries 97-8, 105
Matteo di San Giuseppe OCD (Pietro Foglia) 110, 202, 215
Matthee, Rudi 67
medicine, practiced by missionaries 97-8, 108-10, 114, 283-4
Mekhitar of Sebaste 157-8, 163-4, 271
Mekhitarists 155, 163-4, 271
Melchisedech, coadjutor to Catholicos David IV of Etchmiadzin 135-6
Meneses, Aleixo de, OSA 75, 85
Mercier, Claude-Ignace, SJ 160-1, 181, 185, 202, 211-12, 249
Michel, Pierre-Victor 23, 87-8, 117, 147, 172, 181, 184
microhistory 2, 293-4
Milan 52-3
Miliński, Władysław, see Dionisio di Gesù OCD (Władysław Miliński)
Minerva, Decio, see Stefano di Gesù OCD (Decio Minerva)
Mingrelia 188
Mīr Dāmād, see Muḥammad Bāqir Astarābādī, Mīr (Mīr Dāmād)
Mīr Muḥammad ʿAbd al-Wahhābī, see Muḥammad ʿAbd al-Wahhābī, Mīr
Mīr Muḥammad Bāqir Astarābādī, see Muḥammad Bāqir Astarābādī, Mīr (Mīr Dāmād)
miracles, and magical practices 111-12; definition 110-11, 317; healing 105-15, 165, 283; healing of Muslims 105-7, 112-15, 283
Miranda, Diego, SJ 75
mission and the Enlightenment 1, 4-6, 11, 257-82
missionaries and Armenians 123-65; Catholic churches in New Julfa 6, 140-3, 148-50; first contacts 127-8
missionaries and Eastern Christian monks 124
missionaries and Muslims 118, 120, 229-30, 266-8. See also missionaries and Shi'a scholars
missionaries and Protestants 1-2, 4, 9, 176-7, 185-218, 283-4, 286; arbitration in an affair of honor 199; baptism and godparenthood 168-9, 173, 206-10; correspondence with Protestant scholars 195, 252; disputation 93-5; exchange of worldly services 168-9, 185-99; funerals 210-12, 260; invitations to church festivals 200-201; marriage 173, 201-2, 204-8; mass in private homes 201-4; Protestants as protectors 167-9; relations with a Protestant neo-martyr 165; relations with the Boutet de l'Étoile and Rousseau families 173-4, 197-8; spiritual services 168-9, 199-218
missionaries and Shi'a scholars 92-105; cooperation 89; disputations 81, 92-5, 99-102, 120, 179, 254, 268; help 101, 104; mutual personal respect 103-5
missionaries, ambivalent image in Catholic Europe 4, 219-20; and the Quran 89, 94, 96, 100-102, 266-8; as medical practitioners 97-8, 108-10, 114, 283-4; as translators and interpreters 88-92, 284; dealings with Indian financiers 246-9, 291; diplomatic assignments 84-8, 224-7, 231; divisions among missionaries 21-2, 138, 143, 150, 178-81, 186, 206, 219; knowledge of Armenian 127-8, 162; limited knowledge of the Armenian Church 125-8; local social integration and observance 223-35; mathematics and natural sciences 97-8, 105; multiple social roles 1, 4-8, 119-20, 283-4; Muslims as servants 229-30; participation in financial dealings 51, 236-7, 245-51; participation in trade affairs 236-7, 240-5; perceptions of Persia 79, 81-3, 96-7, 104-5; perceptions of the Ottoman Empire 82; prohibitions on intervention in political matters 225; relations with dervishes 115-16, 120, 194; relations with Vardapet and later Catholicos Moses 131-4; writings in Arabic and Persian 89, 95-6, 100-102

missions, Catholic, and cultural relativization 251–5, 257–60; as sites of particular law 24, 30–1, 181; economy 219–20, 235–51, 290–1; economy, Roman norms 236–7; key role of the regular clergy 8, 220, 288; limited funding from Europe 235–9, 249–50; pluralization as an undesirable outcome 257, 278
Missions étrangères de Paris 22, 179–80, 183, 186, 196–7; and Jansenism 180, 183; in Hamadan 7, 22, 181–2, 197; in New Julfa 7, 22
missions, Protestant 3, 296
Molina, J. Michelle 37–8
monasticism, early Christian 124, 131–2
Monox, Edward 190
Montalbano, Francesco, *see* Alessandro di San Silvestro OCD (Francesco Montalbano)
Monte, Luigi del, *see* Eugenio di San Benedetto OCD (Luigi del Monte) 131–2
Montesquieu, Charles-Louis de Secondat, Baron de La Brède de, *Lettres persanes* 258–9, 312
Montheron, Jean de 82
Morães, Simão de, OSA 75
Moses III, catholicos of Etchmiadzin (1629–32) 131–4, 137
Mostaccio, Silvia 38
Mouton, Laurent, *see* Élie de Saint-Albert OCD (Laurent Mouton)
Mughals, religious patronage 95
Muḥammad ʿAbd al-Wahhābī, Mīr 100
Muḥammad Bāqir Astarābādī, Mīr (Mīr Dāmād) 99
Mullā Ṣadrā Šīrāzī, *see* Ṣadrā Šīrāzī, Mullā
Muscat 217
Muzaffar b. Muḥammad al-Ḥusaini aš-Šifāʾī 109, 252

Nādir Šāh, shah of Persia (r. 1736–47) 70, 73–4, 83, 148, 196
Nahapet, catholicos of Etchmiadzin (1691–1705) 146–7
Nakhchivan 125, 137–9, 162, 229
Naples 25, 237–8
Naudé, Gabriel 343

Nazar, Ḥwāǧa, *kalāntar* of New Julfa 129
neomartyrs 165
Neri, Filippo Romolo, CO, *see* Philip Neri
Netherlands 216, 251–3, 279–80
New Julfa, Armenian merchants 70–4; Armenian churches 72; Catholic churches 6; decline as a hub for Armenian trade networks 153; European laypeople 169–77; printing press 144, 146; school at the monastery of the Holy Savior 144–5; school run by the Jesuits 160–1. *See also* Capuchins in New Julfa; Discalced Carmelites in New Julfa; Dominicans in New Julfa; Jesuits in New Julfa; *Missions étrangères de Paris* in New Julfa; Sceriman family
Nicole, Pierre 123
"nihil esse respondendum," *see* decision-making practices in the Roman Curia, "nihil esse respondendum"
Nobili, Roberto de', SJ 259, 265–6, 287
Nointel, Charles-Marie-François Olier, Marquis de 123

Odescalchi, Benedetto, *see* Innocent XI (Benedetto Odescalchi, pope 1676–89)
Olearius, Adam 9, 200–201
orders, factors of inner cohesion 37–8
Oriental rites 125–6
Orsini, Gregorio, OP 77, 120
Orsini, Pietro Francesco, *see* Benedict XIII (Pietro Francesco Orsini, pope 1724–30)
Osterhammel, Jürgen 3, 295
Ottoboni, Pietro Vito, *see* Alexander VIII (Pietro Vito Ottoboni, pope 1689–91)
Ottoman court, ceremonial 83–4
Ottoman Empire 5, 18, 82; Christian minorities in 5, 177–8
Overschie, Nicolaas Jacobsz 198

Pacifique de Provins OFMCap (René de l'Escale) 79, 128–9, 191, 226
Padroado, Portuguese 6–7, 20–3, 179, 181, 186, 190, 231–2, 242, 265
Pallu, François 146, 162, 164, 170–1, 173, 186, 188

Palma d'Artois, Duca di Sant'Elia, Ferrante, *see* Pietro Paolo di San Francesco OCD (Ferrante Palma d'Artois, Duca di Sant'Elia)
Pamphilj, Giovanni Battista, *see* Innocent X (Giovanni Battista Pamphilj, pope 1644–55)
Paolo Simone di Gesù Maria OCD (Paolo Rivarola) 44, 76, 106, 123, 128, 223, 225
papacy, dual spiritual and secular nature 2
Parigi, Gaspara 276–7
Passeri Aldobrandini, Cinzio, cardinal (1593–1610) 6, 47
Paul III (Alessandro Farnese, pope 1534–49) 15
Paul V (Camillo Borghese, pope 1605–21) 7, 16–17, 131, 136, 203, 262
Pedro de la Madre de Dios OCD (Pedro Jerónimo de Villagrasa) 36–7, 39, 47, 221
Pereira Fidalgo, Gregório 85–6
Peretti, Felice, *see* Sixtus V (Felice Peretti, pope 1585–90)
Pérez de Vargas, Timoteo, OCarm 133
Persian Gulf, *see* Basra; Bandar ʿAbbās; Bandar-i Kung; Kharg Island
Peter II, king of Portugal (r. 1683–1706) 86, 117
Pétis de la Croix, François 109, 252
Philip II, king of Castile (r. 1556–98), as Philip I also king of Portugal (r. 1580–98) 75
Philip III, king of Castile (r. 1598–1621), as Philip II also king of Portugal (r. 1598–1621) 21, 59, 61, 84–5
Philip Neri 257
Philip, catholicos of Etchmiadzin (1633–55) 134
Philippe de la Très Sainte Trinité OCD (Julien Esprit), *Itinerarium orientale* 79, 222; *Theologia carmelitana* 222
philosophy, Greek 92, 95–9, 100–102, 120
Piacentini, Marcantonio, *see* Sebastiano di Santa Margherita OCD (Marcantonio Piacentini)
Piacentini, Vittorio Francesco, *see* Giacinto di Santa Teresa OCD (Vittorio Francesco Piacentini)
Picart, Bernard, *Cérémonies et coutumes religieuses de tous les peuples du monde* 258
Picquet, François 22, 87, 105, 183, 197
Pidou de Saint-Olon, Louis-Marie, CR 22, 48, 87, 143, 150, 152, 180, 193
Piérart, Martin, *see* Corneille de Saint-Cyprien OCD (Martin Piérart)
Pierre de la Mère de Dieu OCD (François Du Jardin) 52
Pierre de Saint-André OCD (Jean-Antoine Rampalle), *Historia Generalis Fratrum Discalceatorum Ordinis* 222, 296
Pietro Paolo di San Francesco OCD (Ferrante Palma d'Artois, Duca di Sant'Elia) 151, 190
Pignatelli, Antonio, *see* Innocent XII (Antonio Pignatelli, pope 1691–1700)
Piromalli, Paolo, OP 114, 137–9, 146, 160, 286–7
Pius V (Antonio Michele Ghislieri, pope 1566–72) 60, 74
Pius VI (Giovanni Angelo Braschi, pope 1775–99) 55–6
Pizzorusso, Giovanni 17
Plato 99, 145
Poland-Lithuania 18, 136–8, 141
pope, limits of his jurisdiction 13–14, 285; *plenitudo potestatis* 13, 21, 285; *primatus honoris* 124–5, 128; reform of procedure for election of 15
Poullet, Nicolas 214
Prescott, Alexander 187
printing press, at New Julfa 144, 146; gift to ʿAbbās I, shah of Persia (1588–1629) 89
Proclus Diadochus 145
Prodi, Paolo 13, 294
Propaganda fide, and privileges of religious orders 20–1, 23–5; and secular rights of patronage 20–3, 286; *Congregatio Persiae* 19; establishment 7, 15–16; expenses for the missions 17–18, 235–9; jurisdictional conflicts with the Holy Office 18–20, 266–7, 270–1; limited capacity to enforce norms 38; limited financial resources 16–18; missionaries' difficulties to access 50, 52–6; personal networks

18–20; relations with regular clergy 47–57, 219–20, 284
Prosperi, Adriano 42
Próspero del Espíritu Santo OCD (Martín Garaizabal) 99–101, 107, 131, 238
Protestants and Catholic missionaries 185–218, 283–4; accounts of Protestant travelers 1, 9, 107, 119–20, 176–7, 219, 232, 284; Boutet de l'Étoile and Rousseau families 171–4; disputations 93–5; gifts and alms 185, 187, 194, 196–7; help along the way 185–8, 284; in the Persian Gulf 167–9; knowledge and relationships 193–6; loans 197–8; mutual professions of respect 188–91, 200–201; mutual visits 188–91, 200–201; postal services 191–3, 284, 287; presence at funerals of missionaries 168, 211–12
Protestants, extramarital relations with enslaved women 168–9; in Constantinople 171–2, 176, 217–18, 280

Qazwīn 189
Qeshm 91
Qizilbāš 66–7
Quran, missionaries and the 89, 94, 96, 100–102, 266–8

Raisin, Antoine 243
Rampalle, Jean-Antoine, *see* Pierre de Saint-André OCD (Jean-Antoine Rampalle)
Raphaël du Mans OFM Cap (Jacques Dutertre) 90–2, 97, 123, 162, 183, 193–5, 200, 202, 212, 216, 226–7, 290; *État de la Perse* 82, 90, 104–5, 194–5; relations with Engelbert Kaempfer 105, 195, 212; relations with Jean Chardin 194–5; relations with Jean-Baptiste Tavernier 194–5, 200
Redempto de la Cruz OCD (Pedro Lagar y Baylo) 79, 102
regular clergy, acceptance of gifts 225; and episcopal authority 178, 181–4; carrying weapons 228–9, 232; food 189–90, 196, 224, 231–5; habit 219–20, 224, 226–8, 231, 253–4, 264; housing 61, 196, 198, 226, 231–2, 249; lay servants 228–32; obedience, its extent and limits 37–8, 57, 220, 288–9, 347; observance 4, 11, 36, 38, 219–55, 287; presence at the local court 88–90, 92–5, 224–7; slaveholding 227, 229–30, 232; social interactions outside the convent 232–5; use of horses 227–8, 231–2, 234; vow of poverty 28, 32, 36, 56, 88, 115, 168, 188–9, 196, 198, 213, 219, 224–8, 230, 235, 243, 254, 288, 290
Reina, Carlo Amatore Adeodato, *see* Cornelio di San Giuseppe OCD (Carlo Amatore Adeodato Reina)
Reinhard, Wolfgang 13, 294, 301
Reinkowski, Maurus 319
religion, as a social phenomenon 258; as a topic of comparative scholarship 258; freedom of 176–7
Renauldin, Jean, *see* Casimir Joseph de Sainte-Thérèse OCD (Jean Renauldin)
Rezzonico, Carlo, *see* Clement XIII (Carlo Rezzonico, pope 1758–69)
Rhodes, Alexandre de, SJ 41, 79, 81, 180–1, 188, 211, 249
Ribitol, Étienne, *see* Jean Chrysostome de Saint-Paul OCD (Étienne Ribitol)
Ricci, Matteo, SJ 264–5
Richelieu, Armand Jean du Plessis de, cardinal (1622–42) 22, 226
Ricouart, Antoine de 22
Rivarola, Martino, *see* Francesco di Gesù OCD (Martino Rivarola)
Rivarola, Paolo, *see* Paolo Simone di Gesù Maria OCD (Paolo Rivarola)
Rocha de Oliveira, António da, *see* António do Desterro OSA (António da Rocha de Oliveira)
Roldán y Ibañez, Juan, *see* Juan Thadeo de San Eliseo OCD (Juan Roldán y Ibañez)
Romanini de Sanctis, Orazio, *see* Benigno di San Michele OCD (Orazio Romanini de Sanctis)
Rosa, Mario
Rospigliosi, Giulio, *see* Clement IX (Giulio Rospigliosi, pope 1667–69)
Rousseau family 214

Rousseau, Isaac 171–2
Rousseau, Jacques 169, 171–5, 202; loans to missionaries 197–8
Rousseau, Jean-François 197
Rousseau, Jean-François-Xavier 174–5, 216; French consul in Basra 175, 215; knight of San Giovanni in Laterano 214; life on the confessional borderlines 214
Rousseau, Jean-Jacques 171–2
Rousseau, Théodore 215
rule from a distance, correspondence 38–42, 53–4, 289–90; limits 56–7, 285–6, 289–90; personal networks 13–14, 285; visitations 33–5, 223
Russia 74, 151–2
Ruzola, Domingo, *see* Domingo de Jesús María OCD (Domingo Ruzola)

sacramental community, *see communicatio in sacris*
Ṣadrā Šīrāzī, Mullā 99
Safar, Ḥwāǧa, *kalāntar* of New Julfa 129
Safavid court, ceremonial of embassies from Christian rulers 63–5, 83–4, 87–8; gifts brought to the shah 75–6, 89, 99, 105; missionaries 83–95, 224–7
Safavid Empire, Christian minorities in 68–70, 174–7; European powers and 60–5; inclusive strategies of imperial rule 3, 59–60, 65–70, 92, 99; merchants and financiers from India 63, 246–9, 291; papacy and 60–1, 65, 74–5, 77; relations with Christian rulers 62–5; relations with other Asian empires 62–5; religious patronage of the shah 92–5; Shi'ism 2–3, 65–7
Ṣafī I, shah of Persia (r. 1629–42) 67, 69
Ṣafī II, shah of Persia (r. 1666–94), *see* Sulaimān I (Ṣafī II), shah of Persia (r. 1666–94)
Sahid, Elias 170
Sahid, family 203
Salus Populi Romani icon 75
San Pedro, Juan de, *see* Juan de Jesús María OCD (Juan de San Pedro)
Sánchez Dávila, Díaz, *see* Tomás de Jesús OCD (Díaz Sánchez Dávila)
Sánchez de Cepeda Dávila y Ahumada, Teresa, *see* Teresa of Ávila OCD (Teresa Sánchez de Cepeda Dávila y Ahumada)
Sanson, François 143, 150, 180, 197
Santus, Cesare 260–1
São Tomé (Madras) 181
Sarhat, Ḥwāǧa 140
Sarterius, Dirck 189
Savory, Roger 295
Sayyid Aḥmad ʿAlawī, *see* Aḥmad ʿAlawī, Sayyid
Sceriman family, Catholic church in New Julfa 6, 74, 140–3, 148–50, 158–9, 164–5, 274–5; in East Asia 153–4; in Goa 154; in Livorno, 152–3; in Russia 151–2; in Venice 152–3, 155–6; investments in Italy 152–3; mixed marriages 275; relations with Élie de Saint-Albert OCD 140–3, 148, 154, 183, 235; trade networks 151–7
Sceriman, Arutiun, *kalāntar* of New Julfa 111–12
Sceriman, Basilio 152, 155, 158
Sceriman, Gasparo 140, 152–5, 158
Sceriman, Leone 153
Sceriman, Lorenzo 154
Sceriman, Marcara 140, 154
Sceriman, Michele 140, 154
Sceriman, Murat 140, 152
Sceriman, Pietro 153–4
Sceriman, Sarat (Giacomo) 154
Sceriman, Stefano 154–6, 158
Sceriman, Zaccaria 140
Schipano, Mario 100, 130
Schlögl, Rudolf 258, 341
Schorer, Nicolaas 210
Scotland 18
Sebastiano di Santa Margherita OCD (Marcantonio Piacentini) 43–4, 70, 148, 168, 182
secularization processes 278–82
self-examination 35–8
Sherley, Anthony 60
Shi'a scholars and missionaries 92–105; cooperation 89; disputations 81, 92–5, 99–102, 120, 179, 254, 268; help 101, 104; mutual personal respect 103–5

Shiraz 7, 31–2, 99, 180, 187–8, 192, 195, 228, 230, 234, 238–9, 242–4, 247, 284
Sicard, Claude, SJ 163
Sicily 45
Silva y Figueroa, García de 85, 89–90, 228
Simeon of Julfa 144–5
Simon the Zealot, apostle 123
Simon, Richard, CO 268
Sixtus V (Felice Peretti, pope 1585–90) 15, 29
slaveholding, by missionaries 227, 229–30, 232; East India Companies and 168–9
Soares, Belchior, *see* Belchior dos Anjos OSA (Belchior Soares)
Soares, Manuel, *see* Manuel da Madre de Deus OSA (Manuel Soares)
Soccioli, Giovanni Battista, *see* Epifanio di San Giovanni Battista OCD (Giovanni Battista Soccioli)
South India, "tropical Catholicism" 5. *See also* controversies, Malabar rites
Spanish monarchy, composite structure of 85
Stadler, Johann Rudolf 165
Standaert, Nicolas 211
Stefano di Gesù OCD (Decio Minerva) 114
Stephan, Armenian bishop of New Julfa (1683–96) 145–6
Stroumsa, Guy G. 297, 341
Sufi orders 1, 66–7, 69, 92–3, 99, 103, 115–17, 120, 194
Sulaimān I (Ṣafi II), shah of Persia (r. 1666–94) 92
Sulṭān Ḥusain, shah of Persia (r. 1694–1722) 69, 73, 147–8
Surat 73, 186, 192–3, 200
Sylvester I, pope (314–35) 124, 133–4

Tabriz 7, 147, 188
Ṭahmāsp I, shah of Persia (r. 1524–76) 60, 64, 66, 74
Tani, Antonino, OP 64–5, 90
Tavernier, Jean-Baptiste 9, 90, 97, 171, 187, 194–5, 199–200, 258
Tbilisi 188

Teresa of Ávila OCD (Teresa Sánchez de Cepeda Dávila y Ahumada) 2, 25, 27, 36, 221–2, 306, 318
Thiessen, Hillard von 179, 294
Thomas Aquinas OP 145, 265
Tilhac, Jacques, SJ 195, 226–7, 235
Tomás de Jesús OCD (Díaz Sánchez Dávila), *De procuranda salute omnium gentium* 221, 262
Tonelli, Giacomo, *see* Dimas della Croce OCD (Giacomo Tonelli)
Torosowicz, Nikol, Uniate Armenian archbishop of Lviv 136–8
Toussaint de Landerneau OFM Cap 191
transconfessional relations, Western Europe 215–16
Tridentine Catholicism (concept) 2, 285, 288
Tripoli (Lebanon) 239
Tripoli (Libya) 209–10
Trivellato, Francesca 293
Typographia medicea, Arabic translation of Euclid's *Elements* 75, 98–9; Arabic translation of the Gospels 75, 89

union of Eastern churches with Rome 123–6, 132–4, 136–8, 141–2, 151–7, 163–4; Armenian trade networks and, 151–7; Armenians in Poland-Lithuania 136–8, 141; negative consequences for business 156–7; profession of faith 132, 134, 141–2, 162; trade privileges for Uniate Christians 151, 153–4
Urban VIII (Maffeo Barberini, pope 1623–44) 17, 20, 22, 24, 65, 136–7, 237, 266
usury 250–1, 339. *See also* missionaries, participation in financial dealings

Valentin d'Angers OFM Cap 104, 138, 173, 179, 194, 201–2, 204, 206–8, 220
Valerio di San Giuseppe OCD (Giuseppe Landriano) 114
Van Leene, Joan 91
Van Reede tot Drakenstein, Hendrik Adriaan 215

vardapet 131
Verenigde Oost-Indische Compagnie (VOC), *see* East India Company, Dutch
Vicente de San Francisco OCD (Juan Gambart) 34, 40, 93–5, 131, 228–9, 233, 236
Villagrasa, Pedro Jerónimo de, *see* Pedro de la Madre de Dios OCD (Pedro Jerónimo de Villagrasa)
Villotte, Jacques, SJ 98, 115, 164, 180, 188–9, 212, 260

Wassilowsky, Günther 294–5
wine, consumption by Muslims 119, 243–4; consumption by the shah 84

Xenophon, *Cyropaedia* 82

Yepes Álvarez, Juan de, *see* Juan de la Cruz OCD (Juan de Yepes Álvarez)
Yerevan 147, 227
Yovhannes Mrkuz 72

Županov, Ines G. 5, 56

www.ingramcontent.com/pod-product-compliance
Lightning Source LLC
Chambersburg PA
CBHW071237300426
44116CB00008B/1076